W9-BXA-776

The
WAR IN THE PACIFIC
Japanese conquests to August 1942

PACIFIC OCEAN

MIDWAY

MONDAY   SUNDAY

HAWAIIAN IS.

OAHU
Pearl Harbor
Honolulu
HAWAII

WAKE I.

INTERNATIONAL DATE LINE

ENIWETOK
MARSHALL IS.
KWAJALEIN

MAKIN
TARAWA

GILBERT IS.

EQUATOR

IRELAND
SOLOMON
EW BRITAIN
BOUGAINVILLE
CHOISEUL
SANTA ISABEL
RGIA
GUADALCANAL
SAN
CRISTOBAL
SANTA
CRUZ IS.

PACIFIC OCEAN

RAL SEA
NEW
HEBRIDE

NEW CALEDONIA

Japan
at War

Japan
at War

An Oral History

HARUKO TAYA COOK
and
THEODORE F. COOK

New York   1992

The New Press

Published in the United States by The New Press, New York.

**Distributed by W.W. Norton & Company, Inc.
500 Fifth Avenue, New York, NY 10110**

LIBRARY OF CONGRESS CATALOGING-IN-PUBLICATION DATA

Cook, Haruko Taya.
    Japan at war : an oral history / Haruko Taya Cook and Theodore F.
Cook.—1. ed.
        p.   cm.

    ISBN 1-56584-014-3
    1. World War, 1939–1945—Personal narratives, Japanese.   2. World
War, 1939–1945—Japan.   3. Japan—History—1926–1945.   4. Oral
history.   I. Cook, Theodore Failor.   II. Title.
D811.A2C62   1992
940.53′52′0922—dc20   92-53731
[B]   CIP

FIRST EDITION, 1992

Book Design by Helen Barrow

For Taya Toshi, Haruko's mother,
who brought the family
through it all.

ACKNOWLEDGMENTS

WE WOULD FIRST like to thank the men and women who agreed to speak in this book and share their stories with us. They all consented to talk on the record, and we hope they feel we did justice to our time together. We also wish to express warm appreciation to the many, many people who were interviewed but who do not appear in these pages. Unsparingly sharing their time and memories, they contributed to this book in ways only the authors know.

André Schiffrin saw the need, expressed the faith, and extended the resources to make this book possible. As publisher, he involved himself from the earliest stages, and his suggestions, admonitions, and assistance were instrumental. No one could ask for a better, fairer, or more demanding editor than Tom Engelhardt, and we owe an immense debt to him for his continued encouragement and dedication to the project. Stacks of tapes in Japanese had to be rendered into text and then translated into English, and throughout, again and again, he was there when the stories threatened to escape or seemed to defy our abilities to extract them. He worked tirelessly and supportively, and through all he has been a friend.

An oral history depends on a chain of introductions, for those who agreed to open their lives to us often helped introduce others. Leads to people willing to speak came from friends, family, acquaintances, and helpful outsiders. Without them this book could not have been made. Only a few can be acknowledged by name, but in naming the following we wish to express our gratitude to all: Teshigawara Heihachi, Nagasawa Michio, Takeda Eiko, Suzuki Sotoo, Kim Kyong-Suk, and Sasayama Takashi. Special thanks to Yue-him Tam for reviewing Chinese names used in the book. Our friends and families in both Japan and America often encouraged us as this book progressed. Haruko's sisters, Taya Kuniko, Suzuki Hiroko, and Hasegawa Nobuko, were special scouts and supporters.

At The New Press, Dawn Davis and Kim Waymer served us well, shepherding the book through all its stages. David Frederickson proved a keen and cunning editor of copy. A thank you too to Sowon Kwon, who read early drafts and made valuable suggestions.

We are of course responsible for any errors of fact or interpretation which remain.

CONTENTS

ACKNOWLEDGMENTS   vii

INTRODUCTION TO A LOST WAR   3

PART ONE · *An Undeclared War*   21

1 / BATTLE LINES IN CHINA   29
A Village Boy Goes to War · NOHARA TEISHIN   29
Pictures of an Expedition · TANIDA ISAMU [1]   35
Qualifying as a Leader · TOMINAGA SHŌZŌ [1]   40
Gas Soldier · TANISUGA SHIZUO   44

2 / TOWARD A NEW ORDER   47
"War means jobs for machinists." · KUMAGAYA TOKUICHI   47
"I wanted to build Greater East Asia." · NOGI HARUMICHI [1] 50
Manchurian Days · FUKUSHIMA YOSHIE [1]   56
Dancing into the Night · HARA KIYOSHI   61
Bringing the Liberals to Heel · HATANAKA SHIGEO [1]   64

PART TWO · *Have "Faith in Victory"*   69

3 / DECEMBER 8, 1941   77
"My blood boiled at the news." · ITABASHI KŌSHŪ   77
"I heard it on the radio." · YOSHIDA TOSHIO   78
On Admiral Yamamoto's Flagship · NODA MITSUHARU   81
In a Fighter Cockpit on the Soviet Border · MOGAMI SADAO [1] 83
Sailing South · MASUDA REIJI [1]   86
A Failure of Diplomacy · KASE TOSHIKAZU   90

4 / GREATER EAST ASIA 95

Cartoons for the War · YOKOYAMA RYŪICHI [1] 95

Building the Burma-Siam Railroad · ABE HIROSHI [1] 99

Keeping Order in the Indies · NOGI HARUMICHI [2] 105

"Korean Guard" · KASAYAMA YOSHIKICHI 113

5 / THE EMPEROR'S WARRIORS 121

Maker of Soldiers · DEBUN SHIGENOBU 121

"As long as I don't fight, I'll make it home." · SUZUKI MURIO 127

Zero Ace · SAKAI SABURŌ 135

6 / "DEMONS FROM THE EAST" 145

Army Doctor · YUASA KEN 145

Spies and Bandits · UNO SHINTARŌ 151

Unit 731 · TAMURA YOSHIO 158

PART THREE · *Homeland* 169

7 / LIFE GOES ON 177

The End of a Bake Shop · ARAKAWA HIROYO 177

Burdens of a Village Bride · TANAKA TOKI 181

Dressmaker · KOSHINO AYAKO 184

8 / WAR WORK 187

Making Balloon Bombs · TANAKA TETSUKO 187

Forced Labor · AHN JURETSU 192

Poison-Gas Island · NAKAJIMA YOSHIMI 199

9 / WIELDING PEN AND CAMERA 203

Filming the News · ASAI TATSUZŌ 203

War Correspondent · HATA SHŌRYŪ 208

Reporting from Imperial General Headquarters · KAWACHI
UICHIRŌ [1]   213

10 / AGAINST THE TIDE   221
Thought Criminal · HATANAKA SHIGEO [2]   222
"Isn't my brother one of the 'War Dead'?" · KIGA SUMI   227

11 / CHILDHOOD   231
Playing at War · SATŌ HIDEO   231

12 / ART AND ENTERTAINMENT   240
"I loved American movies." · HIROSAWA EI   240
Star at the Moulin Rouge · SUGAI TOSHIKO   248
"We wouldn't paint war art." · MARUKI IRI AND MARUKI TOSHI   253

PART FOUR · *Lost Battles*   259

13 / THE SLAUGHTER OF AN ARMY   267
The "Green Desert" of New Guinea · OGAWA MASATSUGU   267
Soldiers' Deaths · OGAWA TAMOTSU   276
"Honorable Death" on Saipan · YAMAUCHI TAKEO   281

14 / SUNKEN FLEET   293
Lifeboat · MATSUNAGA ICHIRŌ   293
Transport War · MASUDA REIJI [2]   300

15 / "SPECIAL ATTACK"   305
Volunteer · YOKOTA YUTAKA   306
Human Torpedo · KŌZU NAOJI   313
Bride of a Kamikaze · ARAKI SHIGEKO   319
Requiem · NISHIHARA WAKANA   327

PART FIVE · *"One Hundred Million Die Together"* 337

16 / THE BURNING SKIES 343
"Hiroko died because of me." · FUNATO KAZUYO 343
At the Telephone Exchange · TOMIZAWA KIMI AND KOBAYASHI
HIROYASU 349

17 / THE WAR COMES HOME TO OKINAWA 354
Student Nurses of the "Lily Corps" · MIYAGI KIKUKO 354
"Now they call it 'Group Suicide.'" · KINJŌ SHIGEAKI 363
Straggler · ŌTA MASAHIDE [1] 367

18 / IN THE ENEMY'S HANDS 373
White Flag · KOJIMA KIYOFUMI 373

19 / "A TERRIBLE NEW WEAPON" 382
Eight Hundred Meters from the Hypocenter · YAMAOKA MICHIKO 384
A Korean in Hiroshima · SHIN BOK SU 387
Five Photographs of August 6 · MATSUSHIGE YOSHITO 391
"Forgetting is a blessing." · KIMURA YASUKO 395

PART SIX · *The Unresolved War* 401

20 / REVERSALS OF FORTUNE 407
Flight · FUKUSHIMA YOSHIE [2] 407
From Bandung to Starvation Island · IITOYO SHŌGO 411
"The Army's been a good life." · TANIDA ISAMU [2] 416

21 / CRIMES AND PUNISHMENTS 420
Death Row at Changi Prison · ABE HIROSHI [2] 420
"They didn't tell me." · FUJII SHIZUE 427

22 / THE LONG SHADOW OF DEATH 432

The Emperor's Retreat · YAMANE MASAKO 432

"My boy never came home." · IMAI SHIKE 438

23 / REFLECTIONS 441

Teaching War · IENAGA SABURŌ 441

Meeting at Yasukuni Shrine · KIYAMA TERUMICHI 447

Lessons · MOGAMI SADAO [2] 453

A Quest for Meaning · ŌTA MASAHIDE [2] 458

24 / ENDINGS 462

Homecoming · TOMINAGA SHŌZO [2] 462

The Face of the Enemy · SASAKI NAOKATA 468

Imperial Gifts for the War Dead · KAWASHIMA EIKO 469

Royalties · YOKOYAMA RYŪICHI [2] 471

"I learned about the war from Grandma." · MIYAGI HARUMI 472

The Occupiers · KAWACHI UICHIRŌ [2] 477

Back at the Beginning · HAYASHI SHIGEO 478

NOTE ON NAMES AND SPELLING

IN THIS BOOK Japanese names are presented in the normal Japanese fashion, i.e., surname first and given name second. The only exceptions to this are in English-language bibliographic references where the order is reversed in the original.

Macrons have been placed to indicate all long vowels, except in the case of place names which are well known to the Western reader: e.g., Tokyo has been left in the normal Western spelling rather than written in the linguistically correct but visually disturbing form Tōkyō.

Since the majority of Chinese terms used here are references to the war years, Chinese names and words have been rendered in the modified Wade-Giles system then in use rather than the more modern Pinyin: e.g. Nanking rather Nanjing, Chunking rather than Chongqing, and Chiang Kai-shek and Mao Tse-tung rather than Jiang Jieshi and Mao Zedong.

Korean names are rendered as used by the speakers.

Japan
at War

INTRODUCTION TO A LOST WAR

J
APAN was defeated in its last war decisively and completely. Approximately three million Japanese died in a conflict that raged for years over a huge part of the earth's surface, from Hawaii to India, Alaska to Australia, causing death and suffering to untold millions in China, southeast Asia, and the Pacific islands, as well as pain and anguish to families of soldiers and civilians around the globe.

Yet how much do we know of Japan's war? The experiences of individual Japanese caught up in that enormous conflict seem somehow never to have emerged from collective images of a fanatical nation at war. What was the war like for Japanese soldiers, sailors, workers, farming wives, factory girls, and schoolchildren? How did they survive, what motivated them, and what did they learn from their ordeal? Certainly, the texture of the Japanese experience is absent from most American discussions of the Second World War in Asia. But so, too, is it generally missing from Japanese treatments of the war. In Japan, one can encounter a powerful, generalized hatred of war, a strong belief that wars should not be fought, but little appreciation for or understanding of the reasons why Japan was at the center of that global conflict a half-century ago.

In fact, perhaps the most common feeling we encountered while studying the Japanese war experience was a sense among those we interviewed that the war, like some natural cataclysm, had "happened" to them, not in any way been "done" by them. All around us were people who had lived the most intense moments of their lives in that era, yet we were often acutely aware that many desired the experiences of that war to remain forever lost. It was as if no framework existed within which those who had lived through that time of war could release their personal stories into the public realm. Yet, feeling that that Japanese war could not be allowed to pass beyond memory without some effort to record what wartime life was like for the Japanese people, we had to ask ourselves, Where does one go in search of a lost war?

One particular encounter captured for us the strange state of the Second World War in Japanese memory today. We were examining the wartime records of a small village in central Japan in 1989 when we turned up a document showing that a man still living in the area had had two brothers killed in the war. Acting on the kind of impulse that was to serve us well, we went directly to his home, a sprawling farmhouse set in a grove of ancient trees on the side of a hill. A man in his early fifties, he greeted us and, on hearing why we'd come, invited us in. Willing to talk, but tense and unsure where to begin, he finally focused on his eldest brother, who had died in October 1937 during "the China Incident"—as the Sino-Japanese war that began July 7, 1937, was known in Japan.

"At that time," he explained, "not many people had been killed in action, so everyone in the hamlet showed great compassion. Eldest Brother was called a 'military god.' My parents even went to Yasukuni Shrine in Tokyo on the occasion of his enshrinement there. The nation treated the family members of the war dead with such care then, that their families almost felt grateful to their sons for having died."

The second brother—our host was the third of five sons—went into the navy in 1942. "That was the year I entered elementary school. This time, my parents were worried. They even bought a radio, something we couldn't afford, because they felt they had to hear the news. We had no idea where he'd gone. Whenever there were *gyokusai* (sacrificial battles) reported, at Attu, Tarawa, or Saipan, my father was subdued all day long. My brother was actually killed at Truk in 1944."

At this point, our host retired to another room, and after a few moments returned with a packet of cards and letters, carefully bound with twine. Tenderly selecting one, he held it out to us, "This is my elder brother's final card home. His last words are 'It is my long-cherished desire to fall [like the cherry blossom]. My brothers, raise our family honor by becoming military men!' " Suddenly, our host halted, drew his shoulders together, and seemed to wince with pain. Then he broke into sobs, tears streaming down his face, falling onto his hands, which clutched his knees. Gradually, he controlled his tears, and continued in a choked voice, "On the day the war ended, my parents cried out bitterly, 'Two of our sons died in vain!' But afterwards, my father never criticized the country, never spoke about militarism or anything. He just talked about what good sons they'd been."

He now served us tea. He seemed more relaxed, and almost as an afterthought, he wondered whether we'd like to see some of his eldest brother's things. He led us into a tatami room, along one of whose walls were displayed grainy photographs of a young soldier in a fur-lined hat, sporting the insignia of a private first class, and a sailor, with the name of the destroyer *Tachikaze* on the band of his cap. Next to them were crisp photographs of two old and weathered faces, their parents. From deeper in the recesses of the house he returned with a large square box made of wisteria wood. Inked on it in bold brush strokes were the characters, "Box for the Belongings of the Deceased." Inside was an official description of the circumstances of his eldest brother's death, and a map, bearing the seal of his brother's commanding officer, showing the exact location of his final moments. Beneath it was the "thousand-stitch belt" —said to ward off bullets—that his sister had sewn for him before his departure for China. Our host pointed out the brown stain from his blood.

At the bottom of the box was a heavy album. The embossed lettering on the cover immediately told us it was the official album of his eldest brother's unit, the Thirty-Fifth Infantry Regiment, commemorating its service in Manchuria. After the obligatory photographs of Emperor Hirohito and Empress Nagako, of the Imperial Standard, and the tattered regimental banner, the portraits of the medal-bedecked hierarchy of the Japanese Army in Manchuria, and of the regimental commander, came the shots of vigorous, fresh-faced young men on their first trip overseas —"going ashore" at Dairen near Port Arthur, "in front of the memorial to the Japanese dead of the Russo-Japanese War," and "competing in a Japan-Manchukuo athletic meet."

The last pages of the album were blank to accommodate whatever snapshots a soldier might want to add, and many had been pasted in. Here was the youth whose portrait hung on the wall behind us in informal poses, a handsome young soldier with his friends and his mess mates. Here were shots of Chinese women with bound feet and wild Manchurian landscapes. Here also was an official-looking photo, entitled "Bandit Suppression Operation Commemorative Picture," showing soldiers in combat gear going into action, followed by a series of candid shots revealing the fate of "bandits" in the operations his eldest brother had clearly taken part in. One showed three severed heads, one with eyes still staring, balanced on a fence; another, a soldier holding a precisely severed head by its hair, the face turned toward the camera; yet another of a Chinese, his arms bound tightly, is captioned in his eldest brother's hand, "his life hangs by a thread." The last few pages contain the family's photographs of their eldest son's grand funeral in his village when his remains were returned from China.

As our host closed the album, he turned to Haruko and said calmly, but with concern, "I don't know what to do with this box. When I die, there's nobody to protect these things. My other brothers died while still young. My sons and my daughter have all left the hamlet for the big city. I don't think any of them want to come back. I've been airing the box out each year to preserve it." Then he added, "I'm sure my brother would be happy that you've seen these things. But please don't connect our name to those photos. It's just that it was that kind of time. It was war. It wasn't like today. Today's peace, I feel, is founded on those sacrificed then."

During our years of interviewing in Japan, that box and its contents haunted us as a symbol of what that war was and what it has since become to the Japanese: a man with a box containing both memories of a brother he adored and evidence of the crimes of war; love and atrocities bound together and hidden from sight; a man who desires to preserve what he, indeed, what his whole family shies away from acknowledging. For that box holds an accurate self-portrait of a young Japanese man who went to war and did what in those years his country, his community, and he felt had to be done. While our host is prepared to air out the objects in the box each year, he refuses to give the meaning of the contents the public airing it demands, and yet if we cannot speak of what actually happened then, can the preservation of the past have any meaning?

Every August 15—the anniversary of the day in 1945 when the Japanese Emperor accepted the demands of the Allies and announced to his people that the war was over—Japan officially recalls "the war" with a government-sponsored "Day Commemorating the End of the War." It is not a national holiday, but on that day the Nihon Budōkan hall in Tokyo, normally the site of concerts, professional wrestling matches, and martial-arts events, is transformed into the venue for a "National Ceremony to Mourn the War Dead." Seated facing great banks of white and yellow chrysanthemums, the prime minister, government figures, local officials and selected representatives of the "families of the war dead" are among the several thousand invited guests. The Emperor reads a short statement broadcast live on radio and television, and a minute of silence is observed precisely at noon. This brief observance, unlike those of that long-ago war, contains no religious elements.

Although conducted at the highest level of government, the ceremony is not used to discuss the reasons for the war, nor to debate its causes, costs, or consequences. It is accompanied neither by ringing speeches in honor of the valiant men and women who fought for Japan, nor in memory of the bravery and suffering of those who died at home or endured agonies in the war's wake. No apologies or regrets are offered to the millions throughout the Asian-Pacific region who survived the depredations of the Japanese, and no one seems to consider anything to be amiss in that. In an uncompromisingly solemn tone, the ceremony to remember the dead confirms the participants in their generally mute and unaroused state. The hall is full of the faces of people who lived through those years and who by the rules of invitation must have lost a family member in that war. Yet how those war dead died or what caused their lives to be lost, are not questions to be raised on such an occasion. There is no way for an onlooker to know what stories these relatives of the dead might have to tell. Nonetheless, we often wondered about them as the annual event rolled around and we, like so many others, took a few moments off to watch the ceremony, or at least to view clips of it on the evening news.

In that strangely disembodied official ceremony, the lost war seems anchored in neither time nor public memory. In fact, for younger Japanese—the vast majority of all Japanese were born long after August 15, 1945—the day to mourn the war dead has become a "seasonal event" signifying high summer, like the cry of the cicada or the hawking of the goldfish seller. For us, the ceremony in its historical opaqueness seemed to capture much of what was both tantalizing and initially forbidding in our decision to try to do an oral history of the Pacific War from the Japanese point of view. We wanted to ask the wives, brothers, sisters, or the few remaining parents, aunts, and uncles of those whose lives had ended half a century or more ago for their stories, and for those of their dead relatives, and we wanted to do the asking before those with direct memory of the war years themselves died.

But was it possible to inquire of such faces? Or even to find them? Where to begin? And if we succeeded, would any of them truly speak to us, or speak truthfully to us after so many years? Haruko had her own doubts. She had lived through the war as a small child in a village to which she had been evacuated with her mother (while her father worked as a civilian employee in the Palembang oil fields in Japanese-occupied Sumatra), and she knew from personal experience how little the war years were a spoken part of postwar family life. But she was also aware of an impulse to explore those wartime experiences she herself could hardly remember. That was why she had made the war the subject of programs she produced for Japanese television and radio in the late 1960s and why she later made the lost literature of that war period the topic of her research into Japanese literature. She suspected that others, too, had this desire to uncover those years so long locked away inside. Ted, whose mother and father met in the Pacific theater during the war, had, thanks to his research on Japanese military institutions and the place of the military in prewar Japanese society, a certain confidence in the willingness of the wartime generation to speak of those days. He had been struck by how many army and navy officers had proven willing to talk with him of their careers and lives, and he hoped it would be possible to expand such contacts to soldiers and sailors and their families.

Just to find interviewees, however, proved a daunting experience in ways that reveal much about how Japan has dealt with its war experience. In fact, our first attempt at an interview, with a respected professor of political science, someone we already knew, whom we hoped might both tell us about his own wartime experiences and direct us to other interviewees, went not at all as anticipated.

After discussing the war generally, he began, with seeming reluctance, to speak of his own war experience as a university draftee who had used all his family's influence to avoid call-up until he was finally tapped for coastal-defense duty late in the war. One day in July 1945, he went on, the intensity of his voice increasing with each sentence, he found himself in charge of an emplacement of ancient coastal guns just as an American flyer parachuted into Tokyo Bay. As the downed American swam toward his position, the youthful candidate-officer found his mind racing. What should he do? Kill him, or take him prisoner? Suddenly, he was spared the choice, for right there in middle of the bay, a U.S. submarine surfaced, scooped up the pilot, and submerged again, taking him to safety. At that moment in his story, the scholar broke off almost breathlessly, and said, "You see, that's the only kind of thing you'll hear. Pointless stories. It's too late to talk about crucial issues. All the people in decision-making posts are long dead." He than assured us in unambiguous terms that people's memories of those years had long faded, and emphasized again that the important stories, those that moved events in the war years, were no longer obtainable. Terminating the interview, he said with some condescension, but at the same time a hint of embarrassment, "You should read more."

It was a shock to hear the premise of our project rejected. Was it truly no longer possible to go beyond what was already in the history books to probe the experience of individual Japanese by seeking out and listening to the stories of those who had lived through the war years? As we thought about it later, we realized that he'd just told us a story which had revealed something of the dilemmas faced by Japanese in the war: How a young man balanced duty and desire; the strange moment when he himself faced the decision of whether or not to kill; and, as he told his story, the sudden insight it gave him into what his life would have been had he killed an American prisoner-of-war in the last moments of conflict.

So we began anyway, knowing that August was the best month for war research in Japan, and that August of 1988 was both a fortuitous and propitious one in which to launch our project. It seems that every year August 6 and August 9, the dates Hiroshima and Nagasaki were devastated by atomic bombs, and August 15, surrender day, serve as a focus for some reminiscing about the war. Television documentaries are aired, and newspapers often run series of short articles or letters by those remembering their wartime experiences. As if by general agreement, booksellers use August as the month to set up displays on the war years, exhibiting the latest military volumes and personal memories or collections of reminiscences, often published that month. Even old movies from the war years are sometimes revived by tiny movie houses in Tokyo, where they play to small audiences of mostly elderly patrons.

We were fortunate that as we began our work, a spate of memory pieces had begun to appear in the large daily papers in Japan. Most were only a few paragraphs long, snapshots in time, capturing a moment of crisis, or release, or realization, or horror. These pieces, fragments of released war memories from otherwise ordinary Japanese who clearly had lived silently with their war experiences for decades, were a little like flashes of lightning briefly illuminating bits of a dark landscape. They convinced us that the stories we sought were there and could be found. We began to search for our storytellers. A newspaper printed a haiku that used a line about the war to signify the season, which led to a poet-soldier willing to talk; tiny public notices of a meeting of veterans of an island campaign turned up a unit's sole survivor; a bulletin board carrying notice of a woman's search for the fate of missing childhood friends produced a tale of wartime bombing; and a classified ad appealing for even a few words about how a man's brother might have died led us to a family unable to forget for even a day. (Of course, obituaries often reminded us that the clock was ticking.) On such small clues, we began our search.

Interviews were usually arranged as one-on-one affairs. Indeed, we soon learned to avoid interviewing more than one person at a time, if at all possible, since group sessions tended to yield comfortable consensus rather than personal disclosure. It quickly became clear that the intense intimacy of the process was greatly enhanced by the ability of the speaker to share his or her story in seeming confidence. The interviews were usually conducted by Haruko. Occasionally, Ted also participated. We wanted to elicit from each person his or her individual memories and impressions of that time. We usually did not proceed with a set list of questions, but over the course of an interview tried to offer the interviewee full freedom to remember in his or her own way. This often took many hours. A pilot of a "human torpedo" told Haruko, "I've never talked this much before. Usually they just want to know, 'What's it like to go on a suicide mission?' Before I've said anything I wanted to say, the interview's over." We learned to listen, but not all were willing storytellers. A few who agreed to meet us found they could not bring themselves to describe what they had experienced, even when they clearly felt obliged to speak. Of course, others simply did not want to unearth what they considered unpleasant subjects. In such circumstances, the tone of an interview could become almost adversarial, but the answers thus elicited provided something of the missing picture. Indeed, *not* telling all was itself sometimes part of the story.

Whatever our methods of interviewing, the moment we chose to begin our project was serendipitous. In the Japan of the late 1980s, there seemed at last to be a growing willingness on the part of ordinary people to speak of their wartime experiences, and speak not just as if they had been the victims of a calamity, but to talk about what was done to others in Japan's name. Certainly, the end of the Shōwa era, on January 7, 1989, with the death of Emperor Hirohito whose reign had lasted just over sixty-three years, contributed to the sense of an epoch passing. For some, that date underlined their own mortality, and left them with a desire to release what they had been holding inside—if not to confess, at least to confide. At the same time, others took the Emperor's death as a moment to put the whole war behind them rather than to reflect on its meanings.

It may be hard for an American—used to a war with a distinct and accepted public story with a clear beginning (Pearl Harbor) and a clear end (Hiroshima and Japan's surrender); a war with its public monuments, from the *Arizona* memorial in Hawaii to the Iwo Jima memorial near Arlington National Cemetery in Washington; with numerous special museums and libraries dedicated to the war; with its exhibitions of public pride and public memory, its proud veterans ready to recount the exploits, glories, and horrors of various campaigns, and its decades of movie and TV retellings—to imagine the state of the war experience in contemporary Japan. It must be said that, for the Japanese, their war has almost none of that public quality. Films made during the war years are virtually never screened. The art and literature of those years—denied, denounced, and repudiated even by many of the artists who created it— is locked away. Often it is even omitted from an artist's "Complete Works," as if the fifteen years from 1931 to 1945 had never existed. The war as seen on television, despite valiant efforts by some independent producers to introduce critical questions into dramas and documentaries, still focuses mostly on Hiroshima and Japanese suffering in the years of defeat.

There is no national museum or archive to which children can go to find out about the war, or where students can freely examine wartime documents; no neutral national setting where one could study wartime art, explore major photo collections, or examine artifacts of daily life.

Although there are certainly displays in local museums devoted to those years, there is no concerted national effort to preserve, accumulate, and reconstruct the war from an historical perspective. Indeed, the only significant large collection of war memorabilia is held in the memorial hall at Yasukuni Shrine, which itself served as the focal point of the cult of the war dead in prewar and wartime Japan. Without a neutral public space for public investigation of, or reflection on, the war experience, scholars of today—and more importantly, those who wish to study the war years in the future—must depend on what little private documentation reaches the public.

As odd as it may seem, almost half a century after the conclusion of the conflict, the war doesn't even have a single nationally agreed-upon name. Throughout the course of our interviews people spoke of "the Pacific War," "the Greater East Asia War," "the China Incident," "the Japan-China War," "the Fifteen-Year War," or explained how the war in Asia was different from the rest of the "Second World War." The choice of name implies a choice of chronology—a given name might place the beginning of the war as early as 1931, or as late as 1941. Choice of name often also indicates ideological perspective. "The Fifteen-Year War"— generally a term of the left—emphasizes the imperialist origins of the war, beginning with Japan's seizure of Manchuria in 1931. "The Greater East Asia War"—now generally a term of the revisionist right—shows the speaker either still caught up in images of wartime, or still displaying a sympathy with the war's goals and objectives. (The term, which came into use immediately after December 8, 1941, was so closely linked with the concept of the creation of a Greater East Asia Co-Prosperity Sphere, declared to be one of the great objectives of Japan's war with the West, that it was specifically excluded from official publications by the Allied Occupation authorities after the surrender.) Most commonly chosen was probably "the Pacific War," the widely used term of the Occupation years and the name which most clearly differentiates between the open warfare that began in China in 1937—called the China Incident at the time, now sometimes called the Japan-China War—and the war with the U.S. and Britain which began in 1941. Using the Pacific War, in fact, freed many speakers from the need to refer to those years of combat and conquest in China at all. Most interviewees, however, preferred "the war" to any more elaborate name. On the most personal of levels, we came to see that each individual has his or her own notion of when that war began. To speak of "the war," meaning the Japanese conflict with the Soviet Union, for instance, could even mean a war that did not begin until August 9, 1945.

As it turned out, to make this book was to discover how hidden the memories of "the war" really are in Japan. To find the people who speak in these pages meant plunging into a half-hidden world of "sources" as well as an underground world of memories. At times, we were passed almost furtively along a chain of individuals, by private introduction, and in an atmosphere of hushed approval. Most of the time people approached individually agreed to speak only for themselves. Indeed, many emphasized their refusal to speak for anyone else, claiming that they knew only what they themselves had experienced.

Meetings often had a secretive quality to them. Many of the hundreds of people interviewed for this book had difficulty even deciding where they would feel safe to tell their stories. For most, it was clearly an issue of some import. Sometimes people chose the most impersonal or deserted of public settings, and so we interviewed on benches in the corners of busy railroad stations, back booths of underpopulated coffee shops, hospital cafeterias, paths separating flooded rice fields, the lobbies of hotels or clubs, or open areas in public parks with barely a bench to sit on. Other times, people felt safest inviting us not just into their homes, but into the shrine-like rooms within those homes that they had set up to remember the dead in utter privacy. More than one person described such a room or alcove, safe even from their own families, as "my *sanctum sanctorum*" or "my museum." Such a space might be simply adorned, with only a few personal photos from the war years set by a Buddhist altar, or packed from floor to ceiling with memorabilia, documents, books, photographs of lost friends, models of wartime ships and planes, or flags signed by long-dead war comrades. Letters, wills, professional blow-ups of treasured and well-worn photos of beloved relatives, poems, wartime diaries, military notebooks, even "souvenirs" from wartime China might be in these places. Bottles of sand and pebbles from a beach in the South Pacific, or stones from a mountain in Burma, brought back from more recent trips to the site of military disasters, were regularly a part of the interview environment.

Not surprisingly, people were often at a total loss for where to begin their stories, since the war in Japan has no generally accepted beginning point. Nor did people—except for the survivors of Hiroshima and Nagasaki, where there has been general agreement on ways to relate the story of what happened there—quite know *how* to tell their stories to another person, a public person, an outsider. Consequently, each interview proved less an experience in which a speaker could plug his or her story into an ongoing narrative than a struggle to create a structure for the tale as it was being told. This is why many of the stories—particularly of the years of defeat—have the feel of wanderings in a shapeless terrain.

Again and again, people halted, sometimes in midsentence, as if to question their own words, as if they could hardly believe that what they were telling us had actually taken place, or that they could have been the central characters in their own stories. "You can't believe me, can you?" they'd ask, only to continue, "But it was true." Or they would say, in almost the same words in interview after interview, "I know it seems impossible now, but that's what we truly thought then. We really believed that, from the bottom of our hearts." A nod of confirmation, an assurance that we did indeed believe them, was usually enough to send them back into the past.

For almost all of the people interviewed for this book, the experience of telling about their years at war was an incredibly fresh one, often an extraordinary return to memories held in privacy and silence for up to sixty years. As a consequence, almost *every* interview involved incredible outbursts of emotion. Tears were a commonplace—of sorrow, of bitterness or grief, of loving memory, of chagrin or even horror over acts committed. Voices choked. Bodies were convulsed with sobs. There were actual groans of pain and anguish, even the literal grinding of teeth. Loud voices boomed from small frames and old shoulders were squared, fists clenched, in anger and outrage. Laughter was rare, although sometimes ironic chuckles and self-deprecating smiles broke moments of great tension. One of the hidden obstacles to securing interviews with some of those who agreed to talk proved to be family members "concerned" that remembering would only cause pain. Perhaps the interviewees themselves, aware from a moment or two long ago, of what emotions might be released if they really let themselves recall their past, dreaded talking about it. When we shared their emotions, even cried with them on occasion, they took that as confirmation that they had communicated their own feelings, and sometimes even expressed gratitude for finally having been able to reveal themselves to another.

In this book, their stories have been arranged in rough chronological order, to convey a sense of the duration, scale, and course of the war as experienced in Japan. It was, of course, a conflict between nations, but for the soldiers, sailors, or airmen, no less the factory girls, farming wives, or workers in the Homeland, the experience was ultimately an individual one. We have selected people from general to private, prison-camp guard to journalist, dancer to diplomat, idealistic builder of "Greater East Asia" to "thought criminal," who talk revealingly of *their* wars. As the reader

approaches these individual accounts of wartime Imperial Japan, we feel
it might be useful to keep in mind four ways in which the Japanese
perception of the war differs from the American experience.

First, Japan was defeated, and there is no well-established narrative
form for telling the tale of the defeated. In war histories and literature
alike, the tale is often told most convincingly by the victors, even when
they shade the story in neutral tones. For the Japanese, even the victories
at Pearl Harbor and elsewhere in December 1941 and early 1942 do not
contribute the beginning of a narrative, as in America's war stories. When
asked, each interviewee can recall precisely where and how they learned
the news of Pearl Harbor and how they felt, but few of their own accord
make it the starting point for even a brief narrative of victory, of euphoria
and excitement, of successful battles won on land and sea. Pearl Harbor
is usually hardly mentioned in their stories. This omission perhaps
indicates how thoroughly the overwhelming defeats that came later
invalidated the obvious narratives of Japanese victories that otherwise
might have been told by the participants.

With neither a decisive beginning nor an ending point, Japanese
memories of the Pacific War can have a structureless quality in which the
individual wanders through endless dreamlike scenes of degradation, horror, and death, a shapeless nightmare of plotless slaughter. This formless
narrative of defeat—of soldiers overwhelmed in battle, or girls escaping
a Tokyo air raid, of a student nurse's living nightmare in Okinawa, or a
desperate mother's flight for her life in Manchuria—is how they tend to
see their war, at least in the instant they are recalling it. The country so
often portrayed in the West as a fanatical, suicidal nation, united in
purpose by their Emperor, looks more like a collection of confused,
terrorized, and desperate individuals beaten down by overwhelming
force.

So little in the public sphere stands between their war memories
and the moment of their telling decades later that the language of
those war years comes immediately back to their lips. Again and again,
such terms as *gyokusai* (sacrificial battles), *okuni no tame ni* (for the
country's sake), *tokkō* (special attack) and *kamikaze* (divine wind),
kempei (military police), *Tennō no sekishi* (the Emperor's children) are
used with immediacy, and specialized wartime words—*akagami* (red
paper, a call-up notice for military service), *sanpachijū* (Type-38, the
standard infantry rifle), *imonbukuro* (comfort bags, gifts for soldiers sent
from the Homeland), *bōkūzukin* (air-defense helmet, the padded
cotton headgear universally worn in the cities by women and children
late in the war)—pop into sentences as if they were current slang. For

instance *gyokusai*, whose literal meaning, "crushing the jewels," comes from ancient Chinese, was used widely in the war years to glorify dying and to create a heroic image of courageous soldiers charging into a cruel and overwhelming enemy force. A *gyokusai* battle like Saipan was as often as not a miserable slaughter of starving soldiers with nowhere to go, soldiers under iron-clad military orders forbidding them to surrender. While some of our interviewees used the word with a certain perspective simply to evoke the wartime atmosphere, many others used such antiquated, and historically discredited euphemisms at face value. For them, the postwar period had failed to coin new words that described the realities of their war.

A second point which should be remembered while reading the following accounts is that war responsibility is not clearly established in the minds of many Japanese today, no matter how certain the rest of the world may be about it. The Japanese people were not, in fact, held responsible for the war by the Allied occupation forces, who tried, convicted and executed selected Japanese leaders and military figures for plotting an "aggressive war" and for condoning and encouraging war crimes. The nature of Japanese responsibility for the war was further muddied when Emperor Hirohito, revered during the war as the figure from whom all authority to act was said to derive, was never charged. In fact, after declaring himself in January 1946 to be a human being and not divine, he was continued in office under a new postwar—and present—constitution as "the symbol of the unity of the people." In Germany, the Nazi Party and Hitler were linked and the dead Führer provided the focus of postwar attempts, however attenuated, to cleanse the society. While Japanese "militarism" in the form of military institutions could be abolished, and the new constitution might renounce war, there was no clear focal point for efforts in Japan to look at all the links between those who had power and wartime behavior.

The reader may then find the war memories presented here extremely personal in focus. Millions of Japanese who supported the national war effort to the last day without any active substantive resistance against their government or military found themselves amid the devastation of a defeated land reeling from personal loss. The war experience was largely shoved out of public view, buried beneath private pain. Larger questions of causality and responsibility were either passed along to the small group of convicted military leaders, politicians, industrialists, and bureaucrats singled out by the Allies, or deferred to the Occupation forces who replaced the authority of the military government. Sorting out the war experience, with some notable individual exceptions, found little place in the public sphere in a country where all that now seemed to matter was rebuilding and starting again. The issue of Imperial responsibility for the origins and execution of the war was left largely unexplored.°

Emperor Hirohito never discussed the war with his own people. As a result, in the forty-four postwar years of his reign, the Emperor whom the wartime generation had been taught to worship as a living god, and in whose name so many had died, never clearly accepted or assigned responsibility for the decisions which brought about the war or the acts which occurred during it. Despite the fact that the war was fought under his command, very few of the people in this book mention him when they explain their experience, except for those who were in elementary school in those years, and grew up thinking of themselves as the "Emperor's children." When he is mentioned, it is usually only with reference to his war responsibility.

Third, in some of these interviews, people introduce the notion of "a Good Defeat." That defeat can bestow benefits is not a concept likely to occur to an American reader attuned to seeing the war from the perspective of an unconditional surrender forced on an implacable foe, in which there could have been no substitute for victory. The idea today takes much of its impetus from postwar Japanese economic achievement and is founded on the position Japan today holds internationally. This complex and sometimes conflicted "lesson" of the war is seldom a fully resolved one for any of the people who used it. For example, Zen priest Itabashi Kōshū, who attended the naval academy in the last year of the war, summed up the war's legacy by saying, "If Japan had stopped that war after taking the Philippines—you know, gotten a decent settlement —it would have ended up with Taiwan and Korea, but even they would eventually have been separated from Japan. How long that would have taken I don't know, but it would have been a long struggle. I believe because Japan lost, today's prosperity exists." He was quick to add, "Now, I'm not saying it is better to lose a war, I'm only saying that if you fight a war seriously, its impact remains. We fought the war thoroughly, with all

---

° Perhaps the most notable exception was the Japanese Communist Party, whose members, most released from jail only in 1945, were among the first to criticize the entire prewar and wartime regime and to denounce the Emperor's role in the war. Progressive scholars of various political persuasions, including the political scientist Maruyama Masao, also tried to address crucial wartime issues, and there were, as well, creative works that questioned the nature of the war—novels like *Zone of Emptiness* by Noma Hiroshi and *Fires on the Plain* by Ōoka Shōhei, films like the *The Human Condition* by Kobayashi Masaki, and the mural paintings of Maruki Iri and Maruki Toshi [see Chapter 12];—and rare individuals like Ienaga Saburō [see Chapter 23] who has conducted a one-man crusade on the subject of how the war should be treated in school textbooks. But on the whole, such efforts did not kindle widespread debate or reassessment.

our energies, and we lost. It was better to do it that way than to take an intermediate path. I am prepared to say aloud, it is good that we lost. We have to pray for the war dead. We must pray for the victims of the war."

Many of those we interviewed rejected the very idea that nothing good came out of that terrible war and those awful "sacrifices." Many felt impelled to find in it something to give meaning to their efforts. Almost inverting the more common theme, the younger sister of a navy Special Attack officer took solace from the knowledge that her brother had died in an accident. "That means," she said, "he never took anyone's life, although he died in the war." There was also a desperate sense that even defeat must have had a purpose, that it could not all have been in vain. Often this took the form of speaking about Japan's release from militarism. As Haratani Ichirō, the ninety-four year-old retired chairman of one of Japan's largest corporations, put it, "Swaggering military men and rigid bureaucrats! If they were ultimately victorious, where would that have led?"

A fourth point that may give the reader pause is how rare are Japanese invocations of the enemy, or of hatred for the enemy, and how nearly the war becomes almost an enemy-less conflict. Rather than seeing defeat coming at the hands of the American, Chinese, or other Allied peoples, the Japanese here are far more likely to attribute defeat to Allied production processes, to blame materiel more than people. When they speak of enemies, they may use the slogans of war—"Anglo-American demons," for instance—in a limited way, but rarely do these bear the sting, the fervor, the racial hatred of terms like "the Japs," often encountered in Western reminiscences.

It may also be important to note here what this book is not. For the most part, there is little discussion of war strategy and only occasional mention of Japanese planning for the war. This is not—as that political science professor who was our first interviewee predicted—a collection of Japanese political or military leaders reflecting on *their* war. There emerges here no clear overview of the war. Very few of our interviewees looked back and tried to reach conclusions about the overall experience of war. Rare indeed was the person able or willing to put his or her own story into the larger context of the war, no less the global situation of that time and its implications. No elegant and simple assessments appear here. The conclusions of most Japanese about the war are "small" and personal, and it may not be going too far to say that a summing up of the war experience has yet to happen in Japan.

Fifty years after the war, the generation that was in charge of Japan's political, military, and industrial apparatus is largely gone, and only a few who held prominent positions spoke to us. Others who could have spoken refused. The industrial barons who profited from Japanese expansion in the prewar era, whose factories produced much of Japan's war supplies, and whose firms have found their way back into leadership in today's economy are not represented here. This book cannot claim to be all-inclusive, but those people whose stories are here were selected from among all our interviewees for the widest possible spectrum of experience.

In the course of the many conversations and interviews conducted for this book, we realized that these memories of wartime have rarely been sought out. For much of the Japanese public, memories of the war that ended in defeat seem too unpleasant, too embarrassing, too barren, too futile, too painful, and as a great many people told us, "too stupid," to be dwelled on. They derive no comfort from such memories. For many, their thoughts seem frozen in the past, a state that precludes giving new meanings to, or seeking out new interpretations of, their emotions and acts of the war years. Two incidents may illustrate how the experiences of the past are still locked up inside people of the wartime generation.

One Saturday in September 1989, Haruko was invited to attend the annual reunion of the "Changi Association." She had already interviewed several of the group's members, military men convicted of war crimes in 1946 and 1947 and subsequently imprisoned in Singapore's Changi prison—itself the site of many atrocities during Japan's occupation of Singapore. The meeting was to take place at Tokyo Daihanten, one of the capital's most famous Chinese restaurants. Arriving there, she immediately noted in the lobby a prominent "Changi Gathering" sign of the type used for wedding parties. It seemed inappropriately open for a group of men convicted of war crimes in Southeast Asia. In the small private dining room, two large round tables had been set up and men in suits and ties, about twenty in all, were already greeting each other quietly. The tables were well-supplied with appetizers, and the first bottles of beer and Bireley's orange soda were just being opened as the chairman, Dr. Wakamatsu Hitoshi, rose to convene the meeting. He assured the group that he had fully recovered from pacemaker implantation, and then spoke of two men who had passed away since their last meeting, and of one other who was unable to attend because of illness. He then led the group in a toast to the members' health, "Kampai!" and everyone plunged into dinner. Conversation bubbled up about travels made, grandchildren born, and children promoted. The Changi veterans laughed, drank, and repeatedly filled each other's beer glasses, but through all the meal's courses, no one referred to the war or mentioned Changi. The meal over, money having been collected for the dinner, and the necessary bows of farewell exchanged, the men went their separate ways. By eight o'clock, less than two hours after the meeting began, Haruko found herself alone in the room with the Changi veteran who had invited her. He seemed to note her bewilderment, and said softly, "As I told you, all that brings us together is that we all spent time at Changi. Most of them never reveal anything about their trials. They seem ready to take all their memories to their graves."

Even those who went through the scrutiny of investigation, trial, punishment, and years of imprisonment do not to this day seem able to fully share the past with each other. They may, however, find in those who did share something of their experience a comfort, a warmth of familiarity, which protects them from feeling absolutely alone with their memories. Inside the group, they are free not to ask questions of themselves, not to examine their most basic assumptions. Turning inward towards those who share, at least in time or place, a similar experience, can provide a way to sustain something of that time. Within the group, there is the possibility of clinging to values attached to memories of friends and comrades lost in the war.

For example, a woman whose husband had died forty-five years earlier as a *Tokkō*, a member of the Special Attack Corps, told Haruko of her friends, "We four or five widows of Tokkō pilots—there are so few of us, since they all died so young—we see each other once a year, at a memorial ceremony to the Tokkō. In March, April, and May, all of us get strangely restless, because they all took off around that time. The season of cherry blossoms is the most painful time for us. We chat over the phone about things that happened more than forty years ago as if they took place yesterday." With a conspiratorial air, and yet almost playfully, she confided. "My closest friend and I secretly pledged to each other that we will have a tiny piece of our cremated bones released into the ocean after we die." She believes that those bones, after a journey of many millennia, will eventually reach the sea off Okinawa, where their husbands plunged to their deaths. "We are going to do it in secret, because it's illegal to scatter a person's ashes without permission from the Ministry of Health and Welfare." Quietly she added, "I don't know if my husband actually crashed into the enemy, but some did. I want to believe that he didn't die in vain."

Like the Tokkō pilot's wife, like the veterans of Changi, those who remember the dead of those years do so in private, in hushed tones, or in surreptitious or silent communion. But it is our belief that the living will not rest easy in the public sphere until that increasingly ancient, but still living, war is no longer avoided, but instead faced and examined in public, and until the complex Japanese experiences of the war are opened to all and become a matter of public discussion and public understanding, in both the U.S. and Japan. Our hope is that this book will help begin that task.

PART ONE

An Undeclared War

By the august virtue of His Majesty, our naval and military forces have captured Canton and the three cities of Wuhan; and all the vital areas of China have thus fallen into our hands. The Kuomintang Government exists no longer except as a mere local regime. However, so long as it persists in its anti-Japanese and pro-Communist policy our country will not lay down its arms—never until that regime is crushed.

What Japan seeks is the establishment of a new order that will insure the permanent stability of East Asia. In this lies the ultimate purpose of our present military campaign.

This new order has for its foundation a tripartite relationship of mutual aid and co-ordination between Japan, Manchukuo, and China in political, economic, cultural, and other fields. Its object is to secure international justice, to perfect the joint defense against Communism, and to create a new culture and realize a close economic cohesion throughout East Asia. This indeed is the way to contribute toward stabilization of East Asia and the progress of the world.

—Statement by the Japanese Government of
Prime Minister Konoe Fumimaro, *November 3, 1938*

JAPAN'S WAR did not begin with Pearl Harbor. For almost four-and-one-half years before December 7, 1941, Japan and China had been embroiled in an undeclared war of continental proportions. That war raged from Manchuria in the north to the borders of French Indochina in the south, and from the international port city of Shanghai for a thousand miles up the Yangtze River, past the capital, Nanking, to Chungking —which General Chiang Kai-shek, China's president, had declared his new capital in the face of the deep advances of Japan's armies. By 1941, nearly 300,000 Japanese soldiers had died in China, and over a million were deployed across the country, occupying most of its major cities, all of its ports, and most of the rail lines connecting them. Millions of Chinese had perished, and still no end was in sight.

The precise start of this war is by no means easy to pin down. From the early years of the twentieth century when central imperial authority collapsed, China was a country in near chaos, wracked by civil wars, divided among warlord regimes, and prey to foreign encroachments. In the wake of the Sino-Japanese War of 1894–95, the Boxer Rebellion of 1900, and the Russo-Japanese War of 1904–05, Japan forced the Chinese to grant them special privileges, and economically it penetrated China's ports and internal cities (as had the Western powers before them). Japan took advantage of the First World War to improve its position at the expense of the West, but the Japanese did not move decisively to take control of Chinese territory until the Manchurian Incident of September 1931.

Japan's army had three years earlier secretly assassinated Chang Tso-lin, the warlord of vast and mineral-rich Manchuria, which bordered Korea (already annexed to Japan in 1910), in the vain hope that the area would not declare its allegiance to the Nationalist Chinese government in Nanking. In 1931 they moved to wrest control of Manchuria from Chang's son, Chang Hsieuh-liang. The Japanese forces responsible for railroad security themselves blew up a section of the line outside the Manchurian city of Mukden, and then, blaming the Chinese, sent in troops.

The extent of Japan's involvement in creating the "incidents" (always blamed on Chinese "aggression") that led to the taking of Manchuria was unknown to most Japanese, whose news was already managed by the government, but the results of the Manchurian Incident were for the most part widely welcomed. In 1932, Manchuria was proclaimed the independent state of Manchukuo—"the Country of the Manchus"—with Pu-Yi, the "last emperor" of China, installed as its ruler. But "his" country and government were largely fictions in a land run by Japan's

Kwantung Army, which garrisoned the territory, ostensibly to protect Japanese rights and property.

To many Japanese, Manchuria promised to be a foundation for Japanese economic recovery in a world grown hostile and unstable in the midst of the Great Depression. Manchuria was viewed as a new world to be settled and developed. Its coal and iron and its potential for abundant agricultural produce were considered essential for Japanese economic development, and its vast territory was seen as a vital outlet for Japan's burgeoning population. The "natives" were thought of largely as temporary impediments to final control, or as a source of cheap and obedient labor. Through the early and mid-years of the decade, Japanese-controlled Manchukuo seemed an oasis of stability, troubled only by a few unruly "bandits," while beyond its borders, the rest of China continued to be wracked by widespread internal strife. In these years, the Chinese Nationalists launched their "extermination and encirclement" campaigns against the Communists—whom they regularly referred to as "bandits" —eventually forcing Mao Tse-tung and the remnants of his People's Army to embark on their Long March from the south to Shensi province in the north, far from China's heartland, but close to Manchuria.

Fighting between Japanese and Chinese troops broke out near the Marco Polo Bridge outside Peiping in northern China on July 7, 1937. Instead of being resolved at the level of local commanders, as had happened so many times in the past, usually with the Chinese conceding territory, this time armed clashes spread. Open warfare was soon raging across North China and it quickly flared in central China and the edge of the great international city of Shanghai, where the Nationalist Armies committed their best troops. Neither side declared war officially, but the Japan-China war had begun. It would not end for eight years.

In the years of war on the continent that preceded the war Americans are most familiar with, one can recognize several aspects of Japan's behavior that were to become fully obvious after Pearl Harbor. First was miscalculation. The war that would not end presaged the even more disastrous military and power miscalculations to come in the war against the Western allies. That the one war led to the other (because of Japan's need for vital resources such as petroleum), rather than deterring it on the most pragmatic grounds, shows how unrealistic Japanese decision-making was at the end of four frustrating years caught in the China quagmire. Japan's war aims, which in 1937 seemed to be to chastise China and perhaps nip off a province in the north, had already, a year later, swollen to embrace the creation of the "permanent stability of East Asia." From then to the onset of the Pacific War, the grandiosity of

Japanese aims continued to inflate while Japan's measurable capabilities seemed to reach their limits.

Second, in the Japan-China war, one can recognize a complex—and in the end self-defeating—mixture of attitudes toward other Asians. Although Japan wanted to control lands belonging to other peoples, it preferred to conceal that control behind a mask of liberation. The forms of Japan's post-1941 Greater East Asia Co-Prosperity Sphere were first seen in Manchukuo and then in the new "Nationalist" Government the Japanese set up in occupied Nanking in 1939 under Wang Ching-wei—a leading civilian defector from the Chinese Nationalist Party. In each situation, Japan tried to employ a fiction of normality in the areas where Japanese troops were deployed, ceding a form of government to the "natives," and promoting slogans like "Asia for the Asians." Yet its unwillingness to hand over actual power, much less anything faintly approaching "independence," led to puppet regimes that offered no real vehicle for channeling local energies, or anti-Western sentiments, into support of the Japanese cause. They were empty shells.

The Japanese people, and the army in particular, were also steeped in a deep sense of superiority to other Asians. Japan was paternalistic in the best of times—it often presented itself as an elder brother "leading the newly emerging members of the Asian family toward development." Such feelings, and a code of behavior that placed little value on the rights and privileges of an enemy population, left Japanese soldiers and civilians capable in wartime of committing shocking and widespread war crimes —of the sort recounted in the following pages—without a prevailing feeling that these were morally reprehensible. They were simply seen as acts integral to the process of war itself.

Of the war crimes, perhaps the most infamous was the "Rape of Nanking." Accounts of Japanese soldiers wantonly murdering Chinese civilians and prisoners in an orgy of violence lasting weeks following the capture of the city December 12, 1937, were recorded by Chinese survivors and foreign diplomats, missionaries, businessmen, and journalists. Those accounts, widely distributed throughout the world—but kept out of Japan by a tight net of censorship, except for a small article or two in local papers—contributed to the revulsion felt by many outsiders at the notion of Japan's "cause" in China. In Japan, however, the news was all about the capture of the enemy capital, and the fall of Nanking led to euphoric marches, celebrations, and parades. Surely the war was now virtually over, and it was ending in the anticipated Japanese victory—or so the Japanese public believed. But the Chinese did not sue for peace.

During the conflict, the undeclared war on the continent was, of course, not portrayed to the Japanese people as a war of brutal or naked aggression. Victories were said to be the product of hard struggle, loyal service, and dogged devotion to the cause of the nation. But the true nature of the conflict was clear to the soldiers who fought in it—men from all parts of Japan, all classes, and all walks of life—and many of those men did return home when released from service, though they were often called up again. The events of Nanking were replicated in everyday ways throughout the war years in China, and later in southeast Asia and the Pacific—the product of arrogance, frustration, and a military system that placed little value on the lives of foreign natives or prisoners, and ultimately, in the final stages of the war, even on those of the Japanese themselves.

The third major way the war in China indicated what lay ahead may be seen in how Japan marshaled its people and resources for the war effort. The war—or at least a certain presentable version of it—was used to mobilize and control the Japanese people and to repress any opposition, not just to the prosecution of the war, but also to the government, the army, and the Emperor.

Newspapers, journals, and picture magazines were filled with stirring reports and images from the front. Newsreel cameras recorded dramatic footage of battles. There seemed to be a mountain of news, but what was permitted to be said was tightly controlled from the earliest moments of the "China Incident," as the war continued to be called even as it dragged on. Scenes of slaughter, Japanese casualties, and the realities of the dirty war "behind the lines" were censored. The public was urged, indeed driven, into mass expression of its support. Those who expressed any doubts, not to say opposition, soon found themselves under attack. Ideological opponents of the Emperor system were completely excluded from political life. Most members of the Communist Party either had been imprisoned or been forced to "change their views" after arrest. The few still at large were in hiding. Progressive thinkers, writers, and professors who did not wholeheartedly embrace national policies were immediately attacked even for showing concern over how village widows and orphans of those who had died in the war would survive or for raising questions about the inflation that resulted from massive war expenditures.

In a phrase already coming into use, this war was *seisen*, "sacred war" conducted under the leadership of the Emperor himself. The war in China was proclaimed not merely justifiable, but also all but won, even though ten months after the capture of the enemy capital should have led to a negotiated surrender, there was still no sign that China was prepared to yield. The war was protected from all criticism. Not everyone in Japan was convinced that its "sacredness" was justification enough for fighting such a costly war, particularly when the total of one hundred thousand killed in action was reached in 1940. A few voices called for an explanation, but when Diet member Saitō Takao asked for a more concrete reason for the nation's sacrifice, he was expelled from the house for insulting the objective of the sacred war and the spirits of the war dead, and most of his offensive questions were expunged from the record. This mobilization offered a strong taste of what was to come after 1941 when the government bent all its powers to create a nation of a hundred million people prepared for death.

When the Second World War broke out in Europe in September 1939, the effects were felt in East Asia as well. After the fall of the Netherlands and then France to Hitler's armies in May 1940, supply routes to China through British Burma and French Indochina were temporarily closed, but at the urging of the United States, once the crisis of the Battle of Britain had passed, supplies again went through overland to Chungking. To Japanese military and government figures, resolving the conflict with China now seemed to require control over an even broader area. The "South" came to seem more and more attractive to Japan as the source of all the vital raw materials the Western nations threatened to deny Japan in pursuit of its war in China. The only way to control China, it seemed, was to control East Asia as a whole. When the Japanese army moved to occupy southern Indochina, despite American warnings, the government had already calculated that the only way to break the stalemate in China was to risk a war with the whole world.

To this day, not only is the Japan-China war the part of the war least known to the Americans (who naturally tend to date the war 1941–1945), but it is also remarkably ill-defined and poorly understood by Japanese as well. And yet the Second World War in the Pacific began in China in 1937, with its roots in 1931. The China front, pinning down a million Japanese troops and claiming by 1945 a total of about four hundred thousand Japanese war dead, remained the war that would not go away until August 1945. Then, in a matter of days, Soviet troops overran Manchuria, where it all had begun. ∎

1 / BATTLE LINES IN CHINA

A Village Boy Goes to War

NOHARA TEISHIN

Seventy-four years old, he sits in front of an open hearth in the center of the tatami room of an old farmhouse in Toga, a remote mountain village in Toyama prefecture in central Japan. The mountains and ridges visible through the open windows are midsummer bright green, their rounded tops wreathed in clouds.

He brings out an ink stick and an inkstone. "I 'requisitioned' this from a Chinese house," he says. Then he spreads out a large Sun Disk Japanese flag, which has a small bluish purple stamp in the corner stating: "In Commemoration of the Fall of Nanking. Field Post Office." It is dated December 13, 1937, the day after the Japanese army entered the Chinese capital of Nanking.

My father made charcoal. We didn't have enough wood on our mountainsides for our ovens, so we had to buy other people's trees, and then haul the charcoal to town using our horse and cart. The mountains here are so steep that terracing fields for rice took too much labor. We ate millet and buckwheat instead. I remember Grandmother, exhausted from her day's labor, dozing off while turning the millstones to grind those grains. White rice was something I ate only three times a year—at the O-Bon festival for the dead in August, at the village festival, and at New Year's.

Every winter, my father had to go far away to work in a copper mine in Tochigi prefecture, because we get such heavy snowfall here. It comes right up over the first floor. My mother was taken away from me when I was only two. My grandparents brought me up. Grandmother opposed my going to agricultural school, because, as she said, "No one who's gone to school from this village ever came back." So I only had six years of elementary education.

In 1934, I walked the twenty kilometers down to Inami, then took the train to Jōhana for my military physical. All my classmates from Toga Village were there. Well, actually, one was missing. We heard he'd killed himself in Kyoto, but since they'd never found the body, he was still on the army register.

Of the forty from our village, ten were passed as Class A, fully fit for military service. I was one of them. After the exam, the administrators told us that two of those examined had achieved scores at the level equivalent to middle-school graduates, Kasahara Akira and Nohara Teishin. They said that about me right in front of everybody! I swaggered a lot, I guess, though the whole town was praised for ten A's.

In the evening we returned to Inami and stayed in an inn where the village mayor and village assemblymen held a party for us. The night of the physical was a time for celebration. The A's were seated on a dais at the front of the room, and we could drink as much saké as we pleased. But I've never been much of a drinker. I like tea. We returned to the village the next day.

I entered the Thirty-Fifth Infantry Regiment in Toyama in January 1935. All recruits got ordinary combat training. In addition, we had to learn one of the special skills for which we alone would be responsible, jobs like using and detecting poison gas, firing a machine-gun, or launching grenades. My speciality was communications. I had to learn to send signals by flag, hand, telephone, or telegraph. The least popular speciality was bugler, because you couldn't really get to private first class from there, and you didn't want to be assigned to look after the horses, since then you hung around waiting for some officer who needed a horse. Medics and stretcher-bearers didn't make private first class in peacetime either. Now, the gas soldiers, they really needed a brain to identify the types of gas, so they were promoted first. In communications and signals, if you were sharp, you could get ahead, too, but you had to get that Morse code into your head. Dah-dah-dit, dah-dah. You sent telegrams by numbers, and at first I didn't think those numbers would ever sink in, but somehow I learned.

It was still peacetime when I first went to Manchuria at the end of 1935. We worked to maintain the security of Manchukuo by suppressing bands of bandits who each day picked a new place to plunder. They were just thieves. They used small Chinese ponies to carry off the things they stole. Women, especially young girls, were prime targets. The Japanese pioneers built walls around their villages to keep the bandits out. Their fields were beyond the wall. Though some places had their own independent garrisons, we in the army were supposed to provide security so that the people could live in peace. But China is a vast country, wider than you can imagine.

We marched and marched from valley to mountain. Marching was our job. We'd go out for about a month at a time, rest for a month or two, then go out again. Normally, we'd go out in company-size expeditions of about two hundred men, leaving the rest of the unit behind to garrison the base.

On bandit-suppression operations there were times we got into fire-fights and actually saw them face-to-face, but we were always in the mountains. I was fed up with mountains. Bushes and underbrush reached your chest and you had to push them out of the way. You quickly became exhausted. After a month, you could hardly move. Those of us from mountainous areas had the stamina to endure that, but quite a few soldiers from the cities, who had made their living with paper and brush, weren't able to keep up with us.

I returned home at the completion of my term of service in December 1936. Back in the village, all we talked about was when our next call-up would come. We followed the newspapers and listened to the radio about the war in China, which began in July 1937. I was drafted the tenth of September 1937 and was sent straight to Central China. I was in the Fujii Unit of my old Thirty-Fifth Regiment. My speciality was still signals. There were nine or ten men under my command. We went into action the night of October 3. We crossed a granite bridge spanning a creek to string wires from the brigade all the way to regimental head-quarters. I was at one end of the bridge directing things and some of my soldiers were connecting wire on the bridge when a trench-mortar round exploded. Shrapnel hit one soldier, blowing a big hole in his chest. He died instantly. Another was hit in the arm. It was dangling limply. I tied it up with a towel and bound his hand so it wouldn't flop around. A third man was hit in the leg. I was the leader of the first squad to suffer casualties in Toyama's Thirty-Fifth Regiment in the China Incident.

You had a heavy responsibility when you laid wire. You had to figure out the distance between the positions you were going to link. That determined how much wire each soldier would have to carry on his back besides his rifle and other equipment. Often it was more than humanly possible. We stretched wire as much as we could. Bullets would some-times hit the wire and cut it. A dead telephone line meant I had to have soldiers run back without equipment to find the break, and then detach men to go back and repair it. After all, we were the link between brigade and regimental headquarters.

At the beginning of the war, the enemy was quite strong, and Japanese soldiers simply formed a line and, when officers gave the order, advanced. Our Thirty-Fifth Regiment was almost annihilated that way in the early battles. At a terrible place we called Susaku Seitaku, we had our toughest fight. The enemy was under cover, shooting at us through loop-holes in walls, so our dead just piled up. We were in the open fields.

"Charge! Forward! Forward!" came the orders, so you'd run a bit, then fall flat, calm your breathing, then charge again. Out of two hundred men, only ten or so weren't killed, wounded, or just worn out. Soldiers were expended like this. All my friends died there. You can't begin to really describe the wretchedness and misery of war.

The regimental commander called to find out why Colonel Shinkai, Third Battalion commander, hadn't taken the position yet. Shinkai told him these methods wouldn't work, that the Imperial Army wasn't marching across China in a flag-taking competition. "If you expend your soldiers here, you cannot continue afterwards." Thanks to Shinkai, from then on, even if it took two or three days to outflank a position, we adopted new tactics. He made us dig trenches all around. It was a kind of mole strategy, attacking only after approaching in trenches. First and Second Battalions also copied our tactics.

But the battles were always severe. There are many creeks in Central China. The dead Japanese and Chinese would just fall into them and get tangled up on the surface. Many hundreds at once. It was a gruesome thing. The corpses would block your way. If you pushed at them with a stick, they moved easily, the whole mass floating away. We drew water from those creeks to drink and cook our rice.

Cholera soon spread. The men with cholera we'd put in a bamboo grove. The grove was surrounded by a rope and the patients promised not to leave. Nobody really prepared food for them. So I'd take my friend's rice and cook it for him. It was said that if you got too close, you'd be infected. But I passed things to him on the end of a bamboo pole. He'd beg, "Give me water, give me water." I had to do something. I boiled water in my mess kit for him. When we were at rest I could do something, but when we went into battle, I had to leave him. I don't know how often the medics came to take care of them. I just felt pity for my own friend. Many died. My friend did, too.

We fought our way to Nanking and joined in the attack on the enemy capital in December. It was our unit which stormed the Chunghua Gate. We attacked continuously for about a week, battering the brick and earth walls with artillery, but they never collapsed. The night of December 11, men in my unit breached the wall. The morning came with most of our unit still behind us, but we were beyond the wall. Behind the gate great heaps of sandbags were piled up. We cleared them away, removed the lock, and opened the gates, with a great creaking noise. We'd done it! We'd opened the fortress! All the enemy ran away, so we didn't take any fire. The residents too were gone. When we passed beyond the fortress wall we thought *we* had occupied this city.

The Thirty-Fifth Regiment received a citation from the general staff, but the citation stated that the Twentieth Regiment had occupied the gate and the Thirty-Fifth had only then passed through. That same night, a scouting party of two or three officers from the Twentieth Regiment—they were from Fukuyama and Kyoto, and were next to us on the front line—had made it to the gate and written on it that it had been seized by their unit. So we were robbed of the flowers of glory, because we hadn't scribbled anything on the gate!

The next day, a Japanese pacification unit arrived and memorial stamp pads were made. I used the stamp on my Japanese flag, as a souvenir. There were hardly any Chinese people about, only the ones who could barely move. We gathered them later into a single area where they weren't in our way. We didn't kill them. I'd say we made them live a "communal life."

Nanking was a grand city. Chiang Kai-shek had kept it as his capital. I saw the tomb of Sun Yat-sen, where the father of modern China was buried. It was really regrettable that most of the town was practically destroyed, from the shelling and air raids. This was the capital of China —like Tokyo in Japan—so we had to do it, but it was still a shame. All the buildings in ruins. Bombed areas were uninhabitable, not even a store anymore. Wherever you went there were Japanese. All military. Hundreds of thousands of troops converged on Nanking. This many people couldn't really remain in there, so the Thirty-Fifth Regiment was ordered to return to Soochow.

The Japanese army was now strung out all over both North and Central China. We in the Thirty-Fifth Regiment were supposed to be mountain men, so we got orders to march on Hsüchow directly through the mountains in early July 1938. We faced tough situations regularly. On one occasion I was in the regimental office when a final call from a sergeant-major came in. "We're under attack. We regret that we're running out of ammunition. Our soldiers have kept a last bullet for themselves in order to make our final decision." Then the phone went dead. Even now my heart aches and I choke up like this when I remember that there were moments like that.

I took part in a "ceremony for the cremation of the dead." Among the dead men was one from this village, from this very hamlet. All you did was pull down any house nearby, pile up the wood, then lay on bodies. It was like baking sardines. You just set fire to it and let the flames consume the wood. Then you took up bones from the parts that burned, put them in a bag, and filled out a tag with the dead man's name. You said a silent prayer, sure, but there wasn't any "ceremony." It was war, so you couldn't help it. When it rained you couldn't even really burn them, so say the battalion commander had died, you'd burn just his body and distribute bits of his bones to the rest. You can't tell this kind of truth to the families of the deceased! So you burn what you can quickly. You just do it, keep going. Ten. Twenty. You have to move fast. The further behind you fall, the faster you must march to catch up. Every soldier wants to get back to his unit before it's too far away. That's how soldiers think.

Once we crossed two mountains in pursuit of the enemy. There wasn't one tree, not one blade of grass, and we had horses loaded with radio equipment and wire. We went to farmers' houses and requisitioned —pillaged, actually—clothing to wrap the horses' legs in, to protect them from the rocks. Those horses were strong climbers, but the descent, that gave them real trouble. They'd slip, going down, even though I had my men carry the equipment.

Stealing of horses began there, I think. They'd break their legs, or become unfit for service. You'd need a replacement. Horse-handlers were each assigned their own horse, but when the soldier was asleep the rope restraining the horse could be cut and the horse led away.

This happened to us. We had only a single horse left to carry all our gear. I ordered the groom to tie himself to it overnight, but the rope was cut anyway. When he came to tell me, it was already after dawn. My squad couldn't move out. I told them to wait and I went hunting. Soon enough, I came across a horse tied to a tree. It belonged to a cavalryman. He was a slight distance away. He looked like he was taking a shit. I ran up, untethered it, jumped on, and rode away. I had become a horsethief in broad daylight! I cut the horse's mane here and there to change the look of the horse. That was how it was in China. We stole horses, even within our own regiment, but we were responsible for moving our own equipment, so how else could we fight the war?

When we came across wounded Chinese soldiers or those on the verge of death, we'd kick them out of the way. I didn't harbor any ill feeling toward them. Wounded Japanese soldiers were lying all over the place. That's war. I had no way to take care of them. I had the feeling that before long I would be one of them anyway. Sometimes I spoke to them. Other times I didn't. If I recognized a face, I couldn't help but say something. Even if a soldier was from your own hamlet, all you could say was "Do your best. A medic will get here soon. Hold on." Then you'd keep going.

There are songs about war comrades who never desert each other. But China was no song. The fallen don't say, "Please go on ahead." They're hurting and ask for help. But you have to advance to carry out your duty. The ones left behind, maybe they're collected later by a medic and get treatment at a temporary dressing station, or maybe they're even taken to a hospital, maybe not. I feel lucky that I was never on a stretcher. My unit "returned home in triumph" after two and a half years.

When I got home, how could I tell my friend's parents that he'd died of cholera? I told them he'd been killed by a stray bullet. I came back without a scar. I worried they might think I'd been hiding myself. There was no place to hide. China was really flat. I was assigned to the responsible position of squad leader. I never acted in a way that others could accuse me. In the field, we often talked about "luck with bullets." There were two or three like me in that unit of two hundred, who didn't get even a scratch. I didn't even take a day off for a cold.

I went back and forth two more times after that. Each time I was discharged I came home thinking I'd be sent back again soon. They simply let us rest a little, that's all. Four times I went in, if you include my active duty. Nobody fights a war because they like it. "Nation's orders," "Emperor's orders"—that's what they said. What could you do but go? If an order was issued and you didn't go, you were a traitor. There's not one soldier who ever died saying *"Tennō Heika banzai!"* [Long Live the Emperor!] I was with hundreds of men when they died. The dead lay with grimaces on their faces.

My prime time, my youth, was all spent in the army. I reached the highest enlisted rank, but I always thought it was a lot better sitting at home here in Toga than being a sergeant-major.

Pictures of an Expedition

TANIDA ISAMU [1]*

On the wall is a picture of his father in the full uniform of a lieutenant general of infantry, his chest full of medals and awards. Next to that is his own picture. In it, he is wearing his army uniform, but displaying no honors. He was a lieutenant general of the engineers. He is now ninety-three years old.

"I commanded the largest number of engineers under one man's command in the history of the Japanese army during the Kwantung Army Special Maneuvers of 1941. I was given a special unit for the task—six regiments, thirty companies. I was the commander of the engineers, but engineers really belong to other people—regiment, division, and corps commanders—so at the time, I wasn't too thrilled by this job; but I'm

---

* A number of the interviews have been divided into two segments. Tanida's interview continues in Chapter 20.

very, very proud of it now. I just can't really boast openly about it because it was only an exercise for operations against our hypothetical enemy the Soviet Union. We never got to actually do it. I would have been bridging the Ussuri River, and the Amur, too—the Black Dragon, one thousand three hundred meters wide!" He points to a framed photograph showing a great river and a tremendous pontoon bridge stretching out onto it. "I took that photograph with the Leica I purchased during my study trip to Germany."

He wants to talk about the factional battles within the Imperial Army in the 1930s, on which he considers himself the sole surviving and leading expert. After recommending his book on the subject, he holds forth on the topic for several hours, in a most animated manner, until the subject of the war finally comes up.

I was a lieutenant colonel at the time of the China Incident in July 1937, and I was a staff officer in the Tenth Army during the landings and seizure of Hangchow Bay on November 5, 1937—part of the critical flanking move around the Chinese positions in front of Shanghai that led to their collapse and the capture of the Chinese capital of Nanking.

The Kaikōsha (the former army officers' association) recently published a book about Nanking. You were there in China when Nanking was captured, weren't you? How many did the Japanese Army kill there?

It's said that hundreds of thousands were killed. That's a lie! I haven't seen the Kaikōsha book yet, though I've ordered it. It's really thick. You should read it. I don't really know what the figures are.

You actually entered Nanking, didn't you? What do you think? How many died?

I don't really know. The Kaikōsha talks about the problem of numbers, and they give a number. I went there to discuss it a few days ago.

At that time, how many people did the Japanese Army think died?

[He stands up and walks to his bookshelf and selects two large albums from the many there and brings them to the coffee table. He opens one.] This is a photograph of the city of Nanking taken immediately after we entered the city, December 14, 1937. I entered the city on my birthday. In the afternoon I took a squad of sentries and marched all around the city. See this gate? I took this photo at three or four in the afternoon.

You don't see any dead bodies, although the gate is damaged. [*He jabs his finger at the photo.*] This is the spot in the other side's books where they claim ten thousand bodies lay. Right here. You don't see any bodies, do you?

Tanida-san, on this page opposite, right here, you've written, "About one thousand confirmed bodies, 4 P.M.," haven't you?

We started about three o'clock. It must have been about four o'clock when we got here. This is in front of the gate. It's still burning. Smoke is still rising. Here I wrote "more than one thousand," but actually two or three thousand dead were probably there. If you move toward the river-bank, about three hundred meters from this gate, you come to this location. [*Turns to next picture.*]

Are the white things in the picture bodies?

I wonder what those white ones are? Something white must be spread out there.

You were an army staff officer, of the Tenth Army, a colonel. And you saw the whole city of Nanking, didn't you? This picture is labeled, "December 14, 1937. Shimonoseki Pier."

No, that place's name was pronounced *Shakan*. We entered before noon and we stopped by a bank. There were a lot of banks in Nanking. We entered the bank, ate our lunch, and then loaded a squad of guards from the army headquarters onto a truck. It was really dangerous, as you can imagine. We then went around to check out the situation. We had no idea what was going on. That's when I took those pictures. [*He points out several in succession.*] In this one, we'd gone just two or three hundred meters inside. This side was burning. Here there were actually several thousand corpses. Chinese books say there were ten thousand right here, but there aren't any in this one, see. This is proof.

The Chinese say the killing extended to civilians, to women and children.

The Kaikōsha wrote the book on Nanking to tell those who claim there were hundreds of thousands killed that they're full of shit! [*He pauses.*]

Now, this picture is a drawing of the offensive plan of the Sixth Division to breach the great walls of Nanking. Are you with me? [*He's *back in command.*] Twelfth day of the twelfth month of the twelfth year of the Shōwa era, twelve noon. [December 12, 1937, noon.] Four twelves lined up. Unfortunately it wasn't twelve minutes past the hour. It was 12:20. Eight minutes late. But still, four twelves were lined up, and the flag of the sixth division went up over the city. I watched this from army headquarters on this mountain. [*He points it out on the map.*] I was in a shelter trench. We'd advanced here from the rear. We had an artist with us who painted this scene. The day we actually entered was the fourteenth. This photograph with the man waving the flag on 12/12/12/12 was taken with my Leica.

This picture is the Tenth Army entering Nanking and advancing down the street on the fourteenth, the day I was born. This is the wall we took. Now, this one is a picture of all those who were there being addressed by battalion commander Miyake, who was describing the assault on the gate. The one who went up first, he's holding a map and talking about it. Section leader Nakatsuru is talking about the assault. This is December 16. In this one we're actually on top of the wall. We climbed up the ladder, crossing the water, and Nakatsuru gave a talk. This one is of Nakatsuru climbing up a ladder. Below you can see two or three bodies.

Now, this picture was taken in 1938, when a touring company came to cheer on the troops. Among those who came were the women entertainers Watanabe Hamako and Koume of Akasaka. This fat one here's Koume. She still lives in Yokohama. I sometimes meet with her even now. She'll perform for small groups of military men. Nowadays she's really skinny. This picture here, that's me, explaining something on the gate. This one is a year later, on the anniversary of the date we took Nanking. I'm giving a talk. This is a field party outside.

We decided to make a park there. We gathered an engineer company in 1939 and built a park. I made this speech at the opening when it was completed. We built a great stone monument, more than ten meters high, to commemorate the Japanese occupation of Nanking. We even had an airplane fly-over for the ceremony, just as in the Homeland. This is the party afterwards. We gathered all the Japanese beauties of Nanking for this one. The area around the park was all devastated, but the park is still there today. That's because one of the company commanders with some brains built a Tomb of the Chinese War Dead there first. The local people were very pleased with this and even sent young men out to help us build it. Thanks to this, the park remains today. This last picture shows me giving a little talk on December 12, 1942, three years after the opening of the park, five years after we took Nanking.

Starting December 12, 1937, the Japanese forces occupying Nanking conducted a several-week-long terror campaign against the civilian population of the city. Brutality, rape, and the wanton murder of unarmed Chinese were widespread. The victors naturally had no interest in counting the dead, and the conquered no way to accurately total up their losses. Outside observers of many nationalities were shocked by what they saw occurring within their own limited fields of vision, and their reports, letters, photogaphs, and even films became the foundation for what the world was to learn during the war about the Nanking Incident. In the fifty years since, diaries, letters, maps, and military documents have surfaced which have built on the testimony and evidence presented at the time and at the war-crimes trials after the war. The full extent of this atrocity can probably never be ascertained.

The controversy over the Nanking Massacre, or the Rape of Nanking as it became known during the war, has generally become a dispute over numbers—how many Chinese, whether military (including prisoners of war, captured deserters, and guerrillas) or civilian (especially women and children) were assaulted or killed by Japanese forces. In China today, the Nanking memorial to the massacre and official histories speak of 300,000 dead. In Taiwan, many Nationalist historians use a similar figure. Leading Western histories of the war, while mentioning the Rape of Nanking, usually give no definite estimate at all. Not surprisingly, even the most liberal Japanese sources quote far lower figures than do the Chinese. In Japan, answers to the question "How many were killed?" range from as few as 3,000 to 6,000 made by individuals whose accounts have been discredited to as high as 200,000. * One of Japan's leading historians of the war in China, Hata Ikuhiko, wrote in 1986 that "illegal murders" at Nanking ranged from 38,000 to 42,000. †

Volume one of the two-volume work referred to by General Tanida, Nankin senshi [History of the Nanking Battle] *published by his officers' association, the Kaikōsha, in 1989, chooses to give no total number of Chinese killed at Nanking. ‡ While it does not flatly deny that a massacre took place, it dismisses completely the idea that 200,000 to 300,000*

---

* Fujiwara Akira, *Nankin daigyakusatsu* [*The Nanking Great Massacre*] (Tokyo: Iwanami, 1988), pp. 49–52. Fujiwara adheres to a figure of approximately 200,000.

† Hata Ikuhiko, *Nankin jiken: Gyakusatsu no kōzō* [*The Nanking Incident: The Structure of a Massacre*] (Tokyo: Chūō Kōronsha, 1986), p. 214.

‡ Nankin Senshi Henshū Iinkai, ed., *Nankin senshi* [*History of the Nanking Battle*], 2 vols. (Tokyo: Kaikōsha, 1989). The two volumes are entitled *Nankin senshi* [*History of the Nanking Battle*] and *Nankin senshi, shiryōshū* [*Collection of Documents on the History of the Nanking Battle*].

Chinese were murdered there. Volume two, a 789-page document collection is appended and readers are left to reach their own conclusions. Although the association of former Imperial army officers was in a unique position to come to a judgment concerning one of the principal war-crimes issues still left over from those years, their willingness to leave the question open is evidence of how little those involved are, even today, willing to acknowledge responsibility for what happened in that war.

Qualifying as a Leader

TOMINAGA SHŌZŌ [1]

"Then, university-student status still brought with it a deferment from active duty. After my graduation I took my professor's advice and headed for Manchuria to work for a company in charge of grain distribution all over Manchukuo. It was a good life. I could afford to get married. When the army caught up with me, I was almost twenty-six. When I reported for my physical in Manchuria I was rated Class A. I wasn't particularly keen about going into the army, but somehow I never questioned my duty."

The war in China was four years old when he was sent there in the summer of 1941. More than half a million Japanese had been killed or wounded on the continent since the China Incident began. There was no end in sight. He was assigned to the 232nd Regiment of the Thirty-Ninth Division from Hiroshima, which had been dispatched to Central China. The division was stationed at the most advanced part of the front line, up the Yangtze Valley toward Chungking.

It was July 30, 1941, when I reported in. They took me to the infantry company where I had been assigned as a second lieutenant. I was fresh from officer school. "These men are the members of the second platoon" was my only introduction to those who would be under my command. I'll never forget meeting them—about twenty men; the other half of the platoon were away from camp, on the front line. When I looked at the men of my platoon I was stunned—they had evil eyes. They weren't human eyes, but the eyes of leopards or tigers. They'd experienced many battles and I was completely green. I'd seen nothing. How could I give these guys orders, or even look into those faces? I lost all my confidence. Among the men were new conscripts, two-year men, and three-year men. The longer the men had been at the front, the more evil their eyes appeared.

The day after I arrived, a special field-operations training exercise was announced for all twenty-two of the new candidate officers. For a week Second Lieutenant Tanaka, our instructor, took us to the scenes of battles that had been fought in our area. He pointed out the battlefields where things had gone well and then he showed us the sites of battles lost, with tremendous damage and carnage evident everywhere. We walked over the ground, or ran over it at his command, looking at the physical features, trying to apply our book knowledge to a geography real war had touched.

The next-to-last day of the exercise, Second Lieutenant Tanaka took us to the detention center. Pointing at the people in a room, all Chinese, he announced, "These are the raw materials for your trial of courage." We were astonished at how thin and emaciated they looked. Tanaka told us, "They haven't been fed for several days, so they'll be ready for their part in tomorrow's plan." He said that it was to be a test to see if we were qualified to be platoon leaders. He said we wouldn't be qualified if we couldn't chop off a head.

On the final day, we were taken out to the site of our trial. Twenty-four prisoners were squatting there with their hands tied behind their backs. They were blindfolded. A big hole had been dug—ten meters long, two meters wide, and more than three meters deep. The regimental commander, the battalion commanders, and the company commanders all took the seats arranged for them. Second Lieutenant Tanaka bowed to the regimental commander and reported, "We shall now begin." He ordered a soldier on fatigue duty to haul one of the prisoners to the edge of the pit; the prisoner was kicked when he resisted. The soldier finally dragged him over and forced him to his knees. Tanaka turned toward us and looked into each of our faces in turn. "Heads should be cut off like this," he said, unsheathing his army sword. He scooped water from a bucket with a dipper, then poured it over both sides of the blade. Swishing off the water, he raised his sword in a long arc. Standing behind the prisoner, Tanaka steadied himself, legs spread apart, and cut off the man's head with a shout, "Yo!" The head flew more than a meter away. Blood spurted up in two fountains from the body and sprayed into the hole.

The scene was so appalling that I felt I couldn't breathe. All the candidate officers stiffened. Second Lieutenant Tanaka designated the person on the right end of our line to go next. I was fourth. When my turn came, the only thought I had was "Don't do anything unseemly!" I didn't want to disgrace myself. I bowed to the regimental commander and stepped forward. Contrary to my expectations, my feet firmly met the ground. One thin, worn-out prisoner was at the edge of the pit, blindfolded. I unsheathed my sword, a gift from my brother-in-law, wet it down as the lieutenant had demonstrated, and stood behind the man. The prisoner didn't move. He kept his head lowered. Perhaps he was resigned to his fate. I was tense, thinking I couldn't afford to fail. I took a deep breath and recovered my composure. I steadied myself, holding the sword at a point above my right shoulder, and swung down with one breath. The head flew away and the body tumbled down, spouting blood. The air reeked from all that blood. I washed blood off the blade then wiped it with the paper provided. Fat stuck to it and wouldn't come off. I noticed, when I sheathed it, that my sword was slightly bent.

At that moment, I felt something change inside me. I don't know how to put it, but I gained strength somewhere in my gut.

Some of the officer candidates slashed the head by mistake. One prisoner ran around crazily, his blindfold hanging down, his head gashed. "Stab him!" Tanaka ordered. The candidate officer swung and missed again. "You fool!" Tanaka scolded. This time Tanaka swung his sword. All of us did. Everyone got covered with blood as we butchered him.

We returned to our companies. Until that day I had been overwhelmed by the sharp eyes of my men when I called the roll each night. That night I realized I was not self-conscious at all in front of them. I didn't even find their eyes evil anymore. I felt I was looking down on them.

Later, when the National Defense Women's Association welcomed us in Manchuria, they mentioned to me that they had never seen men with such evil eyes. I no longer even noticed. Everybody becomes bloodthirsty on the battlefield. The men received their baptism of blood when they went into combat. They were victimizers. I joined them by killing a prisoner.

Every March, new conscripts came from home. The men who'd been there a long time sometimes completed their period of service, but they usually stayed. Those who were conscripted in 1939 couldn't go home until the end of war, because of the huge losses. Six years.

A new conscript became a full-fledged soldier in three months in the battle area. We planned exercises for these men. As the last stage of their training, we made them bayonet a living human. When I was a company commander, this was used as a finishing touch to training for the men and a trial of courage for the officers. Prisoners were blindfolded and tied to poles. The soldiers dashed forward to bayonet their target at the shout of "Charge!" Some stopped on their way. We kicked them and made them do it. After that, a man could do anything easily. The army created men capable of combat. The thing of supreme importance was to make them fight. It didn't matter whether they were bright or sincere. Men useless in action were worthless. Good soldiers were those who were able to kill, however uncouth they were. We made them like this. Good sons, good daddies, good elder brothers at home were brought to the front to kill each other. Human beings turned into murdering demons. Everyone became a demon within three months. Men were able to fight courageously only when their human characteristics were suppressed. So we believed. It was a natural extension of our training back in Japan. This was the Emperor's Army.

The first time I saw combat myself was late September and early October 1941. That was the time of the Changsha operation. Fighting went on day and night. Three battalions were engaged in our attack. I participated in the platoon on the left side of the company on the extreme left flank of the Third Battalion. At first, we advanced covered by light machine guns, while artillery shelled the enemy position. Our strategy was to charge at bayonet point, once we got within fifty meters. There was nothing to cover us on our approach, and a brick pillbox was right in front of us. We couldn't advance until a shell exploded near the pillbox, sending up a cloud of dust. I took the opportunity to lead my men forward, shouting "Charge!" Halfway to the pillbox, the dust suddenly settled, and the enemy started shooting at us again. Dust now kicked up at our feet. We were completely exposed. Strangely, we weren't hit. I was running with the thought that I might fall at any moment. It was only fifty meters to the pillbox—maybe ten seconds, yet it seemed I'd never reach it no matter how hard I ran. When I looked up I noticed a huge loophole for a machine gun and a gigantic muzzle spitting fire right at me. "It shouldn't be this big," I thought. I closed my eyes and fought my way into their position. Half the enemy escaped, but we took about ten prisoners. I was so excited that my mouth moved uncontrollably. I didn't mean to say anything, but words seemed to pour from my mouth, berating my men. A reserve force relieved us, and we went to see the company commander, taking the prisoners with us. We learned that we had been the first to charge into the enemy line and had started the enemy's collapse. There was an assessment of services rendered during the battle. I was the one who received the most praise and honor for my action. But at the time I didn't know that at all. This was my first battle. My first charge.

With experience, I learned to judge whether the situation was dangerous or not. The more experienced I was, the more fearful I became. At the beginning I didn't know anything, and it was like being delirious. A platoon leader always led his platoon in a direct assault. You charged because there was no choice. It wasn't a matter of courage. My only thought was to do my duty. Platoon leader was the position of utmost danger. A company commander could remain behind the front lines, sending one or two platoons out to the front, except in a night attack when he led the whole company forward in the darkness.

Eventually, I served as a company commander myself. It was relatively easy. When the company left on an operation, they gathered first and saluted me. I wondered how many might not return. That was the feeling I disliked most. In a large operation, roughly a third to a half of the company wouldn't return. They weren't all killed, but many were wounded. When there were casualties, other men had to carry them. It took four men to carry one man unable to walk. There was no way to evacuate the wounded if a battle was being lost. Then we evacuated only the ones able to walk, and only as many as we could. The rest of the injured were expected to kill themselves, but some Japanese were captured because they couldn't take their own lives.

Massacres of civilians were routine. They cooperated with the enemy, sheltered them in their houses, gave them information. We viewed them as the enemy. During combat, all villagers went into hiding. We pilfered anything useful from their houses or, in winter, burned them for firewood. If anyone was found wandering about, we captured and killed them. Spies! This was war.

Tominaga Shōzō discusses the consequences of his acts in Chapter 24.

Gas Soldier

TANISUGA SHIZUO

He brings out his military handbook in which are recorded the dates of his promotions and the units he served in. One column gives his speciality as "gas." When he was away from the front, he worked as a clerk in the office of a poison-gas factory.

"We used poison gas in China from the very beginning. It wasn't employed openly, since the Geneva Convention forbade it. We took special care to pick up the expended canisters and remove all traces of its use from the battlefields. I've been studying this as a member of the Poison Gas Workers' Association. We're seeking compensation from the Japanese government for the injuries we suffered while making all kinds of poison gas during the war—choking gas, sneezing gas, and mustard gas." Looking into his notebook, he continues, "I've been able to document when gas was used in China. Nine times in 1937 and 185 in 1938. There were 465 *times in 1939 alone, 259 in 1940, and 48 in 1941. It was employed there all the way through 1945."*

At the end of July 1937, my regiment from Fukuyama was mobilized. This was just after the Marco Polo Bridge Incident at the start of fighting in China. I was a new-minted soldier then, one of the last who received his military training in peacetime. Before the war, we specialists had only four or five days of gas training. We relied on *Defense Against Gas,* a text drafted in April 1937. It hadn't yet become an official manual. Our training focused on mastering how to decontaminate areas where mustard gas had been used. We were given a large bag containing maybe ten kilograms of bleaching powder to spread in front of us. We were supposed to be dealing with mustard gas, so we had to have complete protection— rubber boots, rubber trousers, jacket, gloves, and a head cover. Just putting all that on in the summer made you break out in a terrible sweat. We called it "octopus dancing." The glass lenses on the mask instantly fogged up. It was probably the most hated training in the army.

I was a private second class in the Second Battalion, Forty-First Regiment, Fifth Division. When you spoke of combat then, you were still talking about killing the other side with rifles, machine guns, maybe a little artillery support. That was the normal way we soldiers fought. Occasionally airplanes supported us with bombing. I wasn't sent to China until 1939, after Peking, Nanking, and Hankow had fallen. Most of the work we had was pacification or punitive missions intended to suppress anyone who showed themselves.

Each squad carried two or three "Red Canisters," filled with a gas that induced coughing. They were about twenty centimeters long and five centimeters in diameter. At the top of the canister was something like the tip of a match. A tiny cover fit over it, and it was wrapped in cotton too, so that it wouldn't be set off accidentally. It functioned as a fuse. The second you lit it, smoke would come out. That was the poison gas. If you threw with all your might, you could toss it maybe fifty meters.

Poison gas had little effect when the weather was mild. Updrafts caused the smoke to dissipate. The best time to use it was immediately before a rainstorm, when air pressure was low and the wind was blowing slowly and steadily in the direction of the enemy. I learned how to measure wind speed as part of my training.

Once I got the command "Use Red Canister!" when I was at the front in China. I held up a piece of tissue paper and watched how it fluttered in the wind. I was glad to see conditions were favorable—the weather cloudy, wind blowing toward the other side. "Perfect," I thought. I shouted the order, "Take out the canisters!" I had the men put on their gas masks and fix bayonets, then ordered them to crouch down and wait. One after the other, I threw the canisters toward the enemy. I could see the white smoke come out, spreading across the ground. I ordered the men to charge into the village. Their soldiers, and most everyone else, had already run off.

An old grandmother had failed to get away because of her bound feet. She was trying her best, but she looked like a duck, taking tiny clumsy steps and shaking her tail as she ran. She was wracked by coughing. "She's not even dead yet," I thought to myself. "How strange." Of course, it was a sneezing gas. It wasn't supposed to kill, only immobilize the enemy. I don't think the Chinese had complete gas masks. Usually if you attacked an enemy position frontally, you had to take them at bayonet point. With gas, they'd just run. It was easy. Funny to use that word, but it was true.

I myself used gas just that once in combat.

I went to work at the secret poison-gas plant on Okunoshima island when I finally got home from China. I was there when the war against America broke out. That morning I had just crossed to the island to work, when I heard that radio broadcast: "Today the Japanese army and navy have entered into hostilities with the forces of America and Britain in the Western Pacific."

There had been signs before December 8, but I couldn't imagine Japan would ever really go to war with America, the great power. War meant national suicide for Japan. That's what I truly thought. We'd just started our morning shift. The shock! I'd never had such a feeling in my life. I couldn't sit still. I went to the latrine in the back and thought about what would happen. Tears came to my eyes. I felt this would mean the end of my life. No matter how Japan boasted, it had used up almost everything in the China Incident. How could such a country win with America and Britain as opponents?

The announcements kept coming. Attacks on Pearl Harbor. Singapore, too? Then they played the "Battleship March" on the radio. I was stunned. Everything was described in such optimistic terms. "All's going well," the reports said. And so it seemed, as the news came in over the next weeks. One by one, we were taking places all over.

But I knew all about official military announcements. I had had experience with war. I knew that there had to be lies in these announcements too. They couldn't all be true. In the China Incident they'd say, "We took such and such a place," but they'd never mentioned that we'd used poison gas or that the fighting there was still going on, and on, and on.

2 / TOWARD A NEW ORDER

"War means jobs for machinists."

KUMAGAYA TOKUICHI

He has lived for fifty years in the same small wooden house in the industrial city of Kawasaki, a manufacturing center since long before the war. Seventy-two, he spent almost his whole life on the factory floor before retiring from Isuzu Motors.

You know, the Japanese had a close, warm kind of feeling toward soldiers. Sympathy, you might say. They were sacrificing themselves for the country and I felt a sense of gratitude for their hard work. People knew that military duty was as hard as a prison sentence. They knew, because ordinary people shared the soldiers' hardships. Every autumn, after the harvest, large divisional maneuvers took place in the local rice fields. The soldiers were billeted at ordinary houses. When I was a boy, all of us in the neighborhood played soldier, using sticks for rifles and swords. Very often, the grown-ups encouraged us to do it. And if you ever saw an actual soldier, you automatically addressed him as *Heitai-san*— Mister Soldier.

Many of us common people really cheered the soldiers during the February 26 Incident of 1936. I thought, "They've done it! Fantastic!" People were looking for a breakthrough because times were hard and no one thought of war in a realistic way. Even after the rebels backed down, I imagined that a single shot from our army would just blow the Chinks away. We went to war with light hearts in '37 and '38.

My father had worked at the army's arsenal in Tokyo making rifles and bayonets. He was a laborer of the lowest class. No education. He couldn't read at all. Although he found work at the armory for a while, he could never have become a machinist, because he couldn't understand blueprints. Even the old guys who'd been around the plant for years started to study English so they could read the names of the machine parts on the plans. No matter what my father did, he never knew anything but hard work. Arsenal workers were always laid off as soon as the possibility of war receded, so my father did all kinds of odd jobs. He even tried peddling. Our family lived in one of the many row houses in Tokyo. The house had two small rooms: one was four-and-a-half mats in area, the other just three. It was really crowded—my parents, three elder sisters, one elder brother, a younger brother, and me all packed in.

Most of our kind of people served as apprentices in shops and factories. After sixth grade, my sisters got jobs in a government printing office. At that time, there weren't many people like us going on to higher schooling. Maybe five or six out of a class of fifty pupils. I was one of them. I finished higher elementary school at fourteen, and entered a medium-size machine factory called Hokushin Denki that made thermometers for the high-temperature processing of iron. We also turned out rangefinders for coastal artillery.

I walked to and from that factory every day, about an hour each way. Train fares seemed wasteful to me. My sisters used to wear wooden clogs and walk along the unpaved roads just to save five *sen* of bus fare. Ordinary factory workers worked seven to five, but my factory was on an eight-hour day, first and third Sundays of the month off, because of its semimilitary status. We had four holidays a year: New Year's Day, the Emperor's Birthday, the Anniversary of the Birth of the Meiji Emperor, and the Anniversary of Emperor Jimmu's Accession to the Throne— National Foundation Day. I worked more than two hours overtime every day and was paid for it. At ordinary factories, the workers usually didn't get overtime pay. Instead, they got a suit or a crested kimono when they went on active duty in the army.

We respected the white people who'd produced the advanced machinery we used and had an advanced culture as well, but we looked down on Chinese, calling them *Chankoro,* and Koreans—they were just *Senjin* or *Chōkō.* People didn't lease houses to Koreans in decent places. Instead, they built their own shacks with sheets of corrugated iron. Neighborhood children gathered to watch them eating rice from big bowls with red pepper all over it. They smelled funny at the public bath. They made the place reek of garlic.

I started reading *Red Flag,* the paper of the Communist Party, because of Yoshida, a turner at my factory, who was a year ahead of me in school. I drank cocoa for the first time in my life at his house. He handed over *Red Flag* with the cocoa. I wasn't particularly interested in ideology, but I was attracted to the Communist Party because I was very poor. To tell you the truth, though, I didn't understand it at all. "Down with the Emperor!" sounded all right to me, because poverty had made me distrust authority generally, and I didn't think their rules were doing me any good. I never thought, even as a young boy, that the Emperor was a god.

I was hauled off by the military police—the Kempeitai—because I did "repo" work—that's the job of receiving and passing out the papers on the street at an assigned time. I'd been reading the party papers for two years by then. The Kempeitai asked me what the Communist Party did. I told them I didn't know, that I was just doing it for the cocoa. The interrogation wasn't hard at all, maybe because I was only a youth of about twenty. They kept me for two weeks and then released me. But I did end up losing my job at that factory, and Yoshida was indicted.

I took the conscription examination in 1936. I was graded Class B-2 —backup reserves. When the war with China broke out the next year, the first-line reservists had to go, but I wasn't even trained until 1939, when I took a course as a tank mechanic and then qualified in armored cars.

Machinists welcomed the munitions boom. We'd been waiting anxiously for a breakthrough. From that time on, we got really busy. China news was everywhere. Even my father subscribed to *Asahi Graph,* since every issue carried lots of pictures of soldiers in China. By the end of 1937, everybody in the country was working. For the first time, I was able to take care of my father. War's not bad at all, I thought. As a skilled worker, I was eagerly sought after and earned my highest wages in 1938, '39 and '40. There were so many hours of overtime! I changed jobs often, each new job better than the one before. In 1940, a draft system for skilled workers was introduced to keep us from moving around.

New factories were being built so rapidly. One where I worked only had about twelve or so workers when it moved from Kameido to Kawasaki in 1938. Soon, there were two or three hundred employees. Because of the war, I made as much as a section chief in a first-class company— about 120 yen a month. In March 1940, I got married. At the age of twenty-three, with a substantial income, I was independent enough to set up house. The happiest thing was that I didn't need to worry about finding a job.

I remember the day the navy attacked Pearl Harbor. I was just off the night shift and out with my wife buying a wooden horse for my eldest son. She had him on her back when the news of the attack came over the radio. It was around 9:00 A.M. "We did it! We did it! The war's really begun!" That's what we shouted.

My elder sister asked me, "Toku, do you think Japan can actually beat America?" "I've no idea" was my answer. To tell you the truth, somehow I knew what was going to happen. Those who dealt with machinery realized what a gap there was between us and the Americans. At that time, most of our advanced machinery came from America, England, or France. Japan was unable to manufacture precision tools like polishing, grinding, and milling machines. I don't know for sure, but I suspect Japanese airplane-engine manufacturing plants used American machinery, and it wasn't just oil America had embargoed. They'd stopped exporting machinery to us, too.

I guess we had a kind of inferiority complex toward the Westerners. We called them "hairy ones," but we felt a kind of admiration turned to prejudice. We didn't want to lose to the whites. Like a lot of people, I didn't hate Americans. That's why the government had to make up slogans to promote hatred. They said the Americans and the British were the Anglo-American Demons. We fought a war against America without any genuine hostility. Maybe the professional soldiers felt a strong rivalry, but not us workers.

Looking back at the war years, many people claim they supported the war only because there was no other choice. I think that's a lie. Intellectuals, journalists, educated people, all supported the war actively. The only exceptions were the Communists, and they were in prison. Nobody truly thought Japan would lose. It was taken for granted that we'd stop the war at some reasonable point. Shouts of *"Banzai!"* sent off everything from soldiers and military horses to trains and airplanes. We held so many lantern parades to celebrate our victories! Why have we forgotten that in defeat?

"I wanted to build Greater East Asia."

NOGI HARUMICHI [1]

Yatsuo is a quiet town, one hour by train from Osaka. His study smells of the fresh-brewed coffee he has just brought back from a trip to Indonesia. Very tall and handsome, he is a retired real estate agent.

The idea of creating an economic zone wherein all the nations of Asia could develop in concert was widespread in Japanese academic and political circles in the late 1930s. Of course, Japan was seen as the natural leader of such a regional realignment. Foreign Minister Matsuoka Yōsuke made the first official use of the term "Greater East Asia Co-Prosperity Sphere," in August 1940. The resources of the Dutch East Indies, particularly its petroleum, became increasingly vital to Japanese industrial and military planners as Japan's war in China led to deteriorating economic and political relations with the United States.

A student in 1940, Nogi Harumichi joined the Patriotic Students' Alliance at his university and was gradually drawn into the shadow world

of semiclandestine rightist groups, preparing themselves to play a role in
"liberating the Indies from their Dutch masters."

The man who really got me all stirred up about colonialism was Professor Imamura Chūsuke. He was the founder and head of the Department of Colonial Economics at Nihon University, the private college we called Nichidai. He'd say in class, "I've been to Shanghai where signs say 'Dogs and Yellow People—No Entry!' I've been to the South Seas, an area controlled entirely by the white man." He'd ask us, "What are you going to do to knock down this structure?" He had studied in America and was a professor of current events, but he devoted himself to rousing speeches like this. My feelings resonated with him. I burned with a desire to act. "Given an opportunity, I want to go to the front. I want to go to China. I want to do something myself!" That's what we all said.

America and Britain had been colonizing China for many years. Japan came to this late. China was such a backward nation. At the time of the Manchurian Incident in 1931, we felt Japan should go out there and use Japanese technology and leadership to make China a better country. What was actually happening on the battlefield was all secret then, but I felt sure that the Greater East Asia Co-Prosperity Sphere would be of crucial importance to the backward races. Japan and Germany would only have to combine forces to break the Anglo-Saxon hold on Asia, and redistribute the colonies. That's how we felt then.

Beginning in 1939, Hitler's newsreels were shown every day. When I played hooky, I always went to see them. I'd watch those stirring movies about Hitler and wonder, "What's the matter with the Japanese army in Manchuria? Why can't they just annihilate the British or the Americans? Hitler took all of Poland and united it with Germany!" Then I bought Hitler's heroic autobiography *Mein Kampf.* Japanese youth at that time adored Hitler and Mussolini and yearned for the emergence of a Japanese politician with the same qualities. We wanted decisive action.

Hashimoto Kingorō, a former army officer, and Nakano Seigō, a politician who advocated the "Southern Advance," were two who took after Hitler and copied his style. I went to their speeches, all of them. Sometimes I'd be thrown out. Their supporters would demand to see my student ID and then say I wasn't old enough. Somehow, they didn't like students. So I'd take off my school uniform and sneak in. The meetings were held at the Hibiya Public Hall. Whenever extreme right-wing talks were given, on subjects like "Attack Britain and America," enormous crowds came. People brought box lunches and formed long lines from six in the morning to get in and hear Nakano Seigō endorsing the liberation of Asia. Even then, sometimes you couldn't get in. This was in 1940 and early '41, before the war. When you heard these talks, you felt as if your burdens had been lifted. You were satisfied. The audience would be carried away with enthusiasm for the ideals and theories of the Co-Prosperity Sphere.

Nagai Ryūtarō was another brilliant orator and people loved his tone. He, too, advocated Asia for Asians. I loved the atmosphere of his talks. When Britain lodged a protest with Japan because a British gunboat was sunk by Japan in China, they denounced the British, saying, "While they're engaged in aggressive acts, how dare they complain about the Japanese army there?" They called on us to protest against the British Empire. I myself once went to a demonstration at the British embassy where I joined in shouting, "Britain get out of China! Stop your aggression! What are you doing in the Orient?" We couldn't accept their presence in what they called the Far East.

You would be shocked by what we were taught. "Democracy" meant you could do whatever you pleased. If we found ourselves where we had to fight America, we were assured we would not have to worry. America was a democratic nation and so would disintegrate and collapse. That was common talk. In America, they can't unite for a common purpose. One blow against them, and they'll fall to pieces.

I was studying law and accounting. It bored me, just adding up and recording taxes or looking up interpretations of existing laws. I felt I couldn't stand doing that my whole life. It was at just such a moment that the branch chief of the Patriotic Students' Alliance at Nihon University pulled me aside and said he had a request to make of me. "We have work to do, but it must be carried out clandestinely. That's why I've selected you. If you don't wish to participate, don't say a word to anyone. If you wish to join us, contact me within a week." Then he told me he would introduce me to a "boss." At most of the universities and higher technical schools there was a branch of the Patriotic Students' Alliance. It was founded by right-wing groups and was part of the so-called International Anti-Communist Alliance. I now realize they played the role of skirmishers in agitating for war, but then I was concerned that they might be a gangster group. What if the assignment were to assassinate somebody? I confronted the branch chief and asked him for assurances that it wouldn't be anything like that. He assured me that the work would involve the independence movement in Indonesia. Indonesian independence? That sounded exciting. Even thrilling. I decided to join in early 1940.

They had a private academy located at the home of a businessman, near Meguro in Tokyo. He had a big hall for *kendō* fencing behind his house. The head of the private academy, Kaneko, was a disciple of one of the right-wing leaders, Iwata Ainosuke. He'd gone to Indonesia in early Shōwa, soon after 1926, and had spent years there, wandering around. He was like one of the "China *rōnin*," masterless Japanese samurai who had worked mostly on their own initiative with the Chinese nationalists to overthrow the corrupt Ching dynasty before China's revolution in 1911. I guess I should call him a "Southern *rōnin*."

When I arrived at Meguro, this man came out wearing a formal man's kimono. He looked like Takasugi Shinsaku, the hero of the Meiji Restoration. He was only about thirty-six. Twenty of his students had returned from Indonesia. They were my age, just youths who, on graduation from elementary school, with no real prospects for jobs or work in Japan, had been sent to Indonesia. There they worked in large department stores in cities like Surabaja, and all were able to speak Indonesian fluently. My Indonesian was only what I could pick up at Nichidai while studying colonial economics, but now I burned to go somewhere overseas.

I believed in the Greater East Asia Co-Prosperity Sphere myself, but I couldn't really discuss that with these other students. Perhaps it was because they didn't have the educational level required, but we did talk about what was best for the Indonesian independence movement and focused on how to develop better relations with Indonesia. We saw Indonesia as a nation with great natural abundance, but a nation lagging behind in development. Japan should go there to help them use their wealth. It was a very utilitarian view. Gradually, I sensed that we were being groomed as reserves for the military. Despite that, I thought that it would be wonderful if we were to take part in the independence movement and liberate Indonesia from the Dutch. Even if our army didn't do it, we would, I thought. But gradually we came to believe that perhaps the military was going to do it.

That Twenty-six-hundredth Anniversary of National Foundation! A great moment in Japanese history. We were mobilized for that in the summer of 1940. We students were assigned tasks like guiding people around and preparing their schedules for ceremonies and events. There was a grand meeting of overseas Japanese all under one roof—representatives from Latin America and even from the U.S.A. We took them to military ports and accompanied them to the Imperial Palace for an audience with His Imperial Majesty. Just a year before the outbreak of the war, efforts were made for the total mobilization of overseas Japanese. They were told Japan would not lose if it came to war. These affairs connected with the anniversary, and conducted by the government, were intended to raise the Imperial Army and the Navy high on a pedestal and to demonstrate Japan's dignity and prestige to overseas Japanese, as much as to the nations of the world as a whole.

I participated in what was called the Sumera Study Group. It was a play on words. *Sumera* in Japanese means both the Japanese Emperor and the Sumerians, the Middle Eastern people who were the founders of human civilization. Several scholars founded the group at the beginning of 1940. The organizers gathered student leaders from all the colleges and schools, including the imperial universities, not just the private ones like Nichidai. We met on the second floor of the Shirakiya Department Store. We were even given money when we attended the lectures. We were taught that Japan had to be more aggressive and told how we might expand the nation for the sake of the Emperor. From experiences like this, I'd say almost all the students of that time were caught up in militarism in some way.

I sometimes ran errands to the navy's Military Affairs Section for our academy, bringing them lists of people who resided in the South and things like that, without really knowing much about what I was doing. One day, the head of the group told me, "You're going into the navy. Get your application in order." I was a little surprised since I hadn't even taken an exam. I didn't realize that by then I was already deep inside, that our group was closely tied to the navy's "Advance to the South" faction.

I did have doubts at times, but on such occasions I believed that these thoughts surfaced in my mind because I was lacking in patriotic fervor and spirit. I felt I had to drive myself forward. If a nation decides to take action, everyone must move along with the decision! And, of course, I can't deny that I thought about what advantages might come to me. One can protect oneself best in the company of others.

In November 1941, one of the members of the academy, Yoshizumi Tomegorō, suddenly disappeared. The head of the academy didn't mention it. We'd sensed that preparations for war were on-going and we were just waiting for it to start. Whenever we asked when, they only told us to wait. Wait. They refused to give us any date. Our school year was shortened. We would now graduate in December. I got permission to leave the academy temporarily in order to study for my university graduation examinations and was allowed to board outside the academy if I agreed to join the navy. When I returned to the academy grounds at the beginning of December to take my preliminary physical and the navy written exams, I found it virtually deserted. All the young men had left. They'd mainly been assigned as interpreters for our landing forces. I later learned Yoshizumi had actually landed in Indonesia as a spy for the military.

The day the war broke out in victory, a great pot of sweet red-bean soup was prepared and we took it to the men in the Eighth Group of the Military Affairs Section who'd planned the Southern Strategy. The boss and I served each man in turn. "Congratulations, congratulations," we said. The normal impression you got from navy staff officers was of a cold distance. They hardly ever spoke, and they had the bearing of men supremely confident in their secret mission. But that day, while their faces were still composed, they had a sunny look about them.

What was supposed to happen had finally taken place. I felt a sense of relief at that moment more than anything else. Maybe all of Japan felt that way. Suddenly the constraints of deadlock were broken and the way before Japan was cleared. Yet I still harbored some doubt inside: Was it truly possible Japan could win?

I received notification that I had passed the examinations for the navy on January 15. I was told to go to paymasters' school. There were only six people present, including students in Indonesian language from the Tokyo Foreign Language Institute, a student from Takushoku University, and me, though they'd accepted three hundred. The others, we learned, were on a year's training course somewhere in Chiba prefecture. We six just waited around at the Military Affairs Section. They told us to prepare ourselves until the occupation of the Southern Area was completed, which would be very soon. We didn't even know how to salute. I'd been a student until the day before. Literally. Now I was in a navy uniform with the single gold stripe of a cadet ensign.

In the navy, everything had gone so well that they were already planning Australian operations. In preparation for landings there, they summoned people who'd lived in Australia, made long trips there, or just recently been repatriated. Every day we sent telegrams to them to come to the headquarters. They were asked to confirm the accuracy of tactical maps. We cadet ensigns were invited to observe. A lieutenant commander from the Navy General Staff would question them, asking about the beach line at Sydney Harbor, or inquiring about the depth of the water. You could get an overview of an operation just by listening. Finally, I asked the lieutenant commander, "So are we going to land in Australia?" He just blew up at me. "*Never* will you ask such a question again! Questions are forbidden! And you must never mention a word of what you've heard here outside this office!"

We received orders to leave for Indonesia at the end of March, aboard the *Tatsuta maru*. I was overjoyed with the idea of finally going to the scene of my dreams.

Manchurian Days

FUKUSHIMA YOSHIE [1]

As lively as her sparkling white suit with pink polka dots and its matching pink hat, she alternately laughs and chokes with tears as she speaks in a rich Kanazawa dialect, with Russian, Chinese, and Manchurian words popping up to punctuate her points.

She was one of more than eight hundred thousand Japanese colonists who moved to Manchuria after the region, as vast as the entire Northeastern United States, was severed from China by the Japanese army beginning on September 18, 1931, in what was called the Manchurian Incident. "Ruled" by the newly installed Pu-Yi, the last Emperor of China, who had been toppled while still a child in 1911, the new state of Manchukuo was created in 1932. It attracted "pioneers"—bureaucrats, soldiers, farmers, shopkeepers, industrialists, thugs, and idealists—from all over Japan seeking to make new lives and to carve out an empire on the Continent.

I wanted to be a pilot when I was in sixth grade. Whenever an airplane flew over, I'd rush out of class to look and was often scolded by my teacher. I was a "militaristic girl," I guess. I thought I had to fly a plane or do something! I loved Joan of Arc and I wanted to be like her. I was so scatterbrained and bubbly. I don't know why, but I thought I had to go to Manchuria. I had a strong sense of mission. I even got an award from the *Hokkoku* newspaper for selling flowers to raise money for our soldiers.

My father was a retired navy man and ran a shipyard in the small town of Nanao in Ishikawa prefecture. I had eight brothers and sisters. My father urged us girls to become Red Cross nurses. "What soldiers appreciate most are good nurses," he kept saying. Japan was a very militaristic state back then, so my five elder sisters became nurses. They didn't have to pay for their training. In fact, they were actually paid for going to school.

My dream was to be a kindergarten teacher. I studied one year at the Nursemaid Training School attached to the Metropolitan Education Association in Tokyo. My parents struggled to support me during my training. I returned to Nanao and wanted to pay them back for my education fees, but there was only one kindergarten in town and nobody would take me on. Still, that's what I wanted to do, so I was ready when a schoolmate of mine told me of a chance she knew about. She was from

Manchuria. "Furuko-san, you have to come," she said warmly. "They're building a kindergarten there." I brushed aside my parents' opposition and went to Fushun, Manchuria. I was so full of enthusiasm. I wanted to do everything. I believed "we have to take care of the children of Manchuria because Manchuria has been taking care of Japan." I thought I might even marry someone in Manchuria.

My mother was the daughter of a temple priest and married a military man. She hadn't been able to do what she had dreamed of doing, but she supported me in going out on my own. I was nineteen. She gave me one hundred yen without letting my father know. It cost sixty or eighty yen for the boat and rail fare to Fushun. That was a lot of money. Mother told me, "However good a man or a woman may appear on the way, don't be taken in by them. Go all the way to your destination at Fushun." Beginning on the boat from Shimonoseki to Korea, I felt anxious. So I was completely silent. I ignored everybody, all the way. On the boat and on the Chōsen Railway and on the Manchurian Railway, you got your way by using Japanese. You always went unchallenged.

At Fushun, the South Manchurian Railway Company had an open-pit mine outside the town that produced good quality coal. A large number of foreigners worked for the Fushun mine. The company had various businesses—mines, hotels, railways. The town was quite well developed. There were about a thousand women working there. That was still a time when married women stayed at home. Many were from the Homeland, including those who, like me, had jumped at the chance to come, and those who had come, relying on their relatives. The children in my care at the kindergarten were all from the Fushun office of the railway company. I loved them. After about a year I lost my voice and developed a slight fever. The head of the kindergarten and the head doctor of the children's section of the Fushun South Manchurian Railway Company Hospital examined me and ordered me to be hospitalized immediately. I made no real progress, so they told me to return to Japan. There was nothing I could do about it, so I went back to my hometown. I was heartbroken.

Back in Nanao, I was hospitalized in Kanazawa City and cured in two months. It was pleurisy resulting from the dryness. As soon as I was cured, I yearned to return. I was on leave of absence status from my job. Again I ignored what my parents said and I was soon on my way back to that kindergarten in Fushun. When you boarded a train and traveled across the wilderness of Manchuria, the red sorghum fields stretched on for an eternity and the evening sun set far, far away. It was so magnificent. I was seduced by that great expanse called Manchuria.

December 8, 1941, came during my second stay in Manchuria. It was a bitterly cold morning. Everything was frozen. When the children came in and said good morning, one child—by coincidence her name was Tōjō, Tōjō Eiko—said "Japan and America have started a war." I told her that couldn't be, but she said she'd heard it on the radio. I was shocked. I knew America was large. I wondered why Japan would start a war against such a large country. But our lives were not much affected then.

Miss Iwama, the head of the dorm where I lived, was such a warmhearted person. She loved the Manchus. She used to take me to Manchurian villages. "Let's go and play, Yoshie," she'd say, and we'd go to all kinds of filthy places. Whenever she found children, she'd pat their heads and play with them. She was good in their language. She took me to small local theaters and on the way home we'd eat melons and things. I really came to love Manchuria, but it didn't seem to love me. Once more I came down with pleurisy and had to part from her and the children in sorrow.

I had gone to Manchuria twice and now Manchuria seemed very close to me. But I realized that my physique was not really suited to it and I knew that each time I fell ill I caused many people much hardship. Again home in Nanao, the subject of marriage came up. The kimono-shop owner had a nephew who lived in Manchuria and wanted a bride from Japan. The only conditions he set were that she had to be physically healthy and capable of using the abacus. I loved the abacus. His nephew was really dear to him and the shop owner asked me to marry him. He showed me his picture. He looked like a nice person. The nephew was returning to Japan, and so a formal meeting was arranged in his uncle's drawing room. We talked for two or three minutes, then I wanted to go to Manchuria so badly, I just told him, "I'll go."

When I was about to be married, my mother's elder sister came all the way to Nanao by boat and train to see me. "Yoshie," she said, "are you really going to Manchuria? Do you know what's happening to Japan now? It's the middle of a war." I just answered that Manchuria's all right. It's full of Japanese. The Soviets are good friends. Then she said gravely, "If Japan loses the war, you won't be able to get back." "Don't say such things," I told her, but she wouldn't stop. "If you managed a temple as I do, it would be clear to you. The temple had to donate beautiful Buddhist altar fittings and temple bells to the country for metal. Recently, even the hangers for mosquito nets have had to be contributed. Everything's vanished. I donated my own gold rings. Can such a country win? If Japan loses, Manchuria will be divided up. If we're going to lose, it's better to die together here." At that time, deep inside me, I thought, what outrageous things this old aunt says! I told her Japan will not lose! My father said so. Anyway, the marriage was already arranged.

Again I set out for Manchuria. It was 1943, in the middle of the Greater East Asia War. My husband had started his business in Tōnei, in the northeastern province of Manchukuo, after being discharged from the army there. Tōnei was the closest town to the Soviet Union, along the northeastern border of Manchuria. It was a special area, subject to special laws and controls. There were about three hundred thousand troops along that border. Maybe fifty thousand additional Japanese people, like railwaymen, bankers, schoolteachers, and their families, were woven in among them.

His store was well established. It had a signboard out front saying "Authorized Military Vendor." I still remember the phone number— Tōnei two-five-three. There weren't many phones in those days. Here and there were empty houses. Those people must have gone home, thinking it would be dangerous. Maybe that means we were the only ones who didn't know what was coming.

The hamlets of the Manchurians were separated from us Japanese. We had four hired helpers in our store. One was Chō-san, who was fluent in Japanese. He had a long, oblong face. He was in charge of dispatching and supervising the shipping. Two youngsters—we called them Boy-san, twelve and thirteen—worked for us too. Sweet kids. We also had a girl who did laundry for me. *"Taitai,"* they'd call me, *"Okusan"* in Japanese. Up to that time I had always been the one who'd been used to do others' work. Now I was Madame.

On New Year's Day we were invited to Chō's house for a feast. He was the leader of his hamlet, but my husband bought many of the things they made there. He called my husband *"Jiangui,"* meaning "Leader." My husband told me not to confide in Manchurians. Treat them kindly, warmly, he said, but in your heart, you cannot completely trust them. My husband said, "They're likely to have vengeful feelings towards Japan." Even the kids who worked for us would sometimes blurt out to me that Japan was bad for taking away their land.

My husband bought a large dog from the army, a German Shepherd named Esu. It was a good dog and watched over me while my husband was away. My husband told me that they trained the dogs to bite only Manchurians. They'd dress someone in Manchu clothes and they trained the dog to attack when he came into a room, taking a big bite of his calf. The man's life wouldn't be endangered, but he couldn't move. He could then be investigated to determine if he was a spy. Esu was brought up in that way. We told Chō-san never to wear Chinese clothes. My husband didn't tell me everything, but there must have been many other things he knew, because he had twice been a soldier.

We had a big house. Since we had many large rooms, my husband invited anyone he met from Ishikawa prefecture to come by for dinner. The principal of the school was the head of an Ishikawa Association and my husband served as its secretary. The head of the tax office was also from Ishikawa prefecture. People from Ishikawa stuck together. We had all the food we wanted—cans of bamboo shoots, dried tofu without limit, and shiitake and other mushrooms. Whenever people came, I fed them. It seemed my purpose in life and I enjoyed it. I soon became pregnant. I was ecstatic at that, too.

In Japan there was so little already. Clothing was rationed and food had begun to disappear. Simply having so much food made Manchuria attractive. My husband would get purchase orders from the military for items specified and go on purchasing trips to places like Shanghai. If he thought those things would sell well, he'd buy large quantities and bring them back. He bought from Japanese trading companies and sometimes from the Manchurians. "Authorized military vendor" really meant "broker." He made a great deal of money. I was amazed you could make so much money from the military. I was brought up in the family of a poor military man. When my father died from an accident at the shipyard, we got eight hundred yen in life insurance. My mother said that money came to us from our nation. It seemed a huge sum.

I told my husband, "This must be a dream!" "Why?" he asked me, and I pointed to our bankbook entries showing deposits of three thousand yen, five thousand yen. My husband would order fish roe, yellowtail, or pickled radish from Mukden by the boxcarload and they'd ship it to us. I just couldn't believe you could get money this way. I wondered if I might not be punished for eating things like pound cake.

Soldiers came to relax at our place and I'd make simple country dishes that would delight them. One might ask me, "Okusan, what would you like to eat?" I'd say, "Pound cake!" "Great, I'll get it!" and he'd go to the commissary and buy butter, flour, sugar—the military had lots of everything, anything. If I said, "I'd like cream puffs," someone might bring four or five. They took good care of me! The chance to eat Japanese food and talk to a Japanese woman was enough for them.

There I was, a real country girl, without pretense, like their elder sister or somebody's wife, really almost a high-school girl who chatted on about all kinds of simple things. They appreciated it. My husband's business was booming and he delighted in making people happy. And I enjoyed it, too. I had no idea what lay ahead.

Dancing into the Night

HARA KIYOSHI

He's at the Ōtemachi Cultural Center, with a class of ten students. Here, on Tuesdays and Saturdays, he coaches prospective entrants in ballroom-dance competitions. Today they are in the midst of the tango. He glides effortlessly, his shoulder-length hair swaying as he dances. Small, very thin, and seventy-six years old, he's known as Hara of the Waltz, after his specialty. "I'm getting old, I suppose, but all the dancers are physically so much bigger today. They tire me out."

Once the shooting started, everything was cut and dried. It was a very prosaic, barbaric time. Dance was completely prohibited. Before the war there were about eight official dance halls in Tokyo, and four more in Yokohama. I taught "British-style" ballroom dancing. I'd taught myself from a book by the British world champion. I looked up words I didn't know in dictionaries. I translated it phrase by phrase. Later I found out I'd made a lot of mistakes, but that's how I learned. I chose it because it was *British*. I was a student of design, especially drawing. I had a job at the Matsuzakaya Department Store, but it was just mixing dye for *yūzen* dyeing on kimonos. I quit because I was making a lot more money teaching dancing on the side—one hundred and twenty yen a month as an instructor at a time when a Tokyo Imperial University graduate made forty-eight, an Art School grad got forty-seven, and a Waseda man earned just forty-five.

I was still a student when I first taught dancing in Mita in a kindergarten building that was free in the evenings. Neighbors complained: "It's unforgivable for men and women to embrace each other in a kindergarten!" The police issued a warning, ordering us to remove ourselves from there. It was that kind of era, so I started a membership dance hall near Shibuya. My start as a true professional, I guess. That was 1925.

I remember the night the Taishō Emperor died. It was December 25, 1926, Christmas night. We were dancing. All of a sudden, the police stomped in. We didn't know the Emperor had died. Under Japanese law, it was forbidden to dance and play music on such a day. The owner of the hall and I were hauled off to the Shibuya police station and kept there for a day—all for holding a Christmas party. Special editions of the newspapers had been issued, and the hawkers had been calling out the news, but we hadn't heard them, since we were making our own loud noise. Some newspapers wrote we had danced while holding the special editions!

Of the eight dance halls in Tokyo, the most famous was the Florida. A lot of literary people gathered there. There was one called the *Nichi-Bei* Dance Hall—the Japan-America—at Nihonbashi, but whatever names they adopted, they all did British-style dancing. Those places were run on a ticket system. Patrons would pay an entrance fee and buy tickets on arrival. The girls were all lined up along the wall. You picked your partner and put your ticket in a box on the wall. An expensive place cost about fifty *sen* admission, then ten *sen* a dance. You could also go as a couple on special "pair tickets." If you wanted to dance with a particularly popular partner, you might have to wait ten numbers. A dance hall would hire maybe fifty or sixty dancers. Good ones were light on their feet and could do any dance. I trained them for about two months. The halls paid their transportation fees to the lessons. While they were working, dancers got about a forty percent of the ticket moneys in the expensive halls and a fifty-fifty split in the cheaper places.

The public morals of the dancers were subject to great scrutiny. Each girl had a time card on which she had to write down the hour and minute she left the hall and the exact time she arrived home, with her parents' seal affixed when she got there. The next morning she had to show that to the manager at the hall and get his seal too. In Yokohama there were cafés where sailors went. Mostly foreigners. Those places didn't work on a ticket system. More American-style. A lot of the sailors were Americans. The cafés usually had a dance floor, and a counter functioning as a bar. We sometimes went to one and danced into the early morning hours. We'd splurge on a one-yen taxi, but they'd do it round-trip for one-yen-fifty. Real luxury. I personally never drank while I danced, so I was very popular among the dancers.

Girls who liked to go dancing were true *moga*—"modern girls." The most advanced were the telephone operators. Next came the typists—not those in Japanese, but those in horizontal languages. You know, English and the like. The third most modern were theater girls. I taught those kinds of people to dance. Men were a little different. A lot of sportsmen, rugby players in particular, especially from Waseda. I guess they were often invited to foreign countries, so they came to learn just before going abroad. Tennis players, too. I can't seem to recall ever getting any baseball players, though. Professional dancers also took lessons at my place.

And Imperial Navy cadets. They went on a long overseas cruise when they graduated and it was felt that it wouldn't look smart if Japanese officers just stood along the wall when they received one of the frequent invitations where they might be required to dance. Maybe the navy knew more of the world than the army, or perhaps they were just more relaxed, but beginning five or six years before the war, they always came for lessons prior to sailing. "Make them dance," I was told.

They would come on Wednesdays and Fridays, accompanied by a superior officer. But we didn't have enough girls at my place for all of them at once, so I had no choice but to teach some young officers the male steps and others the female steps, and then pair the lads off. I taught them the waltz, the Bruce, the quickstep, and finally the tango. If we ran out of time, we'd skip the tango. I'd just show them how to do it. A tango was usually only played once in an evening, so you really didn't need it unless you were going to Argentina. I guess this was how I introduced classroom instruction in ballroom dance into Japan for the very first time.

I sometimes even went to naval officers' clubs. They had really good record collections, some even I didn't have. Even jazz. They went overseas so often and got a free pass through customs, so they could bring anything in.

A couple of years before the war, it was decreed that patrons of the dance halls had to give their name, age, profession, and address when they checked in. Then we received a notification that instructional halls were to close within a year. Dance halls were given a two-year warning. The final day of the dance halls was the last day of October, 1940. They were packed. We were given permission to remain open until two A.M. Even on Christmas nights we'd only been allowed to stay open to midnight. The last melody was "Auld Lang Syne." All the girls were weeping. Understandably. From the morrow they no longer had jobs.

Visits to the officers' clubs were also cut back, but in the early days of the war, people who loved dance still got together secretly at home and danced a little. I was invited to the estate of the owner of a great railway company to give private lessons. They still held dance parties, never more than ten people, but they were even given a warning for that. The police kept their eyes peeled for everything.

On December 8, 1941, my wife and I had gone to Hibiya to see a Western movie. As we left the theater, shouts of "Extra! Extra!" were everywhere. When I saw the news, it suddenly came to me why, for six months, navy students hadn't appeared for their regular dance lessons. I guess it wasn't necessary anymore.

Bringing the Liberals to Heel

HATANAKA SHIGEO [1]

Sunlight streaming in warms his study this February day. Books dating from the nineteen-thirties that survived the air raids of the war cover the walls from floor to ceiling. Speaking very quickly and forcefully, with great determination, he says, "I sold all my really good books to make ends meet afterwards, so there's nothing much here."

He was forced to step down as editor of Chūō Kōron *[The Central Review], one of Japan's leading monthly magazines, and then he was arrested, in this same room, for alleged communist activities in 1944.*

I had hoped to work for *Chūō Kōron* from the time I was at Waseda University. Its editorial policies were founded on what was called "liberalism"—which meant the same as "democracy" today, including the political left—and its conflicts with the military had a long history. In 1918, *Chūō Kōron* opposed the Japanese course of action in the Siberian Intervention with a lead article by Tokyo Imperial University professor Yoshino Sakuzō that was really a call to debate. By the time the Japan-China War began in 1937, of course, we couldn't really let our opposition to the military show on the surface, or we'd all have been taken away.

We did, however, give those who were accused, imprisoned, then released under the Peace Preservation Law a chance to present their case. In order to deceive the authorities, we also carried some writings by military men. Had all our writers been leftist or centrists, *Chūō Kōron* would have been crushed far earlier. We called the military men our "magic shields," as they were supposed to ward off bullets. Unfortunately, it didn't work. It just made us feel a little more secure a little while longer. Not once can I recall *Chūō Kōron* really agreeing with or supporting the military. Sometimes it did speak paradoxically, sounding as if it were going along, but only on the surface in an editorial or in a style which might have appeared to be right-wing.

We had a circulation of a hundred thousand at our peak, and censorship was always a possibility. In the early stages of the war, we submitted our magazine for approval only after distribution. If there was a problem, they'd tell us then. The editor responsible would be summoned. The issue was already at the bookstores when you faced the problem of having to delete something. The local police were responsible for collecting the magazines from the stores. They would be piled up in the office of the

Tokkō—the Special Higher Police—at the local police station. They were the thought police. Then we had to go there and, holding a ruler against the so-called "bad pages," tear them out. Everybody had to throw themselves into this—managers, printers, even the waiters in our cafeteria. You rented automobiles and raced to each police station. Once you'd got a seal of approval from the thought police showing that pages had been deleted, it was up to you to take them back to the bookstores.

The most extreme example of this was our March 1938 issue. Ishikawa Tatsuzō's novel *Living Soldiers [Ikiteiru Heitai]* was censored. It described the soldiers' cruel behavior in China. Ishikawa had actually been dispatched to the front by *Chūō Kōron* to write for us, and had been there the previous December when the Nanking Incident occurred. More than one hundred pages had to be ripped from the issue, but the issues still sold out. I was really moved by that. You couldn't even lower the price, and the magazine was thinner on one side, so it was obvious that pages had been cut out, and, anyway, we had to affix a seal: Revised Edition. The cut-out pages were left at the police station as proof you'd done it. Yet, even without a discount, *Chūō Kōron* sold.

I don't know how many times we were summoned to talk things over with the military. In May 1939, the Press Section of the Army Ministry "invited" us to meet at the Ryōtei Kōraku, the restaurant in which the rebellious officers had barricaded themselves during the February Rebellion in 1936. They said dinner would be on them, and they wanted to be sure that all the principal editorial staff attended, because everyone from the army would be coming, from the head of the Press Section on down.

Our president, Shimanaka Yūsaku, was a really courageous person. He spoke out first: "You military men have only to give the command, and the ordinary people will face right or left, as you please; but we have complicated intellectuals to deal with. If you want to convince them you must reason with them." This was, of course, a sound argument. Immediately, though, the head of the Press Section jumped up and shouted, "What do you mean by that? You can't run a magazine according to those ideas!" and all of them began to shout. When military men drink, some turn violent. Fortunately, just as they started to get rowdy, the serving girls came in and managed to calm them down.

A few months later at a "gathering" of publishers staged by the Cabinet Board of Information, we were told to submit our editorial plans and lists of anticipated writers for upcoming issues. From this time on they simply requested the withdrawal of certain projects and authors, and began to openly interfere with our editorial policy. We were given a list of authors who were considered "holders of leftist ideology" or who were "pro-American" or "holders of liberal ideas." I recall some sad occasions when I had to visit authors to notify them that we were withdrawing their writings.

"It's finally come" was all I thought when I heard the news of Pearl Harbor. From the onset of the war, I thought Japan would lose. It had no mobility and no material strength. One day after Pearl Harbor, a special meeting was called in Tokyo by the Cabinet Board of Information. The real reason for the war was the enemy's egotistic ambition to control the world, they told us. The New World Order would now become "Hakkō Ichiu," "Eight Corners of the World Under One Roof." Publishers were to emphasize Japan's superior position in the ongoing war and they should strive to instill a deep hatred for America and Britain in the minds of the people. These were only a few of the instructions issued.

Beginning December 19, 1941, the Army Press Section held a meeting on the sixth of each month at a restaurant in Shinjuku or Kōjimachi to set the tone for support of the war in all magazines. Attendance was taken. A formulaic description of the war situation was given. Active-duty officers commented on each magazine and general requests were made by the army. "Requests" meant "orders." Chūō Kōron, Kaizō [Reconstruction], and Nihon Hyōron [Japan Comment] were frequently denounced.

In these meetings people from other magazines hardly said anything. If they tried to defend us, they thought they themselves might be accused next time. Frankly speaking, they were also thinking, "It serves them right!" Their competitors were being reduced by one. Take Kōron [Review], a fairly right-wing magazine, which did just what the authorities recommended. Surprisingly, left-wing people had gotten together to found Kōron, and then did nothing but urge on the war effort. It was written like an ancient text full of the Japanese myths. It didn't sell at all. Less than a third of our sales. For them, readership might increase with our disappearance.

We also had a regular gathering of the editors of the general-circulation magazines, Kaizō, Chūō Kōron, Bungei Shunjū, Kōron, Nihon Hyōron. The editors-in-chief or their assistants met about once a month to talk things over. At one meeting, we at Chūō Kōron were practically told to slit our bellies open. They criticized us by saying our president Shimanaka lacked an "understanding of the war" and that a liberal like him shouldn't be the head of a magazine. The editor-in-chief of Kōron, who accused us in right-wing terms then, wrote erotic novels after the war when that kind of thing prospered. You really can't do much about changes in the masses, but at least people who pretend to be intellectuals shouldn't change the color of their coats depending on how they calculate their immediate advantage. There seemed to be so many people like that! Really, it was pitiful, those swift shifts from left to right to nothing.

Honestly speaking, nobody said openly that they opposed the war. If you said that you'd have been killed immediately, or taken away and killed later. The editorial division did what little we could. We met with the military, but they didn't listen to us. We argued that we honestly loved our nation, but that without convincing the intellectual class, victory would not be possible. They said that way of thinking was wrong. "Everyone must put their minds to war" was their slogan. To them, that meant run up the flag, sing military songs, and cheer loudly! Even a nihilistic attitude toward war was wrong. They said they could tell if we were sincere just by looking at the color in our faces.

We never could relax our guard completely. We were always worried that something would become a problem. For instance, the censor didn't give us any trouble with Tanizaki Jun'ichirō's novel *Sasameyuki* [published in English as *The Makioka Sisters*]. It appeared in our January and March issues in 1943. It didn't say anything antimilitary, and there weren't any erotic scenes, so it appeared as printed. Then the army became directly involved! "What kind of book is this?" they said. "Here we are, in a life-and-death struggle, when each soldier at the front is fighting hard and bitterly, and out comes this story about the marriage proposals and wedding negotiations of the daughters from the Senba commercial district of Osaka. When nobody has proper clothes, why make such a fuss about unimportant issues like arranging marriages? How dare you print such frivolity? It's totally individualistic. And it's only about women's lives anyway!"

That's how they attacked us. *Chūō Kōron* must be opposing the war. At that level, unless you're really courageous, anti-militarism isn't really possible. In 1943, all Japanese magazines were asked to place the slogan "*Uchiteshi yamamu!*" ["We'll never cease fire till our enemies cease to be!"] from the eighth-century *Record of Ancient Matters* on the cover of their March issues to commemorate Army Day. If we'd done that, it would have been embarrassing. People who'd be excited by something like that wouldn't be reading *Chūō Kōron*. But I knew there'd be a big fuss if we didn't put the phrase in someplace, so we printed it just after the editorial. That wouldn't do! We were the only magazine that didn't obey instructions.

It wasn't good to have any doubts about the war. Japan was always right. It was inconceivable to glorify democratic nations like America or England. We had to say Japan was virtually the chief of Asia and would be the future leader of world peace. Liberals' manuscripts were no longer acceptable. Shimizu Ikutarō was a "liberal" whose article "Americanism as the Enemy" we were prepared to publish in April 1943. The original title was "Americanism," but I myself added the rest out of caution. The article stated that we should study the dynamism of America as a social system, that Japan needed to know about that. They interpreted this as praising America.

I was the chief at the time. I couldn't really stay in the editorial section after that, no matter how much I explained. I was forbidden to enter the Army Ministry. A postcard came from the head of the Army Press Section bearing his seal. He formally broke off personal relations. If relations were broken off, a magazine had no way of continuing. Had I stayed, the magazine itself would have been crushed. I submitted my letter of resignation, but my president wouldn't accept it. In the end it was put out that I had personally accepted responsibility *and* the present *Chūō Kōron* editorial section was dissolved.

I was temporarily suspended. The July 1943 issue was withdrawn from circulation "voluntarily." This was the first time such emergency action had had to be taken since the founding of the magazine. The issue had already been printed and was ready to be bound. Just to look at the titles of the articles now is embarrassing, they sound so right-wing, but even they were not acceptable.

All of us at *Chūō Kōron* shared the same thoughts. There wasn't a single one of us who wagged his tail for extreme militarism. We didn't need to explain our strategy. It may sound like I'm exaggerating, but our idea was to figure out how to push social justice and keep liberal thought alive without glorifying militarism. Our readers during the war were far more progressive than we were. They understood even without our saying it. If we just suggested something, they grasped our liberal intentions. We could substitute empty circles for the dangerous words—words like *Communism*—and our readers were able to fill them in for themselves.

We had to pay careful attention to the word *Emperor*. Whenever it appeared at the bottom of a line, it had to be brought to the top of the next line. Neither could you divide the two characters that make up the word. We had to insert a special space, reserved for the His Imperial Majesty alone, above the word whenever it appeared. People would laugh about it today, but then we had to take it all with deadly seriousness.

PART TWO

Have "Faith in Victory"

I am resolved to dedicate myself, body and soul, to the country, and to set at ease the august mind of our Sovereign. And I believe that every one of you, my fellow countrymen, will not care for your life but gladly share in the honor to make of yourself His Majesty's humble shield.

The key to victory lies in a "faith in victory." For 2600 years since it was founded, our Empire has never known a defeat. This record alone is enough to produce a conviction in our ability to crush any enemy no matter how strong. Let us pledge ourselves that we will never stain our glorious history, but will go forward. . . .

The rise or fall of our Empire and the prosperity or ruin of East Asia literally depend upon the outcome of this war. Truly it is time for the one hundred million of us Japanese to dedicate all we have and sacrifice everything for our country's cause. As long as there remains under the policy of Eight Corners of the World Under One Roof this great spirit of loyalty and patriotism, we have nothing to fear in fighting America and Britain. Victory, I am convinced, is always with the illustrious virtues of our Sovereign. In making known these humble views of mine, I join with all my countrymen in pledging myself to assist in the grand Imperial enterprise.

> —PRIME MINISTER TŌJŌ HIDEKI
>
> *December 8, 1941,* in an address in Tokyo carried by radio at 1:00 P.M. local time, about ten hours after the attack on Hawaii began on the other side of the International Date Line.

THE JAPANESE PEOPLE first heard they were at war with the United States and Great Britain on the early morning of Monday, December 8, 1941. The news that blared from radios, while electrifying in its suddenness, was largely greeted with consternation, stunned silence, and not a little confusion in the streets of Japan's capital and across the Empire. This initial announcement, for one thing, gave no indication of how the new war was going, but only made clear that Japan was now fighting not only a China that refused to surrender, but the world's two greatest naval powers and its premier industrial nation.

The possibility of such a war had been growing for months. Japan had joined the Axis Pact in September 1940, becoming an ally of Britain's enemies Italy and Germany. In December of that year, the United States embargoed exports to Japan of scrap iron and other war materiel. Japan signed a nonaggression pact with the Soviet Union in April 1941, freeing Japan to turn southwards, though it still kept six hundred thousand troops deployed along the Manchukuo-Soviet border. Finally, in July 1941, Japan moved into the southern part of French Indochina to cut off supply routes to China, leading to the freezing of all Japanese assets in the United States and the imposition by America, Britain, and the government of the Dutch East Indies of embargoes on the sale of petroleum and steel to Japan. Under these dark clouds, negotiations between the United States and Japan seemed to grow ever more bitter. The talk in Tokyo was of the American-British-Chinese-Dutch East Indies encirclement of Japan—"the ABCD line"—which, if not broken, threatened to strangle the nation. When Lieutenant General Tōjō Hideki was named prime minister on October 16, 1941, heading a cabinet in which he also served as Army Minister and Home Minister, most political observers took it as a clear indication that Japan was preparing to fight.

It was, however, one thing to talk about refusing to yield to unwarranted American demands and to bluster about the nation's unwillingness to let the British continue to supply China overland through Burma. It was a very different matter to actually be fighting such a war. On hearing the news, many asked themselves, "How can such a war be won?" Yet the government moved swiftly to establish the proper tone for the conflict. Solemnly the Imperial Declaration of War, issued as an Imperial rescript bearing the seal of Emperor Hirohito, placed responsibility for the conflict on the United States and England for supporting and encouraging the Chinese in "disturbing the peace of East Asia" in pursuit of their "inordinate ambition to dominate the Orient." The rescript stated that it had been the Emperor's profound hope that peace be maintained. "But Our adversaries, showing not the least spirit of conciliation, have unduly delayed a settlement; and in the meantime they have intensified the economic and political pressure to compel thereby Our Empire to submission . . . Our Empire, for its existence and self-defense, has no other recourse but to appeal to arms and to crush every obstacle in its path." ° To a people long assured that Manchuria was vital to Japan's survival, and that the war dead in China were just Japan's latest payment in blood to ensure its vital interests on the Asian continent, this was a believable explanation. It seemed only natural to seek some way to continue.

The Emperor did not, of course, address his people directly. His status was considered far too exalted for that. Instead, his prime minister delivered an address after the rescript was proclaimed, also carried live by radio. Tōjō did not promise swift victory, but issued a call for the nation to join him in self-sacrifice. Indeed, he declared, "Our adversaries, boasting rich natural resources, aim at the domination of the world. In order to annihilate this enemy and to construct an unshakable new order of East Asia, we should anticipate a long war." †

The people of the Japanese capital responded to the news as might have been expected, given decades of patriotic education and public exhortation, reinforced by many years of wartime reporting and mobilization. Doubts, fears, and concerns remained largely unvoiced; instead, there were well-prepared rallies and marches to the Imperial Palace. By evening, official patriotic fervor found support in banner "extra" edition headlines followed by news of Japan's "great victory" at Honolulu over the American fleet. This was the first real news of the war. As word of the sinking of American battleships spread, a feeling of relief and elation swept the country.

News of other triumphs soon poured in—landings across a broad swath of southeast Asia including Malaya, the Philippines, Guam, and Burma, as well as the destruction of two British capital ships by Japanese aircraft. Within a few weeks of Pearl Harbor, places that had long been symbols of Western supremacy fell one after another to Japanese forces: Guam, Wake, Manila, Hong Kong, Rangoon, the "impregnable fortress" of Singapore, Batavia, the capital of the Dutch East Indies, Bataan in the Philippines, and Mandalay in Burma. Finally, on May 6, 1942, the last American resistance in the Philippines ended with the surrender of the

---

° See Ienaga Saburō, *The Pacific War: World War II and the Japanese* (New York: Pantheon, 1978), pp. 136–37. Robert J. C. Butow discusses the wording of the rescript and Tōjō's speech in *Tojo and the Coming of the War* (Stanford: Stanford University Press, 1961), pp. 409–11.

† Tōjō's remarks as translated by *Japan Times & Advertiser*, Monday, December 8, 1941, pp. 1 and 4.

island bastion of Corregidor. Within six months of the start of the war, Japanese imperial forces had swept away the British, American, and Dutch empires in Asia and in the Central and South Pacific. Japan was now master of conquests as grand as those of any Western empire-builder. Japanese armies stood at the borders of India and were poised for a descent on Australia. Japanese fleets had raided deep into the Indian Ocean and appeared to control the Western Pacific. Although fighting in China continued, the realization of the Greater East Asia Co-Prosperity Sphere seemed at hand. Who could challenge an army and navy that had so brilliantly planned and achieved these conquests? What could possibly stay Japan's hand now?

If one harbored secret doubts, news photos of seemingly endless fields of British, Australian, and Indian prisoners captured at Singapore, and paintings of Americans humiliated and surrendering on Wake Island or at Corregidor, and of British generals humbled and yielding to General Yamashita in Singapore, seemed vivid assurance that Western domination of Asia had been destroyed and that the future was Japanese.

The new lands in the south, often referred to collectively as the Southern Area by the military, were virtually unknown to most Japanese. Nevertheless, the image of a strong Japan, leading its noble younger brothers in their efforts to free themselves from centuries of backwardness and Western domination, had a powerful resonance for people who were well aware of the sharp policies of racial discrimination of the Western powers. "Asia for the Asians" may have seemed an empty slogan in the West, but Japan's Greater East Asia Co-Prosperity Sphere ended Western European or U.S. control over Sarawak, Borneo, Sumatra, Java, the Celebes, the Moluccas, northern and western New Guinea, the Solomon Islands, the Philippines, Malaya, French Indochina, Burma, the Andaman Islands, Guam, Wake, and the Gilbert and Marshall Islands. Tens of thousands of soldiers from India among the British armies captured in Malaya and Singapore enlisted in a new Japanese-controlled Indian National Army.

In the new Imperial domains, the Japanese Imperial forces, who had long been taught that there was no greater shame than to be taken prisoner, now found themselves in possession of tens of thousand of captured enemy solders and civilians. One of the great tragedies of the Second World War in Asia was just about to begin. Allied soldiers, sailors, and many civilians who had fallen into Japanese hands now stood at the virtual gates of Hell. Their plight was eventually revealed to the world in shocking terms by belated news of the Bataan Death March and the show trial and execution of some of the captured Americans pilots from the daring April 1942 air raid on Japan. But the vast majority of those held were beyond the reach of Allied influence for the duration of the war. Thousands of these officers and men were to die from abuse, neglect, disease, starvation, or outright murder at the hands of Japanese troops or Korean camp guards—themselves on the lowest rung of the Imperial Army's ladder of prestige. Of some 61,000 British, Australian, and Dutch prisoners captured by the Japanese in Southeast Asia in 1941–42, for example, some 12,000 died working on the building of the Burma-Siam Railroad during the war.°

Within a few days of December 8, the conflict was officially anointed "the Greater East Asia War." Unlike the seemingly interminable China Incident, the Japanese government openly declared this to be a total war and few Japanese could doubt that it required total mobilization. Men who in prewar days would have been immediately shunted into the lowest levels of the reserves, now found themselves bound for training units and then the front as millions more were brought into the armed forces. Reservists, including veterans of campaigns in Manchuria and China, were recalled to the colors. Volunteers as young as eighteen and "Youth Soldiers" in their middle teens were actively recruited, and within a couple of years they began to be assigned not to training tasks, but to combat.

Enmeshed in a total mobilization for war, each Japanese nonetheless went to war alone. Many had complex feelings, hopes, dreams, and doubts at the moment they passed into the military world, and few seem to have been prepared for the almost unbearably brutal life of a Japanese soldier—for brutality was the essence of Japanese military training. This system of rigid discipline, beatings, harassment, degradation, and mindless hierarchy was intended to instill into each recruit an unquestioning obedience to orders, any orders. Those orders were considered to come not merely from the superior soldier or officer who gave them, but the very pinnacle of the Imperial state, the Great Field Marshal Emperor himself. In the early months of the war, as Japan's forces surged across Greater East Asia, little attention was paid to anything but the achievement of total victory in the name of the Emperor. Whatever was necessary for that was permissible—indeed, required—and in the final analysis, virtually any act, no matter how cruel, insensitive, or horrible was, in fact, committed. An army on the advance—particularly an army brutalized and relieved by higher authority of all sense of personal responsibility—is not afraid of consequences.

Contempt for Chinese and Koreans, long present in Japan, was

° John Keegan, ed., *The Times Atlas of the Second World War* (New York: Harper & Row, 1989), p. 205.

actively fostered on the China front. As Chinese military forces became less and less able or willing to meet Japanese forces head on, the war took on more of a hit-and-run character, and "pacification" operations were carried out under the "Three-All" policy—"Burn All, Seize All, Kill All." It was hardly surprising that Japanese forces—some transferred directly from the China front—took similar attitudes and tactics with them into the "liberation" of southeast Asia and applied them not just to the defeated prisoners of the Western powers, but to the very populations they were "liberating." Japanese forces, now at the end of supply lines stretched almost beyond capacity, were ordered to resupply themselves by "local requisition." In war-torn regions, where fields and people had already been laid waste, or in isolated pockets of human habitation which found themselves the focal points of military operations, supplies were soon exhausted or nonexistent. Liberated peoples, who had often welcomed the Japanese initially, soon became, in Japanese eyes, conquered "natives" who dragged their feet and plotted against them. As in China, no act seemed unjustified in the pursuit of victory over an intractable enemy who refused to submit. ■

3 / DECEMBER 8, 1941

"My blood boiled at the news."

ITABASHI KŌSHŪ

He entered the naval academy in late 1944. The war ended before he could graduate. "I was there only ten months, but the impression it made on me was very powerful. Were I young and able to live my life over again, I would still want to go. That kind of education—rigid discipline —is no longer available anywhere in the world. Everything was in order. You acted flat-out, with all your power, every day for one goal. I was full of ardor to abandon my life for the sake of the nation."

Today, he is the Head Priest at Daijōji temple of the Sōdōshū sect of Zen Buddhism, located on the outskirts of Kanazawa City. He wears the full paraphernalia of his office. A heavy rain beats down on the roofs of the enormous temple. Despite the summer season, the dampness is carried in on a chill breeze from the moss gardens below.

I was in the second year of middle school that day, Pearl Harbor Day. "Well, we really did it!" I thought. The sound of the announcement on the radio still reverberates in my ears. [*He hums a few bars from "The Battleship March," the unofficial navy anthem played on the radio to set the tone for victory announcements.*] "News special, News special," high-pitched and rapid. "Beginning this morning before dawn, war has been joined with the Americans and British." I felt as if my blood boiled and my flesh quivered. The whole nation bubbled over, excited and inspired. "We really did it! Incredible! Wonderful!" That's the way it felt then.

I was brought up in a time when nobody criticized Japan. The war started for me, in the brain of this middle-school student, as something that should happen, something that was natural. Every day, we sent warriors off with cheers of *"Banzai! Banzai!"* War was going on in China. "Withdraw your forces," America ordered Japan. If a prime minister with foresight had ordered a withdrawal, he probably would have been assassinated. Even I knew that withdrawal was impossible! There was the ABCD encirclement—the Americans, British, Chinese, and Dutch. They wouldn't give us a drop of oil.

The Japanese had to take a chance. That was the psychological situation in which we found ourselves. If you bully a person, you should give him room to flee. There is a Japanese proverb that says, "A cornered mouse will bite a cat." America is evil, Britain is wrong, we thought. We didn't know why they were encircling us. In Japan, nobody was calculating whether we would win or not. We simply hit out. Our blood was hot! We fought. Until the very end, no one considered the possibility that Japan could lose. We were like Sergeant Yokoi and Lieutenant Onoda—the men who emerged from the jungles, one in Guam, the other in the Philippines, in the 1970s—who couldn't imagine Japan had been defeated. That's the way the whole country felt. Today's youth can't conceive of such feelings.

I was at the First Middle School in Sendai, the best school in Miyagi prefecture. I never really thought about becoming a military man. I was thinking about being a doctor. But the whole nation was at war, everyone was for the war. You don't feel that you want to preserve your own life in such an atmosphere. I guess I was simpleminded, but I thought if you have to go into the military anyway, better to go someplace good. I didn't think I'd make it, but the naval academy was smart, attractive. I took the entrance exams in my fifth year of middle school. Until then, only two hundred or three hundred were taken from the whole nation each year, but in our time, two or three thousand were admitted. It was as if they were using a bucket to scoop us up.

There was no sense that you personally might be hit by a bullet. You fought for the sake of the nation, for the sake of justice, whenever or wherever the Imperial Standard led. We didn't even think of the pain of being blown to pieces. The objective of war is always these things. No wars have ever been fought for any other reasons. For "the sake of His Imperial Highness" seemed to embody everything—nation, history, race, and peace. That's why it served to inflame passions and cause everyone to seethe with fervor. For Japan, that was a sacred war. Japan claimed it would unite the eight corners of the world under one roof. If Japan had declared it was fighting only to add territory, I don't believe we ever could have gone as far as Borneo.

"I heard it on the radio."

YOSHIDA TOSHIO

Tōgō Jinja, the Shintō shrine dedicated to Admiral Tōgō Heihachirō, naval hero of the Russo-Japanese War, is a green refuge at the end of a warren

of trendy Tokyo back-street hangouts for young Japanese at Harajuku.
Behind the shrine is the Suikōkai, the former navy officers' club. Today,
officers of the Maritime Self-Defense Force are numbered among its mem-
bers along with former Imperial Navy officers. Inside, a large painting of
the super battleship Yamato *hangs near the entryway. By the reception-*
ist's window is a small stand selling replicas of the painting, naval hats,
nautical books, and models of Tōgō's flagship Mikasa.

"My father was in the navy. I was crazy about battleships as a kid
and was raised in Sasebo, the great naval base. So I ended up an officer
without really thinking much about it." He wears a jacket the color of
young leaves, and dark green trousers. He exudes scholarliness and cer-
tainly looks as if he could have written his thirty books. As we talk, he
sometimes nods to other graduates of the Imperial Naval Academy passing
through the lobby.

"The Imperial Japanese Army and Navy have opened hostilities with
the United States and England in the Western Pacific." I was on my way
to my office at the Navy Ministry when I heard that announcement. That
was how I learned of war for the first time. I, a full lieutenant in the
Intelligence Department, Navy General Staff, assigned to the English
Section, didn't even know they were planning it. I got off the train at
Shimbashi Station. From a restaurant called the Shimbashitei, a radio was
blaring the news. I felt like someone had poured cold water on my head.

I knew Japan shouldn't fight a war. I looked at Japan like an outsider.
A chill cut right through me. I can feel it now. I ran to the Navy Ministry.
Those who had known about Pearl Harbor were all smiles. The people in
my section didn't know anything.

Every time I remember that day I am seized with the same feeling
of disappointment. In the next couple of days, information about the
attack on Pearl Harbor, that afternoon of December 8, came pouring in.
Soon everyone knew. "Victory, victory!" Things became raucous with the
news. But people like me thought from the beginning that Japan would
be completely defeated. I was stunned by our success. Those in the
Operations Section told us, *"We* planned this!" They were swaggering up
and down the halls, swinging their shoulders. Full of pride.

I was supposed to be an insider. I was in a section which had to have
a critical mode of thinking, which had to try to look into the future. For
about seven months just prior to the outbreak of the war I had been in
Indonesia, in Surabaja and Batavia, trying to purchase oil. Japan had been
cut off by America, so we were trying to get some petroleum from the
Dutch East Indies. But Japan's authorities failed in "risk management."
You can say that just by looking at that time with what passes for common

sense today. The leaders looked only at their pluses and paid no attention to minuses. When looking at weapons systems, they only measured offensive capabilities, not defensive requirements. They held that if you attack, the path of opportunity will open up naturally. If you try to defend yourself, you will lose. "Advance, advance" therefore became the only objective. But what would happen when you advanced? What situations would arise? These things were not in their minds. It was almost a philosophy. Manage risks to prevent a collision between countries? Protect your interests by preventing risks? That was not something they cared about. As in *bushidō,* whether you lived or died was not crucial. Individual autonomy or independence? *Not* important.

Our stock of petroleum was kept completely under wraps. It was an absolute secret. Where we obtained oil, how much, and at what price, were also kept Top Secret. The section that had that data was the Fuel Section in the Navy Ministry. We on the Navy General Staff couldn't get that data. They just told us to go to the East Indies and buy oil. I was part of a delegation led by Yoshizawa Ken'ichi, an envoy from the Foreign Ministry. There were five or six from the Foreign Ministry and attachés with staffs from the army and navy. I was the bottom-most member of our naval group of four. The attachés each had residences in the capital of Batavia, so from time to time we'd get together there and talk, and once in a while we all met together at the consulate general in Batavia. But I hardly knew anything about how events were moving. It was just "Hey, Yoshida, do this," or "Take care of that, Lieutenant."

There wasn't any chance at all that the Dutch governor general of the East Indies was going to agree to sell us oil after all these negotiations. The war in Europe had already begun. If the Dutch sold petroleum to Japan, the American embargo on oil sales to Japan would have become meaningless, so the American consul general was right on top of events, making sure they didn't. But I guess even we who were there didn't fully realize that at the time. "Somehow things will work out for Japan"— that's what we thought. That was because Japan saw itself as so strong. It was more over-confidence than self-confidence: "If we go to Indonesia, everyone will tremble in fear and awe and bow down before us. All we have to do is say 'This is necessary for Japan. Moreover, this will make you happy, too.'" We tried to cover our desires with talk of the Greater East Asia Co-Prosperity Sphere.

We had plenty of intelligence information. I got information from the Foreign Ministry, from newspapers, and we received telegrams. People brought back information from many places. We had lots of files. But nobody looked at them. We didn't have much of a staff. The navy didn't spend money on intelligence. Nobody really looked into these things. I wonder why that was the case? Everybody there was a graduate of Etajima, the naval academy. These men were considered qualified to be vice-admirals or full admirals. They had all made their way to the Center—as we called the heart of the navy—since they'd finished at the top of their classes at the academy, taken the exams for the naval staff college, passed, and been there for two years. Everybody said these were the most "excellent" officers in the Imperial Navy. I've often wondered since what that word *excellence* meant to them.

On Admiral Yamamoto's Flagship

NODA MITSUHARU

While the majority of the warships of the Imperial Japanese Navy were steaming toward their battle stations, Admiral Yamamoto Isoroku, Commander-in-Chief of the Combined Fleet, was aboard his flagship, the battleship Nagato, *riding at anchor in Japan's Inland Sea, preparing to give the final order that would commit Japan to war and the navy to the attack on Pearl Harbor.*

Present at the beginning, Noda Mitsuharu was a sailor during the war. He ended up ashore on the island of Saipan and took part in the Japanese garrison's final "banzai" charge July 7, 1944. Wounded, he was one of the few survivors. When he returned home after the war, his gravestone had already been erected.

I was assigned to the Headquarters Combined Fleet as a scribe first class, a clerk in the paymaster's branch of the navy in April 1941. I don't know why I was assigned to headquarters, except that my record at naval training school was good. When I graduated in June 1939, I was sent around the world, or at least half of it, on a training cruise. When we got to Honolulu they didn't let us into Pearl Harbor, but we did go ashore for a one-day "home stay." The crew of the ship was taken care of by the various Japanese prefectural associations on Oahu. I'm from Ibaragi, which unfortunately had no group, so the one from neighboring Fukushima prefecture took care of me.

That day, the daughter of the host family came to meet me in a car! She was a high-school graduate working at the Dole Pineapple factory, like her father and her elder brother. What surprised me most when I got to her house was that there were two other cars! That was astounding. Just laborers at a pineapple factory—not noble offspring of immigrant barons—but each had his own automobile! What a grand country, I thought! In those days, in my hometown of Mito there was only one taxi company with about ten vehicles. Town hall and the police station each had a few more, and maybe one or two families in the whole city had private cars. The roads we took on Oahu were all paved. In Mito there was only a single hard-top road. When the family took me back to my ship, they dropped off cases of Dole pineapple cans for us sailors to take with us.

December 8, 1941, I was serving aboard the battleship *Nagato*, flagship of Admiral Yamamoto Isoroku. We were still in the Inland Sea, in touch with the whole fleet by wireless. Orders and commands to the fleets at sea were all in special codes. If it was *"Niitakayama nobore"* [Climb Mount Niitaka], it meant war with America was going to begin and the attack on Hawaii should proceed. There were all kinds of four-digit numbers with special meanings, listed on a mimeographed sheet, so that if they were sent by telegraph, the officers would know their meanings. We scribes were the ones who made up those lists, duplicated them, and then distributed them.

That day was a very special one for us. We were authorized to purchase saké at the canteen. In the navy, on special days like the Emperor's Birthday, we used to have a special feast, with every sailor receiving fish and celebratory red rice, but that day, with fighting still going on, we didn't have the food. Telegrams of celebration and congratulations poured in from the entire nation addressed to Admiral Yamamoto Isoroku personally. Letters and encouraging post cards came to the *Nagato* by the sack. I took care of them, opening every letter and handing them over to the admiral personally. He ordered me to have extra-large name cards made up bearing the inscription: "Combined Fleet Commander-in-Chief Yamamoto Isoroku." On each, he wrote in his own brush hand, "I swear I shall conduct further strenuous efforts and shall not rest on this small success in beginning the war." His handwriting was truly exquisite.

Even when the chief of staff and the other senior officers had retired to their cabins, the Commander of the Combined Fleet's office light still burned. I wondered what he was doing, until I realized he was still writing those responses. As long as the admiral was up, we sailors couldn't go to bed! After December 8, I'm sure he wrote hundreds—no, thousands—of letters. I respected him greatly for this. I put them into envelopes after affixing the admiral's official seal.

Yamamoto Isoroku had been naval attaché to Washington when he was still a captain. He himself wrote how foolish it would be to fight a war against America, particularly after he saw the automobile plants in Detroit and the oilfields of Texas. I served him up close. He loved gambling, cards in particular. He sometimes lost his whole uniform at the table, as the other officers bet for saké. Yamamoto loved *shōgi*—Japanese chess—and he played that constantly. We nicknamed one officer on his staff "the Staff Officer for Chess" because it seemed he was there far more due to his ability to play *shōgi* than for knowledge of logistics, his official assignment.

The Admiral also loved women. He was famous for his geisha lover from Shimbashi. Everybody knew about it. We knew her, too. When the *Nagato* was anchored in Yokosuka, she and her friends all came aboard the battleship. A launch was sent to convey them to the ship and the ship's captain went to the gangway to meet them. The ship's band played popular folk dances. If the army had ever seen that, it would have caused quite an incident! Yamamoto was really a worldly man, flexible, and approachable.

I know these things, really. I knew him, his personality, well. That "sneak attack" was not his intention. We had a special liaison staff officer, Fujii Shigeru, responsible only to the Combined Fleet staff. When they emerged from the operations room after drafting that final order for the general offensive across the Pacific, I witnessed Yamamoto confirming once again: "Without fail, the Americans have been given notice, have they not?" I saw that with my own eyes. This was not supposed to be a sneak attack. The proof of that is the special liaison officer. He was there to keep us in contact with Imperial General Headquarters and the Foreign Ministry. The Americans were supposed to get our note just before the attack.

After the successful attack on Pearl Harbor, we sailors talked about the opportunities we might get. My dream was to go to San Francisco, and there head up the accounting department in the garrison unit after the occupation. All of us in the navy dreamed of going to America. I don't think anybody wanted to go to China.

In a Fighter Cockpit Near the Soviet Border

MOGAMI SADAO [1]

Manchuria's long border with the Soviet Union was the responsibility of the Kwantung Army, as Japan's forces in Manchukuo were known. Even after the China Incident began, there was no stand-down. There were frequent border clashes with the Soviets which even erupted into open warfare. Japan suffered a disastrous defeat in a pitched battle at Khalkin-Gol (Nomonhan) between July and September 1939. Although

*the scale of the defeat was kept secret—more than 20,000 dead—it led
the Japanese army to reevaluate what was required for a war against
the Soviets.* More tanks, more planes, more men were sent. In the
summer of 1941, as the Germans were sweeping across the western
regions of the Soviet Union, the Kwantung Army may have numbered
700,000 and Japanese air strength had doubled to 700 planes.†*

*Mogami Sadao is now an official of the Kaikōsha, the association of
graduates of the Imperial Army's military academy. He graduated in
1940, a member of the fifty-fourth class. In his dark-brown striped suit,
he looks more like a retired businessman than a former fighter pilot.*

In June 1941, my fighter unit was deployed near the eastern border
of Manchuria as a part of special large-scale maneuvers held by the
Kwantung Army. In reality, this was mobilization for war against the
Soviet Union. There weren't even barracks out there. We dug trenches
and dugouts. We made holes in the ground into primitive sleeping quarters. Our orders were to prepare ourselves to be ready to go into combat
against the Soviets on three minutes' notice.

"Three minutes' notice" means you sit alone in the cockpit of your
plane. You eat meals there, brought to you by your ground crew. After
you do that for three days, the next shift takes over. Now you prepare to
scramble in thirty minutes. You wait in a *pisto*—a ready room—near the
airfield, where you chat with your fellow pilots. You do that for three days
and then you get three days completely off duty. On those days I lived in
Jamusu, a pretty large Manchurian town. The hotel was the very best, a
real luxury place, run by Japanese. For three days, all I did was play.

I didn't have even the slightest idea we were going to fight America.
I had only the Soviets in my thoughts. In my education at the military
academy we'd touched on America in class for only a few hours. Something about American military administration. I didn't know anything
about the structure of their air force. Of the Soviets, I knew everything. I
had maps of Soviet airfields at Vladivostok and Khabarovsk on my walls.
I'd memorized them so that I could recognize them on sight in preparation for our attacks. It was like naval pilots learning enemy battleships, or
the layout of enemy harbors. We were there in Manchuria to attack. Our
assignment was to attack on X day in Y month. We were just waiting for

---

* Alvin D. Coox, *Nomonhan: Japan against Russia, 1939*, 2 vol. (Stanford: Stanford
University Press, 1985), is the definitive source. On pages 1123–25 he tabulates the casualties
on the Japanese side from the myriad incomplete sources available.

† Mikuni Ichirō, *Senchū yōgoshū* [*Collection of Phrases Used During the War*] (Tokyo:
Iwanami, 1985), pp. 10–11.

numbers to replace the letters. We sat in our bunkers thinking about anti-Soviet operations and training daily. I was a first lieutenant then.

At the beginning of December, I was sent off to the city of Tonka to take receipt of a sturdier new type of light attack fighter, Type-98, to replace the Type-97s we were then using. At Tonka, I found that Kikuta, one of my classmates at the military air academy, was supposed to be the instructor training us, but we'd been trained together in Type-98s. He said he couldn't teach me anything I didn't already know, so he told me to drop off my ten men in the morning and then enjoy the town. That's what I did each day.

The morning of December 8, I took my men to the field as usual, but it was snowing hard, so they were assigned to classroom training using a blackboard in the hanger. I had to stay. Kikuta came in during the class, pulled me outside the hanger, and told me the Japanese navy had attacked Pearl Harbor. I was shocked beyond belief! "What! War with America! Can we win against America?" was what I actually said. I didn't know anything about the famous U.S.–Japan negotiations. I had spent my days training and my nights drinking saké. We didn't even get newspapers on the Soviet border. War with America! I was astounded. The foreign language I'd studied was Russian. I'm sure there were reasons why that war couldn't have been helped, but even those like me, men who had made the military their career, didn't know a thing about it. That should tell you what the army's state of preparation was like!

We stopped our Type-98 training and returned to our unit, but our mission didn't change. We still continued to prepare for hostilities against the Soviets. Who would be first to carry out a surprise attack, we or the Soviets? That was what we thought about. Our air wing had twenty-seven planes, with three more in reserve. The Soviet's latest planes were MIG-3s. I didn't know anything about American planes, not even their names. Of course I didn't know a damn thing about their capabilities. But we were very confident of our abilities when compared to the Soviets.

Yet news of the battles with America came in. The army landed in Malaya and began an attack on Singapore. Units from Manchuria were mobilized and sent to the South. We felt we'd been left behind in Manchuria. We wanted to go, too. Get into action on the southern front right away. In August 1942, our unit was finally ordered to Peking, then to Nanking, then to Canton. From Canton we took part in the attacks on Kweilin. Our opponent was Major General Arnold's American Volunteer Group. We encountered the P-40 for the first time. In those early stages of the war, Japanese air power was still superior. The enemy were even outnumbered by us. Our reconnaissance planes would photograph their base at daybreak, rush home, and develop the pictures. The news came, "They're there!" "Go get 'em!" came our orders, but even when we knew they had been at the base at dawn, they were usually all gone when we got there. Evacuated somewhere to escape our attacks. We couldn't even get into combat when we wanted to.

They knew we were coming more than an hour before we arrived. But when they were coming in our direction, we didn't know of their approach until six or seven minutes prior to their arrival. Even at the early stage of the war on the China front, when you looked at a map while you were in Japan, it appeared as if Japan had occupied all of southern China, but in fact Japan held only individual points on the map. If you said Japan held Canton, that only meant Japanese army units were placed in an area within forty kilometers of the city. The other 360 kilometers from Canton to Kweilin was all enemy territory. They fired large cannons to relay the news across the countryside that we were on our way.

We upgraded our planes to the Hayabusa [Peregrine Falcon]. Their maneuverability was excellent. Unless taken completely by surprise, we could circle back on the American planes. They were heavier than we were, so they couldn't really stay with us in a turn. Some exceptionally brave pilots of theirs tried to chase us, but we'd turn inside on them and shoot them down. If they ran away, though, we couldn't overtake them. P-40s were faster in a dive than our Hayabusas, so if they didn't follow after us, we couldn't run them down.

Once we came up with the idea of using P-40s captured in the Philippines. Several of them were taken to Tachikawa air base outside Tokyo. If we had P-40s ourselves, we could shoot theirs down without fail, we thought. We sent a request to higher headquarters to release the captured P-40s to us at the front so we could put our red sun emblem on them and then turn them against the Americans. At first headquarters agreed, and we actually went back to the Homeland to pick up the three planes. But then they changed their minds. They didn't think it was proper to put our national symbol on the planes of the enemy.

Sailing South

MASUDA REIJI [1]

"I was in love with the sea. From the time I was a child I'd heard there was something called 'the comradeship of sailors,' which transcends nationality. But the war came before I had experienced it myself."

In December 1941, the Japanese military embarked on the greatest

*combined land, sea, and air operations ever attempted. From the
Hawaiian Islands to Malaya, and on Wake, Guam, the Philippines, Hong
Kong, and Borneo in between, Japanese fleets and planes made coordinated strikes. These were followed up by landings everywhere but Hawaii.
Tokyo is 3,904 statute miles from Honolulu and 3,490 miles from
Singapore. Japan's fleet base at Truk in the Caroline Islands was 2,341
miles to the south of the Japanese capital. The great prize was to be the
riches of the Indies. All the positions Japan held at the beginning of
hostilities, and all the new bases and garrisons, armies and airfields,
depots and anchorages, would have to be supplied by sea.*

Back then, we were taught that war was unavoidable. This was particularly true at the Tokyo Higher Merchant Marine School, where I
began studies in the fall of 1937. The students were all reserve naval
officers. I guess the navy thought it would supply its wartime need for
officers by drawing on the merchant marine. When I became an apprentice in 1941, I was assigned to the *Arizona maru*, a freighter of 9,683 tons
that had just been impressed into the army as a troop ship and was now
designated *Air Defense Ship Number 830*. She was undergoing a crash
round-the-clock refitting program at the Innoshima dock of the Kure
Naval Arsenal. Two guns were put at her bow and four antiaircraft guns
in the stern. On both the port and starboard sides, on the bridge, and in
the stern we also had pom-pom guns, about ten in all. There were also
stables for hauling horses and crew quarters. I sensed a great urgency in
this work.

Refitting was completed on the twenty-eighth of October and we
sailed for Ujina, in Hiroshima prefecture on the Inland Sea. The whole
port was full, three to four hundred ships, mostly former merchantmen
now under army control. Many were camouflaged troopships with soldiers already on board. The *Arizona maru* was a crucial air-defense ship.
An army antiaircraft-artillery unit came aboard the first of November.
The next day, we crewmen went through the ceremony of being officially
called into the army as civilian employees.

We could tell something big was about to begin. Rumor had it that
the Japanese army was going to advance into French Indochina. Soldiers
practiced antiaircraft and machine-gun fire every day. Twenty-five-milli-
meter single-mounted guns seemed to be a new weapon for the army.
Platoon commanders had copies of its gun manual in hand as they trained
their men. On November 13, regimental commander Ōtsuka boarded
our ship and we sailed to Itozaki, a secret storage depot, in order to load
three thousand drums of fuel for the army. I saw the great battle fleet of
the Imperial Navy as we passed Itsukishima in the Inland Sea. We took

on a mountain of coal for our boilers. We had many steam leaks. Even at night we had to crawl all over the ship's boilers, candles in hand, in temperatures of sixty or seventy degrees centigrade, desperately looking for leaks.

We finally headed south early on the nineteenth, full of excitement and selflessness. We reached Takao on Taiwan on the twenty-third and found the wharves jammed with great piles of supplies—horses, men, trucks—all being moved back and forth as we loaded through the night. It was there, too, that we first got bananas and other tropical fruits. After working all day in the scorching heat, we told each other we'd never tasted anything so delicious. Maybe this, we thought, would be our final taste. On the twenty-sixth, about thirteen hundred infantrymen came aboard. We still didn't know where we were going. On the twenty-ninth we were finally told. We were carrying forces to invade the American Philippines!

We had a clear view of majestic warships and a huge convoy when we put in at Bakō, and small naval launches and army motorboats plied back and forth across the harbor. The battleships *Kirishima* and *Haruna,* the heavy cruisers *Ashigara* and *Haguro,* and six destroyers weighed anchor on December 4, their main guns held at a forty-five degree angle. Bugles sounded and "Depart Harbor" echoed across the water. Our whole crew turned out on deck, at least those not on duty, and waved their caps in salute. The decks of all the ships were soon filled with soldiers and sailors cheering, waving Japanese flags and ensigns. It was a stirring scene.

Arizona maru received orders to depart on December 7. We were part of a six-ship convoy responsible for landing forces at Aparri on the island of Luzon in the Philippines. Our primary escort, and flagship, was the light cruiser *Natori.* There were fifteen ships in all. We arrived off the Philippines coast before dawn on the tenth. The ocean was very rough, with high waves. We lowered the boats with great difficulty and around daybreak the attack force headed for the beach. Bullets zipped toward us. This was the beginning of my Greater East Asia War.

Enemy planes swooped down on our convoy. We put up a severe antiaircraft barrage to meet them. An enemy submarine attack began. The *Natori* seemed to be hit. There were casualties. *Arizona maru* carried out a determined forced landing and disembarkation operation under enemy fire, then returned to the north, escorted by three destroyers, and took on more soldiers. This time we were carrying the Manila Attack Force! An enormous convoy assembled from Takao, Keilung, and Bakō —eighty-four ships in all, sailing together in two long lines extending beyond the horizon in both directions. We were bound for Lingayen Gulf. This was the largest Japanese convoy of the war.

Our hold was full of soldiers, horses too, all packed in. About two thousand men. On December 22, we entered Lingayen Gulf and immediately began landing operations. The swells were high. It was terribly difficult to load soldiers and supplies on the bobbing boats. Enemy planes struck us at dawn, aiming primarily at the beachhead. Bullets from strafing planes chased our boats to the shore. *Arizona maru* poured fire into the sky. We saw enemy planes spiraling down, trailing smoke. Our ship was rocked by the concussions of exploding bombs and the force of walls of water striking our sides. Most of the ships, however, unloaded successfully and the land force began its drive on Manila. We returned to Takao for our next mission. Losses: just one ship, to an enemy sub.

The *Arizona maru* left Takao again on January 30. Destination, Java. We spotted a periscope on February 1, two hundred meters to starboard. Three torpedoes were launched against us. One struck the ship below the waterline, but it didn't explode! It seemed to pass along the hull, scraping the keel, and continued on the other side, emitting great clouds of bubbles before finally sinking to port. On our ship, all was in turmoil. The antiaircraft cannons in the bow were aiming at the surface of the sea, firing at an elevation of zero, so one shell exploded over us, not the sub. A soldier had made a mistake in setting the fuse. The bridge was showered with shrapnel. About ten crewmen were wounded, but we sailed on and escaped further damage.

Again, we headed south. On February 27, after sunset, off Surabaja, the Battle of the Java Sea began. The thunder of big guns, flashes of light, flares in the dark sky, columns of fire. Right in front of our eyes a lurid sea battle was being waged. I thought this might be the last day of our convoy, because if they got through our warships, we were sitting ducks. But when the firing stopped, the Imperial Navy had achieved an overwhelming victory. The next morning we saw flotsam scattered over the surface of the sea, and large numbers of white and black sailors were floating on rafts. We sailed on without stopping—we had to put our force ashore—but I heard that they were later picked up by our sub-chasers. A combined American, Dutch, and British fleet had been annihilated by Japan.

We went on to Singapore, which had just fallen to us—the fuel-storage tanks were still blackened shells—then to Indochina where we took on a cargo of Saigon rice, and then made for Japan. We reached Ujina and home on April 12, 1942. The cherry blossoms had already bloomed. My apprenticeship was over. I was now acting third engineer.

A Failure of Diplomacy

KASE TOSHIKAZU

By the spring of 1941, relations between the United States and Japan had reached a critical stage. Japanese pressure on French Indochina led to warnings from President Roosevelt that America might take action beyond the limitations on trade enacted the previous winter. In Washington, negotiations were in the hands of Secretary of State Cordell Hull and Japan's new ambassador, Admiral Nomura Kichisaburō.

From 1940 to war's end Kase Toshikazu was chief secretary to all of Japan's foreign ministers throughout the war years, except for the three months between July and October 1941 after his mentor, Matsuoka Yōsuke, was forced from office.

We meet in the Royal Lounge of the Palace Hotel. He has his own table in a corner of the lounge, with a fine view across the moat of the Imperial Palace. His long silver hair is beautifully combed. He does not look like a man born in 1903. He is elegantly dressed in a bold blue-gray silk suit, perfectly fitted. Even his cigarette lighter matches his blue ensemble. His back is ramrod straight. He still looks the man who served as Japan's first Ambassador to the United Nations when Japan reemerged diplomatically from the Occupation after the war.

Ambassador Kase prefers to confine his remarks to a technical exposition of the processes of diplomacy, despite the enormity of the consequences of the events that were set in motion that spring and summer.

I am a diplomat by profession. The work of diplomats is to avoid conflict as much as possible. War represents bankruptcy to diplomats. However, if you carry on, thinking only, "We must prevent war," you may end up inviting war. The heaven-sent task of the diplomat is to conduct friendly negotiations to the mutual benefit of both sides.

From that perspective, the Japanese-American negotiations in 1941 were, for me, a matter of the deepest regret. We tried not to sacrifice Japan's national interest, while also respecting America's. We sought compromise. Although we faced the greatest obstacles, we never gave up hope, not until the last moment. When we finally realized it was not possible to avoid the outbreak of war, I felt a disappointment I cannot express in words.

In truth, I often ask myself, was it good to conduct those negotiations or not? We started in April of the year the war broke out. At that time I was chief secretary to Foreign Minister Matsuoka Yōsuke, which would be equivalent to *chef de cabinet* in America. Matsuoka was an extraordinary man. Really a genius. He took me under his wing and served as my patron. We worked so closely that we were sometimes spoken ill of by others. It was said that all you needed at the Foreign Ministry were Matsuoka and Kase.

If you go back further in time, Japanese-American relations turned completely sour from the time Japan entered the Tripartite Pact, forming the Axis with Germany and Italy in September 1940. Matsuoka became foreign minister that summer. Relations were already at a critical stage. I was then a secretary in the Japanese embassy in London. My ambassadors were first Yoshida Shigeru and then Shigemitsu Mamoru. Both of them were extremely eager to improve relations with America. That was my goal, too. I studied at Amherst and Harvard. I was a *cum laude* graduate. I joined the American section of the Foreign Ministry in 1930, had many friends in America, and had served in Washington. I was viewed as one of those who knew America best. I had long cherished the view that for Japan to survive meant getting along with America.

In Japan, I was considered an Anglophile. "Such a man cannot be used," was a common opinion, yet Matsuoka sent a cable calling for me to return quickly to become his chief secretary. I can tell you that I was very popular in London. When I left for Japan, all the British papers covered it on their editorial pages. It was very rare for them even to write an editorial about the return of an ambassador, let alone a man of lower rank.

In Tokyo, the tilt was already toward the Axis. This feeling was not limited to the military. Even in the Foreign Ministry, they were intoxicated with the Axis. Britain, they felt sure, would soon meet its downfall. A diplomat with a high reputation in England was something of a disgrace. Knowing this, why did Matsuoka make me his chief secretary? It was Matsuoka's idea to improve relations with Britain, and then with America, using me. According to ministry regulations, as chief secretary I could be involved in confidential issues from which section chiefs or bureau directors were excluded.

Cabinets fell, one after the other, over the issue of the Axis alliance. The military tried to get that pact at any price. The army in particular acted just as it pleased. Matsuoka's idea was to craft a Tripartite Pact that would not damage Japan's ability to reach agreements with England and America. Then the Foreign Ministry would be able to recover leadership in foreign affairs. Diplomacy, he felt, should be carried out by the Foreign Ministry, not by the military. So it was he who negotiated with the German ambassador, Heinrich Stahmer, in a two-week period in

August, without any consultation with the army or the navy. He had that kind of personal authority and real power.

The Matsuoka mission went to Europe in the spring of 1941. I accompanied him. People thought we were just going to meet Hitler and Mussolini and to celebrate with them, but our hidden goal was to meet Stalin and improve Japanese-Soviet relations. Britain was already fatigued by the war and could provide little assistance to Chiang Kai-shek in China. His prime benefactor was the Soviet Union. By negotiating with the Soviets, we hoped to put a stop to Soviet assistance to China and deal Chiang a severe blow. Matsuoka then would go to America and meet Roosevelt.

Then Chiang Kai-shek would be in trouble. Japan would present a generous, acceptable proposal to him, and convince Roosevelt to tell Chiang that the proposal was good, that he'd been at war for too long, and that he ought to listen to Matsuoka and get on board. That was Matsuoka's plan. Matsuoka had studied in America and he had many friends, like Howard of the Scripps-Howard Institute. Before we left for Europe I wrote letters to these people with the hope that these contacts might lead to improvement in relations. This was the Matsuoka style. A "hidden line."

I attended all of the meetings in Moscow. Matsuoka was the kind of man who gave you your head once he trusted you. His was a man-to-man approach. He was easily moved to tears. I personally liked him a great deal. The American ambassador to Moscow was [Laurence A.] Steinhardt, who was a good friend of Matsuoka's. They'd gone fishing together at Gotemba, near Mount Fuji. Steinhardt had the trust of Roosevelt. In other words, he was able to send cables directly to Roosevelt, not through Secretary of State Hull.

We met with Stalin and negotiated with Molotov. In between, we met Steinhardt three times. I was there, so I can report that Matsuoka would tell him, "Hitler said this," or "Mussolini's opinion was this." From Steinhardt's point of view, Japan was a dangerous country. I'm sure he was curious about the nature of the conversations taking place between the foreign minister of a country welcomed both by the Axis and by the leaders of the Union of Soviet Socialist Republics. I even took the minutes of the meetings and showed them to Steinhardt myself, going over them with him. Our third meeting occurred at the time the Japan-Soviet Treaty of Neutrality, a nonaggression pact, was about to be signed. In that meeting we actually told him that, though we couldn't even mention it to the newspapers yet, a neutrality treaty with the Soviets was to be signed. Steinhardt asked, "Is such a thing actually possible?" "Yes, indeed," Matsuoka responded. "And the Soviets will cut off aid to Chiang

Kai-shek." Matsuoka then told him that with Chiang in trouble, Japan would offer terms of reconciliation that would surprise Chiang. At that time, Matsuoka added, Japan would like to have Roosevelt's support. Steinhardt responded that such events would be truly extraordinary.

We signed the Nonaggression Pact on April 13, 1941. Stalin personally came to the station to send Matsuoka off. We boarded the Trans-Siberian Railway. While we were on the train we received a telegram from Steinhardt. It said, "Talk with Roosevelt went well" —meaning that Roosevelt would meet with Matsuoka. The foreign minister's chest was really puffed out. We arrived in Dairen, Manchuria, with feelings of great optimism. Matsuoka had been head of the South Manchurian Railway, so he was treated practically like a god there. Matsuoka and I stayed at the official residence of the president of the Manchurian Railway. The other members of our delegation stayed at the Yamato Hotel.

We soon received a phone call from Prime Minister Konoe. A very important proposal had arrived from America. He wanted us to return quickly. If the truth be known, Mr. Matsuoka wanted to see the faces of the geishas in Dairen, but he believed this to be Roosevelt's response to his discussion with Steinhardt. So in high spirits he returned home.

The morning of April 15, the Ministry had received a telegram from Admiral Nomura, the ambassador to Washington. It purported to be a proposed draft understanding between the United States and Japan. When Matsuoka returned to Tokyo April 22, Konoe urged him to read the proposal quickly. All the senior ministry officials were gathered there at the foreign minister's official residence. They showered him with congratulations on the conclusion of the pact with the Soviet Union. Matsuoka handed me the telegram. It was quite thick. I went into an adjoining room, locked the door, and read it. I assumed that the original text was in English and this was a translation, very poorly done. I asked the head of the telegraph section to bring me the original immediately. He assured me he didn't have the original. I was puzzled. In diplomatic negotiations, it was useless to send something in translation. You have to have the original text. I did my best to understand anyway: America, it seemed to say, will approve of Japanese actions in China and permit free emigration of Japanese to America. It was a list of good things that would result—if you read between the lines—once Japan had ceased to be a member of the Axis.

Matsuoka felt the preparations he'd done in Moscow had now borne fruit. Something far beyond his expectations had reached him. Ambassador Nomura claimed that Roosevelt knew and approved of this as did Secretary of State Hull. He claimed what we had was an official American proposal, and we believed it was, because our ambassador to Washington said so. We learned only after the war that the thing that reached us as an official American proposal was something Roosevelt barely knew about, and that Hull may have known about but didn't take seriously, not believing it was really attainable.

Prime Minister Konoe and the key military officials didn't read what was behind the words. The atmosphere was "Let's accept this as quickly as possible so relations will improve." After receiving and offering many toasts, Matsuoka met with me. He asked how I read it. This cannot be done, I told him, unless we leave the Tripartite Pact. "Well read," he said. Mr. Matsuoka was a professional.

Nomura called Tokyo every day from Washington. When the minister wasn't available, he spoke to me. He kept saying, "You must accept it quickly. If you don't act quickly, like a fish, it will spoil." No matter what, an ambassador has to be honest. Even if the American government said something which the Japanese government would abhor, that should have been conveyed back honestly. It is a stain on the ambassador to send something as official when it is not. That's unforgivable. This proposal was received April 18. Mr. Matsuoka and I spent many sleepless nights working on it, trying to work out our response to "their proposal." At the beginning of May, we sent our "response" to America. They did not imagine that it was a response to "their proposal," because they had never offered one. Because the process started with a lie, we found ourselves building lie upon lie.

By July, I found it all very suspicious. Matsuoka was a sharp-minded person and he, too, felt something was very wrong. In mid-July, Konoe decided that Matsuoka was opposing his idea of accepting this "American proposal." Konoe chased Matsuoka out of the cabinet and made Admiral Toyoda [Teijirō] his new foreign minister. The trade of military men, of course, is to fight war. If your foreign minister is an admiral and your ambassador in Washington is also an admiral, you have an all-navy battery. When military men start acting as foreign ministers or ambassadors, jobs they really don't know, they eventually lose their way. The negotiations gradually strayed. Konoe was under great pressure and many Imperial Conferences were held.

Finally, on October 26, General Tōjō Hideki became prime minister. I again became chief secretary to the new foreign minister, Tōgō Shigenori. Eventually, on the twenty-sixth of November 1941, Secretary of State Hull dispatched the Hull Notes. When we got the unvarnished American position, Japan made the decision for war, abandoning all hope.

In the end, it was Nomura who was wrong, and Konoe was wrong to believe him. Tōjō, who believed Nomura to the last, was also wrong. As

Japan's ambassador, Nomura went to Washington bearing a letter of appointment from His Majesty the Emperor. Who could doubt a man of that station? That man, Nomura, who didn't know diplomacy and misled Japan, helped all these errors to build up. This resulted in Pearl Harbor.

Those negotiations were cursed from the start. Such a record of irregular, abnormal negotiations cannot be found elsewhere in world history! I often wonder why we went through such hardship and made such efforts. I must declare that had we not started those Japanese-American negotiations of 1941, war would not have broken out. The negotiations damaged peace to that degree.

Thinking back on it now, I'd say I don't believe it would have been possible to have avoided war at the final Imperial Conference when it was formally ratified. Events sometimes overwhelm you, surge around you, and carry you along. You can't always move them. One man's will alone is not enough to do anything. War has a life of its own. Even Prime Minister Tōjō himself could not have stopped that war.

4 / GREATER EAST ASIA

Cartoons for the War

YOKOYAMA RYŪICHI [1]

Cartoonists, too, were mobilized for war by the government. In May 1942 they formed a single new association "dedicated to serve the nation" by implementing official themes like improving fighting spirit, hating the Anglo-American enemy, and exhorting people to make do with less. They held exhibits and appealed to the public to support the war.

At eighty years old, he is one of the Japan's best-known cartoonists. Two tufts of white hair seem glued to the sides of his head. His comic strip Fuku-chan *ran in the* Asahi *newspaper from 1936 until nearly the end of the war.* "Little Fuku was a young boy—me, really—but the readers weren't children, they were wives living at home. It appeared on the family page. I didn't have much interest in social issues and such. I never went to university, I just graduated from middle school and started drawing cartoons to support my family. I couldn't afford to draw anything that might get me admonished for ideology, and I never *was—either by the Communists or the police. I guess I didn't really try to know."*

When the war began, I was at home asleep. That day, the eighth of December, Pearl Harbor Day, my wife woke me with the words, "War's broken out!" I was thrilled. Happy. All the indecisive gloom cleared off just like that.

Before December 8, the army had me locked up in an inn with two other illustrators. We were there finishing some drawings for "paper plays" intended to teach Japanese soldiers about the customs of Indonesia and the Indonesians about Japan. For example, we'd draw that Islamic hat they wear there, and then show a person touching it, and there'd be a big black cross next to it because that was something you weren't supposed to do. A man who'd spent a lot of time in that country kept describing what we were to draw, and we kept drawing. I have no memory of what I drew for the Indonesians. The captions were all in Malay. But that's where I learned for the first time Japan was going toward the South.

They let us go home for a bit just before the war began and gave us few days off at New Year's, too. It was as if I'd been requisitioned. In fact, I had received a call-up, a "white paper." I wasn't to be a soldier, but I had to do work for them. I never got any awards or honors. No money, either. They just used me and then threw me away after the war.

I was taken to Indonesia. I guess you could say I actually went to war, but I never saw anything cruel. I showed paper plays to people in Java. Skits about how strong and just the Japanese military was. It was an advertising job.

When I was told I was off for the South, I bought a military sword. I was surprised how expensive it was. I hung it from my belt in a leather scabbard, but it dragged along the ground because I'm so short. I had to have the sword cut down, but when I went to a shop outside the Azabu regimental base, they were going to cut off its tang, which bore the swordmaker's name. I shouted, "Hey! Please leave that on. I paid a lot of money for that sword!" The smith just snorted, "Shōwa swords don't have names of importance," and cut right through. So much for my great weapon!

I had that sword hanging on the wall of a gymnasium in a school on Taiwan where we stopped off for a month or so on our way to the South. A member of my unit, a *kendō* master from Kyushu, told me "Yokoyama, you have to take care of your blade." The sword was in a white wooden sheath, and wrapped in a leather scabbard. It looked great from the outside. But after he said that, I tried to look at it. I couldn't even draw it out. I pulled and pulled. Finally I jerked it free. The sheath went flying and the blade was rust-red. Everybody around broke into hysterics. Since I was quite famous at that time, because I was drawing *Fuku-chan,* rumors soon spread that Mister Yokoyama had only a theatrical sword made of bamboo.

War is something like that. It's a carefree thing. Horrible as it may be, it's true. There was nothing to do in Taiwan. I wondered, Is this war? There, soldiers taught me that when you go into action you cannot even stop to eat, but everybody else practically dies of boredom. "People like you write in the picture books 'Charge! Charge!' but that's not real war," the veterans said. Waiting, waiting, with nothing to do. Dull. That's real war, I came to realize.

When I reached Java, it was more tedious than you can believe. Our job was pacification. But when you'd won, there was nothing left to do. We were dispatched there to calm down those people who would be irritated at the beginning. Educators and administrators arrived from Japan, and were coming and going. Occupation policy was thoroughly established. All we could do was get the military into trouble. Maybe it was called war, but I had a relaxed and easy time. We'd won.

The army used radios for short-wave broadcasting back to Japan. Then there wasn't any way to record things, so it went out on the air live. The author Takeda Rintarō, cartoonist Ōno Tateo, and I did a radio show. Ōno just said whatever he wanted. He spoke of how abundant things were in Java. How great it all was. Even said, "I'm wearing a loincloth made of tiger skin." While we were in the middle of the show, we got a telephone call from the military. They bawled us out good! We were trying to depict the situation pretty accurately, but they told us, "People in Japan are barely eating, you shouldn't flaunt things here."

I went out with Takeda to give a talk to some military unit in Java. He told me all I had to do was describe how my comic strip *Fuku-chan* was written. That sounded easy, so I went along with him and talked for about thirty minutes. When I'd finished, I received a beautiful book of Van Gogh paintings from the unit commander as a gift. Great! I'd never even dreamed of getting my hands on a book like that. In Batavia they'd all been bought up by the Japanese. Whenever I got outside the capital, the first place I'd rush was to a bookstore. I found Michelangelo, Lautrec, things like that. I found books I couldn't imagine in remote mountain areas. I was so happy. I shipped them all back and they arrived safely.

During the later days of my stay, I collected toys, things like trains, and tried to figure out some way to get them home. There were already shortages of towels and socks in Japan, so I collected them and thread, soap, and toiletries. Foreign things. One of my mates was an expert in brand names, so he pointed me in the right directions. Towels? Cannon. Toothpaste? Colgate. I followed his suggestions and I was never sorry. I bought a cheap leather trunk and stuffed it full of toys, using towels and things for packing materials. On top I painted Fuku-chan's face in enamel, hoping that if anyone should find it, they'd deliver it to me. I sent it by ship. Long after I got back to Japan, I went down to the regimental headquarters and there it was. It had many tags hanging from it. Nanking, Canton, and so on. I opened it. My toys were still there, just as I'd put them in, but the towels and everything else were gone. Still, I was pleased to get it.

We made the rounds of Java for about a month. We showed Japanese movies to the locals, and together with Indonesian actresses and dancers entertained our troops. We had a small unit assigned to us as an escort. I'd say I was able to have a pretty good trip at the military's expense. I didn't really want to stay there, though. I met with Indonesian painters on business, but I never tried to be friendly with them. I got too tired. If they loved me and asked me to stay on, I'd be in real trouble, I thought. I couldn't talk to them. They spoke Malay. I didn't want to just sit around there. Ōno Tateo was different. He got really close with them and spoke in sign language and Japanese. He was held over in the South. He only returned to Japan after he'd become a prisoner of war.

I landed in March and left in June 1942. I was able to wangle my way aboard the *Asahi* plane, though it was officially under navy control, since everyone at the navy in Batavia knew me. When the pilot turned out to be the same one I'd given a bottle of whiskey to during my earlier trip to China to entertain the troops, he saw to it that I was signed on officially as crew so that I didn't have to deplane at Singapore. When I got back to Japan I was released. I wasn't really in the army, so the commander just said, "You've done your bit. You can go home." So, I was back. I kept drawing and writing *Fuku-chan.*

I didn't draw cartoons to truckle with the military. I simply swallowed the military's pronouncements as they were. I never doubted them for a minute. Never really troubled at all. I believed Japan had been doing what was right. My comic strip became the *Fuku-chan Unit.* I guess I was playing at war. In those wartime days, just *Fuku-chan,* the character's name, seemed too weak. Then the newspapers were full of reports of unit this and unit that. That was the atmosphere of the time. A unit meant a group activity. The popularity of individual action declined. As a whole, individualistic things weren't approved of. Organized behavior, like the neighborhood associations, were unit behavior. It had nothing to do with the contents, but it made a good title.

There were all kinds of slogans. Things like "We will put off desire until victory." I used them. But that wasn't my true feeling. In fact, I'm always full of desires. Fuku-chan didn't have much strength of character because the person drawing him wasn't all that committed. Yet I ended up being head of my neighborhood association and had to work with the wives of our neighborhood in all kinds of exercises. I pleaded with them not to excel. "If you are best, we'll have to go all over and show ourselves as examples," I said. I also begged them not come out on the bottom, because then we'd be singled out for criticism. "Where should we be?" they asked me. "Oh, I don't know, maybe third from the bottom would be safest," I answered. That's my philosophy. To excel might be a good thing in the abstract, but in wartime, to stand out brings nothing good.

Building the Burma-Siam Railroad

ABE HIROSHI [1]

In 1942 Imperial General Headquarters ordered the Southern Area Army to build a rail line connecting the prewar railroad systems of Burma and Thailand across southeastern Burma. This would facilitate the transfer of men and supplies to support Japan's large army in northern Burma, which faced the British from India and the Chinese and Americans from Yünnan in China. They were given eighteen months to complete the task. The 265 miles of mountainous jungle and malaria swamps between Tanbyuzayat and Ban Pong proved some of the most inhospital country in all of Southeast Asia. Laborers from Burma and Malaya, approximately 250,000 strong, were brought in to build the line, together with some 61,000 Allied POWs. About half were British, a quarter Australian, and most of the remainder Dutch, with about 700 Americans. The line was completed in November 1943. Approximately one-fifth of the POWs died building it. Although the exact total is unknown, upwards of 80,000 of the local people also perished. °

I was surveying track for the Ministry of Railroads' newly proposed super-express between Tokyo and Shimonoseki when I was called to active duty in the army on January 10, 1941. In little more than a year, together with twenty-one other young officers just like me, I went from raw conscript to budding second lieutenant in the Fifth Rail Regiment

---

° Precise figures are impossible to determine. See Joan Blair and Clay Blair, Jr., *Return from the River Kwai* (New York: Penguin, 1979), pp. 15–16, and Basil Collier, *The War in the Far East, 1941–1945: A Military History* (New York: William Morrow, 1969), pp. 331–32.

under the army in Burma. About six hundred not-very-young soldiers, almost like my uncles, made up our regiment. Many were former rail-unit soldiers who had completed their active service and returned home, only to be recalled to the colors.

We left the port of Ujina on a four-thousand-ton freighter bound for Burma on August 15, 1942. They gave us officers a cash advance of six thousand yen to take these six hundred soldiers south. We consulted about what we should buy for the trip and decided beer would be best. We ordered it at headquarters and began loading it on the freighter. Beer soon filled the hold. The ship's master got angry, but when he asked, "What's the matter with this unit?" we just told him to shut up and keep loading. We were sure that those cases would get us to Rangoon.

On the trip, soldiers could purchase all the beer they wanted for twenty-five *sen* a bottle. Since there was nothing to do on the boat, they were soon clamoring for beer. All twenty-four thousand bottles were drained by the time we got to Takao in Taiwan. So we bought more beer with the money the soldiers had paid. We sailed from port in good spirits. We were dry again by Singapore. There we reloaded with Tiger Beer. We still had two or three bottles per head when we approached Rangoon on September 8. That was the end of our beer-drinking days. We didn't get another drop until the end of the war.

"Go into the jungle and build a railroad!" That was practically the only order we got in Burma. The jungle was incredible. It was deep, dark, and dense, with giant trees like you wouldn't believe. There were no roads. There were no reliable maps, only a primitive chart made by the British army long before. Here and there it had the names of hamlets. You could tell roughly where the mountains were, but that was all. Yet we got things underway. We first surveyed the area on elephant while the weather was still good and recorded the basic topography. We felled trees and estimated roughly whether and where track could be laid.

The Burma-Siam railroad was to be four hundred kilometers long. I was largely responsible for Songkrai, the border area between Thailand and Burma. You started by felling trees at the foot of the hills and then you cut a road for vehicles and brought in other materials. For a while we had gin, whiskey, and cigarettes, thanks to the British at Singapore. British tobacco was so good. Navy Cut was the best! When food didn't reach us by elephant we'd explode dynamite in the river and pick up the stunned fish. Frogs, snakes, and lizards were our normal provisions. When lunchtime approached, about ten men would be assigned to chase down lizards. They were real big and you caught them by hitting them on the head with a stick. The beautiful pink meat was delicious.

We reached the stage of laying a trackbed by September 1943. That's when we brought the prisoners in. There was a camp for prisoners every five kilometers along the line, fifteen hundred men each. Separate guard units were in charge of them. I had to build a wooden bridge ninety meters long over a river gorge thirty meters deep. Without the elephants we couldn't have done it. For a year and a half, I had my own elephant.

The Burmese workers in the Burmese Construction Volunteer Corps were paid one rupee per head per day. We paid two rupees per elephant. Everyone took good care of the elephants. Even Japanese soldiers who beat up Burmese never took it out on the elephants. In the early stages, all our food and equipment came by elephant. We had about ten elephants per platoon. They'd be left free in the mountains in the evening, a chain hobbling their front legs. They'd search for wild bananas and bamboo overnight and cover themselves with dirt to keep from being eaten up by insects. In the morning the Burmese mahoots would track them down from their footprints. They'd usually be no more than one or two kilometers away. Then they'd get a morning bath in the river. Each mahoot would scrub his own elephant with a brush. The elephants looked so comfortable, rolling over and over in the river. It took about thirty minutes. Then they had full stomachs and were clean and in a good mood. Now you could put the saddle mount or pulling chains on them and they'd listen to commands and do a good day's work.

Once the trees were there, our soldiers who'd been carpenters in civilian life took over. The Burmese cut beams thirty-by-thirty-centimeters square, five to eight meters long. You needed sixteen of these beams for every five meters of bridge. That meant we had to prepare an almost astronomical amount of lumber. That was the hardest thing, because a solid-looking type of tree might be devoured by insects in a month. I didn't know a damn thing about trees, so whenever we found big thick trees, I just issued the order "Cut 'em down!" The elephants pulled down the trees that we'd sawed almost through, moved them away, and stacked them up with their trucks. In the beginning, we found trees nearby, but later we needed so many that we had to look further and further away.

That enormous bridge at Songkrai was my first time planning and actually building a bridge. Made of wood on a rock base! All through the dry season, when the river level was low, we dammed up the river, exposing the rocks. We drilled holes for the beams. I implored the regimental commander to find cement for me. At long last, some came. We put the pilings into the holes and filled them in with cement. It made a big difference just having a little cement to anchor them. We then built boat-shaped structures about a meter high around the piles, and packed them with stones. That was to help deflect the water and protect the foundation when the river was flowing strongly in the monsoon season.

We erected the bridge on that base. The rains began. But it held. It was a magnificent sight! The bridge gradually began to take shape as we laid beams from both ends. It grew level by level, rising from the river.

We did it with human labor alone. With rope, pulleys, and some iron bars. We were able to reach the top without even one injury. I didn't let the prisoners touch the bridge. It was too dangerous for them. All the handling and laying of lumber on the bridge was done by Japanese, and we did all the clamping of boards ourselves. Sometimes you had to go into the water. Struggling against the current, tying our bodies to the pillars, we'd set the metal fittings. I did have the prisoners help pull on the ropes. But I couldn't have them clambering on the beams and spans in their leather shoes. At a height of twenty or thirty meters, you'd die if you fell. We did it all with ten to fifteen Japanese.

Burmese and Japanese soldiers worked as one. Perhaps even the British officers thought the Japanese army had done a great job, considering the tools at our disposal. We worked in a drenching rain, wearing only loincloths. British officers in rain cloaks watched us with an expression that seemed to say, "Good show!" Every British officer had a swagger stick and sometimes they'd salute us in a funny way with it. I'd just shout at them, "Get lost! You're in the way! We're not putting on a show for your entertainment!"

The bridge looked massive and solid when all sixteen spans were in place. A trial drive was made. A C-56-type locomotive came up from below, belching smoke, blowing its whistle. It weighed a hundred and fifty tons. It couldn't drive very fast, because the tracks were not yet completely set. Finally, it reached our bridge. My battalion commander was aboard. "Abe," he shouted to me, "you get up here too!" All I could think was "If the bridge collapses, I'll have to die together with him." I hung onto the outside of the cabin and gave the order "Forward! Advance!" The locomotive inched ahead. I listened for any unusual or ominous sounds, but the bridge didn't even shudder.

"*Banzai! Banzai!*" shouted our soldiers. "*Banzai!*" the Burmese yelled, too. Even the captives let out something like a "*Banzai.*" It was unbelievable that a chugging locomotive could possibly be operating in this wild area previously untouched by man. And we had built it in a single year!

Everything railroad soldiers had to do was dangerous. After completing the tracks you had to lay gravel. Only Japanese soldiers were allowed to blast rock for the gravel off nearby mountains, and then dynamite the big boulders to make them smaller. Our captives were only given the job of turning the pieces into rocks of just the right size or digging up soil. Physically weak, they couldn't do much, but they didn't intend to work, either. They didn't get anything in return, even if they cooperated with the Japanese army. On the contrary, if they weakened themselves, they ended up losing their lives.

That movie, *Bridge on the River Kwai*, is complete fiction and idealizes the behavior of British prisoners on the Kwai River at that time. In the movie, the Japanese rail unit was in charge of managing captives. That wasn't the way it was. Our unit specialized in building bridges and only borrowed prisoner labor from a prison-camp unit. We'd go there and ask, "Can we have three hundred workers today?" The guard unit would then provide prisoners and guards for them. We'd assign them to different tasks—a hundred for digging, fifty for cutting wood. In the movie, the British volunteer to build the bridge for us. They say, "The Jap army's way of doing things is all wrong. Let us do it!" Nothing like that happened and they never built us a great bridge. William Holden and his team were supposed to have sneaked behind the lines and blown the bridge up. That didn't happen either.

After the Burma-Siam Railroad was completed, our Fifth Rail Regiment was assigned to transport and maintenance of other rail lines in Burma. There were enormous Japanese forces in northern Burma and we had to get supplies through to feed them. From January to December 1944, we were on the Myitkyina Line, which stretched north from Mandalay towards the Indian and Chinese borders. The British, approaching from the east, attacked it practically every day. In daylight the British planes bombed, and we repaired the lines all night. The trains would have to pass through before dawn. We had to count the exact number of bombs that fell and keep track of the explosions, because they'd drop delayed-action bombs which would blow up while we were working. All we could do by day was sleep in the jungle. We had to change our camp every two or three days. The British didn't even have to worry about Japanese planes anymore. They spread fountain-pen mines all along the rail lines. If you stepped on one, a bullet shot straight up through your foot. Sometimes the enemy dropped leaflets identifying us by our military code numbers. It gave us a weird feeling when the British army, which we hated, knew all about us.

We were protecting a bridge near Meza when Wingate's British airborne troops, the Chindits, landed about thirty kilometers from our position. They came in gliders, but were armed with heavy machine guns and mortars. Overhead, warplanes, patrolled to protect them. The rail line was cut near Mawlu. A division of ours was up there in the mountains, cut off. We couldn't just let them dry up and die without food. We were given the order "Advance!" All we had were our own rifles and maybe two or three hand grenades. We weren't trained in combat. It was broad daylight. Heavy machine-gun bullets flew by just above our heads. Then "Bam! Bam! Bam!" trench mortar explosions came toward us. "Forward!" I shouted. "Advance, or we'll be trapped by them!" To my right, airplanes were dropping bombs. Behind me I saw red flames, shooting out of what looked like a giant Bunsen burner. We were just a hundred railroad soldiers crawling across rice fields, armed only with single-shot rifles. We didn't even have enough bullets, and they had flame-throwers!

I came face-to-face with seven British soldiers. The moment they saw me, they opened up with automatic weapons. I dove behind a tree. I saw them preparing to target me with a rifle grenade, and rolled away from the spot just as a grenade went off. I took twenty-two pieces of shrapnel all over my body, badly enough in the left leg that it should have been fatal. One, just above my knee, went in so deep that it was there the rest of the war. Thirty of us were killed, thirty wounded. Two officers were among the dead.

I was picked up and carried to the rear on March 18, 1944, and spent all of April in the hospital. My wound was still oozing pus in early May, but the enemy was all around, and they needed officers, so I reported back to duty.

Around the time I was wounded, tens of thousands of Japanese were ordered into the deep mountains of Burma, where there was nothing to sustain them. They just piled rice and ammunition on carts and hauled them along. When they could no longer move them by cart, they divided the supplies up and carried them on their own backs. No matter how far they went, it was just jungle. There were swarms of mosquitos. They caught malaria. If the water was bad they came down with diarrhea practically instantly. There was no way for units to keep in touch with each other. There was no ammunition. No food. The soldiers ended up defeated stragglers. The bones of hundreds of thousands of soldiers were abandoned in Burma.° The lieutenant generals and generals should have taken a stand and said there were no artillery shells and nothing to feed the soldiers, no matter what the Imperial headquarters told them to do! But the generals just issued their orders and took care of their own safety first, fleeing by airplane while urging the troops on. The top commander in Burma was executed by the British, but the "great men" in the middle-level commands went home as if nothing had happened.

About January 8, 1945, we received an order to go to a place we called Chōmei on the line to Lashio. North of that point there was much fighting, but my job was to get two divisions out by rail. Every night we marshaled cars into trains and moved them down the line. This went on

---

° Japanese war dead in Burma and the invasion of India totaled over 160,000.

until the beginning of March. The soldiers we were evacuating kept the enemy from overwhelming us, but finally we couldn't hold them off any longer. On March 8 we put a hundred and forty sick soldiers onto the train for Mandalay and pulled out. Just as that train left the station, the enemy arrived.

I limped all the way back to Moulmein. By then my knee had swollen up and was bright red. I couldn't move. An army doctor sent me back to Bangkok to enter the hospital. I asked the train taking me to stop at Songkrai. My orderly carried me on his back to where I could see the bridge for the first time in more than a year. It had been the target of heavy bombing, but had suffered no direct hits. The bridge spanned a gorge so closely surrounded by steep mountains that a bomber couldn't make a direct run at it. It was still there, exactly as I'd built it. I was ecstatic. I went on to Thailand by train, arriving in Bangkok around July 20, 1945. But I went carrying that memory with me. Many of our soldiers withdrew to Thailand over the Burma-Siam Railroad during our disastrous defeat. Many men's lives were saved because of that bridge. I feel that I played a great role.

Abe Hiroshi was charged with war crimes for his part in the Burma-Siam Railroad. He tells that part of his story in Chapter 21.

Keeping Order in the Indies

NOGI HARUMICHI [2]

The Dutch East Indies were central to Japan's vision of a Greater East Asia Co-Prosperity Sphere. From the islands of Indonesia would come petroleum and other resources vital to Japan's military economy. Stunning military successes throughout the Dutch and British holdings in the Indies brought the oil-rich areas of Borneo under Japanese control—Balikpapan fell January 24 and Bandjarmasin was taken February 16. Sumatra and Java were conquered in April 1942.

Indonesia—unlike the Philippines, Burma, Thailand, Manchukuo, the so-called Nationalist government of Japanese-occupied China, and the "Free India Interim Government"—was not "invited" to the Greater East Asia Conference, which opened in Japan on October 5, 1943, to proclaim the realization of the dream. For the Indies, direct military administration, quickly established, with the army and navy each having its own distinct geographic sphere, seems to have been the solution preferred. It was only in September 1944, as defeat loomed, that Prime Minister Koiso Kuniaki promised Indonesia independence "in the near future."

Nogi Harumichi was in the navy's administration, which included southern Borneo, the Celebes, the Moluccas, and Lesser Sunda. "I was sentenced to thirty years' hard labor by the Americans for what I did in Indonesia during the war. When I walked out the gate of Sugamo Prison in 1955, my sentence commuted, I felt that freedom was the only thing I wanted. I was then thirty-seven years old."

In 1942 I thought occupying a country was a wonderful thing. When our ship arrived at the Celebes, in Indonesia, I saw wide stretches of uncultivated soil. "We can develop this land and introduce Japanese technology here," I thought. We were billeted in the houses built by the Dutch colonizers. We didn't take anything from the Indonesians, only from the Dutch. On any given day we might receive the order "Bring your buckets for distribution of wine" or "Officers, prepare to receive whiskey." Johnny Walker whiskey was everywhere. Until confiscated by us, these things had been the property of the exploiters, so most of the time I felt it was fine for us to liberate them.

We had no idea what the four of us new-minted naval candidate officers would be used for. All they said was, "We'll train you on site. Be ready." We made up lists of Dutch prisoners of war who were gathered on the grounds of a former school. Mr. Itō and I met with the Dutch commander, a lieutenant colonel. We issued him orders: "Make a list of prisoners. We will examine it." We were told to gather books from evacuated houses in the city of Macassar, where military confiscation and requisition announcements were posted. We found refrigerators fully stocked, cupboards loaded with whiskey. Western clothes were hanging in the closets. Automobiles sat in front of the houses. We gathered all the books using trucks. Itō was very good with books. He separated and classified them. While we did such miscellaneous tasks by day, we began basic officer training at night, learning such fundamental things as naval regulations, boat handling, and how to command men.

My mental image of the South was really based on a comic strip called *The Adventures of Dankichi*. No matter what I had learned in school, no matter how many pictures I saw of modern cities with wide boulevards like those in Holland, I just couldn't get those images of Dankichi's South Sea islands out of my head. Even when I listened to lectures about life in Surabaja, in my imagination I saw small desert islands with naked black natives under palm trees. When I saw how things really were I was actually shocked.

The building we used as our headquarters had housed the offices of the Netherlands governor general. It was in Greco-Roman style, enormous fans turning overhead in each room. It even had running hot water. Japan didn't have such things. In this occupied area I learned for the first time how developed Europe was. Grand refrigerators were manufactured in Europe, while in Japan we still used iceboxes. Here the Japanese military was full of people who'd come directly from farming villages, never even been to Tokyo. Many didn't even know how to urinate in a Western toilet. A lot of them stood on top and blasted away. A distant anxiety grew in me: "Can Japan win?"

A Civil Administration Department was established in August 1942. I was assigned to its legal section. I was thrown in there, even though I was still just a cadet ensign. Well-educated Indonesians were assigned to each section. They'd been working for the government since the Dutch period and could bring out a great book of documents and records whenever I asked them a question. Japan recreated exactly the same structure the Dutch had used. If we'd removed that, we couldn't have administered the country. This was true even at the lowest levels. Each local district had its own head, with its own system of self-government. It was almost completely feudalistic and practically universal. In the Celebes, the Dutch had controlled only the population of the city of Macassar, and the village headmen were in charge elsewhere. The Japanese military authorities followed the same pattern. We used the feudalistic system as it was.

One of my first jobs was to go with the chief of the the telephone-communications section to inspect facilities needed for public order and security, including prisons, police, and telephones. We traveled through the southern part of the Celebes by car. All seemed to be functioning well, and we Japanese were being treated as liberators who had expelled the Dutch for the Indonesians. The haughty Dutch who had lorded it over the Indies found themselves prisoners overnight. When I got to areas where Japanese forces had never been, village chiefs welcomed me. I wore a white military uniform, but concealed my pistol. They waved the Sun flag and the Indonesian flag too. I felt we were doing something wonderful there. To me, at least, they looked as if they favored us. This lasted through the end of 1942. Then the military demanded an allotment of the rice harvest from the depths of the Celebes. There was a stirring of tension among the locals and troops had to be mobilized to control it.

Allied bombing started in 1943. Macassar was hit practically daily. Casualties began to mount up. Mr. Sumida—today chairman of the Bank of Japan, then a lieutenant, j.g., representing the Civil Administration Department—a naval lieutenant commander, and I were in charge of civil defense. Just before each air raid, it seemed a flare would be sent up, showing our location. Spies were suspected, but the efforts I led to catch them in the act failed. I can't say that there was an organized independence movement acting against us. I sensed resistance in town, but I couldn't pin it down. At first, the pedicabs had stopped the instant I called out to them. Now they kept going as if they didn't hear.

Large-scale arrests of foreigners, persons of mixed blood, and intellectuals were carried out by the Police Affairs Section of the Civil Administration Department, together with a unit of the Navy Special Police, the Tokkeitai, set up at the end of 1943. I worked with them as an interpreter, but refused to continue participation when I realized the charges were invariably trumped up. I disliked the police mentality shown by the unit's inspectors, but the men at the top were deadly serious, so I didn't dare criticize them. I simply told them I didn't have such skills as an interpreter. All Japanese who were involved received death sentences after the war.

I also became aware that right-wing financial groups and the military were in league in our area. Of course, that's not the way I would have described things then. The head of my old private academy had come to Indonesia with his wife. He now headed up the Southern Awakening Construction Company. It even had a Southern Awakening Friendship Association attached to it. When the military built a road to an airfield, an enormous amount of money was appropriated for the job. This construction company would then take the whole job. It didn't really matter what they charged. All the budgets were special military expenditures. With that money, the commanders and the rightists went out drinking. Restaurants with Japanese names were built all over. The ones in Macassar were constructed from beautiful and expensive wood. Tatami mats were brought in on warships. They were really gorgeous, but people like me couldn't really go there. They were for senior staff officers and cost too much. There were serving women there, though no real geishas. On rare occasions, our commander might declare, "I'll take you all. My treat." I'm sure he had special expense money for that. Kaneko-Sensei— my teacher, the academy head—was hanging out with the captains and colonels. I wasn't much use to him, only a lieutenant, j.g., so I had little to do with him in Macassar, but I heard that when he invited high officials to his home, he'd say, "Nogi's one of my boys. Been at my academy. Take care of him."

When you've been in the navy for two years and are promoted, they'll ask you where you want to go. If you remain in the same post after your promotion, you lose dignity. Mr. Itō and some of the others requested transfers back to the Homeland. I requested a transfer to the front lines. I'd started to wonder what I was doing there, military man that I was. I don't think I was motivated any longer by a desire to win the liberation of Indonesia, but I wanted to be sent somewhere where there was intense combat. I was fed up with being a bureaucrat.

I was put in charge of the Tokkeitai special naval police on Ambon Island, closer to New Guinea, and, by then, virtually on the front lines. New Guinea was under attack and American forces were sweeping toward us. I'd never studied the laws that applied to police work. My commander was a naval captain who issued me orders. We were in charge of enforcing military discipline and regulations over our area, including controlling things within the military itself.

I posted two slogans in my Tokkeitai office: "We Are The Emperor's Subordinates" and "The People's Mind Is Our Fortress." I never thought of the Emperor as divine, but I have to admit I used His authority. I really did believe, and told my men, that we dared not lose the local people's mind in the course of accomplishing our duties.

Soon after I'd reported to Amboina, I received a telephone call from headquarters ordering me to go to an ordinary house. When I arrived, I found my *sensei*, Kaneko, this time with Vice Admiral Yamagata and his chief of staff. They had a large bottle of saké. The former head of my academy spoke to me as if I were one of his gang: "I got the go-ahead from the local commander, here. We're gonna build a training base for our boatmen. You're picked to run it. I'll give you the best petty officers as teachers. All right?" Boatmen were necessary for Southern Awakening Construction's ferry service, running back and forth between the islands. They were now going to get the military to train the crews for them. I was startled that such a decision was being made in this kind of place. The commander himself asked me directly, "Well, how about it?" My reply was, "I'll do it if it's an order."

From then on, I was in charge both of the special naval police and the boatmen being trained. They gathered the sons of Indonesian village heads and young local officials too. They were all smart. They were to be taught simple sailing techniques, Morse code, and hand signals. I had to teach them ideology, trying to explain why we were fighting this war, why they had to cooperate with us. My argument was that if Japan lost, their nation would remain a colony, and I asked them to cooperate until victory was achieved.

I didn't truly believe those arguments any longer, but I used them anyway. I felt we were only turning them into our own colony. I had once imagined we would be leading Indonesians in singing their independence anthem, "Indonesia Raia," but now we banned it. I even received an order that all nationalist movements were to be prohibited. We put local people into various key positions and then ordered them to report even the tiniest rumors to us. We dispatched unit members to the houses of suspected local nationalists, but until the end of the war we hardly ever found any.

Among the Japanese forces the atmosphere became more and more brutal. Violent incidents occurred regularly. Superiors were beaten up by drunken soldiers. A naval captain beat up a civilian administrator, accusing him of being presumptuous. There was even a murder that was hushed up. The victim, it was said, "died of illness," and when I tried to investigate anyway, I was told the case was closed. The captain in charge cursed me out: "Stupid fledgling! Don't poke your beak where it doesn't belong. A battle of annihilation is imminent. If we punish this man, we'll be reducing the fighting strength of Japan!" He then suggested that I leave the police unit. "How'd you like to be in charge of an air-defense unit?" This was a threat. If you commanded antiaircraft guns you were the target of an avalanche of bombs. This incident convinced me the military was a capricious organization not worthy of my trust. From then on, I no longer encouraged the men under my command to track down crimes.

The Indonesian people knew, thanks to their illegal short-wave radios, that Japan was losing in New Guinea. When we caught locals whispering about it, we seized them for spreading groundless rumors and undercutting morale. Just listening to short wave—well that was enough reason to execute them. It was in military law and was accepted. We had such cases.

I was cautious, though. I never did anything before the eyes of the locals. Even when we had to do something, I never, never let them see. This wasn't a humanistic matter for me. It was tactical. It would have been bad strategy to stir them up. I judged that I would get stronger negative reactions if we tried to make examples of violators than if we didn't. In other areas they did make examples. But in my area, when they knew we'd captured someone for acting against us, I always had a notice sent to their village informing them that the party had escaped. Even when he'd actually been executed. Often we had trials first. I knew that our military occupation would be powerless if the locals began guerrilla activities against us.

During this period, in 1944, American pilots fell in our area. Army and navy staff officers came to interrogate them, bringing maps on which they could pinpoint locations. After they had extracted the intelligence they wanted from them, the order came down, "Process them." I knew it was illegal. Because I'd studied some law, I knew international regulations. But every day, those two-engine Lockheeds would come and run wild, doing what they wanted. All our planes had been destroyed. We could offer no resistance. We were enraged and frustrated. When you lose your own fighting capability and can only suffer under their attacks, you become vengeful yourself. We'll get them! They'll pay for this!

"It's illegal," I thought, "but the only choice for Japan is total annihilation or victory. If we go on losing like this, we'll never return home alive. Will I be questioned on my responsibility? Not likely. We'll all be dead. If we win, there's nothing to worry about because it was ordered from above." Welling up within myself I felt sentiments like "How dare they bomb us! We can't give them special treatment just because they're prisoners. I can never forgive them."

When I appeared at my trial as a war criminal I didn't say that, of course. I said I had no choice but to obey orders. But the truth was, I wanted to kill them. Still, when I saw their faces, I pitied them. They were as young as ours. The soldiers who'd prepared the ground for the execution, and who'd dug the graves, all watched me. Saying this today I feel ashamed. I had a strange vanity. I didn't want to embarrass myself in front of the men. If I didn't make a good show of it, I'd be a laughingstock. If I analyze my psychology today, I would say I killed them because of that. They were very pale. Their eyes were blindfolded properly. You had to have an actual document, a written sentence and an order of execution, to do it. But there was no trial or hearing. I knew this was illegal, but I announced: "You have been sentenced to death." They asked, "Why?" If I'd listened to them, my own spirit would have been dulled, so holding my sword I made them kneel down.

There were three of them. We used our swords, because it was risky to use pistols. The sound of shooting could have stirred up the local residents. That's why we didn't use a firing squad. We took them deep into the mountains where not even the locals could observe us. Americans. Whites. Pilots. I don't remember their names. The ones who interrogated them surely must remember, though.

Why did we do this? Those who fell from the sky at the front all got killed. Their presence was undeniable evidence that Japanese forces were collapsing, and the Japanese commanders didn't want this known even among their own troops. I think that's why such killing took place. I suspect that such a policy was applied broadly, but I have no hard proof. But consider the fact that this happened all across the front. It can't have been due simply to spontaneous orders from the local commanders. Something had to have come from higher up. Yet, even today, field-grade officers and such never say anything disadvantageous to themselves. I sometimes have occasion to meet them, and I ask them while we're sharing saké, but they still won't speak of it.

The reason I didn't have my subordinates do it in my place was that all of them were former police officers. They had wives and children.

They weren't young. I felt sorry for them. I felt it best for me to be the executioner. By the end, I feared the whole unit would be executed, but only two of my subordinates were tried. One was sentenced to death, but all the others made it home and got their old police jobs back. The one who was executed had killed by torture.

After the war, the Dutch did not charge those who had followed official military legal procedures carried out by the Japanese army and navy. They did not question them even if there were horrible things in the trials. And so, although the Dutch came to investigate these martial-law sentences, they never filed complaints against me. Half of all the Navy Special Police units in the southern theater, commanders and simple unit members, were sentenced to death. This also showed that many cases did not go through proper trial procedures. Nevertheless, the Americans made me dig up the bones of the men I'd killed. When I did, they were still fresh, like corned beef, although it was nearly a year later. Horrible. I washed the bones, together with Chief Petty Officer Yoshizaki, who had assisted me.

Near the end, when we even had to grow our own food, we found ourselves fighting over local laborers, pulling them this way and that. The army tried to pinch ours, threatening to use the Kempeitai. Our food ration was reduced by forty percent. Half the unit worked to build military positions, the other half were farmers. We were really hungry, but we couldn't say so. We just had to endure. We paid local residents for their labor, but it was in military scrip, virtually worthless.

The navy had grudges against the army for not providing sufficient provisions. Right there at the front lines, the Japanese army and the navy fought just like enemies. Had the war gone on six months more, I'm sure they would have started shooting at each other, trying to grab the other's provisions. I myself felt the local Kempei unit had been acting outrageously. Cooking up false cases, just to get points for doing something. They were dragging in village heads one after the other. Calling them spies and then executing them.

Many of my fellow members in the Amboina War Comrades Association view me as someone who took all the responsibility and became a casualty or victim. Officers and men both think that of me. I don't ask them what they did on the islands, because each knows what he did. They don't speak about it, but they remember. It is not possible to forget. I ask them, "If foreign forces did what we did there, right here in Japan, wouldn't you be angry?" They often say they agree with me, but I don't know how they behave after leaving the meeting. I suspect many still fear that what they did at risk of their lives would become a disgrace if they admitted to themselves they were fighting a dirty, aggressive war.

They deny what we actually did. I myself admit that the trials for our war crimes were good. What I went through was good. If I'd gone straight back home, forgiven for what I did, it would been even more frightening for me. Had I gone right back, I would have probably run for the local assembly, become a local official and eventually a conservative party official whose reputation is marred by corruption. If what we did in the name of national egoism were to be accepted, that would be horrible. The leaders of Japan today are all of my generation.

Today, Japan's government justifies what the military did during those war years. I'm saying this because I'm receiving a pension today. The time I spent in Sugamo prison as a war criminal is included in my service. This is the Japanese state saying, "Thank you very much for your efforts. You acted for the sake of Japan." Although I was given thirty years by America for a crime I committed, it's treated as just a foreign sentence, unimportant. After I left Sugamo, nobody looked at me strangely.

"I've been back to Indonesia seven times. Indonesians try not to show us the war museums. If I specifically ask, they will take me, so I finally got to the Djakarta War Memorial, but I wasn't allowed to bring in a camera. They display many photographs of Japanese suppression of Indonesians during the war. Indonesian politicians today must go to the Japanese for economic aid, and they seem to feel it is just better to take the economic assistance and avoid disturbing the Japanese."

"Korean Guard"

KASAYAMA YOSHIKICHI

He introduces himself as Kasayama, the name he adopted during the war years. His Korean name is I Gil. His hands are clenched fists on top of the table. They tremble slightly as he speaks, but, otherwise, he shows little anger or other emotion. His Japanese is excellent, rich in vocabulary, with only a trace of his native Korean. He belongs to the Dōshinkai, an association of the forty or so Korean B- and C-class war criminals living in Japan, men charged and convicted after the war for committing crimes against Allied prisoners. Most, like him, were technically civilian employees, employed or conscripted by the Japanese army for the lowliest tasks, including the guarding of captives.

Workers in our neighborhood of Seoul sometimes vanished in the middle of the night, only to turn up again six months or a year later.

When you asked, "Hey, where've you been?" they'd only say, "Don't ask. I can't tell ya." I got one of them aside, a man about my age—just the two of us, drinking. All I could get out of him was that he'd been grabbed by the military for forced labor at a military port. I thought, my time might be coming soon. If you're gonna be dragged off secretly as a laborer, maybe it made sense to go someplace more publicly, so in 1941 I took and passed the exams to become a "uniformed civilian" in the Japanese army. Although it might look like you'd volunteered, force was behind it. There were even neighborhood associations telling you that if you didn't present yourself as a "volunteer," they'd cut off your rations.

When it seemed like I might be going to the East Indies, I went to the Maruzen bookstore in Keijō, as Seoul was called then, and bought an English book on the Indonesian language and studied on my own. I entered the military officially at the port of Pusan in June 1942. We were searched at the induction inspection, and when they discovered that book I was berated by the sergeant: "From now on people all over the world will get along in Japanese. What'll you do with Indonesian and English?" He beat me up to teach me I was a dumb bastard with "Western thoughts." They didn't take my book away, though, and I kept studying on the boat. By the time we arrived in Surabaja on Java, I could greet people in Malay.

Japan was victorious then, and we all shared in the uproar and excitement. If you wore a Japanese star on your cap, you were really something. I was a bad driver, so when I drove, I zigzagged all over the road. They got out of my way in those days. I was in a prisoner-guard unit. On the surface it looked like a regular military unit, but we didn't have any ranks. My duty was to guard prisoners and assist in the operation of the camps where they were held, not to fight battles. There were about thirty of us Korean guards. Above us were a Japanese lance corporal, a sergeant, and an officer, usually a first or second lieutenant. We simply followed their orders, which were absolute. They always said orders came from His Majesty. Not to follow a noncom's orders meant to disobey the Emperor himself.

We took about two thousand prisoners from Java and moved them toward New Guinea, dividing them among the three islands of Cerabu, Amboina, and Haruku. The strategy, as I understood it, was to build airfields and bases for an attack on Australia. I was on Haruku. When we landed on the island there were no huts, no barracks, nothing. We slept in the blankets we brought with us. In three minutes you got soaked. You caught cold and had diarrhea within hours. There wasn't any firewood to cook rice. We chopped down green trees and burned them with the little fuel oil we had. We built frames for huts from bamboo and laid some kind of floor, then used dried palm for walls and roofs. Gradually we improved living conditions by building things. We called this a camp, but there wasn't even a fence. Because it was surrounded by the sea, there wasn't any place to run. About one hundred prisoners lived in each long, rectangular shack. There was an aisle down the middle and they slept on spots on the floor we called beds. The only clothes they had were their own military uniforms.

I was in that camp with Dutchmen, British, Australians, a few Americans, and some East Indians. Two thousand all mixed together. The majority were East Indians and Dutch. Among the Dutch, there were some administrative officers and doctors. Officers had separate blocks. The British were really haughty when compared to the Dutch. Among the prisoners were a few specialists skilled as Japanese interpreters.

There were fifteen to twenty officers and noncoms on the Japanese side in the guard unit. Hardly any Japanese on the island spoke English, even though some of the officers were military-academy graduates. I could speak a little English since I had studied composition and grammar at the YMCA in Seoul and taken conversation from an American missionary. My grandfather's antique store—The Korean Curio Shoppe, located just in front of the Chōsen Hotel—was aimed at tourists, so English was crucial.

Every morning each work unit came to take out prisoners. My responsibility was to hand over the number they wanted. Sick prisoners were kept in the hospital facilities. All others had to work. The prisoners' own doctors determined who was to be in the hospital. Sometimes Japanese doctors came to check, and if the numbers approved for labor by the prisoners' doctors were too low, they'd say, "This one's fit enough to work. He's not so sick." The prisoners worked from nine o'clock in the morning until five o'clock in the afternoon. Rest breaks at ten and three. There was a large "kitchen," where the prisoners did their own cooking. We cooked for ourselves, too.

The airfield-construction unit had many more tools than we did. They used bulldozers looted from the Dutch army. Japanese soldiers didn't know how to operate them, but Indians in the British army did, so they drove 'em. Their job was to make the airfield flat. It took the Japanese military four months using a thousand laborers to build one airfield. Sure, we beat and kicked prisoners in order to make them work. But their principle was to work as little as possible. Some strong ones would finish their work quickly and then just sit there. That's where we'd clash. Short-tempered Japanese soldiers would slap the prisoners. The prisoners would do what they weren't supposed to do—steal things, hide things, and pilfer from the work unit they'd been assigned to. Even one missing tool was treated by the construction unit as if it had been a weapon bestowed directly by His Imperial Highness. Some of the things they stole were consumables like paper and food. Our clothes were too small for them, so they didn't steal those. When we caught them, we beat them.

I handled the office work and I was also frequently in charge of purchasing, so I went to the villages, and picked up stuff for myself at the same time. I didn't smoke, so I took my cigarettes and exchanged them for food which I hid away in the storeroom and ate when I got hungry.

All the locals were cooperative, on the surface. What else could they do? We designated merchants who could deal with the military. I was the middleman between the military commissary and the village dealers. I took orders from the prisoners, checked them, then passed them along. When the prisoners worked, we paid them money, as regulated by inter-national law. The officers got the same money as Japanese officers, but just the base salary, nothing special like family allowance or combat pay. If you gave the money to them all at once, they'd use it to escape, so we made them save. They received minimum monthly spending allowances to buy fruit, sugar, and things like that. All the rest went to compulsory savings. We used military scrip.

The guards' wages were also in scrip, and most of our money was sent home for savings. They didn't want us to have much either. We got to keep only ten yen, or ten *guilder,* using the Dutch word. But if you had cash, you'd go buy women and drink. On the island there were "comfort women"—Japanese, Koreans, and locals. There weren't so many women that we could afford to let the prisoners go to them too.

Demands for food and medical supplies came from the prisoners, but we didn't have any "main course" either. We had only rice and the leaves of the tapioca plant. We made some soup with those leaves, a little garlic, salt, and a bit of butter. Our superiors were in the same shape. There was nothing to eat and nothing to give. Japanese army regulations specified that we were to feed the Japanese first, then the locals, and what was left was for the prisoners.

Death often came from dysentery. Even when they recovered, there wasn't enough food to give them, so malnutrition appeared. They'd get really thin. Their lips would get completely dry. Their eyesight blurred. The prisoners made a kind of eyeglasses out of colored gelatine paper to shade their eyes from the sun. The sick got worse. If we'd had food and medicine, many of them could have been saved. There wasn't enough salt, either. "Give us more salt. Five grams a day is absolutely necessary," their doctors would say, but we couldn't come close to that. Without salt, humans can't survive. Unlucky captives like ours had been sent to a terrible place. Lucky ones were left in the middle of cities with good facilities, even hospitals. You can even say the same thing about the guards.

Every day they died. There was no time to dig graves. We couldn't dig deep holes because the soil was sandy and the sides collapsed right away—and anyway, there weren't any tools, just shovels and axes. So we put up a hut, called Rest in Peace. Of course, prisoners did this job. Who else would do it? When you put several hundred corpses in one place, the whole island reeks with the smell of rotting bodies, the stink of death. The captive soldiers died more frequently than officers. The officers only supervised the labor. We didn't use them for "heavy labor." That's forbidden by international law, as you know. We did use the noncoms, though. But the officers still said we slaved them, though they hardly worked at all.

The Japanese war situation grew worse. Supplies became scarcer and their arrival more sporadic. We tried to get medical supples from the main islands in Indonesia, but shipments were sunk by Allied subs. There were days when we had to make do with fifteen hundred calories, although a minimum of two thousand calories was required. I was the one who had to go and convey the orders of the Japanese army, the orders of the officers, to the prisoners, telling them what to do. The captive officers heard from Kasayama, the Korean guard, not from the Japanese officers. They thought fifty out of a hundred orders were mine. When the war ended, this came up at the trial.

I might have been better off if I'd never studied English. Because I knew English, I interpreted and had to stand between the POWs and the Japanese army and bear the blame for someone else's crimes. Yet, because of language, I got the easier jobs. I could always say, "I'm busy with paperwork," when I was in the office and so get out of heavy training. We used interpreters, but many of the Japanese "Malay interpreters" couldn't communicate at all—not a bit. We "civilian employees," numbering three thousand all together—collected from all over the Korean peninsula, and spread throughout the South—learned Malay quickly. It was the only way you could do anything. Besides, since I talked to the prisoners, I learned much from them.

Radios were prohibited in the camp. Yet they had them—the prisoners would dismantle them and each prisoner would have one part concealed somewhere. Whenever they moved, we'd search them and try to find the radio, but it was impossible. When they'd moved and settled down, they'd put it back together. They had technical specialists in the camp who could do this right there in the jungle. In the Japanese army, only special units had these skills. So they communicated safely with the outside world and knew they were winning. We guarded them, but we didn't know anything. I sometimes talked with their officers. We'd almost joke about who would win. One brightly moonlit night, planes roared overhead. We went out and looked up. I saw two lamps on each of the planes. The RAF colonel I often spoke with said, "Kasayama, do you know what those are?" "Japanese flying boats," I replied. "You don't know anything," he said. Insulted, I shouted back, "What do you mean?" "They're Lockheed P-38s, planes with two tails. They're here to scout us. Why would Japanese navy planes fly over at night?" I let him talk more. "You'd better listen!" he said. "Very soon, within two weeks, bombing will begin."

Ten days later at about ten A.M., we were bombed. Strangely they avoided the camp, bombs falling only outside the perimeter. Some five hundred local people died in the raid. This was my first experience of bombing. I had to go see what had happened to the prisoners who were working on the airfield. I rode a bicycle through burning trees, my eyes closed, pedaling down the middle of the road, and made it to the airfield all right. I found them there, gathered safely. They weren't even shaken up.

At the end, it wasn't a matter of giving food to the prisoners or not giving it. There wasn't any food even for the Japanese soldiers. It was wretched. Sometimes Japanese soldiers whose transport had been sunk reached the island practically naked. They didn't even have mess kits or swords. In such pitiful conditions, there was nothing you could do for prisoners of war. We ate rice gruel. There was hardly anything to go with it. Some vegetables, but very few. Meat was water buffalo and a few fish.

When we'd almost completed our airfield, we were ordered back to Java. Japanese planes never used that field. On the way back from Haruku, we were bombed again. We were in a convoy of small boats. The boat I was on was jammed with maybe four hundred people. They came straight down from the sky, flying very low, and opened up with machine guns. *Dah-dah-dah-dah!* I was sitting between two friends. I jumped into the sea. Everybody else jumped too, and the boat tipped over. I couldn't swim. I was hanging onto the side of the boat when I saw the planes circle over us, making a figure-eight, and *pon-pon-pon,* they were shooting again. Of course, the prisoners also jumped into the sea. If the British had had a flag to show who they were, the shooting might have stopped. As it was, two or three prisoners died, and so did my two friends.

It took almost sixty days to reach Surabaja, even though it was hardly any distance at all. The boat was just a wreck. It could make between five and seven knots. If the wind blew against us, we stopped dead in the water. In this hulk we took cover in island coves and sneaked along the coast. Of course, lots of prisoners died of illness during those sixty days. We buried them at sea—attached sand-bags to their legs and laid them out on a stretcher and lowered them into the water. A body sinks at first, but several days later gases come out of the body, the stomach fills, and it bobs up to the surface. Then it really stinks, and you have to attach another sandbag to make it sink out of sight again. We didn't have any fresh water along the coast. We used that polluted water to wash and cook our rice, drawing it from the sea in buckets. Hardly anyone was healthy. We were malnourished, and many suffered from beriberi. Your legs felt terribly heavy, and your flesh swelled up and lost its resiliency. I had a mild case. We got back in November 1943. Of the two thousand we took, about eight hundred made it back.

After Surabaja, we went to Bandung. There, we had good facilities, since it was a former Dutch military installation. Abundant food. You could eat until your stomach was full. Even the prisoners' camps were good. Good climate. The prisoners had plenty of food, too. Many former colonial civil servants were now among the prisoners, so they knew what kind of medicine was available and where it was located. They knew which medicine cured which diseases. For a little more than a year it was an easy life for us. Duty was no longer our primary concern. We went whoring and drinking. Raising hell was our main interest. In Bandung we had money, even after the deductions were sent home. We used the black market. We bought things like watches cheaply from the prisoners, and sold them to the Chinese for high prices. Using our "commission," we ate and drank. If you're gonna die, what difference does it make? We abandoned thoughts of going home.

I didn't write home. It was pointless. Even if you had a broken arm, you had to write, "I'm well, I will give my life to the nation. Long Live the Emperor! *Tennō Heika banzai!*" Japan's war situation got worse and worse, and we were hit by raids of eighty or more American planes. The Japanese began to worry that these Koreans might cause a rebellion. So they took our thirty-man squads and broke us into little groups of three or four. We were physically a lot stronger than the Japanese—better in the head, too. That was because they chose only three thousand out of thirty or forty million of us, only the best, while they were the dregs. I myself never thought of rebelling, but some did. The Japanese even tried to "reeducate" us. They built an education unit to indoctrinate us Koreans to be loyal subjects of Japan, but things were so bad that shots were even exchanged. One just missed an officer's head. After the first couple of years, we didn't hide our feelings any longer. When they wouldn't let us go home as our contract promised, there was no point pretending. "Do you think we're going to let you shit on us till we die?" we demanded. All we thought about was squeezing a little more pleasure out of the time left. "Do your best for the military! Do your best for the nation!" That stinks! "We can't sink any lower than we already are. Come on! If you wanna fight, let's see what you can do." We had rifles now, too.

Sometimes we bumped into Japanese soldiers at some canteen. A Japanese soldier would say, "You're Koreans, *Chōsenjin*, aren't you? We're here as official conscripts. We have our Red Papers." We'd answer back, "So what?"—you get courageous when you have a few drinks—"We're here with our White Papers. We're volunteers! The war's the same for both of us, isn't it? Don't give us any crap!" We'd take one into the toilet and beat him up. Two or three of us jumped him and hit him. When he was out flat, we left him there and closed the door, paid our bill in a hurry, and left. They couldn't really be sure who'd done it. We did the same thing in prison later. The Japanese apologized and groveled when they didn't have rifles.

"I knew about the surrender three days before we heard it officially. All the prisoners came out of their barracks in the Bandung camp. They each wore a victory 'ribbon' on their pocket. We had to feed them every day until the Allied forces arrived and the camp was dissolved. The amount we fed them increased suddenly. Now we had to give them food even the Japanese didn't get because they were the victors. They knew all about the Potsdam Declaration and unconditional surrender. It was a complete surprise to us. They told us we had to salute them now, because they'd won. We had to do it. We were the defeated.

" 'I'll rush back home,' I thought. But about four days after it ended, a lieutenant colonel told me I was under arrest as a war criminal. Two Gurkhas grabbed me—one from each side—and dragged me off to the guardhouse. I was tried and convicted. I started serving my life sentence in Changi Prison in Singapore and was then sent to Sugamo Prison in Tokyo in 1951. That was the first time I'd ever been to Japan. When I was paroled in 1955, I had to stay to report in with the Japanese police. I've lived here ever since."

5 / THE EMPEROR'S WARRIORS

Maker of Soldiers

DEBUN SHIGENOBU

"In December 1939, I returned from my active-duty service. I had been at the China front as a cavalryman for six months. You could say it was the last victorious welcome-home conducted by Japan. The streets were full of people cheering and waving flags. We thought the China Incident was a winning war, so we marched bravely behind our commander, who was on horseback, from Kanazawa Station to our camp clear across town. War is something you should stop at the appropriate time."

Widely spaced houses, each surrounded by rice fields, are the distinctive features of villages in the Toyama plain. His home is set off by a line of tall cedar trees. The village from which he went to war is now part of Tonami City.

"There were 10,521 military-affairs clerks in Japan. I was one of them. I was the only one who preserved the actual documents, despite the orders we received to burn them when Japan surrendered." All military records that might be of use to the enemy were ordered destroyed. With a great guffaw he adds, "I am a serious criminal." A wiry man, about five feet tall, he speaks in a loud, vibrant voice with a sense of mission. One of the lenses from his reading glasses often pops out as he bangs the frames down for emphasis, but that hardly interrupts his discourse. He rushes back and forth, to and from his storeroom for boxes of materials, all meticulously arranged, concerning the soldiers he had sent to the front, and he illustrates his points with the appropriate documents.

A man's life, it was said then, was worth only one *sen* five *rin*—one point five percent of a yen—to the prewar military. This was the price of the postcard that many thought was all that was involved in conscripting them. But that's not how it was. I knew well. I was in the village office. I served to provide the military with soldiers and sailors. I also had to follow the appointed procedures when a soldier was killed in action. I did everything. I was rated number-one military-affairs clerk in Toyama prefecture. I even received an award from the commander of the Ninth

Divisional District headquartered in Kanazawa City, incorporating regimental headquarters across the whole Hokuriku region, including Ishikawa, Toyama, and Gifu prefectures.

I ask you—which was superior, the German military system, renowned throughout the world, or the Japanese system? Our system, which could raise large-scale units in less than twenty-four hours, was world-class! No one had a more thorough and efficient system for mobilizing soldiers to the colors than Japan.

All males had the obligation to report for a conscription exam at the age of twenty. But after serving your active duty, you were still eligible for later call-up. As early as the Russo-Japanese War, it had already been decided that liability for military service would extend to the age of forty. In case of war, those with experience would be of great use. Veterans know how to shoot guns, so preparations to summon these people to what was called the National Army were made way back then.

Records had to be maintained prior to active duty, and afterwards for reservists and others still subject to call-up. The soldier himself didn't really know what kind of documents had been gathered about him at the village office. But let me assure you, they were very thorough, very complete, and so clearly entered that even a third person could read them accurately. The military provided a glossary of the precise terms to be used in preparing such records.

If we look at just this one example it should be clear. In 1925, this man, Hakusan Shin'ichi, took the conscription examination. He was rated Class A in his physical—that is, in the best qualified group. He was assigned to the infantry. He was appointed an infantry second lieutenant in 1927. At that time, he was placed on the reserve list, having completed his active duty. In the next column, reserved for remarks, we can see he was mustered again for the Pacific War, called up in 1944, and served in Unit 48 in Japan's Eastern Region.

That is the most basic information. But the next column gives the address of the person to whom that second draft notice was delivered. Ōkado 1229 was the address of his father, Hakusan Jisaku. The responsibility was thus clearly assigned to the father. He was the one who received the red call-up paper. His obligation to inform his son was defined by law. If his wife was there, in the absence of a man, she would have had to convey the news to her son. If she did not discharge this responsibility, she would be charged under military penal law. The government undertook to pay the person's transportation cost back to Toyama from wherever he was when he was informed of his call-up. The actual military unit that was responsible for paying that fee was recorded on the red paper itself. This process was truly the finest in the world.

This system and preparation were nationwide. With a single red paper, all unit organization could be accomplished. Each man's physical condition, work situation, classification according to his military status— all these things had to be memorized by the military-affairs clerk. The clerk usually bore responsibility for investigating each and every person, and reporting any changes to regimental district headquarters. This wasn't just for fifty or a hundred people. It had to be done for several hundred people in two hundred and forty households. In peacetime, not just wartime, one had to be fully apprised of the situation of each individual, know every one of them, including the village youths. You had to know conditions in their families, too. Many children were evacuated to this area from Tokyo. Teachers, too. If there ever was a final battle in the Homeland, like the ones in Okinawa, teachers were to take the lead, so I also assumed control over their military registration.

I often walked around in the village to learn what the villagers were up to. Even those walks belonged to the realm of military secrets. I couldn't say, "I came to check on you," so I'd just ask, "Your son who's working in Osaka as a barber—how's he doing?" In that way I would find out. Then I'd send a letter directly to the man. A person couldn't really lie about their physical condition, in a time of war, so he'd write back, "I'm fine." They always responded like that, without fail. Even those who were classified Class C wouldn't get a doctor to write they had infection of the lungs or whatever. Each man knew how to behave. This was wartime.

It wasn't the military-affairs clerk who stuck somebody with their red paper. But the preparatory work he did was huge. There was no way Toyama regimental headquarters could know about the individual. Yet when a man entered the army for the first time, everything was recorded, including his thoughts. The military-affairs clerk had to investigate these things regularly. When a soldier entered a unit, the military-affairs clerk sent the military a complete report—including the soldier's family background, whether it included a criminal or not, the size of the family's rice fields, the value of their properties—but the individual had no idea what has been sent to the unit. They never really saw it. From time to time officials came from the regiment in Toyama, or from the division in Kanazawa, to inspect the documents.

Most of the time, notifications came in the middle of the night. An envelope was delivered to the village police chief from military headquarters. The police office then phoned the village mayor. I heard that at the beginning of the China Incident it was brought to him under the guard of a policeman, but later the military-affairs clerk had to go from the village office and pick it up because the police station had gotten too busy. I would open it in the presence of the mayor. Until that moment, even I didn't know who was going to be drafted. I'd make notations on the various documents and then call on a person to deliver it. For most of the Pacific War, I delivered them myself—whether they were conscription notices or official notifications of a soldier's death in battle—because if some accident should happen to it on the way it would be a disaster.

This often happened very early in the morning. For example, this record shows that it was delivered at four-forty-five. If it was July when daylight hours were long, that wasn't too bad, but in winter it was really tough. All this was to prevent spying. The mustering of soldiers was a military secret. It wasn't good to incite disturbances among the general population, and you didn't want to give the enemy information about how many soldiers Japan was calling up or where they were assembling.

Once, thirteen red papers arrived in our village on a single day, August 25, 1937. The China Incident had begun July 7. I had to report to the police the exact time when I handed the call-up paper to the family of each of the conscripted. The military-affairs clerk was always sick with worry until the moment the conscript actually entered his unit. At that time, I was only a deputy. When thirteen draft notices arrived at once, I could only pray. If, by chance, one of them didn't turn up or refused induction, the village mayor and the military-affairs clerk would be reprimanded by the military. These things weren't spelled out in criminal law. Maybe the conscript himself would bear the legal responsibility and get punished, but things were seldom that simple.

I learned of the declaration of war on December 8, 1941, via the radio. Preparation had begun in July. We were ordered to call up men, but they were to report carrying a fishing rod, or with a beer or cider bottle hanging from their belts, and dressed in a light summer kimono. Those instructions weren't indicated on the draft notice. They came on a separate sheet. I thought something was strange, but I knew immediately that it was a military secret. We couldn't even send these people off at the station in broad daylight as we'd done for the war with China. But we had a sending-off ceremony at the school.

The families started making "thousand-stitch belts" after the draft notices arrived, but there was very little time. If you wore one of these *sen'ninbari*, it was believed bullets would not hit you. Even when nothing was available, no matter the expense, people would buy a sea bream, prepare red rice—trying to show, on the surface, at least, what an auspicious occasion this was. All the people would then send the conscript off, offering congratulations and felicitations. No one could reveal their deepest emotions. The drafted man had to formally request everyone to take care of his family after he was gone.

All across Japan, village mayors would always say to each of them, "Please do not worry after you leave. If you fall in action, we will enshrine you in Yasukuni." He was speaking for the whole government, the whole people of Japan, promising their spirit would find its way to the great national shrine in Tokyo for those who had fallen in defense of the Emperor. Schoolchildren would stand there in front of the conscripts. The village people, their relatives, everybody would be assembled for them. Prior to the Pacific War they even raised banners, declaring in wide bold letters: "Congratulations On Being Called To The Colors" or "Prayers For Your Eternal Success At Arms," and displaying the inducted man's name. A village youth climbed the tallest cedar by the house and put up a sun-disk flag. For some families, three or four flags flew over the house. Those flags stayed up until the day the man returned. If a soldier from that family had been killed in action, a black streamer would fly beneath. Some families had two or three flags with black streamers.

The public sent them off with cheers. *"Banzai! Banzai!"* "Congratulations! Congratulations!" You had to say it. I remember one man of a fairly advanced age, with children, who was filled with concern over how his family would live after he was gone. In front of the mayor, he had some saké, and a box lunch was served. The village people came one after another to pour for him, and he drank immoderately, sopping it all up, until he could no longer walk straight. Then he came over to me and said, "I don't want to go." He was weeping. "I just got back from the front, and now I've gotten another call-up notice. Why?" That man was killed soon after, at the time of our landings in the Philippines. A postcard I received from him was his last word. Then, the box with his remains arrived. His name was on it, but it was empty. All I could do was give that postcard to the family of the decreased.

In a unit where three or four men died at the same time, even when their remains came back over one or two months, the funerals would be held together. A condolence speech would be delivered by the mayor, and in this area, where the Pure Land sect of Buddhism is strong, a priest from the temple usually came. Among those who died, there were people who had been at the front for eight, nine, or almost ten years. They got caught up in it when they were on their active-duty service, and never got out. When you think about it, the ones who fight wars are the people. Each soldier fought the war. The history of war is not only armies occupying territory.

At the peak of the Pacific War, in 1944 and 1945, the village received an order to get several tens of volunteers for the navy among the youths under conscription age. There weren't any bullets or guns anymore, but still the order came: Make the boys volunteer. It was so absurd. So unreasonable. I'd been to war once, myself. I knew whether there was ammunition or not.

At that time, the village chief told me, "I will get my second son to volunteer. You get the middle-school boy in your family to volunteer." It was expected. His boy volunteered for the Special Attack Corps from Waseda University. He never returned.

My brother was in his third year at Takaoka Commercial School. He was still a fifteen-year-old child. He cried and said, "I don't want to go." But I told him he must. I brought out this very table and a razor and made him cut his finger and write a petition on the finest paper to volunteer in his own blood. His blood dripped into a saké cup. He had to squeeze more out from his finger to finish writing it, since the paper so soaked up the blood. We submitted the petition to the prefectural governor. He was enrolled as a a junior trainee pilot. My parents were silent. It had to be done because I was the military-affairs clerk. I had to send men to the front. Even just one man more.

My brother asked me to give him a military sword when he was about to leave. We went and bought it together. If the war had lasted two days longer, he would have gone, loaded with bombs, as a member of the navy's Kamikaze Tokkōtai.

When I needed volunteers, I walked again and again through the entire village. A grandmother opposed me, saying, "It's too early. Let him wait for his conscription physical at twenty." That boy was killed. The grandma berated me. "You sent him to be killed!" I apologized to her afterwards: "Please, I beg you for forgiveness."

The one who encouraged him to volunteer was me. The man who had to inform his family that he had been killed was me. So many soldiers were sent off this way. Falling for the country, dying for the country. And then, after we lost, they ordered the burning of the records. Was nothing to remain despite all their sacrifice? That was too harsh, I thought. The dead died thinking of the nation. I couldn't bear my feeling of pity for them; that's why I knew I had to keep the documents, even if it was only my village alone that preserved them.

By war's end, I was the only man left in the village. Even those who were in poor physical condition or slightly disabled had been taken. Even those classified C or D had been called up. At the end of the war, I was twenty-eight years old. One of the best-kept military secrets was that military-affairs clerks would not be called up. They were classified with

Imperial National Diet members, mayors, and village headmen and deferred from military service. But finally in 1945, in the extremes of the Pacific War, even mayors and assemblymen were called up, leaving only us military-affairs clerks. The army couldn't raise soldiers without us.

At the end of the war, Shōge village had two hundred and forty-six households and three hundred and eighty-eight serving soldiers. The number of war dead was fifty-three. We gave that much weight to our country. I had to do the job with the belief that it was for the sake of the nation, for the sake of the military. Otherwise, the divisional commander wouldn't have rewarded me for my service. There were many villages and towns in the Toyama regimental district for the Kanazawa division. I was the one singled out for an award. This really shows how much I did. When the military told us how many should go, we had to produce them without fail. I didn't want to shame the village chief. It would have embarrassed the whole village, wouldn't it?

"As long as I don't fight, I'll make it home."

SUZUKI MURIO

Speaking gently in the accents of Osaka, he recalls, "I wrote many poems in China. Whenever we made a major redeployment, the Kempeitai would come and confiscate our notebooks and papers, so I had to put my poems into my head. When I got onto a boat, I'd write them down again. The brevity of haiku was very convenient:

> Kaze no naka,
> Kompai no akaki kawa nagare.
>
> *Amidst the winds,*
> *The anguished red river flows.*

I spent nearly two years in Central China, and that river, the Yangtze, was the center of everything.

> Nete miru wa.
> Tōbō arishi.
> Ama no gawa.
>
> *I lie on my back looking up.*
> *A desertion took place.*
> *There's the Milky Way.*

I wrote many haiku about deserters then, but I never really deserted myself. Too weak-willed."

Now a well-known poet, he heads his own circle working in the seventeen-syllable haiku verse form. He is a professor at Osaka University of the Arts.

I was a bottom-ranked soldier straight from the Homeland when I joined the Thirty-Seventh Regiment of Osaka in the Central China theater. It was 1939. I was put into a heavy-machine-gun company. The guns weighed more than fifty kilograms each, so they were disassembled and packed on horseback for transport, but when you approached the battlefield, four men put the gun back together and carried it. Two men actually manned it in action. Each man in the company was assigned a number, and all the numbers one, two, three, and four were assigned to the guns, while everyone else, from numbers five on, were in charge of the ammunition. Number Two fired the gun. Because a heavy machine-gun is a large weapon, Number Two could hide himself behind it. He was supposed to fire the gun with his hands, but, bent over, he usually pressed the fire button with the top of his steel helmet. "Da-da-da-da-da!" Number One had to load the belt, so his whole side was exposed to the enemy. Ones got killed at a fearful rate.

No matter what country you're from, when soldiers talk about "suppressing enemy fire" they mean getting the enemy's heavy machine guns. A single soldier's rifle puts out one bullet at a time, but by pushing just one button, you can send thirty rounds—a whole ammo strip—out of the barrel of a machine gun. By the time you'd fired ninety rounds you had to change position or they were sure to find you, but since you had to rise up to do that, and you were moving right in the face of the enemy, even though you were zigzagging like a lightning bolt, you often died right there.

If you'd ever attracted anyone's attention, the machine-gun company was where you were thrown. Not just men, either. Even the horses that carried the machine guns were outcasts. In an ordinary stable, horses stand with their faces peering out from their stalls. In the military, the other end's out. A horse that kicked wildly was marked with a red piece of cloth on its tail. Those that bit had a blue piece on their stirrups. Horses that tried to grab you with their front legs had a red cloth on their breasts. Our horse was marked with all three. Yokosaku was his name, and he was one damned shrewd horse. He'd paw the air in camp, full of energy. Outside, when he'd been walking just a kilometer or so, he'd hang his head to the ground and play sick. Since the army had to pay money to requisition horses, but could get soldiers just by sending out a conscription notice on a piece of red paper someone in charge would say, "Maybe the horse is sick. You men carry the load." So we'd have to carry everything on our backs. There really wasn't any love lost between the soldiers and the animals.

I wasn't the "dedicated soldier" you were supposed to be. In fact, three of us were even transferred to a regular infantry unit. Booted out of the machine guns! One was from Waseda University. He soon disappeared somewhere. Escaped. That left two of us, Yamada and me. I'm sure there must have been something in Yamada's background; he was so glum and melancholy. I'm the only one who survived the war. My "spiritual component" was most deficient! Veteran soldiers taught me the tricks: how to get into hospital, how to wangle a tour at the training camp, how to get the best jobs. I was thrown into one training camp after another. There were special camps to instill *"Yamato damashii."* * Some soldiers who wanted to make the army a career were trained there too, but most assigned didn't want to go back to their units. After three weeks, if you'd gotten the Yamato Spirit, they'd make you go to the front lines, so we'd urge each other to stay a while longer.

There was one kind of duty, called liaison, where you were a courier, carrying messages between units. You were told where to go, and when you left you asked if a reply was needed. The answer was usually no. You were to just hand over the message and come back. Sometimes you caught a ride on a truck that departed maybe once a week or so. In China, as far as you could see there was nothing. You were completely exposed and there weren't any guards on the truck either, if you were lucky enough to have a truck at all. The weapon you were carrying yourself was your only defense.

If you didn't move along with the main force when you were out in the countryside, there was always the possibility you'd be captured. Everyone was scared of that. We were all exhausted. Usually the road was just a straight stretch connecting hamlet to hamlet, no crossroads at all. Still, I thought, if they were going to jump out and capture me, they could do it whenever they wanted, even out among the fields of sorghum, so I just strolled along, taking my time. I took things as they came, worried about them only if they happened. I still have dreams where I'm walking alone on the continent, and there's never anyone around me.

Battlefields are weird places. Once you left your unit, unless you told them your location, they wouldn't come to pick you up, at least not a

---

* *Yamato damashii* [the spirit of Yamato (Japan)] encompassed the purportedly unique qualities of the Japanese people, invoked to explain the courage and dedication of the Japanese fighting man. Such spiritualism was a key element in military training.

lowly soldier like me. As long as the headquarters of your unit was in the district, and you could prove which unit you belonged to, any unit would let you stay and feed you for as long as you liked. But when your unit made a major move to an entirely new area, this wouldn't work anymore. "Your unit's not in Central China, get lost!" was all they'd say. You did have to get back to your home unit once a month or so. If you were asked what happened to you, it was enough to say "the situation was really bad," or "I got lost." If your goal was to avoid shooting bullets, this was the only way. While roaming around the continent, I learned a lot.

I came down with malaria fairly early, and was put into the malaria ward at a hospital thanks to a deal I worked with a doctor. When I eventually did return to the front, though, I had no choice but to go into action. I was in the ninth company—the last company—in the third battalion of the regiment, and in the third squad of the third platoon. We weren't exactly the best of soldiers, but our casualties were low. I guess we fought well enough. Generally it was said that the casualty ratio in China was one killed to six wounded. A company was roughly one hundred and eighty men, so if thirty were killed, you could say the company had been "wiped out," its combat capability reduced to zero. While I was hiding myself in the hospital, my unit suffered near total annihilation. When the survivors came back, I asked, "What about the commander?" "Died." Practically anyone else—"Dead" was the answer. Twice this happened while I was away from my unit in the two years I was on the China front.

I met all kinds of people. Every unit has people who don't like being soldiers. You can spot them immediately. Slackers were put into all kinds of places for "training," but we'd always hear when they'd finished their stint. It was practically like gangsters coming out of the pen. The news would spread that someone had "come out" on the other side of the Yangtze River, so I'd go down to the Hinoki Unit—that was the embarkation office of the ferry unit that carried troops back and forth across the river, same name no matter where you were—find out who was actually being released, and go meet him when he landed, for a "coming-out party."

One time we started drinking saké at three in the afternoon at one of the bars run by Chinese. They were long and narrow like an eel's bed. My companion's unit was assigned in a big city, where units were under the internal administrative regulations of the army, the same as back in the Homeland. If a soldier went out, he had to be back in barracks by eight in the evening. Suddenly, we realized he'd missed roll call and would already be considered a deserter. We rushed to his base, but the back gate to his barracks was locked. Even the front gate was closed, and a sentry stood there with a rifle, bayonet shining. Then we noticed an automobile marked with a medical officer's blue flag coming. Should we stop it? If professional soldiers who'd just graduated from military medical school were in it, they'd shoot us dead. But we decided to take a chance. Luckily, it only contained the driver, a private first class whose boss was out on the town somewhere. We begged him to take us through the sentry line in return for a case of beer. The car approached the main gate. They opened the barricade to welcome back their doctor. All the sentries lined up. The driver stepped on it and charged past them.

Some Japanese were known to have been captured, some deserted, sometimes we fought among ourselves. Everybody was whipped up to a fever pitch. There were people who bullied others. Weak ones might resist by using their hand grenades. They'd pull the pin and hold it, while everybody flew off in all directions. We all had the tools for murder, but if anybody got killed, the case was just left alone until there was combat. Then the death would then be recorded as died-in-action or missing.

The military is an amalgamation of human beings. Some you can get along with, others you can't. There are a lot of backstabbers. Sincere men attract sincere men. Easygoing men seem to get together. Birds of a feather.

Shanghai itself wasn't so bad. You got a special pass when you went to Shanghai, like a wooden card you put in your vest pocket, which gave you a little leeway to return after the normal nine-o'clock curfew. I'd ask sentries from my own unit when they were going to be on duty. Sometimes I went out drinking alone in Shanghai and didn't come back until two or three in the morning. Shanghai was the base for the Liberation Army, so you weren't supposed to walk around alone. Even the Japanese Shanghai Naval Landing Force patrolled in pairs, carrying rifles. Even during the day, there were snipers. I borrowed a pistol and took it with me, hidden, the safety catch off. The main streets of Shanghai bustled with crowds, but if you took one step off into an alley you might see five or six corpses no matter which way you looked.

I was often drunk when I got back. Normally I brought a bottle of whiskey as a gift for the sentry. But when you're drunk, you sometimes think the sentry's one of your own. You just walk up to him, and say, "Hey, I'm back," holding out the bottle to him. Once, I was hauled off to the commander of the guard. He kept berating me: What was I doing out that late. Why was I alone? You should be courtmartialed! "You gave me permission," I kept repeating. In the end all he could do was shout, "Let the bastard in." He kept the whiskey.

Soldiers like me had no idea why we were fighting this war. We were treated as nothing more than consumable goods. The men ordered to fly in the kamikaze planes had only one route open for them. On the continent, at least, it was wide open. It all depended on an individual's own character. I thought it would be enough for me if I stayed alive. I wanted to return home, though I didn't particularly strive for that. I didn't have the courage to engage in antimilitary activity, but on that desolate continent I lost the purpose of that war. The feeling grew in me that it was ridiculous to die there, fighting the Communist Eighth Route Army, or the Nationalist Army, or even sometimes finding out that it was the Japanese Army who were shooting at you. There were times I thought I might die at any moment. Tomorrow was far, far away. In that mood, I'd written a haiku in the corner of a military postcard addressed to a friend back in Japan:

> *Me tsumureba*
> *Tani nagare*
> *Chi no akaki nado.*
>
> When I close my eyes,
> I can see valleys
> Flowing blood red.

But that attracted attention. I was caught in a random mail search and they threatened to send me to the Kempeitai. I was told if I changed the part about "blood red" to "pure blood" [*chi no kiyoki*] the censor would let it pass. What could I do but agree? I changed it back to red when I published it in my book years later.

If you are in that kind of place for long, you become nihilistic. I think at the basis of such a nihilism is an abiding humanism, though quite different from the nothingness a Buddhist priest asserts is humanism. I still can't see myself connected to any large entity like a country or state. I can't view war macroscopically. I feel I can write about battlefields, but I don't think I can write about war. If you talk about things like the Greater East Asia Co-Prosperity Sphere, that's too grand for me. I can touch only a sphere as large as I can warm with my own body heat.

After the Pearl Harbor attack, from the next day on, things became really strict. I'd often been told, "We're sending you to the Kempei!" If they really had, the Kempei would have half-killed me. There were officers who were always drawing their swords and crying out, "I'll take his head myself!" Usually military-academy graduates, twenty-four or twenty-five years old. Commanders made out the Spirit of Yamato. If you got stuck in a unit like that, you were really in trouble. Since I wasn't usually at my own unit, I'd take off the first chance I got.

In March 1942, we knew we were about to be sent to the Southern

Area because we were wearing summer uniforms in the midst of the falling snow. We shipped out of the port of Wusong. On board the ship, they spread out a map of the Philippines, so for the first time I knew where we were headed. They also gave us two or three mimeographed sheets titled "Pan-Ocean Operations." We were moving as an entire division in a convoy. This leaflet told us, "Don't panic when your ship is torpedoed! It will take many hours before it sinks." So they said! But when I went down deep into the bowels of the ship to try to find a former schoolmate, I found fifty-kilogram shells, stacked up like huge tuna fish, with only their fuses removed. I asked a sailor how long it would take to sink if we were torpedoed. "Maybe twenty minutes," he answered, "but since we're carrying shells, probably less." They'd lied to us again. Even worse, in Shanghai I'd been one of the three from my regiment sent to take the course in submarine-lookout training!

In the Philippines, the enemy showed himself to us. On the Bataan peninsula, my unit was "in reserve." To say it was a "reserve unit" might make it sound easy, but it was like Japanese chess. In *shōgi* a piece you take from the enemy as prisoner may be turned around and placed right back at some crucial spot on the board as your piece. Just so, they dropped us down right in front of the enemy machine guns in the hottest part of the fighting.

By the time we approached the front line, we were already exhausted. "Fall out!" they said, and you'd collapse for five or six minutes. Lie down and try to catch your breath. In the dark you can't see well, but there was a horrible stench. I threw myself down on what turned out to be the belly of a dead horse. Probably from our artillery. Later that night we were given another short rest, but it was such agony to get up once you'd sat down that I tried to sleep standing up. I leaned against something. It smelled terrible and was soft, but I couldn't see it in the dark. I found out it was a breastwork made of corpses. The Americans had piled up native bodies like sandbags. The heads were facing toward us. On the other side there was a firing step. They shot from inside. Our enemy was an allied army of Americans and Filipinos, but the corpses in the wall were all Filipino.

Our main forces kept in close contact with the enemy and pressed them back. Our whole army was advancing toward the sea, since Bataan was a peninsula. But we bogged down because there were pillboxes up in the cliffs above. They had Czech-type machine-guns. *"Kan! Kan! Kan!"* Those air-cooled guns hammered away with bullets as big as rolled hot towels, and we were their target. We were halted in our tracks. It was April 5, 1942. MacArthur was still at Corregidor.

My group of seven didn't know where to go. We thought we'd be best off if we charged to the very bottom of the cliff, where we'd be in the "dead angle," out of the sweep of the machine guns. In the rush I was hit. The person in front of me just wasn't there anymore. Killed instantly. There was one medic assigned to each company of a hundred and eighty men. I had befriended ours and I'd asked him to be sure to save me if I was ever wounded. I often poured extra saké for him. He was with me when they got me, but while he was treating me, orders came from the commander, "Medic, to the front!" Men were being hit up ahead and he had to go forward. I still have thirty bullet fragments in my body. Two of them are as big the bones of my little finger, lodged in my bones.

But as soon as our main forces had pushed on, enemy soldiers came out of the jungle where they'd been hiding. Our forces couldn't sweep the whole place. I once thought all humans were good by nature, but there we were, left behind on the battlefield, jammed up under that cliff, when a force of maybe sixty or seventy Americans and Filipinos appeared perhaps twenty meters from our position. We had to decide immediately if we would open fire or not. Hamano, the light machine-gunner, and I were the only two who were against shooting. I had to talk the others out of blazing away. I told the men we could probably kill five or six, but stressed that there were sixty or seventy white soldiers and black soldiers. We'd be shot so full of holes we'd look like honeycombs. They glanced in our direction, but kept moving cautiously, passing us by. We were gambling, but we won our bet. They didn't fire either. We didn't shoot, and they didn't announce to anybody that they saw several Japanese over by the cliff. They probably knew the tide was running against them. Maybe they felt, Why die when you've already lost? I guess if you've been long on the battlefield, you know instantly whether the enemy's going to shoot or not. Anyway, that was my philosophy: As long as I don't fight, I'll make it home. I believed in that. Besides, I'd already been shot! I was sent home in June 1942.

A nation has to have great confidence in its own strength to go outside itself. Setting aside any question of motives, in the time of my youth, my physical strength coincided with the strength of my country. There was a strong tide running, and I was swept away in it without any chance to accede or dissent. If you ask me if I have any war responsibility, yes, I believe I do. We walked right into somebody else's country, their home, with our boots on, and we didn't even have visas.

Zero Ace

SAKAI SABURŌ

His study is a museum of Japanese naval aviation. Models of Zero fighters and several American planes, including a Grumman Wildcat and a Hellcat, are suspended from the ceiling. Paintings of Zeros and an oil portrait of young Sakai in a flight suit adorn the wall, together with an impressive array of gifts from American air units, both military and civilian. In one corner a tiny Buddhist goddess of mercy stands by a small cup of water and several oranges.

His book, Samurai, *published in English in 1957, has made him world-renowned among fighter pilots and airplane buffs. He is seventy-three years old. He says he frequently gives talks on leadership to companies in Japan, including such giants as Hitachi, Nissan, and Toyota. He seems smooth and well prepared, but his tone abruptly changes as we speak.*

"It is now more than forty-five years since the end of the war. I believe it is proper to tell the truth about the air units in the Pacific War to those want to know the truth. Well, I'm going to tell you what it was like." His compact frame, packed with energy, vibrates as he moves from somber reflection to anger. Frequently, his voice cracks with indignation when he speaks of the way the Imperial Navy fought that war.

When you've gotten used to combat, shot down one plane, two planes, ten planes, then the moment you face an enemy plane you know instantly the skill of your opponent. You can pigeonhole him into Class A or Class B. "Oh, this one's gutless. He's timid!" you may think. But still you can't always hit him. So you shoot out a stream of bullets. The Zero had two 7.7-millimeter machine guns mounted in front of the pilot, firing through the propeller. The main guns were two wing-mounted 20-millimeter automatic cannons two meters away from the center of the pilot's seat. The only time you could be sure to shoot down a plane was when bullets hit the pilot, or the engine, causing it to malfunction, or the fuel tanks, causing a fire. You're not aiming at the pilot; that's impossible. But if you're lucky, you might get him.

Aerial combat between fighter planes occurred at speeds of between one hundred and two hundred meters per second as they twisted and turned in the air. Hitting a target with machine guns under these conditions was like trying to thread a needle while running. If it weren't so difficult, a pilot would never have enough lives to fight at all, let alone shoot down another plane. Centrifugal force is also at work. Your eyeballs seem to press into your head. The pressure of the explosion driving the bullet from the machine gun is a constant, but the weight of the bullet leaving the barrel increases by up to five times. We called it "pissing bullets," since they bent down instead of going straight. In today's jets, computers calculate the fire for you, but we had to calculate the G-force in our heads and measure the distance with our own eyes. It was impossible to hit anything if you didn't know exactly what you were doing.

It was murderous combat. Kill the opponent before he killed you. That's why you fired too early. It was the same with feudal samurai engaged in a duel with real swords. The master teaching his apprentice says, "Unsheathe your sword in a wide arc. Jump back, separating yourself from the opponent. Then inch yourself toward him, grunting aloud with all your spirit as you move. Approach so closely that you believe you can hit your opponent's forehead with your own hands. Then strike. You will hit him between the eyes with the tip of your blade." At three hundred meters, the opponent's plane seems to be right next to you because unless you shoot quickly, he'll blast you.

Veterans were strong. Within four or five months after the Pacific War began, fighter planes flew in three-plane formations. While one plane was attacking, the other two defended your tail. Whoever discovered the enemy first had the advantage. I was usually the first to spot the enemy. Then you let the flight commander know. Later we didn't take even that extra time. It was "Follow me!" and you'd assume the role of commander the instant you spotted them. You didn't radio, since the worst thing about Japanese fighters then were the radio-telephones. Too much static. You couldn't hear a thing on the one band allotted. I'd kick mine before I took off, so I could report it "out of order." Worse, you had a wooden antenna sticking up behind you. I asked my ground crew for a saw and cut mine off. My group commander caught me at it. When I told him, "I can shoot down an enemy with that extra knot of air speed," he asked me to remove his, too!

Prior to the Pacific War, we received many instructional documents and capability tables for the fighter planes of America, Britain, France, and Australia. They startled me. All of them showed some capabilities superior to those of the Zero. I thought the planes of such advanced nations, moved by the spirit of the Wright brothers, would be magical in their devil-like strength, and that certainly, their pilots would be outstanding, too. But I resolved that if I could spot them first, I could defeat them, no matter how good their planes were, so I worked to train my sight. I was constantly searching the sky. My fellow pilots used to ask, "Are you forecasting weather again, Sakai?" Everyone laughed at me then, but I was able to see stars in daylight by the time the Pacific War broke out. I refused to let myself be killed! I had the same basic training as the other pilots, but there's no limit to what a flyer can do to strengthen himself when he isn't in a plane. Warriors fighting on the land or on the sea are on a flat surface. They must observe left and right, back and front. But aviators fight in a sphere. The soles of your feet, along with the back of your head, need eyes, too.

I fought from the beginning of the China Incident, and then from the start of the Pacific War until the very end. I never lost a single wingman in almost two hundred engagements. I'm prouder of that than of my record of enemy planes downed. Sixty-four by official count. I remember every combat. Each of them was kill or be killed. Some I recall as moments of extreme danger, of terror, and I marvel that I survived.

When I was hit over Guadalcanal, I was flying to save a man under my command. As a reward, God did not take my life. [*He produces a battered old leather helmet with built-in goggles, and a bit of dirty brown silk rag.*] I wore this flight helmet and these goggles in that battle over Guadalcanal in which I was wounded. After shooting down two planes, I charged an eight-plane formation single-handed. They were bombers, and I found myself facing concentrated fire from their rear gunners. Twelve thousand bullets a minute! No way to avoid their fire! I hit two planes, which exploded violently, sending billows of flame and debris directly at me. The canopy on my plane was blown away. At that instant I felt a shock to my head. A bullet hit here, above the bent metal on the goggle of the right eye. It skip-jumped and exited here, making this hole in the helmet. A fraction of an inch lower and I'd have been dead. Another bullet entered through the glass of the goggle. I can't find where it went out, but it must have exited somewhere. I was half-paralyzed. The right side of my head was hit, my left side ceased to function.

I was losing lots of blood. Both eyes were temporarily blinded. Blood was pouring down into them. This is the scarf I used to stop the bleeding. All the triangle bandages and bits of towel I had were whipped away by the wind. I cut the scarf into pieces gradually to stanch my wound on that flight back to base. This scrap is all that's left of my white silk scarf. It's brown like this only because it was soaked in blood. I got back in that condition, completing a round-trip flight of one thousand one hundred kilometers in a single-seat fighter. It took me four hours forty-seven minutes to return. Sometimes I flew upside down. At times I seemed to black out. It was an impossible feat. It is more for that flight than for having shot down many planes in combat that I'm remembered now.

Yet the Zero could make such flights. We flew five hundred and sixty kilometers from Rabaul to Guadalcanal, fought, and then returned to base. Eleven hundred kilometers round trip. Normally six hours in the air. At that time, the range of American planes was limited. From Guadalcanal's Henderson Field to Buin on Bougainville, that was it. They couldn't believe we did it! Some military histories still have such flights as the attack on Port Darwin in Australia being made from carriers, but land-based Zeros hit them.

In the early stages, I can't give most of the American pilots high marks. Dating back to the days of the China Incident, our fighter training was extremely rigorous and our planes had beat even the vaunted Claire Chennault's Flying Tigers. When I go to America, I often talk with American aces and they say, "At the beginning, Saburō, you and your pilots seemed to enjoy shooting down our planes. At the end of the war it was the same for us. We enjoyed it. It was almost like shooting turkeys. I never had so much fun! I understand your feelings well." America was at first startled at the appearance of the Zero. Yet they produced new, powerful fighters one after another to "Beat the Zero!" Japan couldn't produce new planes in any numbers since the country didn't have the industrial strength. More than ten upgrades of the Zero weren't enough.

Yet, if I can speak openly, even in 1945, if I were the one gripping the stick of a Zero and soared into the sky, I could meet their Mustangs or Grumman Hellcats and shoot them down. The combination of the human pilot and the Zero fighter was its true fighting strength. When Japan started the war, the level of our pilots' skills was reasonably high, but within a year the average level declined sharply. Veteran pilots were killed, leaving us like a comb with missing teeth. The development of planes fell behind, and the training of pilots lagged. The skill of the American pilots far surpassed ours by war's end.

Formation aerial combat should have almost Buddhist spiritual ties among pilots. However, the real situation in the Japanese navy was very different. Of one hundred pilots in a unit, eighty to eight-five were non-commissioned pilots, like me, who had worked their way up from being sailors through hard training. The remaining fifteen were officers. When we were at the base, even aces who had knocked down twenty or thirty planes, if they were noncommissioned pilots, ranked lower than those who had just finished their schooling. If they had the gold stripes or two stars of a lieutenant, well, they were "Honorable Lieutenant, Honorable Officer." We were billeted out in the drafty common room, while the nation put them into their own individual rooms, as if they were in a hotel. They were young kids, fledgling "Respected Ensigns," who'd never seen combat, fresh from the Homeland, who'd never be able to get themselves or their Zeros back if they went into action. There they were, drinking Johnny Walker Black—spoils of war—while we wouldn't even get beer full of preservatives! "You dirty swine!" I wanted to shout.

Meals were completely different, too. Veteran aces were fed with food and provisions best fit for horses, while those who hadn't done anything were given restaurant meals. They were even provided with orderlies. Can you believe it!

Let me tell you about Rabaul as an example. The quality of the food declined for everyone; it was all poor. But even then, a distinction was maintained. I was the senior pilot, so I was to look after the complaints and problems, physical and mental, of all the pilots. And where were the officers? They were in the town of Rabaul, four or five kilometers away. Not one of them knew what their highly valued subordinates were up to. None of the noncoms knew any of their honorable leaders, or even where they were honorably living, or what they had at their honorable meals. I knew only because as senior pilot, I was summoned up there for liaison with them.

When we were at the airfield, our ready room and the officers' ready room were separate. When were we going to "consult"? When were the leader officer and the noncoms in the second and third planes in our groups to get to know each other's souls? When were we to develop the unspoken understanding needed for aerial combat? We didn't even drink tea together. They came from far away in the morning. Even then, they didn't mix with us. Even when they were preparing to take off, they hardly spoke to us.

You couldn't fight hungry, so when we were on a four- or five-hour mission we would take lunch with us. It was called a "kōkū bentō"—an airborne box-lunch. You won't believe this, but even in the same formation—with each pilot responsible for the nation's fate, not expecting to return, several hundred miles from base, linked to other formations, all going into battle—even there, what the officers ate and what the noncoms ate was different! And still you were supposed to think in combat, "I can depend on you to cover me"? What a farce! This was the shape of the Imperial forces.

I never learned anything from those officers who graduated from the naval academy about how to search out and spot the enemy, or how to outmaneuver and shoot them down. Instead, we learned from fellow noncoms, and the noncoms learned from the old noncoms, and the old noncoms learned from the warrant officers who were themselves learning from the special-service officers at the bottom of the officer heap. We became like brothers, looking after each other. Yet those officers— graduates of the naval academy, unskilled, lacking in any technique, *they* were officially our leaders. The nation does not know this. How many of their precious men were killed because of the misjudgments and lack of military acumen of those men! It was horrific, let me tell you!

There, at Rabaul, I often gave inspirational speeches before we took off: "Do you know what wars you're fighting?" "One against America and one against Britain," someone answered. "You idiot! There's only one enemy out there, but there is another one you face. Right here, on our own side. It's the graduates of Etajima, the officers who come from the naval academy! In the Homeland, in peacetime, we're oppressed and tyrannized by them just because of rank. Luckily, although this Pacific War is a matter of great misfortune, we're given a chance which comes but once in a thousand years. Who is stronger? The noncoms who fought their way up from the lower ranks, or them? We don't know whether we'll win or lose this war, but if we lose out to them, we'll continue to be despised. The gods have given us the golden opportunity to show who is stronger and more skillful, us or them." That's what I said.

Distinctions by rank were made even at the flying school at Kasumigaura, the home of the naval air corps! The noncoms there were all veteran pilots who'd defeated fleets of enemies! They didn't want to be there flying training planes. Yet they were to teach Honorable Lieutenant Junior Grades. In Japan, there's an ancient saying: "You should never step on your teacher's shadow"; better to step back three paces as a sign of respect. But at the navy's flying school, what kind of attitude did they take? Because they were Honorable Lieutenants, they'd shout at you: "Hey, you! How's my skill coming along?" They weren't joking. The noncommissioned officer would answer, "You are doing exceptionally well, Honorable Lieutenant." That was all you could say. You couldn't instruct them. But when it came to teaching our younger brothers, the new noncoms, we'd be as strict as possible, hoping and praying to impart to them all the skill we could, no matter how tough we had to be.

My squadron commander at Rabaul was Lieutenant Commander Sasai Ryūichi. Sasai-san was the sole exception. He and three others came to our unit after finishing Flight School. My commander gave me an order: "You are senior pilot. Train these four to become full-fledged pilots. They pretend to be officers, but they're useless. Don't hold back. Work them over! Make them skillful." I did that. I trained Sasai thoroughly. Sasai and Sakai became a famous duo in Rabaul, paired in pincer movements and attack operations. When Sakai wasn't doing well, Sasai wouldn't go up. When Sasai was indisposed, perhaps from drinking too much, I didn't fly either. We'd fought together for a long time. He fought savagely and I protected his back. When I was wounded, I insisted that I wouldn't go back back to Japan. Sasai urged me to return. I kept refusing, but eventually maggots infested my eyes and my sight clouded over. I finally agreed to return home for treatment only on the direct order of my commanding officer. I was just a lone petty officer, but they arranged for a four-engined flying boat to take me home via Saipan!

Sasai came to the harbor at Rabaul to send me off. He shed tears and tore from his own belt the silver buckle with the design of a tiger, which had been a present from his father, a Navy captain. He'd told his sons, "War is not just dying. Come back, even with only one hand or one leg, like the tiger." It's said in the East that a tiger goes out a thousand leagues from home and always returns. Sasai told me "Please return here again. I will do my best here alone until that time." Sasai was killed on my birthday.

I underwent operations on my eyes, even incisions on my eyeballs, without anesthesia. I was put in an occupational-therapy section to learn massage, because there were no other jobs for blind men. My right eye was completely sightless. The vision in my left eye was poor, too. I was removed from the active-duty list and transferred to the reserves. While there, I learned that the fighter squadron from Rabaul had returned to Toyohashi in Japan for reorganization and rebuilding. One night, I escaped from the hospital. I was a deserter. Ordinary deserters would run for safety, but I was looking to get back into action!

The officer in charge of my old unit took one look at my face and said, "You're a sick man. You look like a green squash." I begged him to let me come back. "Can you see with one eye?" Yes, said I. "Well, if he can see with one eye, he can see better than most young pilots," he told the doctor. We got special permission from the Navy Ministry for me to join the unit. But a one-eyed pilot has a lot of trouble! I was forbidden from going to the front and was assigned to flight training at Yokosuka. I was told that in my condition I couldn't go to the front, but I finally convinced them that I had to prove myself.

My first engagement back was June 24, 1944. It turned out to be the greatest aerial combat of the war up to then. Two hundred planes on each side. I had been out of combat for a long time. What's more, now I had only one eye! The battle lasted for one hour and twenty minutes in the skies over our base on Iwo Jima. It was carried out over, through, and under the clouds. After just one pass, planes were spread all over the sky.

At the start, I lagged behind a little, so I was below the clouds. I shot down two planes and found myself alone. In front of me was a beautiful formation of planes. I breathed a sigh of relief and sped to join them. Damn! They aren't Zeros. They're Grummans! I gasped. I tried desperately to escape. From an altitude of forty-five hundred meters I dropped to the surface of the sea. I was blessed with the secrets of the art of escape, as well as the mysteries of shooting down the enemy. Poor pilots started shooting from seven or eight hundred meters away. When I was about to be hit, I'd slip my plane off to the side for an instant, avoiding the fire. Then the next plane would come. One after another. Sweat was pouring from me. I descended right to the deck. The altimeter showed zero meters.

The enemy came at my Zero from every side. The water just in front of me burst with white spray from their bullets. There's a way of flying called "sliding," which gives the illusion you're flying straight ahead, while you slip off to one side or the other. "If I can just survive a little longer, they'll reach their time limit for returning to their carrier." I was chased for fourteen or fifteen minutes. My throat was parched. My hands were practically claws from gripping and pulling the stick. Yet I was not hit even once. I asked the antiaircraft machine-gunners on Iwo Jima for help and one battery opened up on my pursuers. On that day, I shot down five enemies and became a one-eyed ace.

Soon after, we were ordered out on a suicide mission. Continuous aerial combat had reduced us on Iwo Jima from over two hundred planes to only nine Zeros and eight torpedo bombers. At the end of those battles we were even hit by naval surface bombardment. We were the first in the Japanese navy to be deliberately organized for and ordered to make a suicide attack on the enemy fleet. Bombers were ordered not to jettison their weapons. We fighters were told not to engage in aerial combat, even if attacked, but to attack the enemy ships, when found, by plunging into them with our bombs.

We took off from Iwo Jima on July 4, 1944. The commander was a naval lieutenant, a graduate of the naval academy. I was named leader of the second flight. Mutō Kaneyoshi, known as the navy's Miyamoto Musashi—after the great sword master—led the third flight. The navy selected such outstanding pilots to lead a suicide attack!

I called to Mutō, a close friend from our China Incident days, and asked "They say 'go'; what do we do?" "What do we do, you say? It's decided," he said. "We go." "We can't live long anyway. You're right, let's go," I chimed in. I never thought, "Long Live the Emperor!" To bring the nation to victory was our thought, and what was that nation? The land of my parents, younger brothers, and sister. Can we bear seeing our country invaded by outside enemies? That's what was on my mind. We were innocents.

My engine was overheating. Normally, I would have landed immediately. But now there was nothing I could do. We flew south-south-east, one hundred sixty-three degrees. I was prepared for death at any moment, but still I looked back over my shoulder. I saw Iwo Jima gradually falling below the horizon. But that pipelike mountain, Mount Suribachi, was tall and it remained visible. "My country's still there," I thought, until it finally disappeared after about thirty minutes. I told myself, "It's time to do it."

We were at about thirty-six hundred meters. I looked at my watch. In about twenty minutes, sixty miles off, the U.S. fleet would be there, waiting for us. The torpedo bombers had navigators, so they began to plunge toward the sea in order to be ready to attack. I wondered whether we were already caught on their radar. We had no accurate radars of our own. I stared up at a towering mass of cumulonimbus clouds about a thousand meters overhead. I was hoping there would be nothing there when a glint caught my eye. One, two, three, four, five . . . I counted to fifteen. They passed us. "Serves you right, you bastards!" They could tell the distance, but they'd miscalculated the altitude. I was the first to spot those enemy planes, me with one eye. So I prepared to attack them. I signaled my flight. All of our planes acknowledged and started to follow me. Then in front of Mutō's group, about thirty planes suddenly materialized, bubbling up from below. Well, we certainly couldn't "avoid aerial combat" now! Instantly, our bombers were targeted. They couldn't do anything because they were carrying torpedoes. Two or three fighters attacked each of them, and they exploded immediately. A circle about twenty-five to thirty meters in diameter spread in the water where they fell. They looked like the smoke rings on a can of Bishop's tobacco.

We met the enemy with an attack in a formation loop, going in all together. In a counterattack I hit one of them and sent it spinning and knocked it down. I recovered myself and looked up and saw Shiga Heizō's plane, with his engine cover blown off. A Zero without an engine cowling is a rare and strange sight. "Don't get separated," I signaled him, checking to see if he was all right. "Fine," he signed back. All of the planes were gone. It had been less than two minutes. Gradually darkness was falling. In front of my eyes there was a large cumulonimbus cloud, billowing up to eleven thousand meters. Underneath it was a severe squall. The American fleet was hiding somewhere in that area. As the light faded, only three of our planes were left. What should we do? We'll smash into them, just the three of us. We dove down to the surface of the sea and looked for the enemy fleet in the driving rain and near darkness for about fifteen minutes. We couldn't locate them. To search until we ran out of fuel would be a vain death. A wasted life. I will take responsibility, I thought.

We reversed course—not simple on the open ocean with nothing to guide us. We were a one-way attack force, so we hadn't done any navigation. We'd never thought of fuel consumption. I had watched the ocean surface instinctively on my way to this point. All I had to rely on was my experience of many years. The surface of the sea was like crepe. We were at seventeen or eighteen hundred meters. I calculated distance from what I thought was that cloud we'd seen before, though it had already changed shape. Soon it was ink black. There was no sense of speed. When I looked left and right I could see purple exhaust coming from the the engines of the two Zeros on my wings. I could tell the pilots were there because of the ultraviolet light on their faces. One hour passed. Two hours passed.

Iwo Jima is just a dot in the middle of the ocean. All five of my fuel gauges showed empty. My wing-men too must have run out of fuel long ago. I thought, "So this is the day I die. Here. Now." In front of me, before the cowling of my engine, my mother appeared. "This way, this way," she said. I had been awakened once before by my mother's voice when I passed out after my wounds over Guadalcanal. Now there she was again. I received the silver watch for graduating first from aviation school. The newspaper clipping that describes that was the first thing I ever did for my parents. My mother, back in Saga, on Kyushu, was shocked and surprised. The poorest boy in the village had gone and won a watch from the Emperor. That rascal Saburō who did nothing but run wild! I'd even stolen my parents' seal so I could enlist in the navy underage in 1933.

I was ready to die. I thought I would plunge into the sea with my two companions when the time came. But if my calculations weren't wrong, we should be approaching Iwo Jima. In the cockpit, even on a pitch-dark night, there is some starlight, and that light can be reflected from the sea. If there's no reflection, if there's a dark spot, specialists like me could tell that an island was there. I was watching my clock. Soon our engines would simply stop. "Show yourself!" I cried out to the island. According to my calculations, it was time. I was searching the ocean, looking over the leading edge of my wing, when I saw that something black, like a tadpole, seemed to be running across the surface of the sea. This was impossible. Things couldn't be working out this well! I pinched myself. It hurt, so I wasn't dreaming. There it was, again, the dark spot had traveled under the wing. "That's Iwo Jima!"

We descended. At lower altitude it was nearly pitch dark. Three planes returning. On the ground they thought that American planes from Saipan might be carrying out a night attack, so they had the base completely blacked out. We had to get down quickly, but neither of my wing-men had ever carried out night operations. We were too busy to practice night take-offs and landings. You need lamps on the ground to mark the place you are to land. There was nothing down there, just darkness. I was afraid we might not have enough fuel for a second pass. I could just make out the coastline south of Mount Suribachi, where the

Americans later landed, lit by the luminous sea creatures that glow phosphorescently when the waves break. That's where we wanted to go. I took our planes at a direct right angle to that beach. At that moment, one lantern, lit by a ground-crewman, shone forth. Just an empty can with waste oil in it. Not normally enough for a landing, but I was desperate, so I went in, *"Zu-zuuu. Do-don."* We were back, but we were considered dead. When we returned to our billets, wooden tablets bearing our posthumous names had already been erected. But we'd lived to fight again.

Somehow I survived the war. I never thought of staying in the military after it. I didn't want any more to do with fighters. I only had one eye, after all. I'd had enough of organizations. In Japan it's what school you attended, not what you did, that counts. It's still so. Golf is now my hobby. I've made three holes-in-one. My goal is to get five—become an ace—before I die.

---

6 / "DEMONS FROM THE EAST"

Army Doctor

YUASA KEN

He was imprisoned in China for crimes to which he confessed after the war, and returned to Japan after his release in 1956.°
He now works in a clinic and lives near Ogikubo in Tokyo.

° The three men in this chapter, and Tominaga Shōzō in chapters 1 and 24, are all members of the *Chūgoku Kikansha Renrakukai* [The Association of Returnees from China], a voluntary group of those arrested as war criminals and held in the People's Republic of China after the war. Some were first confined in the Soviet Union, before being handed over to China. In 1956, Chinese military courts formally indicted forty-five for crimes, and the remainder, about eleven hundred, were set free after their confessions. By 1964, all had returned to Japan. None were executed by the Chinese Communists.

The members of this group publicly admit that they took part in an "aggressive war" and were retained in China because they were "war criminals." The group takes the collective position that its members, "due to the generous policies of the People of China," having reflected upon the crimes they committed against humanity, wish to contribute to peace and friendship between China and Japan. To that end, unlike most Japanese who served in that war, they write of their acts as "victimizers" and speak out about their crimes. They also openly raise what they consider to be the war responsibility of the Shōwa Emperor. They have been denounced by their detractors as "brainwashed."

My father had his own practice in Shitamachi, the old district of Tokyo. I became a doctor myself in March 1941. I took the exam to become a short-term army doctor in the fall. Everyone passed. You can't fight a war without doctors. In December 1941, I entered the Twenty-Sixth Regiment in Asahikawa, Hokkaido, and within two months was promoted to first lieutenant. We were a privileged elite, treated as if we were different from the rest of the people.

I was soon dispatched to a city hospital in the southern part of Shansi province in China. I arrived there January 1, 1942. It was still bitterly cold that day in the middle of March when, just after lunch, the director of the hospital, Lieutenant Colonel Nishimura, summoned everyone together. Seven or eight MDs, an accounting officer, a pharmacist, and a dentist. All officers. He excused the housekeeper and other women. After they'd left, he said, "We'll be carrying out an operation exercise. Assemble again at one o'clock." I was chilled to the bone, but it wasn't the weather. I'd heard in Japan before I went that they did vivisections there.

The hospital building adjoined a courtyard and a requisitioned middle-school building. Our patients were in there. There were nearly a hundred employees. Ten nurses, fifty to sixty technicians, some noncoms, too. I'm the kind of man who usually agrees to whatever I'm told to do. A "yes man," you could say. I remember that first time clearly. I arrived a little late; my excuse was that I had some other duties. Usually the compound was full of Chinese coolies lounging in the sun, but that day nobody was around. Everyone knew what was going on, though they all pretended they didn't.

A solitary sentry stood guard. He saluted me the moment I opened the door. I then saw Medical Service Colonel Kotake and Hospital Director Nishimura, so I snapped to attention and saluted. They returned my salute calmly. I approached Hirano, my direct superior. That's when I noticed two Chinese close to the director. One was a sturdy, broad-cheeked man, about thirty, calm and apparently fearless, standing immobile. I thought immediately, that man's a Communist. Next to him was a farmer about forty years old. He was dressed as if he had just been dragged in from his field. His eyes raced desperately about the room. Three medics were there, holding rifles. Nurses were adjusting the surgical instruments by the autopsy tables. There were some fifteen or sixteen doctors present.

You might imagine this as a ghastly or gruesome scene, but that's not how it was. It was just the same as any other routine operation. I was still new to it. I thought there must be a reason for killing those people. I asked Hirano, but he just answered, "We're going to kill the whole Eighth Route Army."° I pretended to know what he meant. The nurses were all smiling. They were from the Japanese Red Cross.

The director said, "Let's begin." A medic pushed the steadfast man forward. He lay down calmly. I thought he'd resigned himself to it. That was completely wrong. As a rule, Chinese don't glare at you. He had come prepared to die, confident in China's ultimate victory and revenge over a cruel, unjust Japan. He didn't say that aloud, but going to his death as he did spoke for itself. I didn't see that back then.

I was in the group assigned to the other fellow. A medic ordered him forward. He shouted, "No! No!" and tried to flee. The medic, who was holding a rifle, couldn't move as fast as the farmer, and I was a new officer, just arrived in the command. I was very conscious of my dignity as a military man. The hospital director was watching. I never really thought, if this man dies, what will happen to his family? All I thought was, it will be terribly embarrassing if I end up in a brawl, this man in farmer's rags and me dressed so correctly. I wanted to show off. I pushed that farmer and said, "Go forward!" He seemed to lose heart, maybe because I'd spoken up. I was very proud of myself. Yet when he sat on the table, he refused to lie down. He shouted *Ai-ya-a! Ai-ya-a!* as if he knew that if he lay down he was going to be murdered. But a nurse then said, in Chinese, "Sleep, sleep." She went on, "Sleep, sleep. Drug give" —Japanese-style Chinese. The Chinese of the oppressor always bears that tone, as if to say, "There's no possibility you will fail to understand what I'm saying." He lay down. She was even prouder than me. She giggled. The demon's face is not a fearful face. It's a face wreathed in smiles.

I asked the doctor who was about to administer lumbar anesthesia if he wasn't going to disinfect the point of injection. "What are you talking about? We're going to kill him," he replied. After a while, a nurse struck the man's legs and asked him if it hurt. He said it didn't, but when they tried to get him to inhale chloroform, he began to struggle. We all had to hold him down.

First, there was practice in removing an appendix. That was carried out by two doctors. When a man has appendicitis, his appendix swells and grows very hard. But there was nothing wrong with this man, so it was hard to locate. They made an incision, but had to cut in another place and search until they finally found it. I remember that.

Next a doctor removed one of his arms. You must know how to do

---

° The Communist army active in North China.

this when a man has shrapnel imbedded in his arm. You have to apply a tourniquet, to stanch the flow of blood. Then two doctors practiced sewing the intestines. If the intestine or stomach is pierced by bullets, that kind of surgery is a necessity. Next was the opening of the pharynx. When soldiers are wounded in the throat, blood gathers there and blocks the trachea, so you need to open it up. There is a special hook-shaped instrument for field use for cutting into the trachea. You drive it in, hook it open, then remove it, leaving only a tube behind. The blood drains out. It all took almost two hours. You remember the first time.

Eventually, all the doctors from the divisions left. Then the nurses departed. Only the director, the medics, and those of us from the hospital remained. The one I did, small-framed and old, was already dead. But from the sturdy man's mouth came, "Heh. Heh. Heh." One's last gasps are still strong. It gave us pause to think of throwing him, still breathing, into the hole out back, so the director injected air into his heart with a syringe. Another doctor—he's alive today—and I then had to try to strangle him with string. Still he wouldn't die. Finally, an old noncom said, "Honorable Doctor, he'll die if you give him a shot of anesthesia." Afterwards we threw him into the hole. This was the first time.

Japan's occupation of China was no more than a collection of dots and lines in a vast theater of operations. When a man suffered from appendicitis, you couldn't bring him to a hospital. His appendix had to be removed right there at the front line. But there weren't enough surgeons available. Even ophthalmologists or pediatricians had to be able to do it, and they didn't know how, so they practiced. Doctors weren't in China primarily to cure illness. No, we were there so that when units clashed, the leaders could give orders to the soldiers and say, "We have doctors to take care of you. Charge on!" We were part of the military's fighting capability. It was easier to get men to fight if they thought there was a doctor to treat them when they were hit.

The next time we did it, we were practicing sewing up intestines for bullet wounds that had passed through the stomach. I remember the dentist was there, too, saying, "Oh, I've got his teeth!" The urologist removed the testicles. The hospital director said, "I will instruct you myself in this technique." He cut into the intestine and then sewed it back up. At that moment a phone call came for him, and he left the room to take it. One doctor observed the director's work and noticed something wrong: "It's sewed up backwards!" We all laughed. When the director returned, we were still snickering, but when he asked "What is it? What's the matter?" we just couldn't tell him. I remember fragments like this.

Orders for such exercises went from First Army headquarters, through the army hospital, and out to the divisions and brigades. In the beginning, exercises were conducted only twice, in the spring and the autumn. But by the end, we were getting doctors who couldn't do a thing, couldn't even handle instruments. Old men. I felt, we have to do this much more often. We should do it six times a year. I took the initiative and sought permission from the hospital. It was necessary to improve the technique of the army doctors. I did that as a loyal servant of the Japanese military. I felt I was willing to do anything to win. Doctor Ishii Shirō, the director of Unit 731, came to our hospital many times for education.* "If the only way to win a war against America is bacterial warfare, I am ready. I will do anything," I thought. "This is war."

Besides training, I also treated patients. Sometimes they were wounded soldiers, but half suffered from tuberculosis. Infectious diseases, malaria, typhoid, dysentery, and liver diseases were common. I really enjoyed my work. When I went out to town, I could swagger, you know, swing my shoulders as a Japanese officer, feeling I was serving the nation, and watch people treat me well because they were afraid of me. Everybody saluted an officer. All the girls addressed me as "Honorable Military Doctor." If anybody showed even a trace of resistance, we could send him directly to the front. It was easy at the hospital. We had no worries about being killed. We had plenty of saké. Anything we wanted. I felt I ruled the whole country. At morning roll call, they saluted me. I had only to say, straighten up that line, and they'd do it. They'd move back and forth until I told them to stop. I did it only for the sake of my own ego.

In late 1942, at the time of the battle for Guadalcanal, we realized things weren't going to be too easy. About forty doctors were gathered in the city of Taiyüan for a meeting. We were told to assemble at Taiyüan Prison, where I ended up myself a few years later. There, two men from the judicial corps brought out a couple of blindfolded Chinese. They then asked the doctor in charge of the meeting if everything was set. At his nod, they suddenly shot the Chinese, right in their stomachs, four or five times each. We then had to remove the bullets. That was our challenge. Could we remove them while they were still alive? That was how they measured the success or failure of the operation. When asked, "Want to do it?" I said, "No. I do this all the time." But eventually everyone got in on it, helping to control the bleeding or whatever. They both died.

We also carried out medic training. It was in 1944, at a time when

---

* Unit 731 was the army unit near Harbin in Manchuria that specialized in bacteriological-warfare experimentation using humans as guinea pigs. Tamura Yoshio talks about this later in this chapter.

we already knew we were going to lose. Those soldiers! Skinny and hardly able to write at all. I was in charge of education by then. I decided there was no way to teach them except by practical experience. I went to the Kempeitai and asked them to give us one of their prisoners. We practiced leg amputation. The one I got bore no traces of torture. I remember how surprised I was. "This one's real clean," I thought. I remember one soldier fainted.

Another time they sent us two for educational purposes. We didn't have many doctors at the time, so we were able to do all we had to do on just one of them. But we really couldn't send the other one back. So the director chopped his head off. He wanted to test the strength of his sword.

We received requests from a Japanese pharmaceutical company for brain-cortex tissue. They were making adrenocortical hormones. We cut tissue from the brains and sent it along. We sent one bottle. Then a second request came from the company for ten bottles, which we filled. This was a "private route." Everybody was involved.

We forgot these things. We actually forgot what we did! After our defeat, I thought about whether or not I should go back to Japan. There in Shanshi, there were some six thousand Japanese. Half were enlisted men. It was an area controlled by the Nationalist Army. We were impressed into that army. I was a doctor, so I established a hospital for those who were staying. I even thought it might be all right for me to stay there, as if it were Brazil or someplace. I didn't know anything about the situation in the Nationalist-Communist war. I'd probably just as easily have gone with the Reds, had I been in an area under the control of the Eighth Route Army.

Then the civil war began. It went on for three years. Some returned to Japan, but I couldn't leave my patients there. Besides, as a doctor, you feel you can survive anywhere. I ended up a POW with three or four thousand others. Then I was released for a while and went to work in a city hospital.

Finally, they came for me. Those who had committed serious crimes, about one hundred and sixty of us, were taken to the prison at Taiyüan, Shansi. It took four years for me to remember what I had done and to confess. I was imprisoned until 1956. That's when I returned to Japan.

All the doctors and the nurses who had been with me at that hospital in Shansi came to Shinagawa station to welcome me when I returned to Tokyo. The nurses said to me, "Doctor, you had such a hard time. We're so sorry for you." One man said, "Doctor Yuasa, I hope you did your best to assert your Emperor's policy was just and Communism was wrong." That's what they said! I told them, "Don't you remember? I did those things with you. You did them, too." The man I said that to seemed to shudder. Suddenly, for the first time, he recalled that he was a murderer!

It is scary. It's outrageous to murder a person. Yet it's far worse to forget that you've done it. That's the most horrible thing imaginable!

I did about ten men in three and a half years. Six times, all together, I took part in exercises to improve the technique of medical doctors. Removed brains, testicles. Most doctors did that, in the divisions, or in hospitals, all over China. Yet all keep quiet! Why do they forget? Everybody did it. At that time we were doing something good. That's what we let ourselves believe. But they still keep their mouths shut. If they were to recall it, it would be unbearable. That's why they are silent. It was "because of the war." That's enough for them.

Spies and Bandits

UNO SHINTARŌ

He arranges our meeting as if it were a clandestine rendezvous. He is to be recognized by the red handkerchief in the vest pocket of his suit. He picks a crowded spot "by the bronze lion" in front of the Mitsukoshi Department Store on the Ginza and then chooses a quite public coffee shop as the site for our conversation. His long pale fingers are always in motion, clenching and unclenching, frequently mimicking the grip and motion of a man wielding a Japanese sword.

On his return from China, where he was a prisoner of war, he put his Chinese-language skills to work in a small trading company at a time when the major Japanese firms were barred from taking part in the China trade by politics. "I really believe the Chinese Communist Party were the ones who spared my life. In that sense, they were quite different from America and the Allies, who hanged one thousand sixty-eight." *

I was born in the Japanese Concession in Tientsin, China. When my father returned from the Russo-Japanese War, he wasn't able to make a

---

* Out of 4,000 arrested as war criminals by Allied nations in the Pacific and Asian theaters, 1,068 were executed or died in prison from 1946 to 1951. Only 14 of these were the Class A war criminals like former prime minister Tōjō tried by the Tokyo War Tribunal. Most of the rest were tried separately by the countries where they were stationed during the war. Most fell not into the category of Class A criminals charged with crimes against peace, but were in Class B charged with ordering and directing atrocities, or Class C charged with the actual execution of atrocities. See Kazuko Tsurumi, "The War Tribunal: The Voice of the Dead," in her *Social Change and the Individual: Japan Before and After Defeat in World War II* (Princeton: Princeton University Press, 1970), pp. 138–40.

living in Japan, so he went to Korea and then on to Tientsin, where Japan had extraterritorial privileges. He was a dealer in woolens and had a Western clothing shop, a trade he'd apprenticed in at a high-class gentlemen's clothier back in Kobe. The last Manchu Emperor, Pu Yi, got his morning coats, formal clothes, and everyday suits from my father while he was under Japanese "protection." But my father finally got really angry with him and threatened to quit. Everyone close to "the Emperor of Manchukuo" demanded bribes of those he patronized. Father he couldn't make a profit that way. Finally, the Japanese consul general and some lieutenant generals sent some money his way, so he went back to making the Emperor's clothes. Sometimes Pu Yi came to the ice-skating rink at the Japanese elementary school in winter, and I once skated near him. I was raised by a Chinese *amah* from the time I was weaned. I had my very own, and so did my younger brother, and my sisters. I had this nurse until the moment I went soldiering. She cried when I went off. She asked me, "Why are you going to the army? In China, only poor men become soldiers."

I joined the Forty-First Regiment in Fukuyama, Hiroshima prefecture. You don't need to be a university graduate in the military, as long as you pass the required tests. It's hard dealing with the textbooks at first, but once you learn how to memorize them, it's easy. What orders to issue in what situations, how to arrange your forces in any given circumstance. By the book. As long as you look good doing what you do, full of gestures and enthusiasm, and perform flawlessly, they shower you with praise. Bullets don't fly in your direction during exercises, but the deputy commander checks you off. The more simple-minded you are, the better off you are. The old soldiers gave me a hard time for studying after lights-out for the candidate reserve officer examination, but I passed. I'd done it!

After a few months of active field operations in China at the rank of corporal, I was sent back to Japan, to First Kurume Reserve Officer School, where I graduated thanks in part to sumō wrestling, judō, bayonet fencing, swordmanship, horsemanship, and gymnastics, all of which also counted toward graduation. Then I was assigned to the military police, the Kempeitai, at an infantry regimental headquarters in China.

There really wasn't any concrete training for intelligence-gathering or pacification operations. I was only told that I would serve in intelligence when I got to the field. In China, it was all case-by-case. I had to do my duty based on my own judgment. There were several ways the Japanese military gathered information about the enemy. One was supposed to be scouting. A noncom or an officer would go out with a minimum force, approaching the enemy position as closely as possible.

There they would observe them with binoculars and note details about their positions, organization, and combat conditions. Sometimes you could use sophisticated radio receivers at headquarters to intercept signals from Chungking.

The major means of getting intelligence, though, was to extract information by interrogating prisoners. They don't say anything if you don't ask. Even threatened, they often didn't speak. If you torture them, some will talk. Other's won't. Torture was an unavoidable necessity. Murdering and burying them follows naturally. You do it so you won't be found out.

I worked near and for regimental, battalion, and company commanders, and when battles took a turn for the worse, they grew tense and irritable. They had to decide whether to attack or not, and they needed intelligence. How to get the information for them became my problem. You had to show results. We compared the information we had extracted to that we received from higher headquarters. If ours seemed superior, we would act based on our own information.

Getting good intelligence information for our punitive expeditions and offensive operations was a very, very difficult problem for us. We hardly slept at all. Adjutants drafted plans and proposed them to the regimental commander. You have to have reasons for mobilizing your soldiers, and we contributed. We had to contribute to the decision-making process. We tried to secure the needed information by using torture. I gathered capable soldiers and noncoms who understood Chinese and trained them. I was sure this was my purpose for living. I believed and acted in this way because I was convinced of what I was doing. We carried out our duty as instructed by our masters. We did it for the sake of our country. From our filial obligation to our ancestors. On the battlefield, we never really considered the Chinese humans. When you're winning, the losers look really miserable. We concluded that the Yamato race was superior.

An intelligence officer also uses spies and pays out rewards for information. Baiting the trap properly was the key to success. Spies were generally gangsters. Bright gangsters. Paper money had no value for them. They wanted opium. In big cities or large villages, there were always pariahs. We'd find them and train them, threaten them, cajole them. We'd tell them, "If you take the wrong course, we'll kill you, but if you do what you're told, you'll have to build warehouses to hold your fortune." We'd then bring out the opium. "I'll do it!" they'd say in a minute. Every day we received large amounts of the drug. Today, you could buy a fleet of automobiles with that! The opium came down from staff level at division headquarters. The better we did, the more opium came. Spies are traitors. The more of a traitor each was, the better information he brought in.

When we got good intelligence, I immediately went to the regimental commander and made my "I-would-like-to-receive-your-seal-for-this-information-Sir" speech. "Sure this is true?" he'd ask. I'd say, "Yes," and we'd call in a signal soldier, who'd send off a coded telegram to division or corps. It might seem a little strange for me to say this about myself, but I was appreciated as an intelligence officer. You couldn't really get much information from watching the enemy though your binoculars, but with opium you could get mountains of it. Some was false, some was true. To differentiate between the two was where my technique was needed. Intelligence officers played a much more crucial role than people think.

I interrogated many people, but two I remember particularly well. Chen Jing was a boy soldier. He was taken prisoner of war in a major operation at the end of 1943. Big as Chen Jing was, he was only sixteen or seventeen. He looked so innocent and naïve that they brought him back without killing him. He soon learned our Japanese songs, and some officers put him to work in the regimental armory repairing weapons. Everyone trusted him.

The regiment received twenty to thirty spare pistols each year. That year they went missing. Chen Jing had stolen them and passed them along to the guerrillas. This was discovered only because, during a punitive strike, dead guerrillas were found with Japanese pistols and the serial numbers matched the newly delivered weapons from the regimental armory. I conducted the interrogation. The most excruciating torture is to tie their hands behind their back with a string and then hang them from a wall by that cord. All their weight is borne by their shoulders. It works better than beating or strangling. If you use this method, ninety percent of them talk. But Chen Jing didn't. When he realized he wouldn't be spared, his attitude changed. I reported this to the regimental commander. He told me to make my own decision about what should be done with him. As Cheng Jing passed by the door of my room on the way to his execution, he shouted at me, "I will avenge myself on you! I did it for my motherland!"

Enemy enlisted men have little information of value. Only the officers know anything of great use. Pi Shu-t'ing, the second man, was a captain, himself an intelligence officer. He looked obedient, as if he'd do whatever we said, but he resisted. We had had a special cell built for the most stubborn ones. I named the torture we did there the "excrement technique." Usually, during your incarceration, your feces were removed from your cell, but not in that room. There, you were covered in your own shit and, sooner or later, you died insane. Occasionally we'd yell in the cell window, "Still not talking?" "Never!" Pi Shu-t'ing would shout back.

Officers and noncommissioned officers all had swords officially issued to them, the so-called Shōwa swords, but besides those, they brought quality swords from home. They'd want to give these a "cutting test." I often got such requests through my senior noncom. One sergeant in particular was looking for a chance to lop off a head. I gave him Pi Shu-t'ing, but told him to do it right. He was dragged from the cell— he could no longer walk—to a hill about seven hundred meters away.

I personally severed more than forty heads. Today, I no longer remember each of them well. It might sound extreme, but I can almost say that if more than two weeks went by without my taking a head, I didn't feel right. Physically, I needed to be refreshed. I would go to the stockade and bring someone out, one who looked as if he wouldn't live long. I'd do it on the riverbank, by the regimental headquarters, or by the side of the road. I'd order the one I planned to kill to dig a hole, then cut him down and cover him over.

My everyday sword was a Shōwa sword, a new one with the name Sadamitsu. My other sword was called Osamune Sukesada. It was presented to me by my father and dated from the sixteenth century. Sukesada was a sword made for fighting. It cut well, even if you were unskilled. It wasn't a particularly magnificent sword, but it was the kind the samurai in that time of constant warfare appreciated. It was the best sword for murder. With Sadamitsu, you couldn't really take a head with a single stroke. The neck was cut through, but it didn't fall. Heads fell easily to Sukesada. A good sword could cause a head to drop with just an easy motion.

But even I sometimes botched the job. They were physically weakened by torture. They were semiconscious. Their bodies tended to move. They swayed. Sometimes I'd hit the shoulder. Once a lung popped out, almost like a balloon. I was shocked. All I could do was hit the base of the neck with my full strength. Blood spurted out. Arteries were cut, you see. The man fell immediately, but it wasn't a water faucet, so it soon stopped. Looking at that, I felt ecstasy. I'm not that way today.

You might ask how it could happen that we'd kill people like this. It was easy. Once, for instance, I got a call from divisional headquarters: "You've made grandiose claims, Uno, but the area you're responsible for isn't secure. How are you going to explain this?" I could only answer that I had no excuse. I then resolved to clean up things. I dispatched our reserve squad, took the village mayor and others captive, and tortured them. They claimed they didn't know anything. I was furious. I'll show them, I thought. I lined them up, nine of them, and cut their heads off. I knew that only two of them would have bent my Shōwa sword all out of shape, so I used my father's sword. As might have been expected, that good old sword did the job with no ill effects. Guerrillas at that time caused enormous losses for our forces. Even killing them didn't even the score! Among the "guerrillas" I killed were military men and a village chief.

The day I did those nine people, you know, I was quite calm. That night I went out drinking at a restaurant. I brought other captives to bury those bodies. We did that in the open field next to the prisoner encampment. We told them not to look, but in a sense, it was better for us if they did. They would realize that if they got out of line, they too might be in danger.

A horse squadron was attached to our regiment. At that time, new-minted recruits, with just one star, arrived straight from the Homeland. The man responsible for their training asked if he could put on a display, as part of their education. We showed them executions. They hid their eyes in their hands, they couldn't look. Right from Japan, without any training. *"Pah-pah!"* I did it, without getting even a drop of blood on my uniform. There's a way to cut them, you see. A sword is not a knife. If you have a fine sword, you merely have to pull it from its scabbard and draw it across the shoulders. It cuts right through. You don't have to expend any real effort. Don't have to swing it from way up high. You just stop after you've cut through.

Most officers did this. If they didn't, their authority was weakened. The men would say, "He's nothing but appearances." Nobody wanted to be called "spineless." It wasn't so bad doing it in the midst of battle, but there's a lot of pressure on you when you cut off a head with everyone watching. We usually had about eighty captives under our control, though sometimes we had has many as a hundred and fifty. Most were captured at the front. According to regulations, captives were supposed to be sent back to headquarters. Company prisoners were to be sent back to battalion, and battalion captives to regiment. Whenever we had about eighty useful prisoners, we'd phone division and send them along if they wanted them. The ones I killed were those there was no point sending on.

Near the end of the war, our regiment was on the line of the Yellow River, but we were ordered to Manchuria, because Manchukuo had been emptied when all its defenders were sent to other fronts. Our unit had a great tradition. "If we're to go into combat against the Soviets we'll confound their plans"—so we thought! Officers like me didn't believe Japan could lose. We were moved by the Yamato spirit.

American were damned bastards to me then. I burned with hatred for them. Even when the navy began to get beaten—we learned of this by radio—we didn't think it would happen to the army even if we were less well equipped than the enemy. I never dreamed the Emperor would throw in the towel. I believed he would share our fate. But he just threw up his hands and quit. Radio reception was poor, so that all we caught were snatches from the Imperial announcement of surrender. We learned its contents only from a stenographic copy of it. I'd already heard that an unprecedentedly powerful bomb had been dropped, but I still believed that in the battle on the beaches Japan would be strong. We would hit back then!

Everyone, including the division commander, assembled on the parade ground. Two regimental flags were there. I was ordered to be the flag officer in charge of burning them. The bugle sounded and I did it with tears streaming down my face. The chrysanthemum seals at the tips of the flag standards were made of brass and would not burn, so we blew them to pieces with explosives. I tied my two swords together, and blew them up along with those imperial symbols. It was August 19, 1945.

I thought the victors would deal with the losers in a gentlemanly manner. But the Soviet forces came and we were hauled off to the Soviet Union. According to international agreements, at the end of hostilities prisoners of war held by each side should be released and allowed to return home, whether victor or loser. For five years, though, we were enslaved. When I was turned over to the Chinese I thought they had nothing on me. But they had people to testify to everything. I admitted to what I had done, or anyway to most of it. I couldn't admit I'd killed nine that one day. I only confessed to six. Our trial lasted about a week. Afterwards I went to a prison cell. Every day I thought tomorrow would be the day I would be sentenced to death. I couldn't sleep at all. I heard my mother's voice. But the Communists only gave me thirteen years. After my sentencing, the surviving families of the Chinese charged the judge, crying out in fury. In the end, I served eight years.

If our meeting today had happened back then, when I first saw your face, I'd have noticed your neck without fail. When I walked into the regimental commander's room, I'd announce, "Second Lieutenant Uno arriving!" The regimental commander might be looking at a map, sitting on a chair. I'd see his neck and forget instantly that I was a second lieutenant, he, a colonel. What a great neck, I'd think. Then suddenly I'd come back to my senses. It was almost like being addicted to murder. When I met people, I often looked at their necks and made a judgment. Is this an easy neck, or hard to cut? I'm not really reminiscing about those days, but that's how you become, murdering people. I regret this. But that kind of reflex impulse is still somewhere in me. Prime Minister

Takeshita's neck is an easy neck to cut. The best necks aren't really skinny or too fat either. Foreign Minister Abe's isn't easy; you'd get caught up in his chin. I'm only joking, but that's how it really is. I ended up like this.

Unit 731

TAMURA YOSHIO

Unit 731, also known as "the Ishii Unit" after its founder-director, Army Medical Lieutenant General Ishii Shirō, was the Japanese army's principal bacteriologial-warfare research and experimentation organization. Built at the village of P'ingfang outside the Manchurian city of Harbin in 1935, both the facility—officially designated a "water purification unit"—and its work were classified top secret by the military. Until its buildings were demolished at the approach of Soviet troops in August 1945, Unit 731 was the site of experiments aimed at developing and testing bacteriological agents and means of delivering them as weapons of war. What this entailed was the deliberate use of live human beings, suffering from no illness, as experimental animals and exposing them to diseases like bubonic and pneumonic plague, epidemic haemorrhagic fever, typhoid, and syphilis in order to obtain data useful to developing the most deadly and effective strains and means of causing infection.

The very existence of such a unit and research program has never been fully acknowledged officially—neither during the American Occupation of Japan, nor now—though an official of the Health and Welfare Ministry admitted before the Japanese Diet in 1982 that Ishii had received a retirement pension.* No firm figures exist for the total number of victims, but they likely numbered in the many hundreds, perhaps thousands. Most were Chinese, but the research allegedly extended to Allied prisoners

---

* The existence of such units was once the center of debate, though it is now supported by overwhelming documentary and personal testimony since the immediate postwar years. Ienaga Saburō's *Taiheiyō sensō* [*The Pacific War*], which was translated into English in 1968 and published by Pantheon, cites many early references. In "Japan's Biological Weapons: 1930–1945," appearing in the October 1981 issue of *The Bulletin of the Atomic Scientists*, Robert Gomer, John W. Powell, and Bert V. A. Röling presented a chilling exposé of the nature of Japanese biological-warfare research and the complicity of Allied, specifically American, authorities during the years of the American Occupation in keeping the extent and very nature of the research secret for reasons of American "national security." See John W. Powell's "A Hidden Chapter in History," pp. 44–52, and Bert V. A. Röling's, "A Judge's View," pp. 52–53. Peter Williams and David Wallace, *Unit 731: Japan's Secret Biological Warfare in World War II* (New York: Free Press, 1989) is the most comprehensive study in English.

*of war—Americans, British, Australians, and New Zealanders held at Mukden. Weapons developed at Unit 731 were reported by some attached to the unit actually to have been employed in Japan's war with China, and at least one claims they were planned for use against U.S. forces on Saipan.**

Determining the full extent and nature of Unit 731's work is further complicated by postwar American policies, which had the effect of allowing the leading Japanese doctors and officials involved—including Ishii Shirō himself—to escape back to Japan and to avoid prosecution as war criminals, in exchange for their cooperation. Their knowledge of bacteriological-warfare techniques and defenses against it, together with the records of their human experiments, allegedly contributed directly to American biological-warfare research after the war. Not only have some of those involved themselves continued to work actively in related fields, but some rose up the ladder in medical-academic circles to become professors at major national universities and research institutes. An expert in freezing has served, for example, as a leading consultant on the Japanese Antarctic expeditions and research.

After declining to talk many times, repeatedly suggesting "Speak with more senior people. Talk to my superiors," Tamura Yoshio finally agreed to meet at a train station near his home on the Bōsō peninsula in Chiba. The rice plants in the nearby fields bend low under the weight of their yellow grain nearing harvest. Our discussion takes place at a roadside restaurant for tourists, nearly deserted in the off-season and eerily quiet. When the conversation turns to his experiences, his words seem to come almost one by one, as if forced out through his lips. Only repeated focused questions, referring to a short article he had written about his experience, break his silence and compel him to take his story to the next step.†

To be honest with you, I don't want to recall what I did a long time ago. But I feel I have to say war is a dirty thing—something one should not do twice. I am a war criminal because of the things I actually did. Not in theory.

I dropped out in the midst of my second year of middle school to go to China. I was the eldest of six brothers. My father, a former policeman, was a small-scale farmer and part-time laborer. My parents didn't

---

* Takidani Jirō, *Satsuriku kōshō, 731 butai* [*Carnage Arsenal: Unit 731*] (Tokyo: Shinmori Shobō, 1989), pp. 17–18 gives a figure of three thousand "Chinese, Koreans, Americans, and Russians" being experimented on at Unit 731.

† His article, *"Saikinsen. 731 butai no bankō"* ["Bacterial Warfare. Atrocities by Unit 731"], was published in Chūgoku Kikansha Renrakukai [Association of Returnees from China], eds., *Sankō* [*The Three Lightnings*] (Tokyo: Banseisha, 1985), pp. 23–40.

approve of my going, but somehow I managed to get them to affix the family seal to my application. And so I became a uniformed civilian employee of the Japanese military, spending a little more than a month in training at the Army Medical College's epidemic-prevention research laboratory in Tokyo before leaving for China in May 1939. I didn't even think about what I was going to do over there. For that month we created cultures for bacteriological research and learned Chinese in the evening. About thirty of us in all. We were together with our friends and things seemed bright and boisterous. We were to be the junior employees for the Ishii Unit. Because we were from Chiba prefecture, the same area as Commandant Ishii, I simply was drawn along by my seniors. At sixteen, I was one of the youngest.

We took the Shimonoseki-Pusan steamer. From Pusan it took roughly four days before we arrived in Harbin on May 12, 1939. As soon as I got off at the station, the first thing I noticed was the smell of horse manure. Horsecarts were racing everywhere. Harbin was an international city. There were many Russian-style buildings dating from the time of the czars. By bus, it took about an hour on the military road to get to Ishii Unit 731. Along the road we passed a memorial to the fallen Japanese dead of the Russo-Japanese War and saw red sorghum fields stretching off into the distance.

In those days, Unit 731 seemed simply a huge concrete structure, several hundred meters long, out in the middle of a field. Just naked concrete. There was only one entrance. That main building, in the shape of a hollow square, was three stories tall and had no windows below the top floor on the inside of the square. There were two two-story buildings within the walls. Experiments on human beings were conducted inside them. Those people who were involved in those experiments were called the Special Group. Production plants for bacilli and the like were located there too.

Lodgings and barracks were built outside the wall after our arrival, and we moved there. Noncoms, and those of us in the youth troop, lived there, while all the other workers came by bus from Harbin every day. There were about ten buses for the commuters. Those who ranked major or above had chauffeured cars, several coming together in a car. If your rank was high enough, you came by yourself. There were many vehicles assigned to Unit 731, and they became more and more numerous. There was even an airport.

We got up at six o'clock, did military drill, and then spent most of our mornings in lectures on bacteriology. In the afternoon we had labs. We really were kept very busy. No time to think about anything. The first thing we were taught was the Military Secrets Protection Law. It was really simple: "Don't look, don't talk, don't listen." The Kempeitai warned us that we would be punished under some article of that law if we even so much as mentioned anything we saw there. This unit, they said, was of primary importance and its work had the highest-level classification. The next thing we were taught was the Military Penal Code, and that said that if we ran away, it would be no different than deserting in combat and we would not escape death by firing squad. We had military police assigned directly to our unit. Under a law calling for the protection of military secrets, when this unit was created, all the Chinese who resided in the area were evicted and confined to a "protected hamlet." They were really practically imprisoned there and used for labor.

At that time all of Japan was very spy-conscious, so I wasn't really shocked by these things. They also gave us an anti-Communist education. I guess the Japanese army was most fearful of the Communist Party. Also, most of those who were kept at the Ishii Unit were Chinese Communist Party members or sympathizers. We were told everything about them was bad. They were "Reds! Reds!" At night, I became aware of the sound of chains, military boots, and military swords jangling when I had been there at the unit for about two weeks.

The thing that first shocked me though—what I remember even now—were the rabbits. They were given injections and they had seizures. Shots of cyanide, nitric acid, and strychnine nitrate. We were told not to look away from those rabbits. I don't think the kids of today could do it. Observing and killing animals was the first step. Gradually we came not to think anything of it, even when conducting experiments on human beings.

I went on to specialize in animals like mice and rats. We did everything at the direction of our superior, like culturing bacteria, carrying out experiments on animals, studying the results, determining exactly what level of each bacterial strain was necessary to kill them. Each experiment stated what animal of what weight died in how many days after an injection of what strength. When an animal died, it was immediately dissected. The heart, liver, kidneys, everything was taken out and cultures made, and bacteriological levels tested and tabulated. That means we were calculating "levels of morbidity." It takes two years to train someone to be able to do this.

Directing us were bacteriological scholars. Most of them had been senior professors at such prestigious universities as Kyoto Imperial University [Ishii's school]. All the army doctors there had studied bacteriology. We, ourselves, without even knowing it, were being raised to be noncommissioned officers, or perhaps even officers, for the unit. When high-ranking officers from the Kwantung Army came for inspections, we lined up and responded as if we were already soldiers. It was almost like being hypnotized. We just drifted down that course, without really being conscious of it. Within two years, many of us, although under the age of conscription, had volunteered to enlist. Later, I also took that step. We sensed that we were becoming an elite, even though we didn't have any real academic pedigrees. They even told us they would send us to college, though only two of thirty ever made it there.

In a word, we were really caught up in it. When we were assigned to the bacterial unit, after the completion of our education, we were designated "chemical-weapon handlers" and began receiving our "chemical allowance," which was bonus pay, so I was getting paid what a university graduate made in those days. We now became official members of the bacteriology unit, though we were still technically civilians. We exerted ourselves to try to make ever-more-lethal bacteria. Of course, if you cut corners in your work, you yourself might be infected. One scratch and you could die. During the first year, two of us died. The dangerous work of handling the animals infected by disease, of course, was carried out by the boys in the youth troop. Our superiors only compiled the data and judged. Given the way rank works in the military, there was no way to escape this except by climbing the promotional ladder yourself.

You had to have special passes in order to enter or leave those two buildings inside the unit's inner court. It took a long time before I qualified, but even then, those of our level didn't go there often. When you did go, you really were appalled. Even for people who had already lost their humanity it was ghastly to see. [*He pauses for a long time, sitting in silence.*]

Where did you go?

Those two buildings inside the square. To get there you went through an iron gate. There was a time clock to record when each person went in. Photographs of those with passes were posted too. I hardly ever entered there alone. I always went with my superior, to assist him.

That was the first time I heard the expression *maruta*. It was a term used by army doctors. At first, I thought of it only as a "log," which is what the term means in Japanese. But in German it has the meaning of a medical experiment. "How many logs fell?" Other people would have no idea what was being said, but among ourselves, we often spoke about how many fell or were dropped. This was only after I started going into those buildings. This use was limited only to us insiders. [*Again he falls silent.*]

In your article you mentioned injecting bacteria. Did you do that yourself?

I didn't do it myself, directly. We tried to have the infection progress naturally. In the case of plague, it was necessary to have the medium of the flea. We used fleas.

If you give as hot, it isn't possible to get the benefit of an experiment. We cultured the fleas, that was what we did when we were engaged in "practice" during our training. We raised them in clean oilcans. Rusty ones were no good. We put wheat, unhusked wheat, about fifteen centimeters deep in the can and then put a rat in a tiny basket, about the size of my fist. The rat couldn't move. You then increased the humidity and temperature above the rat's body temperature and left it for about a month. Whenever the rat died, we'd replace it with a new one. To exchange rats was our job. Sometimes when some fleas were still on the fur of the dead rat we removed them with a dryer. We did it in darkness. We were totally naked except for a white gown. We had nothing on our hands or arms. When the number of fleas reached a certain level, we would dump out the wheat and gather the fleas into a cylinder by putting a red electric light bulb on in the darkness. The fleas ran to the dark side. That was their habit. They disliked red light. To use this in bacteriological warfare, you had to put a live rat injected with plague bacilli in with the fleas. They would then attach themselves to the rat, and then the rat would be dropped from the sky. The rat would die and the fleas would scatter, because fleas won't stay on a dead body. We were told we had to replace the dead rats both quickly and carefully because infected fleas might be present, but we had no way to be cautious. So we were involved in bacteriological warfare, although it was called our "practice."

Before plague can infect people, it first infects rats, so we also had an "animal group," which bred rats and other animals for experiments. They were rats, not mice—not special laboratory rats, but common blacks rats. The ones you used to breed fleas had to be the wild variety. The white mice of the laboratory would be too conspicuous for bacteriological warfare.

We were handling bacteria, so we took a bath in disinfectants when we returned. We took off our uniforms and submerged ourselves in the bath. We reeked of that disinfectant. We got orders, for security reasons, not to allow any smell of disinfectant to cling to us if we left the unit, so we'd take another bath when we got back to our barracks to try to get rid of the smell, but it clung to our bodies. Even going out of the unit gradually became more difficult. We were totally wrapped up in our work. During the Pacific War I don't think we even had Sundays off. There was no place to spend money so it was all saved up. All my friends had about a thousand yen saved up. It was enough money to buy a house, more than a house.

Did the Chinese man you said you worked on in your article have the plague?

Yes, he did. It was done in a way resembling natural infection. The fleas were probably put in some kind of container and tied to his body. I'm not sure. There are many ways it could be done.

How many days did it take for him to develop the Black Death?

It is said the incubation period is generally a week.

Was that man young?

Yes, all of them were. Most were men. There were very few women.

Were you involved with many of these people?

Well, let me see. I wasn't involved with that many, although I saw them. I actually did that to only one. Just that one person.

How did you view those people? Didn't you have any feelings of pity?

Well. None at all. We were like that already. I had already gotten to where I lacked pity. After all, we were already implanted with a narrow racism, in the form of a belief in the superiority of the so-called "Yamato Race." We disparaged all other races. That kind of racism. If we didn't have a feeling of racial superiority, we couldn't have done it. People with today's sensibilities don't grasp this. That's why I'm afraid of the power of education. We, ourselves, had to struggle with our humanity after-wards. It was an agonizing process. There were some who killed themselves, unable to endure. After the defeat.

Did you exchange words with these people? I know you were able to speak Chinese.

Yes, I did. Although they only swore at us, "*Jih-pen kuei-tzu!* Japanese devil!" When you entered there, and had that said to you, there was nothing you could do but ignore it. If you ask, "Did I feel hatred toward them?" I'd say, yes, hatred was there, but I simply had to ignore it. In other words, they were valuable experimental animals. We treated them with civility. Thus, we gave them very good food. It was a lot better than the food we had. If you talk about a "menu," there was a Chinese menu for Chinese people. There was a special cook. They were always taking them food. Unless you provide a certain level of nourishment, they were of no use as experimental materials. When you went into their kitchen, it really smelled good. Nothing but good smells. Yes, that was the way it was. That's why if you call it a crime, it was. Therefore, quite a few of them refused to eat.

Did the ones who were there know what was going to happen to them?

Yes, they did.

Did you let the person live to the very last moment and try to extract plague bacteria?

Yes, that was the objective. Unless you dissected them quickly, extraneous bacteria would intrude.

Did you do it while they were alive?

[He pauses for a very long time.] Yeah. Yes, at the moment when he may or may not still have a breath of life remaining. If time passed, the effect of the experiment would be reduced.

Where did you extract the bacteria? From what part of the body?

From all the internal organs. In order to determine which part is most infected by the disease. You see, from the perspective of bacteriological warfare, it is best if pneumonic plague develops in the lungs, because death comes quickest in that form. Normally, when you are bitten by fleas, the disease develops in the lymph system, which produces boils and sores there. That's bubonic plague. That's what you mean when you speak of the progress of the infection.

So, you removed the lung and used it to culture bacilli to be used to spread the disease outside?

Yes. We used it to make the bacterial culture I spoke of earlier. I was actually there, on the site, doing that.

Did any of your friends catch the plague?

Unit 731 didn't have a hospital, only an infirmary. Those of us who got infected would have had to go to Harbin for a hospital, but if a plague patient appeared in the Japanese military medical system, it would be a severe breach of hygiene. Dysentery or typhus might not cause too much of a stir, but still, action had to be taken to prevent epidemics. That's why they didn't put the patients into an ordinary army hospital. Anybody who got sick was put into the special buildings. I guess they treated them, because they were members of the unit, but I'm not absolutely sure about that either. If they got infected and they were about to die, it was the same, whether they were unit members or not.

Were they too used to make bacterial culture when they passed away?

Yes, yes, they were just the same. We were all experimental material. If you died, you got a two-rank promotion. The unit held a unitwide funeral, and their ashes were taken to Japan. The unit commander himself read a memorial eulogy, shedding tears for the dear departed member—"Your heroic spirit will avenge . . ." and so forth.

Mr. Tamura, you yourself were on the site when your friend's life ended. How did you feel?

I knew the whole truth only much later. I left the unit for active duty as a soldier soon thereafter. Volunteered. Maybe it was because they made me be present there and be involved in that. I don't know. Even at that time I thought, "I can't take any more of this. It's impossible! I can't believe it!" It was inconceivable that he would be used that way. Even I didn't think we would be used that way. I was shocked, but I didn't dare discuss it with the others. If I'd talked I would probably have been accused under the Military Secrets Law.

I left there in 1943 at age twenty. But even in the army, after I completed my new-recruit training on the Manchurian-Soviet border, I was assigned to brigade headquarters and then the medical service. The man in charge of their medical department was from Unit 731 and knew of me. I worked in Chinese hospitals and research institutes in Manchuria. I feel I was allowed to study Chinese for that purpose.

I was never involved in actual bacteriological warfare as a soldier. I never fought with a gun. I was never subjected to an air raid. That kind of war I didn't fight. I was at headquarters and there was no real danger. I was always trying to get out, but never could.

The overwhelming majority who were able to flee back to Japan right at the end of the war were men like that. The men who were caught and charged as war criminals in the Soviet Union from Unit 731 were my superior, Karasawa, and Kawashima Kiyoshi. Five more were charged in China, including me. I don't know much about this, but those in Japan evidently traded their research to America. In return for their research documents, detailing their experiments, they were absolved of any crimes. That's what I heard.

Commander Ishii was managing a Japanese inn and living a quiet life when I returned to Japan in 1955. One of my old acquaintances suggested that it would be better for me if I paid a courtesy call on him one time, but I had no intention of going. I later heard he died of cancer of the larynx.

Most of the people at Ishii Unit 731 simply pretended not to know anything about what they had done. Many had been from top schools and they simply went back to similar places and gained positions quite high up in Japanese medical circles. The Institute for Infectious Diseases, the predecessor to the National Institute of Health, was closely associated with the unit. The leaders of the Ishii Unit even have a close-knit, old-boy network, called the *Seikonkai* [Refined Spirit Association].

Efforts to get other members of the Ishii Unit to talk of their experiences were unsuccessful. When contacted by telephone, the wife of a major, also convicted as a war criminal, said, "My husband is really ill. We've suffered enough. We don't have much time left. Don't torture us anymore. If he talks, memories come back and it's really painful. Other people, more responsible, escaped." She cried and sobbed over the phone. She refused to convey a request for an interview.

Independent reports confirm that he was still an active jogger two years after that call. ■

PART THREE

Homeland

"One hundred million [people], one mind." [*Ichioku isshin.*]
—Slogan used from 1940 on.

"Abolish desire until victory." [*Hoshigarimasen katsu made wa.*]
—Winning entry in the national competition to select an official slogan for 1942, the First Anniversary of the Launching of the Greater East Asia War. Submitted in the name of a fifth-grade girl.

"We'll never cease fire till our enemies cease to be!" [*Uchiteshi yamamu.*]
—Phrase from the *Kojiki* [Record of Ancient Matters] of A.D. 712, chosen as the national slogan for Army Memorial Day, *March 10, 1943*, as translated in the Nippon Times.

FOR JAPAN, the war in China, the need to garrison the lengthy Manchurian border with the Soviet Union, and the scale of the combat and resupply in the Pacific theater, as well as the tremendous task of bringing raw materials by sea to Japan itself, required awesome levels of armaments and war production. Yet, despite the impressive record of industrialization from the late nineteenth century on, Japan was still a country poor in the mineral resources and raw materials necessary for heavy industry—coal, iron, copper, manganese, tin, rubber, and, most crucial of all, petroleum. Indeed, it was to secure such resources that Japan first embarked on its path of conquest in the 1930s. It defies the logic of economic and industrial thinkers on both sides of the Pacific that Japan, with coal and steel production only one-thirteenth that of the United States, should nonetheless have launched the Greater East Asia War. The results were predictable.

That the United States vastly outproduced Japan during the war years is well known. A few figures illustrate this discrepancy: In 1941, Japanese aircraft production totaled 5,088. The United States produced 19,433 airplanes that year—before war was declared. Between 1941 and 1944, total Japanese aircraft production was 58,822, and American production was 261,826. That hardly tells the whole story, since the quality of aircraft produced in Japan declined, while that in the United States rose steadily. In 1944, Japanese output of small-arms ammunition was 6.5 percent that of the United States, and tank production, just 4.7 percent.[*]

When the Greater East Asia War was declared by the Emperor, war became the essential feature of everyday life for the entire population of Japan. If all national resources—and especially human resources—were absolutely required for the war effort, that meant each Japanese was expected to play a part in production, in resource conservation, and in providing enthusiastic support.

At the time of Pearl Harbor, every household was already a member of one of the newly established neighborhood associations, the *tonarigumi,* under the control of the Home Ministry and its police force. These associations of five to ten households each were used to informally blanket the country, facilitating neighbors watching each other and empowering a neighborhood to admonish anyone, whether for letting a beam of light slip out through their black airraid curtains, for failing to buy their allotment of government bonds, or for showing a lack of enthusiasm in contributing gold rings to the war effort. Each association was

---

[*] Jerome B. Cohen, *Japan's Economy in War and Reconstruction* (Minneapolis: University of Minnesota Press, 1949), pp. 209–10, 245.

also directly involved in the distribution of rationed items—which may help account for the fact that the neighborhood associations survived until the final stages of the war, after many other organizations collapsed.

The nation's schools, too, became building blocks in the national mobilization scheme. Even elementary schools, renamed National Schools, were assigned the crucial task of creating "children of the Emperor," willing to "sacrifice themselves" for the sake of the nation. Outside of school, the newly consolidated Great Japan Youth Association, fourteen million members strong by June 1943, regimented young people, from third graders on up to working youths of twenty-five.

The members of various women's associations had from the beginning of the war in China regularly turned out to cheer those sent off to the front—their resolutely happy faces reminding the men of their town or village that their women and children were behind them. In February 1942, all these women's organizations were brought together in one unified twenty-million-member organization, the Great Japan Women's Association. In villages across the country, the local activities of these many different organizations were overseen by the Imperial Military Reservist Association, long the backbone of the veterans' organizations supporting the military.

Rather than bringing huge windfalls to the Japanese people, the military conquests in the South only increased the military's needs. New imports were channeled into the production of military goods, and soon consumer goods all but disappeared from the stores. In early 1942, severe shortages in food, clothing, and all other basic necessities led first to price controls, and then to even tighter rationing. Crucial industries had already been brought directly under the supervision of the government before Pearl Harbor, and the *zaibatsu,* huge privately-owned conglomerates, benefited from the government's protection. Fulfilling military needs became industry's acknowledged priority. In order to meet the military's unrestricted demands, the trend toward a concentration of production and capital, long underway, dramatically accelerated, and small to middle-sized companies were winnowed out in such areas as petroleum production, petroleum processing, steel, shipbuilding, airplane manufacturing, chemical production, and light metal manufacturing. Companies for generating and distributing electric power also underwent drastic consolidation and were now placed directly under government control.

Many small retail shops and stores were soon forced to close simply because they could no longer get enough items to sell, or acquire key ingredients needed to make foods or merchandise they might have been producing for generations. Large numbers of people who lost their means of livelihood this way found themselves seeking work in military plants.

Under intensified national mobilization laws, such "industrial warriors" lost the freedom to move from job to job, while plant and factory owners were strictly bound by rules and regulations created to fulfill the slogan, "Increase production!" Ironically, for a nation which had long claimed that overpopulation was one of its key problems—and used as its oft-repeated justification for expansion abroad—the mobilization of millions of men, first for the South and then for the defense of the Homeland, created ever more severe labor shortages both on farms and in factories.

In the end, military and civilians had to turn to extraordinary measures. To replace skilled workers away at the front, efforts were made first to tap students graduating from school, then to seek workers among the unemployed, and finally among Koreans who had emigrated to Japan. In addition, hundreds of thousands of Koreans, and Chinese from both Taiwan and the mainland, were drawn into heavy labor in mining and construction jobs at which many tens of thousands died.° Sometimes forcibly rounded up in their impoverished homelands by the Japanese military, but often recruited with promises of high wages and good working conditions once in Japan, such workers frequently found themselves virtual prisoners, condemned to work quite literally under the whip until war's end.

Young women and school-age students made up Japan's great untapped labor pool. The conscription of unmarried women into war production began slowly, while married women were never formally conscripted into war industry at all. Policies aimed at increasing the number of children born in Japan—under the slogan "Be fruitful and multiply"—and ideas about the proper role of mothers in the raising of citizens held by leaders in government right up through Prime Minister General Tōjō himself made it extremely difficult to draw on married women for factory work. More and more, however, students supplied labor to replace men drafted into the military. These unskilled young workers, underfed and in fragile health, were soon authorized to work even midnight shifts and work was officially proclaimed to "equal education." By war's end, about 3,400,000 such students had been mobilized into various forms of war work.

Mobilization also meant that the government made extensive efforts to assure that all forms of media carried a uniform view of Japan's objectives in the war and did so with enthusiasm. The means by which

---

° Figures for fatalities among imported laborers in wartime Japan have never been authoritatively determined. Boku Kyong-sik, *Chōsenjin kyōsei renkō no kiroku* [*A record of the forced labor of Koreans*] (Tokyo: Miraisha, 1965), p. 91, estimates that as many as 64,000 Korean workers died in Japan. In addition, about 150,000 Koreans died in military service or as civilian employees of the Japanese military.

Japan's lofty goals were to be achieved were rarely, if ever, spelled out in detail, as such matters were not supposed to be of concern to the people at large. Their overwhelming responsibility was simply to obey and execute the orders they were given, and this was emphasized at every opportunity. Newspapers, magazines, novels, graphic art, radio, movies, and other forms of entertainment were marshaled into the war effort. Strict censorship and—perhaps even more stiflingly—self-censorship were in place. The newspapers were filled with "victory news"—reports of "military gods," "invincible Imperial forces," military harangues meant to stir up hatred of "American and Britain demons," and exhortations to fulfill such slogans as "Heighten hatred of the enemy" and "Be frugal and save."

Organizations of all types were formed to mobilize cartoonists, artists, novelists, and others for the war effort. Well-established painters held "Sacred War" and "Greater East Asia War" exhibitions where they showed propaganda art portraying Japan's early military successes. New movies allowed the Japanese people to experience their military successes through film. *The Battles of Hawaii and Malaya* of 1942 recreated scenes of Japanese planes swooping in to attack the American fleet at Pearl Harbor so real that the audience was pulled right into the moment and shared the pilots' exhilaration at their achievements. Newsreels also moved audiences with concrete images of Japan's new southern empire; shots of navy parachute units descending on the Celebes to the accompaniment of melodies from Wagner were unforgettable. As in the China war, novelists were called up and sent to the front to gather material for their latest works promoting the war. Paper for magazines and newspapers, the film for movie production, and even the paint for the artists' palettes, all came under government control. The authorities could thus instantly close a newspaper or end film production by withholding supplies, but many artists and writers needed no such pressure to succumb to the allure of the early victories.

Japan became a land of slogans: "Luxury is the enemy" ("luxury" might now mean no more than a bar of soap or an extra box of matches); "Saving is the road to victory"; "Let's send even one more plane to the front"; "Deny one's self and serve the nation"; and "Serve the nation with one death." There were nationwide contests to create new slogans that would ever more fire the public's devotion to Japan. Most common were slogans of self-denial "until victory is achieved."

As the war proceeded, everyone was now part of this world of slogans which less and less reflected reality, as the gap between publicly monitored images and private perceptions widened. People spoke in approved formulas: "Congratulations on your husband's going to war." "Thank you very much. He's happy to serve the nation." Each Japanese had a public face which he or she was expected to wear in all public encounters.

As the war successes faded, an emotionalism inflamed by a narrow patriotism overwhelmed the nation. Spiritualism superseded realism, and symbolism took the place of success: people now quite literally trod on stars-and-stripes flags painted on the pavement, while women's-association members skewered Roosevelt and Churchill dolls with bamboo spears to practice "national defense." Liberals who merely questioned the war's direction or the wisdom of its present course had no means to express their thoughts—for behind all the slogans and regulations lay the immense police powers of the state. In the New Order of Greater East Asia, any way of thinking other than the Imperial one was "dangerous thought." America and England could not win, it was said, because of their belief in individualism and liberalism. If the enemy was liberal, then to be liberal was to be like the enemy. Any perception of a lack of enthusiastic support for the war was punished, while even the smallest interference in the war effort led to arrest or retribution. Simply failing to remove one's hat in the theater when the Emperor appeared in a newsreel could mean arrest. It was a risk to put even a few critical words in one's own personal diary.

Yet dissatisfaction was hardly absent in Japan, despite all outward displays of unity. Most people simply felt it was impossible to express dissent, and abandoned any hope of affecting events in any way. All that was left was to endure, to struggle on, trying to stay in step. There were, however, breakdowns in control. Despite all the government rhetoric about equal burdens and sacrifice, the black market became a common feature of towns and cities. People who had connections with top military men or high-ranking officials could find anything they desired. Kiyosawa Kiyoshi, a well-known writer on diplomatic affairs, penned in his diary on April 30, 1943, that the following saying was popular around town: "Only the stupid queue up in the world of stars [the army], anchors [the navy], the black market, and connections."*

The destruction of everyday life left nothing to replace it except an illusion of unity and solidarity. When Japan's strength finally rested on no more than the people's endurance, they showed remarkable resilience and almost unbelievable fortitude, but they could not defend themselves against the arsenal of the enemy, much less carry the war to America.

---

* Kiyosawa Kiyoshi, *Ankoku nikki, 1942–1945* [*Diary of Dark Days, 1942–1945*] (Tokyo: Iwanami, 1990), p. 30.

As individuals, they could neither protect the skies over their cities, nor negotiate peace. The domestic sphere proved the only theater of operations in which Japan's military leaders could exercise unrestrained power and control to the last moment, and they exploited that position to the fullest. There were no revolts, no explosions. The people obeyed and endured until virtually the final moment. ∎

7 / LIFE GOES ON

The End of a Bake Shop

ARAKAWA HIROYO

Rice rationing began in Tokyo and the other five largest cities on April 1, 1940. Miso and soy sauce came under a coupon system in February 1942, two months after the outbreak of the Pacific War. Soon thereafter, fish, eggs, tofu, other grains, and virtually all major food items were placed under ration controls. As shortages grew, the black market flourished.

She's a classic "Edokko," a Tokyo-ite born and raised. She speaks in a clear voice at a staccato pace. She talks of her days making kasutera, *loaves of the spongecake modeled on the Portuguese* pão de Castella, *first encountered by Japanese in the sixteenth century. Long and thin, made without shortening, they are a Japanese favorite.*

We had a shop in Monzen Nakachō in Tokyo's Fukagawa district. We made *kasutera* and took them to movie theaters, playhouses, and to the Takaraya, a shop for passenger boats departing for Ōshima. We sold the loaves for four *sen* two *rin* apiece, and they resold them for about ten *sen*. At Takaraya alone, we sold a thousand loaves a month, especially in the summer. We had about a hundred clients—there were a lot of movie houses in the Asakusa district in those days—We also sold baked squid, buttered peanuts, and deep-fried green peas. Those we just bought in bulk and repackaged into individual bags.

My husband was the master chef. He was the only one who baked *kasutera*. He started making them at three o'clock in the morning. A can of eggs, a can of sugar, a can of flour all went into a machine. *"Clinkety-clank, clinkety-clank!"* What a sound it made! I'm sure our neighbors found it terribly noisy. When the *kasutera* were baked, I helped wrap them individually, just me and one other person, and then put them into a box that could hold thirty loaves. By noon they were piled high. Then delivery men would take them to the theaters. They always stopped off to watch movies. When they finally got back, I had to count the money and do the books. I often fell asleep over those books.

There were many shops along the street—a fishmonger, a tempura shop, vegetable stands, dry-goods stores, a general sundries shop, a paper goods and shōji-screen shop, and a fan shop. Opposite our store was a stand selling croquettes. When we were really busy, we'd just call across to him and order croquettes for dinner. If we hadn't had a war we'd have done really well. We made good money. In those early days of the war, my daughter Nobuko and I used to take a month off to go to a hot spa in Yugawara or Shiobara, or to the shore at Ōiso. We even took along some girls from our neighborhood.

As the war grew hotter, many people we dealt with were called up to the front or drafted for labor service. A bakers' association was formed in the belief that sugar, flour, and the like would be easier to obtain if we cooperated, but the association soon decided that the best course was for small bakers, who used less, to merge with big ones. We had enough sugar, so we were able to carry on on our own, but some couldn't.

We were in the business of selling food, so we didn't really suffer from any shortages then. Somehow people would always have something to bring us—vegetables, toys, or books for Nobuko. We didn't suffer even when things began disappearing from town. If you queued up you could always buy something. Whenever you saw a line, everybody joined, even if you didn't know what it was for. A joke that went around then was that you could join a line and find out you were waiting to get into a funeral.

One day it started to rain. I was worried we might have a serious storm, so I looked out from the second story. A long line of people, all holding umbrellas, stretched to the end of the street. I thought something must be going on at the Fire God's temple, but when I got downstairs, I found out the head of the line was at our shopdoor. They were lining up to buy *kasutera*. When we baked, the smell filled the neighborhood. It seemed that from then on, people came individually and we could sell the cakes directly to them for ten *sen*.

I told the various national-defense women's groups that I didn't want to join. Once you joined, you had to go out all the time, and couldn't do anything in your own place. For me, the work of the neighborhood women's association was enough. The people who joined those other groups were the "Madames" of intellectual families, with housemaids and the like. In our own neighborhood group, we put on our white aprons and the sashes of our association and sent off our soldiers, flags in hand. It didn't seem to happen all at once, but soon you'd notice: "The man of that house is gone," or "He's been taken away for labor." Many shops and businesses closed or were left in the hands of women.

The head of each group had to be chosen from within your group of about ten families. I, too, had to be head sometimes. When you were, people came to you all the time and you had to appear at every function, no matter what the occasion was. If anyone was called up for service, you had to go to that person's house to offer congratulations and bring them farewell money. This happened almost every day, so I'd have real trouble keeping up with my own affairs. You offered congratulations because they were being allowed to serve the nation. You couldn't say, "This is terrible. I'm really sorry for you. Take care of yourself and come back safely." But I'm sure their own families said things like, "Please come home to us" or "Don't get killed." Any family would be ruined if their son or husband didn't return.

For the first year and a half of the war, things were really good. My younger brother used to carry Nobuko here and there to attend victory marches. I didn't really have the time to go. Before long, though, every corner of every street in Monzen Nakachō seemed to have people standing there asking for us to add stitches to the soldiers' *sen'ninbari,* their thousand-stitch belts. People hoped that would prevent a man from getting hit by bullets. Just thinking of that now gives me chills. You couldn't really refuse. I'd ask, when's he going? "Not yet. But we expect his call-up at any time, so we're preparing." The war dead began to return. Everyone lived in dread of their impending call-up.

Four or five men from our neighborhood were called up at the same time, so we got together and held a joint purification ceremony. My own younger brother was drafted. We all went to a shrine and prayed. Nobuko's uncle made a great speech. You wouldn't believe how grand he sounded! "As the flowers of the cherry bloom, I extend my gratitude to the nation for calling me to serve, and I pledge I will work for all of you and for the whole country to the utmost of my ability." He was working at Mitsubishi Heavy Industries in Tsurumi at that time. He'd gotten the job through my husband's cousin's connections and had hoped he wouldn't be called because he was employed there. Jun, my husband's cousin, was a reserve lieutenant or something. Whenever a call-up card came for him, he always came back the next day. Three times—but on each occasion he came right back. He was working on airplanes or something. The big shots always get the best deal.

Military men—not even of high rank, but anyone wearing a manteau or a saber—would sometimes take things from the neighborhood vegetable shop without paying. The grocer told me they'd just pocket it. You couldn't really ask them for money. The police, too, and you couldn't do anything about it, because they were watching out for you. When we were still baking *kasutera,* but only once every two or three days, they'd come by. "Oh, today you're baking? This house sure smells good." You couldn't get by without offering something. That policeman had a fine, high-bridged nose—a very handsome cop.

For a while we had a supply of Shanghai eggs. They were powdered eggs. You added water and mixed it in the blending machine, but they didn't get frothy like real eggs, and the *kasutera* wouldn't rise either. Eventually, even they became unavailable, so we had to change our business to sandwiches. There was no more sugar. We'd buy ten loaves of bread, slice them as thin as possible, fill them with whale ham. There wasn't any real pork ham anymore. We knew someone who worked at a marine-products lab. Those bureaucrats there had unlimited butter. We got butter from them.

Soon enough, bread disappeared for us ordinary people. Even whale ham. We had to give up the sandwich business, so we tried "cut bread." My husband had already been conscripted for industrial work by this time, but at night he taught me how to make it. It was for the army, so we could get plenty of supplies. You kneaded it, put sweet bean paste inside, shaped it like an elephant's trunk, baked it, then cut it into pieces. We took it to a wholesaler in our pullcart.

There were very few men left in the neighborhood. The grandpa in the paper-goods store next door, the old uncle at the bicycle shop, and the old man at the fishmonger's. Most of the shops were shuttered. Only when rationed goods arrived did stores open. When the dried cod came in, then you could go to the fish stand. But people helped each other. I thought human relations were better then.

Eventually we had to deliver our baking machinery to the military because it was made of iron. We didn't get paid anything. Before that we'd had to contribute watches, gold teeth, anything valuable. Foolishly honest people like us contributed whatever we were asked for, while right-wing crooks over in China were making fortunes with those things.

Finally, we decided to evacuate from Tokyo, since we had little left and the air raids were coming more often.

I'd often go to pick up Nobuko at school and hear the roar of approaching planes. I'd dash into the earthen shelters along the embankment by the roadway. After a while I'd emerge and then go on toward the school. There were many military installations and plants in the area we'd evacuated to. Soldiers often came to farmers' houses and built little stoves to cook rice. The big shots would stay at the temples, the lesser ones with the farmers. Then farmers had big houses, so they'd take in three, four, or five overnight. We had lots of soldiers around, so I wasn't frightened. "If anything happens I'm sure they'll take care of us"—that was how I felt.

My house in Monzen Nakachō was burned down in the March 9 air raid. 1945. I heard that the old man at the fishmonger's was killed in that raid. Although our house was gone, we were able to dig up some rice bowls and other household things that we could still use. We also dug out a mixing bowl we'd had, almost as big as a washtub, and brought that back. We used to take baths in it. Everybody was suffering from food shortages. I exchanged kimonos for rice.

There was a German shepherd dog in the neighborhood. A very good dog. It would listen to you. Whenever there was an air raid, even before the warning sounded, it would howl. Such an incredibly sad and miserable noise! Its masters were rich, so they had a fine house. The son of the house was a dentist. They'd kept the dog under their wood floors, but still it barked and barked. The army ordered it killed. Said it was disturbing army communications. They had to poison their own dog.

We never went back to making *kasutera*. But we were still lucky. We didn't have anybody killed by that war.

Burdens of a Village Bride

TANAKA TOKI

The summer smell of the green rice paddies fills the air, which inside the expansive house is stirred by a large fan working at full force. The house, near a small temple at the top of a steep path, seems to hang over the edge of the mountain. The house is nearly ringed by a stone and concrete pond full of young carp, her late husband's passion.

"When you think about it, I guess you'd say everybody had a rough time during the war. If you include my husband's brother, six men were killed in action from this one hamlet of Uebatake alone. There were thirty-three households then." Both of her brothers died in the military. Her father was killed in an air raid.

Straight-backed at seventy-four years old, she moves with vigor, and speaks in the dialect of the region. Two American students from the University of California San Diego are enjoying a three-week "home stay" with the family.

I was twenty when I got married at the end of 1933. There weren't really love marriages then, just marriages between households. On January 20, my husband left for active duty. Went to China in April. He didn't even know when he departed that I was carrying our son.

The bride was in a terrible position in those days. There were lots of children when I came to his family. I guess I was pretty stupid to come here! My husband's family had nine children. Six boys. He was the eldest. Then there were three young girls—ten, three, and one. I knew there were lots of them, but I didn't know how many. I soon gave birth to one of my own. My mother-in-law held all the money. Sometimes I had to go to my father's house to ask him for financial help. There just wasn't enough. During the winter I made straw rope to tie charcoal bags, and I made the bags themselves. In the summertime I raised silkworms. We had to do all that just to get money for so many children.

We hardly bought any food, but ate what we raised at home. Sometimes when a fishmonger came by we bought something. There weren't any shoes. During the winter, when there was deep snow, we made footwear for ourselves from rice straw. We picked fiddleheads and other wild vegetables and grew vegetables on our own land. We had to take care of ourselves. We didn't even have electricity in our village back then.

My father-in-law passed away, and my husband's grandfather the following year, so that left just my mother-in-law and me to take care of a large number of children and the temple. Somehow you had to find some way to earn cash. I worked in the paddies. It wasn't like now, with those big wide paddy fields. Then they were tiny ones, scattered all over in bits and pieces. We kept an ox. I can't really believe it when I think about it now. In the evening I worked as late as there was light to see. In the morning, one person fixed breakfast, while the other had to go out into the fields to work. Your man's in the army, not a single letter comes to you. You don't have the faintest idea where he is.

Then you had the National Defense Women's Association work, too. You had to send off the soldiers and welcome them back. And you had to volunteer to make money to send to the military. On the next mountain over, some of the men still left in the village were making charcoal. We'd go there and carry it down for them. We did things to comfort soldiers. We collected small things to send to them, bought canned goods, made "comfort bags" and wrote "comfort letters." We were the old kind of people, so our handwriting was poor. While working on the second floor, I'd sometimes write a line or two for a comfort letter. I took a lot of time on even a single letter. They were going to soldiers from the hamlet. Because I was doing so much work outside the home, I had to ask my mother-in-law for permission, even though I had no choice about going or not going. I had to ask to be allowed to do anything. I wasn't free.

My second child was conceived in the tenth year of our marriage when my husband was home for a year or so, but she was still in my womb when he went back and he didn't know about her. When he returned to Kanazawa to pick up soldiers, or something, I went there to show him his thirty-day-old daughter. The trains were really crowded and there was no food. In those days, even a single apple was hard to get. I carried her on my back in a bitter-cold wind. He was already a noncommissioned officer, so he took lodgings for us for the night. He told me that because he was a very methodical man, he had risen high in the army. Besides that, I don't recall what we talked about. At that time, clothing was rationed. You could only buy so much per head, all determined by coupons. My husband had gotten coupons for me from some soldiers from Nagano who were still single. Thinking of that now brings tears to my eyes. It's slightly embarrassing. He bought me two pink pieces of underskirt with which he covered the baby on my back. He also bought a toy for her. We parted at Kanazawa Station. He went to the South. I could only cry on my way back.

Letters had come from him when he was in North China, but after he went to the South nothing came for about two years. I thought I had to be strong. If you let it beat you, then you'd lose out. With no men in the family, they'd make light of you. You're only a woman, they'd say. I didn't let that happen to me. I lived so that I couldn't be despised. You never know what people feel about you in their guts. "What's going to happen to that house?" they'd ask. "No letter from the Master. Maybe those women think he's still alive, but he can't be." People were saying things like that behind our backs, and sooner or later you'd hear about it. "I can't be defeated by other people," was what I thought. "I have to do more. I can't be beaten by this."

There were many hardships, but the hardest was to keep the family together. These days everybody's roof is made to shed the snow, but then all roofs were thick thatch, made of reeds. Ours was twelve *ken* long [nearly 24 yards]. It was a tremendous job to gather enough thatch for it and one of the biggest causes of my worries. You had to prepare a huge supply of reeds, a tough job for a woman. First you cut them, then dried them, then bundled them. You piled them up there in the mountains. Later, you had to bring them down on your back, then haul them up and put on the new roof. This had to be done in the autumn.

If you had a family with a man who hadn't gone to the front you were all right. But in those days, there weren't any families with men. Everybody was gone. A few families had an old man around, but they couldn't really help. There was only my mother-in-law and me. My father lived deep in the mountains. One year, I asked him to come and help us. He worked till nightfall and I remember him setting off for home in the darkness.

I had two brothers. One was in the army, a flight soldier. The other was in the navy, in the naval Special Attack forces. They sent him home to bid farewell to his brothers, sisters, and parents. He knew he was going to die. He'd be going down in a submarine, then he'd blow up. He was still unmarried. I'd gone back to my family home to talk to him. I knew it would be better if I could stay until he left, but I had obligations to my husband's house, so I returned and went to work early the next morning.

There was no bus service then, and no private motor cars, either. One truck did go back and forth to the town of Inami with charcoal. The last time I saw my brother, he was leaving for his unit. I couldn't even send him off. I was too busy gathering thatch on the mountain. I could see him from where I was, but he didn't know that. I felt such compassion for my poor brother. It was awful. All alone there, I cried and cried. I could only stop at my work and watch him leave the mountain wearing his sailor uniform, sitting on top of a load of charcoal.

As the war dragged on, we attended the drills of the Reservists' Association. We practiced with bamboo spears on the schoolground under the blazing-hot sun. Some fainted because of the heat. Men made the spears for us and hung up dolls made of straw, shaped like men. We wrapped our heads with *hachimaki* and wore the sash of the National Defense Women's Association across our chests. We did our best. If you opposed anything about war, of course, you were a traitor. You had to say, "yes, yes," whatever the subject. But when I thought about my husband's hardship at the front, doing that much seemed natural.

Dressmaker

KOSHINO AYAKO

Almost immediately after the Pacific War broke out, clothing rationing for civilians was severely tightened. The Ministry of Commerce and Industry announced a coupon system for clothing on February 1, 1942, limiting each person living in a city to 100 points a year, while allotting those living in the countryside 80 points. A blouse was 8 points, a pair of socks 2 points, and a man's overcoat 50. Initially there were additional points allowed for specified items like handtowels. As the war went on, the number of points allotted was reduced and the "cost" of items was officially increased, but in fact most goods simply disappeared from the stores.

"I've now been in the clothing business for sixty-five years." A leading fashion designer, she is busy with final preparations for her upcoming show in London. The phone rings often and her assistants rush frantically about in her Osaka studio. Her three daughters are also internationally

renowned designers and businesswomen, perhaps even more famous than their mother.

Our family were kimono merchants. When I began making Western dresses, there were very few women who would wear them. Most of my clientele were store clerks, like the girls from the Daimaru, Takashimaya, and Shirakiya department stores. Among them, only the most fashionable would have considered dresses. The majority still wore kimonos, sometimes with store smocks thrown over them. Even I still wore kimonos. I was too busy to make a dress for myself.

When the war started, nobody came to dress shops. Even if you'd had a dress made, you couldn't wear it. I remember when skirts were no longer acceptable. So women wore pants with wide legs, called *monpe,* and pants suits, like today. It's very difficult to make those bulky *monpe* trousers from bolts of fabric cut for kimonos, since they're much narrower; you have to match up more than one piece. Cutting out the pattern was the hardest part. Improvising, I introduced darts and devised three types of *monpe.* One was just like pants, with an elastic band at the waist, because some people had difficulty tying a drawstring. I went around to schools at no charge; I had plenty of free time, as my shop wasn't busy. Women's association members would bring whatever clothes they had and I'd instruct them in how to turn them into *monpe.* I usually did the cutting-out for them. I easily did a hundred or more. Some people were very clever and caught on just watching the movement of my hands, but others were slow and couldn't get the hang of it no matter how many times I showed them.

During the war, everything was National Defense Color. That was the army's color, the color of uniforms. Today, if I recommended khaki to a woman who went through those years, they'd hate it. They say it brings back those times. They don't want to remember. But then it was the safest color, fine anytime, anyplace. The streets were full of army color. After the war, that color was in oblivion for a long time, but it's made something of a comeback recently. I guess it seems new.

Anything with any sense of elegance at all was forbidden under the prohibition regulations, even a single line of gold-embroidered thread in a kimono. Kimono sleeves had to be cut short. Your *haori,* the cloak you wear over a kimono, had to be shortened, too. They were supposed to look more gallant that way.

I kept my shop open through the whole conflict. I'd take apart good kimonos in order to make *monpe.* I also made Western clothes from old fabric. There wasn't much to wear. Even when everything was rationed and the coupon system was introduced, we still did pretty well. In the area from Tan'nawa, in Wakayama prefecture, to Sakai, in the heart of Osaka, there were one hundred thirty-two shops charged with distributing clothes coupons under rationing. When rationed fabric came, it arrived in two trucks. One truck was for my shop. The other was divided among the other one hundred thirty-one. We had that many ration points.

The cloth delivered was of all kinds: calico, Fuji silk, crepe, even big flower prints. I wondered why the military had been holding on to flower prints. Maybe they were thinking of making curtains. There was even hand-woven homespun. Rough silk was one point, cotton one point, rayon five points. Each person had a coupon book with tickets in denominations of one to five points. You handed over the coupons and then paid your money. When a truck arrived, people lined up early in the morning. They'd already been standing for more than two hours by the time I opened the shop at ten. I only sold the fabric for the official fixed price. I'd cut the cloth into the standard three-yard lengths. Calico was one yard for three *sen*. Some wanted two lots. If you had a large family you needed it, even just to make shorts. I'd usually have to ask them to stand in line again, but sometimes I'd hand over two without saying anything. The next day those people would come around, bubbling over: "Thank you so very, very much for yesterday." They'd bring rice, hidden under an infant in a baby carriage, or some other place like that. I had rice all the time. We got new rice, onions, *matsutake* mushrooms. I didn't do any black-marketing or gouging. People were really happy with that.

Everything was rationed. Tobacco. Fish. Even a tiny mackerel had to be divided among ten families. Kishiwada is a beach-fishing area; they took the fish in offshore nets. Every evening they brought us some. They wanted white cloth. Fishing is a job that really gets your clothes dirty. They needed cloth for shirts and the like. We had white fabric in abundance and sold it for the proper price. We couldn't even finish all the fish they brought. I spread them around our neighborhood. My relatives all lived far away, so sharing with the neighbors was the best thing to do. People tell me now that they had a difficult time getting enough to eat during the war, but I went through the whole war without worrying about that. I had a life far more luxurious than most.

My husband was called up and died of illness overseas in the army in February 1944. A placard emblazoned with 'A House of Honor' was put up by the entrance to our house. Because of that, even if I'd fancied another man, it was useless to love. I was low-key and discreet. You had to be afraid of the Kempeitai all the time. I never did anything wrong, but I felt my partner was worried about the military police. Marriage was out of the question.

Those war years were a time when we were held in by everything. We had to worry about the country, what the people around us were thinking. We were completely repressed.

Within two or three years of the end of the war, new clothes suddenly appeared again. Wild, large flower patterns, tartan checks, bright colors. I thought, it's my world at last! Finally, I could go wild. Red and yellow became very popular. I loved yellows—lemon yellow, melon yellow, mustard yellow. People said, "Yellow is the color of lost love." I didn't care, I liked it.

8 / WAR WORK

Making Balloon Bombs

TANAKA TETSUKO

This "new weapon," a balloon capable of carrying bombs to attack the North American continent, was conceived and developed after the first American air raid on Japanese cities led by Jimmy Doolittle in April 1942. The balloons were some ten meters in diameter, made of paper or rubberized cloth filled with hydrogen gas. A 15-kilogram antipersonnel bomb and two 2.2-kilogram incendiary bombs could be suspended beneath the balloon. When launched from one of several sites in central and northern Honshu, the balloon was to rise to a predetermined height using an altitude-managing system and sandbags for ballast, and then be carried in the jet stream more than 8,000 kilometers eastward across the Pacific Ocean. Between November 1944 and April 1945, more than 9,300 of those balloons were launched. Some reached the northwestern parts of the United States and Canada.*

During the war, she was a student engaged in making the paper for these balloons. She now works as a volunteer with a group helping Japanese women left behind in China at the end of the war who are still trying to locate relatives in Japan.

---

* See Robert C. Mikesh, *Japan's World War II Balloon Bomb Attacks on North America* (Washington, D.C.: Smithsonian Institution Press, 1973) for a discussion of damage inflicted and the extent of defensive measures taken to counteract this "threat."

My ancestors were samurai who served the feudal lord of this Yamaguchi area. A wall in our home bore a rack for holding spears. My grandmother used to tell me, "You must behave like the daughter of a warrior family." I was always conscious of that, whether in school or anywhere else. Japan was already in the midst of war when I first become conscious of the world around me. Father was a schoolteacher, one of those teaching militarism, and I received a militaristic education. The foundations of that education were "patriotism based on loyalty to the Emperor" and the principle "sacrifice yourself to serve." You weren't supposed to think about yourself: Work for the Emperor, even if you must give up your own life.

The year the Pacific War broke out was the year I entered Yamaguchi Girls' High School. My dream to be a ballerina ended after only a few lessons at school. On December 8 I heard the news on the radio. I was seized with a sense of tension. Amazing! Japan had declared war against America! Such a large country. I wasn't afraid. Japan would win, of course—so I thought, but I sensed it would be a terrible, difficult struggle.

In my first year, we still had classes. English was canceled, though. That was the enemy language. During music class the melodies of Germany and Italy were acceptable, but American and English pieces were banned. Later, school classes practically came to an end and our education became mostly volunteer work. Because men were continually going off to the front, we were sent to help their families—planting rice, weeding the paddies, harvesting rice, growing barley. I carried charcoal down from the mountains. I'd had no farm experience before. It was very strenuous, physical labor, but I never thought of it as hardship. We patched soldiers' uniforms, sewed on new buttons, repaired torn seams for the Forty-Second Infantry Regiment stationed in Yamaguchi. Nobody complained about it. We were part of a divine country centered on the Emperor. The whole Japanese race was fighting a war.

In 1944 an army officer from the military arsenal in Kokura on Kyushu came to our school and told us that we would be making a "secret weapon." The weapon would have a great impact on the war. He didn't say then that we were to be making balloon bombs, only that somehow what we made would fly to America. What a sense of mission we had!

A factory started at our school in August 1944. Stands were placed all over the schoolyard and drying boards were erected on them. Each board was the size of one *tatami* mat and had handles at each end. We covered the board with a thin layer of paste made from the *konnyaku* plant and then laid down two sheets of Japanese paper and brushed out any bubbles. When dry, a thicker layer of paste, with a slightly bluish hue, a little like the color of the sky, was evenly applied to it. That process was repeated five times. We really believed we were doing secret work, so I didn't talk about this even at home, but my clothes were covered with paste, so my family must have been able to figure out something.

The two basketball courts in our schoolyard also were converted to drying space. There was a big ginkgo tree next to them. It was a wonderful spot to take a break when you'd been playing, as I had so often done as a member of the basketball club. That tree was cut down because it blocked the sun.

Our work depended on the sun's cooperation. When it rained, we had to carry everything into the gymnasium. When the autumn showers began, there was nothing you could do. No matter how much they spurred you on with exhortations about your production target, they wouldn't dry, and when they wouldn't that paste really smelled bad. Eventually, we removed all the desks from the classrooms and brought in a large *hibachi* and a pile of charcoal. We practically started a bonfire in class, all the windows and halls lined with drying boards. Sometimes you almost got poisoned by carbon monoxide.

There was another school in Yamaguchi doing the same work, the Nakamura Girls' School. We heard a rumor that they were soon going to depart for the military arsenal. Why couldn't we go too? It was December 1944, and the war situation was intensifying. We knew that if we stayed at school, production would remain low or decline, so we addressed a petition to our principal, pledging ourselves in blood. One of the girls who lived near the school rushed home to get a razor so we could cut our fingers to write in blood, "Please let us go and serve the nation."

We had no idea then that our principal had resisted an order to send us to Kokura, because the arsenal would be a likely target for air attacks. Finally, though, the order to the school couldn't be avoided any longer, so on January 2, 1945, we departed. That was my sixteenth birthday. We marched off in formation, one hundred and fifty of us. Only those who were physically too weak were left behind. We were in high spirits. But we were still children, and some thought this was like a school trip. We all wore white headbands with the characters "Student Special Attack Force" on them. I thought I might not be coming back, so before I left I wrapped up a lock of my hair and clippings from my nails in paper and, together with my last will and testament, left them pressed in a book at home.

When we arrived I was shocked by the size of the factory. Everywhere, metal drying boards were revolving on steam-blasting machines that dried them. The noise was deafening. We were taken to the place where the balloons were actually assembled and tested. There stood an enormous balloon, perhaps ten meters in diameter. When we saw this we were thrilled. This was what we'd been making! It fired our determination. Six hundred of our *tatami*-sized sheets were required for just one balloon.

That night we moved into our dormitory. There was no heat. To keep us warm, we had only the blanket we had been told to bring. The factory provided nothing but blue cotton sleeping mats. The first morning we awoke to the strains of the "Cuckoo Waltz." At four-thirty! We ate breakfast and left for work at five. From the dorm to the factory took fifty minutes on foot. We formed four lines and marched there wearing our headbands and singing military songs. We had *tabi* socks and *geta* clogs on our feet. Of course, we wore our *monpe*. Each of us had one of those cloth air-raid helmets, and an emergency bag strapped across our chests like so many warriors. We didn't wear anything white, because that could have made us targets.

When we arrived in front of the factory we had morning assembly. A young military officer, a graduate of the military academy, maybe a captain, gave a speech of admonishment, something like, "You will be defeating America with these arms. Work to your utmost. Achieve your quota!" Then we all recited aloud the Imperial Precepts for Soldiers and Sailors. All I can remember now is "soldiers and sailors should consider loyalty their essential duty," but I used to know them all.

At six o'clock, we relieved the shift that had been on duty through the night. Those were the girls from the Nakamura School. The floor was muddy with the extra paste that always streamed off the drying boards. From above, steam, condensed into water droplets, fell on us. Each person was in charge of two drying boards. The paper dried very quickly, so you shuttled back and forth between them like a crab. If it got too dry then it would crack and fail the quality test. That was unforgivable, so we ran barefoot across the pasty floor.

I can't recall ever eating lunch. One very meticulous person kept a diary. According to her diary, we were so hungry that we ate our lunch at the same time we ate breakfast, since that was so spare. We worked twelve hours straight—no breaks except to go to the toilet, which was outside the factory building. It was filthy. There was no electricity, even at night, and no lights because of the blackout. Most of us tried not to go there if possible.

During the night shift we got a special issue of two rice balls at midnight. We were happy to have them. We ate them standing. At that moment, the machinery stopped briefly. We were also given two white tablets. Some thought they were nourishment pills. Others thought they were pep pills. You only got those tablets on the night shift. Later I heard that at Kyushu Imperial University they were experimenting with tablets to keep pilots awake, and we were being used to test them. One thing was sure, we didn't get sleepy when we took them. When we couldn't complete our quota we had to stay longer. I don't recall how many we had to do, but I do remember running and running and then just meeting my target. Gradually, the weaker girls fell behind.

When we returned to our dorm we gulped down our food, little as it was, and then rushed to take our bath, because it was bitter cold. The steam warmed the factory, but outside it was freezing. Besides, you marched back to the dorm in damp clothes, gusts of wind tearing at you. The bath was pretty large. I was usually one of the first ones there, which meant I usually had enough hot water.

There were about ten people in my group. I don't even remember who they were. I can only remember the girl next to me. That's how exhausted we were. We had sweet potatoes that were sometimes old and had turned black and smelled strange mixed in with rice. You got one rice bowl full of that and one cup of *miso* soup, nothing added. No vegetables, nothing. It wasn't enough food to sustain us at the work we had to do.

We changed shifts on Sunday. All day on Sunday we slept like corpses. It was washday, too. Our *monpe* were rigid with paste. The laundry had a roof but no walls. It was completely exposed, bitter cold, and the water was cold, too. Sometimes our families came to visit, but left having seen only our sleeping faces. I had four younger ones at home. My mother told me she wouldn't be able to come to visit me. I understood. Our parents worried and tried to send food. When one of our neighbors came, my mother gave her sweet bean cakes for me. I was so happy that I still remember the taste of them, seasoned with salt from my tears.

We did our best. Our spirit was in it, but whenever we got messages or packages from home, we always broke down. In the beginning, we shared things which came from the families, but gradually, even when you thought you ought to share, you just couldn't. There were closets on both sides of the room. Girls would put their heads into the closet and start eating. You just stopped caring about other people.

We didn't have any newspapers. No radio. We didn't even hear the news announcements made by Imperial General Headquarters. We just pasted paper. The balloon bombs we made were launched from Chiba or Miyagi prefectures. They rose up into the jet stream and were carried across the Pacific Ocean to the west coast of North America. When seasonal winds died down in March it was difficult to launch them, so our work at Kokura stopped at the end of February. I was there only two months. By then, we were out of materials. There was no paper. Not even any *konnyaku* for paste.

When the war ended, we felt that what we had done, all that effort, everything we had suffered, had been in vain. I was overwhelmed by a sense of emptiness. I didn't really want to think about the days we spent there. There wasn't anything good to remember.

The book into which I placed my will turned up thirty years later when my parents' home was about to be rebuilt. My mother brought it to me and said, "We just found this," with an expression of shock on her face. It seemed almost indecent to me. I threw it away. I'd written, "I'll go to the Kokura Arsenal and do my best for the sake of the nation." I had asked my parents, "Please forgive me for going [dying] early." Finding that will was a terrible embarrassment. It reminded me of how I'd been.

We only learned some forty years later that the balloon bombs we made had actually reached America. They started a few forest fires and inflicted some casualties, among them children. Five children and a woman killed on a picnic in Oregon in May 1945 when a bomb dropped earlier exploded. When I heard that, I was stunned. I made those weapons. Until then, I had felt only that our youth had been stolen from us, and that I'd missed my chance to study. I thought we were victims of the war.

Some of us got together and felt we would like to organize an effort to apologize. I started with my classmates, but encountered strong resistance. They didn't want to think of themselves as victimizers. America dropped bombs on us, atomic bombs on Hiroshima and Nagasaki. If you are going to talk about victimizers, some said, it should be those who led us. I was deeply disappointed. There are alumnae of the balloon-bomb factories all over Japan and the experience has too often been beautified —young girls doing their utmost for the sake of the nation, toiling with all their energy to make secret weapons. Too many of us don't want to look back on what that means.

Forced Labor

AHN JURETSU

Korea became an important source of labor for a Japan desperately short of the manpower needed for its war effort. With enhanced authority from the National Service Draft Ordinance of 1939, Japanese officials rounded up large numbers of workers. Reportedly between 670,000 and 1,000,000 men were brought from Korea to Japan during the war to work in coal mines, on construction sites, and at other difficult tasks throughout the country. An unknown number of women were also pressed into service in Japan and throughout the Empire, in many cases forced to become "comfort women," working in primitive brothels to serve the Japanese troops and administrators from Manchuria to the islands of the East Indies.

Seventy, Ahn Juretsu looks very frail, but his voice is forceful and loud. He has severe difficulty hearing due to injuries sustained during the war when he was enrolled in labor service for the government that had annexed his native Korea in 1910.

Korea was a colony. No human rights at all. We were just the same as slaves. You have a mouth, but can't say what you want. You have a mind and a body, but can't think or do what you want. I'm from Chūsei Hokudō, in the middle of what's today South Korea. Because we were farmers under Japanese government control, the conditions of our lives were so poor, you can't imagine it. Just like beggars today. Out of about eighty households in my hamlet, only three children went to Korean elementary school. The school fees were sixty *sen* per month. We couldn't afford that. I went to school for three years, but had to drop out. Even at that, I didn't go into the first grade until I was thirteen.

I then went to work in Keijō, Seoul today, and got a job in a spinning plant. Managed by Japanese. There were exams to get in. They didn't normally hire ordinary people, but those from my province had a reputation as good workers. You entered the plant at seven A.M. and worked to seven P.M., all for seventeen *sen*. Japanese—even women—who patrolled the plant in white hats, earned two yen a day. In those days, an egg cost one *sen*. For seventeen eggs I worked all day long, covered in oil.

It was 1940, the time of the twenty-six-hundredth anniversary of the founding of the Japanese Empire. I remember singing songs about that. But rapidly the war got worse. For the first time, they called for volunteer soldiers, Korean soldiers. I was the eldest son. I thought, if I die, my whole family will be extinguished. I tried to quit my job at the plant, but they wouldn't let me leave. I had to have my parents send a telegram saying one of them had died before they let me go. I was seventeen. I returned to my province and got a job mining gold, tunneling into the mountain with a chisel and hammer. If you worked in a gold mine in those days, everyone thought you were as good as dead. You never knew when a shaft would collapse on you, but you made sixty *sen* a day.

When the Greater East Asia War began in 1941, the state considered iron and coal more crucial than gold, so the mine was closed. If you didn't have a job in the countryside, you were rounded up as conscript labor, and taken off to Japan. There were cases where the police grabbed a man in the middle of rice-planting—went right into the paddies and dragged him away. The police knew I'd been let go from the gold mine, so they came and told me I'd been drafted for Japan. We were hauled off to the provincial capital. In front of the provincial office, the governor made a big speech: "I want you men to go to Japan. Work for His Imperial Highness. Lay down your lives."

That's how we got here. That was 1942. Six hundred Korean youths, put on a train from Shimonoseki, the windows nailed shut so we couldn't get out. All the way north to Aomori we went. When we wanted to take a piss, they wouldn't even let us go to the toilet. "Piss off the rear platform," they told us. We had to stand there on the moving train doing our business while they held on to our sash.

We were put in an "inn" at Aomori, prior to boarding the boat for Hakodate on Hokkaido. It was equipped with everything needed to treat us like criminals, wired shut once you got in. No escape possible. People who looked and acted like today's *yakuza* came to meet us. They dragged us off to Ken'nenbetsu, where they were building a naval airfield. We were assigned to what was called the Hirano-gumi Construction Company. They never gave us an address. Never. We were just "Airfield Construction Unit X."

The governor's farewell speech was grand, but when we got here, things were completely different. We were beaten up every day. Knocked around brutally. They'd shout. *"Bangō!"* More than half of us didn't know any Japanese because they'd never been to school, didn't know it meant "Count off," didn't know what that was anyway. When nobody did anything, they'd beat us mercilessly. I'd had a little school, so I could understand a bit.

The next day, all our luggage was taken from us. "To be put in storage," they said. "You'll be here for three years. We'll give it back then." We arrived in about April, but it was still bitter cold up there. The north winds blew in from the Chishima Islands. They didn't let us wear more than a pair of shorts; they said, "You'll run away if you're dressed." Everyone worked shivering with cold. We first leveled the ground. Digging into the hills and filling the depressions. We carried the dirt, huge heaps of dirt. Next we laid down volcanic ash and stones, then covered it with asphalt. Our hands were rubbed raw. It was a rush job. Planes from America were coming! Japan had to be ready to launch planes, too! A year's work had to be done in three months. I tell you, we were made to slave there. If you treated men humanely, doing that kind of work that quickly was impossible. The *oyakata* had swords hanging from their belts, and pistols, too. They were our overseers and the top bosses. For the smallest thing, they'd pull out their swords and wave them threateningly. We were all terrified. The rest of the "staff" had whips. They're the ones who beat us. I can't tell you how painful that was!

We didn't have shoes. They gave us straw sandals. Three sets. You put one on your feet, tied the others to your belt. When you got back at night they'd all be gone—used up. You ran around madly—beaten, whipped, pushing and carrying earth and rocks. The winds of Hokkaido were really strong. It was foggy in the morning; then the dust swirled around us, blackening our faces. On our way from our barracks to the site and back again, we shouldered our shovels and had to sing military songs. They beat us if our voices weren't robust enough. "Thinking about escaping, are you?" they'd scream.

When we got back to the barracks, there was a physical inspection to check if we had stolen anything. We were only wearing shorts. You wouldn't even treat criminals that badly. At night, at dinner time, they made us sing, "A drop of water is a drop of heaven and earth. A grain of rice is a gift from the gods." Then we had to express our thanks for what we were about to eat: *"Itadakimasu."* They scooped up one rice bowl worth of rice and dumped it out onto a plate. And a piece of pickle. No soup. Nothing else. They fed us like this and yet we worked. Even friends couldn't recognize each other's faces, that's how thin we were growing.

At the bath, they'd yell, "Change!" and you'd run to climb in. From the second you were in you waited, crouched down, ready to leap out on command. They beat you if you were even an instant too slow. Nobody knew what they wanted. Just do it—Now! At night, when we slept, we put down our straw mats and then spread out our *futon* head to head, separated only by a space enough for one staff member in heavy work boots and carrying a wooden sword to pass through. If we talked to each other they beat us with that stick. "What are you saying? Damn you!"

Many died. Couldn't take it. Too little to eat. Nothing to wear. Just work. If you didn't have a strong hold on life, you couldn't survive. Within a year, in just our barracks, where a hundred and thirty or forty were housed, more than thirty died. In the morning, we'd see someone lying there, groaning, "It hurts! Hurts! *Idai, idai!*" When we returned in the evening he'd be gone. In Hokkaido, there were many woods, everywhere, so they just dug a shallow hole and threw the body in. Not even a telegram to their families to tell them they'd died.

Letters? They gave us a "model letter" and told us to send one exactly like the example every sixth month. It said, "I'm eating well. My stomach is full of rice. They pay us as they promised. There's no place as good as this. I'm happy I was born." That kind of crap. We had to write that. Then they put them in envelopes, but I don't know if they ever mailed them. If you wrote even the tiniest bit of criticism, you'd be beaten until you were practically dead.

I was almost killed twice. I thought of escaping constantly. Because of school, I knew some geography, the shape of Hokkaido. I was sort of a leader. I talked only to those whose feelings I knew were like mine. Conspiring. Deciding how to escape and where we should go. One night we promised each other we'd make an attempt and set the date. The very next day they discovered our plan. They gave one of our "friends" an easier job. His friends had trusted him. Yet he squealed on us.

They put me at the clearing just inside the entrance where everybody could see me. They gave me no food, beat me, and speared me with wooden swords. There was no one to stop them. Nobody tried. I was half-dead. Then they put a straw mat over me and poured water on it. Everybody thought I was dead. Someone told me later, "In the morning you started breathing again." It was awful.

Another time the same thing—no, worse—happened to me. We were digging up volcanic ash. We were told we'd soon be getting on a truck and if we had any short pants or trousers in our stored luggage, they'd get them for us. I had pants from the gold mine that I told them I wanted. In one pocket I had ten yen in Korean money. I didn't even remember it. When we underwent our physical inspection that night, one of the staff bastards found it. "What's this? You hid money for your escape! You sonofabitch!" They dragged me off again and beat me until both ears swelled up the size of my fists. They didn't take me to a doctor. No medicine. "It's all right if a bastard like you dies. A Korean? Two Koreans? Worth less than a dog!" That's what the overseers said. I lost much of my hearing then.

At the site of the airfield, you pushed earth. If they paired up a weak man with a strong one, the cart would flip over. Then they'd beat you. Let's say the cart in front and in back crash together, catching someone in between. If your leg was broken, they'd murder you. "We're not going to feed you for three or four months for nothing." We'd come back from the worksite and they'd be gone. We knew they were dead.

Wages? They didn't pay us anything. When we left Korea we were told we'd be paid one and a half yen. We never saw even one day's wages. They gave us a ration of tobacco. One pack of Minori brand loose tobacco. But you couldn't smoke when you wanted to. You had no source of fire. When the staff issued the order, "Smoke tobacco!" everyone rushed to light their pipes on the one bright shining coal they gave us. More than a hundred men tried with that one bit. If you weren't quick and smart, you couldn't smoke even when they let you.

I finally escaped in 1943. Because our place was a construction barracks it had thick board walls, almost like concrete, and the latrine had spikes at the bottom, to keep you from escaping that way. Some people had actually leapt down and tried to swim out through the shit. I was always looking for a way to escape. We had no tools, but whenever I went to the toilet—I went there only for that—I looked to find a place to dig my way out. One night, I found it. I dug and dug, finally making a hole big enough to get through. All in one night. I had a friend I'd shared all my hardship with. I wanted to bring him along. I went and woke him up. It turned out he, too, had a friend. Twenty of us ended up breaking out together.

It was about one or two o'clock. The staff were asleep. They'd spent all day beating us up, so they were exhausted. We stole everything hanging in their room, from clothes to pocket watches. We knew that if we were all together, we'd be caught and wouldn't come back alive, so once outside, we separated.

I slept in the mountains by day and walked at night. Most of the food I ate was potatoes. It was after the October potato harvest, so I'd dig them out from where they were stored, make a fire, and bake them. I ate pumpkins too. Hokkaido pumpkins taste real good. I walked for seven days, taking the railway tracks, since I thought they'd catch me along the roads. I sold the watch and got some money. I knew this rail line would eventually take me to Hakodate. But I was really lucky. Along the track I found a ticket. It was for Osaka! Someone must have dropped it when they were in the train's toilet. That's what saved me. My fate.

I reached Umeda station in Osaka. It must have been obvious I was a worker. I was carrying a bundle of the clothes I'd taken when I escaped. A man came up to me immediately and asked if I'd like to work, so I got a job at the Sakurajima Hitachi Shipyard. Quite a few American POWs had been hauled there to work. I found myself working side-by-side with them. They had numbers painted on the backs of their shirts. We were making pipes and fittings for ships, filling the pipes with sand, heating them, and then bending them to shape. The American prisoners were really pitiful. I felt sorry for them. But they never said they were going to lose. "What you think about Japan?" I asked. They answered only, "Japan hate. Little food. Much work." They said, "America will come to free us."

When I gave one a cigarette, he said, "Thank you, thank you." If I'd been caught I'd have been beaten. I had a friend there, also Korean. We used to tell them, "Not Japanese. Korean. Korean." They didn't seem to understand, so I drew a map. Pointed to Korea. That they seemed to understand. We shook hands.

Air raids began in Osaka. I thought I might be killed by planes if I stayed in the city, so I went to Gunma, where my uncle was doing some kind of subcontracting, and got work. One night I was in Takasaki City when we were hit by an air raid. I learned then just how frightening they were. I ran to the Buddhist temple in the middle of the night. That's where I met the end of the war. That raid was on the night of August 14, 1945.

When Japan lost I was so happy. I jumped up and down, thinking, "I'm going back home to my own country!" I went to Shimonoseki the next year, intending to take a boat home, but I met a man I knew who'd gone back, only to return. He told me, "Don't go back to South Korea. It's even worse than here. Syngman Rhee has returned. It's all controlled by America. First we suffered as a Japanese colony. Now we're becoming an American colony." So I decided not to go. I thought, "I'll oppose American control of the Republic of Korea." Even now I cannot go to the Republic of Korea. I believe Koreans should handle Korea. Americans and Russians, get your hands off Korea! That's what I've thought.

As soon as Ahn leaves the room to meet a bus bringing his granddaughter home from nursery school, his wife, Ezure Setsu, a Japanese woman he met after the war, who has sat quietly throughout the interview, begins to speak in a low voice, but with an almost startling intensity:

"Even today, my husband is not yet allowed to go to South Korea. He's one of 348 executive committee members of the General Federation of Korean Residents in Japan [Chōsen Sōren] and he can't go home unless the country's reunited. He's worked for that his whole life. His ideology is North, but his home is in the South.

"When we quarrel, have differences of opinion, I sometimes feel he thinks of me as a 'Japanese bitch'—just one of them—that's why he causes me so much trouble. No matter how hard I work at our pachinko shops, all he says is 'it's for the sake of the organization.' He never says 'for the sake of the family.' I never went to bed before two A.M. I rose before six. I had to save money to honor the checks he wrote, sometimes six months to a year in advance! I adjusted and set the pins in the pachinko machines myself. For thirty-five years I never took a day off. All I wanted was to have a leisurely sleep just once. We never saved any money. He always took what we had. Because I'm Japanese, he's getting revenge, that's what I think sometimes.

"I'm still a Japanese in my residency registration, but I've lived with my husband now for almost forty years. I think of him as if I were a Korean myself. I want to take him to his motherland, even if I must hold his hand to guide him. Sometimes he says he will live only two or three years more. I encourage him, 'Your mother is still there,' I say, but if he

dies here, I will gather all his ashes, every bit, and take them to his motherland."

Poison-Gas Island

NAKAJIMA YOSHIMI

Okunoshima is a small island in the Inland Sea in Hiroshima prefecture. It was selected in 1927 by the Japanese army to house a plant to manufacture various types of poison gas. It was easy to maintain security on the island, and its isolation from surrounding towns by water was considered important in the event of accidents. The several families who had lived there were evacuated to make room. Okunoshima was Japan's only plant for large-scale poison gas production. When manufacture of gas munitions was stepped up at the onset of war with China in 1937, the gas was also taken elsewhere to be put into munitions. The facilities on Okunoshima expanded rapidly between 1938 and 1940, employing up to six thousand workers. Secrecy surrounding Okunoshima was extremely tight. Indeed, the island itself was removed from Japanese maps in 1938, leaving only blank sea, and it did not reappear officially until 1947. *

Nakajima Yoshimi is now eighty-two years old. His thin, almost bare-boned body lies on a bed in a small room he shares with three other patients in Tadanoumi Hospital, the only facility in Japan that treats diseases caused by poison gas. About twenty like him are hospitalized here. Many more visit as outpatients. He suffers from chronic bronchitis because of his years making poison gas. The first conversation with Mr. Nakajima was cut short by a fit of coughing.

The next day is a "good day" for him. It seems to take his whole strength to voice his thoughts and he strains in a harsh voice. It is extremely difficult to hear what he says, yet he wants to talk. He refers knowingly to production processes that he does not have the energy to fully explain to an outsider. His wife very quietly passes Kleenex tissues to him whenever he needs them.

I was really happy when I started that job. When I was hired, I didn't know exactly what I was going to do. Didn't know much about poison gas. There was little work around because of a recession, and this was a

---

* Japanese poison-gas production is not widely covered, but is the subject of Takeda Eiko, *Chizu kara kesareta shima Okunoshima* [*Okunoshima, the Island Wiped from the Map*] (Tokyo: Domesu Shuppan, 1987).

job which would last as long as the Imperial Army lasted. So I went to the island.

We made suffocating gas, mustard gas, tear gas, and asphyxiating gas there. One breath of that last one and you were dead. We knew which we'd be making by the raw materials. Hydrochloric acid, sulfuric acid, table salt. There was a place called "the chamber," a glass-enclosed room, where you actually worked with the gas. I was mainly engaged in the making of yperite, a mustard gas. This gas was persistent, meaning it didn't disperse easily. When we made it, we had to wear complete protective suits—"octopus suits," we called them. They were unbearable in summer.

The air in the chamber was supposed to be kept clean by an exhaust system, but the poison was really strong. It corroded the fan, which often broke down. When it wasn't working, the chamber was full of gas. Even when you were wearing gas masks, you inhaled some. Even with rubber gloves, suits, and trousers on, gas got in through the cracks or joints and reached the skin.

When they were blowing, those fans made a tremendous sound of rushing wind as air was evacuated from the factory building. When the air pressure was down and the clouds were low, that air hung over the island. If it rained, the exhaust fell to the ground. The pine trees behind the mustard-gas factory withered and died.

From 1937 to 1944, I worked here. Nearly seven years in Chamber A-2. About twenty of us were making mustard gas. We really had no time off. No Saturdays or Sundays. Twelve hours a day. Sometimes I had to work through the night. We couldn't take a day off unless the doctor excused us. This wasn't voluntary. It was by order of the big shots. The head of the factory was a colonel. The Kempei were there, too. They even got into the same bath with us. It was a secret factory.

The production from Building A-4 was brought to the Vacuum Distillation Building and put into the tank there. It was a tall building off at one end. It was heated by burners, and the pumps started. When all three were going, the temperature in the tank would reach the point where the gas would begin to appear in tiny bubbles. A complete vacuum had to be achieved. If there was even the tiniest leak, we couldn't get anything done. They'd call out, "The vacuum's not working; Nakajima-san, please check it out," and I'd have to go into the chamber and examine it to find holes. I'd smear coal tar into any I located. I did this for them many times.

I got blisters on my hands and legs. Under a thin layer of skin, water built up. If you broke it, it was painfully sore for a long time. I'd go to the infirmary and they'd put on some talcum powder to treat it, but it didn't have much immediate effect. The skin was broken and blood and pus oozed out. The hardest thing about it was the chest cough the poison gas gave you. On top of that, sometimes at home the chest pain was terrible. Suddenly, I couldn't breathe! That happened four or five times. If I grabbed my pillow, sat up, and tightly clutched it to my chest and stretched, then I could breathe, just barely. If I took in bits of air very slowly, that is. I was young then, that's why I didn't die. Even when something like that happened, I went to the factory the next morning.

I went by bicycle to the station, by train to the boat, and by boat to the island. Five or six boats were lined up in rows in the little Tadanoumi harbor to take workers over. I don't know how many, maybe five thousand worked there. I got to work about eight o'clock. We all exercised to the radio, then went to the job assigned for that day. It could be laying in supplies or making product. That vacuum distillation process! There was large tank, taller than a man. A spiral tube enveloped it. It was very hot in there. I always wore a protective gas mask and suit. Stocking was the easiest job, since it was done outdoors. You might be given the job of separating gas from waste liquid. It looked like thick, dirty mud. The product was then filtered using four layers of glass, then put into a fifty-kilo drum, and then the inspector would come. Using test paper, he'd see if it passed.

In summer, when the temperature exceeded thirty degrees centigrade, the containers of Yellow Type-1 B would sometimes burst, so about ten of us would have to go there to release the gas that built up before that could happen. There was a rumor that this gas was taken to China. It's quite clear it was taken away somewhere. We who made it got blisters on our skin and the skin would sort of rot off, so I knew what would happen if it was used. The biggest blisters could be five or six centimeters across. The small ones were as big as the mark you leave when you push your finger on your arm.

My family knew what I was doing, although I had signed an oath of secrecy, saying that I would not tell even them. My skin was all rough and raw. Blood seeped out sometimes. Even internal organs were harmed. My face turned really dark, almost black. We wore gas masks, but . . .

Whenever I got on the train, even if the train was full, as soon as I came near, people moved away, giving up their seats. They thought I was a leper. They didn't know I worked at the factory. My testicles were really raw. It was like that all over my body.

We'd work in those masks and that suit, for up to two hours. Then we'd take a bath. What a wonderful bath! Big and deep. We ate in the factory dining hall. Lots of food. That's because it was a military factory.

Sometimes, we went to visit a shrine near Mishima. My body was damaged. It hurt to walk. I felt weak, coughed all the time. My face was black. My skin was peeling off, all over my body. I've still got patches left. Like this one under my arm. [*He pulls back his* yukata *to show a black scaly spot, about the size of a half dollar. It is hard to the touch.*] On my back too. They're black, rough.

When senior army leader General Hayashi Senjūrō came to visit the factory, two other workers and I showed him our hurt bodies. Took off our shirts to let him see. Those two died coughing up blood after the war. All the friends I worked with have died. Some had to have holes opened in their throats just to breathe.

When I did bonus work, I'd make two hundred yen. More than a school principal. When I made mustard gas, I'd get paid a "gas bonus." The pay increased for working the night shift. I'd buy everything with coupons at the factory store. Sweets and saké. Not real saké, synthetic, but in the town there was no sugar, nothing like that. So I never had much left when they handed out the cash.

I was on the China front as a soldier for a year. Then, in 1943, I went into training with a tank unit. Almost immediately they told me, "Go home. Your body's been wrecked by poison gas." They all went to Iwo Jima eventually. Gave up their lives there. I can't stop crying even now when I think about those men. Then I cough.

I got another call-up in 1944, and went to Hiroshima. Field artillery. Then ordnance school in Chiba. Then the war ended. We lined up to listen to the radio. To hear the Emperor's message, you know. I fainted. A couple of people carried me off. It really made me sad. We worked to win without rest. That's why we did it. Now, it was for nothing. All of it was meaningless.

Whenever I cough I remember all the terrible things.

It takes fifteen minutes by boat from a harbor near the hospital to reach the island of Okunoshima. Today the island is a resort, dotted with tennis courts, bicycle paths, palm trees, and an unpretentious four-story "people's inn." Many signs give directions to fishing sites and campgrounds, but none show where the remaining gas-storage buildings or the electric relay station may be. There is a Poison Gas Archive, newly opened to public, but there are no visitors. Even the attendant is absent. A postal-savings passbook, belonging to Nakajima Yoshimi, is displayed in a glass case. Brown with age, it records his purchase of war bonds and shows a cap on the cash withdrawals permitted. One gas worker's uniform and several pieces of broken equipment are also on display.

9 / WIELDING PEN AND CAMERA

Filming the News

ASAI TATSUZŌ

"Whenever I go to the memorial hall at Yasukuni, I see so many statues and displays of people I filmed. I find myself saying, 'I got him. Him too! A lot of them.' It's pretty hard on me. I went to every battlefront over nine years of war. My camera and film were rifle and bullets for me. But all the film I took was seized by MacArthur. Eventually, the United States returned them to us, and now the films are stored at the National Film Center, or someplace. But they won't let us see them. The Japanese officials say they don't have enough money to show them, but that's just bureaucratic bullshit. Those are the people's films. They have no right to keep them from the public."

His long white hair falls onto his shoulders. Tall and thin, he exudes the aura of an artist. He often illustrates a story by holding up a phantom camera and panning or changing angles with his hands.

When the China Incident broke out I covered Japan for MGM, but Hearst's Metro-Tone News show *News of the Day* was our main customer. We were damn busy, sending in one or two stories a week, covering everything from the fall of governments to train wrecks—anything just to introduce Japan—but since we worked for a foreign news service, we weren't allowed to follow the army to China. After the Marco Polo Bridge Incident of July 7, 1937, Dōmei News, Asahi News, Yomiuri News, and all others began offering nationwide coverage of the events in North China. We had to ask for dupes from the other services and then sent those on to our office in America.

In August 1937, when the story jumped to Shanghai, news people went crazy trying to cover the war. Dōmei News Agency was so new that they didn't have any veterans, just regular still photographers trying to carry around movie cameras in Shanghai. When they asked me if I'd join them, I jumped at the chance. I spent the next six years based in Shanghai.

I went everywhere. It was incredible, I can tell you. I flew with bombers about ten times as they attacked Chungking. I got Wang Ching-wei when he fled from there, before he became president of Japanese-occupied China. I even covered the battles of the unit I'd have been called up to serve in if I'd stayed in Tokyo. That was the Kanō Unit from Tokyo. It was the first to land at Shanghai and had a terrible time. Two days after I went to their headquarters to cover them, Commander Kanō himself was killed. It was a real shock to me.

A large number of special correspondents soon arrived—reporters, photographers, movie-news people. I had to send home at least two or three reels a week, and Shanghai was a stalemate. The lines didn't move for four months. For days, weeks, men couldn't move. Often, when soldiers were waiting to go forward to relieve those in the trenches, they'd tell you something like, "God, I love sushi." Or they'd speak about home. That's all they cared about. Sometimes they'd ask, "Are we winning this war?" They often asked me to come over and sit with them awhile. Under conditions like those, they had no idea what was going on.

Shanghai itself was a jungle of concrete. Long, low tenement houses were everywhere. If you went into the alleys between them you'd be shot, so the soldiers broke through the inner walls, room by room, in order to move forward. My camera and I went with them. Once, I went into an alley, crossed the street in order to shoot them coming from the vantage point of the other side. The enemy was shooting at me from ten feet away. I got a good shot of bullets hitting the brick wall right next to me. Then the naval landing force I was covering came out through the wall, carrying a heavy machine gun, and opened up. *"Bam, bam, bam, bam, bam!"* The bullets were slamming into the wall over my head. I realized then that the enemy soldiers were just above me, shooting back at the marines. My camera was pointing at our troops. I got wonderful shots, taken from the enemy side. They were real. I was actually over there *on* the enemy side. Later I turned cold just thinking about it. I didn't know anything. That's the only reason I could do it.

I followed that famous Nishizumi Armored Unit, of movie fame. Tank Commander Nishizumi was named a war god for his bravery. I went right to the front with them. You dug a foxhole under the tracks of your tank and slept there. Then, even if a mortar were fired at you, you wouldn't be hit. You gradually learned how to deal with such situations if you were at the front long enough. Cameramen fresh at the front, covering troops for the first time, often got killed. They didn't know how to stay alive.

I was once on my way back to Shanghai after a battle, when I came to a field hospital at the mouth of a tributary of the Yangtze. As we passed in our car, I saw a wounded soldier squatting down on his heels looking like "The Thinker." He was dressed in hospital white. It was evening. I was just returning from horrific combat. The tranquillity struck me. I wanted to capture it on film. As I got closer, I saw that a destroyer was leaving the port. The soldier was watching it go. Waves from the ship's wake lapped the shore by his feet. I took a shot showing that soldier looking out across the river, the destroyer in the distance. Then I shot the wave and panned to the soldier's face. I sent nearly a hundred feet back to Japan. You could have put an antiwar caption on that! Just as it was. I didn't have to ask the soldier how he was feeling. I just took the shot and left. The head of the moving picture division raved, "Asai, you sent the greatest footage I've ever seen! Everybody else just turns in war scenes. It's not that I don't want to use your film, I just don't know how." I heard they finally showed just a brief cut on the news, but I still remember it.

Back home, people were desperate for news from the front. They formed long lines to get into the news movie theaters that showed only newsreels, just war, but it was all *"Banzai, banzai!"*—just emotion. I didn't take that kind of film myself, though I'm not denying its value. For example, in *The Soochow Operation,* the soldiers in the most advanced unit go in and occupy the city. Then those who come in later go to the city gate and raise cheers. For a still photo, that might be OK, but I wouldn't have staged anything for my pictures. I wanted to show only what the camera saw objectively. That's what I call "news." It's my bad habit!

I marched from Shanghai to Nanking with the troops, carrying my camera. It weighed roughly thirty kilograms. Not too bad for those days. It was an Aimo, a hand-held job made by Bell and Howell. Real good. Nothing like that in Japan then. I repaired it myself when the mainspring broke. We used Fuji Film. I shot only the film I wanted to shoot. I even wrote my own captions. I was often able to decide the cuts and their order.

But you know, when the fighting was really heavy, you couldn't even look out of the trenches. Once I crossed a creek, crawled through the trenches, and peeked over the edge of a parapet. All I could see was a swath of ground covered with the corpses of Japanese soldiers. They'd risen from the trench at the command "Charge!" and been mowed down by enemy fire in a moment. You couldn't even recover their bodies. If soldiers received the order "Advance!" they had to go. No choice. I was a cameraman. I could say no, stay behind. I just couldn't let my camera roll on that scene. All those Japanese bodies! I took shots of the soldiers crossing the bridge over the creek later, but you can't really direct your camera at the corpses of your own kind. Even if you did, you couldn't show that. Don't you agree?

I didn't really shoot pictures of Chinese corpses either, though there were hundreds of them. I was there at Nanking. At the time of the Nanking Massacre. I didn't go out to take pictures. I never saw them killing, but I saw the corpses. More than several hundred. A lot more. But I didn't film them. You couldn't have shown them, either.

Just before the Pacific War broke out, I was called back to Tokyo to be a member of the Navy's press corps. As early as October I knew war was coming. By November, the cameramen from Shanghai were already being transferred to the South. They showed me the funny paper money they'd been given, bills from the places the army was going to land. All over Southeast Asia.

Everybody got so excited at the news of the attack on Pearl Harbor! The senior cameraman, Ueda Isamu, who'd returned from Hollywood, didn't think it was so good. "Listen, Asai," he told me, "America won't take it this way for long. They'll really do something." The soldiers didn't know America, but I'd worked for MGM, so I had some idea. I thought I might not come back alive this time. I was twenty-seven. I didn't get married then because I didn't want to make anyone a widow. I went everywhere with my camera. Singapore, Sumatra, New Guinea. I even met Prince Takamatsu twice.

We knew a lot about the war situation. We learned we were gradually losing. It was after Midway that things got bad. Before that operation, I was in Sumatra. Someone told me, "Planes are being transferred," so I wangled my way onto one. Something must be up. We flew back to the Homeland, but then we kept on going north, to Paramushiro Island, near Soviet Kamchatka, then with a scouting mission flew over Attu and Kiska in the Aleutians. When I went out, the plan for the invasion of Midway was being implemented in the Central Pacific. When I got back, everyone looked so deflated. So glum. The staff officers at headquarters kept saying, "This is terrible. A disaster."

Staff officers hardly ever went out to the front themselves. It was a real event when they did. Usually they just sat with their legs apart, looking tough, engaging in desktop strategizing in Tokyo. The army especially was like that. They'd land thousands of men somewhere, but there'd be no supplies coming from the rear. "Use local requisitioning," they'd order them. The local people would be growing barely enough to feed themselves, and here would come thousands of Japanese to take away what the natives had. It was that kind of armchair strategy! Those staff officers didn't do a single thing good.

I was in Rabaul for about a year and a half, assigned to the 705th Air Unit. I went on bombing missions. I flew to New Guinea. I saw planes hit around me. I didn't really film our planes going down, though. Only once, a plane in our formation catching fire and going down wreathed in flames. I sent that film in separately, about a hundred feet of it, wrapped in red tape, indicating it was secret. I was told it was forwarded to the air office of the Munitions Ministry, where it was used for research into where our planes caught fire.

The film I most remember taking was the last footage of Admiral Yamamoto Isoroku. He came out to Rabaul. It was his first trip there and it became his last trip, too. Even our headquarters didn't know his plane had been shot down until the announcement was made in Tokyo. I couldn't send back the film I'd taken by an ordinary flight. The last film of the navy commander-in-chief? What if it got lost? I thought I'd better take it myself, but we weren't allowed to leave the airfield or say anything. I sat tight, holding onto my film. After two weeks or so I was told by the base commander, "Go ahead, Asai. We'll give you a plane." I flew straight to Tokyo. We put out a newsreel, *The State Funeral of Yamamoto Isoroku.* My footage of the living admiral was played just before the footage of his funeral. I took about four hundred feet, maybe four minutes of thirty-five millimeter. Isoroku arrives at the airfield by car. Base commander is waiting for him. He gets out of his car. He goes to the site of the ceremony. The attacking unit waits for him. The unit takes off, Yamamoto cheers them off, waving his hat. I actually had a meal with him. Sat just a few meters away. But he never came back, like so many of the other fliers there at Rabaul.

Dōmei News Agency was disbanded and dissolved by the Occupation soon after the end of the war, and I went to work under the U.S. Signal Corps. I was assigned to film the Tokyo War Crimes Trials, the International Military Tribunal Far East. I was there for three years, from the time they started to build the courtroom in Ichigaya. I thought the Tokyo trial was just victor's justice, a monkey play, a kangaroo court. They didn't even mention they'd dropped the atomic bombs. But the news reports shouldn't reflect your feelings. People who watch the news should reach their own conclusions about what's going on. That's the way it should be, isn't it? I tried.

War Correspondent

HATA SHŌRYŪ

We meet in a noisy room on the ninth floor of the Press Club in central Tokyo. He is in a dark-blue pin-striped "power suit." His postwar career included time as the Asahi Shimbun's *Moscow correspondent, chief editor at its Osaka head office, and a member of the board of directors.*

Asahi Shimbun, one of Japan's most prestigious papers, dispatched about six hundred reporters to the war areas and had sixty casualties among them. The paper's circulation was two million during the war years.

I was ecstatic when I was hired by the *Asahi* in 1936 on my second try. I grew up reading it and loved the tone of its editorials. They'd warned voters in 1928, at the time of the first election with universal manhood suffrage, "Don't be deceived by the government authorities." My father was so proud to be voting. When the authorities rounded up the left-wing scholars and politicians soon thereafter, I knew from the paper's democratic tone that terrible things were being done, so I too was critical. At the time of the Manchurian Incident of 1931, a group of us at school produced our own four-page newsletter which mimicked the *Asahi*'s "nonexpansionist" line, and at the Osaka Foreign Language Institute, I again took my cue from the paper and felt I must oppose the growth of fascism in Japan. I was a cub reporter assigned to the Nada branch office in Kobe when I got my call-up for active military duty in January 1937. I joined my regiment in Manchuria for basic training, returned to Japan for officer-candidate school, and went to the China front. I was there until 1939. After a period training recruits in Kanazawa, I was released in August 1940 and rejoined the *Asahi*.

I was shocked on returning to find the newspaper so wholeheartedly supporting the war. They were ultranationalistic! The atmosphere of the paper was more jingoistic and militaristic than what I'd experienced in the military itself as a first lieutenant in the cavalry. The views they held on the Emperor are an example. We in the military didn't really think about the Emperor in any complicated way, but in the newspaper, they were stone-headed about the *Kokutai*, the "National Polity." The newspaper also conducted activities to raise contributions for military aircraft, solicited poems and songs, and composed patriotic marches. I can't say I really had any views critical of the war at that time, but I wasn't charging full speed ahead, either.

After my return from the front, I was still able to write pretty freely at the local office in Shimonoseki. Censorship of articles really began only after the start of the Pacific War. Newspaper circulation grew greatly with the war. Each newspaper company competed keenly with the others in reporting the war. "Extra! Extra!" was the newsdealer's constant shout. The extras were called "Never-to-be-published-again-extra" since the news that appeared in them didn't appear in the regular daily papers. That practice had started even back after the Manchurian Incident, as competition in reporting news fast became more severe. *Asahi* had its own planes. They flew to the south, too. How speedily news could be reported from the battlefront was crucial. The technology for speedy news reporting developed with the war.

All the newspapers published local papers in the occupied areas, dividing them up into spheres. The *Asahi* published *Java News* in Javanese; *Yomiuri* published *Burma News* in Burmese. The *Nichi-Nichi* and the Dōmei News wire service did the same thing. These were intended to lead the people in the new territories. In this sense, newspapers were at one with the nation and the army.

When the war was going at full tilt, the authorities had the fewest complaints with the *Asahi*, so we became the model for all the others. Of course, our own inspection division examined articles before they ever reached the military to ensure that they didn't break the rules. This wasn't the section for editorial revisions, mind you, but was set up to deal with things *before* they could get the paper in trouble with the Home Ministry. This was the same thing as self-censorship and was set up immediately after the Pacific War broke out. It existed at all the newspapers.

I was sent to the Rangoon office in 1943 and was in the south for *Asahi* until the end of the war. I was probably freer than the correspondents assigned directly to the army and navy; they were really considered to be in the service, even though their pay came from their newspaper. At the branch office we had good food, so those other correspondents often came to our place to eat well. We had *go*, mah jongg, and *shōgi*, and we had a car. They might have a military car assigned to them, but we had our own. Otherwise, things weren't too different for us. We, too, wore khaki-colored trousers. Everyone in Japan was wearing khaki in those days.

While we could contact local people, it was rare to reach the point where we could actually trust each other. There were good people, of course. One who taught Japanese language was honest and beseeched us, "Frankly speaking, the Japanese Army liberated us, but now they're pushing horrible things on us." I didn't report that.

It is often said that the navy had a broader view than the army, while within the army, the cavalry had a broader view than the regular infantry. Well, the air forces had a broader view than either. The Fifth Air Division, which I covered, was very concrete about things. Victory and defeat for air units were determined by altitude, speed, and firepower. No matter how much you asserted *bushidō* there, if you didn't have the speed you couldn't escape or overtake your opponent. Japan lost because it didn't have any of them. They tried hard and fought well, but they didn't have what it took. I wrote about that, and I was really scolded by the paper's East Asia Division chief. "Hata, what's the matter with your articles? You always talk about altitude, speed, and firepower. You're only writing about numbers. But true combat power is arms multiplied by fighting spirit. If one of them is infinitely strong, you will succeed." But if you wrote only about the Yamato Spirit, then the front-line soldiers would have said, "Mr. Hata, you shouldn't write such stupid things." On the front lines, they were witnessing the war, and they could see everyone was dying.

The Fifth Air Division strongly opposed the Imphal Operation to invade India in 1944. The division commander, Tazoe, went to Singapore to present his objections to the Third Air Corps commander. The operation would be reckless, and even success would be problematical. The Third Corps reported to the Imperial General Staff that the operation would be "difficult." But the government ordered it carried out anyway. I heard that, but I didn't report it. If I'd written it up, they wouldn't have mentioned those things to me anymore. They told me the air force had strong doubts about the operation, but it was "off the record." I was a young front-line reporter. I could have mentioned it to the head of our Asia Division, but I couldn't really have written it.

Although it was still early in 1944, first and second lieutenants in the field were already saying that they couldn't win this war, though they didn't say they would lose. Such thoughts weren't limited only to lieutenants. Even regimental commanders, staff officers at headquarters, and division commanders of the air corps knew. They trusted us reporters and told us everything, but we didn't write it in our papers. We only wrote articles as if we were winning. I learned later that word of this had even reached the ears of the Emperor, and that he questioned his staff, citing the concerns of the air-corps commander about Imphal, but he let the decision stand. Once decided, they all had to obey, so the area air forces threw all their efforts into it. Young men died one after the other.

When I look at my own articles today, I have a sense of shame about the terms I used. I described the Japanese planes as "land eagles" or "wild eagles." When they were shot down, I wrote "all the planes blew themselves up." I'm embarrassed by those things now, but as for the articles about the overall war situation under my byline, even looking at them today, I don't feel I have to crawl into a hole to hide.

Everyone there had Yamato Spirit, but with Yamato Spirit you couldn't create extra air speed. Captains, lieutenants would all be together at the mess tent prior to an operation. The next day nobody'd be there. They hadn't come back. We had days like that all the time. Yet they didn't look particularly sad. Maybe it was the education in those times. When the men went into combat, the Spitfires and P-51s met them. They were knocked down almost immediately. Some fighters were just gone; some landed in the mountains and the valleys across the border. Some crews came back on foot. Units were often below half strength.

I observed this process of defeat. The closer you got to the front, the less often you found a burning and unflinching belief in victory. The further away you were, the greater the arrogant confidence. This was true of newspapers, too. The people in the main office were the most arrogant. It may not be a nice thing to say, but it is important. We were in Rangoon. The people who were covering the army sometimes came from the political desk at headquarters in Tokyo. They burned with an unflagging faith in victory. They hadn't done anything in the war. They had simply covered the Army Ministry in Tokyo, while I was covering the front. That was the only difference between us. But when we had to take cover in the air-raid shelter, they were the first to dash in. We colleagues argued the issue of how the war might end. They looked at me incredulously, "How will the war end? In our total victory! Without doubt!" Rear-line guys, even among newspapermen, swaggered about.

I really don't think I valued my own life so very much. I did pieces called "ride-along articles," which purported to be written by reporters flying with the bombers. But our division commander wouldn't let reporters go on the bombers because it was so risky. When our planes went out in the direction of Assam they were fine new aircraft. None of them returned. A correspondent from Nichiei, the news-film company, went down with them. I was spared because of our commander. I *wanted* to go, though. I never even imagined I might actually die. I don't think I was alone in this. There were many who wanted to go. I think that's one of the reasons journalism has a responsibility for the war. We contributed to the creation of a certain kind of atmosphere, where people would go without questioning, unthinkingly. Day in, day out we repeated the same basic story. I wrote such articles almost every day.

Reporters, whether overseas or in the homeland, came to believe that promoting and conducting the war were our obligation. We thought that Japan was liberating Asia from the West, and entering the company of the imperialists. Japan and Germany didn't have anything, did they?

The colored people of Asia had been exploited by the "have" nations of Europe and America, so this was a war to liberate Greater East Asia. We mesmerized ourselves with such arguments. They were quite appealing, actually—and if you didn't agree, you couldn't survive.

The whole nation became that way. At the request of the military, I came back to Japan in the summer of 1944 to give a series of talks. More than half of all factory workers then were women. It was really difficult for me to say to them, "Please make good airplanes." I knew it was impossible. At that time, there was no fuel. Schoolchildren were cutting pine roots and trying to extract fuel from them. What I told them was that their young airmen were fighting well and needed good planes. When I said anything even slightly unfavorable to Japan, or remotely unpleasant, it was like throwing a wet blanket over the whole audience. But when you told a story with even a glimmer of good in it, everyone got excited. A story of a young boy shooting down a B-24 lit up the whole place. Neither the speakers nor the listeners wanted to hear unpleasant stories.

This can be said about newspaper articles, too. There were Japanese reporters in Berlin, Rome, Stockholm, Lisbon, and Buenos Aires. They could have written more freely and said, "In Japan the cheers are 'Banzai! Banzai!' but when viewed from outside, things appear quite different." Berlin was an Axis capital, so I understand the men there, but from Lisbon and Stockholm, they should have sent in different things, even if they weren't welcomed. Every reporter ended up wanting to submit articles that would be printed and would please the Japanese people.

When I was in Rangoon, the British reporters who were on the other side went on strike and left in protest over censorship of their work by the local military command. On the Japanese side, severe competition continued among the newspeople, but our competition was not over the quality and accuracy of the reports that would be left to history, but rather over how most effectively to rouse the public. Because of this pressure and competition, there were reporters who wrote total lies.

There was the extreme case of the Three Human-Bomb Heroes. In 1931, three sappers carried a lighted charge at the end of a long pole right into the enemy barbed wire entanglements and were killed in the explosion. The truth was that they simply didn't make it back as fast as they had intended. But the army made them "military gods," men who were willing to kill themselves for the nation. All newspapers gave this story sensational coverage and many movies were made about it. That was a complete fabrication—but many, many lies, both big and small, were written then. Even those who scorned lying didn't really write the truth themselves.

If I reflect on that period as a journalist, I not only didn't write any articles critical of the war, but actually was active in writing militaristic ones. As a local reporter, I sometimes accompanied the "Orphan Trains" —specially reserved excursions for families of men enshrined in Yasukuni Shrine after dying in battle, which went from Saga, Yamaguchi, and other cities to Tokyo. I wrote beautified descriptions, flowery lines dripping with insincerity. "Father, I'm so full of energy and I'm studying so hard," I quoted the children saying to the spirits. I wrote such articles thinking I was sympathizing with the children. Looking back now, I don't believe that was true. One of my senior reporters tipped me off: "When you go to interview a 'wife-of-a-military-nation,' she'll probably wail and cry. If you write only that the woman said, 'I'm proud to be the wife of a warrior who died in battle,' that would be a lie. You should write, 'Although she sobbed and cried, she said . . .'" I grasped his point and adopted that style as my own.

I was in Singapore at the end of the war. After hearing the Imperial broadcast, one colleague said that Japan should fight on. Another reporter in Saigon told me, "Hata, we're committing national suicide. Like the Inca Empire, it will be said, 'Long ago the Great Japanese Empire existed here.' Japan has already perished, so let's leave its name behind in the annals of Romance." Many of my colleagues were brainwashed in this way.

Reporting from Imperial General Headquarters

KAWACHI UICHIRŌ

A newspaper and television journalist. He is today known as the producer of Eleven P.M., *the Japanese equivalent of* The Tonight Show.

"At the end of the war I was a military correspondent, accredited to Imperial General Headquarters, the Daihon'ei. *All the official war news came only from us. There are now probably fewer than ten left of all those I knew. We felt we were a chosen elite—a few each from the national dailies like my* Yomiuri Shimbun, *and the major local papers. The Dōmei News Agency wire service was represented, but the radio—NHK—only sent someone over to broadcast official announcements. Many of those who covered the army later went on to become board members at their papers. I didn't get that far, though."*

It's been a long time since the war. When time passes, memories seem to grow weathered, and even hardships can seem like happy times.

But even now, almost fifty years later, when I walk along the Ginza, suddenly I see a place and think, "I clung to this wall and hid myself here during the bombing."

I began my career as a reporter in Osaka. When the public announcements of the war dead came in, you got in a car with a list of addresses and rushed to the family's home. I spent whole days in that car visiting families. You assumed that they knew, but often they hadn't heard anything. They'd wail and cry. It was awful. There was a small placard at the entrance of each house where someone had died that said, 'House of Honor.' Some houses had three of them out front. Our going there meant that a fourth member of that household had just been killed. Before the Pacific War broke out, the casualty reports weren't piling up yet, so we'd always go out and try to get a story on each one. We'd get a photo of the dead soldier and we'd get a family member to talk about him. Usually we'd submit a story filled with fixed phrases like "They spoke without shedding a tear," no matter how much they'd cried. Every paper competed for a picture. Photographs weren't common like today. In those cases where there weren't any, we still had to get one, so we'd even take his face out of a childhood school graduation shot. Sometimes you'd borrow the family's only picture of their son and it would get lost in the paper's print shop. It was very hard to have to go back to the family to apologize. Even though it wasn't a big story, with the family picture it always made the paper. That was a job they gave to the new boys.

We told a lot of tales about laudable virtues when I was on the city desk. We called them *bidan*, beautiful stories. When a series of ten articles was planned for the paper, all the participating reporters would discuss themes and the style each would use. "I'll use the 'small mother' voice." "I'll use the 'struggling, yet gallant mother' type." Like this we'd establish a theme for the series.

I might be assigned "weak boys from the city who nonetheless fight hard at the front." It could start like this: A soldier's unit bombarded by enemy guns is surrounded and defeated. In the midst of a hail of enemy fire, our soldier, the only survivor, sabotages his rifle so the enemy can't use it. Then he dies. We'd get the outlines of these stories in from the front, then go to see the mother to find out what kind she was. Of course, a rifle wasn't much of a weapon. Even if captured, it wasn't going to reveal any great Japanese secrets, but in the atmosphere of those times this was still a *bidan*.

There were lots of styles. You could write the story any way you wanted. You'd have a mother who had been weeping, mourning for her son, crying so hard and long that her face was swollen and her voice was choked. Her dead son would appear before her and beg her, "Don't cry,

Ma. When you cry, it only hurts me to see you so sad." Then she'd stop. That's what we'd write. We couldn't repeat the same thing every time, so we'd have to change it around.

I recall one about a widowed mother and her only son. The boy comes back on leave from the army. The train tracks pass near the house. Just hearing the sound of the trains makes him bawl at the thought of going back. That'd be our lead. We'd push that for all it was worth, right at the top of the story. The point was, even this kind of kid fights well when he gets into action. He never comes home again. We'd make it clear that he hadn't done anything particularly heroic, just his duty. We'd focus on the fact that he wasn't the son of a particularly courageous mother, only the boy of a humble, ordinary, lonely mother, a "small mother."

Once, when I was covering Yasukuni Shrine, I spotted a family that had come for the ceremony to enshrine a soldier recently killed. The younger brother was hugging a huge bundle of rice stalks, whole plants, ripe from the harvest. I asked him why he held them so. "They were planted by my older brother," he answered. If you just look around, something will always catch your attention. Of course, there were made-up stories too.

The assignment to cover the regional military headquarters was a great job! In those days we couldn't really go abroad freely, but I was able to hop back and forth all over the place. I saw a lot. I even had a chance to go aboard a German merchant cruiser, a Q-Ship, the *Michael*. It was 1942, the year my son Kyōtarō was born—he's a *Yomiuri* reporter himself now. This ship had brought a cargo of German weapons and other supplies to Japan to exchange for things we had. I heard after the war that it also brought rocket blueprints, including those for the V-weapons used to bombard England, information on other new weapons, and plans for radars, all as part of a regular shuttle between Japan and Germany. It was absolutely secret.

The ship looked like a tramp freighter by day, but it had tremendous speed and four large guns, a scout plane, and torpedo tubes like those on a U-boat. It displaced only 4200 tons, but had a crew of four hundred. They had flags from everywhere in the world. They'd surprise and capture Allied merchant ships, unload the cargo, take off the crew, later to put them ashore on an uninhabited island; then they'd scuttle the prize. The funniest thing about the ship was that since they'd left Kiel, they'd taken American, Canadian, and British merchantmen and confiscated their stores. They had every kind of food imaginable! Monday was "American food day," Tuesday was "British food day." I don't think they ever killed anyone. I boarded in Singapore and stayed on board for two months. By day, they'd hide inshore by an out-of-the-way island. At night, they'd slip out to sea and hunt. It was scary. I thought we'd be caught and be sunk for sure.

I wasn't aboard as a newsman. My status was equivalent to a "PK," pronounced "*Peekaa*"—an officer in charge of military reports, not a Japanese journalist. I didn't even get an article out of the experience. I wrote some, but when the *Michael* blew up in the port of Yokohama after I'd gone ashore at Kobe, the story was killed. The cause of the explosion remains unknown.

When articles by war correspondents began to appear in the paper, the profession of correspondent became very popular. I remember it was like being a star. I was now assigned by the *Yomiuri* to the Imperial General Headquarters. The Kempeitai checked you out before you could be appointed. The army made us wear a uniform created specially for us. Maybe they just wanted to control us, I don't know, but the drab uniform they provided sure wasn't much to look at. They certainly didn't have to worry about us outshining them in those uniforms. The collars buttoned up to the top and could choke you. Yet, I've got to admit they were easier to work in since you didn't have to explain who you were all the time. But we didn't have any ranks to show off, and we didn't get any medals either.

There was a special ritual for issuing Imperial General Headquarters announcements. Today, they'd use word processors, but then, they came and read the announcement first for NHK radio. Then, they'd read it for the newspapers, explaining practically every word or phrase in the text. We'd telephone the announcement in to our head-office desks, but that wasn't really enough. We had to be safe, so we'd ask for a messenger to take the text to the paper. A mistake in a single Chinese character could mean your neck—these were "the Emperor's words" after all—so we wanted to be sure the phrases got through exactly as they announced them. Messengers on motorcycles from all the papers circled the building while we in the second floor pressroom were getting the text together. When we had our story, we'd stuff it in an envelope and throw it down to our man, so he could zoom off to the head office. There, the typesetters would compare it with the type they'd set from our telephone call and correct any mistakes. What a waste it all seems now, but it was life and death then!

General staff officers from the front often came back to report to the army minister. We'd be asked to meet them, and then we wrote up the accounts we heard, as if we'd been there ourselves. "Kawachi, Special Correspondent with Unit X at the Front" would be my byline. I went to a lot of exotic places that way! At times, things got complicated and contradictory. Yesterday I was at Attu island in the Aleutians, and today

I'd be in the Marianas. Officially, for the record, I'd actually been there, even if I'd never set foot outside the capital. When my report appeared in the *Yomiuri*, I'd be credited as "*Yomiuri* Special Correspondent." When it appeared in the *Asahi* or other papers, I was "Kawachi, Army Special Correspondent." The army press officers knew that if they talked to certain journalists like me, their stories would appear on the front page. Then they, or their units or their commanders, would get a lot of exposure, while somebody else might only get them a line or two.

I remember once when Colonel Shiroishi asked me if I would be willing to go the Southern Area. Instinctively I knew what he meant and I agreed. My wife had been evacuated to the countryside near Osaka. It was almost impossible to get a train ticket to visit her at that time. It wasn't a matter of money, since tickets were cheap for us; it was just transport control. I was given a special transport voucher, with the red Army stripe across it and a seal on it, which could be converted into a ticket practically anywhere. I then went to the "Southern Area," spending four or five days with my wife in Osaka. People who didn't know this thought I was off in the South Pacific! This was normal procedure. I wrote up a bunch of stories about conditions there—not dramatic accounts of our victories, but relations between the Japanese and the natives, that kind of thing. They were pretty good stories.

People tend to think that every report was censored and that it was impossible to write anything critical of our wartime situation. In fact, though, depending on who was doing the writing, many things got through the censor. You learned the tricks. I knew how to write reports late at night, when few people were on duty at the press-corps office. I could call up the colonel in charge, tell him the outline of the story, and sometimes he'd tell me his seal was in his desk drawer and I could use it to pass the story. Of course, he trusted me and knew I wouldn't go too far.

In hindsight, a lot of the announcements from the Imperial General Headquarters look like nothing but lies. It wasn't that they tried to lie from the start, just that there usually wasn't enough information available. In order to make an official announcement it was necessary to get the Imperial seal on it first. This was the official procedure. It's what made the headquarters "Imperial." Back then it was inconceivable that the Emperor could make a mistake. He was a god. You couldn't change what he'd said and explain that it was in error. Once something had been announced, they'd have to try to justify it, and one lie would lead to another, until the whole thing became a big lie.

It didn't always start out that way. For example, there was an uproar when it was reported that the American fleet had been wiped out in a battle off Taiwan, just prior to their planned landings on Okinawa. The ecstasy of the moment, the relief at the thought that the special attack forces had turned the tide and crushed the Americans swept everyone along. A colonel from the Press Office burst into the press room with a large bottle of saké. "Here comes a torpedo," he cried, swinging it as if he were launching it from a plane. "The moment we've been waiting for has come!" He was shouting. For the first time, the army had joined the navy in a coordinated joint air attack at sea, and they'd been victorious. They were exultant. "It's the Divine Wind, the Kamikaze!" The colonel bounded up the stairs, calling for everyone to toast the victory. When all the saké was gone he ordered junior officers to rush out for more. His joy was real.

By the next day, we knew differently. This was the first time army planes had gone out to attack ships. They really had no idea about the sizes of their intended targets, they simply charged into the antiaircraft barrage, which was terrific and something they'd never seen before. They tried to duck in under the ack-ack, to breach that wall of fire. Every ship looked enormous up close. Everything happened so fast. They had hardly any training in this kind of attack. Whenever a plane dropped its bomb and an explosion sent up a pillar of flame, the pilot thought his plane had surely scored a direct hit. When smoke rose from a ship, even if it hadn't been hit fatally, even if was just superficial, it was reported sunk. Many pilots thought they'd obliterated their targets. The reports poured in of the annihilation of the U.S. fleet. These raw reports coming into head-quarters were issued over the Imperial seal. In fact, it was soon clear that only a frigate or two had been hit, and even those ships in the outer picket circle were able to proceed under their own power—but you couldn't take back the official announcement. Officers then had to cover up the mistakes. Theirs weren't intentional lies, but rather signs of the acute anxiety, the desire everyone felt for something good to happen. They jumped at the prospect and their fragments of news were immedi-ately seized on by the newspapers, which glorified the "story."

Even military strategy sometimes changed as a result of such stories. At the time of the American invasion of the Philippines, General Yamashita Tomoyuki had planned to fight a defensive battle until he received news of the complete Japanese victory over the U.S. fleet which encouraged him to move against Leyte. The Japanese defeat there might have begun with this. In a sense, I'd have felt better if Imperial General Headquarters had lied intentionally, had deceived the people on purpose to force a final sacrifice. But the fact—so much the worse, it seems to me —is they were really uninformed and didn't know the true situation of the war they were responsible for fighting.

I went to airbases to get stories about the Kamikaze, the special attack forces. They were just tales of courage and bravery at first. You'd describe how they took off without shedding a tear and things like that. I remember one group of young Kamikaze pilots who spent a night in Matsudo City in Chiba before departing for their attack base. They knew they were going to the front, but their families didn't know they were leaving as special-attack pilots. Reporters were told to be cautious in speaking to their family members so they wouldn't find out prior to their missions, so we made a lot of noise and had a merry time, lots of drinking and singing together. The next day they departed, dipping their wings as they flew south. At that moment I looked back and saw a mother and father praying, holding a Buddhist rosary. They knew. Nobody told them, but they knew. The *Yomiuri* photographer didn't dare take a shot of the parents with that rosary. Planes dipping their wings in parting were really a heartrending sight, even sadder than human beings waving good-bye, particularly in the case of the Kamikaze. They were bound for Taiwan or the Philippines. From there they would plunge into the enemy. I covered such events and went to get that kind of story so often that I guess I got used to it.

Once I focused my story on how they spent their last hours. They knew they were going to die, so they really didn't lose control. They didn't even get drunk or rowdy. All were young and innocent. They must have been really scared. They had to imbue themselves with their death, make themselves blind to other thoughts. When it rained and delayed their flights, they didn't know how to spend even one more day of life. They had to soar into the air instantly, without lingering. Any hesitation could make it all unravel. On rainy days they ended up writing terrible poems. I can't even talk about them, they were so bad. At that time, I remember thinking that they shouldn't be writing this awful stuff. Now I look back on it and think it was all right. They weren't writing for literary posterity or for the critics. They just wanted to leave something behind. I suggested that instead they might leave their handprints, but they told me they weren't sumo wrestlers. They were imagining an ink print of their hands on Japanese paper being hung in their school auditoriums for other students to see. They didn't think their own hands impressive enough. They wanted some kind of flashy legacy. They wanted to die a "good death."

I slept there with them. Sometimes I joined them all in the common bath and had my back scrubbed by a boy who was going to die on the morrow. I never met one of them who came back alive. They were all so young. Every one of them looked like he had a girlfriend. Each had a pure-white silk muffler. Almost all of them practically reeked of perfume.

Some even wanted to have their teeth fixed before they took off, because they wanted to die in perfect shape. They were going to die anyway. What difference could it make whether a tooth was fixed or not?

I went to many departure ceremonies. The commander would pour a cup of saké for each of them in turn. It was called the Farewell Cup. He'd drink with them. When an airplane gains altitude, each cup does the work of three or four cups on the ground. Those among them who were not able to hold their drink very well must have staggered through the skies. I don't know if they consciously planned it that way, but this was the ritual every time.

During the Tokyo air raids, I lived in the *Yomiuri* dormitory in Ochanomizu. Tokyo was a charred wasteland. You sort of got used to people dying. Hundreds of thousands were killed in the air raids. There were bodies lying all over the city. A man dying meant nothing. I didn't really contemplate my own death, didn't give the situation any serious thought, and yet felt a kind of emptiness, a kind of anxiety about the future.

You couldn't tell what was really going on. A place on a map would be declared Japan's "life-line." Then we'd be defeated and that place was no longer a "life-line." We'd use the phrase "point of decisive battle" to describe a place like Leyte. Then it would change. It was constantly changing. When you're a correspondent at Imperial General Headquarters, and you've been reporting things like that, you become embarrassed. "Special Correspondents to Decisive Battles" is how the head-office reporters started to refer to us. We'd even issue reports of air raids that said, "The damage was light," despite the evidence of our own eyes. At the last stage of the projected battle for the Homeland, the army planned to fight on from the huge underground complex they built in the mountains of Nagano. They were going to move the Emperor there. They even told us reporters about it, and asked us to come with them.

10 / AGAINST THE TIDE

THE "Yokohama Incident" involved the imprisonment of a total of forty-nine people—intellectuals, authors, journalists, and publishing figures—including five associated with each of the magazines *Kaizō* and *Chūō Kōron*. They were accused of secretly plotting to revive the Communist movement in Japan. Four died in prison, and two more soon after being released.° From 1942 until 1945 many people were arrested and detained at various police stations throughout Kanagawa prefecture and the prison in Yokohama. There was no single incident or action, but the affair was spread out over several years and takes its name from the fact that the arrests were coordinated by the Yokohama branch of the Home Ministry's Special Higher Police, the dread Tokkō police. These investigators worked to enforce the multiplying laws against dissent and "thoughts crimes," which built on the Peace Preservation Law of 1925.

The Peace Preservation Law prohibited organizing groups or movements that had as their objective the alteration of the "national polity"— meaning a state headed by an Emperor—or those who opposed private property. Under that law, Communists, labor organizers, and members of allegedly radical groups had been arrested by the thousands and convicted long before the war began.† Many eventually recanted their views and were released, but six months was the minimum time any person convicted under the Peace Preservation Law was imprisoned.‡ Those arrested were frequently subjected to beatings and other forms of torture. Some died while under detention.

Repeated revisions of the law made its interpretation broader and the punishments heavier. In 1941, a total revision applied the law to liberals, intellectuals affiliated with no party, and people holding religious beliefs at odds with the state religion of Shintō. Harboring such

---

° Hatanaka Shigeo, *Nihon fashizumu no genron dan'atsu: shōshi.* [*Suppression of Free Speech in Japanese Fascism: An Abridged History*] (Tokyo: Kōbunken, 1986), p. 178.

† Between 1928 and the end of 1943, a total of 68,508 persons had been arrested in the Japanese Homeland—excluding Korea and Taiwan—under provisions of the Peace Preservation Law; 6,227 had been tried and convicted. See Nihon kin-gendaishi jiten henshū iinkai, ed., *Nihon Kin-gendaishi jiten* [*Dictionary of Modern and Contemporary Japanese History*] (Tokyo: Tōyō keizai shimpōsha, 1986), p. 408.

‡ Hatanaka, *op. cit.*, pp. 177–78. See pages 190–91 for a complete list of those arrested.

"dangerous thoughts" was determined to be a crime. Between 1941 and the end of 1943, a total of 2,069 persons were arrested and 627 prosecuted for such crimes.° ■

Thought Criminal

HATANAKA SHIGEO [2]

He was editor of the magazine Chūō Kōron [Central Review] *before his arrest.*

I was sitting here, right in this room, when they came. Four detectives who declared they were from the Kanagawa Special Higher Police. They were the "thought police." One sat on either side of me. I wondered why they'd come. It was January 29, 1944. When I wanted to go to the toilet, one of the detectives followed me inside and stood there when I was doing it. They started turning all my books inside out. They even looked behind the picture frames. They didn't say why they'd come. They just showed the summons. Written on it was "Suspected of violations of the Peace Preservation Law."

I thought there must have been a mistake. I never imagined they'd come in that way. Because I was so hated by the army, I always assumed they'd take me as a soldier to the front. There were such precedents. A *Mainichi* newspaper reporter once wrote, "Can Japan defeat America with bamboo spears? We have to build more airplanes." That offense, the "Bamboo-Spear Incident," left Prime Minister Tōjō Hideki white-hot with anger. He ordered that reporter drafted. The man was almost forty years old, nearly the upper limit of service in the second reserves, but he was sent off to some regiment until the navy rescued him, and made him a "special correspondent to the South."

The thought police put all the bound copies of *Chūō Kōron* I had, even those dating from before I went to work there, in a great pile, wrapped them up in *furoshiki,* making three or four large packages, and took them away. My wife tells me they came back three or four days later and stirred everything up all over again. They took me to Yokohama on the commuter train, and from there by taxi to Hodogaya Police Station. They said, "You won't do anything foolish, will you?" I wasn't handcuffed. Then they put me into a small detention room, where I waited.

° Elise Tipton, *The Japanese Police State. The Tokkō in Interwar Japan* (Honolulu: University of Hawaii Press, 1990), pp. 156–57.

Finally, I was hauled into an "investigation room," a cold-looking tatami room. The windows were covered with a black curtain. Their tone and attitude changed instantly. From then on the "terror" began. They told me I had to confess that I'd carried out Communist activities. "Do you know Kobayashi Takiji died?" they asked. He'd been a novelist, a Communist who was killed in police custody. They told me nobody cared if the police killed a Commie. After beating me, they affixed my finger-print to a statement saying that I'd been involved in Communist activities. I was then thrown back into the detention room and left there, in a world shut off from everything.

On that same day, thirty-odd people in addition to those of us in publishing were hauled away, including a research group from the Manchurian Railway. Because there were so many, they were spread out among the various police stations. Compared to some of the others, I was hauled off late. Three other men from *Chūō Kōron* were taken before me, and two of them died. The torture of people arrested prior to me was really terrible, it seems. Because I was arrested later, the protocol was already written up. The written document existed and all I had to do was approve it. If I hadn't agreed to it, they would have continued to torture me. According to their preliminary examination I was "Communist Hatanaka Shigeo," who had caused other people to act "under the direction of Communist Hatanaka Shigeo." I don't like saying this, because those people were killed, and they were nice young men, but because of horrible torture, they were forced to declare that I was a Communist. I found that I "had used articles in *Chūō Kōron* to spread the Communist way of thinking in the world," and "used *Chūō Kōron* as a weapon in the Communist movement."

The interrogators asked me, "What is Communism? How was the Comintern developed? What were the origins of the Japanese Communist Party?" This is what they called "seeking understanding." The process was supposed to get the accused to recognize what they had done. I didn't remember anything about those things. So then they'd say, "Here, read this," and just showed me the answers written on a piece of paper. They said the editors of *Chūō Kōron* and *Kaizō* [*Reconstruction*] had run their magazines to lead the country in the direction of Communism, which was against the Peace Preservation Law. They said I'd been involved in activities to support Communism, which opposed the Emperor system and denied private property. That, too, was in violation of certain articles of that law.

In the end, it became more trouble than it was worth to deny what they said. I was physically weak. The torture I received may have been less than what the earlier ones got, but I'd had enough. At first, there were no outside supplementary rations allowed and no visits by anyone. After about four months or so, they finally allowed food to reach me from the outside. I was permitted to receive changes of clothes, too. One day, the head of the thought police told me to look out the window. I could see my wife and father coming towards the building, but they didn't know I was watching. This was one of their tactics, playing on human emotions. The Special Higher Police from the Kanagawa prefectural office were real bastards.

The hardest thing is torture. You can't really explain it with words. I can't describe it. There were many kinds of torture. In my case, I was in a room about the size of six *tatami* mats. It was like in one of those *Yakuza* movies on TV where they chop off their fingers. You know, tough-looking detectives sit cross-legged all around you and literally beat you, kick you, pull your hair, throw you around by your head. They put a pencil between your fingers and press down. That really brings the pain home to you! [*He suddenly cries out in a loud voice, almost a scream.*]

Aoyama-san, one of the Yokohama Incident victims, still had swollen fingers because of that, right up to his recent death. They also beat you with a bamboo sword. They pressed lit cigarettes to your body. I escaped this one, but some were turned upside down and forced to hang from the ceiling. The food wasn't decent. It was only some kind of chopped noodle and a couple of pieces of cooked burdock stem, so you soon began to suffer from malnutrition.

The cells at the station didn't have decent facilities. No heat at all. There was a tiny hole, probably an air vent, high up on the wall that they never closed no matter how cold it got. When it snowed, I was sometimes awakened by snow in my cell. My body was covered with lice. When I was finally sent somewhere else pending trial, it was October 17 or 18, and I'd been arrested January 29, so I'd had no bath for about ten months. One of the regular policemen who watched us felt sorry for me and let me wipe my body with a cloth and water. We didn't have a barber, so they took us out to have our hair cut. The barber was so shocked. He said he'd have to take off my whole scalp to get rid of the dandruff.

While I was still at Hodogaya station, most of the prisoners there were petty thieves, perverts, or rapists. Yet even the lowest policeman had a kind of special hatred for thought criminals—working for the Commies in the middle of war! They hated us, so they tortured us. The other prisoners thought we were something pretty special. They called me *Sensei* [Teacher]. "You're having a tough time, aren't you, Sensei?" one said with concern. I asked him what he'd done, and he just said, "Oh, I'm a petty thief." He was released once, but he was soon back inside.

It may be an indelicate thing to say, but they didn't remove the urine or excrement from the cell. You'd be eating your lunch, and right next to you somebody would be taking a piss. That may seem inconceivable, but when you get hungry you can eat. You descend to that shameful condition.

In the police station they had only communal cells. I felt relieved when I was transferred to a real cell pending trial, although my fate was still undecided. In prison you might get a solitary cell, with its own running-water toilet. When you were examined, you were taken from there to the court. On rare occasions, the prosecutor would come out to investigate us at the prison, but usually we were taken to him.

When my draft notice came, I was in prison. I didn't even know it had come, but my wife was shocked and went to the military-affairs clerk at the town office with that red paper. He asked, "Is he 'economic' or 'thought'?" An "economic criminal" was someone who had violated one of the wartime economic regulations, like selling pork illegally. When my wife said "thought," he replied, "Well, then you can go home and forget about it." That was it. Thought criminals belonged to the Tokkō, the Special Higher Police. On the same day that my draft notice came, Mr. Yokawa, who was the managing director of *Chūō Kōron,* got his. He was summoned to the same unit as me and was killed in action in Okinawa. If I'd been outside, I probably would have died there, too. I was tortured and I hated it, and in the end I surrendered to them, but I might have been dead if I'd been drafted. I might not have lived through the war. So in the end, they may have gone out of their way to protect this "unfaithful Japanese." This is irony.

Once the prosecutor completed his investigation, then the preliminary investigation for the public trial officially began. There really wasn't any "investigation." It was just the same as at the police station, only without the torture. All I had to do was approve what they wrote down. I tried to say those things were extracted under torture. "Is that so? Well, then, I'll have to send you back to the police for further investigation." That was enough to get me to drop the idea of speaking out. It's meaningless to be killed in a place like that. "Probably I should spill whatever they want. This kind of Japan won't win, anyway." Those were my thoughts.

The prosecutor and the preliminary judge were just the same. They didn't ask any questions. Things simply proceeded to the trial. We were placed on the second floor of Building 3 of the prison. There all the inmates were like me. I could tell by their voices. I had only a tag with a number preceded by *tsu;* that meant "thought criminal." In the cell next to mine was a man from *Kaizō.* Nearby were two men from *Chūō Kōron.* They never used our names. When we went out for exercise or when we went to court, we could see them, but we were not allowed to talk to them. If we tried, we were beaten up. Punishment there was really severe. Any transgression against the rules and they'd dunk you into a tub of water and leave you there. Two died. You could hear their screams. They'd beat you with a thick cord; you'd be wearing only your underpants, and that too really hurt.

I knew that war conditions had taken a bad turn, but we were inside. Then one afternoon a young guard opened the door, looked into my eyes, and said, "I don't like it. I don't like it. I can't stand it. 'Unconditional surrender'?" That's how I knew the end of the war was near. Two or three days later, one of the janitors, a prisoner who did manual jobs, told me, "Japan's like this!" and held his hands up over his head in the sign of surrender. I also heard a voice calling out *"Banzai! Banzai!"* in a cell near mine. It was a Korean with a Japanese name. The guard didn't even get angry at him. If things had been normal, they'd have tortured him to death. The amount of food we received suddenly increased. Thought criminals were now allowed to enter the mixed bath and meet other prisoners. I met Hosokawa Karoku—a fellow journalist—there. He'd been arrested in September 1942. We exchanged greetings and expressed joy that we'd survived. But nobody really said, "Japan's lost."

Our trial took place on September 3, 1945. After the war was over. We boarded a prisoner bus, tied together in a chain. We were shocked to see Yokohama completely gutted by fire. One day, we'd heard the sound of bombs and smelled things burning, but we'd never imagined this. Our prison, which was wooden, remained untouched; not even one incendiary bomb hit us. We joked later that they must have intentionally spared it to have a place to put war criminals!

This is only a guess, but I think the Yokohama judicial police and the bureaucracy burned all records of the police and preliminary investigations on August 26, just before MacArthur landed in Japan. Now, more than forty years later, we're asking for a retrial, but that's been denied by the Yokohama District Courts and the Tokyo High Court. They say there's no way to reopen an investigation without documents of any kind to investigate. They burned the documents because it was convenient to them! They say they are convinced we won't do anything like that again! What do they mean "again"? We have no proof of our own innocence!

Sure, I said what they told me to say. I wanted to get out even one day sooner. I agreed to say anything, but I never committed any crime. It had all been decided before the trial. I talked to a lawyer for the first time just prior to the trial. I was to get two years' penal servitude and three years' probation. That's what they gave me, officially, but I went on probation directly. Everybody got the same sentence, except for the

Kaizō editor-in-chief. I don't know why, but he got two years with six years' probation.

We later sued because we'd been tortured. Most of the torturers denied it and escaped indictment, but three police inspectors who tortured us were sentenced to two or three years at hard labor a few years after the war. They were pardoned just prior to their imprisonment, on the occasion of the San Francisco Peace Treaty.

Chūō Kōron and *Kaizō* were completely suppressed on July 19, 1944. That last issue of *Chūō Kōron*, after fifty-nine years, was number 682. It was dissolved "voluntarily" and was forbidden even to pass on the company name. After the war we made a comeback and again I became editor-in-chief.

But, you know, I didn't really resist the war. I was simply chased after by the police. I only wanted to keep from doing what the military ordered me to do. I gave opportunities to former Communists and others as often as possible, but they weren't writing Communist propaganda. Had they, I'd have cut them. But just giving them the opportunity was the problem. I abhor military men. I consider them a separate race of humanity because of education. Military men put on ceremonial uniforms for special occasions. Theirs is childish, simple-minded thinking.

It was really a miserable era. I wish such a period had never existed. But because Japan lost, we are able to speak like this. This, too, is a paradox. If we'd won then, we might have been more miserable. Maybe we should thank America.

"Isn't my brother one of the 'War Dead'?"

KIGA SUMI

The smells of medicines and food mix in the dining room of the hospital in Saitama where she spends most of her time these days, since her husband has been hospitalized here for three years. "I was going out with the man who'd become my husband when my brother Wada Kitarō was arrested. He accompanied me partway on the days I went to visit Kitarō in the detention center. He encouraged me and told me I had no reason to be ashamed."

She speaks in a low voice, seeming to reach deep inside herself to pull forth memories. She selects her words with great care.

"My mother died the year before last, at the age of ninety-six. I have now taken over for her. This is a case where the state trumped everything

up and I want them to take it back. Along with others who were charged with my brother in the Yokohama Incident, we're seeking a reexamination of his case. Just the other day our request was thrown out of court. We do not have very bright prospects for success, but we are not going to give up. I want to recover his honor."

The Wada family had been doctors in a farming village in Kyoto prefecture for generations. One of my elder brothers should have succeeded to the practice, but none of them did. I told my father that I wanted to take after him, and he seemed to like that idea, but he passed away when I was in fourth grade. Even in his will it stated that Sumi should become a doctor, but when the time came, I faced the fierce opposition of everyone. My eldest brother in particular, ten years my senior, believed that women should be trained as brides and then be married off. Back then those feudalistic ideas were still strong. I threatened to kill myself if they didn't listen to me. In the end they relented and allowed me to go study pharmacology.

My other brother Kitarō studied French literature at Keiō University and then went to work at *Chūō Kōron*. I got on better with him. He was gentle and kind. We talked together often, but still he was five years older than me. In fact, the time we spent together was very limited. Because we lived in the country, he left home when he entered middle school. He returned for summer vacations, so we spent those months together. I remember him making all kind of funny sounds when he was studying Russian. I suppose you could say he was a "literary youth."

My graduation from the Imperial Women's School of Medicine and Pharmacology was moved up because of the war. I graduated in September 1942, six months early, and remained at the school to do research as a lecturer. By then, all three of us kids were in Tokyo. Kitarō and I used to keep in touch by telephone. He always spent what little money he had on books. One day when I called, they told me he'd taken the day off, so I called his boarding house. They told me he wasn't there. This, too, was in September 1942.

I soon discovered that my eldest brother and my uncle were also looking for him. He'd disappeared. We tried everything, looked everywhere. Finally, we found out that he'd been taken to a police station in Yokohama. The three of us went there to see him, but it was terrible. They swore, "We'll never let you see that traitor." They berated us, abused us with foul language, treating us as if we were traitors. We had to return home without seeing him. The place we'd gone to was the Special Higher Police Section, so I was able to deduce that his was a "thought crime." Beyond that we knew nothing.

He was then moved to the detention house in Sasage in Tokyo. I finally received a notice that I would be permitted to see him. My eldest brother wasn't sympathetic to him at all. He suspected him of actually being some kind of thought criminal, and blamed him for it. I thought, Kitarō has only me. I took all the responsibility on myself. Every month, once a month, I went to see him. I brought back his laundry and I noticed blood on his underwear.

I wasn't allowed to go on weekends, so I had to talk my professor into letting me go during the work week. There were three of us lecturers, and while I can't say they were actively on my side, I think they understood.

When you got there, you faced a tiny barred window. On my side was a chair where I waited until he was brought in by a guard. Every time I visited he looked skinnier. So pallid. He apologized to me, his younger sister. He shed tears in front of his own little sister and kept repeating, "I'm sorry, so sorry." There was nothing I could say to him. I was heartbroken. There he was in prison garb handcuffed, even while we spoke. The guard stood next to him the whole time. We exchanged words about our health. I told him about mother. I begged him to take care of himself. What else could we say? He probably wanted to tell me—would have told me—how he came to be arrested, why he was there. I wanted to ask him, but I couldn't. I was given about ten minutes.

I was allowed to provide him with food while he was held pending trial. Kitarō told me he was so hungry he could hardly stand it. There were a couple of box-lunch shops in front of the detention house which were authorized suppliers. They could send food in to him. One of them, Asanoya, seemed to value thought criminals particularly highly. It was a little strange, but I spoke to the wife there. She told me they were undergoing terrible torture. You can tell just by the atmosphere when a person is on your side. You know. The kindness comes through and is truly welcome in the midst of a world where everything seems stacked against you. The people at the detention house! How can I describe them? Arrogant to the world? They didn't treat me as if I were even human. When I spoke with that woman, I was able to calm myself down.

Kitarō's call-up papers arrived from the village office. My eldest brother, my uncle, and I, the three of us, again went to the prosecutor's office and asked them to release him because he had been drafted. Again, they denounced us. "How can we possibly release this kind of traitor!" They poured spite on us and chased us out of there. Because of this the village learned of his arrest. They all knew. They had been waiting for him to return for induction, preparing his farewell party with Japanese flags hoisted. He didn't show up. Notice was sent to the village office, informing them of the reason. Mother told me villagers started throwing stones at the rain shutters of the house at night. Until that moment, they were warm and showed their best faces toward our family. They would say, "Doctor Wada saved my life. He was a wonderful physician." That changed overnight. We were now all traitors. My mother was there alone and had nowhere to go.

It was my bad luck that an airfield intended for Special Attack forces was being constructed in our village. When I returned and walked the path of the village, people didn't greet me, but looked away. The rumor started that I was a spy. I was supposedly back to take pictures of the airfield. They spread word that, after taking pictures, I had sent a telegram from the station. They repeated these things as if they were plausible.

Kitarō was tried alone. He was separated from the others who were charged. For that trial our mother came to Tokyo. The four of us sat in the rear gallery of the courtroom. We were so far away. The sound of Kitarō's voice barely reached our ears, and we were unable to hear what he was actually saying. We didn't even understand what he was being tried for. We didn't know what the charges were. Kitarō's sad, lonely-looking back is burned into my mind's eye. He looked so small, so far away. The only thing I heard distinctly was him confirming his own name.

Very recently, after more than forty years, the charges in this trial were disclosed. For all those years we knew nothing. When it came out, it was all so ridiculous. How could they dare sentence someone to prison for attending a study meeting? That was it. Kitarō himself didn't tell me this. I heard it later from others who'd attended. It seems as if everything was made up by the authorities. Even if you went to have a cup of coffee after work, they made it into "The Meeting with X." He was listed as having been present. For that they sentenced him to prison. I believe it was a two-year sentence. He wasn't a Communist Party member. Maybe he harbored Leftist sympathies. Once he was sent to prison I was unable to visit him anymore. I never saw him again after the trial.

The following year, on February 7, a bitter-cold morning, I heard someone call out, "Telegram! Telegram!" The telegram read, "Kitarō died." I cannot describe my feelings at that moment. I didn't know the cause. Maybe illness. Maybe he shortened his own life!

I dashed to the prison, dropping everything. I was escorted in. "This way," they said. On the concrete floor a straw mat covered him. A man removed that cover. "Please confirm it." He was lying naked on the concrete floor. It was just as if it were the corpse of a dog or cat. I'll never forget that feeling. Misery. I was there alone. His face was swollen. His eyes were open. I squatted down and tried to close them. I couldn't.

I don't remember what I did afterwards.

I view my brother as one of the "war dead." He didn't go to the front, but he was murdered, tormented to death. I believe he actually was murdered. For many years I searched for the cause of his death. I wanted to know why he died. One of the guards at the prison told me, "Mr. Wada didn't come out in the morning. I found him dead in his cell. It was very cold that day. Maybe he froze to death."

He did nothing wrong, but he was made into a criminal and he died that way. Had he survived, he would have been able to vindicate himself, through his own pen. Kitarō's anguish, the anguish of a man who died in prison! My heart reaches out to him.

I still go back to our village in Kyoto. My brother's tomb is there, and my mother's. The house is still there, though nobody lives in it now. Going there stirs complex feelings in me. It's not Chekhov's *The Cherry Orchard,* but the family that had prospered so is now all ragged and run down. I don't take pleasure in going back.

---

11 / CHILDHOOD

Playing at War

SATŌ HIDEO

Like so many schoolchildren, he was evacuated to the countryside when the threat of American bombing of Japan's cities grew critical. The precise number of children evacuated, as individuals or with their families, is not known, but about 450,000 children enrolled in the third grade and up were sent to the countryside in group evacuations from twenty cities by April 1945.

He is now a scholar at the Japanese government's National Language Research Institute. His current research is on how the Supreme Command Allied Powers conceived and implemented educational reforms during the Occupation of Japan after the war. "I've visited America six times and been to twenty-six of the states," he proudly declares.

I was born in 1934, the youngest of five brothers and sisters. Around that time, my father was dispatched twice to China by Dai-ichi Bank, where he had worked since graduation from Tokyo Imperial University in 1927, though he had wanted to go to Europe. I remember he brought back English chocolates as souvenirs. I hadn't known there was anything that delicious in the whole world. The box, beautifully printed, astonished me. I was also given a letter-opener paperweight shaped like a Chinese broadsword. The sword could be drawn out of its scabbard. I still have it. Things like that, made of metal, were rare objects by then. When I played with the family miniature trains, I just connected the rails together in a straight line, with a stack of books at one end. I'd set the rails at an angle from the top of the book pile and let the engines slide down the tracks. That's when my brothers would tell me, "When we played with them they used to run with electric motors." The motors were broken, and there were no parts available to repair them.

We lived in the suburbs of Tokyo. At the outbreak of the Pacific War, I was a second-grader. I'm not certain that I actually listened to that special broadcast announcing the war—I've heard recordings of it so many times since—but I do know it was quite cold that day. I remember the principal of our school speaking to us at the morning assembly, full of exhilaration that we—that Japan—had entered a great war. "At last!" he said. In his talk, the word "Honolulu" came up. All I remember thinking was, "What a strange name!"

The number of female teachers at our school increased as the male teachers gradually were called to military duty. The men going into the service would extend their greetings to us at morning assembly, a white sash with a red sun across their chests, but the war didn't really seem close to me then. In third and fourth grades I had an extremely young male teacher who stammered quite severely. I was a very naughty child. During breaks I used to jump up onto the teacher's platform and imitate his way of talking. It's funny, but I ended up a stammerer myself. I don't believe that a man like that would have been able to teach in peacetime.

I also had an experienced teacher, Matsukawa-sensei, who was a great storyteller, extremely popular when I was in fourth grade. He was in his forties. Although he wasn't the teacher of my section, he sometimes taught ethics to all of us together. I remember vividly the story told about the Harvest Festival, November 23. His Imperial Highness is a living god, he said. When he makes crucial decisions, he withdraws to the Imperial Sanctuary and there communes with Amaterasu-Ōmikami, goddess of the Sun, and other gods, in pitch-black darkness. He told the story so convincingly and dramatically that we kids sat there, eyes round with wonder, and felt in our heart of hearts that it must be true. You know there's a saying "he lies as if he saw it"? He was very adept at addressing himself to children. In teaching composition he told us we should write freely exactly what we thought. He didn't really preach at us and he didn't beat us. While the content of his ideas was militaristic and nationalistic, he taught it using the techniques of "new education" he had mastered in the Taishō era of freer education in the nineteen-twenties. Each child in the room was riveted to his every word.

Some graduates of our school who had become Youth Air Soldiers came back to visit after completing training, before they left for the front. This was part of an effort aimed at recruiting future volunteer pilots. They would stage a fly-over. The time was always set right before lunch hour, just when I was hungriest. We all had to gather in the schoolyard. Sometimes it seemed they wouldn't show up no matter how long we waited, but eventually we'd hear the drone of airplanes. They would fly above us and dip their wings in salute, then wave before they flew on. Once, immediately after one of these visits, we were allocated soft rubber balls. There was no rubber available for such frivolous things then. I had been using hand-me-downs from my brothers, treasuring them. When they burst or leaked, you refilled them by sticking an old syringe into that belly-button-like point on the ball. But these were brand new rubber balls. At least some of them descended via parachute from one of the planes that flew over our school. This was immediately after the advance into Southeast Asia in 1942 and Japan's capture of the rubber plantations there. But when I think about it, that rubber probably couldn't yet have found its way into our balls. I guess they did it to draw us children into the war effort. Whatever the facts, I only know I was in ecstasy when it was my turn to go up to receive my very own ball.

From the end of my fourth grade, from 1943, I began to hear the word "evacuation." My whole home was going to move, and even to my child's mind, this gave rise to uneasy feelings. One day, three or four large trucks came and began loading up our household belongings. Mother was told she must arrange all our things into boxes they gave her, and just like that, acting in great haste, we left Tokyo for Shimozuma in Ibaragi prefecture. The last day of our school classes in March, I was forced to bid farewell. Everyone said, "Satō will be evacuating." Only three out of fifty of us left at that time, so I felt exceptionally lonely. All my other classmates were evacuated later to Nagano.

The thing that sticks with me most about my time in Ibaragi was the bullying we evacuated children faced. I was persecuted thoroughly. My whole fifth year at elementary school was spent that way. We didn't have any relatives there. We were total strangers with no connections to use to get extra food. My lunch was full of barley and other rice substitutes. The kids sitting next to me brought "silver rice"—pure-white, shining rice. They were from farming families. My lunch box was made of "aluminite," though, while theirs were just wood. I guess I had a feeling of superiority, believing we were on different cultural levels. The clothes I wore were different. Mine were Keiō-style, dark blue, double-breasted, with a white collar, modelled on the Keiō University elementary school uniform, with short pants and high socks. During the cold winter, I wore stockings under my shorts. My leather shoes had metal buckles. These were all hand-me-downs from my older brothers, but at that elementary school in Ibaragi, the majority wore common kimonos. Even those who wore Western-style clothes had very rough things.

This isn't really one of my best memories, but I recall that during one of my national-language classes I was pushed in the back by the boy behind me. Maybe it wasn't during class, but at a break. Anyway, I turned and told him, "Such behavior is simply *banyū*." "What's that mean?" he asked. I wrote down the *kanji* characters for the word, showed him, and then told him it meant "brute courage, the valor of savages." From that moment on he stopped bullying me. I had older brothers and sisters, and my father had many books, too. I'd read novels by Herman Hesse even before I was evacuated, so I guess, for a young child, I knew a great many characters.

Perhaps my feelings of superiority were the cause of the bullying, or maybe being bullied made me think of them as country bumpkins. In any event, they often beat me up. They made the weakest-looking among the locals pick fights with me, while they hung back. If I looked as if I were going to fight back, or if it seemed I was about to come out on top, they'd rush out, two or three of them, and join in, giving me another drubbing. One day, as summer vacation approached, they ambushed me on my way home from school. There were five or six of them facing me. This time I was ready to die. Without holding back, I launched myself against the most muscular one. I was third-smallest in the class, so I had quite a physical handicap. When I charged into him, my mouth only reached his stomach. All we were wearing was thin summer clothing, and his shirt was coming out. When I crashed into him, I bit him. He started pounding on my head, but I thought it was all right to die right there, so I just chomped down harder. I felt something lukewarm in my mouth—the blood of my opponent. I bit even harder. It was then he started crying. I'd been crying from the beginning. Still I kept biting until the blows stopped landing on my head. Eventually, my teeth met and I came loose. I guess I took a piece of him with me. I think his mother lodged a protest at my house. I got the reputation: "He's scary when he bites."

Month by month, the number of transfers from Tokyo increased. As the objects of bullying grew in number, the intensity of my own suffering slackened. Those of us who were evacuees came together. In our breaks we often talked to each other. I learned a lot about various parts of Tokyo in school. I learned, too, that flattering or currying favor with your superiors was an option for some. One boy learned Ibaragi dialect surprisingly fast. Soon he became *"kobun* number one," the chief flunky of the biggest bully in the class, and was taking part in the bullying himself. I was astounded by that remarkable skill he displayed in transformation. You know, years after the defeat, when I found we were both students at Tokyo University, he didn't even recognize me. The side that bullies soon forgets, but the side which is bullied will never forget.

In Ibaragi, some among the teachers were experts in beating. Everyone dreaded them because they seemed to beat students half for pleasure. But we children, too, were skillful in receiving beatings. You'd resign yourself to them. If you averted your face, they declared that you were rebelling against the teachers. You got an extra two blows, rather than the just the one you expected. You simply bore up under it, your teeth clenched. The blow would then fall on your cheek and that limited its damage. When you were called into the teachers' room, you had to announce, "Sixth-grade pupil third class Satō Hideo has business for Teacher Yamada. May I enter?" The teacher would respond, "Enter!" It was just like in the army. If we encountered our teacher on our way to school, or on our way home, we had to stand at attention and salute.

The thing I hated most was the habit of slapping among the pupils themselves. Again it was just like the military. All these customs entered our lives in 1944 and 1945. Everything then was done by group. If one member of the group forgot something important, or didn't do his homework, everyone in the group was responsible. We'd be made to line up in the hall, two lines facing each other. The teacher would order us to deliver a blow to the student standing opposite us. I hated that. But students knew what to do. You caught the other's eye and then you slapped. If you didn't do it at full force, both of you would be beaten by the teacher, so you had to pretend to strike with all your might. But you stopped swinging at the moment you heard the sound. If you stopped then, it wasn't too bad.

I wasn't among those who had poor scholastic records, so I was often appointed class leader. If you held that position, hazing let up some. As class leader, you not only had to issue orders, you also had to hoist the national flag. Two of you did it together, while a recording of the national anthem was played. You had to work in tandem. In a poor group, the flag reached the top of the pole with a stanza still remaining. Afterwards, if the teacher was one of the scary ones, he'd beat you for your timing. So when you raised the flag, all your attention was focused on ending exactly on the last word, on the last syllable. Today, I go with my children to school athletic meets, and am chagrined that they still raise the flag, though that practice began only in 1931 or 1932. But now the children are quite terrible at it and they never seem to get it right. I'm glad for that.

In our classroom there was an enormous map of the Greater East Asia Co-Prosperity Sphere. We pasted Japanese-flag markers on the areas occupied by Japan when big battles were fought, and when Japan achieved glorious war results. I was crazy about geography from the time I was young. I really memorized the map of Asia all the way up to India. Places like the "Malay Peninsula" and "North Borneo" rang with hidden meaning. I could draw them all in the air back then.

The last great "victory" I remember was the battle off Taiwan in January or February 1945. The "Sea Battle off Leyte" was described lavishly in the newspapers—how many enemy battleships were sunk within how many minutes, how many sank later, how many were damaged. I knew all the "facts," though they turned out to be false. I drew pictures of all those battles, and of all the planes and battleships. I can still sketch a Zero fighter pretty well. I remember the grand photographs of battleships appearing in the newspapers. One New Year's Day it was the battleship *Yamato.* It was such a smart-looking ship. Battleships up until then had their main superstructure stacked in a way that looked somehow clumsy, and their main guns were arranged in pairs. But this new battleship had guns arranged three to a turret. I remember when we went to New Year's services at the shrine, we talked about this. "Did you see those battleships? Great, aren't they? State of the art!" The names of the ships weren't printed in the paper then, so we didn't know they were called *Yamato* and *Musashi,* but their pictures appeared on the front pages to inflame our fighting spirit.

The year of the defeat, 1945, I was a sixth-grader. We no longer had many classes at school. The main thing we did was dig an antitank ditch in the corner of the schoolyard. "Dig a hole," they told us sixth-graders. The older children were no longer around. From April 1945 on, everyone above us was mobilized daily for work in war plants, while we spent days building "octopus holes." That was terrible work for an elementary-school kid. It took three days to hollow out a single foxhole deep enough so that when the teacher jumped in, it would be over his head. We were assigned the task in groups, and each group was responsible for completing theirs.

Harvesting fodder for military horses was another of the jobs assigned to fifth- and sixth-graders. Today Shimozuma is a city, but then it was a tiny town. This was the Kantō Plain, no real mountains nearby, just Mount Tsukuba off in the distance. So we went out in the flatlands to cut grass in groups. Prior to departure, our teachers would tell us over and over again, "Cut grass only from areas under trees, otherwise planes from American carriers will target you." It was easy to spot us because we wore white short-sleeved shirts in those hot days of May, June, and July 1945. But we paid no attention to our teachers' preaching. We were responsible for feeding military horses. We only had a fixed time allotted to the job, roughly two class periods, every other day. The grass under the trees was short. It was extremely inefficient to pick there. Since all wood was being used, many areas were now treeless, and where the trees had been cut, the grass grew much taller. We'd assign one person to stand watch. His basket would be filled by everyone else while he watched the sky. We kept our ears pricked for the sound of airplanes. American planes constantly flew over. You could hear them start to circle, a high-pitched *"Kuuuuuun!"* The lookout would shout, "They're banking!" Aiming for us, they'd turn and begin their approach. Now they'd be coming at us—Grummans, F-4Fs, or those Corsairs with their bent wings. Carrier planes.

When they began their descent, they dove precipitously. Even a child instinctively knew who their targets were. We'd scatter in all directions at the shout, "They're coming!" trying to get into the woods. If you were too far from the trees, first you'd run with your back to the plane. Then, you'd turn to face it. Bullets streaking out in a line. You'd try to get your body between those streams of bullets.

You'd just throw yourself flat, and raise your head to watch the plane. If you were watching, you might be able to roll away and escape at the last moment. The plane comes in low, a cannon on each wing, right toward you, at enormous speed, but still it takes time. You can tell if they're aiming at you. Then you see sparks fly. The sound comes afterwards. You learn to judge from experience the angle of the sparks. When they flash at forty-five degrees, they're most dangerous. Then you closed your eyes instinctively. They often called it strafing, but it wasn't with machine guns. They were machine cannons, twenty millimeters, and they had explosives in each shell. It wasn't like in the movies, when you see those little puffs of smoke. Across the rice paddies the dirt flew up, and at the root sparks shot up, and explosions went off, *"Boom!-boom!-boom!-boom!-boom!"*

The instant you knew they'd missed, you'd stand up and start running. They were so low that the pilot sometimes opened his cockpit window and leaned out—American pilots, looking out at us, wearing airplane goggles. I even waved at them. This happened to me more than ten times. On our way back home from school we were strafed, too. Then we'd jump into the dividers in the rice paddies. Nobody blamed us for getting our clothes dirty on these occasions. As far as I know, none of my classmates were hit by strafing, though I saw an ox blown apart in a field.

Children can easily adjust to war. It almost becomes a sport. It's just an extension of naughty games they all play anyway. You would put your courage to the test. On hearing the planes banking, you'd see how long you could go without flinching. How brave could you be?

The army built an airfield near our school in the fall of 1944. Even my mother went there for volunteer mobilization work and dug bunkers to conceal military planes. We, too, were called in to carry the soil used to cover them over. We boys knew the names of all the planes and could reel off which types were where, but if we were caught doing it, they shouted and told us not to look! Our teachers instructed us not even to tell our families what we'd seen, for then we'd have been in violation of national security regulations!

From March 1945 on, we experienced air-raid warnings and actual raids every day. Eventually, there ceased to be any distinction between them. They came about an hour after sunrise. When the preliminary warning sounded, all the planes at our airfield would take off, one after another. They would get into formation just over us and fly off. At first we thought they were going to intercept the enemy. But we overheard the adults talking, "They're just going to hide in Tochigi." When the all clear sounded, we could hear the roar of the planes as they returned. We came to feel strongly that the Japanese military were not protecting us, that they thought only about themselves.

When I was still in Tokyo, and in the early period of my evacuation, I really believed the army was going to protect us. But when I watched them more closely, I could see that they were dirty, full of fleas, that their discipline was loose. Now, I saw a lot of dull-looking, grizzled soldiers at my school, looking more like men of my age today than the young warriors they should have been. They often congregated in a corner of the yard, smoking cigarettes and obviously loafing. In this way, I caught my first glimpses of the world of adults.

Just after I had become a sixth-grader there was a terrible air raid and the local airfield was destroyed in a single day. When we passed by a couple of weeks later, on another labor mobilization, the place was in ruins. A few bunkers and shelters were left, but the silver airplanes we had been told not to gaze at were completely annihilated.

Throughout the war years, though, the Emperor remained special. Our image of the Emperor never flickered. I was repelled by the army which I saw with my own eyes, but I never extended those thoughts to the Great Field Marshal Emperor who existed in the inner recesses of that army. Whenever I saw a picture of the Emperor riding his white horse, I gushed, "How wonderful!" We weren't even allowed to step on a newspaper that bore the Emperor's image. We couldn't wrap our lunch in such a paper, because juice might leak on the Emperor's face.

The defeat wasn't such a grave thing to us sixth-graders. The idea that I wouldn't be strafed any more was a relief. Until then, America had been a nation of demons. I really mean that. I liked drawing, so I often drew caricatures of Churchill, Roosevelt, and others, copying them from the newspapers. Our teachers told us that Americans were monsters and lowly creatures. They told us of the *gyokusai* battles on Tinian and Guam, where it was said wounded Japanese soldiers were bound together and plowed under with bulldozers. The B-29s were coming from airfields built on their graves. I couldn't imagine such cruelty. Much of our knowledge of the Americans came from what the teachers said, of course, but I think what really sank in were the war paintings, like the works of Fujita Tsuguji, colored double-spreads, which appeared in newspapers and magazines aimed at children. In the paintings of Fujita, the fearfulness of war was given immediacy through the visible cruelty of the American forces. So fear of war was turned into fear of American soldiers. Because we were strafed, we had a real sense of fear, too.

I was born in war. It was always around. But war is fun. Boys like war. War can become the material for play. All our games were war games, except ones with cards. In one we played at school, we dove under barbed-wire fences at full speed, and I missed, getting severely scratched. I still have that scar today. Whenever boys of about the same age got together, we always divided into two groups and played against each other. One game was called "Destroyer–Torpedo." Torpedoes beat battleships, destroyers beat torpedoes, light cruisers beat destroyers, heavy cruisers beat light cruisers. If a person who was a torpedo was hit by a destroyer, that person would be taken to your camp. Then, the other side would have to come rescue him. I loved playing at war.

When the war ended, we just turned around, almost without even noticing it. Overnight. I experienced no real inner conflict. At the end of my sixth-grade year, we painted out the passages in our textbooks which the American occupiers considered offensive. Up to then, textbooks had been something you felt fortunate to have. You bowed to them before you opened them. Now we cut out pages and blackened out whole passages with ink. Yet I never felt any humiliation as some said they did. I simply obeyed the order I received from my teachers.

Even the same wartime experiences take on different colors and shapes as you grow up. It's just that way with my brother. Satō Seizaburō and I had exactly the same experience. He's just a little older, yet he was one of Prime Minister Nakasone's "brain trust." We experienced the same things in childhood, yet he could serve Nakasone, who in the early 1980s was able to describe Japan as an "unsinkable aircraft carrier." My brother never talks of his wartime experiences. Absolutely never.

---

12 / ART AND ENTERTAINMENT

"I loved American movies."

HIROSAWA EI

A well-known screenwriter today, he was third assistant director of Kurosawa Akira's film Seven Samurai. *In 1974,* Sandakan Brothel Number Eight: Nostalgia, *his powerful rendition of the story of Japanese prostitutes in Southeast Asia early in the twentieth century, won him wide acclaim in Japan.*

He frequently consults small notebooks in which he has recorded every film he's ever seen since his childhood, where he saw it, and his contemporary reactions. "In 1942, the thirty-three hundred and fifty theaters in Japan were divided into just two groups, Red and White, and movies were allocated accordingly. There were some German films because Germany was Japan's ally, but no matter where you went, they were showing the same movies."

I've spoken to my own children about what war is. War's been with me since my childhood, almost like the seasons—spring, summer, fall, and winter. It's part of me; impossible to think of myself without war. What I mean is this: the Pacific War had an overwhelming impact on my life. I, who was born in 1924 and raised as the son of a bookstore owner in the small town of Odawara, was forced to examine concepts like "Japan," "the Emperor," and even "War" itself because of my experience. I've been writing about war ever since. Some of it became movies, some didn't, but either way, that Great War became the baseline of my life as a writer.

In 1931, the year I entered elementary school, the Manchurian Incident occurred. It was a plot by the Japanese army. The interminable

Fifteen-Year War had begun. I remember the three soldier-boys who were billeted at our home overnight at about that time, a private first class who had a red shoulder patch with three stars, and two privates with two stars each. They were on military maneuvers. I got really excited. I was so swept up in my admiration for soldiers as a young boy. They interlaced their rifles so skillfully, making a tripod by the door. I timidly approached those Type-38 rifles and saw the chrysanthemum crests on them. "That shows they were bestowed on us by the Emperor," one of the soldiers told me.

Soldiers had a unique smell, a mixture of sweat and leather. When they removed their uniform blouses, white, crystalized maps from dried perspiration were on their khaki undershirts. I stared at them in surprise. From their sunburned faces, from smiles showing white teeth, came an explanation, "We've been marching since dawn." The next morning, still in darkness, the three soldiers snapped to attention, formally saluted my father and me, and declared loudly, "Thank you for your kindness." They left with quick steps. Through the morning mist I could hear the sounds of their unit marching off.

I've been fond of movies since I was a child. I was deeply touched by the simple heroism shown in movies about the Three Human-Bomb Heroes. That's a story from the Shanghai Incident of 1932. Three Japanese sappers carry a lighted charge at the end of a long pole and dash right into the enemy barbed-wire entanglements and are killed in the explosion. It made my boy's heart pound. Those soldiers were played by actors wearing stiffly ironed pale-colored uniforms, each crease etched in as they struck dramatic poses. Those were silent pictures and were accompanied by an ensemble of Japanese musical instruments. It seems strange today, but the sound of the samisen, koto, and *tsuzumi* drum played at the theater seemed to match their image well.

I loved the American movie *The Lives of a Bengal Lancer*. I saw it in 1936. Gary Cooper's the hero of that action drama set in India under English colonial control. He's an officer in the cavalry. In the climactic scene, he fights his way through the enemy camp until he reaches the tower containing their ammunition magazine, sets fire to it, and dies in the explosion. The same theme as the Three Heroes movies! What sticks in my mind is that I first saw this movie on the beach at Odawara. On summer evenings, they used to erect a tent there. A white cloth was hung as a simple screen, and people sat on either side of it. The movie, though only projected onto one side, was visible from both. That evening I made the mistake of sitting on the wrong side, so all the subtitles were backwards, but it was an action drama, so I could follow it pretty well anyway.

Some army bigwig was there that evening, a lieutenant general, and he sang its praises: "What a wonderful motion picture! Just like the Three Heroes!"

From then on, I became a fan of Gary Cooper. I saw his *Beau Geste*, *Dawn Patrol*, and *Morocco*. Even though he wore a uniform in *Morocco*, it wasn't about war; it was a romance. In *Farewell to Arms*, I couldn't understand why Cooper tore off his military shoulder patches, took off his uniform, and escaped. I didn't know then that the censor had chopped the film up before it was shown in Japan. Still, the hero who dies for the nation and the hero who dies for love both became images of heroism to me. I was thrilled by each of them.

Newsreels now began to come to us directly from over there in China. They were talkies. *"Peww, peww,"* the sharp whiz of rifle bullets, and the *"dah-dah-dah-dah"* of machine-gun fire punctuated them. The image of those soldiers who'd been billeted at our home, of sweat and leather, began to appear on screen. Even fiction had to match that reality, so the distance separating us from the soldiers now narrowed.

A true-to-life image of soldiers emerged in the movies *Five Scouts* in 1938 and *Earth and Soldiers* in 1939.° *Five Scouts* was considered to be of great educational value, so all of us in school were sent to see it. There's one scene in which a soldier sent out scouting doesn't return. All are concerned. At dawn, he comes back. Some of his comrades-in-arms start singing *"Kimigayo"*—the national anthem—and it ends in a chorus, as they express their deep emotion. That's what the Education Ministry today wants our children to sing in school. Of course, when I was a boy, I was made to sing that song at all ceremonies without fail. I was astonished then that the song appeared in a movie, that they sang it together spontaneously, as if to celebrate their friend's return. The comradeship and close rapport between soldiers seemed real to me, but somehow that one thing just didn't ring true.

Earth and Soldiers left quite an impression. Soldiers trudging on forever. I realized that what those soldiers had told me in my own home was true. That movie was just marching. Marching to Hsüchow. I was kind of appalled at the thought that I would have to march that much if I became a soldier. About the same time the military drill we had at middle school became more severe and we had to march a lot too. Soon their fate would become mine. I suddenly felt as if I were suffocating. I hated war because it approached me.

They showed *Nihon News* before the features. That was the beginning of state press control. What a title opening! The Japanese golden

---

° *Five Scouts* [*Gonin no sekkōhei*] and *Earth and Soldiers* [*Tsuchi to heitai*].

eagle stretches its wings over the globe. Then the command, "Remove your hats!" appeared on the screen in huge characters, followed by "Imperial Family News." You had to face the screen directly, bareheaded. Since people were sprawled on the tatami floor of the little theaters waiting for the show to start, when the command came on screen, total confusion reigned as everybody tried to get up and arrange themselves appropriately. "His Imperial Majesty Bestows an Imperial Tour on the Kansai Region" might then appear. That was the subject of the first *Nihon News*, June 11, 1940. The Emperor's Mercedes-Benz comes out of the Nijūbashi Gate of the Imperial Palace. Cars carrying security men flank it. They arrive at Tokyo Station. The Imperial Carriage is seen leaving the station. That was all. Nothing to the story, but the narrator used such difficult words, all reserved for His Imperial Person. Next followed "War News."

In 1941, we heard that Universal, Paramount, Twentieth Century–Fox, Columbia, and MGM were all going to close down their offices in Japan after completing the projected runs of the films already imported. *Mr. Smith Goes to Washington* and *The Life of Edison* were among those. Excellent movies. I felt desolate, thinking I wouldn't be able to see American movies anymore. Carefully held back for the 1942 New Year's showings were *Gulliver's Travels* and John Ford's *Gunga Din*. I was really looking forward to *Gunga Din*. Of course, I couldn't see it because of December 8.

I went to see *Mr. Smith Goes to Washington* on October 26, 1941, at a time when America and Japan were on the verge of war. It sticks in my mind as a result. It truly captures a feeling of humanity. People are willing to let even a stripling like Smith work his will. We lived in the same world, but in America, a young person's will was valued so much that if James Stewart began to speak in the Senate, nobody could prevent him from finishing. This was "democracy" and something called "social justice." I hadn't known these terms, but they must be good things, nevertheless.

On the Sunday of November 2, 1941, I thought I might be getting my last chance to see American movies. I asked my mother for two meals of rice balls and caught the first train on the Odakyū Line for Shinjuku. There, I ran from theater to theater, seeing *Stanley and Livingston, The Ghost Goes West, The Condor,* and *Stagecoach*. Sitting in the darkness, I ate my rice balls and sipped water from my canteen. The last film was *Stagecoach*. I'd seen it twice already; still, I watched until the last possible moment to rush for the final train back on the Odakyū line. I rose from my seat, checking my wristwatch. At the door, I looked back and saw the stagecoach dashing away into the distance, then I bolted for the station.

Those American and British movies really formed my mental character. For example, in *The Citadel* (1938), directed by King Vidor, Robert Donat played the role of a young doctor who went to a Welsh mining town, discovered the cause of black-lung disease, and then fought desperately to make the truth known to the world. Because of this movie, I read the original novel by Archibald Cronin, and, thanks to that, I learned the meaning of "humanism" for the first time.

I remember the day the war started against America and England. I was still a middle-school student, commuting from Odawara to Yokohama by train. It was a cold winter morning. Tajiri, my friend who boarded at Fujisawa Station, told me that according to today's news, our military's entered into a "situation of war" in a place called "the Western Pacific." It was December 8, 1941. I knew relations had worsened, but I didn't think war with America and Britain would ever come. They were great nations for which I was filled with respect. "Is it all right to fight a war against such countries? Can we possibly win? What would victory mean? Raising the *Hinomaru* in Los Angeles? But even then, what would happen next?" I couldn't imagine. That was the way I felt as a boy of seventeen.

I wanted to be a graphics artist, a designer, but everything had changed and that kind of job didn't exist anymore. The whole country was caught up in loyalty to the Emperor and patriotism. Among my classmates some took the examinations for military-related schools and others crossed the sea for Manchukuo. I didn't know what to do myself. I was in complete disarray.

"When I graduate from school I'll be sent to the battlefront. Certain death awaits me. There must be something I want to do before that. But what?"—These were the heavy thoughts I was considering on my commute to school. Suddenly, a man shouted, "Hey you! Why don't you stand up?" Leaning over me was a man with a square, clog-like face who wore a national uniform and a brown fighting cap. He boarded the train every morning at Ninomiya Station and shouted, "In the midst of the final battle, young ones must stand! Students stand!" and he made all the students stand up. Then he'd turn to some man also dressed in national uniform and say, "Soldier of industry, please be seated. Thank you very much for your great work for the nation." He was so imperious. He blocked my path and shouted. "Hey student! What's that smirk on your face? Want me to beat the crap out of you?" I stood up, silent, wondering to myself, On what authority does this man do this kind of thing? Why?

I had the thought that war makes people abnormal. Drives them to madness. My father put it this way: "The Great Kantō Earthquake of 1923 couldn't be helped, but the thing called 'war' was caused by Man.

There should be some way to prevent it. War is so much more horrible than the Tokyo earthquake because it is avoidable." Dad was a merchant. He left me a legacy of freedom, maybe from the era of Taishō Democracy. There was nothing like that in my school education.

The Japanese film industry was in a terrible state just before the war, thanks to the introduction of the Movie Regulations. The content of movies was controlled by the government. Examining human character or entertaining audiences were secondary issues. The primary purpose of movies were the "theses" given by the state.

At the scenario stage, movies were censored—and the completed movies were censored again. The people who did this were high-ranking government officials or senior Kempeitai officers. They said whatever they thought, and what they said became orders. "Add this! Take out that! Do it this way! Put in something of that!" Even comedies had to include slogans supporting the war effort—things like "Be frugal to carry out the war properly." Movies thus became incoherent. Military men and government officials led a splendid existence, like gods, but geishas and saké-serving women were not to appear on the screen, they now said. Eventually, it wasn't good to show men and women walking together. Such stupid rules were now enforced. There were no longer credit titles because it was necessary to economize on film. Movies bore only the company name and a title, and they became very short. The length of the feature was predetermined—roughly one hour and twenty minutes.

At the beginning of the war with America and Britain, on the other hand, the variety of images expanded and new scenes appeared in news-reels and films—parachutes blooming in the sky over tropical areas, military flags whipping in the wind over the Aleutian archipelago. These shots, moreover, tended to confirm the reports we'd already read in the newspapers, as if to say, "You see, there it is." Since you couldn't obtain any other kinds of information, the newsreels had real value. It made you believe what you saw. If you give the national flag to Indonesian kids and tell them to wave it, and then show that in a film with the narrator saying, "Thus goes our Greater East Asia Co-Prosperity Sphere," people natu-rally think that's what's happening. But movies describing soldiers at the front could no longer raise negative aspects of life there. Only the positive things could be described. There's no drama if you only look at the positive. Making war movies under such restrictions, what could you do but describe the outstanding heroics of men? In *Torpedo Unit Depart for the Front!* [1944]° for instance, Fujita Susumu plays an air officer who purposely draws the enemy's fire, providing an opportunity for his unit to

---

° *Torpedo Unit Depart for the Front!* [*Raigekitai shutsudō*].

launch its attack. If this now looks almost like a forerunner of the special-attack forces, that's only because reality went so far beyond fiction when the Kamikaze Special Attack units were actually created. Japanese movies soon fell behind events and went off track.

Several months prior to my active duty, my wish came true. In May 1944, I was hired by Tōhō Movie Studio as an assistant director. My call-up was scheduled for September, so I knew I had only a very brief time. I was assigned to a movie, *The Sea Rose Spy*, about a female spy of mixed blood, Chinese and Japanese, played by Todoroki Yukiko.* She's sent in by the U.S. military from the submarine *Sea Rose*. Although she does terrible things, at the end of the picture, she repents after she's run over by a car, or something. On her deathbed she realizes the error of her ways and gives the secret code to her interrogator as she "comes to understand the true meaning of the Greater East Asia Co-Prosperity Sphere." She is impressed by a warmhearted member of the Kempeitai. Have you ever heard of anything so stupid? Understanding the meaning of the Co-Prosperity Sphere and then dying? You can't make *that* into drama. Too cerebral a plot. The Kempeitai was featured in the picture, rounding up a nest of American spies. It's all right to give the military police a leading role, but how could a human being who came here with the idea of spying, reform herself so easily? I couldn't write such junk, even if you ordered me to!

All the movies had objectives like this. The purpose in making any film was more important than its scenario, and that purpose had to be stated clearly. *The Sea Rose Spy* was to be made "to emphasize the firmness of national defense and arouse the public to prevent espionage." In that way they pushed for impossible things. The soul of the Japanese movie industry was stolen by submissive acceptance of these changes. In other words, the heart of the industry was lost to the bureaucrats.

During filming, military-police officers came to the studio to see the movie. They were my age, and seemed extravagantly arrogant. Each wore an armband with the words "Kempei" on it, and a military sword, its scabbard polished to a high gloss, which jangled at his waist. They looked quite smart. They treated the set as if it were their own. Most of the chairs on the set were just props. I told them once that they couldn't sit on them. They looked at me fiercely and one said, "How dare you tell the Kempei what to do!" They were people who aspired to something completely different from me.

I saw Charlie Chaplin's *The Great Dictator* while I was making that picture. It had been confiscated in the Philippines and brought to Japan.

---

* *The Sea Rose Spy* [*Kanchō: Umi no bara*].

It was screened at the company's private preview room, packed with people on a hot summer afternoon. There were no subtitles. It was his first talkie, and at the end, Chaplin talks on and on. One man in the room who understood English gave us a translation in a soft voice, and all around him people listened. As I, too, listened, I thought, "What marvelous things he's saying, accusing fascism and Hitler. What am I doing here, when he's really doing something, conveying frankly his true inner mind?" That's why his movie's so strong.

I saw *Gone With the Wind*, too. Also confiscated in the Philippines. For sound effects alone, I thought it was fantastic. The theme of Tara kept on playing all the way through the intermission, using so much film, while we in Japan had to economize so much that we couldn't even give the director's name. I had the feeling of extravagance and luxury in *Wind*, especially when Atlanta was burned, but Chaplin's words had a much greater impact on me. He spoke directly to each of us: "Hannah, the dawn is near." That really hit me.

My call-up came on September 5, 1944, when I returned from Kobe, where we were shooting *The Sea Rose Spy* on location. We were nearly done with the thing when I went to say farewell to the film people. They all wrote greetings and words of encouragement on a large sun flag made of silk. Even people who had no connection with me. Yamada Isuzu-san —I only knew her by sight, yet she, too, wrote her name under a slogan "Congratulations on going to war."

I wanted to write a scenario before I went, as a proof of my existence and of my desire to be a movie maker. I wrote desperately in the heat of those summer days. But you couldn't really write a screenplay with a deadline like that looming over you. You needed to have your mind free and your ideas firmly arranged. I burned everything I wrote in the corner of the yard.

I was assigned to a field-artillery unit. We dug foxholes in the sand. From there we were supposed to run out and set charges on the sides of enemy tanks. I was supposed to be a human bullet. To die as one of the Emperor's limbs.

My thoughts were severed like a broken film on August 15. The war ended. It was like a daydream. Had it really lasted fifteen years? No, it wasn't a dream. It was all because of the voice of *Chin*, the Emperor, which I heard for the first time that day. His voice spoke difficult words but it conveyed the end of war. I felt faint, filled with pleasure and relief at no longer being one of His Majesty's limbs. I realized I would be able to see American movies again. I would now be able to live. Today, the only document I have that shows I was a soldier is this military notebook I carried.

Everyone made war movies. I did too, although I was little more than the clapper boy. We all had some concern about being punished for our wartime activities. Despite those worries, we immediately started making movies again. Even while our hands were raised in surrender, we got on with it. I went back to my company on August 20. They were already working. I wondered what that meant. I still wonder what the war really meant to us. Mori Iwao, one of the board members, put up a sign with the slogan, in English: "New Face, New Plot, New Treatment." They'd been so tight with the military, they'd worked so closely with them. Now, they could erase it all with those few words! I wondered if it were possible.

It was good that Japan lost, but I couldn't understand why the American military men who now supervised the movies acted so pompously. They, too, stuck their noses into every detail: "No swords, no 'feudalism.'" We had handed our hearts over to the bureaucrats during the war, and now I felt we were doing it again. What a difference from the image I'd gotten in *Mr. Smith Goes to Washington*! Why were these Americans so arrogant?

Still, I did believe it was our era. The movie houses that survived the fires might not have had any seats—all "standing room only"—but we could now express our feelings freely. The creation of drama is based on exactly the free thinking that war prevents. I feel very strongly about this. For me, that war was the starting point of everything.

If I were asked, "What were you during the war?" I would answer, "I was a victimizer, although I was a victim, too." I made that movie, *The Sea Rose Spy*, I played the role of lantern carrier, helping the military spread the word, and I was a soldier. That I didn't do anything really wrong was just an accident. I was posted to the beach in Chiba. Had I been sent to the China front, I would have done whatever I had to.

Star at the Moulin Rouge

SUGAI TOSHIKO

She is the founder of her own school of classic Japanese dance, called Gojōryū. Whether she sits or stands erect, hers is the posture of a model. She seems ageless in a blue and white kimono with embroidered butterflies at her shoulders. She lives with her husband, the owner of movie theaters in Sapporo, the capital of the northern island of Hokkaido. "The present mayor of Sapporo was a great fan of mine when he was a Tokyo Imperial University student during the war. So was my husband."

My stage name was Ashita Matsuko. It means "waiting for tomorrow." My adoptive father, who was the founder of the Moulin Rouge in Shinjuku, thought that suited me to a T, since I was still a little girl when I started. Those early years of Shōwa, beginning in 1926, were still the era of *Moga* and *Mobo*—"Modern Girls" and "Modern Boys." "Flappers!"—all the latest trends—were still pouring into Tokyo and we had a grand time.

The Moulin Rouge building was three stories high. On the roof was a red windmill with turning blades. There weren't many tall buildings then, except for a few department stores like Mitsukoshi, so you could see it clear across town at night. It was a Tokyo landmark. When it opened in 1931, you couldn't advertise like you can today, so Mother and Father went to the baseball stadium and paged themselves: "Will Mr. Takanawa of the Shinjuku Moulin Rouge please return to your theater immediately." When they went to the public bath, they'd tell everybody, "The show running at the Moulin is really funny." News spread by word of mouth. Mom worked in a high-class supper club frequented by many authors and writers. She supported my father in those early days when Dad thought he saw a real opportunity to make it big in comedy, despite his background in opera and classical music. Mom even pawned many of her best kimonos.

The year I made my debut was 1933. By then, the Moulin had already gotten off the ground and was doing very well. People formed long lines to get in. My father put on a mixed program of light entertainment—songs, short plays, and dance. You had to be able to do everything to play there. The audience was largely made up of intellectuals and students. The local university was Waseda, but Keiō students came too. And well-educated salarymen. We had many fans who were writers, real men of letters. There were a lot of learned *sensei* out there in the audience cheering us on.

Every morning the whole staff assembled and we all had to read the newspapers. The day's program was ad-libbed from the day's news. That's why we were so popular among students. It was social satire. Spicy, too. In 1934, we ran a story of the corruption of a government minister and right-wing terrorism. Another show, called "Cats and Taxes," was a farce about a government worker who took bribes, a cabinet minister's wife who loved cats, and the cats themselves.

My father didn't even mind closing the show for one day so we could go and learn. He always went for something new, original, and funny. Usually our daily bill had one "variety show," two "modern" plays, and a "classical" play. In the evening, we offered a discount ticket that let you see half of the show. A xylophone would sound a few soft notes, *"Ping pong bing bong,"* indicating discount time, and the students would pour in. The variety show, rich in satire, was always included in discount time.

What we called "minute plays" were a specialty of ours. Short skits that took on any and all topics. In one, Hitler appeared. He comes out making that salute, arm straight out, marches to center stage, clicks his heels together, and stands at attention. He's wearing a dignified military uniform and a solemn expression on his face. The audience falls silent in anticipation. Suddenly, he shouts, " 'Hi-ray' Hitler!" ducks through a split in the stage curtain behind him, and disappears. Stage lights down. The place erupted in laughter. Just a play on words, "Enter!" [*haire*] instead of *"Heil!"* [*haire*], but it did the trick.

One of our regular features was called *"Mū tetsu"* or "Moulin philosophy," I suppose. They were riddles and word gags. I used to play the headmaster, and wore the academic robe of a professor of philosophy as I pranced around with that day's lesson. It was a smash. Students used these on each other all over Tokyo. If you didn't know what *"Mū tetsu"* was, well, then you were only passing yourself off as a student. I think the Japanese word-gag humor so popular today really started there at the Moulin. Everything was original. Music and scenarios. Samisen and Japanese drums were played with Western instruments, and punctuated with the xylophone. That, too, was the start of the mixing of the two kinds of music.

Although things were going great, we had a premonition of what was coming. Censorship of the scripts grew stricter and we couldn't throw in ad libs as freely. We had to reserve a special seat right in the middle of the theater for a policeman. If he declared, "No further!" we had to shut the curtain and stop the play. He'd complain, "What you just said is different from what the censor passed." I remember my fellow actors and writers complaining that things were getting boring when they got back from the censor's. Sometimes half a script would be slashed out. "All the good parts were cut," they'd grumble. Sometimes the policeman would let us go on with the show, but other times we weren't permitted to continue. On days when the policeman wasn't there, we all thought, "Today, we can speak freely, let's really let go." And we did. There was a degree of understanding between actors and audience. They understood what we were up against.

Gradually, the scenarios and the shows themselves took on more of a wartime coloration. Yet I don't think we ever put on any Damn-the-enemy!-Go-get-'em! type of plays. I remember one I liked in particular called "The Youth Unit." The protagonist was a Kyoto weaver's son. The boy's father goes to the front. No more work at home. The boy's bullied by local toughs, "Your old man ain't around no more," they taunt. He looks lost. The scene's a temple yard. Ginkgo leaves are falling. There's also a young girl who feels affection for the boy, but that's just extra. One day he receives a letter from his father. It says, "Your dad is doing his job in good spirits. He was the first soldier to breach the enemy line." The boy reads that to everybody. The other kids now defer to him. "Tarō," they say, "you're in command today." Tarō leads the boys' unit around the stage. They're all carrying bamboo rifles. That was a popular skit. I played the boy.

Costumes! They could be a problem. Today, they're really skimpy, but when I was doing it, you had to wear panties that came down at least three inches on the inside of your thighs. You couldn't expose your legs too much. Even the way you raised them was controlled. In a chorus line, you know, like in the can-can, you wanted to kick your legs as high as your head, but it wasn't allowed. "Just as far as your knees." Those were the rules.

The great author, Shiga Naoya-*sensei,* who is often pictured as one of the most dignified men imaginable—well, he often came to our shows. He used to tell us "Watching you people inspires my creativity!" What we did wasn't really all that sexy. It wasn't erotic, but he often came backstage to tell us how sprightly we were. In those days, the spirit of "self-denial for the sake of the nation" was everywhere. I thought I was doing that, comforting all of them from the stage, and that everyone drew strength from that. They used that strength for Japan.

We sometimes went on "comfort trips." The real front lines were too dangerous. They recommended we not go there, but we were allowed to go to Manchukuo. We went in the summer. The Moulin Rouge had so many student fans that summer vacation was our slack time anyway, so we closed down and the whole troop went off to Manchuria. There were maybe a hundred of us. It was like a big expedition. Musicians, actors, actresses, stage hands. Our audience was soldiers and Japanese residents out there, and we always played to packed houses. They were starving for that kind of entertainment. We, in our turn, were exhilarated. I felt we were on a worthwhile mission. It seemed to be the very reason we were alive when we felt their response.

I always looked forward to getting fan letters, but none ever came. I learned much later that Mother kept them in the office. Eventually, she showed me some. Many were full of praise. Some wanted to have tea with me. Others said they would be waiting at a particular place. I understood then why Mom hadn't shown them to me! Only later did I realize that when I'd affixed my seal to the company contract, I'd agreed to a clause leaving the job of dealing with outside letters to the office. That was Moulin policy. It was very strict. On our trips, we had to press our knees together when we sat. I never went out for tea with a man. Oh, of course I knew the men in my group, my backstage "brothers" in the company, but they weren't *men* men.

Actors started to get their call-ups. Our teacher of calligraphy was drafted. Then a scenario writer. We sent off lots of the men from the company. Our conductor, too. They stood right at center stage and were applauded by the audience before they left for the front. One of them from the cast—he played bit parts—told me that was the only time he'd ever felt like a star. Some never came back.

Students who were going off to the front came to see us for the last time the night before they left. Sometimes, while I was on the stage, I'd hear shouts from the house, "Ashita Matsuko *banzai!*" I was very innocent. I liked being on the stage and I knew they liked seeing me out there. Even with the air raids, people would come, like ants gathering around sugar. They arrived with their steel helmets, or their cotton headgear. When air-raid warnings sounded, the audience would scatter like baby spiders. They'd fill the nearby shelters and the space under the elevated tracks in Shinjuku Station. We would run into the underground room we had backstage. When the all clear sounded, we'd pick up the show where we'd left off. Between shows we practiced our "bucket relays," civil defense exercises to put out fires.

All the great, large theaters either closed, or like the Kabukiza, were burned out. The players from the Kabuki theater came and played for us, even in our tiny space. We stayed there in Tokyo until May 25, 1945.

Even that day, I was on my way to Shinjuku. The trains didn't run into the center of Tokyo by then, so I had to get off at Ryōgoku Station, where the sumō tournaments used to take place. I walked from there through Kudan. Clear across town. The asphalt under my feet was still hot from the night's fires. I passed Yasukuni Shrine, all burnt down. Ichigaya, Yotsuya, Shinjuku Gyoen. Walking all the way until I saw the Dai-ichi Gekijō theater. It was still there. So I thought, "The Moulin will be all right." It wasn't called Moulin anymore, of course. Foreign names had all been banned, so it was named *Sakubunkan,* or the "Composition Hall." It was right next to the Dai-ichi. But when I turned the corner I didn't see it. It was gone. Only part of the facade, made of reinforced concrete, was still standing. The back, all wooden, was completely burned. I shuddered and my strength drained away. I was just a little past my twentieth birthday. One of the prop men came up to me. "Ashita-san, I'm so sorry. There's no excuse. Forgive me. We tried to put out the fires, but we couldn't." He was brokenhearted. He said this with all Tokyo burned down around us.

I appeared in some movies after the war and in some plays in Kyoto, but I ended up quitting the stage completely when I got married. The world had changed so much! Strip-tease became so popular! I could *act*. Nobody cared about that. Nude was enough. I really didn't feel much regret about retiring. Looking back on it all now, I'm happy. I was loved in those years. I'd made the war a little brighter.

"We wouldn't paint war art."

MARUKI IRI AND MARUKI TOSHI

Sheltered in a woods of bamboo, ginkgo, and maple, the artists' rambling Japanese-style farmhouse is separated from the Maruki Art Museum by an uncluttered garden, through which a few colorful Japanese chickens roam freely. A two-story modern concrete and tile structure, the museum was built to house and display their works. They are widely known as "the painters of the atomic bomb."

Iri was born in 1901 and Toshi, his wife, in 1912. They rushed to Hiroshima three days after the atomic bomb exploded because Iri's family lived there. What they saw then, and a fear that there would be no visual record of what actually happened, led them to begin painting the A-bomb experience. While each is individually a well-known artist, their collaboration, mixing his Japanese-ink-and-paper style and the Western oil-painting and portrait traditions in which she was trained, has produced a series of huge multipanel mural paintings, mounted without rigid frames or permanent backing for ease of transport.

Over the years, their concern over mankind's cruelty has led them to paint not just the Hiroshima and Nagasaki bombings, but among other horrors, the Nanking Massacre, Auschwitz, and the Minamata mercury-poisoning disaster. A new painting about the crushing of the Chinese students at Tiananmen Square had just been completed when we spoke.

MARUKI IRI: Painters were forced to paint pictures that supported the war. Unless you drew war paintings, you couldn't eat.

MARUKI TOSHI: They wouldn't give us any art supplies. Those who drew war pictures received money, paints, brushes. All the things they needed.

IRI: It wasn't that they rounded you up and threw you into prison for not painting. We didn't want to do that kind of painting. We did oppose the war, but we never ended up in a detention cell, and we never went to jail. I guess we didn't do much to oppose it, since many were taken to prison by the police.

TOSHI: We dodged one way, then the next. Tried to avoid them.

IRI: Our painters' group was called the Art Culture Society. Fukuzawa Ichirō was its head. He was an outrageous man. Today, if we talk negatively about the Emperor, his mood sours. Yet in those days, he was actually imprisoned. Spent years inside.

TOSHI: Most of those in the Art Culture Society didn't do war paintings. Mr. Fukuzawa got arrested. He was kept in a police cell for more than a year. He probably couldn't resist any more. He ended up painting a large picture of the "Annihilation of the Americans and British." I am sure he was the kind of person who knew what art is.

IRI: The art critique Takeuchi Shūzō went to prison. A lot of people who are not well known now went to prison then. It was that kind of time.

TOSHI: Graduates of art school were immediately called up by the military and ordered to paint for and cooperate with them. They never had time to oppose the war. They marched directly from student life into war work, and school education itself had been directly tied to the military. When told to paint something, they were already painting before they were thinking. Those military men came to us and asked us to paint, too. When we told them we couldn't, they said "You're really oddballs."

When people were imprisoned, they were beaten up, treated horribly. If they couldn't bear it anymore, they might end up painting pictures of the annihilation of America and Britain. I feel it would be enough, then, if they just said "I'm sorry, sorry for what I did." You can't help it during wartime. But none of them have said that. None have shown that kind of pure-heartedness. What they did with utmost sincerity was wrong, but they couldn't avoid it. Now they feel embarrassed about it. If only they'd say it, they could go on, paint their next painting.

IRI: Human beings change. It troubles me deeply.

TOSHI: We didn't resist. At least not enough to be thrown into a cell. We didn't resist openly. We lived in a place called *Atelier Mura*—Atelier Village. A person who had gone to America and made a lot of money there before his return built these for artists. We lived in Pantheon Number Three. Our unit was really damp. We tried to dig an air-raid shelter there, but it filled with water. We finally decided that if anything ever happened, we'd just pull up our *tatami* and hide underneath them.

Painters who had hometowns and native villages to return to began to leave Tokyo. Before long, people who were not actually painters came to live there. One faucet was shared by four families. The faucet across from our place was where everybody came to get their water. Some people painted war paintings, some didn't. There were all kinds, but we never really quarreled over it. I remember a sculptor making a statue of a pilot soldier. I didn't think there was anything bad about it. In fact, I didn't think about it at all. Most of us were equally poor, so we could understand each other's feelings. That's why we didn't really quarrel. Even if you don't paint war art, you could feel good for those who did. It was good for them. I find that very interesting. You didn't think, "Their ideology is wrong"; you just felt happy they could eat.

A woman in our unit became friendly with a policeman. She began living with him. It was right near us. Policemen must be awfully clever, or else people gave him things, because they lived very well. They came to the faucet to wash their rice. We could hear the sound of them washing white rice.

I'd gone to the Soviet Union. I think it was 1941. Afterwards I did an exhibit of my Soviet sketches. We used to carry our paintings on a cart from our Pantheon all the way through the Hongo district, down the steep hill toward Ueno. That cart practically pushed us down the hill as we stood in front of it. Most people had given up trying to show their art, but we were tenacious. People we didn't know would ask us, "Where are you going with your cart?" "We're holding an exhibit of our paintings," we'd answer. "Where?" "At the Seiryūsha," we'd shout. Sometimes they'd even come.

We held many such exhibits right up until the most terrible of the air raids. It wasn't true that everybody ran away from Tokyo. People came to see our paintings from all over. People hung in almost to the last moment. The war gradually approached. It comes closer and closer to where you are, but you can't uproot yourself, move out of the way. Finally we did move to Urawa, in Saitama, where we grew sweet potatoes. We had quite a harvest. I remember inviting people from the Art Culture Society to come eat potatoes with us. Being farmers kept us busy. We didn't really paint much.

IRI: Yet we still painted. That's how painters are.

TOSHI: Painters always want to paint something. If they ordered you to paint, most painters probably would, even war paintings. That kind of decision determined whether you collaborated in the war or not. For instance, Fujita Tsuguji ended up painting for them, but he was such a brilliant painter that if you look at his *The Day of Honorable Death on Saipan,* you can almost imagine this is a painting opposing the war. The truth comes out, presses forward in the picture. *The Final Attack on Attu* is the same. His war paintings show the misery of war. It seeps out. I sometimes wonder whether or not he really did paint those to sing the praises of war.

IRI: Fujita Tsuguji! That's *all* he thought about!

TOSHI: He was probably a pure nationalist!

IRI: He painted war art with all his energies. Then he ran off to America. Then to France.

TOSHI: After the war he was a sensation! We denounced him as "the number-one war criminal among war painters." We actually said that.

IRI: We, of course, opposed war itself. All my friends were called up during the war. I didn't go to war.

TOSHI: But he was a borderline age. Forty-five.

IRI: I lived thinking a notice might come at any moment. One of our friends, Aikō, was younger than me. He was a truly stouthearted man, but so gentle to others. We held a send-off party for him when his red paper came. We told him, "You're such a good painter. Everybody knows that. Say, 'I'm a great painter,' when you go in the army." We told him he'd be assigned to paint for the unit commander. There was lots of work for painters in the army. Painters got officer treatment, even those who weren't very good at painting, if at least they knew how to boast. But Aikō wouldn't say these things. He went to the front lines, fell ill, and died in a field hospital somewhere.

TOSHI: Don't you remember the man with the saber who came to suggest to us that we'd be better off if we painted war paintings? His saber clanked along. "Don't be hesitant. Don't delay. Paint war pictures." That was how he talked to us. He came to the Art Culture Society office. It was difficult not to paint under such circumstances, with such "encouragement."

IRI: Looking back on it now, it all seems a lie. In war there's no food. Maybe it was different for real farmers, in the countryside, but people like us really had nothing. Everything disappeared. People actually died of starvation. I was brought up in the countryside near Hiroshima. I was quite good at catching fish in rivers, and could tell immediately whether there were fish in a stream or not. When we evacuated to Urawa there were several small rivers, but no fish at all. Even fish disappeared.

TOSHI: I ate snails. I found them and ate them. I found them crawling along the fence. I grabbed them and brought them home. I made a charcoal fire. I still had some charcoal then. I put them on a screen over the fire. They crawled away. I guess they were hot. I caught them and put them back, roasted them, and ate them.

There wasn't any salt. The salt ration had stopped. Evacuees from Tokyo didn't know anyone in the area. You couldn't find anyone who'd share some rice with you. People with kimonos were better off. You could bring one to a farmer's house, and ask to exchange it for rice. But I didn't have anything, nothing to offer.

IRI: Even if you painted, paintings can't turn into money.

TOSHI: I don't know anybody who was ever able to exchange a painting for rice. I didn't even try. However, I was asked to illustrate passages written by a leading author, Niwa Fumio. I was to accompany him to the South Seas. I was told I would have a good life. You'll be sending those back to Japan, they said. They'll be in print. They asked me point-blank. I thought to myself, "I'm really in trouble now. How can I refuse?" I found a doctor among my relatives and asked him to certify that I wasn't physically fit to go overseas. He agreed. So I got a lung infection and avoided going. If you didn't respond favorably to the "request"—the order—from the military, you'd end up "unpatriotic," a traitor.

At the end of the war, people were crying, *"Boo-hoo, boo-hoo,"* when they heard the Emperor's words. Tears didn't come to me. I just thought, "The war's ended. With this, the air raids will stop." I don't think I was particularly happy, even about that. It didn't occur to me that I'd narrowly escaped death. I didn't have that thought.

IRI: Me? I was exuberant!

TOSHI: That's because you're a man.

IRI: I'd managed to make it through without getting killed. If I'd been taken off to the war, I'd be dead.

TOSHI: You would have died. You'd be dead, definitely.

IRI: My life had been saved! That's what I thought.

PART FOUR

Lost Battles

Umi yukaba, mizuku kabane,
Yama yukaba, kusamusu kabane,
Ōkimi no he ni koso shiname.
Kaerimi wa seji.

Across the sea, corpses soaking in the water,
Across the mountains, corpses heaped upon the grass,
We shall die by the side of our lord.
We shall never look back.

—*"Umi yukaba,"* by Ōtomo Yakamochi from the ancient *Manyōshū*
poetry collection, used as a phrase of parting by soldiers going to the
front. Set to music in 1937, after 1943 it preceded radio announcements of battles in which Japanese soldiers "met honorable death
rather than the dishonor of surrender."

ETWEEN THE SUMMER OF 1942 and 1945, the Japanese military suffered an almost unbroken series of tactical, operational, and strategic disasters, virtually unparalleled in history. After brilliantly executed advances in the first six months of the Pacific War, the Imperial Japanese Navy suffered its first crushing reverse at Midway in June 1942. Few battles have so completely exposed the fragility of a nation's position. The loss of four of the country's aircraft carriers and many irreplaceable flight crews forced the Japanese navy, still strong in surface ships, onto the defensive. From then on, initiative passed at dizzying speed to the U.S. Navy. The Allied counteroffensive began almost immediately at Guadalcanal in August 1942. Although the Japanese won an overwhelming victory against an American cruiser force at Savo Island on August 8 and subjected American troops protecting their vulnerable airbase at Henderson Field to frequent nighttime naval bombardments, Japan was unable to effectively reinforce or resupply its own troops on the island or attack the Americans by air or ground in sufficient strength to dislodge them.

If seesaw naval battles raged off Guadalcanal for most of the remainder of 1942, this was only a six-month interval before the industrial strength of the United States weighed fully into the balance. New American airplanes, fresh crews, fleets of warships including aircraft carriers, escort carriers, battleships, cruisers, and destroyers, packs of submarines, and hundreds of support vessels soon appeared in the Pacific. The Americans continued their drive up the Solomon Islands chain to New Georgia and Bougainville in summer and fall 1943, closing in on the Japanese main base at Rabaul. American and Australian forces soon went on the offensive in New Guinea, too, and from the summer of 1943 on began to chop up and annihilate the Japanese forces on that island. On land and sea, under the sea, and over it, Allied forces held the strategic initiative, and this gave them the tactical advantage around almost the entire arc of the Japanese "defensive perimeter." They were soon able to concentrate their forces and strike with overwhelming, largely unanswerable strength, wherever and whenever they chose.

The notion of "perimeters" and "front lines" proved largely a fiction in the broad Pacific reaches, as American submarines hunted freely to the very coastline of Japan itself. With the Imperial Navy largely driven from the seas or forced into making high-speed shuttle runs under cover of darkness, and with Japan unable to support its overextended garrisons, the Allies took on the task of the piecemeal elimination of Japan's land forces. The numbers of troops actually engaged in fighting on either side at any moment were relatively small, but the length of the supply lines for both sides was unprecedented. It was in this logistics war that Japan's war machine was exposed for the hollow shell it was. Without supplies, food, ammunition, medicine, reinforcements, or information, no modern military can maintain even a semblance of capability for very long. Japan's military position disintegrated precipitately, and with it the prospect that Japan could secure a settlement on favorable terms—which seems to have been Japan's initial definition of "winning the war."

The war went from "victory" to defeat so quickly and with such decisiveness that the Japanese high command seems never to have fully come to grips with its altered strategic situation. Having launched the war on a logistical shoestring to acquire supplies, and having achieved a success that must have been beyond its own most optimistic expectations, Japan's military greatly overreached its ability to protect and support forces in the newly conquered possessions. A few figures tell the disastrous story of the consequences of American domination of the sea routes between Japan's Southeast Asian possessions and Japan itself: in 1942, 40 percent of all the production of the captured oil fields reached Japan; in 1943, 15 percent; in 1944, 5 percent; and in 1945, none at all.° Looked at another way, Japan's crude-oil output, which had stood at 24 million barrels in 1940 (22 million barrels imported and 2 million produced domestically), was reduced in 1941—largely by the Allied embargo—to only about 5 million barrels (3.1 million imported) and achieved a wartime peak of only 11.6 million barrels in 1943 (9.8 million imported, 1.8 million domestic), less than half of pre-1941 levels. Japan's domestic petroleum production declined during the war years, falling to just 809,000 barrels in the first half of 1945.† The most frantic efforts to produce synthetic and alternate fuels, including stripping hillsides of trees to make pine-root oil, could do little to produce the fuel needed to keep Japan's planes flying.

The strategic decision to scatter men and planes throughout the conquered regions left garrisons isolated when the Americans chose to penetrate the vaunted "defense lines" in the Pacific. There were almost no strategic decisions available to the high command that could have altered the course of the war as it seemed to bear in on them. In fact, the Japanese high command was torn between irreconcilable strategic alternatives. Withdrawal from overextended positions, while theoretically possible, was exceptionally difficult to execute in the face of Allied power,

---

° Philip Knightley, *The First Casualty. From the Crimea to Vietnam: The War Correspondent as Hero, Propagandist, and Myth Maker* (New York and London: Harcourt Brace Jovanovich, 1975), p. 299.

† Jerome B. Cohen, *Japan's Economy in War and Reconstruction* (Minneapolis: University of Minnesota Press, 1949), p. 134.

though some forces were extricated from Guadalcanal in February 1943, and Kiska in the Aleutians was evacuated after the garrison on the nearby island of Attu had been annihilated. But evacuation was seldom possible, and withdrawal from one position simply exposed others to attack. The only course of action appeared to be to stand in place and die.

Although actual events relegate the very idea to the realms of "alternate history," there was always at least one alternative theoretically open to the Japanese high command: Japan might have accepted defeat and sought a settlement on unfavorable terms. A Japanese surrender in 1943 or early 1944, no matter how bitter, would certainly have saved millions of lives, and would have been a recognition of the actual strategic situation of the war when Japan had almost no means of altering its course. Moreover, a peace in the Pacific in early 1944—as long as it appeared to be unconditional—might still have held major attractions to the Western Allies preparing to invade Fortress Europe. A "Badoglio option"—a surrender led by the military, as occurred in Italy in 1943 under Marshal Pietro Badoglio—would have been an alternative to the slaughter that was by then predictable. The war was lost, and yet following the loss of the islands of Makin and Tarawa, which opened up the central Pacific to American advances, Prime Minister Tōjō told the Diet on December 27, 1943, that "the real war is starting now."[*]

Cut off from reliable sources of resupply, small island garrisons braced for invasion, in the face of which there was no escape. And just as the troops on tiny Tarawa atoll faced extermination, so, too, did the large Japanese armies deployed in New Guinea, the Philippines, and Burma, which found themselves forced into inhospitable mountain and jungle wildernesses by Allied troops—who loathed the fighting conditions as much as the Japanese did, but in sharp contrast were generally well-supplied and well-supported. Huge numbers of Japanese, cut off from military supplies and often literally starving to death, found themselves totally unable to live off the land at the expense of the local populace, as they had been able to in agriculturally rich China. Whole armies of men from Japan's towns, cities, and villages—from a relatively advanced country economically—were trapped in the most primitive of conditions. To make a virtue of such a horrific disaster, Japan's leaders invoked the concept of *gyokusai*. Japanese soldiers were urged to fight to the last man; they often did, striving to die in a final attack on the enemy rather than in surrender.

The reality of these final battles was that starving, exhausted, even

[*] Courtney Browne, *Tojo: The Last Banzai* (London: Transworld Publishers, Corgi Books, 1969), p. 185.

weaponless soldiers "charged" into the enemy—often actually limping or crawling—and were blown to bits by artillery or mowed down by machine guns in the infamous "banzai charges" of Allied war stories. Often, however, "fighting to the death" meant nothing more "glorious" than holding on desperately to life until one was located by American flame-throwers or satchel charges, or until the proper moment came to detonate a hand grenade and kill oneself. Yet the reports broadcast and printed in the Homeland told only of the splendors of honorable death and faithful service. The suicidal rush of the few survivors at Attu and the total annihilation of the garrison of Tarawa were portrayed as glorious victories of the Japanese spirit, in which "the garrisons died heroically to the last man." Beautified death, beatified suffering, glory in destruction —this is what the Japanese people as a whole were being prepared for through such accounts, as the enemy inexorably approached the Home Islands.

The Japanese soldier had little prospect of escape. He was locked into a military system that specifically forbade surrender. As the Field Service Code of January 15, 1941, stated, "Meet the expectations of your family and home community by making effort upon effort, always mindful of the honor of your name. If alive, do not suffer the disgrace of becoming a prisoner; in death, do not leave behind a name soiled by misdeeds."[*] Such an ideology of dishonor in surrender was to lead commanders in hopeless military positions to dismiss the possibility of surrendering in order to save their men's lives, thus repeating at a local level the course Imperial General Headquarters was setting for the nation. In an era of total war and mass armies, where an entire people could be mobilized in service to their Emperor, and where each and every soldier was expected to live according to a code once reserved for the samurai military caste, gyokusai battles were "logical," however rare it may have actually been in Japanese history for the common fighting man to take his life when his lord was defeated. Many felt they knew very well, from their experience as victors in China and in Southeast Asia, what it meant to be a prisoner; and they had also heard terrifying tales of what the Allies did to those few Japanese who had tried to surrender in the early campaigns in the South Pacific.[†] Entire garrisons, divisions, virtually whole theaters of operation were pressed to take their own lives, assist their comrades in suicide, and exhort or command any Japanese civilians in the area to join them. In a

---

[*] [Tōjō Hideki, Army Minister], Senjinkun [Field Service Regulations] (Tokyo: The Army Ministry, 1941 [reprinted by Bōei mondai kenkyūkai, Tokyo: 1972]), chapter 2, sect. 8.

[†] "These Japanese fears were not irrational," according to John W. Dower, War Without Mercy. Race and Power in the Pacific War (New York: Pantheon, 1986), pp. 68–71.

war in which defeat, position by position, was essentially unavoidable, this was virtually a formula for the suicide of an army. Tarawa was typical. Out of the 4,700 defenders, only 100 prisoners were taken.

"Suicide" became more than an escape or a desperate tactic. It became a national strategy. Individual Japanese soldiers, and Allied ones as well, had employed suicidal tactics on a number of occasions during the war. Diving a damaged plane into an enemy ship, crashing into an enemy plane rather than plunge meaninglessly to one's own death, or making a final rush into an enemy position—these were acts seen often enough in the war and glorified in war propaganda on both sides. But only Japan, late in the war, turned to an official strategy of suicidal attack. This began with the organization of a "Divine Wind Special Attack Corps," the *Shimpū* (or *Kamikaze*) *Tokubetsu Kōgekitai,* by the Imperial Navy during the Japanese defense of the Philippines. Escorted to their targets by fighters, the pilots were instructed to plunge their bomb-laden aircraft directly into enemy ships. The first such attack occurred on October 25, 1944, during operations off Leyte Island, and the tactic met with some success. The *Tokkō* (as the attacking army and navy planes were called by Japan) were usually referred to as Kamikazes by the Allies.[*] From that date to the end of January 1945, in the Philippines, for an expenditure of some 378 kamikaze aircraft and 102 kamikaze escorts, 22 U.S. warships were sunk, including two escort carriers and three destroyers, and 110 ships were damaged, including 5 battleships, 8 fleet carriers, and 16 light and escort carriers. By way of comparison, conventional air attack sank 12 ships and damaged 25 more in that period.[†]

"Success" encouraged repetition. At the same time, the notion of an enemy so dedicated, so fanatical, so self-destructive that he was willing to smash his plane, boat, or submarine into you, chilled the bones of the Allied men—especially those who faced this threat with even greater intensity in the Okinawa campaign, but at far greater cost to the Japanese.

Measures were soon worked out, however, to minimize the chances of a *Tokkō* slipping through to the heart of the fleet. But this mattered little to the Japanese high command, for like the typhoons that destroyed Kublai Khan's invading Mongol fleets in 1274 and 1281, these new Divine

---

[*] The Japanese use *Tokkō* (an abbreviation of *Tokubetsu kōgekitai* [Special Attack Forces] to describe a broad range of special weapons and tactics used by both the army and navy, not just suicidal aircraft. See Chapter 15, "Special Attack."

[†] Richard O'Neill, *Suicide Squads. Axis and Allied Special Attack Weapons of World War II: their Development and their Missions* (New York: Ballantine Books, 1984), p. 157. See also Denis and Peggy Warner, *The Sacred Warriors: Japan's Suicide Legions* (New York: Avon, 1989), pp. 323–334.

Winds had quickly ascended to a mythological altitude. This miracle-to-come, which would sweep all enemy fleets away from the sacred shores of Japan, was by 1945 a constant refrain in what was left of the Empire, and tales of the heroic sacrifices of the men who were the embodiment of the *Tokkō* spirit were recounted everywhere—stories which fused images of suicide and deliverance. By August 1945, the Imperial high command was preparing to stake virtually all remaining Japanese air and sea power on desperate mass attacks prior to an Allied invasion of the main islands.

As many of the following interviews indicate, for the individual soldier or sailor (no less the civilian in the Homeland under attack), the experience of loss was an almost inexplicably bewildering one. Unlike Allied memories of a desperately hard-fought progress through the Pacific to ultimate victory, Japanese narratives of the Pacific War often descend precipitately from brief tales of victory and joy (or relief, or even anxiety) into a shapeless nightmare of plotless slaughter. ◼

13 / THE SLAUGHTER OF AN ARMY

The "Green Desert" of New Guinea

OGAWA MASATSUGU

He was in China when his unit, the Seventy-Ninth Regiment of the Twentieth Division, was transferred to New Guinea in January 1943.

"When the families of the dead come to see me, they always confront me with the question, 'Are you really the Mr. Ogawa who came back from New Guinea?' They have in mind a powerful image of a strong, sturdy man who returned alive. A man who could kill without hesitation. When they see my true physique, people can't even believe I played baseball in college. My position was shortstop." *His large eyes dart back and forth behind his glasses as he speaks. An extremely thin and small-framed man, he walks very slowly around his house because of a painful back condition brought on by carrying his pack in the war. He is now a professor of medieval Japanese literature.*

South of the equator and north of Australia, New Guinea is a huge island, more than three times the size of either Great Britain or Honshu, Japan's biggest island. Japanese forces landed at many points on its north shore early in the war, but efforts to seize the city of Port Morseby on the southeastern coast by seaborne assault were turned back in the Battle of the Coral Sea (May 5–6, 1942). This initiated a bitter struggle, pitting Japanese against Australian and American troops in battles that ranged across the ridges and valleys of the towering Owen Stanley Mountains and along the island's sweltering coasts. At least 148,000 Japanese troops were to die on New Guinea in the course of the war.

Ogawa Masatsugu's regiment finally was in the eastern area of the island when it was caught up in an offensive—Operation Cartwheel—launched in June 1943 by General MacArthur's forces. At the coastal town of Finschhafen on September 22, Australian troops defeated a numerically superior force of Japanese and drove them away from the coast. The Japanese army was then forced to conduct a "fighting retreat" through the mountains, harried by the Australians and Americans. Ogawa Masatsugu's book based on his experiences,

Human Beings in Extremis: The Island of Death, New Guinea, won a major literary prize.[*]

After the main force had passed over the gorge, they blew up the suspension bridge. The thousands who trailed behind were left to die. We were at the end of the line. Soldiers who had struggled along before us littered the sides of the trail. It was a dreadful sight. Some were already skeletons—it was so hot that they soon rotted—or their bodies were swollen and purple. What little they wore was removed by those who had less. Wearable boots were instantly taken, so most of the dead lay barefoot. The worms crawling over the more recently dead gave them a silver sheen. The whole mountain range was wreathed in the stench of death. That was what it was like.

Our own forces blew up the bridge before we could cross it! We marched for another month because we were one day late. We'd already been marching for nearly two months by then, ever since the many battles at Finschhafen, and we'd almost gotten through the mountains to the coast. It was about the tenth day of February 1944. Behind me there were more thousands, completely dispersed, scattered. Many had gone mad. I couldn't get over the fact that, delirious as they were, they still continued to march in the same direction. Nobody, no matter how insane, walked the wrong way. The dead bodies became road markers. They beckoned to us: "This is the way. Just follow us corpses and you'll get there." That was true until we came to the gorge where the bridge had been. Now, we had to find the way for ourselves.

New Guinea was green, full of greenness, all year long. If it had been any other color, you couldn't have stood it. The green provided some relief, but it was a desert of green. The advance units had quickly eaten all available food. The rest of the column had to survive on what little was left after they'd passed. The soldiers who fell by the side of the mountain trail increased rapidly, so mixed together that you ceased to be able to distinguish their units. When we left Finschhafen, we had already passed the limits of our energy, and yet we had to crawl along the very tops of ridges and cross mountain ranges. It was a death march for us.

It had rained for more than half a year straight. Our guns rusted. Iron just rotted away. Wounds wouldn't heal. Marching in the rain was horrible. Drops fell from my cap into my mouth mixing with my sweat. You slipped and fell, got up, went sprawling, stood up, like an army of

---

[*] Ogawa Masatsugu, *Kyokugen no naka no ningen: "Shi no shima," Nyūginia* (Tokyo: Chikuma Shobō, 1983).

marching mud dolls. It went on without end, just trudging through the muddy water, following the legs of somebody in front of you.

As you marched, you lost comrades from your unit. Usually, you just flopped down by the road, rested together, then moved on. But sometimes the one you were with would say, "I'll just rest a little longer." You'd lose the will to stand up if you sat too long. "Let's get going. Come on!" I said to one. He was sitting at the edge of a cliff. He only lifted his glasses and wiped his face. He looked utterly exhausted. I never saw him again.

The worst was the jungle at night. Even if you attached a white cloth to your pack, it couldn't be seen. You'd have to follow the person in front of you by pushing lightly up against his pack. You had to keep your mind focused only on that. Sometimes you'd move swiftly. At other times you slowed to nothing at all. Then you'd shout, "Get going!" and find yourself pushing against a tree. If you tried to rush, you'd stumble, as if your feet were grabbed or clutched at by something. You weren't supposed to call out. The enemy might hear. Each step, you had no way of knowing if there was going to be ground under your foot when it next came down.

At times the rain was heavy in the mountains, not like in Japan. It was more like a waterfall. You'd have to cover your nose or it would choke you. A valley stream could turn into a big river instantly. If you got caught there washing your face, away you went. People could die of drowning while crossing the mountains. I climbed mountains four thousand meters high. Dark black clouds swirled around us. I had the feeling the heavens were glowering down at me. Beyond the clouds, you could see stars even in daylight. It was like being in the eye of a typhoon, suddenly seeing those stars shining behind the dark clouds. It was a weird experience.

For a time after the bridge was blown up, military police, the Kempei, were stationed here and there on the trail, ostensibly to protect the security of villages along the way, and to direct stragglers. Soldiers often grumbled about them. One day I encountered a Kempei. He demanded that I salute him, even though he was a noncom. "I'm a sergeant too," I insisted, "even though I don't have any stripes." "You must salute the Kempei forces!" was his only response. We didn't even salute officers in those conditions. "You're alone?" he asked. I replied that I had a companion, but he was a little behind. "Why didn't you kill him, then?" he demanded. "You can't get out of these mountains if you wait for stragglers. It's all right to kill them. One or two of you doesn't mean anything." He looked two or three years younger than me. The dark shadow of the Kempei disappeared from the mountains about half a month after the bridge went down.

In the army, anyone over thirty was an old man. Twenty-six or twenty-seven, that was your peak. The young soldiers, serving for the first time, didn't know how to pace themselves and died quickly, though there were many strong men, fishermen and farmers, among them. If you were older, you knew what you could do and what you couldn't. I was in what was called the regimental "labor company," but it was really a special unit organized for all kinds of difficult missions. We blew up enemy tanks with saucer-shaped mines. We'd approach moving tanks from their blind side and attach the charge directly to their hull. We'd trap them in tank pits. We were sometimes called the Special Attack Raiders. The heaviest casualties were in our labor unit. We were like a small engineering unit, building bridges and destroying enemy strongpoints, but we took pride in being like tiger cubs, the most valuable unit in the division. Our primary weapon was a flame-thrower.

One thing that surprised me when I went into the military was that the majority of the long-service soldiers had only gotten through elementary school. Many of the conscripts were well educated, many beyond middle school. You could recognize conscripts by their glasses. Regular soldiers often said, "draftees have glib tongues, but are useless in action." When I was a corporal, I once got into a fistfight with a sergeant for saying that there wasn't any difference between a regular soldier and a conscript when both are on the same battlefield risking their lives.

I turned down the chance to become an officer candidate. When they told me I had permission to apply, I said "I don't like the army. If I liked the military I'd have gone to the military academy in the first place." They beat me mercilessly for my impudence that time, I can tell you. You see, I didn't want to kill subordinates with my orders. I could watch out for myself, but I didn't want to determine what others should do. Eventually I reached the rank of sergeant, but it didn't mean much in New Guinea. Nobody ever seemed to rank below me, since reinforcements never reached us. I was always near the bottom.

I heard later that our high command considered the battle at Finschhafen a turning point of the Pacific War. It seems they had an expectation that a victory there could have reversed the tide of war. In fact, we did rout the enemy easily—at first. I was amazed how weak the Australian soldiers seemed. Their infantrymen ran before us when we attacked. The next day, though, their artillery and airplanes bombarded us from all sides. Only when we were totally exhausted did their infantry return to mop up at their leisure. Our side had no fighting capability left.

The bigger the scale of the battle, the less we riflemen had to do with it. Cannons and machine guns dominated then. As you can imagine, in infantry battles, machine guns were the stars. Five machine guns blaze away, spewing out six hundred rounds a minute. The bullets just come "*Ba-ba-ba-ba, dah-dah-dah-dah!*" You want to dig into the earth even just five or ten centimeters more. You can't raise your head. You know how well they know your position by the height of their fire. When the bullets come low you can't move. Your back is heated by the bullets. You can't fire your single-shot, bolt-action Type-38 infantry rifle. You'd feel too absurd. It's like a kind of symphony coming from both sides. You'd get intoxicated by it. An hour of firing like that and my whole way of looking at the world around me was different. I was transformed, along with Nature itself.

I came to feel the Australian military was very strong indeed. They didn't want to have infantry battles. They wanted to leave the fighting to mechanized power. The Japanese military only had infantry. Our artillery had almost no ammunition. If we fired even one shell, hundreds came back at us. "Please don't fire at them," we'd pray to our guns from our trenches. I had a sense then that one day war would be fought without humans. Just airplanes and artillery. War in which human beings actually shot at each other, where we could see each other's faces, that was over. What were we infantrymen there for? Only, it often seemed to me, to increase the number of victims.

The "enemy"? I often wondered what that meant. We didn't hate the enemy. We seemed to fight them only because they showed up. I sometimes wondered why either side was there. It was like a plot by both sides to fight in this place. In China, at least, when our soldiers were killed I sensed they had been killed by a real enemy. There, two sides, similarly armed, grappled fiercely with each other, man-to-man.

In New Guinea, we didn't know what was killing us. Who killed that one? Was it death from insanity? A suicide? A mercy killing? Maybe he just couldn't endure the pain of living. I remember that war as mainly one of suicides and mercy killings. Once, as I was trudging along, a soldier by the road caught my eye. He'd lost his voice. He just pointed at my rifle and with a bent finger signaled that he wanted me to pull the trigger. I couldn't. My mind was still mired in some kind of lukewarm sentimentalism. I knew he had no hope, but I couldn't shoot him. Another time, I saw a man kill his younger brother. Love is such a cruel thing. That's what I felt then. The younger brother had gone insane, although he was the physically stronger of the two. They were in different units, and met by chance in a shack in the mountains. The younger brother was cackling madly when we came upon him. The elder one slapped him across the face and shook him, calling out his name. He just kept laughing. Finally, the elder brother shot him dead. I didn't even raise my voice. The brother and I dug a grave for him.

I knew an army doctor, about thirty-five years old, who volunteered to shoot all those who knew they couldn't survive. This I consider "sacred murder." Often subordinates asked their superiors to kill them when the main force was about to depart. If you were left behind, that was the end. A man who had the strength left to pull the pin could always blow himself up, so everyone tried to keep one hand grenade until the last moment. Even those who tossed away their rifles never threw away their last grenade.

My three years in New Guinea were a succession of such horrors. Everything was beyond my control. Planes roared directly overhead. We could smell their thirst for blood. No matter how many flew over, you knew the one that was after you. Once, I was just aiming my rifle when an enemy bullet actually got stuck in my barrel. If it had been a touch off line, the umpire's call would have been "You're out!" A bullet went through a man's helmet, spun around inside and exited through the same hole. Around his head was inscribed a bald line where the bullet had gone. How can you explain something like that? You move your body just a little and immediately the place where you've been lying is hit directly. Luck? Accident? That just won't do it. I was forced to learn the limits of human intelligence. Things you'd think would logically be best for you often proved to be the worst. "If you're going to die anyway, die gloriously," I'd think. I often volunteered for special missions. Yet again and again I'd come back and find it was the main unit that had been wiped out while I was off on a dangerous assignment. I felt something was controlling us.

I never really killed anyone directly. I shot my rifle, so I might have hit somebody, but I never ran anyone through with my bayonet. In China, soldiers were forced to practice on prisoners, slashing and stabbing, as soon as they arrived for training. "Stab him!" they'd order, indicating an unresisting prisoner. I didn't move. I just stood there. The platoon leader became enraged, but I just looked away, ignoring the order. I was beaten. I was the only one who didn't do it. The platoon leader showed them how, with vigor. "This is how you stab a person!" he said. He hit the man's skull and knocked him into a pit. "Now stab him!" They all rushed over and did it. I'm not saying I determined it good or bad through reason. I just couldn't take the thought of how it would feel, running a man through with my bayonet.

The New Guineans seemed immaculate. To get help from the natives in the mountains was the only means left to us. I was so happy to see that they accepted words without twisting them all around. We could communicate directly. When I first caught a glimpse of black people, I thought we'd never be able to communicate, but one of them spoke

Pidgin English. That saved me. Because of Pidgin, I was not afraid. I understood German, French, and English, but I was amazed how useful a few simple words could be. I was impressed by how beautiful human beings could be, too. An old native once left a mixture of roots and water and a little salt by my head when I'd collapsed flat on my back in the trail. And a village headman went himself to tell other Japanese two kilometers away that I had fallen ill, even though his people thought I was already dead.

I think the natives and the Japanese got along well. They'd dance in a circle when the moon was full. Those of us who were from farming or fishing villages would casually join in and dance, too, as if they were dancing in the Japanese countryside. They'd borrow drums and do it pretty well. The natives seemed really pleased by this. The whites never approached them; they merely frightened them with their guns. With the Japanese, they shared living. Sometimes I wonder why they cooperated with an army that was disintegrating. The Australians would win them over with goods, things like canned corned beef. We never had anything to return to them. All we could say was, "Thank you." Yet their kindness lasted to the very end of the war. Some village chiefs were executed after the war because they provided us with food. They were accused of "hostile action" by the Allies. The enemy organized them to work as irregular guerrillas against us. Indeed, the thing I most regret about New Guinea is the incidents I learned of later where New Guineans were killed by Japanese. It makes me despondent to think that we could have killed people like that chief who saved me.

In the world we lived in on New Guinea, you had no use for the language or knowledge you had accumulated before you went there. Literature, which I'd studied at Keijō Imperial University, meant nothing. I sensed that the extremes of existence could be reduced to the human stomach. Lack of protein, in particular, fostered a kind of madness in us. We ate anything. Flying insects, worms in rotten palm trees. We fought over the distribution of those worms. If you managed to knock down a lizard with a stick, you'd pop it into your mouth while its tail was still wriggling. Yet, under these conditions, a soldier offered me his final rice and a soldier I met for the first time gave me half of a taro root he'd dug up.

We had other fears on New Guinea. Near the end we were told not to go out alone to get water, even in daytime. We could trust the men we knew, but there were rumors that you could never be sure what would happen if another of our own soldiers came upon you. We took precautions against attack. I once saw a soldier's body with the thigh flesh gouged out, lying by the path. The stories I heard made me shiver and left me chilled to the bone. Not all the men in New Guinea were cannibals, but it wasn't just once or twice. I saw this kind of thing. One time, when we were rushing along a mountain trail, we were stopped by four or five soldiers from another unit. They told us they had meat from a big snake that they were willing to share with us. Their almost sneering faces unnerved me. Maybe we were thinking too much, but my companion and I didn't stop. "Thank you, maybe next time," we said, and left. I knew that if it were really snake, they'd never have shared it. They were trying to pull us in to share their guilt. We never talked about it afterwards, but when we reached the coast other soldiers warned us that there were demons in the jungle. Maybe this was just wild fear, but I can still visualize it clearly.

I didn't really have a future while I was trudging along in those mountains. There was no tomorrow, no next day. All I could think about was falling asleep, or following pleasant memories back into the past. Still, when a staff officer showed up, gathered maybe fifteen of us together, and told us to prepare for our final battle and issued us our final rations, I felt that the future had been foreclosed. I was now completely uncoupled from anything to come, in a closed universe. I thought if I could just drag myself a few steps further, I might actually grasp the situation a little better, know where I was, but I couldn't even climb the slightest incline without crawling on my hands and knees. Near the end, everything was called *gyokusai*. In the end, I never did it, but whole regiments were used up in those attacks, protecting us as we trudged through the mountains on our fighting withdrawal. This can be interpreted as a comradeship of which we were unaware.

Human beings can be divided into two extremes. I collapsed from fever many times. Sometimes a soldier who happened to pass by carried me on his back to the next village. One time a soldier I didn't know told me he had two *gō*, just a handful, of rice in his pack. "It's no good to me now," he said. "You take it." Some people are like that. They become extraordinarily lucid in the face of death. I was deeply moved, in a sense, but I couldn't say, "All right, I'll take it." After all, each of us kept that two *gō* of rice for the time of our own death, so we could say, "Now I'll eat my last meal."

Another time, when we were climbing from Kali into the mountains, I was hailed by a soldier unable to move. He asked me to cook some rice porridge for him with the rice in his mess kit. I got water but asked one of our men to make it for him, since I was such a bad cook. By the time the rice was ready, darkness had descended in the jungle. At last somebody guided me back to where he was. "Your porridge is ready!" I said as I shook him by the shoulder. He simply fell over. Already dead. I wonder what on earth he must have been thinking while that rice porridge was cooking. Maybe "That guy ran away with my last rice!" I did my best and it was no good. I felt wretched. The soldier who'd guided me there opened the dead man's mouth and put some of the porridge in. All he kept muttering was "What a pity, what a pity." I saw the two extremes of humanity. I don't know what divides men that way. There's something murky and filthy in human beings. If you've seen this, you might find yourself at one or the other of the poles.

One day natives brought in a soldier on a stretcher. I couldn't tell who he was at first, but he was from our special unit. He told us his name. We'd last seen him when we were going over the ridge line more than a year earlier. On the very day they carried him in, he was shot as a deserter. The man who shot him still regrets doing it. But if you were ordered to do it, you had to. If they had gone strictly by rank, it would have been my job. I was officer of the day, so in one way, I'm the one most responsible, but the warrant officer didn't pick me. I'm grateful for that and I feel guilt and responsibility toward Yoshimura, my friend, who had to shoot him. "Forgive me, Nagayama," Yoshimura said twice in Osaka dialect, and then shot him. This took place after the end of the war, but just before we became prisoners.

I understand there were many such deaths by execution. For example, you'd get an order to "take the message and report back in three days no matter how difficult." You might have to travel a distance as far as from Osaka to Kobe in that time. But malaria was like a time bomb. If it went off you just collapsed and couldn't move. That happened to me. So a week later, you return and you're charged as a deserter. Even many officers were ordered to kill themselves for the crime of desertion. They'd go out on scouting missions, find themselves unable to get back in time, and so leave death poems behind. What a bitter feeling they must have had before being shot. The military was a place where only results were weighed, not reasons.

We didn't know anything about the war situation outside our bit of jungle. One day at the enemy camp we saw two flags go up, the Union Jack and the Japanese flag. We heard *"Banzai! Banzai!"* in Japanese. We'd never seen anything like this before. We then had three days of silence. Planes flew over and dropped leaflets proclaiming, "Peace has come to the Orient." Even the regimental commander didn't know about the end of the war. This must have been about August 15, but even that I don't know exactly. It would be a lie if I said I felt sad, or happy. I can't analyze my feelings at that time. I just felt, "Well, so it's over."

Our Seventy-Ninth Regiment had sailed from Pusan, Korea, on New Year's Day 1943 with 4,320 men. Including reinforcements, 7,000 men in all were assigned to our unit. Only 67 survived. My own company broke camp in Pusan with 261 men. I was the only one who boarded a transport ship bound for Japan and home after the war. I was told that of about 170,000 officers and soldiers in eastern New Guinea, 160,000 died. When we were imprisoned as POWs on Mushu Island, after the war had officially ended, a dozen or so men died every day. The island was all coral, so we couldn't dig graves for them. We didn't have the strength, anyway. They had to hasten our repatriation because they couldn't keep us there any longer. We were shells of men, completely burned out. Even on the way back to Japan, the transport had to stop several times to commit the latest dead to the sea. They were only one step away from home.

It's such a long time ago, so it's probably all right to put all this down about individuals, but I often wonder what the family members of the deceased will feel. You can't call how their relation died "glorious," and of course they'd like to believe that if they had to die, at least they died accomplishing a soldier's duty, not in a ditch by the trail, through madness, by their own hand, or eaten by their fellow soldiers. Relatives of those whose deaths I can confirm with the evidence of my own eyes still ask me, "Isn't there any chance he could have survived?" When I was being held as a POW, even I thought that one day soldiers might begin to pour out of the jungle. But it didn't happen.

All battlefields are wretched places. New Guinea was ghastly. There was a saying during the war: "Burma is hell; from New Guinea no one returns alive." Former company commander Captain Katada told me after the war that when his ship stopped in Korea, he went as far as my parents' home, intending to tell them about me. He paced up and down in front of it, but couldn't bring himself to let them know where I was, so he never went in. I guess people at home already realized that there would be no return from New Guinea.

Soldiers' Deaths

OGAWA TAMOTSU

"I refused to apply for a military pension for a long time, although I was eligible. It was a way of expressing my feelings about the experiences I had had. I haven't spoken to anyone about these things for forty-five years." He apologizes for his local dialect—*rich in the accents of northern Japan's Akita region*—and for drinking saké the whole time we talk at

*a restaurant near a company dormitory in Yokohama City, which he
and his wife have managed since his retirement from Nissan Motors.*

*His face contorts with pain; at times he breaks into uncontrollable
sobs, or a wail of anguish escapes him.*

I was at the front almost six years, in China, and then in the South
Pacific. The final year was the most horrible. It was just a hell. I was a
medic in a field hospital on New Britain Island. My unit was stationed at
Tsurubu, in the western part of the island, when the U.S. forces attacked.
I remember—it was December 26, 1944. Just after Christmas. Only the
night before we'd been talking about what "they" did on Christmas night.
From the time they landed, we were on the run through the jungle,
heading for Rabaul. Our movement, though, was called "changing direction," not a "rout." Words are convenient, aren't they? Our wild flight for
five hundred kilometers was for the army "changing direction."

Until that moment, I'd managed the war fairly well. I was young and
simpleminded. I really believed it my duty to serve as a Japanese soldier
—one of His Majesty's Children. As a child, when you were asked what
you would like to be, your answer would always be "a cabinet minister,"
or "a general," or "an admiral." I dropped out of school as a teenager,
thinking that since I'd have to enter the army at the age of twenty anyway,
I might as well go help my father, who was a mine administrator in Akita.
Soon I had my own subordinates, maybe fifty or sixty of them, and spent
a lot of time whoring and doing all the other things a young man does. I
didn't think much about war. It certainly never crossed my mind that I
could die in war. All I wanted was to leave a child behind when it was my
time to go off to fight. My eldest son was in fact born soon after I entered
the army.

I was tough and found it easy enough to get around the officers, so I
wasn't beaten up much by the old-timers. Even better, when I got sent
to the China front, my company commander turned out to be a relative.
He *really* took care of me. I was even ordered to remain behind when
the unit went on "punitive-force expeditions," so I was a pretty damn
lucky guy. I've got to say that. But I was never promoted. Maybe it was
because of my attitude. I was kind of arrogant for a private second class.
So those two stars on my collar remained unchanged for a long, long
time, long after some others got their third star. Eventually, I was
chucked out of my unit—"reassigned" they called it, to a newly organized
combat unit being sent to the South Pacific.

The unit concentrated first at Shanghai. Japan was still doing all
right, or so we thought anyway. Immediately prior to boarding a transport
bound for the South Seas, I was asked to serve as an orderly to a medical

officer. I had only two stars, but I'd been around for a long time, so at first I said no. I couldn't see myself as anybody's lackey. In the end, though, I agreed. To be frank, I was thinking of that good food the officers got, so I was assigned to another ship. That transport—the one I would have been on—was sunk just outside Shanghai harbor. Most aboard were killed, so you can say I was lucky.

I was on New Britain for three years, and here's what I learned: Men killed in real combat are a very small part of those who die in war. Men died of starvation, all kinds of disease. They just fell out, one after another while on the run in the jungle. Amoebic dysentery, malaria, malnutrition. The ones without arms or with only one leg had to walk on their own. Worms and maggots dropped from their tattered, blood-soaked uniforms. Men suffering from dysentery walked naked, with leaves, not toilet paper, hanging from their buttocks. Malaria patients staggered along with temperatures as high as 103. It was a hell march, and the whole time we were attacked by the natives. They were the enemy's sharp stingers.

We set up our field hospital again and again at different locations. The mark of a field hospital, a red cross superimposed on a green mountain shape, was supposed to represent succor and respite for those who came to it. Our relief section consisted of a medical doctor and five or six medics like me. We would simply cut down trees to use as poles and roof the place with nipa palms. We medics truly tried to save men's lives. Gangrene set in unless an amputation was performed quickly, so the doctors operated on men using only partial anesthesia, because lumbar anesthesia took time. We were true medical men, but we didn't consider the consequences, not there. After all, how could we take the legless with us? We left an enormous number of them behind. There weren't any stretchers, so the more or less mobile ones were given a few days' rations and just told to take off, get away from the hospital, get lost. The immobile ones, they were left behind.

We had only a few hand grenades and a little medicine. Soon this was used not to cure but kill our own men. I killed, too. We were five or six medics with one to two hundred patients to care for. What could we do with those without arms or legs? Carry them on our backs? Left behind, they'd have been massacred by the natives. It happened. Instead, we'd give them a shot of opium and then inject a 20-cc solution of corrosive sublimate into a vein. It took only a few seconds to die. I could tell from their eyes they knew what we were doing. "Please," one soldier begged. I guess he was asking me to take him along, but what could I do? I was sure I'd die soon, myself. I was sure it was only a matter of time.

In the beginning it was hard to do it, then I got used to it and didn't cry anymore. I became a murderer. I killed men who didn't resist, couldn't resist. I killed men who only sought medicine, comrades I was supposed to help. Naturally the fucking officers didn't do it themselves. They left it to the orderlies. We did it under orders from the company commander, then covered the bodies with coconut palm leaves and left them there.

Lack of food left men on the run with not even the strength to boil water. From unboiled water came dysentery. More vigor lost. Walking caused thigh sores. Some men fell behind their units and some were swept away crossing rivers. Some starved. Dead bodies were everywhere. Somehow, the dead called out to the dying. They often lay together in the raised huts of the natives, so airy and cool. Three kinds of bodies: skeletons concentrated in the center of the hut; then two- or three-day-old bodies, huddled together, all swollen with gas and beginning to decompose; finally, at the edges, the ones about to die. White worms covered the bodies. Millions of worms in human shapes, rustling just like reeds. You'd see a dead man's glasses moving because of worms, moving as if he were alive.

We staggered through the jungle at night, because if the American planes caught sight of even one soldier in daylight, they chased us mercilessly. When we heard worms rustling in the dark, we told each other there were dead men nearby.

If we knew the division commander was going to pass through our area, a field hospital would quickly be set up, complete with signpost, and we'd be told to find patients. It was easy enough to gather up a hundred patients. As soon as the commander disappeared, so did the hospital. It was then that we killed the immobile ones. And I killed a sixteen-year-old child there. This I clearly remember. He'd been drafted into the army locally after swimming ashore from a bombed merchant ship that sank off Bougainville. The only survivor. His whole family had been on the ship. He was suffering from malaria, though he looked fine when the fever was down. He had real cigarettes hidden in the fuses of an anti-aircraft shell and gave some to me at a time when I was already mainly rolling and smoking ginger leaves. When I went out to give him the injection, he was asleep. It was the commander's order. The medical officer was watching me. I accepted his cigarettes and, in return, I killed him. We were under severe attack from the Americans at the time. We were made to believe the enemy were demons. It was a kind of brainwashing.

I got amoebic dysentery myself and had to walk naked, without trousers. Barefoot, too. I took some cotton from a life vest, tied it in a roll with a vine, and hung it down my back. I suffered terribly from diarrhea.

Only mucus came because I wasn't eating anything. I was unable to keep up with the unit. All I wanted to do was sleep, just be left behind to die. Once I remember sitting down by the shore, feeling strangely well. It was like I was in heaven. The coral reef stretched way off till it disappeared. The waves washed over my body. I was able to see islands silhouetted in the distance. One must have been Bougainville. I can still see those shapes clearly. I wondered, must war always end like this? It was then that the commander's orderly stumbled upon me. I didn't even know him. In order to drag me back to the unit he had to hide his commander's belongings in the tall grass.

At the sight of me, two or three soldiers cried, "Ogawa's come back!" I wept, too. I was back from the dead. However, someone stole the commander's stuff, including his private stash of rice, and he beat that orderly until blood gushed from his nose. This, I thought, is a commander who values his goods more than one of his men, and I hated him for more years than I'd like to say. I thought I'd never forgive him, but time changes human beings. That commander and I get along today like relatives.

Our flight lasted a whole year. The natives acted like a shield for the Americans. They drove American trucks, wearing Japanese swords. There were two kinds of natives, the Kanaka and Nyugya tribes. When things were still going good for us, our army used the Kanaka tribe. Somehow their women were attracted to us Japanese because we looked so young and fresh to them. They attacked us! Sex with them was somehow strange. But when you were away from Japan for so long, even black jungle women were women.

The natives were the enemy. Americans were the enemy. Even our own soldiers became the enemy under such extreme conditions. Sometimes, at night, a smell of coffee drifted through the jungle. That was a scent my nose will never forget. The enemy sentries having coffee from some kind of portable coffee pot. At night, men often disappeared. They went right over to the enemy camp to swipe some food. Mainly what they got was canned goods, but they couldn't tell what they were taking because the labels were in English. They brought back all kinds of stuff. Facing starvation, one could do anything.

We were shocked when the Americans built an airstrip overnight. We had never seen bulldozers before. Then we saw all their warships. A fleet of transports and cruisers lined up so thick they blotted out the horizon. "Japan's lost," I thought for the first time. The only one who wept at the actual news of Japan's defeat was the commander. I listened to the news, laughing. I was going to be able to return to Japan! I could hardly contain myself. I'd live!

Now, here I am drinking beer and saké. That one year, it was only one of sixty-seven for me. Sometimes, when I look back, I even get a sense of fulfillment that I survived. Sometimes, though, it's all nothingness. I think to myself: I deserve a death sentence. I didn't kill just one or two. Only war allows this—these torments I have to bear until I die. My war will continue until that moment. I'm alive. What a pity I can't do anything but weep. I know tears don't erase my sin. It's karma. I'm an atheist, but if there's a God . . . No! I don't believe in God. I did it myself!

I don't hate Americans now. I don't bear a grudge against anyone with the exception of one person. I cannot speak his name aloud. That person is still alive. He had an excellent education and was able to judge for himself. He was in a position to stop the war at the Imperial Conferences. I don't care what other people say. He cannot avoid the responsibilities of the war.

[*Emperor Hirohito died January 7, 1989, about four months after this conversation.*]

"Honorable Death" on Saipan

YAMAUCHI TAKEO

Saipan was the home of many Japanese colonists who had emigrated to the Mariana Islands when they became Japanese trust territories after the First World War. Saipan's airfields, and those of the nearby island of Tinian, lay in the path of the American navy, which was advancing by stages across the Central Pacific. Beginning in November 1943, powerful task forces of aircraft carriers, bombardment groups, and amphibious landing forces, operating together, assaulted Japanese-held islands in the Gilbert and the Marshall island groups. Although fighting was bloody for the attackers at Tarawa, Makin, and Kwajalein, the defenders were virtually annihilated in each case, and the island-hopping Americans secured the important airfields and supply bases needed to continue their assault.

Saipan and Tinian were strategic points in the Pacific because their possession would make possible for the first time the large-scale bombing of the Japanese Home Islands by four-engine bombers from bases far closer to Japan than the ones in China. Their importance was recognized by the Japanese military, and Prime Minister Tōjō Hideki declared Saipan to be "an impregnable fortress."

Yamauchi Takeo was a student of the Russian language, clandestinely sympathetic to socialism, when called into the army. "Once you're in the military, what you thought on the outside becomes meaningless. They reshape and remold your very nature. They make a human being who fits into the mold. One who will move as ordered, like a chess piece." He was sent to Saipan in May 1944, just before the battle.

He points out relevant photographs and maps chosen from American books of the campaigns on the Marianas while he speaks. "I've now reached an age when I don't have much hope for myself. That makes it easier to admit that I'm a man who acted contrary to his own beliefs. I didn't disclose my views in the military. I fired my rifle despite my principles, and I survived only by surrendering." He is sixty-eight years old, one of three survivors from his company of two hundred and fifty men.

On May 14, 1944, the freighters carrying the Forty-Third Division left the Tateyama harbor in Tokyo Bay, escorted by five warships. We were told for the first time that we were going to Saipan. We were laid out on shelves like broiler chickens. You had your pack, rifle, all your equipment with you. You crouched there, your body bent. You kept your rubber-soled work shoes on continually, so your feet got damp and sweaty. Water dripped down on you, condensation caused by human breathing. The hold stank with humanity. A few rope ladders and one narrow, hurriedly improvised stairway were the only ways out. We expected the ship to sink at any moment. We were told to put our watches into rubber bags. We had a little food to nibble for survival at sea. Yet we reached Saipan without incident on May 19. The second group of the Forty-Third Division, which sailed after us, was hit by American subs as soon as they left Tokyo Bay. Five of the seven ships sank.

The impression I had when I landed was that they had made no preparations for defense at all. Along the coastline there were only a few partially dug trenches, like earthworms laid out on the sand. I noticed no concrete gun emplacements. I heard some noise coming from high above in the mountains, and was told that they were constructing heavy artillery positions up there. We came ashore at Garapan, a built-up port, and we were stationed for defense at the village of Oreai, five kilometers away. I was leader of a squad with thirteen men under me, all late call-ups. They averaged twenty-eight or -nine years old. I was the youngest at twenty-three. Even marching was arduous for them. Two or three times American planes flew over on reconnaissance while we were relaxing. Our guns and equipment were still piled up at our landing points. About thirty-two thousand Japanese troops were spread out all over the island.

On June 11, we were on guard duty at battalion headquarters. I was the duty sergeant that day. We received reports that morning that American carrier task forces were approaching. American reconnaissance planes flew over Marpi Mountain at nine A.M. At noon, sirens sounded, and suddenly antiaircraft artillery began to blast away, *"Bam, bam, bam."* I looked up. Right in front of my eyes appeared huge numbers of American planes, and the air attack started. Men must face war suddenly, men who've not yet done anything fun in their lives. On Saipan there were many towns like Garapan and Charan, where they had women at comfort houses, but the war began before we even got a chance to go.

Around four o'clock the air attack was broken off. Whole sections of the mountains were burned black and the island was dark with smoke. Thirteen or fourteen naval-defense planes had taken to the skies to meet the Americans and were quickly shot down in air-to-air combat. I actually saw them falling. After that, no Japanese planes flew over Saipan. They came back the next morning at four-thirty. The primary ammunition-storage depots and anything that stood out were strafed. We tried to shoot at American planes with our rifles. Not many Japanese antiaircraft guns remained. I saw a few American planes explode in midair, but there was no effective fire from the ground anymore.

The third day, June 13, I was eating a large rice ball when I heard a voice call out, "The American battle fleet is here!" I looked up and saw the sea completely black with them. What looked like a large city had suddenly appeared offshore. When I saw that, I didn't even have the strength to stand up. The first platoon, the second platoon, and the machine-gun platoon, two hundred men all together, were on the very first line. I was in the third platoon, three hundred meters behind the coastline, directly under battalion HQ. We were the reserve platoon. From noon the naval bombardment began. The first salvos exploded along the beach. The extreme intensity of those flashes and boiling clouds of smoke still remain in my mind today. They went sixty meters straight up! Huge guns! From battleships. A total bombardment from all the ships. The area I was in was pitted like the craters of the Moon. We just clung to the earth in our shallow trenches. We were half buried. Soil filled my mouth many times. Blinded me. The fumes and flying dirt almost choked you. The next moment I might get it! Miraculously, nobody in my platoon was killed. The bombardment went on all day long on the fourteenth. We were still there! Alive! On the fourteenth, we had nothing to eat, not even a rice ball.

The morning of June 15, I thought, would probably be the same, until I heard, "The American army's coming!" I lifted my head a little. They advanced like a swarm of grasshoppers. The American soldiers were all soaked. Their camouflage helmets looked black. They were so tiny wading ashore. I saw flames shooting up from American tanks, hit by Japanese fire.

All the men in front of us were destroyed on that first day. Only distance saved us. The Americans got to within eighty meters of us. We were firing at them from our trenches, which were behind rocks at the top of a slight slope. At about two P.M., a vice-commander from battalion headquarters, a second lieutenant, ordered me to attack. This adjutant stood right behind me, demanding, "Why don't you charge?" I told him I hadn't received orders from my platoon commander. "Everyone else has charged! I order you to charge!" I didn't sense any of the other squads going forward, but he drew his sword, took a violent pose, and again shrieked his order, "Charge!" I was in terrible trouble. Finally I announced, "We will now attack the enemy position!" I gave directions to each man, then I ordered, "Charge! Advance!" It was so obvious that we'd be mowed down. I burst forth from my hole and slid in amongst the small rocks in front of me. Next to me was Gotō, a bachelor. Private First Class Tsukahara, the machine-gunner, was on the other side. Nobody else. I was terrified. Bullets were ricocheting off the rocks in front of me. I fired at an American soldier who seemed practically on top of me. I suddenly felt something hot on my neck. Blood. I'm hit, I thought. But it was just a graze. I was too petrified to move. I couldn't even shoot anymore.

"We'll try to get back to our trenches," I called to Gotō, but he didn't respond. He probably died right there. I had seen Tsukahara shooting at first, but he didn't answer my call either, so I dashed back to our trench alone. The adjutant wasn't anywhere around. I don't know why he came and gave me that order. I found Tsukahara in the trench, too, his right eye wounded, his face all red. His machine gun was hit and broken. I asked the others why they hadn't obeyed my order—they just apologized.

We stayed there until nightfall. I ordered Private First Class Nakajima of my squad, newly married, to stand watch. He had a "Colman," a beard modeled after the famous American actor Ronald Colman. As I was moving to another part of the trench, he suddenly called out, "Honorable Squad Leader!" Then, "Ow!" He was slumping down. I found a hole in his arm, clean through. You're all right, I told him. But he cried, "My stomach!" His stomach looked okay, until I saw that his back was carved out to the bone.

My 136th Regiment was strung out along the coast right in front of the American forces. On it depended Japan's defense. The regimental flag was brought up. I was summoned by my platoon commander and told that our platoon, being directly under battalion command, would not take part in that night's offensive, but that the rest of the regiment would drive the Americans back into the sea. We were ordered to remain in our trenches.

We could hear men shuffling, trying to keep quiet, as they moved up. When the enemy put up their flares, it was as bright as daylight. As soon as it darkened again, the men inched forward: *"shuffle, shuffle."* The American forces were only a hundred meters in front of us. The clash should have broken out immediately, but nothing happened. I dozed off.

A tremendous volley from what seemed like the whole American army jolted me awake. Arrows of fire flew across the trenches. All at once. Tracers. They were beautiful. *"Dah-rah-rah-rah-rah-rah-rah!"* went the machine guns of the American forces. The Japanese machine guns went *"Tan-tan-tan."*

While we waited in our trenches, Japanese soldiers fled through our lines, rustling as they moved to the rear. Silence fell after about an hour. I could tell the night attack had failed. "What should we do, Squad Leader? Shouldn't we fall back?" my men asked. I was thinking, "Here's where I want to be captured. In order to survive, I will become a prisoner." But my men sought my commands. When I didn't respond, eventually they all withdrew.

My intention was to stay where I was. When the American forces came into our trenches I was going to pretend I was dead and wait for an opportunity. I had heard that Americans would fire bullets into even the corpses. But I had to chance it. If I missed this opportunity, I wouldn't get another. I lay face down. Morning came. I was sleepy. I hadn't had anything to eat. I was dozing, when someone poked me. "Are you wounded?" In Japanese! I looked up. Bloodshot eyes looked right into mine. "What are you doing?" a Japanese soldier asked me, then he shouted, "Get out of the way!" I was blocking their flight through the trench. I didn't have much choice. I, too, fled, crawling on all fours. I dumped my bullet case—still with a hundred bullets in it. Dropped my rifle, too. That way, I could crawl more freely. My elbows, knees, hands were all scraped raw by rough coral. Fifth Squad Leader Corporal Aoyama of my platoon appeared suddenly, blocking my way. "Battalion Commander Andō and Adjutant Igarashi are here," he announced. "They're severely wounded and are now preparing to take their own lives. I will accompany them."

Behind me, men were pushing, impatiently whispering, "Hurry up! Keep moving!" I told Aoyama, "The whole platoon's falling back. No point dying here." It was very difficult for him. There were the two of them saying "We're depending on you, Aoyama," but at last, he left them. Together, we moved toward the rear, down the trench, fearing our end was near. "Let's smoke a cigarette," Aoyama finally said. Our last ones. Then we bumped into Nakagami, one of my men who'd fallen back before me. The three of us decided to try to make our way into the mountains together. The area was full of shell holes, like craters. We found a house and a concrete cistern. At the very bottom there was still some water left. We gulped it down. There was a *sawasa* tree. We picked and ate sour fruit. Shells kept exploding near us. Suddenly, Aoyama cried out, "Oh! It hurts!" A small piece of shrapnel was lodged in his stomach. Nakagami had disappeared. Finally, over where the shells had fallen, I saw him wriggling, covered with blood. A direct hit. I didn't even think about rescuing him. All I cared about was putting some distance between me and him. Aoyama, who was groaning loudly, and I ran on toward the hills.

Eventually, a man approached us. "Squad Leader Yamauchi, I was in the first line. Everyone was killed. Only I survived." He started to tell me glorified stories of bravery. "Shut up," I told him. He asked to join us. The three of us wandered in the mountains for five days. Everywhere, bombs and shells were falling. We snarled at each other and quarreled with whomever we met. Until I ran into Lance Corporal Murata, the First Squad Leader. "You made it Murata, wonderful!" That was how I greeted him. He was a graduate of the Economics Department of Kyoto Imperial University, a year older than me, but from the same military class. He and I decided to stay together. Nakayama from our platoon turned up, too. That made five of us. After a while, they began saying such things as, "Imperial military men cannot just act on their own forever. Our company must be assembling somewhere. Let's go find them."

In the middle of the night of the twentieth, we first heard the voice of Lance Corporal Ōmatsu, Fourth Squad Leader, and then saw him emerge from the gloom. He'd injured his palm, couldn't shoot his rifle, and was on the way to field hospital. I say "hospital," but it was just a place on the ground where the wounded were laid out. He told me our platoon commander, Second Lieutenant Kitahama, was there, too. We learned from him as well that the 136th Regiment was on the east coast, the other side of the tallest mountain on Saipan, four-hundred-meter-tall Happōchō. There, the survivors were gathering. We decided to join them.

The five of us moved out, seeking our company. We eventually found them clinging to the valley wall, doing nothing, day and night. A regiment of thirty-two or thirty-five hundred men, now only about four hundred strong. We'd heard that our company commander had gone mad during the battle and disappeared just before the night attack; that day he'd been throwing stones at his men and shouting, "Bullets will hit you if your helmet shows above the trench!" All the officers had been killed in action, and Warrant Officer Furui had taken command of our company. We reported to him, "Five men, including Sergeant Yamauchi, have made it back." He was delighted. I was appointed "liaison sergeant" to regimental headquarters.

There was a good, cool water source there, one of only two on the entire island. We drank until we practically burst. There was nothing to eat, however. After three days we were discovered by American planes. They came in at low altitude. About a hundred of us were killed and wounded. That night we received orders to "change direction." We were to move to a safer location. We formed two columns and the whole regiment fled into a kind of valley on a plateau. One of my men opened a tin of beef for me and promised to take the first watch, so I lay down. When I woke up, shells were already falling. An accounting officer covered himself with a log, trembling. I, too, clung to that log.

Second Lieutenant Takahashi, then the battalion commander, was near by. He issued an order to withdraw. Everybody fled into the mountains, running in all directions like baby spiders. I fled with Private First Class Fushimi, my runner, but he was hit by artillery and died. While I was wondering what to do alone, I ran into a master sergeant and a corporal from my company. I was now under his command. We found a half-cave where we stayed for two and a half days until we learned the location of our company from soldiers who were wandering by.

There were now about two hundred men left in the regiment. The regimental commander and his ilk were dug into a cave in Papotchau Cliff. The men dug their own trenches and were hiding in them. My platoon commander, Kitahama, who'd returned from the field hospital when his wound stopped bleeding, took command of our company. I was assigned to be his liaison noncom. I waited in a hole, ready to carry messages.

Occasionally, we sucked on some sugar cane we picked up. It was so sweet! But no water. From June 28 to 30 we stayed there. Then the decision was made to head in the direction of Radar Hill. The night of the thirtieth rain fell heavily. We drank rainwater with great relief.

We moved in single file. That's when we were hit by a concentrated attack. It was horrific. I was almost killed. My glasses were blown off. I'm shortsighted. In the darkness, I desperately searched among the corpses until I found them. We didn't think the Americans were near, but in fact we'd been surrounded and ran right into their front line. They opened up on us with everything they had and hurled us back in confusion. We lost our way, didn't know where we were. We could hear American soldiers exchanging their unique whistles almost right next to us.

I was sucking rain water off the bark of a tree when I heard somebody talking. "Murata? That you?" It was eerie. Again, I'd bumped into Lance Corporal Murata, the Kyoto University man. Four of us hid behind some rocks for three days. Murata's an intellectual. Doesn't boast about his valor. I thought maybe I can consult him about getting myself captured. But when I found myself alone with him, I couldn't make myself say it.

The American army began firing heavily in our direction on July 3. We couldn't remain there. Below us was a valley about six hundred meters long, filled with corpses. Corpses burned black. Hanging from the branches of trees, tumbled onto the ground. Corpses crawling with maggots. Without passing through that valley there was no escape. In our flight, Murata was hit. Directly, by a rocket from a plane. *"Whooossh!"* He died. It was dusk.

Only three of us made it to a place called Paradise Valley. There we found water. We filled our canteens and stayed until the fifth of July. The Americans again attacked fiercely. About two hundred to three hundred Japanese were there. A hodgepodge force. Many died. Whenever a group of us gathered in one place, we were always attacked. That night, we reached the sandy beach on the coast. I was fed up with the jungle. I thought, it's all right to die. I just wanted to stretch out on that wide beach. I abandoned the rifle I'd borrowed from a soldier when I again became a squad leader. He'd begged me, "Please return it later, Honorable Squad Leader." But I never saw him again. I never fired it, either.

On this sandy beach, too, we were suddenly fired on in the night. We couldn't even tell where the shots were coming from, but fortunately we found a dugout covered with thin iron plate, sand piled on top, high on the beach. It was big enough for three men to crawl in. We stayed there until the eighth of July.

We saw some of our men heading off, single file, in the same direction. "Where are you going?" we asked. "We're assembling at Garapan to attack," they said. "The Americans took Garapan a long time ago. You can't get there," I shouted back. "It's an order!" Fujigaki and Ueda turned to me. "Squad Leader, what shall we do? Don't we have to go?" I told them, "Don't you remember? We went through that already! We don't have to go again." The three of us remained in our dugout.

I soon learned that Lieutenant General Saitō Yoshitsugu, Commander of the Forty-third Division, issued the order for all survivors to make a "general attack" on the morning of the seventh. That included civilians. He then killed himself, or rather he ordered one of his men to shoot him with a pistol.

In those days, Japanese soldiers really accepted the idea that they must eventually die. If you were taken alive as a prisoner you could never face your own family. They'd been sent off by their neighbors with cheers of *"Banzai!"* How could they now go home? "General attack" meant suicide. Those unable to move were told to die by a hand grenade or by taking cyanide. The women and children had cyanide. Those who didn't jumped off cliffs. Ones like me, who from the beginning were thinking about how to become prisoners, were real exceptions.

The attack went off early on the morning of the seventh. Four thousand Japanese charged into the American lines. About three thousand were killed. I didn't take part. I slept during the day. On the night prior to the attack I told my two men that there was no point starving and dying here on Saipan, that Japan would lose in this war, that there would be better days ahead for us. I never brought up my Communist beliefs. But their only response was, "Squad Leader, you're talking like a traitor. Behave like a military man!" I had been rebuked by my own subordinates, a farmer and a city man who'd only graduated from elementary school. They were unflinching.

The American forces passed beyond us on the ninth. At night we moved up to where the vegetation offered us cover. Some sailors and army men were there. On the tenth, we were fired at from the sea. Intense firing. The man next to me was killed. I suggested to my men that we swim out to where the bow of a sunken ship was jutting out of the sea, but they didn't want to act with me any more. They walked back into the jungle to find the company. I spoke to others about swimming out to the ship. That night, we tried, but it proved a simple-minded idea. We couldn't even get close. The waves were too strong, and it was much farther away than it looked. Most of the men turned back. Just one sailor and I were left. Suddenly, an American machine gun opened up on us. I could hear the bullets skipping on the waves. We quit and swam back. That sailor and I fled to the very northern tip of the island where we found a cave to crawl into.

Inside were a Japanese noncom—I thought he must be a master sergeant; that's the way he spoke—several soldiers, and some Japanese women with babies. Maybe twenty of them, altogether. It was pitch-dark at night. I could hear their voices. Babies crying. The sailor and I sat in the corner, in the darkness, without talking to anyone else there. Immediately above that cave ran a road. American forces were all over the place. The sergeant insisted that the babies' cries would alert the Americans. "Kill them yourself or I'll order my men to do it." Several mothers killed their own children.

Now, the Americans began to broadcast surrender advice over loudspeakers. From the sea. "Japanese Forces! Throw down your arms! We will protect the honor of those who have fought hard and who give themselves up. We have water. We have food." Their Japanese was a little shaky. They said they would resume firing after a fixed interval. That was the first time I heard an American call to surrender, but I feared that if I surrendered within sight of our own men during daylight, I might be shot in the back.

Late on the thirteenth, deep in the night, I slipped out of the cave and huddled under a tree at the edge of the cliff. I planned to make my way out when the call to surrender began at daybreak. There were several civilians there, too. A young woman of sixteen or seventeen, a middle-aged couple, and a man, a little older than me. I couldn't tell if he was a civilian or a soldier. I pleaded with them to let me in their group. The girl spoke to me. All her family members had been killed, she said. Her younger brother by artillery fire. Her parents had killed themselves with cyanide. She, too, took something, but nothing happened to her. That's what her parents must have wanted, she said. I told her, "You must not kill yourself. Your parents tried to spare your life that way." I couldn't actively say, "Let's surrender," because I was worried about what that young man might do.

The middle-aged woman offered me some porridge in an old tin can. I hadn't eaten rice for days. I began to wolf it down eagerly, but that man glared at me. I offered him some, and he started gulping it down. This, I thought, was a good chance. "I'm going now," I announced. "Come with me if you want to." I didn't say where I was going, I just stood up.

The American army was only a little ways off. "When I'm spotted by them," I thought, "I only have to raise my hands immediately." I had a cigarette case I'd carried since my student days. Silver plated. I'd scratched a picture of a wood nymph into it as a joke. On the back I'd written, "Workers of the World, Unite!" in Russian. I worried that although America was allied with the Soviet Union, maybe Communism was illegal. I threw it away. I was making my way through the jungle when I heard, "Halt!" An American soldier was pointing his rifle at me. I thought, "I'm saved!" I looked back. Trailing me were that young woman and the middle-aged couple.

I was questioned. "Are you a soldier?" Yes, I said. An American sergeant ordered me to sit down. He told me there were Japanese troops all over that area. "Tell them to surrender. Shout to them." I'd barely been able to surrender myself. I didn't have enough courage to call on others to give themselves up. So I yelled, *"Oooi! Oooi!"* ["Hey! Hey!"] "What's this 'oooi' mean?" the sergeant demanded. "It means 'come out,'" I said. He didn't push me any further. I wanted to say something more to that sergeant, but at first only Russian words came to mind.

Finally, I said, "Will peace come soon?" "I hope so," he answered. I can't tell you how happy I was. I'd achieved my wish. I was going to survive the Second World War. From now, I'd be able to observe this turning point in world history from a safe position! I'd made it out! I was the seven-hundred-fifty-seventh military prisoner-of-war taken on Saipan.

I surrendered on July 14. The American soldiers had been demons on the battlefield, ready to kill me in an instant. Now, here they were, right in front of my eyes. Relaxed. Sprawled on top of Jeeps, shouting, "Hey!" Joking with each other. At that moment, Japanese forces fired at us from the mountain. The Americans started to fire back. I threw myself flat, in an instant. The women just stayed sitting where they were. Indifferent. Seemingly lost.

It was an embarrassment to be a POW. Even though I didn't really feel that way, the others all feared their families would suffer. As the number of POWs increased, we became more and more like our former military selves. Ranks came back. Suddenly, once again, I was Squad Leader Yamauchi. We were taken to Hawaii, then Angel Island in San Francisco, then to a town in the hills near LaCrosse, Wisconsin. Veteran POWs who'd been there ahead of us, naval officers who'd been taken prisoner, had already established complete Japanese military order in the camp. There was no one for me to talk to. "If I speak my mind," I thought then, "I'll probably be lynched." Gradually, I learned that this military order was only a kind of ritual. They were talking to hear themselves talk.

I could read books and work in the hills. Officers didn't have to do any labor, but noncoms did. So out we went to cut down trees in firebreak areas. We took our lunches. That was probably the most enjoyable time for me. Here I was in America. I could read American newspapers—the *Chicago Sun* and the *Christian Science Monitor*. I was able to think about whatever I wanted to think about. Occasionally, thoughts of my parents or family came to mind, but I no longer felt bound to Japan. It may sound strange, but I even thought maybe it would be OK for me to become American. I'd studied Russian, but the longer I was in America, the smaller the Soviet Union seemed to grow. American liberalism came to look better than socialism. Universalism, a world without states, seemed best of all. The nation didn't matter to me any more. It was the best time I ever experienced, one I look back on fondly, even now.

According to a Japanese source, of the 43,682 military defenders, 41,244 died in the battle of Saipan (June 15 to July 10, 1944). Also, approximately 20,000 civilians had lived on Saipan, including Japanese—many from Okinawa—Koreans, and tribal people. Eight to ten thousand of them died in the battle. Approximately four thousand Japanese women, children, and other noncombatants were driven into the northern corner of the island, where most committed mass suicide rather than let themselves be captured by the enemy.° It was the first time American forces had seen civilians take their lives in such numbers. The sight of women leaping from cliffs shocked even battle-hardened veterans. Prime Minister Tōjō's cabinet fell soon after the Saipan defeat and he was replaced by General Koiso Kuniaki.

° Kuroha Kiyotaka, *Taiheiyō sensō no rekishi* (History of the Pacific War) vol. 2 (Tokyo: Kōdansha, 1989), pp. 143–46.

14 / SUNKEN FLEET

Lifeboat

MATSUNAGA ICHIRŌ

He is a graduate of the naval academy at Etajima and the son of a rear admiral. In the summer of 1944, he went aboard the Imperial Japanese Navy's Natori, *a 5,170-ton light cruiser, as chief ship's communications officer, holding the rank of senior lieutenant. The tide of the war had long since turned against Japan. American submarines, airplanes, and warships roamed freely across the vital supply lines of the Empire.*

When the light cruiser *Natori* weighed anchor from Cebu in the Philippines, we thought we were making the last supply run to Palau. It was August 1944. Strategic estimates determined that the Americans would next approach the Philippines. In their way stood Palau. Merchant ships lacked the speed to resupply our base there, so we had begun making runs to Palau at the beginning of July. We even evacuated the women and children. We might not like being a supply ship, but it was vital, and we were committed to carrying out our mission. There were more than 600 men aboard the *Natori,* well over the peacetime complement of 435. The number of crewmen on watch for submarines and the number of antiaircraft machine-gun batteries had been increased, and we were also taking several dozen reinforcements to Palau.

We were supposed to be a fighting ship, but we were weighted down with goods. Our cargo space was very limited. A senior naval officer in Manila even suggested removing the lifeboats to make more room, but Captain Kubota, the *Natori's* commander, refused with the words, "Those cutters are to protect our crew members." Instead, he removed the ship's reserve torpedoes, over the objection of the torpedo officer. The *Natori* might have been twenty-three years old, but she was an Imperial Japanese Navy light cruiser, and we were trained to do battle with the Americans. When those torpedoes were removed, you felt like you'd been sent to the minor leagues. The captain also ordered new lumber taken on board and lashed to the deck with manila rope, not wire.

It took three tries for us to exit the San Bernardino Strait between Luzon and Samar. Word was that the American task forces were lying at sea to the east of the Philippines, and each time we had to scurry back to port. Our breakout was on August 17. We estimated that American submarines would by lying in wait along the direct route to Palau, so the captain set a course more than two hundred miles to the south.

We soon found ourselves in a severe squall. We zigzagged, although we assumed they wouldn't know where we were, but as soon as we left the squall, a little after two A.M., we saw a blue flare from *Number Three Transport Ship*, the requisitioned cargo vessel running with us. That meant "torpedo track sighted." The officer on duty called out, "Starboard watch!" The crewman on watch called back, "Torpedo track! Starboard one hundred twenty degrees." "Right—full rudder. All ahead full!" Before the helm could respond, we were hit by a running torpedo.

I was on the bridge when there was an enormous explosion. The whole ship rocked. A pillar of fire shot higher than the mast. A fire started just astern of the bridge. All electric power was immediately lost. The main generator must have been damaged. All we had to try to save the ship with were hand pumps and primitive hand-held lights. But we successfully flooded the magazines, fore and aft. I ordered a man on the bridge to communicate through voice tube to the forward radio room. He tried, but white, acrid-smelling smoke came out of the tube, and there was no response. I concluded that the four or five men on duty there had died in action.

Thanks to rapid repairs, we recovered boiler pressure and were soon capable of half-speed. Our companion ship had already left the area. The captains had agreed before departure that if either was hit, neither would slow down, even to recover survivors. After about fifty minutes, at 3:30 A.M., we were again attacked by a submarine. We could see the torpedo coming. It had a white track. No evasive action was possible, so it hit us directly amidships. But it didn't explode!

To retain our buoyancy, we cut loose the two main anchors, four tons each. Next went the cargo bound for Palau, including sixteen airplane torpedoes, antiaircraft weapons, food—roughly six hundred tons' worth—all over the side, piece by piece. Gradually, the *Natori* began to settle, bow first. We jettisoned most of the ammunition for the main gun batteries in order to save the ship. *Number Three* returned, and began to approach, but our captain signaled by flare for him to stay away. It circled us twice before departing, signaling by lamp: "Leaving for Palau as planned."

Again the watch cried out, "Periscope sighted!" We couldn't use our hydrophone to locate the submarine because we'd lost electricity. We only had our eyes. The order was given to open fire in the sub's direction. Pillars of water rose where our shells hit. We felt some relief when the sun appeared at last. But by five in the morning, the forward deck was already awash. We were still making six knots, in reverse. At about six o'clock, the Captain spoke with the head of the engine room and then went below. When he reappeared on the bridge, he'd changed into his pure white dress uniform. He was wearing white gloves and held his military sword in his right hand even though there was a magnetic compass on the bridge and no one was supposed to wear a sword there.

He ordered rafts to be made from the lumber we were carrying and had hard tack and fresh water loaded onto the cutters. The boats were lowered and the rafts set adrift. They were ordered to stand clear of the ship itself. He smoked two cigarettes, but otherwise was himself. He then ordered every man up from belowdecks. This was the first time the men had been able to leave battle stations. "Warship *Natori, banzai!*" he announced. "His Imperial Majesty, *banzai!*" Three cheers for each of them. While this was happening, the ship's doctor ordered the injured taken off in the motor launch. Our position was radioed to naval headquarters in Manila. The captain's last order was "All hands abandon ship!" With that, he turned and went into his cabin and latched it from the inside. Five hours had passed since the first torpedo struck.

We all went into the sea, swimming away from the ship as quickly as possible to avoid being pulled under. The *Natori* went down bow first, twisting around to port to show all four screws. The motor launch was caught by one of the screws and was pulled down with roughly fifty men aboard.

The ocean swells were enormous. I swam for the second cutter and climbed aboard. After me came Kobayashi Eiichi, chief of navigation. He ordered me to signal to the others to find the executive officer, who was next in the chain of command. When we couldn't, Kobayashi said, "As third in the line of command, I must now consider the executive officer to have been killed in action. I am assuming command." We located the other two cutters and the two remaining harbor launches. There were several rafts. And many men were still swimming. About eight o'clock, launch number three sank suddenly, with many screams. The sea was so rough, the wind so strong, that we weren't able to row the cutter to them. "Hold on to a raft or wood! Don't swim! You'll tire yourselves out!" I shouted in their direction. When the *Natori* sank, the lumber on its deck floated to the surface. Many men clung to those boards.

We didn't know what to do. We faced the prospect of being hit broadside by the waves and capsized. In the dark, we couldn't even tell which way the sea was running. Suddenly, I remembered, "Sea anchors!" A sea anchor is a device that combines buoyancy with weight. I jumped into the rolling sea to gather some lumber. We used the cutter's metal crane arm for weight. We set the sea anchors and drifted. Between squalls, a friendly plane flew over and dropped a communications canister with the message that two destroyers were on their way to rescue us.

We began picking up the men who had been hanging onto the lumber or lifebuoys since we went down. I was now second in command on the cutter. We didn't have any tools or equipment to indicate our location. No smoke markers or signal lamps. No radio. Senior officer Kobayashi on my cutter determined that we should attempt to reach land by rowing, rather than just waiting for rescue. We didn't have much potable water or food. We didn't even have a compass. The crewmen were all against it. The son of a fisherman spoke up first, alluding to an old saying of the sea that a fishing boat that develops a problem should stay put. He suggested we remain where we were. But the senior officer replied, "That's a peacetime proverb. This is war." The crewmen knew they would be pulling the oars without food or drink.

On the other hand, we naval-academy graduates knew that wooden cutters were unsinkable. Lieutenant Kobayashi—he was only twenty-seven and had graduated a year ahead of me—was unshakable. He told the men, "If we do not reach land, all six hundred members of the crew of the *Natori* will be considered missing. We'll never be able to express our regrets and pray for our war comrades who shared the fate of the warship. We must reach land, whatever it takes." Those who had opposed rowing finally came around to his point of view once they realized they'd just be considered missing, not killed in action. They couldn't bear the thought. To be "missing" allowed for the possibility that you'd let yourself to be taken prisoner. So now they had motivation.

For two or three days the sea remained very rough. The senior officer set policy. How to carry out his orders was now the responsibility of us other officers. What stars would be our "landmarks," how many hours a night would we row—such decisions had to be made. The senior officer decided that men who could navigate by the stars should all be in the same cutter. The other two boats therefore had no choice but to follow us.

I was in charge of rations. Had we done as we normally did, the officers would have had more to eat than the enlisted rankings. But had we done that under these extreme conditions, military discipline might not have held. I had to be careful to avoid any hint of unfairness. I remembered stories of mutinies that were sparked by food in the wake of a shipwreck. My responsibility was to forestall a mutiny. The senior officer said simply, "We'll make for the Philippines by rowing." I had the task of getting us there. I took great pride in my psychological leadership.

We had two kinds of small hard biscuits. One was wrapped in

seaweed, the other plain. I issued one of each per man per day. I slept on the tins containing the hard biscuits, so no one could get at them. We had a dozen cans of condensed milk. I thought they would be enough to adequately nourish one man. The thing I feared most was night blindness. We might miss islands in the distance—if ever they appeared. I suggested to the senior officer that he use the milk. He refused. I certainly didn't think it would be a good idea for me to drink the milk. They'd never have forgiven me. So that condensed milk remained untouched to the end.

Senior officer Kobayashi insisted we must not lie to the men. If we assured them not to worry, "We'll get there tomorrow," and didn't arrive, they'd no longer trust us. Our authority would have ended there.

There were three cutters, each with about sixty-five men aboard. There were no covers for the cutters. We just crossed oars over our heads and covered them with our jerseys. We were all in our tropical fatigues. Just short pants, officers and sailors alike. I read somewhere that American airplane pilots were issued survival kits which included fishing tackle. We had had roughly five hours before our ship sank and it would have been better to bring fishhooks or nets on board, or even bait, but as a naval officer of Japan, I never thought to try to save my own life while my warship was still afloat. We'd make no preparations to extend our own lives.

We had one machine gun in the bow of our cutter. We officers were in the stern. The men's facial expressions gradually changed. They became threatening and sullen. I asked the senior officer whether I should change the location of the gun. His response was, no. If a mutiny were to take place, we'd have no chance, anyway. It would be sixty to four. We'd have to rely on our authority as their superiors, the ones who evaluated them. I thought in my own mind, "I have to do something to prevent mutiny. It might break out at any moment."

We set our sea anchor during the day and raised our cover. They were assigned duty watches. Those on duty would pour seawater onto the cloth. It cooled things down a bit when it evaporated. We tried to sleep. It was hard. We rowed ten hours a night, and ate about half an hour after sunrise. Whenever a squall came we drank rainwater. First we'd hold our mouths open, as wide as possible, but not much went in that way. We stretched out our shirts to collect the water and sucked on them like babies. We were very lucky—that year the rainy season lasted a little longer than normal. We had squalls every day. There must have been lots of American ships in that area. I'm amazed they didn't locate us. If they'd found us, what choice would we have had but to fight?

The crewmen talked about food, all the time. Especially what they ate when they were home. One kept on about the purity of the water at a shrine in the woods behind his house. A former schoolteacher speculated about his pupils, who might already be on summer vacation. Men with families must have thought of their wives and children. Few spoke about them though. Japanese at that time considered such conversation unmanly. I think the senior officer was married, but he never mentioned it.

We planned carefully. The Philippine archipelago stretches twelve hundred kilometers, north to south. We had been sunk three hundred nautical miles east of the Philippines. Even without a compass, if we rowed due west, sooner or later we would reach some part of the archipelago, no matter how we drifted north or south. Our calculation was that it would take fifteen days to reach land by rowing, but we divided the food into thirty days' worth of rations, assuming that some days rowing would be impossible due to rough seas. We were concerned about how long our physical strength would hold up. If we kept the North Star exactly on our starboard, then we knew we were heading west. That we were certain of, but how many days could we go without food or drink?

Each cutter had twelve oars. With two men to an oar, twenty-four men could row. The other forty had to lie flat. If you raised your head, you'd be cracked by an oar. It was hard for those rowing, but it was hard for the others, too. All you saw was sea. We made a sail. Everyone had to contribute a small portion of their uniform. We used an extra oar for a mast, but we were never able to sail with it. Still, we kept hoping, that maybe tomorrow we wouldn't need to row if a good wind came up.

There is a common saying in Japan, that "The foundation of leadership is for the leader himself to set the example." But the leadership style we were taught at the naval academy was different. If I had rowed, I would have been able to offer the strength of only one man. The leadership of the commander was not meant to provide only man's strength, but to bring together the strength of all the others and set them in a single direction. That's why we officers didn't row.

It was sweltering. On the ocean in the South Seas in August, at the peak of the summer's heat, when the sun rose, any exposed skin immediately felt pain. It was like needles were being stuck into you. That pain lasted until the sun began to set. The men wanted to go swimming. We were concerned that they would exhaust themselves, but we were just as worried that if we rejected all their requests, we might face a mutiny. Among the officers, I was strongest, so I tested the idea myself. Having eaten hardly anything for a week, could I still float? I lowered a length of hawser over the side into the sea and let myself down into the water. It felt wonderful! All the heat in my body was drawn off by the seawater. I let go of the rope. I didn't sink. We decided to let the crewmen take turns going.

Some quick-witted sailors spotted some tiny crabs on the bottom of the cutter, crabs the size of rice grains. They gave me three of them. Just eating something alive seemed to send energy flowing through my body.

On the tenth, maybe the eleventh day—I don't remember well—a man shouted, "Butterfly!" It was a tiny white butterfly, the kind you see in cabbage patches. "Land must be close!" Normally, we didn't row during daylight. Now everyone wanted to row, but we found no land. The gods must have sent that butterfly so that we wouldn't give up hope. We often saw birds, but that was the only butterfly.

We were deceived many, many times. "Island! Island!" the man on watch would call out, only to have it turn out to be a mirage. When we finally sighted land, we didn't expect it to be real. I had imagined that an island would look something like a saké cup in the distance that would gradually enlarge. But the land we did at last sight was a ridge line stretching across the horizon. It looked quite close already. Everyone really wanted to row, then. Get there quickly! But senior officer Kobayashi declared, "If we row now, we'll reach land after dark. We're suffering from night blindness. On land there may be Americans with good eyesight. Or natives." Normally, we started rowing an hour after sunset. That night we didn't begin rowing right away. The senior officer thought things through that carefully. Lieutenant Kobayashi was a man of sterling character. He brought out the best in us. That is wonderful leadership.

We rowed for thirteen days without food or water. An unprecedented feat. Almost two hundred men in the three boats made it. Some who'd been burned in the fires on the ship died. A few died from the fatigue of trying to stay afloat in the ocean for so many hours after the sinking. Their corpses we threw back into the sea. We couldn't exactly keep them. It was the South Seas, after all. For a while they looked as if they still had a mind to follow the cutter. Probably the families of the deceased would have liked a lock of hair or a nail clipping, but we didn't have that kind of thing on our minds.

We came ashore on the northeastern tip of Mindanao Island, near Surigao. There, the navy had a tiny torpedo-boat station, some thirty men. The arrival of a hundred and eighty visitors overwhelmed them. When we reached land, we couldn't walk properly at first, but each of us stood up straight and all were able to disembark onto the pier on their own. At that moment, one of the crew members knelt down on the ground, clasped his hands together in front of the senior officer, and said, "I owe my life to you." I believe he might have been the leader of those who had most considered mutiny.

I'm now seventy years old. Three times ships were sunk from under me. I was on the heavy cruiser *Furutaka* when she went down off Savo Island in October 1942 near Guadalcanal, sunk by U.S. cruisers. I was plucked from the sea by a destroyer after about forty minutes in the water. I was on the light cruiser *Naka* when she was sunk by U.S. carrier planes at Truk Island in February 1944. I encountered dangerous situations time and again and returned alive. I wasn't wounded. I wasn't burned. I was very lucky. A lot of people met more horrible and dangerous things than me.

Later, the men who worked during the war were called "professional soldiers," but we weren't doing it to make a living! We served the nation, yet we were permanently purged by the Occupation, prevented from holding office. We had no work. I get really angry about that. We fought for all the people, but after the war, pilots were called "degenerate ex-kamikazes" or "twisted, broken crazies." Those who did not cooperate with the war, they were the ones who held their noses up in the air, boasted about themselves afterwards. That kind of thinking is wrong, I believe.

Transport War

MASUDA REIJI [2]

"In 1971, we were finally able to erect a memorial stone in honor of the merchant-marine sailors killed in the war. More than sixty thousand of them died. It was placed at Kannon-zaki on the Izu Peninsula. You can see the Pacific Ocean from there. The epitaph reads, 'Rest in peace, friends. The waves are quiet at last.' Crown Prince Akihito, today's Emperor, visited there in May 1971."

He served throughout the war on all kinds of ships. He is now dedicating himself to preserving the memory of those who perished forgotten on the sea. "Three million one hundred thousand war dead! Army and navy casualties make up two million of that figure. Between four and five hundred thousand of those two million perished together with transport ships. Some made it to shore, only to be caught in 'death with honor' final battles. They didn't even have any weapons with which to fight."

Not long after my return from carrying forces to the South for the army, I found myself drafted into the navy. I was sent to fight on the navy's destroyer *Asashio*, when the Americans made a counterattack and took Guadalcanal back from us late in 1942. Navy ships have steel furnaces capable of withstanding high pressure. Very different from merchantmen. Their turbines and boilers were extremely efficient. Some transports sailed at eight knots or so, while a destroyer could make thirty.

Truk was the headquarters of our Combined Fleet in the South. The great battleship *Yamato* was there at anchor. We were always being sent to the very front lines, and those battleships never even went into battle. People like us, graduates of the merchant-marine school, were shipped off to the most forward positions, while those bastards from the Imperial naval academy sat around on their asses in the *Yamato* and *Musashi* hotels. Sure, the captains of destroyers and light cruisers were Etajima naval academy graduates, but the chief navigators and engineers were from the merchant-marine schools. All of us came from outside the navy.

We took part in the last evacuation from Guadalcanal. We then were sent to try to keep our troops on New Guinea supplied after the enemy army came up from Port Moresby over the Owen Stanley mountain range and threatened Buna. Japan boarded seven thousand troops on nine transports, guarded by eight escorts and sent them off toward New Guinea. If we could get those troops and their heavy weapons there, they could turn back the Allies. But we were spotted by enemy reconnaissance planes almost immediately. About halfway to New Guinea, ten B-17 heavy bombers attacked us. One transport was sunk.

Finally, on March 3, 1943, we passed through the Dampier Strait, and were preparing to land our force. I was on the destroyer *Arashio* at this time, attached to the chief engineer. Suddenly, we were attacked by more than a hundred thirty planes. Our side had only forty. We didn't have a chance to beat them. While the air battle was going on, the other side swarmed over our transports. They would come in on you at low altitude, and they'd skip bombs across the water like you'd throw a stone. That's how they bombed us. All seven of the remaining transports were enveloped in flames. Their masts tumbled down, their bridges flew to pieces, the ammunition they were carrying was hit, and whole ships blew up. About five thousand died just before the landing.

They hit us amidships. B-17s, fighters, skip-bombers, and torpedo bombers. On our side, we were madly firing, but we had no chance to beat them off. Our bridge was hit by two five-hundred-pound bombs. Nobody could have survived. The captain, the chief navigator, the gunnery and torpedo chiefs, and the chief medical officer were all killed in action. The chief navigator's blackened body was hanging there, all alone. We were carrying about fifty men from the landing force, one hundred and sixty army men, and three special newspaper correspondents. They, too, were all killed. Somehow, those of us down in the engine room were spared.

Because all the top commanders on *Arashio* were killed and the ship was heavily damaged, we were ordered to transfer the crew over to my old ship, the *Asashio*. The chief engineer and I were left in charge of the *Arashio*. We decided to stay aboard, because we could still make way at perhaps five or six knots. Then a second air attack came in. We were hit by thirty shells—from port to starboard. The ship shook violently. Bullet fragments and shrapnel made it look like a beehive. All the steam pipes burst. The ship became boiling hot. We tried to abandon ship, but planes flying almost as low as the masts sprayed us with machine-guns. Hands were shot off, stomachs blown open. Most of the crew were murdered or wounded there. Hundreds were swimming in the ocean. Nobody was there to rescue them. They were wiped out, carried away by a strong current running at roughly four or five knots.

Still aboard were a few sailors, the chief engineer, and I. Eight of us struggled to steer the *Arashio* by hand. Some of those surviving jumped into the sea, saying it was better to take a chance on being saved from the ocean than to remain on such a ship of horrors. Eventually, about seventeen of us did survive, when that night, near midnight, the destroyer *Yukikaze* came to our rescue. But nobody alive knew how to read the lamp signals they flashed at us. We thought if it turned out to be an enemy warship we'd have to kill ourselves with our pistols. We gulped down whiskey. Finally, we heard a voice calling out, "*Ooooi! Ooooi!* This is *Yukikaze!*" We answered as loudly as we could, "*Arashio* here!" They lowered a boat and evacuated us. I was taken off on their second trip. Aboard the other destroyer, I found quite a few soldiers from transports who had been plucked from the sea. *Yukikaze* returned to Rabaul at full speed. My former ship *Asashio*? Sunk almost instantly. Lost with all hands.

Eventually we were sent home to Japan via Rabaul. Back at last in Yokosuka, the first thing we requested was a Buddhist priest to hold services for all our dead. We were confined to base for a month. Couldn't leave or say anything about what had happened. Today that fight's called the Tragedy of the Dampier Strait. I was ordered by the Navy Ministry to report to the heavy cruiser *Mogami*. She'd barely made it back from Midway. She no longer even had her main gun turrets. They'd crashed down into her scout plane hanger deck from bomb hits during the battle. Yet now she was being ordered out on offensive operations. "I won't be coming back again," I thought when I got those orders.

When I boarded *Mogami* I found last testaments written by men who'd perished at Midway. Petty officers had put down things like, "Please, my beloved parents, forgive me for the misfortune I bring you," or "Dear wife, please forgive me." These were left by dying men, men being suffocated by gas during the Midway battle. I found them in the administrative officer's cabin and smuggled them ashore.

I was on the *Mogami* in the counterattacks in the Solomons. We operated out of Rabaul. At Kolombangara in July 1943, we went on a bombardment mission and were ambushed. We went back to Rabaul, only to be attacked by more than a hundred planes as soon as we arrived. All the ships were hit, including our cruiser. We had to limp to Truk for repairs. Then, off we went to reinforce Saipan, where we were routed again. We were now out of oil, so we found ourselves withdrawn to Singapore in the summer of 1944.

Prior to the Leyte Operation, I stood up for my rights as a lieutenant in a dispute with an ensign from the naval academy over who should command the junior officers' mess, and while I was right, I was transferred to *Submarine Chaser Number 21*. I guess this is airing the navy's dirty linen, but long-standing naval customs were not that easily changed. Graduates of the Tokyo Higher Merchant Marine School, university graduates, medical doctors, or those from the fishery academy, were all assigned to the bowels of the ship. Only naval academy graduates were qualified to walk the decks. That was their attitude. There was no sense that you were all fighting together. You can't win with such an attitude. That's why I was transferred off a heavy cruiser and put in charge of the engine room in a sub-chaser.

The Etajima graduates were the elite. I saw plenty of them. There were many opportunities to win in that war, but they were missed. If commanding officers had acted with courage and decisiveness, no matter what branch of service they came from, I believe we could have won more often, but they acted timidly, with their hearts in their mouths. We often needed only one last push.

We still had a substantial fleet left, even in Operation A, our move against Leyte, but we didn't give sufficient weight to the importance of transport ships. When the Eighth Fleet, off Rabaul, tore down to Guadalcanal and annihilated a whole American fleet at Savo Island in August 1942—How long ago our victories seem!—they completely ignored some thirty American transport ships hiding in the shadow of the islands. They just came home without attacking them because no medals or awards were given for sinking freighters, only for sinking carriers or battleships. Fundamentally, the navy viewed transport and supply lightly.

In the end, in 1944, the navy belatedly tried to turn out coastal-defense ships, because so much of the transport fleet had already been destroyed. One hundred eighty-five were built, but we had no airplanes, and without control of the air those ships were sitting ducks. One after another they were blasted out of the water. One hundred and one were sunk. About ten thousand lives were lost there, most of them under merchant-marine-school graduates serving as chief engineers, chief navigators, and captains.

Many records and memoirs exist for the admirals, but almost nothing for the crews. The crews of the merchant ships were the supporting cast, the stagehands behind the stars. Japan lost some twenty-five hundred transports. Eight million tons of shipping. Sixty-two thousand crewmen perished on them. On the American side, six hundred thousand tons of shipping were sunk and only several hundred were killed on transport ships in the Pacific. The difference in strategies between Japan and the United States is crystal-clear in these figures.

For the Leyte Operation all the transport vessels were supposed to converge on Leyte. But my new ship, *21*, was loaded with sugar and military supplies, and got orders to sail to the Homeland. We had the honor of escorting a tanker full of aviation fuel. The other ships we were with sailed off to Leyte and were sunk en route. Their captains were all merchant-marine graduates. We ran into a typhoon near Bakō, so we escaped into Keilung and were actually able to bring that tanker home to Kyushu. At that time, a drop of gasoline was equivalent to a drop of blood. The officers in charge at Kure Arsenal were delighted with our performance.

I was assigned to a coastal defense ship called *Itō*, which was fitting out at Uraga dock. The engine had no reverse! I spoke to the captain there and we agreed, "We can't fight a war with a ship like that!" He personally took his case to the Navy Ministry and was able to get them to upgrade the engine so it could at least reverse the screws. My subordinates were guys who were ten or fifteen years out of the navy. They'd practically forgotten what a propeller was. In 1945 we couldn't even go out into the Pacific Ocean any more. We had no air presence.

In 1967, I took my wife to the Grand Canyon, Las Vegas, and San Francisco. At Fisherman's Wharf in San Francisco we saw a U.S. submarine on display. It had markings on its conning tower, one for each Japanese transport ship it had sunk. That's how they viewed transport ships.

From the very beginning of the Greater East Asia War, I went into most of the battle zones, but somehow I made it through, though all my ships were sunk or destroyed. My body's riddled with injuries. The wound in my back still requires attention. I'm grateful to be here, but we merchant mariners in the Navy were lower than military horses, less important than military dogs, even lower than military carrier pigeons.

That was no way to win a war.

15 / "SPECIAL ATTACK"

T HE DIVINE WIND SPECIAL ATTACK CORPS [*Kamikaze Toku-betsu Kōgekitai,* usually abbreviated in Japanese as the *Tokkō*] is most often associated with the airplane attacks against the American fleets invading the Philippines and Okinawa. But a wide range of other special-attack weapons were prepared by both the army and the navy, and the concept of "special attack" was eventually applied widely to any attack that used unorthodox methods from which the attacker did not expect to emerge alive.

Various aircraft were adapted for the Tokkō missions, from first-line planes to trainers. One special aircraft, the *Ōka* [Cherry Blossom], was a rocket-powered flying bomb. Virtually unstoppable once launched, it had to be delivered to distant American task forces during the Battle of Okinawa by slow, overburdened, and exceedingly vulnerable two-engine medium bombers. In its initial mission all eighteen Ōkas employed were destroyed when all of their mother planes were shot down before they approached launch range. The navy's *Shinyō* [Ocean Shaker] and its army equivalent, the Maru-ni, were powerful motorboats with a large charge in the bow, which were to be driven into enemy ships at high speed. Perhaps the nadir of this type of warfare was reached with the *Fukuryū* [Crouching Dragon], in which men wearing underwater breathing devices and carrying specially designed mines on poles would meet enemy landing craft as they approached the beaches of the Homeland.

One of the weapons prepared to strike at the enemy where they could not be reached by conventional tactics was the *Kaiten* [Turning of the Heavens] Special Attack weapon. This was an improvisation—two of the Navy's Type-93 "Long Lance" torpedoes, enlarged and fused together. Most of the forward part of one torpedo was filled with 3,000 pounds of explosives. A section containing the pilot's seat and the needed controls was attached behind it. Aft of the pilot section was the rear portion of a second torpedo, containing the propulsion system. It was not so much a ship as it was an insertion of a human being into a very large torpedo. Five or six Kaitens could be carried on the deck of a single submarine, each accessible from inside while submerged, through a hatch that was then shut from below. A Kaiten was secured to the submarine with iron bands that could be released on command from the sub's captain. Once launched, a Kaiten could achieve a speed of forty knots. It was a powerful weapon which, if it found a target, was capable of sinking even an aircraft carrier. But if it missed, there was no way to recover it—or its pilot. ■

Volunteer

YOKOTA YUTAKA

He wears a wine-colored beret, a tweed jacket, a pink shirt, and a string tie bearing the face of a Buddhist deity. He seems very shy at the station, but drives his tiny gray car through the narrow streets of Tokyo as if it were a Formula-1 racer. "Don't worry, in thirty years I've never been caught speeding. Except once, when they put up a speed trap."

"This is my room," he says, showing a small room at his house. "I worked hard to clean it up for you." On a shelf is a miniature model of a Kaiten in cut-away, showing the pilot, the only crewman, wedged between two huge torpedoes. It is a gift from a reader of his book.° "I get lots of letters from young girl students. They're my warmest fans." An Imperial Navy ensign blazes on one wall with photos of the parents of members of attack forces he had been part of and memorial photographs of the groups before they departed. Whenever he mentions the name of one of his comrades, tears come to his eyes.

"Your Motherland faces imminent peril. Consider how much your Motherland needs you. Now, a weapon which will destroy the enemy has been born. If there be any among you who burn with a passion to die gloriously for the sake of their country, let them step forward. Mark the paper before you with two circles. If you do not care one way or the other, inscribe a single circle. Those who do not wish to go may throw the paper away. Do not think of returning alive. These arms have not been created in order that you may return alive. Weigh your decision overnight. In the morning present the appropriate paper to your subsection commander."

We heard these words as we stood assembled before the commander

---

° Yokota Yutaka, *Aa kaiten tokkō-tai: Kaerazaru seishun no kiroku* [*Oh, Kaiten Special Attack Corps: A Record of Youth Gone Forever*] (Tokyo: Koinsha, 1971). An English version of his story appeared as *Suicide Submarine!* Yutaka Yokota with Joseph D. Harrington (New York: Ballantine, 1962).

of our school. We were all graduating from Youth Flying Corps, the Yokaren, at Tsuchiura Naval Air Station. At that very moment I decided. "I'm going!"

At the time of Pearl Harbor I had been a sixteen-year-old, finishing middle school, really impressed by the nine war gods of the midget submarines who were credited by the papers with much of the success at Hawaii.° They weren't, of course, actual human torpedoes, but even then, I'd thought to myself, I wouldn't mind dying like that. I was a militaristic youth. I'd been purely cultivated to serve. I wanted to go to Etajima, the naval academy, but I never got in. You had to have perfect parents, above reproach. Mine were always fighting. The Kempeitai, military police, came to investigate our family. I was rejected. I gave up that hope and jumped into Yokaren. But if I'd entered the naval academy at that time, the war would have ended with me still a candidate ensign. I would never have participated in the war. So flunking the naval academy made my life much more fruitful. I am really grateful that I was rejected.

At the time, I was afraid that if I only wrote double circles I might not be chosen, even though I had one of the very best records in our squad and was very strong in *jūdō*. Underneath my circles I added, "Without reservation, I request that you select me. Yokota Kan." I wrote it in big letters and handed it in.

I was picked first.

When selected I felt a slight sense of sadness. My life now had no more than a year to go. But I was already in Yokaren. I wasn't thinking of surviving the war. Rather than getting shot down by some plane, better to die grandly. Go out in glory.

Ninety-four percent, I heard, put down double circles, five percent put a single circle, less than one percent threw the paper away. I was exhilarated. But I remember Noguchi, who held the second grade in *kendō*. They didn't chose him. He dashed up to our squad commander, a desperate look in his eyes. "How could you leave me? Why won't you take me?" He was in tears, "Please make me the one hundred and first." They chose one hundred out of two thousand. In the end, he wasn't allowed to go. But he tried so hard to be one of us.

We trained desperately. You couldn't complain of pain or anything. You had to push on: "If I don't hit the target, if I have to 'self-detonate,' I'll die without doing what I must." It was agony. For everybody. Once

---

° Five two-man midget submarines were lost. Nine men were killed in action. One, Sakamaki Kazuo, was captured by the Americans on December 8, 1941, becoming the first Japanese prisoner-of-war. He was never mentioned by the Japanese press during the war. The other nine men were featured on front-page stories as "war gods."

you become a member of an attack force, you become deathly serious. Your eyes became set. Focused. If you'd had two lives, it wouldn't have mattered, but you were giving up your only life. Life is so precious. Your life was dedicated to self-sacrifice, committed to smashing into the enemy. That's why we trained like that. We practiced that hard because we valued our lives so highly.

Yet despite everything we did, American battle reports credit us with only two ships! Don't toy with us! As sub commander Orita said, "We should storm off to America! We should protest violently."

Even in the submarine I was on, we definitely sank three or four ships. And there were many other subs out there, too. All without result? Don't make me laugh! It can't be! When I went off on *I-47*, Lieutenant Kakizaki and Warrant Officer Yamaguchi were launched, too. While they still had operating time, we heard a big blast, *"GUWWAAAN!"* They wouldn't have self-detonated while there was still time. They must have hit something. The only alternative was that they were hit by a burst of machine-gun fire while on the surface.

Seven- or eight-thousand-ton ships were the ones most often sunk by our Kaitens. We thought that it would be all right to exchange our lives for a ship at least as big as a heavy cruiser. But what we really wanted was a carrier! Lieutenant Kuge and Warrant Officer Yanagiya hit a destroyer. I didn't want to trade my life for anything as small as that, but if they hadn't sunk it, we would have found ourselves under a rain of depth charges. In the midst of its bombardment we carried out a "blind launch," and either Kuge or Yanagiya got him. That destroyer was worth at least as much as a carrier to all of us. If we'd been hit then, I wouldn't be here now.

The morning of our departure from Hikari we said farewell to life. We wore our dress uniforms. They gave us each a short-sword, a *tantō*, just as if we'd graduated from Etajima, and a headband marked with the words, "Given Seven Lives, I'll Serve the Nation with Each of Them." I received my first that day. I still have two of them. This one here's really filthy because you banged your head so often in the crawl space that led from the submarine to the cockpit of your Kaiten, which was strapped to the sub's deck. When I die, I'm going to wear this into the next world. [*He wraps it around his head.*] I'll wear it in my coffin. This is my death costume.

When the motor launch first took us to our mother ship, we jumped onto our own torpedoes and, standing with our legs apart, waved our Japanese swords in circles in answer to the cheers. Before that, let me tell you what I did. I actually kissed the bow of the Kaiten that carried the explosive: "Do it for me. Please. Get an enemy carrier for me." I didn't know anything about kissing then, but I kissed my Kaiten without thinking.

"In a week it's Okinawa! Nothing less than thirty thousand tons! No suicide for any tiny ship!" We all shouted like that. Our voices probably didn't reach other ships in the harbor, but we shouted anyway.

The islands in the Inland Sea were beautiful as we passed through. It probably sounds affected to say it, but we felt, "These islands. These waters. This coast. They're ours to defend." We thought, "Is there any more blessed place to die?" I don't think anyone who wasn't a Kaiten pilot can understand that feeling.

There's an old expression, "Bushidō is the search for a place to die." Well, that was our fervent desire, our long-cherished dream. A place to die for my country. I was happy to have been born a man. A man of Japan. I don't care if it makes me sound egotistical, but that's how I felt. The country was in my hands.

As we passed the Bungo Channel off Shikoku on March 29, 1945, I felt acutely that this was my last view of the Homeland. Even here at the gates of Japan, enemy submarines were waiting for us. We sailed in zigzags. As soon as we left the channel, the sub captain and the whole crew were tense and alert. During the day we sailed at full speed in order to close with the enemy as quickly as possible.

"Please let us meet a big one!" That was our deepest desire. "If we're lucky," I thought, "fortune might bring me a big fat aircraft carrier." In the submarine we joked with each other, played *shōgi*, *go*, cards, too. Ensign Kuge, who was to annihilate an enemy destroyer, was almost a professional in doing magic tricks with cards. One sailor on the sub was an outstanding *shōgi* player. His name was Maejima. Once, I played him. Until the middle game I was doing very poorly; then he started making blunders. I said, "Stop it! Fight to the end. Don't make allowances for me!" "No, no," he replied. "You're very strong." Eventually, he lost. I later learned that he was rated first *dan*, while I was only eighth *kyū*, far below him in strength. Even when I had a chance to talk to him after the war, he still maintained he'd given it his best effort.

Our submarine, *I-47*, with its six Kaitens on deck, was part of a four-sub attack plan, a total of twenty Kaitens in all. But we never made it to Okinawa. We were discovered only two days out, bombed, and depth-charged. Afterwards, our Kaitens looked like they'd been made of celluloid, all bent and twisted out of shape. We had to return to Hikari empty-handed.

I sailed the second time on April 20 for the American supply lines between Ulithi and Okinawa. When we reached the area where we might encounter enemy ships, they gave us pilots a feast. The larger a ship is, the stricter the rules. The petty officers bully the sailors. But on a sub, from the captain to the leastmost sailor, all the meals were the same, though the officers had their own mess. In a submarine, if you die, you all die together. The Kaiten officers were berthed with the sub's officers, and I was with the sailors, but they gave me the best bed. The crew were all young. The captain toasted us: "We don't know when we'll encounter the enemy, so this will be our farewell party. I wish you a most satisfying dash against the enemy."

Warrant Officer Yamaguchi, whose Kaiten was to be launched right next to mine, was a real joker! On a morning when an attack seemed possible, we'd change into our dress for death in our ready room. You had to strip naked before you could put on the proper clothes. One day, I wanted to say good-bye to the reserve officers who'd taken such good care of me, so I was a little late. When I got back, all the others were fully dressed. They all gathered around, leering, giving me a hard time. "Hey, guys, look the other way, I have to change my F-U," I said, referring to my loin cloth. "Yokota, there's nothing to be ashamed of," Yamaguchi said. "No cute girls here. What's the matter, your main gun just a water pistol?" I turned my back and quickly put on my loin cloth. "You stingy bastard!" he said. "Your cannon looks even smaller than my 'side arm.'" "Yamaguchi, you've got two?" asked Shinkai. "Naw. I call it a 'side arm' when things are peaceful." We laughed until our sides ached.

We were young. We often talked about women. Dirty jokes were our stock in trade. We never talked much about "loyalty," or "bravery," or "the nobility of the soul." We were just like brothers. Kakizaki never mentioned it, but he had a girl friend. He had a picture of a woman in his gear. After he'd carried out his mission, a letter from her arrived for him. He never got to read it. I always had a picture of my mother in my pocket. She'd died when I was just four. Whenever I boarded my Kaiten the words, "Ma, I'll soon be there with you," escaped my lips.

"Kaiten pilots! Board! Prepare for Kaiten battle!" The sub's speaker blared. Our time had come. Once again we tied our *hachimaki* about our heads. Because we were men we were vain. It would have been a disgrace to lose composure. "We are now departing," we declared. "Please await our achievements." You clambered up the ladder to the hatch leading to your Kaiten. You didn't have much time, but still you looked back down and forced yourself to smile. "I'm going now," was all you said. You wanted to be praised after you died, just as much as you wanted it during your life. You wanted them to say, "Yokota was young, but he went with incredible bravery. He was dignified to the end." It would be terrible if they said, "He went shaking. So unlike a Kaiten pilot." There was only one like that in our whole group. He was a disgrace to the Kaiten Corps.

I cut him out of the pictures I have of us preparing to depart. But that's not important anymore.

At that moment, you're sitting in the cockpit. "Compose yourself. Gather your thoughts. If you're harried you'll fail. You have only one life. You're going to your mother." I calmed myself like that. "If you get confused and can't really display your ability, out here in the middle of the rough Pacific Ocean, your life will be wasted. You'll be giving it up in vain." Nothing came to my mind except accomplishing our objective. "You must succeed! Absolute success! That's all that I can accept. If I do not succeed, I cannot die in peace. Even if my life is gone, I will not rest."

The crewman who took care of my Kaiten was Warrant Officer Nao. As he closed the hatch from below, he stretched out his hand. "I pray for your success." In that tiny cramped space he grabbed my hand.

When the hatch has been closed from below, the only means of communication is by telephone. "All Kaitens prepare for launch!" came the order. "We will launch number one and number four Kaitens! Others await orders!" Those were Commander Kakizaki's and Yamaguchi's Kaitens. You hear the sound of the restraining belt being released. Then the roar of them taking off, moving away. We were lying side by side. You only hear the sound. Through your periscope, you can see only the pure white bubbles left behind.

After twenty minutes or so we heard *"GUWAAAANNNNN!"* A tremendous explosion. You call out on the phone, "When am I going? What am I supposed to do?" "Only two enemy ships sighted." "What, can't you find more?" "Wait," comes back on the phone. "What'd you mean, wait? There must be more of them. Search harder!" Then they ordered Furukawa to launch. Three had now been dispatched. That was the last launch on that occasion. I was ordered to come back in. *That* was the moment I really wanted to die.

Our third mission, near Saipan, was also the third time I came back unable to make an attack. On my third mission, all members of my attack group had been members of previous groups but had been unable to launch for various reasons. Before we departed, we swore to each other that we would not return. No matter what. But I returned because three of the Kaitens failed. There was a crack in my main fuel-line pipe. The other three launched. Kuge left a letter asking that nobody think of those of us who couldn't go as cowards. He wrote, "When Sonoda found out he couldn't launch, I saw him crying. Please let those three go again immediately. They are going to return. Welcome them back warmly, I beg you. This is my only concern, I who must now leave before them." Kuge himself had returned twice. Once his torpedo drove cold and the engine wouldn't ignite. He knew how we felt. How we wanted to crawl into a corner and die from our failure!

It didn't help. I was really beaten up this time, called a disgrace to the Kaiten Corps for coming back alive! Because of that beating I still have difficulty hearing with my left ear, and I bear scars on my left hand, too. They envied me for having been chosen to go when they had not yet been selected.

One day, a maintenance mechanic told me that Japan had lost. "What are you saying, you filthy bastard?" I couldn't believe it. That night, we were all assembled. The senior commander of the Special Attack Forces told us the news. He was in tears. I left the gathering, and went through a tunnel in the base toward the sea. There, for the first time, tears sprang to my eyes. I cried bitterly. "I'll never launch! The war is over. Furukawa, Yamaguchi, Yanagiya, come back. Please return!" I cried and cried. Not because Japan had lost the war. "Why did you die, leaving me behind? Please come back!" I shouted toward the sea. My tears were not tears of resentment or indignation, nor were they in fear for Japan's future. They were shed for the loss of my fellow pilots. My comrades. I even thought about killing myself as I stared out to sea. I didn't have a gun. I got some explosives, but I didn't have the guts to just blow myself to bits.

I cannot tell you the agonies I went through after the war. Only a few of us went through this, Sonoda, Shinkai, me. Just a few. You go off in a submarine together, like brothers. Real comrades-in-arms. You board a torpedo strapped to the back of the submarine, then they leave, the ones right next to you. Nobody can understand this. Sonoda never speaks about it. He tells me he doesn't want to recall that time. I'm sure he has his own reasons. Even other Kaiten members don't understand. I don't really ask anyone to understand my feelings.

I smoke a lot. I drink saké. I drink thinking it's not written in the Bible that you shouldn't drink. I've been going to church for the last twenty years. I'm a survivor of the Special Attack Forces. One who's distorted. I can say I'm sort of a distorted Christian.

Normally, your memories fade with the passage of forty years. In my case, they seem to come back stronger and stronger. Last January I went to Ulithi Atoll, Guam, Palau, and Yap. From Guam to Ulithi there aren't any planes. So we chartered a tiny eight-ton hulk. On the way back the engine broke down and we spent three days drifting about the reefs of the atoll. Like Robinson Crusoe. We didn't have any water, so we ate coconuts given to us by the village headman on Ulithi. He welcomed us with "Irasshai"—"Welcome" in Japanese. Said we were the first Japanese to return to Ulithi Atoll since the war. I threw flowers into the sea, together with the Buddhist sutras I've been writing for every one of the lost Kaiten pilots for many years now.

We thought it probably was the spirits of our dead comrades that stopped our engine. Kept us from leaving. They were probably telling us, "Don't rush back home. Stay with us awhile." So many fine young men, wonderful men, were killed.

Human Torpedo

KŌZU NAOJI

"I didn't die in a Kaiten. I lived forty-five years after that. Still, up to today I don't know why I was born. Yet here I am alive. Writing my book may be it. I consider it part of my will. But they tell me, 'That kind of book won't sell anymore.' Yet, I feel I must do something, so I keep writing. My heart goes out to those who died so young. I still feel their deaths had some meaning. They didn't die from illness. Each died with a clear purpose in mind."

He speaks softly, with little outward show of emotion.

At the time of Pearl Harbor, I was only nearing the end of my second year at the Higher School. The war was being fought by adults. Students were still deferred from the draft. If everything had gone normally, I wouldn't have graduated from university until March 1946. I was sure I was absolutely safe, and I acted that way.

Then they changed the rules. The first thing they did was reduce the period of study. That happened just before the outbreak of the Pacific War. I was forced into university after two years and six months instead of the normal three years. Then in the fall of 1943, student exemptions were canceled. The day after the announcement was made I went to my campus. Everything was in an uproar at Tokyo Imperial University. Nobody knew anything. Some said, "They'll never take students from the Imperial universities. Not Tōdai and Kyōdai [Tokyo Imperial University and Kyoto Imperial University]!" But as things turned out, that couldn't have been further from the truth. In October I was pulled into the military. Forced in.

I was skinny. I didn't think I'd be able to take it if they got hold of me. I was sure I just wasn't cut out to be a soldier or a sailor. Officers from the army had been attached to our schools since my middle-school days. They were swaggering bastards. I couldn't stand them. The navy looked better from the outside, and I did find myself in the navy, a second-class seaman, the lowest thing it was possible to be. I took the officers' examination. They felt that those of us from the Law Faculty of Tokyo Imperial University had the minimal qualifications to sit for the paymaster exam in the Imperial Japanese Navy.

What happened was that with one exception, everyone in my group who wore eyeglasses became paymasters. In those days, seventy percent of Tōdai students wore specs. Then they called out the names of all those who'd been assigned to gunnery, navigation, torpedo school, but they didn't call mine. Next they announced the names of those who had been selected for service as "defense-specialty reserve students." Mine was the only name called. "Defense-specialty?" At that time I didn't know we were losing battles one after another. I thought, "I don't have to attack! That's great. Things have really worked out well." But in the kind of war they were really fighting, "defense specialist" was a black joke.

I was sent to the antisubmarine-warfare school in February 1944 and was stuck there until the end of October. I was fed up with school by then. "What am I doing in this place?" I asked myself that when they started calling for volunteers who were "full of energy," who were "willing to take on a dangerous job," and "willing to board a special weapon" that would "reverse the tide of the war at once." Why not? It's got to be better than this. I applied for it carelessly. Almost ninety percent of us volunteered.

Since they only wanted forty of us, though, I was pretty sure I wouldn't be one of those selected. They called us out a second time, a third time. Each time some of our classmates hadn't been chosen. In the end, we began dimly to grasp the criteria used in selection. Eldest sons were removed from the list. You had to be a second son or lower. Even then, if you had an older brother at the front, they took you off the list. If you were the third son, but neither of your elder brothers had a chance to survive, you were dropped. I was a second son. My younger brother was still in middle school. My eldest brother was an officer in the navy. I suppose they thought my younger brother had a good chance to survive, so I was picked. But I never imagined I'd be going to a place from which I'd have absolutely no chance to return alive.

So forty of us entered the Kaiten Corps. We arrived at Kawatana on the twenty-fourth of October. There weren't any weapons for us yet. They couldn't even tell us what these secret weapons would be. Highly classified, was what they said. At Kawatana they had these plywood motorboats —they called them Shinyō, "Ocean Shakers." We charged into "the enemy" on those! You fixed the helm three hundred meters before impact, locking the rudder in place. A hand-engaged lever controlled acceleration. Once you let go of it, it didn't automatically let up like the pedal of a car. Then you jumped into the sea. The unmanned boat would then plunge into a target representing the enemy. They weren't telling you you had to die. We *were* wearing life jackets, but you had to wonder if it was possible to survive this kind of attack. I thought it was damned outrageous, but they told us not to worry, the Kaiten would be a much superior weapon. How could I have imagined they wouldn't include any escape system at all?

As we were beginning our training, the first announcement of Kamikaze attacks was made. I think that was October 29. Reading the news of the "Divine Wind" Special Attack Corps in the newspapers— planes crashing into the enemy ships—I was bowled over. Even then, I didn't grasp the true nature of the Kamikaze. I still wondered, "What are they going to do if they parachute down in the middle of the enemy fleet?" Yet there I was. We couldn't share our doubts with each other. We were all drawn from different universities. If I had expressed my disquiet, my university could have been disgraced. I had to keep my own counsel.

Today, I know they deceived us! I know it with all my heart! But then—and for many years afterward—I thought it must have been me. I thought I misheard them. We only received explanations orally. I thought I missed what they said. Even a decade ago, I had some doubts. But in 1987 a document turned up. When I saw that for the first time, I knew. The document had been drafted August 20 and issued August 31, 1944, by the Chief of the Personnel Bureau and the Chief of Education of the Imperial Navy. It bears the seals of Navy Minister Yonai Mitsumasa and his chief subordinates. It sets forth instructions for recruiting and training reserve student officers to fill positions in special-weapons units, and outlines how to select and train them. It expressly forbids touching on the weapon's capabilities or its use. Those doing the soliciting were instructed to say only that if you attack in the weapon you'll kill the enemy without fail. They were told to state that some danger was involved. But that was all. Seeing those words in print, I knew they'd misled us deliberately.

As we were waiting to move to our final staging base at Hikari we received a postcard from one of our comrades who'd gone there ahead of us. On it was "Say hello to Kudō." That was our code phrase for "Escape is impossible." Until that moment we had had no confirmation that the Kaiten was a self-exploding weapon which gave you no chance to escape death.

We'd heard rumors, but I didn't actually see one until I got to Hikari. The body was painted flat black. It overwhelmed a man. A small sail and a tiny periscope located at its center seemed to disturb the harmony of the whole. The rear third was a Type-93 torpedo. A maintenance officer described it to us dispassionately, "The total length is fourteen point five meters. Diameter, one meter. The crew is one man. Explosive charge one point six metric tons. Navigation range seventy-eight thousand meters. Maximum speed thirty knots."

I was supposed to be ready for this, but the shock nearly knocked me down. In the summer of 1946, I recorded my thoughts at that moment: "At last we saw the weapon we would ourselves board. I sensed something larger than the power of a human being glowering down at me. I lost my reason and my emotions. I was dumbfounded. I felt that I had myself turned into something no longer human." I couldn't really tell, at that time, whether what I sensed was higher or lower than a human being, but I felt I now knew why we human beings could no longer control our own destiny.

If you worked at it carefully, you could get out of the Kaiten Corps. All you had to do was fail to operate the Kaiten properly and do the same thing again on your second try. You'd be shouted at: "You stupid bastard! We won't let a dumb shit like you operate a Kaiten!" and they'd take you off the list. But I never thought of escaping myself; that would only have meant somebody else dying in my place. Even if the whole unit had to be replaced, they'd have found others. It was that kind of system. I couldn't bear the idea of sacrificing someone else by quitting. I knew if I did, I'd regret it for the rest of my life, even if I never knew his name. I hated the thought that I'd fail and they'd say, "Those reserve students are no good!" I couldn't do that to the others. I *wanted* to navigate well. Like they say in Chinese, *"Mei fa"*—"It can't be helped." I was resigned to it.

It was horrible to contemplate death in a Kaiten. Many young men charged into the enemy and died during the war—in Kamikaze planes, in Ōka manned rocket bombs, in Shinyō boats. If everything went well for them, and the battleship that was their target was close, looming in front of them, at least they could count the seconds to impact: "Three, two, one . . . ." Then, as long as they kept their eyes open, they'd know the moment of their deaths!

But the Kaiten wasn't like that. You're underwater. You can't look out. You've already determined your course, peering through the periscope. "The enemy position in one minute and thirty seconds will be this. I set my angle of attack at this." You submerge. You run full speed at the estimated enemy position. From the moment you commence your attack, you see nothing. You have a stopwatch. You know how much of the one minute and thirty seconds has elapsed. But you may have made an error in measurement. You keep thinking, "Now. Now. Now!" But you never know when that moment will come. "Time's elapsed," you realize. "I missed the target." You come to the surface. You search again for the enemy. You realize you passed astern. Once more you set your course. But again, you don't know the moment of your death. You may die ahead of schedule. You don't even know that. I can't imagine a crueler weapon. Yet I can't ask anyone how they felt at that moment, because no one who experienced it came back alive.

There were men who returned as many as four times from missions, but in every case it was because their Kaiten was unable to launch from the host submarine, or no enemy was found. Nobody who was launched from a submarine ever returned, so we don't know their feelings. At that final moment a cold sweat must have broken out. Or maybe they went mad. But there are no witnesses. Nothing could be crueler than that. Nothing. Who am I to say that a Kaiten pilot could remain sane at a moment like that? In the book I've been writing about the Kaitens, I couldn't put these thoughts in it. With the families of those who'd perished in mind, I just couldn't say that aloud. Even after forty years, I just couldn't write it. Such a hardhearted weapon! So callous. I have here a list of the dead. All of them. I still wonder how they felt at the moment of death.

In reality, hardly any ever hit an enemy ship. Those who returned following Kaiten launches say they heard the sounds of explosions. They say they heard them just before the mother ship broke off to return home or seek new targets. That must mean they self-detonated. When the Kaitens are released to begin their attacks, the targeted ships are far, far away. The pilots try desperately to overtake them. They fail. They're alone in the middle of the Pacific Ocean. It's possible to open the hatch and climb out. But what would you do in the middle of the Pacific? I believe they thought it better just to blow themselves up. At least I'll die in one blast, they may have thought. That, I don't know. Nobody knows.

The verification of all American ships lost during the war has long been completed. According to their records, Kaitens claimed just three ships sunk or heavily damaged. One at the Ulithi Atoll was hit, two others in the open Pacific. But I'm sure there must be ships not registered by the American military—drafted ships, Australian ships, British ships, others for which records are not complete. Some might have been lost to Kaitens, so I cannot speak with absolute confidence. Still I can't help thinking, with the exception of those three pilots who hit, how must the others have felt?

One hundred and six Kaiten pilots lost. This includes seventeen killed in practice or in accidents. With the three hits, that means eighty-six remain to be accounted for. Two were lost during an air raid on their base. Seven were killed on ships transporting them, others together with their mother ships. The total number of men who were actually able to carry out attacks was very small, I tell you, very small.

There was a plan to build one thousand Kaitens over several months, but in reality only four hundred to four hundred fifty were produced. They assembled one thousand three hundred sixty-four pilot candidates, but manufacturing fell behind. It wasn't that they trained many at once and then selected the best. There weren't enough training boats or instructors for that. You got about four practice runs in basic training. If you survived without accidents, then you were appointed to an attack unit. There you practiced some more and then went on your mission. I first actually boarded a Kaiten in May. It was an "accompanied ride" with an apprentice instructor. How long I'd waited for that moment!

I don't know who selected the attack unit. There were usually five or six men in a unit. When you were selected, the commander of the unit called you up and informed the others, "You will serve in my unit." From that moment on, they considered themselves as one.

One hundred and twenty-one men who had graduated from the naval academy were assigned to our unit. Two hundred and thirty of us were reserve students. We also wore the single cherry blossom on our collars, but the naval academy graduates used to tell us, "You got your cherry blossoms from Roosevelt. You became ensigns after only a year. We spent years earning ours." We thought, "Hell, it wasn't us who wanted these things."

They beat us up regularly. I don't think they used such methods at the naval academy, but with us they didn't hold back. In the navy, they put almost superstitious faith in the belief that brutality and physical punishment made better sailors. Normally, though, officers didn't touch the men under them, but the regular officers in the Kaiten Unit must have believed it was the best way to handle these irregular upstarts, these former students, so weak in spirit. They never let up. "Academy this, academy that"—we didn't give a damn how they did it at the naval academy, but at the same time we thought, "We'll show 'em, they'll see what we can do." I guess that's what they wanted us to feel.

The Kaiten Corps was formed on September 1, 1944, on Ōtsushima. The first Kaiten attacks were made in November and December. The fervor was intense. The Hikari Base opened December 1, and the first attack force left there February 20. Everyone was caught up in a mad rush. By the time the second and third attack forces departed, the frenzy had died down and a sort of normality had taken hold.

Dispatching the attack force was a grand show, let me tell you. It was so thrilling. Probably every man who sent off his fellows was himself carried away with excitement. It was almost like the departure for battle of a great general and his samurai warriors in the feudal age—very different from the pushbutton war of today. There was a sense of man-to-man combat in it. In the army, war had already become a clash of power against power, a battle of tank divisions, or mass war like the Imphal attack in Burma. The individual was obliterated in a war like that. Even air war was no longer the clash of lone warriors. But the Kaiten was still an individual affair. An elaborate ritual was staged, a grand send-off.

"Tomorrow, I'll be the one sent off like that," we thought. "There's no distance separating me, the new arrival, from those departing today and those who have already gone and are now dead." I could send them off without feeling guilt, but how did these paymasters or the superior commanders who were not themselves going to die feel? I can't tell you that. I never thought the Emperor could act on his own. I didn't see myself throwing my life away for him, nor for the government either, nor for the nation. I saw myself dying to defend my parents, my brothers and sisters. For them I must die, I thought.

Bride of a Kamikaze

ARAKI SHIGEKO

We meet by the statue of the Goddess of Mercy dedicated to the Special Attack Forces, the Tokkō Kannon, at Setagaya Fudō Temple in a quiet residential neighborhood of Tokyo. A gathering is held there the eighteenth of every month. Wearing a green dress with a large floral pattern, she looked very young and moved gracefully, as she changed the water for the flowers, lit incense, and arranged objects on the altar. She seems like a daughter, or younger sister of a man who had been a Tokkō, until she is introduced as "the widow of Flight Lieutenant Araki."

At her home, where we later talk, there are many photographs of family members—on walls, on bureaus, and the tops of cabinets. Off by itself in a corner is a photograph of a young man in a flight jacket.

He passed away in 1945. Forty-five years have gone by, and yet strangely the face of the man who died in action remains that of a twenty-one-year-old. My second husband died at fifty-seven with an old man's face, while his is almost like my son's. I guess that's why the yearning gets stronger year by year. It's like the love of a mother cherishing her son's memory.

I hadn't planned to get married so young. We were brought up as brother and sister. When my parents married, they each had a child. My mother brought me with her and my father brought him. He went to Seijō Middle School and then entered the Military Academy. I was studying Japanese dance, hoping to teach. But we were told, "You can't dance this," "You can't dance that." There were so many rules then. We couldn't dance *Madame Butterfly* because Lieutenant Pinkerton was an American.

We lived in Takadanobaba in Tokyo, but when the war started, we were evacuated to Kōzu in Kanagawa prefecture. In Kōzu, I worked at a pressing plant for the navy. We made a kind of starch cake from rice. The plant was in the middle of a field. Every day, from the direction of Sagami Bay, dozens of planes flew over us, heading toward Mount Fuji. They must have been Tokkō, Special Attack planes. You could see the Rising Sun on their wings. We'd go outside and wave flags, or just our hands. One plane, perhaps the leader's, would fly low and dip its wings in greeting. We cried and cried. We knew that would be the last we saw of them. We'd wave frantically until they disappeared, then we'd pray for them. This was our daily life in April and May, 1945.

One night, he came home suddenly, without any warning. It was April 9, about eleven o'clock. It was raining. Everyone was already sleeping. "What's happened? What a surprise!" He told us he'd been given permission to take overnight leave. An air-raid warning had sounded earlier and we were under a blackout, so we moved about the house groping in the dark. He said, "There's something I have to tell you. All of you, because we're a family." He told us he'd been selected as a group leader of a Tokkō mission, that he didn't know when his attack would take place, but it would be soon.

He then said, "I have one request to make, although it's very selfish. I want to marry Shigeko, if possible." For a second I was stunned. I knew at that moment he was going to die. My father and mother were silent. I was silent, thinking. He, too, of course was silent.

"I will do as Haruo wishes," I finally replied.

"It's decided, then. Let's arrange for the ceremony!" Everyone seemed to say it at once. My mother was weeping. She was my mother, after all. There was no saké, but we had some potato liquor. Mother brought it from the kitchen, together with some sweet-potato stalks and a little dried squid. It was all we had. We then performed the nuptial ritual, exchanging toasts three times from a tiny cup. My father started to sing the "Takasagoya" wedding song, but when he got to the part about living forever, he fell totally silent. We couldn't help crying then. We all wept. He knelt in the formal way. I tried to control my tears. My mother ran off to the kitchen. Even now, I can't take that song. I don't like going to weddings. I'm reminded of my wedding and not theirs. I can't seem to keep from crying. At last, my father started again and sang through to the very end.

It was after two o'clock when we finally retired. Dawn came so soon. He didn't say a thing to me, not one word. He probably couldn't say what I should do after his death. I wanted to say something to him, but I couldn't find the words either. At a time like that nothing seems right. I had so many things to say and felt frustrated at my inability to voice my thoughts. There was the air-raid warning, too. If it had only been a preliminary alert, we could have had some light. Unfortunately, it was a full alert. My mother was making some noise in the kitchen. The rain shutters were shut tight. The all-clear probably came about two o'clock. No enemy planes came over, but along the coast the blackout was very strict. Your eyes get used to the dark and you can make things out dimly. I could hear a suppressed sob from my mother. I sat formally. He did, too. I noticed something move and felt his hand grasp mine. I returned his grip. We were so modest. Why were we that bashful in the darkness? We didn't know anything. We rose at four o'clock in the morning. He left home just after five, not telling us where he was going. "When can I see you again?" I asked. He said only, "I'll be back when it rains." He left with those words. We were husband and wife only four hours.

All of us waited for him whenever it rained. From April to June. "He'll be back today," we'd all say when the rain fell. We didn't lock the entrance, so he could come in at any time. We'd wait until the last train, but he couldn't come back, of course. He'd died in action long before. We waited for him, waited and waited for him, all of us, without knowing he was long dead.

Meanwhile, I got pregnant. I found myself throwing up often and wondered why. My mother didn't have any experience. I'd been adopted, you see. My mother was actually my aunt. We thought I was ill. We went to a doctor. He asked cautiously, "Do you have anything to tell me?" I said, "No." "Are you married?" "Yes" "Well, it seems you may be carrying a child."

I was stunned. From that moment on I wanted to see him and tell him. We searched and searched, but we had no clue. It was in mid-June that Takagi Toshirō visited us. You know him, don't you? The famous author? At that time many reporters visited the bases used by the Tokkō pilots, among them Mr. Takagi. "At Chiran, I was entrusted with the last will and testament of Araki Haruo, together with some clippings of his hair and nails," he said solemnly. I was overwhelmed! "He was killed in action on May 11."

Carrying the baby now became my reason to live. It was so for all of

us. We took special care and I gave birth to a son on December 25.
Christmas Day. We named the boy Ikuhisa, taking the Japanese reading
of the characters of his father's military unit, *Yūkyū* ["Eternity"]. We all
worked so hard to raise him. But suddenly, on the fifth of November,
1946, he took ill and within thirty minutes he'd stopped breathing. I was
holding him in my arms. Everything was over and I was only twenty-two
years old.

I'd always fought with him. "I can't stand the sight of you," he used
to say. I'd tell him, "I don't care either. There are lots of boys better than
you. I'll marry one of them." We were the same age. We made good
opponents. He must have always thought he'd marry me. Somehow, I
thought if he became a lieutenant we'd be together, even if we did fight.
I was always conscious of his presence, as if we were engaged. If he'd
married someone else, I'd have been furious.

In his will, addressed to his father, he wrote that he'd flown over our
house at the end of April, circling many, many times. Father was working
in the fields and didn't look up. "Father," he wrote, "I was unable to
catch your attention." We were all wracked with regret. Father was filled
with remorse forever after. Whenever airplanes flew over, he'd always
wave at them and say, "Why didn't I notice the plane carrying my own
son?"

It was such a brief and simple will. The letters I'd received up to
that time had always started, "Dear Miss Shigeko." The will started,
"Shigeko," as I'd hoped. It was addressed to his wife. He told me of his
concern for my long-term future. He said he felt brokenhearted over
that. He told me to live purely, strongly, and correctly. When I think
of it now, I cannot help but cry. He asked me to forgive him for taking a harsh tone with me. Why did a man who was going to die have to
beg my pardon? I was the one who wanted to be forgiven. He asked me
to absolve him for his selfishness and willfulness. Since he showed
concern for my future, he must have wanted to be forgiven for getting
married, too.

Father's was a long letter and covered many subjects. Mine was
really short. He must have written it last. His hand was shaky. Asking to
be forgiven. That is the most heartbreaking for me. I had no way to
respond to his plea. I could only pray. I could only feel sympathy and
misery. My emotions reach out to him. My mother's name didn't appear
anywhere in his wills. She was hurt by this. I comforted her by saying that
when he spoke of Father, he meant her, too.

From June to July, the Tokkō planes were practically all shot down
one after the other as they approached their targets. I don't know if he
actually crashed into the enemy, but some did. There were results. I want

to believe that. I want to believe that he didn't die in vain. Otherwise he still lies at the bottom of the cold Okinawan sea for nothing. I want to raise him even now. I know there's nothing left, but I can't help this feeling.

[*She brings out a small photograph album.*] Would you like to see these? These are photographs taken by Mr. Takagi on the tenth. This is Haruo, he's in the middle. These three men were all group leaders at Chiran, the air base the Tokkō used in Kyushu. They were classmates at the Military Academy, fifty-seventh class. This was really unusual. By chance, they were all assigned to attack on the same day, although they went off at different times. All three were twenty-one years old. Haruo took off in the lead plane, just after six A.M. The headband he wears bears the rising-sun emblem. The students at the girls school near the air base at Chiran had cut their fingers and filled in the red sun with their own blood. This picture shows Haruo giving the final address before take off. He's smiling, conscious of the camera. In this situation nobody could smile naturally. There is another photograph, a group picture of their trip to pray at Ise Shrine. See the tall man? Haruo really stands out, doesn't he?

These are the only pictures I have. We didn't have time to take pictures. We talked about it. "We'll have to take a proper wedding portrait when he comes back." But that chance never came.

I did marry again and bore children. When my children were of grade-school age, I sometimes wondered who I would choose if he returned. Should I go with Haruo, leaving my husband and two children, or should I preserve my family and leave him? I really thought about this, seriously. To be frank, I was somehow relieved after my husband died. I had the thought, "Haruo can come back anytime now." Isn't it odd? You can't believe that, can you? But I never saw Haruo dying. I watched my husband die with my own eyes. My first child died in my arms. There is no way to confirm death in his case. Some members of the Special Attack forces made forced landings or ditched at sea. There are people who did come back. Some who survived wanted to break all contact with their classmates and friends. Even when classmates tried to get in touch, some absolutely refused to meet them. I hear those stories and sometimes I wonder.

In those years, he appeared in my dreams many times. It seems impossible to believe, but he even gave his child a name. "He'll be born tomorrow," he told me, and he was born the next day. After my husband died, I stopped seeing dreams of Haruo. Why doesn't he appear to me anymore? Maybe it's because now he can come back anytime. All that's left for me is to look forward to the day when I meet Haruo in the other world and can say, "I haven't seen you for a long time." He'll be awfully surprised, I'm sure! "Who's this grandma?" Maybe he'll just look aside and claim he has no idea who I am.

"I'll go first. I'll meet you at Yasukuni" is what the lead pilots said to their groups. It was their pledge. To meet at Yasukuni. They were cling-ing to the idea of meeting again. They couldn't help themselves. I believe their courageous spirit is only there at Yasukuni Shrine. I frequently go to Yasukuni, but I go to the graves more often. On the anniversary of his death, or any day when the weather is good, I go. I only end up crying if it's a rainy day. It's a beautiful place. You can see the sea stretched out before you. Mount Fuji is directly opposite. It's high on a hill, surrounded by mandarin-orange groves.

I went to Okinawa about six years ago. I wanted to see that sea, once. I was told it was in the vicinity of Kadena Bay that he made his attack. We don't really know. Anyway, I brought some sand and pebbles from there and put them next to his grave. When I was there, I called to him by name, shouting loudly "Haruo-san!" Sometimes people ask me to go with them to Okinawa, but it's not a place I want to go to twice. Okinawans think they were the only victims. It's amazing how strongly they feel that. That feeling is everywhere. They think Okinawa was cut off and only Okinawans had terrible times. I see such stories in the newspapers and I don't like them. Haruo died to protect Okinawa. I get angry when they consider themselves just victims. Did you hear about the incident where they even burned our flag? I'd hate to set foot on the soil of Okinawa again.

So many memories came back to me like pictures on a revolving lantern. There are times when I wish the Emperor had reached the decision to surrender earlier. So many civilians also suffered. There was so much damage. We were going to do it with our bamboo spears. When they landed we would attack them. We had those spears at our right hand at all times at the factory. "Each one, stab one, without fail!" they'd tell us. "Yes!" we'd reply in unison.

Our spear was about a meter and a half long, with a sharp point cut diagonally across at the end. We practiced every morning, "Thrust! Thrust! Thrust!" I thought I'd definitely be able to stab them. We had the image of the Americans as being gigantic. We were told, "Americans are large and well built, so go for the throat. Stab here, drive your spear up into the throat. Don't look at the face. Stab without looking." We really believed we could do it. Isn't it scary? We often called this "*Yamato damashii*," the "Spirit of Japan." We'd put on our headband with the rising sun emblazoned on it. Then we'd bow deeply in the direction of the Imperial Palace. Next, we drilled with our bamboo spears. Finally, we'd start our work. But I enjoyed it. It was for Japan, it was to preserve and protect the country. We were sending our loved ones off to die to protect the country. It was the least we could do on the home front. It's amazing isn't it? Beyond comprehension today. At that time we had an unbounded faith in Japan. We felt the Yamato race was unequaled.

Even after forty years my memories will not be extinguished. I get really excited when I talk like this. At that time, I thought it was natural that Haruo would die. It would have been shameful for him to go on living. I was half-waiting for his death. But he had assured me he would come back once more. I thought the next time would be the last time. What should be my frame of mind then? I was contemplating what I would do as the wife of a samurai. How would I welcome him? With what words would I send him off? Then he died on me! Just like that, out of the blue. That's what shocked me. It wasn't that I wanted him to die, please understand. But I was waiting for his "glorious and honorable death." If he didn't die, it would be a disgrace. If a family lost someone in action in those days, we would congratulate them. We'd say, "That's wonderful." We really meant it! At least, that expressed half of what we felt.

When at last I learned he'd died, people said, "That's good; congratulations." I replied, "Yes, it is. It's for the country," and then I returned home to cry alone. I let no one see my tears. We were told that with our eyelids we should suppress our tears. We were told not to cry, but to endure. My father and mother showed no tears in front of others. Nobody expressed their sorrow or sympathy for us. They only said, "It was an honorable death in battle, wasn't it?" and we'd agree.

Even between parents and child we never expressed such ideas as "Why did he die?" or "What if he had lived on?" We were simply silent on these things. Nobody held me tight in their arms and comforted me with words of sympathy. But when the baby boy was born, my father cried out in a loud voice: "This is Haruo's reincarnation!" He wept openly. Everyone broke down, the only time we all sobbed, holding each other's hands. The midwife was startled and told us to hurry up and boil some water and stop crying. Father must have held those tears inside for the whole year. We took special care of the boy. When the baby died I thought there was no God, no Buddha in the world. I fainted at the grave when we had the funeral. Just as I was putting Haruo's wooden box and the baby's remains in together.

I have only good memories of him because he died young. If we'd lived together until now, maybe we'd have gotten bored and divorced. That four hours was such a valuable time. It is a time only we know about. I felt I was loved body and soul. We didn't sleep at all. But we didn't speak. It was precious. Truly wonderful. He must have been overwhelmed with sorrow. I thought I would see him again. I didn't think it was the last time. He did say, "If we had a rope, we would jump into the sea off Kōzu, our bodies tied together." I could only say "What?" I didn't know what to say. He went on, in a quiet voice, "I cannot do that now." If I'd told anyone, people would have accused him of shameful conduct for an officer. He was more mature than I was. The room we were in was a Western-style room, about ten tatami. It had glass windows. We were able to see each other's faces in the light from outside. The room where we had the wedding ceremony had paper walls, with rain shutters outside, so it was pitch black. After the stand-down from the full alert, about two o'clock, we were able to turn on a light shielded by black cloth. The light embarrassed us and we turned it off again. The next morning we were still too bashful even to look into each other's faces. We both turned away. Later I regretted not having looked at him closely. I wish I'd studied his features. But I can easily see him the next morning, standing in the hall near the window, looking out, dressed in his uniform. That moment is impressed on my mind. His form took shape in the early morning light.

Breakfast was ready. Then I asked him, "Can I come with you to the station?" "Walk behind me," he answered. I went with him to the train wearing *monpe*, though I wore a kimono for my wedding. It was embarrassing for us. My eyes were on him, but he walked straight ahead, never turning back to look at me. He bought a ticket at Kōzu Station. I tried to glimpse it, just to know where he was going, but he snapped, "You can't look!" I stepped back, startled.

When I visit the graves, I always make it a point to walk along the beach and then visit that house before coming home. It's still exactly as it was, though we sold it and moved long ago. I talk to him. "I'm walking now alone on the road we walked together," or "I'm already sixty-seven years old." Sometimes his image overlaps with my husband's. Maybe I get him mixed up because I married my husband in Kōzu. I may start out talking to Haruo, calling him "Haruo-san," but I end up addressing "Father" or "Grandfather," as the children and I always called my husband. He was a tall, handsome man. A man like that was blown to bits, so that not even a shred of flesh was left. It's all right if he crashed into an enemy ship, but it's possible he is alive if he were shot down on the way. You cannot be certain he was hit in the head or heart. If he'd been hit in the leg or arm, he could have survived. I hate having thoughts like that.

My grandson says, "Grandma always looks up when a plane flies over." I look up because it's as if the Tokkō planes are overhead as they once were, forty-five years ago. That won't ever change. I remember these things as if they happened yesterday. I don't have much of a chance to speak in this way. I try to tell myself not to look back, to keep everything bottled up. But once the dike breaks, it seems like it never stops flooding out.

Later, she asks, "Would you like to see his will?" She brings out a brownish, single sheet. It reads:

Shigeko,

Are you well? It is now a month since that day. The happy dream is over. Tomorrow I will dive my plane into an enemy ship. I will cross the river into the other world, taking some Yankees with me. When I look back, I see that I was very cold-hearted to you. After I had been cruel to you, I used to regret it. Please forgive me.

When I think of your future, and the long life ahead, it tears at my heart. Please remain steadfast and live happily. After my death, please take care of my father for me.

I, who have lived for the eternal principles of justice, will forever protect this nation from the enemies that surround us.

Commander of Air Unit Eternity
Araki Haruo

Requiem

NISHIHARA WAKANA

She comes to the station on a bicycle, a tiny woman with black, short-cut hair, wearing a bright red sweater. When she talks about her parents and her brother, her gaze seems to drift off. Sadness, happiness, and despair are vividly expressed by her passionate alto voice.

She is active in the Association to Memorialize the Students Who Died in War [Nihon Senbotsu Gakusei Kinenkai]—known as the Wadatsumikai. Most of the students memorialized left their campuses when university deferments were ended in late 1943. Many of these highly educated young men were drawn into the special-attack forces. They frequently left behind letters or diaries in which they grappled with issues of life and death which they were facing just as the war reached a fever pitch. Some of what they wrote in their final moments was published in Japan as Kike wadatsumi no koe *[Listen to the Voices of the Sea]* in 1952. *Their thoughts just prior to the moment of death are widely read. Four volumes of diaries, letters, and materials left by her brother have been published.*

In Britain they say "God Save the Queen." With the help of God, the King or Queen can govern. If they do not obey God's will, if they are tyrants, the people have the right to cut down the King or Queen. But in Japan they said, "Die for the Sake of the Emperor." No one could disobey an order to die for him. I've been thinking these issues through for the last forty-three years. I'm no Communist, but I'm convinced that if we hadn't had "The Emperor's Army" they would never have invented a Special Attack weapon like the Kaiten "human torpedo."

I'm the youngest of five brothers and sisters. Minoru was the eldest, so there was a gap of twelve years between us. He was born in 1922. I only lived under the same roof with him in my early childhood. When he left home to enter the First Higher School in 1939, I was six. It was a matter of great pride for the family that he was able to gain admission to such a fine school. He then entered Tokyo Imperial University. Hardly had we celebrated his advancement to Tōdai than he was called to the colors. I remember it well. I was really rather proud of his joining the navy. The year I entered elementary school, they had all become "National Schools," so we received a thorough indoctrination in the notion that we were the Emperor's children, "little patriots." It was entirely natural that we would offer our lives to the Emperor.

Besides, we didn't expect Japan to lose. Even if you went into the military, we believed that would bring brilliant results and we were certain a return home was assured. It never occurred to us to oppose this. On the contrary, a little girl, a third-grader, could brag, "My big brother's going to war. He'll be in the navy." I'm sure my parents felt anxious that their precious son was leaving, but I don't believe even they imagined he would really die.

I was brought up in Numazu City in Shizuoka prefecture. It's a small town and not much information reached us. People in the middle of Tokyo might have grasped the riskiness even for university students called to serve, but we in a provincial city never thought that way. We sent soldiers off to the front in the highest of spirits. When my eldest brother went, the block association marched to the station waving rising-sun flags and wearing white sashes boldly inscribed with the message "Congratulations on Being Called to Service." Some women's-association members in white aprons sang. When other men in the neighborhood had been called, we all went waving our flags. Now, it was brother's turn and I was bursting with pride.

He went to the naval barracks in Tokuyama. He had three sisters and we wrote to him often—everything about the family, large and small. We wrote to him, described how we made *mochi* rice cakes, how much progress we'd made at school, what we studied, what we'd done every day. We took turns sending him letters, so he got them all the time. That enraged his commanding officer. "What's wrong with you, letting them fill letters with such worldly thoughts! I prohibit them to write to you!" My brother addressed a letter to Father asking him to keep his sisters from writing for a while. That's in his diary. Elder Brother was bitter and chagrined by this order. Father told us not to write to my brother anymore. It came suddenly, and we weren't told why we should stop. The intervals between his letters lengthened. Once we were able to see him at Numazu Station on his way to the Tateyama Naval Barracks from Kyushu. I cut a lock from my bangs with a pair of scissors and gave it to him. Looking back now, it amazes me, but I just wanted to convey my feelings to my brother. I wanted him to have something of mine. I think he may have kept it to the moment of his death.

In May 1945, he returned home suddenly. We were ready to retire for the night when the entrance bell rang. It was raining hard, close to ten o'clock. We opened the door and there was my brother! "Minoru-chan's home!" We roused the house. We woke up Mother and Father. My eldest sister had already gotten married, and my second sister was studying at Tokyo Women's College. Just four of us were still at home. Minoru brought a trunk full of canned salmon, candies, and *yōkan* sweet bean cake with him.

We asked "How come they let you come back?" He just said, "I've become important, so they allowed it." I was a child, so it didn't occur to me to doubt the meaning of his words. I took what he said at face value. I clung to him until late into the evening. If I were not careful, I felt, he might disappear. I was so desperately happy! He stayed two nights and returned to the base in Hikari on the third day. This was, according to his diary, his last farewell prior to his departure in a Kaiten.

It took twenty-four hours by train from Hikari to Numazu at that time. On his way home to us he wrote in his diary, "I have no confidence in myself. I feel like I may spill it all if I see my parents' faces," but he didn't give us even the slightest inkling of what was ahead. Only my father may have sensed something, because by May 1945—this was after the Tokyo air raid—the word *gyokusai* (sacrificial battles) was heard everywhere.

The morning after his return I announced, "Elder Brother's back; I'm not going to school." It was a small town, and everyone knew everything about everybody. "Let's go for a walk," Elder Brother said to me that morning. I'd loved going for walks with him from the time I was really small. If I were a dog, I'd have been shaking ten imaginary tails, that's how excited I was—and I hadn't even begged for that walk. He'd suggested it!

Right in front of our house was a pine grove, and just beyond that, the sea. You could hear it at night. With me practically clinging to him, we went down to the shore. We'd always played along the edge of the ocean, skipping stones, trying to get them to break through the onrushing waves. Elder Brother displayed great skill for me that day. He broke the waves three or four times. The memory remains vivid. There is a place called Osezaki across the bay, on the Izu Peninsula, where Tokyo University had a lodge. We could see it clearly from where we were. Brother called out the azimuth, so many degrees, so many minutes. It must have become a habit for him during his training at Hikari. Whenever he saw an island, or a ship, he must have instantly calculated the degrees and minutes with his eye. There, on the shore, we sang a song and then walked to Numazu Park. That was our usual route. Then we strolled into town.

On the way back, we entered a photographic studio. It was so unexpected. I followed him in, filled with delight. Elder Brother first had a picture taken of himself alone. Then he sat and I stood next to him. The photographer told me to put my arm around his shoulder. I was eleven years old, a tiny child due to the malnutrition of the time. He was already an ensign. Because the photographer posed us that way I can tell that he knew this would be the last picture. For a naval officer to come to a photographic studio with his little sister was not a trivial thing. These were the only pictures taken on his last visit. Brother had a camera and it would not have been strange for him to take a picture of the family together, but he must have worried that we would think something amiss. To my brother, I suppose I was really only a little child, too young to know or understand his feelings. That must have been a salvation to him.

Elder Sister was only a year younger than him. The next morning, they went out on a walk, but could say nothing to each other and turned back halfway through their course. I bitterly regret that I didn't notice anything. But, at the same time, I pray that my childish innocence, my inability to fathom his feelings, was a comfort to him.

> Unaware my elder brother's departure [for battle] in his Kaiten
>   was imminent,
> I played with him, skipping stones on the sea.

I composed that poem more than thirty years later. I remember the physical presence of my brother so clearly. How could I have imagined he would disappear forever? I didn't know what it meant when a warrior came home in the midst of war.

Submarine *I-363*, which carried my brother, soon went out on its mission. It wandered at the bottom of the sea for more than a month. Once they actually boarded their Kaitens and prepared themselves for the command to launch, but the American transport ship outdistanced their submarine and the attack was called off. They returned, unable to find their prey. It was like having your head placed below the guillotine, only to be saved just before the blade falls. Brother's comrades say that those people who returned home were like ghosts. There was no way to comfort them. You couldn't congratulate them—"Great, you came back alive!"—No, indeed, for they had to go out again so soon.

My brother stopped writing at that point. I've always been very impressed with how much he did write until that moment. Such a diligent writer, he put down his pen completely when he returned alive from that mission. This probably meant that he had conceived of death up to that point in an abstract way. How could someone prepare his mind for that? He was only twenty-three-and-a-half years old. Perhaps he'd never known a woman. He loved his parents, loved his younger brother, loved his sisters. He played the violin and he wrote poetry. What he wanted to do was infinite. In his diary, until that point, he writes, "This is the last birthday of my life," and elsewhere, "This is my last Imperial Rescript Day." In this abstract way, he was ready for death, but after coming back alive, he confided to his war comrades that he didn't want to die. He told one of them that while he was playing the piano. On another occasion, when classmates were looking through albums together, my brother showed them my picture. "This is Wakana, my youngest sister. See, isn't she cute?" Two of his comrades whom I really trust told me that, so I don't think there's any doubt, he no longer wanted to die. But the date when they would next go into action was already fixed; it was to be August 31.

During morning training on July 25, he and his Kaiten were lost. It was probably due to a steering problem, perhaps a loss of ability to maneuver and control descent, even though that Kaiten had just returned from maintenance. My brother was not an unskillful pilot, but his Kaiten porpoised and must have dived to the bottom of the ocean. They searched desperately for him, but, unfortunately, a large-scale American air attack came in. The Japanese naval arsenal at Kure was the target of regular carrier attacks. It was always best to search for a Kaiten from above, but our side couldn't launch a plane to look for him. From the testimonies of his comrades, I know they worked hard and did their best, but his Kaiten had stuck on the bottom. I was told he might have lived another twenty hours trapped inside.

My family here in Numazu, we didn't know anything at all. The war ended August 15. Numazu had been attacked in a large air raid July 16. Fortunately, my house survived unburnt. Our relatives, from all over Numazu, came to our home. Each family occupied one room. Sometimes as many as seven families were there at one time. We suffered from fleas and stifling conditions indoors when we had the shutters closed because of blackouts. There was little food. It was a horrible month. But by the fifteenth of August, most had left us and we had returned to the quiet, subdued life we had known before. That morning we were told there would be an important broadcast and we were instructed to listen without fail. People from the entire neighborhood came to the house, filling the main room. They must have thought, "They'll have a radio," since by luck, our house was in the one corner of the city that had escaped the fire. We knew from the introduction that his Imperial Majesty would address us, but then we really couldn't understand the high-pitched voice that came next. Today the announcements we hear on television are clear, but then sending and receiving conditions were poor. We hardly understood what was said. I sat there, listening absentmindedly. My father wiped away tears with his fist and groaned loudly, so I became sad and cried.

That night, my father said for the first time, "Minoru will come home!" Of course he'd return! We didn't have any thought that he'd died. Who cares if the country's lost? Minoru-chan will be back! A smile returned to Mother's face. "It's all right to take these down, isn't it?" my other brother said of the black cloth over the windows. He tore them all down. I played piano that night as if possessed. I was so happy. "Minoru-chan will come home!" That's all I could think about. For ten days we waited like that. On August 26, that morning—it's still crystal clear in my memory—I was lying on the porch sofa reading *Mother's Virtue,* Yoshiya Nobuko's version of a famous English story about a mother's love. My mother, who had been sweeping the entrance hall, came to me quietly and said, "Minoru killed himself." My mother's face was ashen. In her hand was a telegram. I glimpsed it, and it said "Wada Minoru Public Death." It was dated August 25. "Public Death," not "Death in Battle." We didn't know the meaning of the term "public death." We thought it must mean Minoru had taken his own life. General Anami and other military men had slit their stomachs by the Nijūbashi Bridge in front of the Imperial Palace.

I took that notice in my hand. My thought was, I must take it to my father. Father owned his own clinic at the time, but he was working in a public infirmary. I borrowed a bicycle from a neighbor because we didn't have one of our own, and carrying that notice, took the road through the pine wood along the shore. It was a sweltering day. The voices of the cicadas were boiling over all around me. Japan had lost, not only that, but my brother, who was supposed to come back, was dead, and we didn't even know what had happened to him, That misery and anger! I rushed into where my father was receiving patients, crying, "Minoru-chan's died!" I was immediately told to go home. It was a terrible thing for an eleven-year-old girl to go home alone, dragging her bicycle. But I had no choice.

Already the neighbors knew. The strength and unity of the women's association was manifest in this situation. Mourners started to call on us instantly and began cooking vegetables for the guests to come. It was like this out in the country. There's a very cynical *haiku* which says if someone dies, someone else comes and starts cooking white radishes, but it's true. When father came home he went and opened the trunk which my brother had entrusted to him. In that trunk were his will and all the letters he sent, neatly arranged. His will and his diaries. They put his will on the family altar and Father sat under the windup clock by the long hibachi. That was always Father's seat, but now he was bowed over, head in his hands. "Why did you die? Why did you die?" That's all he kept saying. Tears fell in big drops from his eyes. If it had been written "Died in an accident July 25," my father would have been spared that lamentation.

My father, who was born in Meiji and brought up with this nation, never grumbled about his son's going to war. If this notice had come before the news of defeat, he would not have grieved in such a way. I came to understand this much later. His was the lamentation of King Lear. He offered his son to the nation, therefore he could accept it if his son died when the nation was engaged in combat. But now, when the nation was defeated, why shouldn't he have come home to complete his duties as the eldest son? Why did he forget his parents, sisters, and brother?

I was more frightened by my father's appearance than by the fact that my brother had died. Until that moment, I had thought children could not die before their parents. I really thought that. "Until this morning we were so happy" was what went through my head. Why couldn't we just reverse time? If we could, just for half a day, I wouldn't mind dying myself. These were the desperate thoughts of an eleven-year-old girl. The next day my father and my other brother went to Hikari. There they found out it wasn't a suicide. After that Father never again showed that kind of emotion in front of other people.

Mother tried desperately to keep herself occupied. For many, many years I followed around after her and clung to her, begging her, "Please don't die, Mother. There are still four of us left. Don't leave us." I felt *I* had to keep my eyes on my mother, or she might just go away somewhere and die. Sometimes she would leave the table in the middle of a meal, disappear. Father would ask me to see how she was doing, and I'd search. Sometimes I'd find her crouched in the corner of the garden, weeding. Perhaps my mother would have wanted to get my elder brother back in exchange for the four of us. Now I have three children. If one of them died, and I was told by the other what I'd said to Mother, I don't know what I'd do. I didn't understand my mother's feelings then. I couldn't say, "I'm here. Don't die, for my sake!" I couldn't say that, even though I was a small child.

I think the utmost crime of man is to use another man as a tool. When the Americans attacked Tokyo in the great fire-bombing, I understand that there were few American casualties. Nine died, and they killed a hundred thousand people. They came in three hundred planes, about three thousand crew members. Some were shot down, but most were rescued by American submarines. They valued lives to that extent. They didn't attack until such preparations were made. In Japan, if you were told it was an order from the Emperor, you couldn't do anything about it. The fact that the Special Attack strategy existed only in Japan means this was only possible in the Emperor's Army. Is there any other country on Earth willing to send its people into a combat from which they could not possibly return?

In May 1944, my brother wrote, "If human torpedoes are being developed, it must be we who will ride them." My brother was not acting for the sake of the Emperor, but for the parents he loved, the brother and sisters he loved, for the hometown he loved. He probably thought the air raids would stop if he went out and sank an enemy battleship or aircraft carrier. I must say frankly that it was a kind of delusion that the whole nation was caught up in. "Eight Corners of the World Under One Roof" was part of it. The belief that this is a godly nation and that the divine wind would blow soon. Japan must have seemed a strange nation, viewed from outside. Iwo Jima, Attu, Saipan—there they carried out *gyokusai*, knowing the situation was hopeless. They should have surrendered to the Americans, but perhaps it was because of the Field Service Regulations. They didn't teach what it meant to be a prisoner-of-war. To become a prisoner made you a traitor. There's no way of knowing how many people died in Imphal, New Guinea, and the Philippines. Why didn't they surrender?

One of my brother's comrades, Mr. Kōzu,° belongs to an antiwar soldiers' association. A couple of its members became POWs at the end of the war. Yet even their colleagues say things like, "How can they speak about war when they ended up prisoners?" After experiencing that war, you'd think they'd all recognize its meaningless stupidity—but still they denigrate those who became prisoners. Even today.

"Two or three million Japanese deaths in the war," "the deaths of six million Jews." We shouldn't make deaths into numbers. They were each individuals. They had names, faces. "Thirty million Asian deaths." One hundred thousand dead in the Tokyo air raid. Hiroshima, one hundred thousand dead. My brother might just be a fraction of several millions, but for me he's the only Elder Brother in the world. For my mother he was the only Eldest Son. Compile the dead one by one. All those precious lives thrown away, most of them nameless and completely forgotten. My brother was one of the most blessed of all the dead in the Japanese military. His memoirs were published posthumously because he was a student soldier, because he was a Kaiten pilot.

At the end of September 1945 there was a big typhoon. The bottom of the sea was churned up and his Kaiten was beached on an island called Nagashima. Some people were still at the Hikari base, finishing up business. Three of them went to the island. Only one Kaiten—his—was unaccounted for at war's end. "That must be Wada," they thought. He was sitting cross-legged, with a small trunk in front of him. He'd died from suffocation due to the lack of oxygen. Decomposition had not progressed very far. I think it was a few days into October, when I answered the call at the door. His superior officer was standing there with a white box. "I've brought your brother's remains," he said.

This ring on my finger is a heirloom from my brother. When he came home for the last time he gave Mother a pin for her *obi*. At that time, he had a pretty good salary, so he bought one with a large pearl in the middle. The pin became worn, so Mother made it into a ring. When she was dying she said to me, "You've done so much for Minoru-chan; you should have this." What I've done, though—it's only because the dead are mute. They cannot speak. The living must act with energy for them. That's all I'm doing.

After my brother learned he was going to war in 1943, he made a recording of himself playing Jules Émile Frédéric Massenet's *Requiem* on the excellent violin Father had bought him when he entered First Higher School. When my daughter married and I'd sent off her things to

---

° Kōzu Naoji, whose story appears above as "Human Torpedo."

her new home, I was overwhelmed by a strange feeling that I was sinking into the depths of the earth. I was washing dishes in the kitchen, and I turned on the radio. That piece of music came on. It was as if my brother was telling me, "Why are you sad at such a joyous time? Think how your mother must have felt when she sent me off to war." This piece of music is the only sound that my brother left for me. When I hear that melody I think of him.

Through the pine wood I race clutching the Public Notice,
While the cicadas of the defeated nation cry out in chorus.

I'm frightened of ideology, of -isms, and of nations. I prefer an unjust peace to a justified war. No matter what the ideals are, if they are going to lead to war, I prefer a corrupt, immoral, unprincipled, unredeemed peace.

I cannot forget my father howling,
Crouched like a wounded beast.

PART FIVE

"One Hundred Million Die Together"

Kūshū da. Kūshū da. Sore kūshū da.
Aka da. Aka da. Shōidan.
Hashire. Hashire. Mushiro da, suna da.
Kūshū da. Kūshū da. Sore kūshū da.
Kuro da. Kuro da. Sore bakudan.
Mimi o fusage. O-meme o tojiyo.

Air Raid. Air raid. Here comes an air raid!
Red! Red! Incendiary bomb!
Run! Run! Get mattress and sand!
Air Raid. Air raid. Here comes an air raid!
Black! Black! Here come the bombs!
Cover your ears! Close your eyes!

—A song for a children's dance to practice civil-defense techniques. From the *Collection of the People's Favorite Songs* [*Kokumin aishō kashū*], widely used in 1944.

IN JAPAN, people had their first glimpse of how truly bleak were their prospects from news reports of the fate of the civilian residents of Saipan, which fell to the Americans in July 1944. Newspapers across Japan, for instance, carried translations of a *Time* magazine article that described women and children committing suicide, and especially the extraordinary sight of young Japanese women choosing to plunge off cliffs rather than surrender to American soldiers. Such awe-filled "enemy" reports were presented by Tokyo as clear evidence of the glory of civilian sacrifices, and portrayed as proof of the "pride of the Japanese woman." Typically, the *Yomiuri* newspaper carried a comment by a Tokyo Imperial University professor that "our courage will be buoyed up by this one hundred times, one thousand times" and exhorted its readers to "sacrifice before our great victory." *

This was fully in keeping with how the defeats the Empire suffered had been described to the Japanese public for more than a year. All such disasters, from Guam to Saipan, were called "great sacrifices prior to Japan's great victory." As the bombing of the Homeland increased in intensity, the press had little choice but to acknowledge that "America's edge in the war of material has been creating difficulty for the Imperial forces." This sort of statement was usually qualified, somewhat lamely, by the claim that "Japan's losses are limited." † It was also always emphasized that America, as an individualistic and liberal nation, had to try to fight a short war in order to keep pacifist sentiments under control at home. The Japanese public was repeatedly reassured by military men, government officials, and their favored intellectuals that if only Japan fought in the true Yamato Spirit, America's will to battle would collapse in rancorous homefront disarray.

While such official calls for sacrifice in the name of victory intensified, the most common topic of conversation in Japan's cities was how to cope with the difficulties of daily life. In the face of an increasingly effective Allied naval blockade and terrible labor shortages among farmers and fishermen, food shortages became acute. The price of rice on the black market soared, and police assigned to "economic" duty were kept busy checking packages and bundles on streets and trains, looking for all sorts of contraband. Even train tickets were impossible to purchase

---

* Kiyosawa Kiyoshi, *Ankoku nikki, 1942–1945* [*Diary of Dark Days, 1942–1945*] (Tokyo: Iwanami, 1990), pp. 220–22.

† Japanese papers were virtually unanimous in their use of these turns of phrase at the end of the war.

without either official or military vouchers. In 1943, Sundays, as days of rest, were abolished.

Military setbacks on the rim of Japan's Pacific empire, no matter how cloaked, gradually brought the Homeland within range of American air attack. Defense schemes against such attacks, though prepared with great energy and involving the whole population, were totally unrealistic. People were encouraged to dig small, nearly useless shelters under the floors of their living rooms, or in the corners of household gardens. By the sides of city streets, slit trenches and person-sized holes were also readied. Everywhere, women sewed supposedly protective headgear stuffed with cotton for themselves and their children, and were ordered to carry these "helmets" suspended from their shoulders at all times, facing severe reprimands from teachers or officials if found "unprotected."

The responsibility for civilian defense fell primarily on women, since most ablebodied husbands, fathers, and sons were either in the military or at factories, which they were often obliged to "defend" in case of attack. Neighborhood associations conducted firefighting exercises, featuring such primitive methods as water-bucket relays and use of damp mops to put out sparks from incendiary bombs. Hand-operated pumps and fire extinguishers—little more than large water pistols—were stockpiled, and cisterns and kettles were filled. A blackout was strictly enforced. Even a lit cigarette in the night could bring a severe admonition. Later in the war, pulling down buildings en masse to create firebreaks was begun in some cities.

Concentrated attacks by American B-29 heavy bombers against Japan began in June 1944 from bases in China. Initially aimed at industrial targets and carried out from high altitudes, they grew heavier in the fall of 1944, when Allied bases in the Mariana Islands (captured in June) became operational. Raids now came regularly, but not until the early morning darkness of March 10, 1945, did the Americans first fully employ new tactics that would in the space of less than three months reduce most of Japan's major cities to ashes. That raid, as recalled by survivors in some of the interviews that follow, likely took the lives of more than a hundred thousand people; the figure will never be known, for almost all official registration records were destroyed in the inferno that consumed one-quarter of the nation's capital in a single night. A million people were rendered homeless at a stroke. Since the overwhelming majority of Japan's urban structures and almost all housing was constructed of wood and other easily combustible materials, no civilian-defense efforts could stop Japan's cities from going up in flames. Those who stayed at their "posts" in an air raid as planned, to defend home, neighborhood, or factory, were simply the most likely candidates for death in the ensuing fire storms that ravaged urban Japan.

Yet official reports and public announcements sought to minimize even this catastrophe and turn it to propaganda advantage. The *Asahi* newspaper of March 11, for instance, carried the headline, "130 B-29s Blindly Bombed Imperial City. 15 Shot Down and About 50 Planes Damaged." In the words of the accompanying article, "the military, government offices, and the people jointly dealt with the audacious enemy's blind bombing. Our accumulation of war power for the final battle in the Homeland will not be blocked by such an enemy attack. Rather, it will stir our fighting spirit and our resolve to destroy the enemy." * Such statements were belied by the facts. By March 18—only eight days after the destruction of Tokyo—the major cities of Nagoya, Osaka, and Kobe had each been devastated by an incendiary raid made by more than three hundred planes.

People learned how to react to these attacks, not from military or civilian authorities, but from their own terrible experiences. They learned that they should flee as soon as the air-raid warning sounded rather than trying to stay to extinguish fires. Although the authorities chided citizens for simply escaping, in air raids on Tokyo on April 13 and on the Tokyo-Kawasaki-Yokohama area on April 15, although 220,000 houses were destroyed, the number of fatalities and other casualties was only one-fifteenth those of March 10, despite a refinement in American tactics—the addition of delayed-action bombs meant to hinder fire-fighting efforts and to leave behind a fear of further explosions even after the bombers had departed.† Such air raids on cities meant an end to any possibility of making a distinction between front and rear areas. Mothers, children, the old—everyone was now in the combat zone. By spring 1945, neither Allied military institutions nor the Japanese military and government seemed to have any desire to differentiate combatants from noncombatants.

The battle for the Japanese Home Islands officially began on April 1, 1945, on the island of Okinawa, the southernmost of Japan's forty-seven prefectures. In early 1945, the people of the prefecture had already mobilized to defend their homes. The *Okinawa Shinpō*, the island's only daily newspaper, asked the army chief-of-staff on the islands, Colonel Chō Isamu, what the residents of Okinawa should do in case the enemy

---

* Saotome Katsumoto, *Tōkyō daikushū* [*The Great Tokyo Air Raid*] (Tokyo: Iwanami, 1970), p. 177.

† Saotome Katsumoto, *Tōkyō ga moeta hi: Sensō to chūgakusei* [*The Day Tokyo Burned: War and Middle School Students*] (Tokyo: Iwanami, 1979), pp. 171–72.

landed. His response was, "Accept the leadership of the military simply and without hesitation. All residents of the prefecture must become soldiers. They must destroy the enemy with such fighting spirit that each one of them will kill ten [of the enemy]." Chō added that a military's duty was to win wars, not lose them in order to protect local residents. By mid-February, the *Okinawa Shinpō* was already editorializing: "Arrogant America targets our South West Islands. Nimitz [Chester A. Nimitz, commander of the American fleet in the Pacific] begins his operation. It's a god-given opportunity to eradicate the enemy. All residents of the prefecture, exhibit your *tokkō* spirit!" [*]

Once the American forces landed, the villages and towns of Okinawa and adjoining smaller islands became battlegrounds. Those residents not able to escape into the island's northern wilderness were directly exposed to what many described as a "typhoon of steel"—naval shelling, artillery, bombs, mortars, machine-guns, flame-throwers, and satchel charges. Soldiers from other parts of Japan assigned to defend the island, Okinawans called into the local defense forces or mobilized to act as guides, student nurses, boy runners, and other irregular forces, as well as women and children, all found themselves huddled together in caves—some natural, others man-made—helpless in the face of America's overwhelming military power. As described by survivors below, the "friendly forces" did not exactly turn out to be protectors of Okinawan residents. Japanese troops routinely ordered mothers with babies out of caves or forced them to kill their crying infants so as not to attract the attention of the enemy. Many local people were executed by their own forces as potential "spies" before Okinawa was declared officially secured by the Americans on June 22, 1945.

The costs of the Battle of Okinawa were enormous. But while many Okinawans still remained in hiding and resisted surrendering, the atomic bombs dropped on Hiroshima and Nagasaki in August ushered in a new level of frightfulness. ■

---

[*] Ōta Masahide, *Okinawa no kokoro: Okinawa to watakushi* [*The Heart of Okinawa: Okinawa and I*] (Tokyo: Iwanami, 1988), p. 65.

16 / THE BURNING SKIES

"Hiroko died because of me."

FUNATO KAZUYO

She was living with her family in Tokyo on the night of March 9, 1945, when the Japanese capital was attacked by 325 B-29 heavy bombers.

The tactics adopted in this raid were a radical departure from those employed previously in attacks against Japan's cities. Most had been high-altitude daylight approaches to pinpointed targets, primarily employing high explosives. The commander of America's air offensive from the Marianas, General Curtis E. LeMay, ordered this raid to proceed largely at low altitudes of between 5,000 and 8,000 feet. Moreover, guns and ammunition were left off many of the planes, so that extra clusters of M-69 jellied-gasoline incendiary bombs could be carried. Each plane could carry 40 clusters, each comprising some 38 bombs, for a total of about 1,520 bombs per plane. The raiders dropped some high explosives and phosphorus munitions as well. Tokyo's residential areas, rather than specific factory complexes, were the intended targets. The dispersal of Japanese industry among small workshops was given as a reason for the selection of the Shitamachi district along the Sumida River as the primary target zone. Studies made of the fires that followed the Kantō earthquake of 1923 and analysis of the construction of Japanese homes and neighborhoods had shown that such tactics would likely start uncontrollable fires. The goal was to incinerate as much of the city as possible.

Today Funato Kazuyo lives with her husband and two sons in Katsushika Ward, Tokyo. Her husband was orphaned in the bombing of Tokyo that day. Recently she wrote a children's book about her experiences. Tears well up in her eyes, and she is frequently overcome as she recalls that night.

Our school seemed to be shaded in militaristic hues. The themes of school pageants were "soldiers," or "buglers at the charge," or "military nurses." In all our compositions, drawings, and in calligraphy, we wrote to the soldiers of our gratitude for their fighting. Teachers became very strict, perhaps in order to bring up "little patriots" who would obey at a single command. My school was new, so it was easily militarized. We were famous for marching. After the morning assembly, we marched, and it made us feel just like soldiers. Martial music blared from speakers as we rapidly formed four lines, then eight lines, all in step. It was thrilling, carrying out crisp moves to the piercing commands of the physical education teacher. We also had air-defense drills. We put on our special fire helmets and, holding our school bags, we hid under the desks in our classroom. You covered your ears with your thumbs and with the remaining four fingers covered your eyes. They said our eyes would pop out and our eardrums burst if we didn't. We also practiced putting out fires by bucket relay.

I had three elder brothers. Kōichi, my eldest, and Minoru, the next, were in pharmacy school and both had been mobilized under the student mobilization law passed the year before. Minoru was dispatched to the Army Medical Supply Depot around March 1944. On August 11, I became the second to leave the family. I was sent to the countryside under the Group Evacuation Law. I was in the sixth grade. There were three younger than me. Baby brother was only three months old when I left. If I'd remained at home I'd have been carrying him on my back, while supervising my younger sisters' play and running errands in our neighborhood. I wondered what would happen to the little ones when I left, but I was quite excited by the idea of going off with a large group. As it was, they evacuated to a relative's house with Grandmother.

We sixth-graders were finally sent home from our evacuation area in Yamagata on March 2, 1945. Six days after we got home came the raid. If evacuation was intended to save lives, there was no need for our return, but there wasn't space for us in the village anymore. New third-graders would soon be coming. I wrote Minoru a letter from Yamagata saying, "Let's meet in Tokyo."

I didn't know my younger sisters were already back in Tokyo. Hiroko had reached school age, so she had to have a physical examination in Tokyo. Grandmother returned with Teruko on her back, saying, "If Hiroko is going back, we'll go too." The idea was to get the whole family together again in conjunction with my return for graduation.

Besides, air raids hadn't been that frequent in Tokyo. We were really boisterous and happy. Yoshiaki, my third elder brother, returned, too. The night of March 9, Minoru came home from the site of his work mobilization. So, by chance, all of us were in Tokyo that night. It was so unfortunate.

A north wind had been blowing all day. It was cold. We were all asleep because those days you retired early, since you couldn't burn the electric lights late. The first air raid came a little after ten o'clock. It came in a flash. There was a preliminary alert—three or four planes—but immediately, the warning was canceled. Just reconnaissance, they must have thought. Then the full force of the raid hit. When Mother woke me, all was in a terrible uproar, great loud noises everywhere. Father had to dash to his duty station at the school with his iron helmet and his haversack, because he was on the medical detail of the Vigilance Corps. At that time we always slept in *monpe,* so I awoke Hiroko while my mother put the baby on her back, and we went into the shelter dug under the shop. My three brothers had gone out to extinguish small fires from incendiary bombs. Suddenly Kōichi rushed in and told us to run in the direction of the school before our escape route was cut off. "We'll come later," he said. When we went out, we could see that to the west, in the direction of Fukagawa, everything was bright red. The north wind was incredibly strong. The drone of the planes was an overwhelming roar, shaking earth and sky. Everywhere, incendiary bombs were falling.

The baby on Momma's back howled. I had Hiroko by the hand. Teruko was staying at Grandmother's house. Minoru went there to get them. When he arrived, incendiary bombs were falling heavily and nobody was around, so feeling himself in great danger, he turned back. Mother, the baby, Hiroko, and I were by then in the shelters behind the school. They were uncovered and were more like lines of trenches. This was where we were supposed to assemble if anything happened.

Incendiaries began hitting near the school and the line of fire was coming closer. People panicked. Running, screaming. "We're all going to die! The fire's coming!" The sound of incendiary bombs falling, "*Whizzz,*" the deafening reverberations of the planes, and the great roar of fire and wind overwhelmed us. "If we stay here we'll die! Let's run!" Everybody danced to this theme. My mother and I, too. Many people who stayed there survived, but almost as if we were compelled to heed those voices calling, "Women and children, follow us. Why are you hesitating?" we jumped out. Somebody was shouting, "If you go toward Sunamachi you'll be safe!" Sunamachi was south of our house. Large bombs had fallen in that area weeks before and many parts of Sunamachi were nothing but vacant lots. Sunamachi was downwind and it was an ironclad rule to go upwind in a fire, but we couldn't go any further in the other direction. A firestorm lay that way. You'd have to go through it, and so many people were running madly away from the fire. "Make for Sunamachi!" We left the shelter and crossed the wooden bridge over the drainage ditch in front of the school. Then we ran into our three brothers. My father, too. The Vigilance Corps had given up. I felt, "At last we're safe."

Nearby was Sarue Onshi Park. Father must have judged that it would be safer to go in there, so we made for it, all holding hands. When we got to the foot of the small Ōshima Bridge they wouldn't let us enter the park. It was already full of people coming from the Fukagawa direction. We had to backtrack through that firestorm. Even two or three minutes was a terrible loss of time.

"Hold on tight, don't be separated," Minoru told me as he took my hand. Kōichi put Hiroko on his back. We ran in the direction of Sunamachi. There are many rivers and bridges in that direction. We reached Shinkai Bridge. Sunamachi lay beyond, but that's where we were all scattered. The wind and flames became terrific. We were in Hell. All the houses were burning, debris raining down on us. It was horrible. Sparks flew everywhere. Electric wires sparked and toppled. Mother, with my little brother on her back, had her feet swept out from under her by the wind and she rolled away. Father jumped after her. "Are you all right?" he screamed. Yoshiaki shouted, "Dad!"

I don't know if his intention was to rescue Father or to stay with him, but they all disappeared instantly into the flames and black smoke. Everything was burning. In front of us were factories, red flames belching from windows. Kōichi, Minoru, Hiroko, and I, the four of us, were the only ones left.

There was thick shrubbery and a slight dip at the foot of the bridge, and we huddled together there. Kōichi shouted that we couldn't go further, and we really couldn't go back. Many people jumped into Onagigawa, twenty meters wide. We could just barely see a roadside shelter from where we were. Ditches had been dug along many roadsides in case of air raids. Kōichi took Hiroko's hand and I clung to Minoru. We dashed across the road through the flames. Hiroko's headgear caught fire. It was stuffed with cotton. The four of us tumbled into the shelter. We tried to remove the burning cover from her head, but it was tied tight so as not to be blown away by the wind. Hiroko tried to pull it off herself, so both her hands were burned. Her hair burned, too. We were finally able to tear it off and smothered the fire with our legs. We lay flat on our stomachs, thinking that we would be all right if the fire was gone by morning, but the fire kept pelting down on us. Minoru suddenly let out a horrible scream and leapt out of the shelter, flames shooting out of his back. Kōichi stood up calling, "Minoru!" and instantly, he too, was blown away. Only Hiroko and I remained.

There was someone else in the shelter, a schoolgirl. I was really saved by her. I don't think I could have endured the fear if it had been just Hiroko and me. There was no cover, and all the surroundings were aflame and sparks rained into the shelter, and Hiroko kept screaming, "It's hot, hot!" We would have jumped out, and my little Hiroko and I would have been killed. The schoolgirl came close to us. "I'm separated from my family. Let's do our best, the three of us." She was perhaps two years older than me. I don't remember if she told us her name or not. She covered Hiroko with her body and then we put Hiroko in between us and lay flat at the bottom of the air-raid ditch. Hiroko was burned very severely. She kept crying, "My hands hurt, my hands hurt. Please give me water, Kazu-chan." I scratched out a hollow in the earth and put her hands into it. She said her hands felt cool and comfortable. We spent the night there, waiting for the fire to pass.

First the sounds stopped. At the earliest signs of dawn the girl said, "Let's go back where it's already burned. Everyone will probably be safe and will return there. You'll be able to go home then." The thought of being separated from this girl made me anxious. I asked her where she was going, and she told me the Eighth District. Our house was in the opposite direction. We left the shelter together. By the Shinkai Bridge many people had perished. Those who couldn't cross the street and make it to the shelter had jumped into the river. Dead bodies covered the water. Some people had tried to escaped by running under the bridge but they, too, had been roasted.

When I separated from the schoolgirl and recrossed the bridge I'd crossed only the night before, I saw charcoal-black people. It was truly horrendous. There were some whose clothes were still smouldering but whose bodies weren't moving. Not just one or two. At the foot of the bridge was a small police station. Only the concrete was left. But I thought a policeman might be there anyway. I let Hiroko lean back against a concrete wall. Then the thought came that Father and my brothers would pass this way, that we'd meet here and go back to the pharmacy together. I was probably afraid of walking the street alone. I waited at the foot of the bridge, but nobody came. Hiroko asked for water. People said she should be taken to a relief station for treatment. Finally, we arrived at the burned-out area that once was our house. I was able to locate it only because in front we had a large concrete cistern full of water. In it was a dead man, half his body in the cistern. He wasn't burnt at all. Many of the glass bottles in my father's drug store had melted down. The store itself was a pile of rubble.

Everything was so quiet. Hiroko and I sat on the concrete steps at the entrance to the store and waited. A young woman from the neighborhood association came by and said, "Your eldest brother's just over there." Kōichi was sitting on a burnt-out truck in the garage of a delivery firm nearby. He couldn't see because he'd run through the smoke. He was trembling. "How could you have come back safe?" he asked. He'd assumed we were all dead. Tears of joy streamed down his face. As he left the shelter, he'd been bowled over and tumbled far down the street.

He regained consciousness flat on his stomach, resting against a slight curb. That little bit of curb saved him.

A little while later Father appeared with Yoshiaki. The people who came back were like ghosts, uttering no words. They simply staggered back, thinking somebody might be where their houses had been. Father said, "Minoru wouldn't let himself die. He's, too strong." He gave us first aid, using Mercurochrome and bandages. He told Hiroko, "You've been terribly burned, but Daddy's here. Don't worry." The five of us then waited for Mother. Quite a long time passed. Actually, Mother was already there, but no one recognized her. She wasn't shouldering my little brother. Her clothes were all charcoal. Her hair, too. She was covered from head to toe by a military blanket and she was barefoot. She was squatting down. Yoshiaki noticed her first, "Mom?" Father said, "What's happened to Takahisa?" My mother was silent. Her back and elbows were severely burned. Those who had run through that fire knew its savagery. We couldn't really ask what happened to our little brother. It was all one could do to save oneself. Mother's eyes were injured because of the smoke.

It's really a cruel thing to say, but I could see she had been holding Takahisa on her back. Where Takahisa's legs had touched her body there were horrible burns. Her elbows, where she was probably holding him to keep him from falling off, were burned so that you could see the raw flesh. She could barely walk. "You made it back, you made it back. That's wonderful!"was all my father could say. We put Mother in the garage and gave her some water and we all huddled together. Neighbors waited here and there for family members who hadn't returned. In my family, nobody else came back.

Near evening, our relatives from the Komatsugawa area, which hadn't burned, came to meet us with a pullcart. They said they'd seen red plumes of flames like lotus flowers in the distance. Father delayed leaving as long as he could. "Just a little bit longer, a little bit longer," he kept saying. Finally, he left a piece of paper from his Vigilance Corps notebook with the address we were evacuating to.

We made it to a farmer's house in Komatsugawa. Mother groaned but didn't say anything about Takahisa. She didn't even cry, just lay flat on her stomach. Father went back to the burnt-out area looking for Minoru, Teruko, and Grandmother. It took two or three times before he gave up. At first, we thought about finding the remains, but we never located them. We contacted Minoru's school in vain.

Hiroko's condition worsened. She asked for water all the time, but couldn't swallow any. Father said it must be tetanus. She had to be hospitalized, but most of the hospitals had been burned down. We were told there was a small one in Komatsugawa, so Father took her there on the back of the cart. As we thought, she had lockjaw. Father was told a serum shot might save her, but they had no serum there.

Hiroko's face was burned very severely and her bandages soon became soaked with blood and pus. There were so few bandages available that we washed hers at home and then took them back to the hospital. That day, it was my day to wind bandages for her. She hadn't been there many days. I walked into the hospital room with the bandages. There was just one bed in a square concrete room. I said, "Hiro-chan, why are you sleeping with your eyes open?" I tried to close them, but they couldn't close. "Hiroko, Hiroko," I called. She didn't say a thing. Usually it was "I want water!" or "It hurts." Father, who had been staying with her, came in and said "Hiroko just died, even though I brought serum for her." I never heard of the tetanus virus before. Now, I learned for the first time that it lived in the soil. I was the one who had put her hands into that hole I dug in the moist ground of the shelter. The tetanus virus must have entered her then through her burns. When I heard this I couldn't sit still.

Many of our relatives were at Komatsugawa, and some said, "Kazu-chan, you were there with her, and you don't even have one burn, but Hiro-chan died." I'd done my best to scratch the soil to make a hole to cool her hands. I'd done it with all my childish heart. They'd praised me then. "You did so well," they said. Now, nine days later, my sister Hiroko was dead and they were whispering quietly about the reason. Father assured me it wasn't my fault. In disasters, tetanus and typhoid occur. But he also said poor Hiroko's life had been needlessly lost.

Although Mother never expressed it in words, I think she had the most difficult time. She had let the child on her back die. We don't know if she left him somewhere, or whether he just burnt up and fell. Once people who were trying to collect records on the Great Air Raid pleaded with us to ask her, but we couldn't. She's now eighty-eight years old. While she was still able to get around I used to take her to pray at their graves. She'd pour water on them and say, "Hiroko-chan, you must have been hot. Teruko-chan, you must have been hot."

At the Telephone Exchange

TOMIZAWA KIMI AND KOBAYASHI HIROYASU

We meet in an impressive conference room at the Nippon Telegraph and Telephone company's headquarters in Shimbashi in central Tokyo.

Miss Tomizawa, eighty years old, is dressed in a gorgeous kimono. Mr. Kobayashi, seventy, wears a blue suit and tie. They appear very formal as they are led into the room by the head of the company's Office of Development and Enterprise. He convenes the interview with the admonition, "Today the company is called NTT, but then it was the Ministry of Communications. We must be careful to make this distinction." Two company representatives remain present throughout.

Between seventy-five and one hundred thousand people were killed by the air raids on Tokyo which began just after midnight March 10, 1945, probably the single greatest loss of life in a single day from military action in that or any war, including the atomic bombings. An additional 40,000 persons were officially reported injured. An area of approximately fourteen square miles was devastated, with sixty percent of all buildings in that area destroyed.

TOMIZAWA KIMI: Back then, there were exactly 8,399 telephone jack sockets for the whole Sumida Bureau. Since I was a supervisor, I'll never forget that number. Sumida Bureau was the largest of the six common battery switchboards in Tokyo's Central Telephone Exchange. At that time, there was probably only one phone for dozens of houses. Unless it was crucial that you have a telephone, you really couldn't get a line installed. Government offices and police stations—they were the top priority. Ordinary households were the fifth and bottom priority.

The year I joined the phone company was 1921, the tenth year of the Taishō era. The only kind of work available for girls like me then was at the spinning mills, as a servant, or as a nursemaid. Being a telephone operator was a very good job for a girl. You could advance and you even got a pension. I was twelve when I started working there.

KOBAYASHI HIROYASU: The administration of all the machinery and equipment was handled by men. Connecting phone calls was the only job open to women. I worked on outside equipment. Even our chains of command were separate, we maintenance men and the operators. I often worked more than twenty-four hours straight. I'd come to work and stay all day long. At night, when the air raid sirens echoed, I'd come to work again, by bicycle. In the pitch dark. It was dangerous to use a lamp.

TOMIZAWA: I didn't know how to ride a bike, so I walked thirty minutes from home to our phone station. I covered my head with my air defense helmet, but I was often stopped by air-raid wardens who'd say, "Women shouldn't walk about under these conditions." They'd make me wait, even when I showed them my identification as a worker in the telephone exchange. It took me a long time to get there.

We did our best. Really. We now wore *monpe*. We were prepared for fire and knew what we should do. We had fire drills with buckets and fire-beaters. We even had military exercises. "Advance! Take your positions! By sections!" They gave us military commands. I was still young, so I could do things easily, but I felt sorry for the older women. When they were ordered to march, they couldn't even keep their left hands and right feet in synch!

Communications were crucial. Even the railroads couldn't work without them. If communication links were knocked out, you had to work around the breaks. If even a single telephone line survived, you used that to restore communications, so crucial messages could be sent. The responsibility for defending and keeping our system operating was shared. It wasn't only taken on by us supervisors. We all shared a feeling that we were accomplishing our duty.

KOBAYASHI: We felt that, too. But when everything was burning there was no order issued to evacuate the office. No order came releasing you. Just defend your position to the death! That's it. The operators were all thirteen- or fourteen-year-old kids! If they had been at home, they'd have been the first to be told to run away. But here, in a sea of flames, they were still at their switchboards, or trying to pour water on the fires. The word "flee" never passed the lips of those above them. An ill-fated job.

TOMIZAWA: That day, I was on day-duty. But from five to eight was always the busiest time, so I stayed around until eight, then I returned home.

KOBAYASHI: March 9, 1945. I was there. Air-raid warnings came every day, so we weren't particularly shaken when we saw red spots far away, but soon the airplanes were flying above us. Places near us were turning red. Over there, it's red. Here, it's red! Some were still at the switchboards. The others were trying to extinguish the flames after the building caught fire. Outside, huge telephone poles, set against the building and meant to protect the windows and withstand any bomb blast, became like kindling under the incendiary bombs. When the poles started burning, there were still some working the phone lines.

TOMIZAWA: Our place had communication lines to the antiaircraft batteries and the fire-fighting units for the whole Shitamachi area. There weren't any wireless communications in use then, so crucial government lines passed through our switchboard. Until the last second, many operators were still working, plugging lines into the jacks.

KOBAYASHI: Parts of the building were still made of wood. The windowframes, for instance, and the rest areas. Wood, covered with stucco. Up on the roof, there was a water tank. Through pipes, it was supposed to lay down a curtain of water over the whole building. But the water in the tank, when it was released, was soon exhausted. We opened up fire plugs, and though water poured out fast at first, everyone was using them, too, so it soon trickled to a stop. We had a small pond, maybe two meters long. It had goldfish we kept for fun. We drained that water, throwing it onto the windows to cool them down. The glass shattered, *"Ping!"* because of the heat. I remember those kids carrying buckets. Helter-skelter. Even the water in the teakettle was used up.

Outside, the world was ablaze. We had no more water. It was all gone. That was it. The operators and the night supervisor, Matsumoto Shūji, were there. Mr. Matsumoto was found dead in the shelter. Burned to death. He was a marathon runner, but he was responsible for them. According to a survivor, Miss Tanaka, they finally did try to leave the building. "Get out, get out!" they were told, but the flames were too strong. They couldn't flee.

TOMIZAWA: Only four of them survived. Fortunate to escape that dangerous situation. The remaining thirty-one all perished.

KOBAYASHI: When we left, we men thought we were the last ones. We couldn't really get the gate open, so we climbed over the side wall. The bridge over the Arakawa was jammed. People coming this way from the far side, and trying to go there from this side. They packed together in the middle and couldn't move. People are greedy. Even at times like that, people are carrying things. Our phone cable was next to the bridge, partially submerged in the water. We took a chance. There was no other way. We hung on to it and moved across hand over hand, our bodies in the water. All the way across the river to escape the burning air. It was like a circus act.

If there'd still been water, water coming from the hydrants, we probably wouldn't have made it. But there was no water. No way to fight the fire. Besides, our line of command was separate from that of the girls. We were later questioned. "Why did only the men flee?" They wanted to know why we didn't take more girls with us. But when they investigated, they found that even the coin boxes on the public phones had melted completely. Then they understood.

Not even a single line was still operational. When I returned the next day, where the thick cables went in, they had melted down. There were no windowframes. All the metallic things had melted in the heat and were bowing down, all bent over. The switchboards, anything made of wood, all burned. Gone.

TOMIZAWA: The interior cables were still hanging in the empty concrete box. A chill went through me.

KOBAYASHI: Some people could be identified. By their stomach wraps. Where it had been tight against their skin a name could be found written on it. It wasn't burned. To tell you the truth, I couldn't tell if they were men or women. They weren't even full skeletons. Piled on top of each other. The bottom of the pile, all stuck together. A few bits of clothing could be found on them. The underpants of Mr. Matsumoto were left. Touching the wall of the shelter. When Matsumoto-san's wife came, nobody could bear to tell her that her husband was not there anymore. "You have to tell her," everyone told me. "You were on night duty together." There's nothing more painful than that. His wife confirmed that they were her husband's underwear.

Even after all the bones were buried, when it rained, a blue flame burned. From the phosphorus. Soldiers stationed there used to say, "Maybe they'll come out tonight," thinking of the ghosts and the blue flames.

I wonder what war is. I wonder why we did it. I'm not talking about victory or loss. I merely feel heartbroken for those who died. Its not an issue of whether I hate the enemy or not. However much you're glorified, if you're dead, that's it. Young kids worked so hard. Without complaint. It makes me seethe. Burning flames, huge planes flying over, dropping bombs. My feeling of hatred—"You bastards! Bastards!" you shout. But there was no sense that you're capable of doing anything about it. If you win, you're the victors. You can justify anything. It's all right if the ones who have rifles are killed. That's OK. But these kids didn't have weapons, they had only their breasts. Those are the ones whose end was tragic.

I wonder, does war bring happiness to anyone? The ones who perished here on duty were merely promoted two ranks. They got a medal from the Emperor. A long time afterwards. Their parents didn't even get their pensions. Only the men with stars are enshrined in Yasukuni. But where are those who perished here? Girls of fifteen and sixteen. Who did their best. [*His voice breaks.*] People even ask, "Why didn't they escape earlier? They should have fled earlier."

TOMIZAWA: They are the ones who should be enshrined.

KOBAYASHI: No! Not that! Their parents want them back!

17 / THE WAR COMES HOME TO OKINAWA

Student Nurses of the "Lily Corps"

MIYAGI KIKUKO

The Himeyuri Peace Memorial Museum stands at the southern tip of the island where the severest fighting of the Battle of Okinawa took place in 1945. It has just opened after eight years of hard work and fundraising by the survivors of the Himeyuri [Lily] Student Corps. It is thronged with tourists and junior-high-school students on their school trips. Hanging on the walls are the enlarged black-and-white photographs of young girls, each with a name beneath it. Some portions of the wall have only names, without pictures. Testimonies of survivors are on display, as are lunch-boxes, fountain pens, combs, writing boards, pencil boxes, and other artifacts, dug out from the caves where the students worked. The museum itself is above one of the caves, but the pathway leading down is blocked off. Okinawa is honeycombed with natural volcanic caves which were incorporated into the island's defenses and used as shelters by civilians and soldiers alike during the battle.

"If that war hadn't happened, all my friends and classmates would have led peaceful lives with their children and grandchildren," says Miyagi Kikuko. At sixty-two, she is one of the youngest survivors of the Himeyuri Student Corps. A retired school teacher, she spends much of her time these days answering questions from visitors to the museum.

Okinawa prefecture had a population of approximately 570,000 in 1945, about 80,000 of whom had been evacuated from the island by the time the battle officially began on April 1, 1945. Many students enrolled in the island's girls' high schools, middle schools, and normal schools were called up to serve in the student corps, with the students from the most elite schools joining the Himeyuri Student Corps for girls and the Blood and Iron Student Corps for boys. About 2,000 students were mobilized in all, and of these, 1,050 died.

In February 1945, just before I was mobilized, I went home to say farewell. I assured Father and Mother that I would win the Imperial Order of the Rising Sun, eighth class, and be enshrined at Yasukuni. Father was a country schoolteacher. He said, "I didn't bring you up to the age of sixteen to die!" I thought he was a traitor to say such a thing. I went to the battlefield feeling proud of myself.

The Himeyuri Student Corps consisted of the fifteen- to nineteen-year-old girls from First Okinawa Prefectural Girls' High School and the Women's Division of the national Okinawa Normal School. I was in my fourth year at the high school. On the night of March 24, to the accompaniment of the loud thunder of guns from the American naval bombardment, we were mobilized straight from the school dormitory to Haebaru Army Hospital. Although called a military "hospital," it was actually in caves scattered around the town of Haebaru. The hospital wasn't really complete, so our first work consisted of digging out the cave where we were to hide ourselves. Outside, it rained shells for five or six days.

We had our graduation ceremony in a crude, triangular barracks on the battlefield. While the bombardment continued, we knelt on a floor lit by two or three candles. It was so dim we could hardly see our classmates' faces. "Work so as not to shame the First Girls' High School" was theme of the principal's commencement address. We sang a song which went, "Give your life for the sake of the Emperor, wherever you may go." Our music teacher, only twenty-three, had earlier written a song for our graduation. It was called "A Song of Parting," and was really wonderful. Not a war song at all. We'd memorized it while digging shelters. I especially liked one verse with the refrain "We shall meet again," but there was no time for it at graduation. It was already after ten o'clock at night. Still, with the reverberations of the explosions shaking the ground, we sang it on our way back to our cave. The next morning that triangular building wasn't there anymore. Three days later, on April 1, the landings began.

In no time at all, wounded soldiers were being carried into the caves in large numbers. They petrified us all. Some didn't have faces, some didn't have limbs. Young men in their twenties and thirties screaming like babies. Thousands of them. At first, one of my friends saw a man with his toes missing and swooned. She actually sank to her knees, but soldiers and medics began screaming at her, "You idiot! You think you can act like that on the battlefield?"

Every day, we were yelled at: "Fools! Idiots! Dummies!" We were so naïve and unrealistic. We had expected that somewhere far in the rear, we'd raise the red cross and then wrap men with bandages, rub on medicine, and give them shots as we had been trained. In a tender voice we'd tell the wounded, "Don't give up, please." Now, they were being carried in one after another until the dugouts and caves were filled to overflowing, and still they came pouring in. Soon we were laying them out in empty fields, then on cultivated land. Some hemorrhaged to death and others were hit again out there by showers of bombs. So many died so quickly.

Those who had gotten into the caves weren't so lucky either. Their turn to have their dressings changed came only once every week or two. So pus would squirt in our faces, and they'd be infested with maggots. Removing those was our job. We didn't even have enough time to remove them one by one. Gas gangrene, tetanus, and brain fever were common. Those with brain fever were no longer human beings. They'd tear their clothes off because of their pain, tear off their dressings. They were tied to the pillars, their hands behind their backs, and treatment stopped.

At first, we were so scared watching them suffering and writhing that we wept. Soon we stopped. We were kept running from morning to night. "Do this! Do that!" Yet, as underclassmen we had fewer wounded soldiers to take care of. The senior girls slept standing up. "Miss Student, I have to piss," they'd cry. Taking care of their excrement was our work. Senior students were assigned to the operating rooms. There, hands and legs were chopped off without anesthesia. They used a saw. Holding down their limbs was a student job.

Outside was a rain of bullets from morning to night. In the evening, it quieted down a little. It was then that we carried out limbs and corpses. There were so many shell craters—it sounds funny to say it, but we considered that fortunate: holes already dug for us. "One, two, three!" we'd chant, and all together we'd heave the dead body into a hole, before crawling back to the cave. There was no time for sobbing or lamentation.

In that hail of bullets, we also went outside to get food rations and water. Two of us carried a wooden half-bushel barrel to the well. When a shell fell, we'd throw ourselves into the mud, but always supporting the barrel because the water was everybody's water of life. Our rice balls shrank until they were the size of Ping-Pong balls. The only way to endure was to guzzle water. There was no extra water, not even to wash our faces, which were caked in mud.

We were ordered to engage in "nursing," but in reality, we did odd jobs. We were in the cave for sixty days, until we withdrew to Ihara. Twelve people in our group—two teachers and ten students—perished. Some were buried alive, some had their legs blown off, five died from gas.

They used gas bombs on May 9. Thrown into the cave with the third-year students—the fifteen-year-olds. Three students and two teachers perished. The way they died! Their bodies swelled up and turned purple. There were no injuries. It was like they suffocated to death. They thrashed about so much we had to tie up their arms and legs like the soldiers with brain fever. That was the cave next to mine. When our teachers returned to our cave, they wept bitterly, even though they were men. A poison-gas bomb was also thrown into the cave where the current Himeyuri Memorial is located. Forty-six of fifty-one perished there.°

About May 25, we were ordered to withdraw to Ihara. All the men we had nursed were simply lying there. One of us asked, "Soldier, what are you going to do with these people?" "Don't worry," he responded, "I'll make it easy for them." Later we heard that the medics offered them condensed milk mixed with water as their last nourishment, and then gave them cyanide and told them, "Achieve your glorious end like a Japanese soldier." The American forces were nearby. Would it have been so terrible if they had been captured and revealed the Japanese army's situation? Instead they were all murdered to protect military strategy. Only one person crawled out and survived to testify.

The road to Ihara was truly horrible, muddy and full of artillery craters with corpses, swollen two or three times normal size, floating in them. We could only move at night. Sometimes the American forces sent up flares to seek out targets. Ironically, these provided us with enough light to see the way. This light revealed people pulling themselves along on hands and knees, crawling desperately, wounded people calling to us, "Students! Students!" I had an injured friend using my shoulder as a crutch. Another friend had night blindness from malnutrition. She kept falling over corpses and crying out. We'd become accustomed to the smell of excrement, pus, and the maggots in the cave, but the smell of death there on that road was unbearable. And it poured rain every day.

Tens of thousands of people moving like ants. Civilians. Grandfathers, grandmothers, mothers with children on their backs, scurrying along, covered in mud. When children were injured, they were left along the

---

° There are Okinawan references to the use of poison gas by the American forces during the battle of Okinawa. As in this case, the way the victims died points to the use of an agent which caused asphyxiation. Miyara Ruri, a survivor from the Third Surgery Cave, describes the moment: "White smoked filled [the cave] at the same time as the sound *Daan, daan, daan,* rang out—I can't see anything! I can't breathe anymore! Breathing is agony—I felt like I was being choked." She regained consciousness after three days. Her story appears in NHK Ohayō Jaanaru Seisaku-han, ed., *Senso o shitte imasu ka* [*Do You Know About the War?*] (Tokyo: NHK Hōsō Shuppan, 1989), vol. 1, p. 81.

roadside. Just thrown away. Those children could tell we were students. They'd call out, *"Nei, nei!"* and try to cling to us. That's Okinawan dialect for "Older Sister!" It was so pitiable. I still hear those cries today.

In daylight we were pinned down. In the wild fields, we clung to the grasses and cried out to our teachers, "I'm afraid." My group were all fifteen- or sixteen-year-olds and the teachers took special care of us. "Bear up! You can take it!" they'd reassure us.

Finally, on the tenth of June we reached Ihara. Ten days for what takes thirty minutes by car today. There the first, second, and third surgeries were reestablished. The second surgery was already completely full. There was only space to sit with your knees pulled up to your chest.

I don't remember going to the toilet after we moved to Ihara, we were so dehydrated. If you put your hand into your hair it was full of lice. Our bodies were thick with fleas. Before we had been covered in mud, now we were covered with filth. Our nails grew longer and longer. Our faces were black. We were emaciated and itched all the time.

We bit into moldy, unpolished raw rice and took great care gnawing on our biscuits. When we ate those, we felt as though we'd had a real meal. Those grains of unpolished rice were so hard that, one day, a teacher said, "Let's go out and cook them." Just warming them up that way actually let them swell a little so you could get it down easier. We got some water and crawled out with the teacher. Behind rocks, we gathered dried leaves and finally warmed the unpolished rice in a mess kit. Then we headed back, at last reaching the entrance to the first surgery cave. When I stood up and put my foot in, the ground felt wet and slippery. It was June 17. I smelled blood. I thought instantly, "They've just been hit!" We lived in darkness and sensed everything by smell. From below I heard my classmates' voices, "I don't have a leg!" "My hand's gone!" At my teacher's urging, I descended into a sea of blood. Nurses, soldiers, students killed instantly or severely injured, among them a friend of mine, Katsuko-san, with a wound in her thigh. "Quick, Teacher, quick," she was crying. "It hurts!" I was struck dumb. There was no medicine left, and near me a senior student was desperately trying to push her intestines back into her stomach. "I won't make it," she whispered, "so please take care of other people first." Then she stopped breathing.

Now, her words chill me to the bone. But a militaristic girl could say such a thing. How could she have been so strong? She was only seventeen. I saw weeping teachers cutting locks of hair from the deceased and putting them in their pockets. They no longer had the faintest idea of how to take care of us. All they could say was, "Do your best! Don't die. You absolutely mustn't die!" They were desperate to protect us, young teachers in their twenties and thirties. I wonder how each of them must have suffered, and my heart goes out to them as I think about how brokenhearted they must have been. Out of three hundred students, two hundred nineteen perished. Twenty-one teachers went to the battlefield and sixteen died. No one imagined so many lives would be lost. Particularly in such cruel ways. The teachers, too, were utterly ignorant of the horror, the terror of war. Japanese of that time were like that. "Victorious battle!" "Our army is always superior!" That was all we knew. We were so gullible, so innocent.

On the eighteenth, the order of dissolution was issued. From then on, they told us, if we behaved as a group we would stand out too much. The U.S. forces were quite close, so we were to "escape" as individuals. Everyone shed tears, but what could we say? We didn't know what to do. And our friends, lying there injured, were listening to the order, too. They knew they would be left behind. There was no way to take them with us. Absolutely none.

We had to leave two students behind with the soldiers as well, because the Americans were so close you could even hear English being spoken. One of the students accepted milk from the medics. She might have been given cyanide, too. The other didn't want to die and forced her immobilized body to crawl. She was still crawling in the mud near Haebaru, when attacking American troops rescued her. They took her to the U.S. military hospital and nursed her with great care, but I heard she died there anyway. That was in May. After the war, one who'd heard her reported that she said, "I hated and feared these Americans, but they treated me with great care and kindness, while my classmates, my teachers left me behind."

Nineteen of us, three teachers and sixteen students, left the cave together. But a large bomb exploded and we lost track of four of our group immediately. We crawled, stood up, then crawled again, always under heavy bombardment. The next morning dawned so soon! It was the nineteenth of June. A severe attack was in progress. We were still in sight of the first and third surgery caves. So close! We'd gone such a little way! Hardly a minute or two by car, today. When we looked around we saw we were surrounded by tanks. Americans were whistling to each other. Tanks moved forward, attacking. Until then we'd had to flee at night. Now, we clung to the edge of the road. I heard a great booming sound and passed out. Eventually, I came to my senses. I was covered in mud and couldn't hear a thing. In front of me, two classmates were soaked in their own blood. Then they were screaming in pain. Third-year student Akiko wasn't moving. She'd died there. Two teachers in their twenties had disappeared. We never saw them again. Already on just that first morning, nineteen people became twelve. Nearby, Japanese soldiers were running for their lives, yelling, "Armor! Armor!" Behind us, the tanks were coming on, spewing out a stream of fire. I was shaking with fear. The vice-principal, the only teacher left, shouted, "Follow me!" and we all crawled after him. My friends were covered with blood. We urged them to keep up and though they were moaning, "I can't. I can't go on. It hurts," come they did.

On the twentieth, the large guns stopped firing and they began burning things with flame-throwers. We were smoked out onto the cliff tops. We friends promised each other, "If I'm unable to move, or you're disabled, I'll give you cyanide." We each kept a hand-grenade like a talisman. "If we stand up, they'll shoot us," we thought, so we stood up. We walked upright with dignity, but they held their fire. We were slightly disappointed. It was weird, eerie. Yesterday it had been Hell; why was it suddenly so quiet? We reached the cliff's edge, an incredible precipice, and we climbed down, soon covered in blood, all the way down to the sea. We were in full view of the ships at sea. If they wanted to, I thought, they could kill us with a single salvo. Yet we reached the breakers. Everywhere the shore was full of people, all civilians. Later, I learned that nearly one hundred seventy thousand people were crammed into that narrow bit of island. People, people, people. They were almost piled up on each other. There was nowhere even to sit, and the waves were coming in lapping at them.

A small boat came toward us from a battleship. Then, for the first time, we heard the voice of the enemy. "Those who can swim, swim out! We'll save you. Those who can't swim, walk towards Minatogawa! Walk by day. Don't travel by night. We have food! We will rescue you!" They actually did! They took care of Okinawans really well, according to international law, but we only learned that later. We thought we were hearing the voices of demons. From the time we'd been children, we'd only been educated to hate them. They would strip the girls naked and do with them whatever they wanted, then run over them with tanks. We really believed that. Not only us girls. Mothers, grandfathers, grandmothers all were cowering at the voice of the devils. So what we had been taught robbed us of life. I can never forgive what education did to us! Had we known the truth, all of us would have survived. The Himeyuri Student Corps alone lost one hundred and some score students in the four or five days that followed the order to dissolve the unit. Anyway, we didn't answer that voice, but continued our flight. We were simply too terrified of being stripped naked. That's what a girl fears most, isn't it? We never dreamt the enemy would rescue us.

So, we climbed back up, but the top of the cliff was being scoured by flame-throwers. We had to cling on midway. When we looked down we saw the white surf. It was the night of the twentieth. Moonlit. Everything was exposed. That was Arasaki Beach. Today it is all so green and peaceful. Our friends who were injured on the morning of the nineteenth were increasingly desperate and bloody, but still with us. Our hands were growing weaker. "Teacher, teacher, I can't hold on!" "Climb up," he'd say. Finally, we clawed our way to the top and just collapsed. Twelve of us. There we all cried out, "We can't take any more." The third-year students cried the most. "Teacher, please kill us. Kill us with a grenade!"

Teacher had always urged us on, but finally even he said, "I guess it can't be helped." We felt great relief at those words. At last, we would become comfortable. "Teacher, here's good enough. Please make us comfortable." For the first time we all sobbed. We all wanted to see our mothers. *"Okaasan!"* came from our mouths. We'd struggled so hard not to speak of our families up until then. [*Her voice chokes.*] I wondered how Father, Mother, and my younger sister were doing on this battlefield. I wanted to see them so badly, but to put such feelings into words was taboo in the cave. That day, for the first time, someone said, "I want to see my mother!" Yoshiko-san, who was an only daughter, clung to me. She was such a lovely person, a sweet person. She, too, said to me, "I want to see my mother just once more." We all said it. "We want to walk under a sky from which shells don't rain." For ninety days we'd been cornered like moles in dark caves. Someone now began singing a song about a home village and "the mountains where we chased the rabbit . . ." Of course, we dissolved in tears. That night we completely forgot we were surrounded by American soldiers.

Arasaki Beach was totally silent on the twenty-first. The military ships were still glaring at us from the sea, but not a shot was fired. I had a hand-grenade, and so did Teacher. Nine of our group were jammed into a tiny hole. Higa-san, Teacher, a Japanese soldier, and I—the four of us—couldn't fit into it. We were nearby. I was sitting facing a warship, glaring back at it, gripping my grenade. A small boat approached and signaled to us. They waved, "Swim out, we'll help you!" I shuddered. I was completely exposed. Suddenly, a Japanese soldier climbed down the cliff. A Japanese soldier raising his hands in surrender? Impossible! Traitor! We'd been taught, and firmly believed, that we Okinawans, Great Japanese all, must never fall into the hands of the enemy. Despite that, a Japanese soldier was walking right into the sea. Another soldier, crouching behind a rock near us, shot him. The sea water was dyed red. Thus I saw Japanese murdering Japanese for the first time.

Out of nowhere, a Japanese soldier appeared and dropped to the ground right in front of me. American soldiers must have been chasing him. He was all bloody. Higa-san and I tumbled into a tiny hole. I saw Teacher and this Japanese soldier fly into the air. Then I heard, "Come out, come out" in strangely accented Japanese. Soon a rain of small arms fire began, Americans firing at close range. They must have thought we were with that soldier. They blazed away in our direction. A senior student, Aosa-san, was killed instantly, as were Ueki-san, Nakamoto-san, and the Japanese soldier. I was now under those four dead bodies. Three senior students were hit by small-arms fire and screamed out in pain. Yonamine-sensei, our teacher, shouldering a student bathed in blood, stood facing an American soldier. Random firing stopped. The American, who had been firing wildly, must have noticed he was shooting girls. He could be seen from the hole where my ten classmates were hiding. They pulled the pin on their hand grenade. So unfortunate! I now stepped out over the corpses and followed Teacher. The automatic rifles of four or five American soldiers were aimed right at me. My grenade was taken away. I had held it to the last minute. The American soldiers lowered their rifles. I looked past them and saw my ten classmates. The night before those third-year students had been calling for Teacher to kill them quickly. Now, there was nothing left of them. The hand grenade is so cruel.

I simply sat there where I'd slumped down. An American soldier poked me with the barrel of his gun, signaling me to move in the direction he indicated. I didn't speak English. I couldn't do anything but move as he ordered. To my surprise, three senior students had been carried out. Their wounds had been dressed and bandaged and they were being given saline injections. Until that moment I could think of the Americans only as devils and demons. I was simply frozen. I couldn't believe what I saw.

It was around noon, June 21. The sun was directly overhead. I staggered, crying, in the blazing sun. American soldiers sometimes called out, "Hey, schoolgirl!" I was skin and bones and covered with filth. My only footwear was the soles of workers' shoes tied to my feet with bandages. "Hey schoolgirl. No poison!" I didn't know what "no poison" meant, but when I got to their camp I was given something called "ra-shon." I didn't really feel like eating. I lay on the sand, crying aloud all night long. I was then sent to Kunagami Camp in the north. For three months I was taken care of by many families I don't know anything about. During the third month I met my father and mother. Mother, barefoot, ran out of a tent in the camp and hugged me to her. "You lived, you lived!" I still remember her crying out loud.

After the war, I refused to go the ceremonies of memorial. I tried to forget as much as possible. Because it was horrible and it was sad, or for whatever reason, I just didn't want to remember. It is only very recently I have been able to speak about it. I decided to get involved in constructing the memorial museum because I felt if I didn't talk, nobody would support it.

Young people sometimes ask us, "Why did you take part in such a stupid war?" For us the Emperor and the Nation were supreme. For them, one should not withhold one's life. Strange isn't it? That's really the way it was. We had been trained for the Battle of Okinawa from the day the war with America began. I hate to admit it, but that spiritual training taught us how to endure. That's why we were able to complete the museum library, don't you think? We still have to grit our teeth a little longer until we repay the huge financial debt we incurred building the museum.

On my way back to Naha from a visit to the battlefields, I mentioned to my taxi driver that I had spoken to one of the Himeyuri Corps. He asked me if they told me that when they moved into caves, all the civilians who had been there were expelled. "You should go see the Second Girls' High School memorial site too, not just the one for them," he said, and took me there. In contrast to the memorial for the Himeyuri, which had been bustling, this one was quiet, and I was the solitary visitor.

"Now they call it 'Group Suicide'"

KINJŌ SHIGEAKI

He is a professor of religion at Okinawa Christian Junior College. The school building where we meet stands on a hill surrounded by fields of waving green sugarcane, the ocean visible in the distance.

He lived on Tokashiki, the largest island in the Kerama archipelago, about twenty miles west of the main island of Okinawa. The island is six miles long, north to south, and about one mile wide. The speed of the American attack on the island made it impossible to launch any of the one hundred suicide motor-boats of the Third Sea Raiding Squadron which had been deployed on Tokashiki for the expected battle for Okinawa.

He has been supporting efforts to tell Japanese schoolchildren through their textbooks about the extent of the Japanese army's cruelty to Okinawans during the fight for Okinawa. He speaks evenly and dispassionately, even eloquently, until he comes to his own personal moment of tragedy. While his demeanor remains unchanged, words and memories come out only in broken fragments, as if, despite his best efforts, he is struggling to recall a nightmare he can only half remember.

"During the war there was no phrase 'shūdan jiketsu' [group suicide]. There was 'gyokusai,' however, a grandiose militaristic euphemism, signifying the 'crushing of jewels,' meaning people giving up their lives joyfully for their country rather than succumbing to the enemy or falling into their hands. It was only after the war, especially in the 1950s, that 'group suicide' came into use. It's a term easily subject to misinterpretation. The state now wants to say these deaths were 'voluntary deaths.' But that isn't the way it was. The people of Okinawa never killed themselves on their own initiative."

The American forces landed on Tokashiki Island on March 27, 1945. We islanders were told by the Japanese forces to gather near a military camp, a place called Onnagawara. From my hamlet, Aharen, to that camp was roughly seven kilometers. A momentous decision had to be made before we started. We had caves for our shelters where we had already determined that we were going to die. Everybody knew that if we all gathered together in one spot the possibility of being discovered by the enemy would be that much greater. It was much safer to huddle in our own shelters, scattered about the island. Despite that, all the residents went to a dangerous place. That proves that an order from the military was in force.

A week prior to the "group suicide," a sergeant gave out two hand grenades each to the members of the village youth organizations and to the young people of the island office at an emergency meeting. They were directed to throw one of them at the enemy and use the other to engage in *gyokusai*. The military-affairs clerk of the village testified afterwards that this was so. It meant that the soldiers and the civilians were to fight as one united body and expend their last efforts together. In short, what was planned was a *gyokusai* of everyone on the island. It's often been argued that the military never actually issued orders to commit suicide, but that's beside the point. You have to grasp here the relationship between the military and the residents as a whole or you'll never understand what happened.

On the twenty-eighth, the American and Japanese forces squared off against each other. It was touch-and-go. The Americans seemed poised to descend on us at any moment. Residents from all the hamlets, about a thousand people in all, had gathered in that one place under the supervision of the village mayor. Women told their children there was no path for them other than death. Weeping, crying people swore that they were going to die together. Women arranged their hair neatly and prepared themselves for their own deaths. This scene remains vividly impressed on my mind. We were told we were to await orders from the military. Hours passed. Then orders seemed to have been issued. Hand grenades were distributed, and began to be used. Fortunately or unfortunately, the number that actually exploded was very small. At this point, we were spotted by the U.S. forces. I think an air attack came first, then mortars.

The concussions knocked me half-insensate. I guess the killing had already started. I sat there quietly for a while. A strange scene began to unfold right in front of me. One of the village leaders, a middle-aged man, snapped off a sapling. I gazed at him, wondering what he was doing. Once he had that stick in his hands, he turned into a madman. Striking his wife and children over and over again, bludgeoning them to death. That was the beginning of the tragedy I saw.

As if by a chain reaction, it spread from one family to the next. We all must die that way. Everyone seemed to think so. People began to raise their hands against their loved ones. I had just turned sixteen. I was with my brother, two years older than me, my mother, my younger brother, and my little sister. Five of us in all. My father had gotten separated from us on our way. He had poor night vision.

My memory tells me the first one we laid hands on was Mother. Those who had blades, or scythes, cut their wrists or severed arteries in their necks. But we didn't do it that way. We might have used a string. When we raised our hands against the mother who bore us, we wailed in our grief. I remember that. In the end we must have used stones. To the head. We took care of Mother that way. Then my brother and I turned against our younger brother and younger sister. Hell engulfed us there.

I don't know how much time passed. My brother and I talked about which of us would die first. A boy about our same age ran up to us. We truly believed that we were the last survivors on the island. He said if we're going to die anyway, let's at least kill one enemy. We knew that if we were captured we'd be chopped to pieces. They'd cut off our noses, our ears, chop off our fingers, and then run over our bodies with their tanks. Women would be raped. That's why we were committing suicide, to avoid capture by the enemy. We determined we would chose a way of dying appropriate for subjects of the Emperor. There were some girls there too, sixth-graders. We tried to chase them away. We told them it was impossible for girls to come with us, but they followed anyway. We left the site of the group suicide, where the bodies of the victims lay piled on one another, and their blood was coloring the streams red.

We didn't know where the enemy was. We carried sticks with which we would charge into them. We simply walked where our feet took us. The first people we encountered were Japanese soldiers. You can't begin to imagine what a shock that was to us. Are the soldiers still alive? Ordinarily, they might have given us a sense of security, but what we felt now was anger and distrust, boiling up in us. Could it be possible that we, alone, had gone through this horror? Our sense of unity with the military —that we would be forever tied together in death, which had reached its peak in those deaths—dissolved completely afterwards. Now, the Japanese more than the Americans became the object of our fears. Those residents still alive were forbidden to go where they might come in contact with the Americans. We were forced to live in one small area, clustered together. This brought up the problem of food. In order to live I drank from the streams colored with blood. It remained that color for days.

I was later to learn that an order was issued to execute all remaining residents of Aharen because they had moved back to their hamlet without permission from the army. These were the survivors of the group suicide. One hundred twenty-four out of about some three hundred from my hamlet of Aharen survived the suicide. In the end, no executions were carried out, and all of us survivors were captured by American forces.

On my island, the military never engaged in combat and survived virtually intact. Only the residents engaged in *gyokusai*. Even members of the special-attack boat unit, the security of which had raised such concern, retreated into the mountains when there was no opportunity to attack. The residents committed suicide quite early, gathered in one place as if they were mice in a sack. On other isolated islands, where there were no soldiers, there were no group suicides.

For Okinawans, August 15, 1945, meant liberation from the Battle of Okinawa. For me, it was supposed to be a liberation from the nightmare of group suicide, but it didn't work out that way.

The coming of peace meant a return to a normal mentality from an abnormal psychological state. But the more I recovered my normal mind, the more strongly the abnormal came back to me. I began to experience indescribable internal torment. I was still a child, remember. I didn't have the mental strength to criticize the state ideology or really think about what group suicide was. All I had were doubts about why my family —my mother, my brother, my sister—had had to meet such violent deaths. All I had was a deep despair. By good fortune I had an encounter with a Christian. At first, I was attracted to Christianity out of a desire to forget my horror. Eventually, though, I came to believe that, as a Christian, I shouldn't forget. Survivors must testify. But it took me more than twenty years before I could speak in public about group suicide. Most of the islanders still would prefer to forget. I understand their pain.

Straggler

ŌTA MASAHIDE [1]

A student at the Okinawa Normal School in Shuri, he was mobilized just prior to the landing of the U.S. forces on Okinawa as a member of the Tekketsu Kinnōtai, the "Blood and Iron Student Corps."

American military histories consider the Battle of Okinawa to have lasted from April 1 to June 22, 1945. Estimates of Japanese losses vary widely, but one source sets Japanese deaths at 65,908 troops from the main islands, 28,228 Okinawans, either from the local defense corps or serving in the Japanese army, and 94,000 noncombatants killed in bombardments, caught in the cross-fire of the armies, slain directly by soldiers of both sides, or dead from group or individual suicide. More than twenty-five percent of the prefecture's entire population, as many as 150,000 Okinawan civilians, may have died in the course of the battle, if those who died of hunger or malaria are included. °

Although Okinawa was declared "secure" on June 22 by the American military occupation (which was to become the Government of the Ryukyus), the battle did not end after the eighty-two-day bloodbath. In the weeks and months that followed, thousands of soldiers and sailors, members of the local population in local defense units, and boys like Ōta Masahide continued to try to survive without surrendering. They considered themselves under orders to carry on the fight. The official capitulation of Japanese military forces on the island did not take place until September 7, five days after Japan had formally signed the instruments of surrender on the battleship Missouri in Tokyo Bay.

The headquarters of the Okinawa Defense Forces were located beneath Shuri Castle. All the leaders were there, Commander Ushijima Mitsuru, Chief-of-Staff Chō Isamu, Operations Staff Officer Ihara, staff officers Jin and Kimura. The Chihaya Unit, to which I belonged, was under the direct command of the intelligence section of the headquarters of the Defense Forces, and we were stationed with them underground. Whenever information came in, our job was to carry the latest on the battle situation to the civilians and soldiers in the caves.

° Eguchi Kei'ichi, *Jūgonen sensō shōshi* [Brief History of the Fifteen-Year War] (Tokyo: Aoki Shoten, 1988), p. 223. There are numerous casualty figures for the battle. Discrepancies result primarily from calculations of the precise number of men who were officially enrolled in the Japanese military forces.

On June 19, the dissolution order was issued to the Blood and Iron Student Corps, the Lily Student Corps, and other such units, but my small group was not to be dissolved. We were designated a "special unit." We were to gather in the north, at Nago, to fight an "intelligence war." A guerilla war, we'd call it now. We were ordered to allow ourselves to be captured by the Americans. Our mission, then, was to move around behind their lines gathering intelligence. A final saké party was held at headquarters that June 19. All the generals dressed in formal uniforms, all their medals on their chests. Staff officers wore their gold braid. I saw that. When it was over, they took off their military uniforms and donned the black kimonos worn by elderly Okinawan women, to make them as inconspicuous as possible. Some classmates of mine in the Chihaya Unit were assigned to accompany them as guides, one for every two staff officers. With one exception, all those who left the caves as guides were killed.

With three other comrades, I left for Kunigami in the north. We tried to pass through the enemy lines. I was soon injured. Although we set out swearing to remain together, whether in life or in death, I lost all track of them. I couldn't walk any longer. I crawled on my belly to the place where today they put up the Memorial to the Vigorous Youth. There was a well there, the only one in the area. So many people were piled up in it that they were floating on the surface. I collapsed on my back trying to reach it. Machine-gun and automatic-rifle fire was pounding us.

That evening—I don't remember the exact date, maybe the twenty-second or twenty-third—a man passed by me, then returned and looked at my face. It was my classmate. Shinjō. I'd visited his home once. In that brutal, savage time, when hardly anyone could play the violin, he was a violinist. His elder brother composed beautiful and famous pieces of music. Shinjō told me he was about to charge into the enemy. "I don't need this anymore, "he said and handed me rice, packed in a sock, and dried bonito. At that time, we put rice in our socks and tied them up. I still had a rifle and two hand-grenades with me, and one hundred twenty bullets. I was wearing a half-sleeve uniform with short pants, but no belt, only a string to hold them up. I couldn't wear shoes because my feet were injured. Besides, my shoes had been stolen. If you took your eyes off something for a minute—food, shoes, anything—they'd all be stolen. I'd lost all my food that way, too.

I didn't have any dressings or medicine, so if I'd put on leather military shoes, walking would have been next to impossible. I needed workman's shoes with rubber soles. There were many natural caves in the Mabuni areas where people from the surrounding farming area were hiding. They were starving. I suggested to one that we exchange some of my rice for such a pair of shoes. He was really pleased, since, not being wounded himself, he could easily take military shoes from a corpse. Thanks to Shinjō's rice I was at last again able to move a little.

Searching for food, I climbed to the top of Mabuni Hill. Below was located the cave where we had previously hidden ourselves. There I found small graves of Commander Ushijima and Chief-of-Staff Chō. They had committed suicide. I suppose you could call them tombs, but they were very plain. Ushijima's was just the length of a man, thinly plastered over with concrete, and above it a slab of wood, probably prepared beforehand, reading "Commander Ushijima's Grave." As I approached it, at first I thought I saw a cross there. I was very moved by it, sensitive teenager that I was, thinking one had been put up by the American soldiers. But soon I realized that rather than a cross, what I was seeing was a short American dagger stuck into the grave marker. Then I noticed scratches on it, too. I didn't understand the meanings of the words written there, then, but I remembered the shapes of the letters. Later I learned they said, "God damn! Go to hell!"

For a long time we lived in a cave as defeated stragglers. My own survival then seemed inconceivable to me. I thought only of how I might break out of enemy territory. I could hardly walk with my injured leg. I took off my short-sleeved shirt and put it inside my helmet. I buried my rifle. Simply to throw away a rifle with the chrysanthemum emblem on it would have been a serious offense! Finally I made it to the ocean, but I didn't have the strength to swim far. Human beings instinctively run into the sea when they are chased into a corner. Everybody was swimming. Before my eyes they sank and drowned. I passed out. I was washed ashore and lay unconscious for two or three days on that beach. I regained consciousness next to a woman lying face down on the sand, holding tightly to a package wrapped in cloth. She was already dead. Maybe she's got food in her carrying cloth, I thought, but when I tried to pry open her fingers one by one, she was holding it so firmly I couldn't do it. While I was struggling with her fingers, the waves came in and carried her body off. I just lay there at the waterline, unable to move, waiting for her to return. When I finally opened the package it contained candles and a comb. No food. Yet candles were very valuable.

Every day American soldiers came to hunt the remnants of the defeated army. Among my companions at this time was a graduate of Bunri University in Tokyo named Shiraishi. He was very gentle, and had the complexion of a girl. He'd brought a Webster's dictionary into the military. He never got promoted. He looked after me and I stuck to him. I told him at one point I was prepared to meet my end right where we were. "No," he said, "let's go as far as we can," and he insisted on taking me with him.

One day from the American warships and from the land, too, yellow and red balls exploded in the air, just like fireworks. At first, we thought it was the Special Attack forces counterattacking and we were glad. But finally Shiraishi pointed out that that was impossible. Japan was no longer in a position to do anything like that. About that time, there were only the two of us, and we had nothing to eat. All around us were the tents of American soldiers. If you threw a grenade, the Americans would run for cover, and you could sneak in and steal some food.

Once, because Shiraishi loved reading, I brought back an American magazine from one of my missions. "Ōta, look at this," he exclaimed. Of course, I didn't understand English. "Japan lost," he told me. "The explosions we saw the other day were American salvos of celebration." Later I learned it was exactly as he said, a salute to Japan's surrender, but at that time, people like us were watching from what we still thought of as battlefields. Shiraishi warned me, "Don't leak a word of this outside, or they'll kill the two of us." The stragglers of a defeated army were on a hair trigger and killed each other over the smallest of things.

Shiraishi read sentences incomprehensible to me. I was moved more by the force of his scholarship and the splendidness of learning language than by the danger around me. Once he said to me, "If you survive, come to Tokyo and study English." Those words altered my life completely. From then on we told each other, "Let's not die in vain. Let's survive."

The hunting for us stragglers was severe. Every day Americans came to the heights of Mabuni with automatic rifles, stripped to their bare chests, and ate lunch. When we went looking for food along the beaches, they would shoot at us from the heights, as if it were sport. We'd watch the Americans leave about seven o'clock at night, then we'd pick through their leftovers. They couldn't eat all they brought. So as not to let them fall into our hands, they'd intentionally pierce any extra cans with their bayonets to cause them to spoil, but even spoiled food was a matter of life and death to us, so we'd try to heat whatever we found, to kill germs. But there was no real kindling. Not a splinter of wood, not one chip. If you gathered up a few soldier's belts, the raw rubber in them would burn enough to cook everything a little. This was how for many months I roamed and scrounged around there.

One day, a "placation squad" of former Japanese soldiers came with American MPs. "We've lost. We were defeated. Why are you taking so long to come out?" they called out to us. In our cave there were then maybe one hundred forty or fifty people, in all kinds of different groups.

They'd all lived separately, but now they came together to consult on what we should do. "This must be fake! We shouldn't go out unless we get real, solid proof of defeat. It's a trap." Some said that. Shiraishi and I kept silent. Gradually, the conclusion was reached that we would demand proof of Japan's defeat. The placation squad consisted of three people. One was a former officer. Another was an Okinawan soldier. I knew him because he'd been a guard at headquarters. When he saw me he asked what I was doing there. "Your friends and teachers are all in a POW camp," he said. When I asked him who was there, to my surprise he cited names I knew.

The next day the officer brought proof. It was the Imperial Rescript. "Read it!" we demanded. Everyone surrounded him, clutching our hand grenades. The officer looked scared. He requested that we leave a route open so that he could withdraw. He read the Imperial Rescript and some asked him to leave for the day. He did. Again they argued about what should be done. Some thought it was fake. For the first time, a medical lieutenant whom Shiraishi and I knew opened his mouth, "Those sentences couldn't have been written by an ordinary person. They're in a unique style. I think it's real." That was a strong statement. Quite a few people resisted the idea. I remember a probationary officer, a Waseda University graduate, fiercely opposing accepting the truth of the document. Finally, though, the first lieutenant's argument was accepted and our surrender was decided upon. We raised one final condition. We wanted to be allowed to wash ourselves, to make ourselves decent, before we became prisoners of war.

We did so in the open air the next day. Suddenly, everybody looked like someone else because until then we'd seen each others' faces only at night or under layers of filth. We felt like we had all emerged from a different world.

I thought the day I finally left the cave was September 23. Actually it was October 23. Nearly four months had passed since Ushijima committed suicide. In the prisoner-of-war camp, those who came from Okinawa were in one tent, those from outside of Okinawa were in another, and the Korean military workers were in a tent alone. Practically every night, there were challenges—those who had been harassed before called out their oppressors, beat them up, made them kneel down, and forced them to apologize. Until then, we'd received "education to make us the Emperor's People." We thought we were just the same as the Japanese, that we'd fought together as one. Now, though, Okinawan soldiers and members of the Okinawa local defense forces talked about how terrible it was, how they'd been bullied. I myself had seen Okinawan mothers thrown out of caves and food snatched away from them countless times. "Why is such a thing happening?"—the thought still stuck somewhere in my brain. Yet I wondered, "What's the difference between Okinawans and people from outside the prefecture?" For the first time I began to be awakened to differences in our cultures. I began to see that I was an Okinawan.

18 / IN THE ENEMY'S HANDS

White Flag

KOJIMA KIYOFUMI

A reserve naval officer during the war, he is a leader of Fusen Heishi no
Kai, *the Soldiers Against War Association of Japan, a group founded in
1988 which has about 250 members.*

*According to the final figures released in 1964 by the relief bureau of
the Ministry of Health and Welfare, there were 127,200 Japanese troops
from the army and navy on duty in the Philippines on August 15, 1945.
Prior to that date, 486,600 Japanese servicemen had died in the
Philippines in the course of the war—368,700 from the Army and 117,900
from the Navy. An additional 12,000 were reported to have died after that
date.*°

I'd ended up a reserve naval communications officer because I'd
tried to find someplace relatively safe when I was at Keiō University.
Instead of being sent to navy accounting school, I received orders to
report to the battleship *Yamato.* I was shocked! *Yamato* was then the
largest ship in the world. Unsinkable, they said. Japan's finest. Everyone
was so envious of me. "The laziest guy in the class! How'd he get sent
there? What's wrong with the navy?"

I was on the *Yamato* long enough to go through the Leyte battles in
September and October 1944. We got the crap kicked out of us and
Yamato limped back to Kure only at the end of December. I went ashore
with orders to report to the Twenty-Sixth Air Fleet Headquarters.
Nobody knew why, or even where it was. Eventually, I discovered it was
in the Philippines. Almost all those who stayed aboard *Yamato* died when
she sank on her last sortie defending Okinawa.

Flying down to the Philippines, I got stuck for five days in Taiwan
because the air was under enemy control. At last a plane took me and
three or four other reserve officers over the Luzon Strait between

---

° Kuwata Etsu and Maebara Tōru, eds. *Nihon no sensō: Zukai to daata [Japan's Wars:
Diagrams and Data]* (Tokyo: Hara Shobō, 1986), p. 21.

Formosa and the Phillipines. The pilot told *us* to watch out the windows for enemy planes! Luckily we made it to Clark Field. But the Americans had gotten to it first. The runway was all pock-marked, and the air was filled with brown dust. Not an intact Japanese plane was to be seen. We dashed for the terminal building, really just a cottage. There, about ten officers with golden shoulders were gathered, men wearing admiral-class rank-boards and staff officers with gold braid hanging down everywhere. They made straight for that plane. All the naval commanders of the Philippines ran off to Taiwan on the plane that brought me to Clark. In short, that last plane was sent out to rescue them, and we were tricked into going along for the ride. They were to "lead the defense of the Philippines" from Taiwan, while their subordinates were left behind.

When I finally reported in to Twenty-Sixth Air Fleet Headquarters, my commander just said, "Kojima? We're not supposed to have any Kojima here." The deputy commander desperately shuffled through a stack of papers, until at last he called out, "Oh, here he is," and he assigned me as code officer under the younger brother of Prince Takamatsu's wife, a lieutenant j.g. with the fancy old Court name of Matsudaira. He was obviously a complete screw-up. There are some people like this among the aristocrats. That night, while I was trying to get to sleep, I heard small-arms fire and was told that every night guerrillas attacked and killed sentries at the headquarters. Next morning at breakfast, I received three miserable little sweet potatoes on my plate. On the *Yamato* I'd eaten white rice with several delicious side-dishes. "What a horrible place I've ended up," I thought. At lunch we had "sweet potato rice"—a few grains of rice stuck on sweet potatoes —and pickled watermelon rind. Dinner was two rice balls the size of Ping-Pong balls, and a tiny sliver of canned beef—*and* some cooked sweet potatoes. I was fed up with sweet potatoes in one day.

The U.S. forces landed in January. About ten days later, after we'd all fled into the mountains, I was summoned to headquarters by name and told to go back to the airfield with a few men. From there, I was supposed to send a telegram stating, "The enemy has reached Clark Field. We are about to withdraw."

Of course, all the bigwigs had been in the mountains for a week, but that wouldn't have looked so good. That's why we found ourselves in the middle of the abandoned airfield waiting for the enemy to show up! It was an eerie feeling. From far away, a cloud of dust approached us. Tanks and swarms of other vehicles were coming in our direction. We had only one lousy truck. There were enemy planes overhead. We couldn't just drive away. Our orders were to confirm their arrival—to send that telegram only when their tanks actually arrived. It was really scary. We finally sent it and in complete darkness we made a desperate dash for it.

Somehow, we survived and made it back into the mountains, but we were navy communications men and had no weapons except for our daggers. We were ordered to make bamboo spears. They told us not to worry, the Americans wouldn't come into the mountains. But if they came we were to fight with spears. The enemy, of course, went anywhere they wanted to go, mountainous or not, and we didn't have the strength to fight hand-to-hand. The fight for the airfield had practically wiped out our army troops and the few naval soldiers we had. The stragglers who escaped were reassembled into a platoon. When the platoon commander was killed, the other men at "headquarters" said they didn't need me around anymore, and ordered me to "take command" of the platoon.

I'd heard the general staff officers and command staff talking, saying it was over, that there was no use dying in such a situation. Now I had to report to "my platoon." Normally, a platoon commander had information about each soldier, like family backgrounds and where they came from. I didn't even know their names. I did recognize one of them as a Waseda graduate, a petty officer, and a fellow intellectual with whom I could have communion, but my other thirty men were all draftees. You can't really use men over twenty-five years old as soldiers. Mine were over thirty. The eldest was forty-seven, there were even two fifteen-year-olds, too. Volunteers. They were the only energetic ones. All were down with malaria or something. Many were shaking. Temperatures over forty degrees centigrade [104°F]. We were in no shape to fight a battle. We had one rifle for every three men. One of them was a school principal. He became my batman. This platoon was part of the "Land Combat Unit" holding the "front" on Luzon!

To be honest with you, I thought I'd been put in the most horrible spot on earth when we were ordered to take up our front-line positions. The units on our flanks were soon hit severely and overwhelmed, but our orders to withdraw never came, and we couldn't pull back without orders. The army unit on our right, which was to be our anchor, disappeared into the night. The naval unit on our left was annihilated. Observation planes circled overhead and dropped white smoke markers. When we were smothered in smoke, the troops said, "Commander, we're in trouble!" They'd already experienced it, so I listened to them and I threw myself into the nearest octopus hole. Immediately, trench mortar rounds rained down. You couldn't breath from the dust and acrid fumes. Dark smoke poured into your hole and almost choked you. When the explosions stopped, I poked my head out. Everyone's face was black. Shells had hit either side of my hole and men were dead. I lost ten men that first night. Two or three days later, we finally fled.

We were now without a home unit, so there was nobody to give us food. Our quartermaster corps was somewhere deep in the mountains. Until then, we'd gotten our meals delivered in large pots. The navy didn't even give us mess kits, so we picked up empty cans, punched holes in the sides, and put wire through the holes. We all had those empty tin cans hanging from our waists, clanking along. They looked miserable and made a sad sound. Soon everyone was skin and bones. Friendly forces began firing on each other because of lack of food. Weak stragglers became the prey of stronger ones. It was horrible. Surrounded, we just wandered in circles in the jungle in worn-out clothes looking for food. Fighting the enemy was the last thing on our minds.

The dead looked so horrible. All their buttons popped off, leaving them naked. Legs swelled up, and turned black. The smell of death was hideous. I just thought that I didn't want to die that way. Yet I was so exhausted that I slept near those bodies. Occasionally I mentioned the word "surrender," but surrendering was absolutely unacceptable though everyone instinctively grasped their real situation. There was no way to survive in these conditions. If I'd explain carefully that there was no way out other than surrender, they would explode with anger. Unthinkable! We must fight to the last second! I withdrew my talk about our surrending. Still too early, I thought.

Many days passed. Now, we had no salt and nothing to eat. We had to eat snails. So I mentioned surrendering again. This time, they said, "Take us in, Commander." There were now just seven of them left—four navy men, two army men, and one military civilian from Taiwan. I recall at that moment looking up into the blue sky and thinking, "I will have no nation from now on. I will be alone." But I thought, too, "Finally, my fight is over." I don't think I was fighting for the Emperor in the first place. If you'd asked me why I was fighting, I guess I would have said, "For my parents, for my younger brothers."

As we came down from the mountains and approached the enemy, the two army men urged the rest of us to go on ahead because they had such terrible diarrhea. I suggested that we all rest instead. Later, they repeated their request. Finally they said they didn't want to surrender. As two members of the Imperial Army, they'd rather "die for the sake of the Emperor." They asked me to leave them a hand grenade as we left them.

The Filipino native defense force was along the front lines. I knew we'd be killed if they got us. They really did kill Japanese men by poking out their eyes and cutting off their noses. So we couldn't afford to give up our arms until the very moment we were captured by an official enemy force. I'd kept our white flag secret, not putting it on a branch until after we were actually approaching the American forces. It was a piece of parachute silk I used to carry things around in. If I'd raised a white flag openly, we'd have been shot by our own forces. The white flag was carried by the Taiwanese. By chance, we stumbled upon an American barracks. Four or five sentries were posted outside. They were holding coffee or bread or something in their hands, their rifles off to one side. Everything went flying as they dashed into the barracks. We were there to surrender, yet we hardly knew how. In a moment, hundreds of them, all in field uniform, were aiming their rifles at us. It was a strange moment. We still had our weapons. I had a pistol in my belt and a sword at my side We were so emotionally wound up, it's amazing we ourselves didn't open fire. I couldn't have complained had they shot me.

The enemy formed a circle around us and drew closer and closer. They were shouting something at us. Suddenly, I realized this wasn't captive style, the way we were, so I told my men to drop their weapons. The enemy still kept shouting. Our hands weren't up. But I honestly didn't know what to do, I'd never surrendered before. Finally, one of them beckoned to us, hand flat, palm up, so we advanced step by step. As soon as we were within reach, enemy soldiers jumped on us and patted us down, touching us all over. I know now they were checking for weapons. Then Filipinos dashed at us, taking away our watches, belts, anything. I had four watches—mementos of dead soldiers—and a good silver buckle with a Japanese helmet engraved on it, but they took that too. It was terrible the way they stole everything, but that's how we were able to officially become prisoners of war.

It was really rare for an officer to surrender with subordinates like I did. Usually, the surrenders were individual. Among the officers in the Twenty-Sixth Air Fleet Headquarters, two surrendered. Both alone. In my case, my platoon were all stragglers, so maybe that's why I was able to do it. Also, we were navy.

My men had eaten nothing for days. They begged me to ask for something to eat. I was embarrassed to ask for food practically at the moment of surrender, but I did it anyway. They told me they'd just had breakfast, and as a front-line unit had to wait for more food from the rear. They were sending us back there in any case. In fact, they put us on two jeeps and off we went. Filipinos were out in the fields. They made chopping motions across their necks to show how we'd soon be killed. They also threw stones. The American guards shot into the air to warn them off. The driver of my jeep offered me a Lucky Strike. I was a heavy smoker, and I hadn't smoked for so long, I was dying for one. I drew it from the pack and thanked him, and he told me to pass it back to the others. The Americans were still holding rifles on us, but when we put our cigarettes between our lips, they lit them for us with a lighter. From that moment on I think I could feel my closed mind opening up. When I finished that first cigarette, he gave me another. He ended up giving me the whole pack.

A swarm of enemy soldiers came out to see us when we reached camp. I guess they wanted to get a look at these funny-looking guys they'd caught. But when I saw them! Blond, silver, black, brown, red hair. Blue, green, brown, black eyes. White, black, skin colors of every variety. I was stunned. I realized then that we'd fought against all the peoples of the world. At the same time, I thought, what a funny country America is, all those different kinds of people fighting in the same uniform! I'd discovered a new kind of country.

We were put out in an open field with everyone staring at us curiously. Two enemy men stood behind me. My soldiers, the four of them, were sitting off to one side, nobody really keeping them covered. I was envious of them, they looked more at home than I felt. When I again asked for food, I was told, "We've just finished lunch." But when I said we'd take anything, even water, they brought us water. When I told them we hadn't eaten for days, they brought us some canned food. I think it was corned beef. It was unbelievably delicious. After all, we'd been eating grasses.

When we were finished, a soldier came up to us, holding out a shovel. He told me to dig a hole. I turned pale. When Japanese soldiers captured enemies, they always had them dig a hole, made them kneel down, and chopped their heads off—so I'd heard, anyway. And it was me they'd brought the shovel to, not my men. I looked around desperately for some place to run, but all I saw was a wall of iron, so I resigned myself to my fate. I stood up shakily and started to dig. I had no strength left and the soil was as hard as rock. My hole was very shallow. I thought, this will never be big enough for me. But the soldier took away the shovel and simply threw in the can I'd been eating from, and ordering me to collect the rest from the others and bury them, too. I guess I looked stunned, so he added that it was a sanitation measure. Honestly, when I saw that shovel! It wasn't only me, all the men reacted the same way. I was the one who'd assured them it would be all right, and now they all thought I'd been wrong.

At the next military camp, out of a sentry box came a nisei, a Japanese in an American uniform. I can't tell you how strange that felt. He questioned us, but this time in Japanese. Until then, I'd been using my very limited English. No one could understand me even when I said, "wa-ta"—that I wanted water. I had to spell it out on paper. The same when I said I was a lieutenant. They did get "hungry" though. At this camp, we were thrown into a detention center and there saw five or six dirty-looking Japanese. Until then I'd forgotten I was a POW. We'd been taught to feel that prisoners are somehow loathsome, and at first I saw those men that way, even though I was one myself.

It was a tiny, iron-barred place. We had no choice but to lie down like sardines. There were so many mosquitos, we finally called out to the guard. He brought out something which he sprayed around, and in an instant all the flying mosquitos were dead on the floor. A tool of advanced civilization! We were so tired we all fell asleep by eight o'clock. Even then, though, I kept thinking I might be killed at any moment, or, if they let me live, I'd be left to farm on some distant mountain somewhere. That's what was going through my mind when I heard my name called. I was taken out of the cell to meet my second nisei that day. He was unarmed. He took me to his own room. "Mr. Kojima," he asked me, "would you like coffee or tea?" Coffee, I replied. Then he pulled out a bag of cookies. We'd been told it was our duty to endure privation to the moment of victory. We hadn't had such luxurious things for years. He just opened the bag and dumped them on the table. "Go ahead," he said. "Please eat."

I asked him his rank, and he told me he was a first lieutenant. Then I asked him the date, and it was then I learned I'd been captured on April 13, 1945. He informed me that his grandmother and grandfather lived in Hiroshima, and asked me what I thought of nisei soldiers. Did I hate them? I realized he was genuinely worried about that, which was why he was being so kind to me. It gave me confidence. "You were born in America," I replied. "You're fighting for your country, America. I have no ill feelings about that." He was like me, and I did the same thing for my country. Then he told me about how Japanese-Americans were horribly ill-treated in America, that they were placed in camps, and still oppressed even though the outstanding record of the all-nisei 442 Regimental Combat Team had changed the situation a little. We chatted until ten-thirty at night, and I learned that there were people who were suffering because they belonged to neither country.

Eventually, I was flown to a camp on Leyte. The novelist Ooka Shōhei [who later wrote Fires on the Plain about his experiences in the Philippines] was among the prisoners there. I became friendly with some American officers, talked every day. Other prisoners asked me why they were "investigating" me. The truth was that the American officers were also college graduates and reservists, and we just hit it off. One gave me a collection of Schiller's works to read and other poetry books, too. Meanwhile, the commander of the Leyte area wanted to meet me. Lieutenant Paul recommended me to represent the Japanese POWs for the area. I told Paul that I was just a low-ranking, lowly junior lieutenant, and that there were a lot of far more impressive people around. The highest-ranking prisoner was an army major, but he was a horrible man. He talked proudly every night about the women he'd raped every time the Japanese army occupied a new area. He was always surrounded by a circle of toadies, raptly listening to him. Paul said to me, "You know what kind of people most of them are. That's why I picked you."

Paul took me to meet a rear admiral. The first thing that commander said was, "The Japanese Army must take responsibility for killing captured Americans on Palawan Island." * He glared at me. What a horrible spot to be put in. I'd been on Luzon, what did I know about Palawan? Paul said something in English, and the topic of conversation shifted. I was asked how we were being treated. What a relief! Then he asked me about the Emperor system. Personally, I told him, I don't think we need an Emperor. I'd seen too many soldiers die at the front in the name of the Emperor.

The next day, Paul assured me that the conversation had been a great success. Said I'd be taken by a navy lieutenant-commander first to Hawaii, then on to Washington, D.C. I had come to feel very close to Lieutenant Paul. He made a great impression on me, speaking such excellent Japanese after only nine months of language training! He gave me an American uniform. We all wore them, with "PW" stamped on the back. This one had no letters on it. I felt as if I were no longer a prisoner.

On my way to Hawaii, I was the only POW among all those American military men. They were curious about me, and came to talk to me. I was then just beginning to understand Americans. A navy ensign came up to me, came to attention, and saluted. Then he asked if I would give him my autograph. When I asked, "In Japanese?" He replied smartly, "Yes, sir."

I was so surprised by their attitude. In Japan, everyone despised a captive. What they wanted to ask me most was when the war would be over. How long would the Japanese forces hold out? When I told them I was a navy man captured in the mountains, they broke into laughter.

In Hawaii I was given a single room with a bed and a lamp. Like in a hotel. That first morning I looked out of the window and saw rows and

---

* The scene of a massacre of Allied prisoners of war.

rows of tents—all Japanese prisoners. It was a shock. I hadn't realized so many POWs had been taken. I thought they had only been surrendering one by one. For the first time I began dreaming that, if there were this many of us, I might actually be able to return home someday.

Because I fell ill with malaria, I never got to go to Washington. I did, however, assist in efforts to make Japan's surrender possible, because I'd seen men die every day in the jungle. Even one more day's combat meant more would die that way. What empty deaths! The attacks on the Japanese Homeland were increasing day by day. I knew that Japan would be completely annihilated. That's why I started making leaflets in Japanese. Until then, nisei had been drafting these. Although they could speak the language, many couldn't write it well. So I began to correct their written Japanese, but that was taken as behavior aimed against my own country. I came in for criticism even among the Americans for that, particularly from the professional military men who saw me as a traitor to my country. Of course, that was how the Japanese military viewed me, too.

I was involved in preparing the leaflets that were dropped over Japan at that time. The most critical issues arose at the time of the Potsdam Declaration [July 26, 1945]. How should its provisions be presented to the Japanese people? The Japanese government was not disclosing them directly. The demands of the Potsdam Declaration for immediate surrender were then the subject of indirect negotiations between Japan and the Allies. We put Japan's response and the American response together in a single leaflet and dropped thousands of copies. One of the leaflets fell inside the palace grounds, and Privy Councillor Kido took it to the Emperor, triggering the end of the war. Or at least there's that story.

I monitored all the Japanese radio broadcasts, swinging from euphoria to despair as I head the news, hoping against hope that the war might end. All through July. The Japanese government was still insisting on protecting the "national polity." The Allies insisted that the Emperor be placed under the Supreme Commander of Allied Forces. Then the atomic bomb was dropped. I remember "Atomic Bomb" in big letters headlining the *Stars and Stripes* military paper. I didn't know what that was, but there was a picture of an enormous cloud. That paper contained a report on the extensive damage, and some other American papers even criticized the inhumanity of the bomb. I thought of that nisei lieutenant's family.

I returned in October 1946. I'd had a post at a big bank, so I had a place to go back to, but it was practically a monster of financial capitalism and I hated that. I soon submitted my letter of resignation and returned to my mother's hometown in Shimane. There, I ran a local newspaper on my own, believing that democracy should start at the bottom. I was very popular among the Occupation forces and even got special allotments of paper. I ran it for ten years before I again returned to Tokyo.

I don't think I have long to live, but I want young people to know how stupid that war was. One other thing, too. I want to make this country a land where people think and live on their own. I was very briefly a captive, and while living as a prisoner of war I learned about democracy and freedom. The impact of that war will last until I die.

While Mr. Kojima does not seem to have been stigmatized in the postwar years for being a POW, many Japanese who were captured before the war ended did suffer discrimination and were torn by self-doubt.

19 / "A TERRIBLE NEW WEAPON"

AT PRECISELY 8:15 A.M. on August 6, 1945, one of a group of three B-29s dropped a bomb over the center of Hiroshima from an altitude of 8,500 meters. The bomb was three meters in length, 0.7 meters in diameter, and weighed 4 metric tons. It was detonated at an altitude of 590 meters. The fission of the 0.85 kilograms of uranium contained in the bomb released energy equivalent to the explosive force of 13,000 tons of TNT.

At the instant of the explosion, a fireball of several hundred thousand degrees centigrade formed, and 0.3 seconds later, the fireball attained a temperature on the surface of 7000 degrees centigrade. Intense thermal radiation was emitted by the fireball for three seconds after the explosion, and some continued to be emitted for about ten seconds. The temperature at hypocenter—the hypothetical point where the bomb would have hit the ground—rose from 3000 to 4000 degrees centigrade. Those exposed to the heat rays within one kilometer were killed by intense burns and the rupture of internal organs. Burns were caused to the bodies of those within 3.5 kilometers of the hypocenter, and clothes and wooden houses were ignited. A huge pillar of smoke and debris rose to a height of 9,000 meters within eight minutes and formed a mushroom-shaped cloud visible many miles from the city.*

An intense blast was also created at the instant of the explosion. Theoretically, the blast at the hypocenter had a maximum blast pressure of 35 metric tons per square meter and a maximum velocity of 440 meters per second. At 1.3 kilometers from the hypocenter the blast attained a force of seven tons per square meter and a wind velocity of 120 meters per second. The explosive wind reached a distance of eleven kilometers about thirty seconds after the explosion. The blast stripped people of clothing, tore off burned skin, and ruptured the internal organs of some victims, and it drove glass and other debris into their bodies. Wooden buildings within a radius of 2.3 kilometers were leveled and over half of all such buildings within 3.2 kilometers were destroyed. Even concrete buildings near the hypocenter were smashed by the blast.

The third major effect of the detonation after heat and blast was radiation. Gamma rays and neutrons emitted within one minute of the bombing inflicted a wide variety of physical damage to people as far as 2.3 kilometers from hypocenter. Those within one kilometer received intense radiation doses. Residual radiation caused many who entered the area within 100 hours of the explosion to suffer exposure to gamma rays.

Moisture condensing on rising ash and dust fell as the "black rain" that began falling within thirty minutes of the explosion and continued to come down for some ninety minutes. It contained huge amounts of radiation that damaged not only humans, but plants and animals as well, over a large area. Long-term effects of radiation, including diseases like leukemia and the development of cancers, are still claiming victims.

Estimates of deaths in the blasts themselves, once estimated at 78,000 in the case of Hiroshima and 27,000 in Nagasaki, are widely acknowledged to have been higher, but accurate figures for the numbers in the target cities have proven difficult to determine. It is estimated that by the end of December 1945, approximately 140,000 persons had died from effects caused by the single atomic bomb dropped on Hiroshima August 6. The blast in Nagasaki three days later had claimed 60,000 to 70,000 by year's end. ∎

---

* There are many histories and physical descriptions of the physical effects of the atomic bomb. Rarely do figures agree precisely. The numbers given here are drawn from both Shōno Naomi, *Hiroshima wa mukashibanashi ka: Gensuibaku no shashin to kiroku* [*Is Hiroshima an Old Story? Nuclear and Hydrogen Bomb Photographs and Records*] (Tokyo: Shinchōsha, Tokyo, 1987), pp. 13–15, and "At the Moment of the A-Bomb Strike," a leaflet produced by the Hiroshima Peace Memorial Museum.

Eight Hundred Meters from the Hypocenter

YAMAOKA MICHIKO

She is a hibakusha—*one who was exposed to the atomic bomb. The term has come to be used frequently to specify this particular kind of victimization, as distinct from more general terms applied to those who suffered from the war. Persons registered with the Ministry of Health and Welfare are eligible to carry an "A-bomb notebook," which officially identifies them and today entitles them to receive the relief medical assistance available only to victims of the bomb.*

We meet in a corner of a large room in the Hiroshima Peace Memorial Museum, a short walk from the Atomic Bomb Dome at the edge of the Peace Memorial Park. "These days I talk to groups of schoolchildren who come to Hiroshima. They seem to listen, but I fear that nobody really understands our feelings."

That year, on August 6, I was in the third year of girls' high school, fifteen years old. I was an operator at the telephone exchange. We had been mobilized from school for various work assignments for more than a year. My assigned place of duty was civilian, but we, too, were expected to protect the nation. We were tied by strong bonds to the country. We'd heard the news about the Tokyo and Osaka bombings, but nothing had dropped on Hiroshima. Japan was winning. So we still believed. We only had to endure. I wasn't particularly afraid when B-29s flew overhead.

That morning I left the house at about seven forty-five. I heard that the B-29s had already gone home. Mom told me, "Watch out, the B-29s might come again." My house was one point three kilometers from the hypocenter. My place of work was five hundred meters from the hypocenter. I walked toward the hypocenter in an area where all the houses and buildings had been deliberately demolished for fire breaks. There was no shade. I had on a white shirt and *monpe.* As I walked there, I noticed middle-school students pulling down houses at a point about eight hundred meters away from the hypocenter. I heard the faint sound of planes as I approached the river. The planes were tricky. Sometimes they only pretended to leave. I could still hear the very faint sound of planes. Today, I have no hearing in my left ear because of damage from the blast. I thought, how strange, so I put my right hand above my eyes and looked up to see if I could spot them. The sun was dazzling. That was the moment.

There was no sound. I felt something strong. It was terribly intense.

I felt colors. It wasn't heat. You can't really say it was yellow, and it wasn't blue. At that moment I thought I would be the only one who would die. I said to myself, "Goodbye, Mom."

They say temperatures of seven thousand degrees centigrade hit me. You can't really say it washed over me. It's hard to describe. I simply fainted. I remember my body floating in the air. That was probably the blast, but I don't know how far I was blown. When I came to my senses, my surroundings were silent. There was no wind. I saw a slight thread-like light, so I felt I must be alive. I was under stones. I couldn't move my body. I heard voices crying, "Help! Water!" It was then I realized I wasn't the only one. I couldn't really see around me. I tried to say something, but my voice wouldn't come out.

"Fire! Run away! Help! Hurry up!" They weren't voices but moans of agony and despair. "I have to get help and shout," I thought. The person who rescued me was Mom, although she herself had been buried under our collapsed house. Mom knew the route I'd been taking. She came, calling out to me. I heard her voice and cried for help. Our surroundings were already starting to burn. Fires burst out from just the light itself. It didn't really drop. It just flashed.

It was beyond my mother's ability. She pleaded, "My daughter's buried here, she's been helping you, working for the military." She convinced soldiers nearby to help her and they started to dig me out. The fire was now blazing. "Woman, hurry up, run away from here," soldiers called. From underneath the stones I heard the crackling of flames. I called to her, "It's all right. Don't worry about me. Run away." I really didn't mind dying for the sake of the nation. Then they pulled me out by my legs.

Nobody there looked like human beings. Until that moment I thought incendiary bombs had fallen. Everyone was stupefied. Humans had lost the ability to speak. People couldn't scream, "It hurts!" even when they were on fire. People didn't say, "It's hot!" They just sat catching fire.

My clothes were burnt and so was my skin. I was in rags. I had braided my hair, but now it was like a lion's mane. There were people, barely breathing, trying to push their intestines back in. People with their legs wrenched off. Without heads. Or with faces burned and swollen out of shape. The scene I saw was a living hell.

Mom didn't say anything when she saw my face and I didn't feel any pain. She just squeezed my hand and told me to run. She was going to go rescue my aunt. Large numbers of people were moving away from the flames. My eyes were still able to see, so I made my way towards the mountain, where there was no fire, toward Hijiyama. On this flight I saw a friend of mine from the phone exchange. She'd been inside her house and wasn't burned. I called her name, but she didn't respond. My face was so swollen she couldn't tell who I was. Finally, she recognized my voice. She said, "Miss Yamaoka, you look like a monster!" That's the first time I heard that word. I looked at my hands and saw my own skin hanging down and the red flesh exposed. I didn't realize my face was swollen up because I was unable to see it.

The only medicine was *tempura* oil. I put it on my body myself. I lay on the concrete for hours. My skin was now flat, not puffed up anymore. One or two layers had peeled off. Only now did it become painful. A scorching sky was overhead. The flies swarmed over me and covered my wounds, which were already festering. People were simply left lying around. When their faint breathing became silent, they'd say, "This one's dead," and put the body in a pile of corpses. Some called for water, and if they got it, they died immediately.

Mom came looking for me again. That's why I'm alive today. I couldn't walk anymore. I couldn't see anymore. I was carried on a stretcher as far as Ujina, and then from there to an island where evacuees were taken. On the boat there I heard voices saying, "Let them drink water if they want. They'll die either way." I drank a lot of water.

I spent the next year bedridden. All my hair fell out. When we went to relatives' houses later they wouldn't even let me in because they feared they'd catch the disease. There was neither treatment nor assistance for me. Those people who had money, people who had both parents, people who had houses, they could go to the Red Cross Hospital or the Hiroshima City Hospital. They could get operations. But we didn't have any money. It was just my Mom and I. Keloids covered my face, my neck. I couldn't even move my neck. One eye was hanging down. I was unable to control my drooling because my lip had been burned off. I couldn't get any treatments at a hospital, so my mother gave me massages. Because she did that for me, my keloids aren't as bad as they would have been. My fingers were all stuck together. I couldn't move them. The only thing I could do was sew shorts, since I only needed to sew a straight line. I had to do something to earn money.

The Japanese government just told us we weren't the only victims of the war. There was no support or treatment. It was probably harder for my Mom. Once she told me she tried to choke me to death. If a girl has terrible scars, a face you couldn't be born with, I understand that even a mother could want to kill her child. People threw stones at me and called me Monster. That was before I had my many operations. I only showed this side of my face, the right hand side, when I had to face someone. Like I'm sitting now.

A decade after the bomb, we went to America. I was one of the twenty-five selected by Norman Cousins to be brought to America for treatment and plastic surgery.* We were called the Hiroshima Maidens. The American government opposed us, arguing that it would be acknowledging a mistake if they admitted us to America, but we were supported by many civilian groups. We went to Mount Sinai Hospital in New York and spent about a year and a half undergoing treatment. I improved tremendously. I've now had thirty-seven operations, including efforts at skin grafts.

When I went to America I had a deep hatred toward America. I asked myself why they ended the war by a means which destroyed human beings. When I talked about how I suffered, I was often told, "Well, you attacked Pearl Harbor!" I didn't understand much English then, and it's probably just as well. From the American point of view, they dropped that bomb in order to end the war faster, in order to create more damage faster. But it's inexcusable to harm human beings in this way. I wonder what kind of education there is now in America about atomic bombs. They're still making them, aren't they?

A Korean in Hiroshima

SHIN BOK SU

Korea House, an office building in the center of the city, is where she wishes to meet. Her accent is rich in the flavors and vocabulary of Hiroshima. Tears occasionally well up in her eyes as she speaks. Her present husband has been hospitalized for about a year. He was also in Hiroshima on that day.

The number of non-Japanese who became victims of the atomic bombings at Hiroshima and Nagasaki is extremely difficult to determine.† But careful estimates indicate that about 50,000 Koreans were exposed to the atomic bomb in Hiroshima. Approximately 30,000 were killed. Of the 20,000 survivors, all but 5,000 were repatriated to Korea after Korean

---

* Norman Cousins, longtime editor of *Saturday Review*, is widely known in Japan for his work in support of the victims of the atomic bombs and other work for the promotion of peace.

† One of the best discussions of the problems encountered in the non-Japanese population is to be found in The Committee for the Compilation of Materials on Damage Caused by the Atomic Bombs in Hiroshima and Nagasaki, *Hiroshima and Nagasaki: The Physical, Medical, and Social Effects of the Atomic Bombings* (New York: Basic Books, 1981), a translation of *Hiroshima no genbaku saigai* (Tokyo: Iwanami Shoten, 1979), pp. 461–83. The best numbers available are for the Koreans.

independence. Chinese, from both Taiwan and the continent, people from elsewhere in Asia, Allied prisoners of war, and Japanese-Americans caught in Japan by the onset of war also became hibakusha.

It was the time of the "unification" of Japan and Korea. Mr. Minami, the governor general, addressing us, said we were now all Japanese. All of us Koreans were suddenly told to change our names. We adopted a Japanese name, Shigemitsu. The characters meant "thickly-wooded," because our family had been living on a heavily wooded mountain. A new school was founded about four kilometers from our village of two hundred and fifty people. I wanted to go. My parents opposed it since they thought it would be too dangerous for a girl. I beseeched Grandpa and finally he relented, so I became a first-grader at the age of ten.

Seven of the ten teachers were Japanese. Korean kids, even when they wanted to go weewee, didn't know how to say that in Japanese. So some kids ended up wetting themselves. But still, when at that school, I felt we had become Japanese. Many Japanese people came to Korea. There were money-lenders, real usurers who lent money at outrageous rates, and when they weren't repaid immediately, took away people's fields and became rich. They had bathtubs in their own homes! Lived in luxury.

Conversations about marriage came up when I was about twenty-three years old and working in an agricultural laboratory. I yearned for Japan. At that time the Japanese were gods. Their authority was overwhelming. When we met Japanese we bowed to them. My husband-to-be came back to Korea from Japan for our *o-miai,* our first meeting. I agreed to it. In three days we were married. He was just an ordinary Korean, a simple, straightforward person. That's how I came to Hiroshima in 1937.

I'd believed that Koreans were living the good life in Japan, but that didn't seem to be the case. But my husband was a subcontractor, part of a subsidiary of Mitsubishi which was using Korean labor. I didn't have to worry. We were able to eat white rice. We had cash too. I was quite happy I'd come to Japan. He bought me my first Western dress a week after we arrived. He was one of the leaders of the Kyōwakai, a Korean people's group. I asked him to arrange for a Korean Women's Kyōwakai. He got the needed permission, and when it opened, all the big shots from the city came. Thought it was a great idea. I became its head. We did volunteer work and also civil-defense and air-defense training. I was occupied from morning to night.

We ate breakfast about seven forty that morning when the atomic bomb fell. Then a warning of an imminent air attack sounded. My seven-year-old son warned my husband's mother, who lived with us, "Grandma, take care. Hurry, or you'll die." "Don't worry about me," she answered, "I run well. I'm fine." With this kind of banter we entered the shelter in our backyard. We all had our headgear on. We left the radio on loud until we heard that the skies over Hiroshima were all clear. Then we came out, removed our headgear, and stripped off our outer clothes, down to our underwear. It was so hot in Hiroshima. I took off the baby's diaper cover. Grandma wore only a band around her waist. She put the youngest on her back, tied on with a sash—he was thirteen months old —and went into the kitchen to wash the morning dishes. The other two children were sleepy because air raid warnings the night before had kept them awake. So I told them to nap awhile, and put out their futon. I hung the mosquito net for them in the six-mat room. From our window I noticed the cistern water was low, so I ran a hose out from our bathtub to fill it up.

Suddenly, *"PIKA!"* a brilliant light and then *"DON!"* a gigantic noise. I looked up. But I couldn't see anything. It was pitch black. I heard Grandma's voice shouting. "Help, help!" "Where are you?" I called. "I'm in the living room. I'm suffocating!"

Gradually, the darkness lightened. I saw that Grandma was on top of the child. Two pillars of the house had fallen on her neck and legs. I looked around and there were no houses to be seen. This can't be a bomb, I thought. I pulled at the pillars, but couldn't lift them off her. They didn't even budge. I shouted to our neighbor, "Help, my child's buried under the house!" He jumped over the ruins of his own house and tried to pull them out. He couldn't move a thing. "I'm sorry," he said, "My grandfather is trapped in the second-floor room. I have to rescue him."

Then Mr. Ishihara, our other neighbor, bleeding himself, gave me a knife with the handle missing. "Mrs. Hirota," he said—that was my Japanese name then—"cut the sash off with this." I ran to them, cut the sash with the kitchen knife, and pulled the baby boy out. The flesh on his left leg was torn. Somehow, with both of us tugging, Grandma managed to wriggle free herself. It took more than an hour and a half. Then Grandma started to run away. She was thinking only of herself! I shouted at her, "Take the baby with you," but she didn't listen. I chased her and caught her. There was a millet field nearby where we grew vegetables because of the food shortage. I got her to sit down and hold the baby in her arms. Then I ran back to the house for the other children.

Where were the children sleeping? Our house was quite large. They had been in the middle. The fire-prevention cistern was still there, so I used that as a point of reference and started digging through the roof tiles. One by one. I shouted, "Takeo! Akiko! Come out!" But I heard no response. I kept pulling off tiles. I heard the droning sound of an airplane! But I no longer cared if I died right there. I just kept digging. Soon it started raining. That was the Black Rain.

My husband returned about the time things started burning. That morning he'd gone to visit someone in the city. He was in a toilet and was buried there. He came back wearing only his shorts. His whole body was covered completely in black soot. I couldn't tell who he was until he said something to me. I cried to him that the kids were still under the house.

The flames were starting to break out from the rubble. He found a straw mat and soaked that in water. He walked over the roof tiles. That straw mat caught on fire while he was trying to move aside as many tiles as he could. A soldier came and insisted that we flee. We were both dragged away. That night we stayed at a city sports ground. All night long people were dying off all around us.

The next morning, we went back to find out what happened to our children. The house had burned completely. All our household goods, so carefully piled up for evacuation, and some rationed food we'd accumulated were still burning. So were the corpses of my children. When I approached, I saw a line of buttons from my son's white shirt. Akiko, my girl, was curled up next to Takeo. Flames were still licking up from them.

I couldn't walk anymore. Pieces of the house were imbedded in my back, and I'd been rushing around so desperately that I'd injured my legs. One of my husband's men took me in a cart to get some medicine. Along the street, I saw men and women all red, burned, someone still wearing a soldier's cap but with a body all scorched. You couldn't tell men from women. If there were breasts, that was a woman. Faces hung down like icicles. Skin in strips from arms held out in front of them. "Water! Water!" You couldn't walk the streets without stepping over the dead. I saw girl students, all dead, their heads in a water cistern. It must have been hot.

About a week later, we were notified that we should come to school to pick up the remains of our children about a week later. There we were given two yellow envelopes. When we opened them, my husband said, "These are from the backbones of adults." Our kids were seven and four. So we released those bones into the river.

My husband had only gotten a small scrape on his knee. I thought we were lucky. But from the twenty-fifth of August his hair started falling out. He went to the hospital and got some medicine, but his mouth turned black. He swore he'd die if he stayed there, cried "I have to go to Tokyo. I must get medicine!" He ran off to a train station. I put my baby on my back and followed him. I just left Grandma there. They'd both made it. We jumped on a freight train packed with soldiers and we reached Osaka that night. He looked as if he were going to die right then. A train heading away from Tokyo came by. I lied to him. I said that it was bound for Tokyo and I took him back to Hiroshima. The next morning he died. His body had turned black. Blood seeped from his skin. He smelled awful.

By then, we were living on the one rice ball a day they brought on a truck. A month passed before the wife of a neighbor told me that if you went to city hall, they'd give you money for the ones who'd died of the atomic bomb. That was good news. I went to the city office. The clerk gave me a form to fill out. I put down our names and place of family registration. "You're a foreigner," he said. Until that moment I'd been Japanese. All I'd done was say my registration was in Korea. "We cannot give anything to Koreans," he replied. "Why?" I asked him. My husband and two children had died because we were Japanese. Who had suddenly decided we were aliens? "I don't know," he said. "The orders came from above."

Five Photographs of August 6

MATSUSHIGE YOSHITO

He is seventy-six years old. He has just given a talk about the atomic bomb to a group of elementary school children at the Peace Memorial Hall in the Peace Park in Hiroshima. He has with him the photographs he took on the day of the explosion. "When I talk looking at these pictures, memories of more than forty years ago come back as if it were yesterday."

I worked for the *Chūgoku Shimbun,* the Hiroshima daily paper. I was a photographer, but I was attached at the time to an army press unit stationed at the army divisional headquarters in Hiroshima. The night before, I went to the HQ by bicycle at the sound of the air-raid warning —about twelve-thirty. It was three point seven kilometers from my house to the division in a straight line on a map. After the warning was lifted, I stretched out on an army chair and caught some sleep. The sun rose and I watched Hiroshima City from the stone walls of Hiroshima Castle, where the headquarters was located. It was a quiet and peaceful morning, so I went home, since it was still too early to go to the newspaper. That became the dividing line between death and life for me. Both the division and my office were nine hundred meters from the hypocenter.

My underwear had gotten sweaty on the trip home, so I hung it out on the clothesline when I got home. I was about to get it when terrific sparks jumped from the spot where the electric lines entered the house. I heard a tremendous cracking noise, like trees being torn apart, and at the same instant there was a brilliant flash of immaculate white, like the igniting of the magnesium we used to use for taking photographs. I couldn't see a thing. I was sitting in a six-mat room, half-naked, my shirt out on the line. I sensed an explosive wind like needles striking me. It seemed only a moment before my wife came in. "A bomb fell," she just said. I grabbed her hand and we ran outside. When I fully came to my senses, we were already squatting down in a hollow in a sweet-potato field across the train tracks from our house. We thought an ordinary bomb had hit our house directly or exploded right near it. It was absolutely black outdoors. I couldn't see my wife's face even though we were pressed right up against each other. I thought my wife and I had been saved, as I felt the warmth of her hand in mine. My heart felt ready to split open, it was beating so fast.

Gradually, the lowest edge of the fog seemed to rise a little, and I could see. A four-story wooden fire station nearby had collapsed in an instant. I had to get to headquarters! I returned to my house to find my camera. The walls had toppled over. I noticed that I, myself, was bleeding from little bits of glass, from chest to face, but my bleeding soon stopped. My wife seemed all right, so I grabbed my camera, a Mamiya Six, Japanese-made, and walked along the train tracks toward the center of the city.

I approached the City Hall, about one point one kilometers from the hypocenter. Both it and the Western Fire Station were in flames. It was a sea of fire. I couldn't make my way to the newspaper office, so I returned to the western side of the Miyuki Bridge and tried to head towards the city center by passing along the bank of the river. But fireballs were rolling down the road. There was nobody to be seen. If I hang around here, I thought, I'll be swallowed up in these fires, so I returned to the bridge.

You had to weave through the streets avoiding the bodies. People's bodies were all swollen up. Their skin, burst open, was hanging down in rags. Their faces were burnt black. I put my hand on my camera, but it was such a hellish apparition that I couldn't press the shutter. I hesitated about twenty minutes before I finally pushed it and took this first picture. The man in this picture might be a policeman giving first aid to people for burns using cooking oil. A can of oil's behind there. This woman's hair was burned frizzy. They were all barefoot because their shoes had stuck to the asphalt. This woman was holding a baby in the crook of her arm. She was half naked. The baby's eyes were closed. Either dead or in shock.

She was running around crying to her child, "Please open your eyes." The baby was probably already dead. You can see in the picture that her legs are slightly blurred. The film was slow then, so you can tell she was running.

I approached and took this second shot. It was such a cruel sight. The viewfinder of the camera was clouded with my tears when I took it. It was around eleven o'clock. The whole area was still under fire and smoke. The bottom of the picture shows the asphalt. People, lying along the upstream railing of the bridge which had fallen onto the surface. They're using it as a pillow. The people on the downstream side of the bridge didn't have that luxury and were lying directly on the road. Their bodies were burned head to toe. They were covered in asphalt. They mistook me for a soldier. "Please Mister Soldier, give me some water," they'd call out faintly. I had an armband on that said "Military Reporter." I could only reply, "The relief unit will come soon, so please hold on."

I returned home, but left again about two o'clock. The fire was dying out. I set my feet towards the center of town again with a mind to go to the headquarters or the office, but corpses were everywhere and smoldering ruins were still sending up plumes of flame here and there. It was hot, I suppose, but maybe my nerves were paralyzed. I didn't feel a thing.

Japanese homes are made of wood and collapsed easily from the force of the blast. So, too, did most of the shops and other small buildings. Many people were trapped under the wreckage. They couldn't pull themselves out. This area was hit by winds with a velocity of 440 meters per second and thermal waves of several hundred degrees centigrade. Fires began spontaneously. Even had the people gotten out, they couldn't have outrun the flames. Many people burned to death. The corpses I saw on the seventh were black and hardened, but on that day they were still burning from below and the fat of the bodies was bubbling up and sputtering as it burned. That was the only time I've seen humans roasting.

I walked on flames to reach the office building. It was made of reinforced concrete, so I was confident that the inside wouldn't be burned down. I'd left my other camera in my locker there. I was ready to enter the building when I saw piles of ash and red coals glowing inside. I took only a few steps in before I pulled back.

Nearby, I saw a burnt trolley car halfway up on the sidewalk. Probably blown there by the wind. I didn't go near it, but walked toward Kamiyachō. There I saw another burned trolley car at a curve. It looked like people were still on it, so I approached, put my foot on the step and peered inside. Fifteen or sixteen people were there, all dead. Kamiyachō had been only two hundred and fifty meters from the hypocenter. They probably died instantly when the pressure of the blast wind caused their internal organs to rupture. Then they burst into flame and burned, together with the car. All of them were naked. I had my foot on the rear doorstep. I didn't really stare at them, but recoiled in shock. The doors and windows were charred. Only the skeleton of that train remained. I don't remember if it was hot or not. I don't think I grasped the doorframe when I looked in. I thought about taking a picture. I even put my hand on the camera. But it was so hideous I couldn't do it.

I did take a picture of people lined up to register for disaster relief. The seated policeman, his own head wrapped in a dirty bandage, was giving them documents to prove that they had suffered a disaster. With this piece of paper they could get rations, or board a train, as victims. In it you can see they're also passing out hard biscuits, one bag per person. I myself received one. We ate it that night. We had no water, no electricity. We had no idea when airplanes might come again.

I returned home about five o'clock. My niece came to the house. Her face and half her body were seriously burned. She couldn't get back to her own place. Her shoes had gotten stuck in the asphalt and come off, so she'd walked barefoot. The soles of her feet were burned and swollen. We had no medicine, so we just fanned her to cool her some. Maggots, like tiny threads of silk, many of them, were already infesting her wounds. Humans were burned, but flies survived. We spent the night sitting on the wreckage of the fire station. I could see fires burning in scattered places toward the center of town.

The next day we took our niece to the house of my wife's brother a little way out in the countryside. I'd evacuated my own child and my parents there a month previously. Luckily, none of us were seriously injured. We were able to stay overnight with my children. I had my camera on my shoulder, but I didn't take any more pictures those days.

I went back to the newspaper office on the ninth. There was no point in taking pictures, since there was no newspaper for them to appear in. But on the eleventh or twelfth of August I developed these pictures I had shot on the sixth. When the sun set I developed the film outdoors in a simple tray.

They appeared in the evening edition of the *Chūgoku Shimbun* a year later, on August 5, 1946. I was summoned to the Occupation GHQ together with the reporter who wrote the article. Despite what we expected, they weren't angry. We were told that it was all right to print those things, since they were facts, but they wanted us to submit them for review prior to publishing them. The American questioning us then asked me how many pictures I'd taken. I told him five. He asked me for copies of them, so I went back and made him prints in B5 size. When I brought them to him, he asked me to sign them. I started to write my name on the back, but he said, "No, no, sign on the front. It's OK to use Japanese," so I signed my name in characters on the face of the pictures taken August sixth.

I didn't feel any particular hatred toward the American or Australian soldiers who came to Hiroshima. I was actually an A-bomb victim, inside my house, but I never suffered directly from it. I am a shade anemic. I find it strange I haven't fallen ill. I'm often asked why I didn't take more pictures. Some even criticize me for that. It makes me angry. How can they ask such a thing? They didn't see the reality. It was too overwhelming. I wasn't the only one who had a camera that day. Other people walked around with cameras, but nobody else took pictures.

"Forgetting is a blessing."

KIMURA YASUKO

"I didn't hate the America that dropped the bomb. It was such a horrible time. I hated air raids. I hated war. To my child's mind, the bomb ended it all."

She now lives in Tokyo, where she and her husband run a small business making socks. We talk in her house next to the factory, where the sound of ten knitting machines, clattering away, can be heard.

Hiroshima was a military capital, full of army and navy facilities. Children in that town were all like minisoldiers. Everything was done to orders. We never doubted Japan would win. We were truly little patriots! When my mother wrote to me at where I'd been evacuated with my school, that I would be able to return home when the war was over, I was unable to forgive her. I was nine years old then. The teachers at the temple to which we were evacuated were very strict. We weren't allowed to take even one step outside the temple grounds except to go to school. Yet, the house mothers were very kind and gentle. That was our salvation. They were local village people, nineteen or twenty years old.

The temple was located on a high hill between Shimane and Hiroshima prefectures. From there we could look out and see the people coming along the road. Following that day in August, we saw many injured fleeing Hiroshima on the road. Somebody said, "Hiroshima's been attacked with a new type of bomb." Our teacher went there and brought back the news that all of Hiroshima had been destroyed.

The three hundred children of Noborichō National School at the evacuation point were all from families who'd lived within eight hundred meters of where the bomb was dropped, the hypocenter. We were part of a group evacuation, kids who had no other place to go. Only the children could be evacuated, so our families had all stayed in Hiroshima. Now we waited at the temple for some word from them. Somehow, some families managed to send messages like "Elder sister lived," or "Father is alive."

On August 15, the war ended. Group evacuation was officially suspended all over Japan, but the children of Hiroshima had no place to go. It was finally decided that they would send back any children who had received word from surviving family members. I remained where I was.

Children boast among themselves about anything. They say, "My grade's better than yours!" At the temple, we boasted about the numbers who had been killed. Those who had lost the most family members were the biggest braggarts. We were called forward by the teachers and told who in our family had died. We'd then go back and say, "I had three." A person who'd lost more could say, "I lost five," and they were superior. I thought, "three, just three." I was somehow envious. I even thought, "Five's better." We didn't know what dying meant. But when our evacuation ended, those who'd been belittled—"Only one of yours died"—well, they had someone to come and take them back early. That's when we learned what it meant to have five family members die. It meant nobody would come for you.

When they could assemble a group of thirty or forty children who had received word, they sent them back by truck and handed them over to relatives who met them in the burned-out ruins of Hiroshima. I got word that my father had survived. Finally it was my turn to go home.

We arrived in the early evening. The reddish setting sun hung in the sky. The ruins from an ordinary fire are burned black, aren't they? But the ruins of Hiroshima were brown, the color of unfired pottery. The glaze of the roof tiles was completely gone and they were spotted and mottled, all reddish brown. The city didn't look as if it had been burned. Yet it was flattened. In the middle of the ruins two buildings, a department store and the newspaper, stood alone. There, my father met me. He couldn't stand waiting at the assigned meeting place any longer, so he walked part of the way to meet my truck. I remember his figure standing there. Behind him was the stone wall of Hiroshima Castle. I remember the tears in his eyes when I met him.

I knew that Mother had died. When I was taken to a relative's house, there was a round flower vase with a piece of writing paper tied with packing twine. "This is Mother," Grandmother told me. It was eerie. Even with all the roof tiles knocked off and broken into bits, there was this completely unbroken vase. Its glaze had been burnt off. Its surface was rough. That, they told me, was her. I was frightened. I couldn't believe it. I drew back instinctively.

Mother must have died instantly, we think. I was told she was standing in the hall along the back of the house. Her ashes were found there. I was told that only bones were left. In an ordinary fire the body is burned black. You can tell that from the pictures of the Tokyo air raids. But here, only bones were left. White bones, lots of them.

That day, my elder sister, in her first year of girls' school, had been mobilized to clear the remains of demolished houses to make firebreaks. Almost all the schoolgirls and boys of the same age as my sister were killed. Perhaps ten thousand. My father searched and searched on the sixth, the day the bomb fell. And all day the next day, too. On the eighth he found her name at a hospital. He was told she'd died the previous day and had already been cremated. They piled all the bodies up, soaked them in gasoline, and then burned them. There really weren't any bones left. According to a nurse, she reached the hospital completely burned and called out, "Mother! Mother!" until the moment she died.

We don't know anything about my younger brother. He was six years old. Later, one of our neighbors told us that he was playing with his children, that he heard their voices until that moment. Even when people were burned to death you could usually find the bones and at least say, this is my house, so this must be them, but we found nothing. They must have been blown away somewhere.

That morning, Father and Grandmother were on the outskirts of the city, moving our luggage from temporary storage. Father entered the city immediately to search for the family, so he was exposed to radiation. My elder brother, who was in the second year of middle school and had been mobilized for factory work, also came into Hiroshima that day.

After I returned, I refused to let myself be separated from my grandmother. Wherever she went, I followed her. I didn't want to be alone. Whenever Granny bumped into someone she knew, before saying hello, they'd ask each other, "What were you doing when the flash came?" That was the greeting in Hiroshima. "How did you survive? How did your family members die?" That's what she asked everyone she met, and that's what they talked about again and again.

Wherever you went, you could see tiny bones. That was horrible. I couldn't stand those bones. The whole area had been burned down. No matter where you went you didn't bother to take the roads. Everything was flat, nothing was standing, no gates, pillars, walls, or fences. You just walked in a straight line to where you wanted to go. Practically everywhere you came across small bones that had been left behind. There just were too many to collect them all.

We moved to Tokyo when I was in the second year of high school. For the first time I wondered what Hiroshima had been all about. I had thought the whole of Japan was like that, but it was only Hiroshima. From then on, I wanted to forget. I was now far away from Hiroshima and in a sense I had nothing to do with it. I never really signed any petitions calling for the prohibition of atomic or hydrogen bombs. I thought it had nothing to do with me. A friend once asked, "Don't you think your mother was murdered?" "No, not particularly. It's the same as dying any other way, isn't it?" That was the way I answered. If you try hard to forget you can forget. If you have thirty years it's possible. I abhorred the word *Hiroshima*. If it came up, I wouldn't mention that I had family members who'd died there. On August 6 I refused to watch television and never read the newspapers.

I did feel some desire to see the place where as a schoolgirl I had been evacuated before the bomb. My life had been saved there. But I didn't make the trip until many years had passed. I couldn't remember anything about that time until I stepped from the car that took me there. It was the season when the rice was in flower, early August, and that fragrance brought everything back to me. In the midst of the rice fields, I had been told that my mother had died. I couldn't help crying. I didn't know why I was crying, but then the memories came pouring out. I began reading books and asking questions of my one surviving brother.

A number of years ago, a group of about a hundred of us went back again to our evacuation site in two buses. But we never asked each other what happened to our families. Nobody volunteered information about themselves and nobody asked. Not asking was the most considerate thing to do. There was no real need to ask. Everyone had someone killed.

That's one of the things about Hiroshima. You can talk about your own experience, but you can't speak for others. When you're able to sort out in your own mind what happened, only then are you at last able to speak of your own experiences. I only lost three. As many as three survived. I was one of the truly lucky ones. My father survived and was able to return and function in society. He brought me up properly before he died of cancer. Only three were killed, but it took me thirty years to reconcile myself to that.

My sister's classmates seem to feel differently from me. They were all mobilized from school and all were supposed to be there. I recently spoke with some of the girls who survived. They apologized to me for surviving. By chance, only those who played hooky and skipped labor service that one day lived. I told them to please go on living. To live life for my sister, too.

My brother is alive, but he was exposed to secondary radiation. It cases terrible pain. He lives in agony. He's a member of a *hibakusha* group. Members younger than he die one by one, and he thinks he'll be next. He takes sleeping pills. Even during the day he gets drunk from them. He's become that kind of drop-out. Even those who survive have their minds torn apart.

I'm sorry I fled from it for thirty years. I was the only one in the family who wasn't exposed to the atomic bomb. Had I actually been exposed, I would have thought about of how my family suffered, or how they died. Instead, I simply ran away.

PART SIX

The Unresolved War

IMPERIAL RESCRIPT

To Our good and loyal subjects:

After pondering deeply the general conditions of the world and the actual conditions obtaining in our Empire today, We have decided to effect a settlement of the present situation by resorting to an extraordinary measure. . . . We declared war on America and Britain out of Our sincere desire to assure Japan's self-preservation and the stabilization of East Asia, it being far from Our thought either to infringe upon the sovereignty of other nations or to embark upon territorial aggrandizement. But now the war has lasted for nearly four years. Despite the best that has been done by everyone—the gallant fighting of military and naval forces, the diligence and assiduity of Our servants of the State and the devoted service of Our one hundred million people, the war situation has developed not necessarily to Japan's advantage, while the general trends of the world have all turned against her interest. Moreover the enemy has begun to employ a new and most cruel bomb, the power of which to do damage is indeed incalculable, taking the toll of many innocent lives. Should We continue to fight it would not only result in the ultimate collapse and obliteration of the Japanese nation, but also it would lead to the total extinction of human civilization. Such being the case how are We to save the millions of Our subjects or to atone Ourselves before the hallowed spirits of Our Imperial Ancestors? This is the reason why We have ordered the acceptance of the Joint Declaration of the Powers. . . . We are keenly aware of the inmost feelings of all ye, Our subjects. However, it is according to the dictate of time and fate that We have resolved to pave the way for a grand peace for all the generations to come by enduring the unendurable and suffering what is insufferable. . . .

The 14th day of the 8th month of the 20th year of Shōwa
[August 14, 1945].

—*Nippon Times* August 15, 1945.

THE WAR THAT BEGAN at the Emperor's command in December 1941 was also brought to an official end by Imperial rescript, broadcast over the radio on August 15, 1945. That day the Japanese people heard the voice of "the living god" for the first time. The Emperor told them, in what qualifies as one of the great understatements in the history of politics, "The war situation has developed not necessarily to Japan's advantage, while the general trends of the world have all turned against her interest." Three years and eight months after his government had declared war, the Japanese were now asked to "bear the unbearable and endure the unendurable."

The conflict between states was ended by an exchange of diplomatic notes between Japan and the Allied governments. The first Occupation forces landed at Atsugi airbase outside Yokohama on August 28, 1945. On August 30 a plane brought General-of-the-Armies Douglas MacArthur to Atsugi so that he could assume his role as Supreme Commander Allied Powers in Japan. The instruments of surrender were signed on the battleship *Missouri* on September 2, officially ending the Second World War. These formalities were accomplished with remarkable ease and no apparent resistance in Japan. The day Japan surrendered to the Allies, in addition to the 4,335,500 men in uniform in Japan itself, there were officially 3,527,100 soldiers and sailors spread over the Asian mainland and the islands of the Pacific. Of these, some 1,125,000 were in China and 665,000 more were in Manchuria. From Okinawa to Burma, China to the Philippines, Japanese commanders took part in formal surrenders and read the Imperial rescript to troops who had until that moment been preparing for their "final battles."

But war does not so readily release its grip on either its victims or its practitioners. As the men and women in this section indicate, for the Japanese, the war—and the dying—did not stop simply because the governments involved had declared it over. In Manchuria alone, where Soviet troops attacked on August 9, 1945, another 180,000 Japanese colonists died or were killed at or after the war's end. For many of them, in fact, the war did not really begin until practically the day the nation surrendered.° Up to 700,000 Japanese—military men and male administrators or colonists from Manchuria—would continue their war at heavy labor in prison camps in the Soviet Union, some not returning

---

° Ienaga Saburō, *Taiheiyō sensō* [*The Pacific War*], 2nd ed. (Tokyo: Iwanami, 1987), pp. 293–95, states that there were 1,550,000 Japanese civilians in Manchuria at the end of the war.

to Japan for a decade or more. In 1990, joint Japanese-Soviet investigations determined that 62,068 of those men died in captivity.°

Elsewhere in an Asia already plunging into a chaotic series of civil wars, colonial wars, and national liberation struggles, millions of Japanese still in the field faced an uncertain future, suspecting that their homes and families thousands of miles distant might already have been destroyed. By the time of the *Missouri* signing, some of these soldiers had been recruited or impressed into Asia's new wars—sometimes as temporary police on the side of the old colonial regimes of Europe reasserting their claims to power in Indonesia, Malaya, and Indochina; sometimes on the side of Asian rebels calling for the "liberation" of their countries. In China, a rekindled civil war between Nationalists and Communists drew in not only Japanese soldiers captured before war's end, but also whole units that surrendered in August. On isolated islands, and in areas completely cut off from the Homeland, some officers and soldiers with no way to receive further orders, and no authority to act on their own, remained determined never to surrender, or to obey their last specific orders to hang on until the Imperial Army "returned for them." A few would hold out for decades.†

Not only the Japanese soldiers and civilians left overseas but those at home now had to fend for themselves amidst the devastated landscape of Japan's cities, the ruin of its industries, and a rural economy stripped of much of its resources in the last frantic struggles of 1945. With the removal of wartime discipline and constraints and the total collapse of a national food-distribution system, starvation became an everyday reality. War orphans reduced to street urchins, homeless beggars, impoverished women driven to prostitution, and abandoned people, physically or psychologically disabled by the war, seemed to fill the country. Koreans, forcibly merged into the Japanese "family" in 1910, now found themselves once more "independent," and thus ostracized as "foreigners" in the country they had toiled for and suffered from, receiving not even the pittance that the new government was able to provide to its own citizens.

For millions of Japanese caught up in a great national effort—who had supported the war for the sake of state, the Emperor, home, or family, out of duty, resignation, or in pursuit of ideals or grand ambitions

---

° *Asahi Shimbun,* June 20, 1990.

† See Hiroo Onoda, *No Surrender: My Thirty-Year War* (Tokyo: Kōdansha, 1974). Lieutenant Onoda, who finally surrendered in 1974 to a young Japanese journalist who found him and brought him orders from his former commander, describes his ordeal on the tiny island of Lubang in the Philippines. Yokoi Shōichi, a sergeant, had emerged just the previous year, after twenty-nine years in hiding on the island of Guam.

—the few final words ending it, while bringing relief or joy at being alive (or sometimes shame at having survived), coincided with a deep sense of abandonment. Without the formal structures that had guided them for so long, they found themselves left alone to pick up the broken bits of their lives. For the vast majority of Japanese—exhausted, hungry, demoralized, and now living in an occupied land—the war experience was somehow shoved out of public view, buried beneath the private pain.

In the defeated nation, larger questions of causality and responsibility were either passed along to a small group of leaders, deferred to the Americans who now ruled the country with their own views of how the war should be explained and interpreted, or left to the silent torment of individual memory. Sorting out the war experience found little place in the public sphere in a country where all that seemed to matter was rebuilding and starting again. Even the International Military Tribunal Far East, the so-called Tokyo War Crimes Trials, seemed to most Japanese to describe a world of elite maneuverings, coups, and plots, of military cliques and cabals, that few people could identify with their own experience of history. In the end, responsibility was affixed to twenty-five senior military men and civilians at the top of the Japanese government —the class A war criminals—who were convicted by the Allied judges of plotting against peace and blamed for inhuman acts and designs. Seven were executed on December 22, 1948, including former prime ministers Tōjō Hideki and Hirota Kōki. Although there were lower-level trials and executions of persons accused of ordering and committing "conventional" war crimes, there was no sense that the Greater East Asia War's causes, or all the barbaric acts inflicted in its name, had been given an airing.[*]

The Allied desire to establish a workable government in Occupied Japan, and the apparent willingness of Emperor Hirohito to work with General MacArthur—symbolized by a renunciation of Imperial divinity in January 1946—left the issue of Imperial responsibility for the origins and execution of the war largely unexplored. The Emperor, in whose name the government functioned and for whom soldiers and civilians had been told they were to die, was retained as a "symbol of the unity of the people" under the new constitution promulgated November 3, 1946.

In the defeated nation, the war that began with the euphoria of the attack on Pearl Harbor and the fall of Singapore and ended in the

---

[*] Kazuko Tsurumi, *Social Change and the Individual. Japan Before and After Defeat in World War II* (Princeton: Princeton University, 1970), pp. 138–40 discusses the fate of the class B and class C war criminals, as well as the more famous class A criminals tried in Tokyo. She states that of a total of about 4,000 persons "arrested as war criminals, 1,068 were executed or died in prison from 1946 to 1951." Just fourteen class A war criminals died, including seven by execution.

rubble of Hiroshima and Nagasaki now seemed more like a natural, or supernatural, catastrophe that had been survived, than a conscious choice of policy, and the earlier undeclared war in China was more or less ignored. Ironically, in the country whose leaders had wanted to mold "One Hundred Million Bullets of Fire" united in common purpose, and which had been excoriated by its enemies as "identical prints off the same photographic plate," * the war became the most individualized of events. Its excitements and terrors, locked within each heart, became a set of memories to be repressed, confronted, or endured, but largely not expressed, even within one's own family, hardly among one's peers, and certainly not explored in the public realm.

Instead of the nation gathering to explain how defeat had come, or working to understand the war in all its terrible diversity and horror, Japan drew no larger lessons or conclusions, and engaged in no real national debate. Each individual found himself or herself alone with only a private obligation to remember the dead to sustain their memories of those years of war. ∎

---

* See Frank Capra's film, *Know Your Enemy: Japan* (1945) in the *Why We Fight* series of films produced during the war.

20 / REVERSALS OF FORTUNE

Flight

FUKUSHIMA YOSHIE [2]

May 30, 1945, the Soviet Union announced that it would not be renewing the USSR-Japan Nonaggression Pact of 1941. War with the Soviet Union now became a likelihood and the Imperial General Headquarters accordingly issued orders to the Kwantung Army to withdraw to a defensive triangle in southern Manchuria, with the Korean border at its base. Troops were deployed southward, and many officers' families were sent south by rail. In northern Manchuria, and in areas along the Soviet border to the east, lived as many as 300,000 Japanese civilians and "agricultural pioneers." No efforts were made to evacuate these people, since the policy was to avoid "provoking" the Soviets.

When the Soviet forces finally entered the war against Japan on August 9, 1945, most able-bodied men among the settlers already had been called up by the Kwantung Army to replace troops dispatched to other theaters of war. Women, children, and old men, left in confusion in towns and villages in the forward areas, were scattered across the countryside by the first waves of the Soviet tank and air attacks. Tens of thousands died in a chaotic flight. Some were killed fighting the Soviets, others committed suicide individually or killed each other in mass suicides, while many others drowned crossing rivers, died of disease or starvation, or fell victim to bandits or Chinese irregular forces, including units of the Communist Eighth Route Army. Large numbers were raped and murdered by Soviet troops. The people of Manchukuo, which Japan had claimed to be the "harmonious land of the five races," turned against their Japanese masters. Many of the people who had been dispossessed by Japanese settlers now wreaked revenge on those who had conquered them.

Fukushima Yoshie, a kindergarten teacher, married a military vendor and settled with him in Tōnei [today Tungning], near the Soviet border north of Vladivostock. Her husband was called up in July 1945, leaving her at home with their infant son.

The ninth of August dawned a beautiful morning. I was giving breakfast to my dog, Esu, when I heard the sound of airplanes. It must be a drill, I thought. Then I heard *"Pa! Pa! Pa!"* and saw silvery things falling, shining in the sun. I telephoned the Kempei office because I knew someone in the military police, but nobody answered. I turned on the radio. It was about seven. An announcer read "News Bulletin! News Bulletin! The Soviet Union has broken diplomatic relations and declared war." The Soviets were coming! My son, Masaaki, had been born on September 25, 1944. He had just begun to walk, but wasn't fully weaned. I put him on my back and grabbed an emergency rucksack I had prepared earlier. I also took a tiny Buddhist sutra with me.

The world had been turned upside down. The residents of Tōnei had no idea which way to escape; everyone just wanted to go whatever way the Soviets weren't said to be coming. Some shouted, "Into the mountains!" Others, "Follow the rail lines!" Someone started off and everybody followed in a long line. But that night, when the Soviets caught up to us, we all fled in different directions. From that first night, you were totally on your own. If you ran into someone familiar, you greeted them and maybe walked together, but soon enough you were separated. I had no idea where we were. Tōnei was far into the wilderness of northern Manchuria. There were no roads, and I'd never seen a map.

It was hell. Perhaps the railway tracks would take us to Mukden. I found them and walked along them. Those who collapsed just died by the roadbed. But it wasn't long before you couldn't walk the rails anymore. The Soviets started using them to take surrendered Japanese soldiers toward the Soviet Union. We had to move into the mountains. They were a wilderness, sometimes even a primeval forest, and there were dead bodies all over the trails.

In the depth of the mountains, my son developed a fever. He had trouble breathing. I had abandoned the Japanese practice of carrying him on my back, and was holding him in front of me by this time. That was so I could see him better and offer him my breast. My son's breathing grew more and more labored and his fever shot up. I was beginning to think I'd have to die if he died, when a group of Japanese soldiers appeared. One of them was wearing the Red Cross insignia. He said immediately, "Measles. He probably won't make it, Ma'am. It's better for you to reconcile yourself to that." I begged to know what medicine he carried. He admitted he had some German-made medicine in an ampule good for pneumonia, but he was reluctant to waste even a child-size dose of it. I clung to his arm and begged him, tears streaming down my face. I wouldn't let go. Finally, he gave my son that medicine. It cured him.

There were many places we passed where the Japanese had fought savagely against the Soviets. We were afraid of being caught. If the Manchus found you, you'd be stripped of all you had. But the Soviet forces were the most frightening. They killed Japanese just for the sake of killing. I saw many who'd been bayoneted. Heaps and heaps of bodies in the wilderness of Manchuria.

Japanese soldiers gave us women hand grenades and told us to die with them if the time came. I threw mine away somewhere in the mountains. It was too heavy for me to carry even one day. They also gave us cyanide. There probably wasn't a single Japanese woman who didn't receive a little packet from military men with the admonition, "It would not be good for a Japanese woman to be raped." But I got so soaked, what with my sweat and the rain, that mine just melted away.

The situation we were in didn't allow anyone to look after somebody else for very long. Some soldiers would look reliable and be very affectionate to my son, patting and playing with him. But when the child cried at night, everybody hated me. The soldiers would ask me either to move away from them or kill my son. I encountered this situation many, many times. I resented the soldiers bitterly, but the day came when I was to see the matter from their side.

I again found myself walking along the railway tracks. I came across a little infant girl in a good kimono, lying on a neatly arranged pile of her things. She even had a little shade on to shield her from the sun's direct rays. Her parents must have died, or been killed, or left her in the hope that someone else would take her. That child was so precious, only about five months old. I held her in my arms, I now had two babies with me. This didn't last even a day. I felt terrible remorse. I left her near a Manchurian village where people would find her. When it comes down to saving your own child, you become like that.

I caught frogs and cooked them on sticks over a fire. Whenever it rained, "escargot" would come out and I'd eat them too. Somehow, my breast milk started to flow again. The leaves of the goosefoot plant were edible and rich in vitamins, so whenever I saw them, I picked them. Then I gathered grass to burn and boiled the leaves in a can. I was given matches sometimes. They were so valuable! I kept them dry no matter what. Without them you felt lonesome at night. You couldn't make a fire even if you wanted to. But I liked nighttime. Sleeping with my son for a few hours, I was able to forget my hardship. I always knew morning would come, though.

I have no idea where or how far I walked. I once got a ride for four days on a bumpy horse-drawn cart to the city of Botankō [Mutanchiang today]. That's where a Manchurian, Mister Ku, asked me to come to his place. He said he owned a theater. "I know people in authority, so come."

He claimed he was pro-Japanese and used to work for the Kempeitai. His Japanese was excellent, and from him I learned for the first time about the destruction of Hiroshima and Nagasaki. "Japan will never recover," he said. "Your husband, if he was a soldier, will probably be taken to Siberia. He will never return. You have a nice child. I want a Japanese child. Please become my wife." I refused. Mister Ku had three beautiful concubines, but their eyes looked strangely out of focus. Everyone at his house smoked opium at the same time each day. He showed me a bed made of ebony. Still I told him no. Again he asked me to marry him. That night around eleven o'clock I put my child on my back and opened the door. It was the end of October. Manchuria was already bitter cold. The skin on my hand stuck to the metal bolt of the gate when I slid it back to escape.

Sooner or later I found a freight train heading in the direction of Harbin. In the boxcar were five or six soldiers, deserters, who'd all gotten a place there by paying money. I was the only woman with half a dozen men. They had warm-looking fur coats. My son and I had only a dirty old blanket. For four or five days we traveled like that. Whenever the train stopped, Russians would come to investigate. One time, the train stopped and the baby cried. The soldiers got irritated, "Why do you let your baby cry? If they catch us they'll kill us." A kind man among them said, "If that happens, we'll just put up some money and pay off the Soviet soldiers." As we feared, the door to the car flew open. When they realized I was a woman they took my baby and tried to rape me. I cried out "*Spirochete, spirochete!*" That means "syphilis" in Russian. Besides, I'm sure they saw I had boils and sores from mosquito bites all over my body. Finally, they left me and the baby alone.

Several days after that, the train stopped for a long time. Diarrhea got really severe. I couldn't eat. Not even bread. My son, too, had diarrhea. I couldn't endure any more. The sunlight streamed into the train. One of the soldiers had opened the door and was going to relieve himself. It seemed like we must be near Harbin. We'd already come quite far south. I looked out the door. It was a long way down to the ground. I held my son and jumped. He was all I could hold. I left behind the few things I still had, including my last pictures of my husband, but I still had the tiny Buddhist sutra inside my clothes next to me.

I don't remember how far I walked before I reached the city of Harbin. The whole area was in total confusion. Japanese beggars, Manchurians, and boastful Russians now settling in to run it, all mixed up together. A free lodging place for evacuees from the distant areas like ours had been set up in the former Musashi Department Store. I took up lodging there. It was quite large, and a great many people were there.

There wasn't any heat—nothing but a pile of sorghum husks. You'd huddle together under them to get some warmth. "Typhus is spreading, so be careful," people warned me. I decided to put up an advertisement announcing that I was here. I'd seen many such announcements on electric poles and walls. I wrote, "Mr. Fukushima Masaichi: Yoshie made it here. Please contact me at the Musashi."

The thing I did most was beg. I think I could be a beggar even now. You simply say, "Help. Please help me." As long as you don't have any pride or feel humiliated, it's easy. Eventually, I borrowed enough cash to go into the business of selling tobacco one cigarette at a time. It was warm in the sun. Carrying my son, I took up a place where lots of Japanese passed by. I would describe my husband and then ask them if they'd seen him. But I didn't even know the name of his unit. His name alone, Fukushima Masaichi, wasn't enough. Yet I did see people find each other that way.

Eventually, my son and I were able to return to Japan. It was February 1947. I remember how green the wheat seemed as we approached the port of Sasebo. My mother-in-law met me at the station when we finally got to Kanazawa, so I knew my husband wasn't back yet. For years I lived thinking alternately that he might be alive or that he was already dead.

One day in 1955, I received a letter from a man in Tochigi prefecture. He wrote, "Fukushima Masaichi, who died in my prison camp four hundred miles from Moscow, might be your husband." He had been dead since May 18, 1946.

Today, I get my own pension and my husband's memorial pension, and my son helps me out. We now run the two nursery schools I've built since I "retired." I have finally achieved piece of mind. But a few times a year, when the Japanese children who were left behind in China come to Japan to look for their families, it all suddenly comes back to me. My son says, "I could have been like that." When I see those people, I feel guilty at the life I'm now leading. I'm this happy and they're still suffering from that war.

From Bandung to Starvation Island

IITOYO SHŌGO

He was an official in the Ministry of Commerce and Industry before the war. "I was feeling pretty important, having been appointed an Imperial official. But I feared I'd be called up as a common soldier, even though I was married and had been classified C in my army physical. So I volunteered to go to the very front line as an administrator. Because I made that choice, I'm alive today."

After the war, he worked at the renamed Ministry of International Trade and Industry. Seventy-one, he is now retired. Ballroom dancing is his hobby.

When I was first in Djakarta, as a general administrator sent from the industrial division of the Ministry of Commerce and Industry, I really didn't need to know Malay. But in October 1944, I was transferred to the Bandung Industrial Laboratory. Malay was essential for that job, and the language studies I'd taken up after my arrival really paid off. There were about one hundred and twenty workers from seven or eight different countries—Germans, White Russians, Chinese, Dutch, and native people from all over. It required special abilities to achieve communication through Malay and win cooperation for the Japanese administration of the occupied areas. Everyone else was hesitant to take this position, but I thought it would be very challenging.

Prior to our arrival, the lab had specialized in testing thread, wire, and other industrial materials for their tensile strength and capacities to withstand stress. All the material and equipment necessary for advanced research were available, but the documentation was entirely in Dutch, and we weren't allowed to use Dutch. Besides, the Japanese army told us, "Basic research isn't needed now. That's for peacetime. Make something useful. This is war." So we went to work making electrodes for use as detonators for dynamite. We also developed high-sensitivity photographic paper for aerial photography.

A Japanese, Hayashi Shūichirō, was in charge of the detonators, and a White Russian named Tiessen was put in charge of photographic paper. We were told Tiessen was very bright, but we were warned to be cautious. It was not clear to what extent he was utilizing his full abilities. The workers had all been there in the Indies from before the war. They often claimed they didn't have a certain essential piece of equipment, or required special supplies, always unavailable. I sensed that they were spending more time making demands than they were working. It was a kind of sabotage.

At home I had a chauffeur, a gardener, a cook, a male servant, and a female servant. I had a grand residence in the best part of Bandung. It was just like when the American forces moved into the finest neighborhoods of Akasaka, Tokyo, in the Occupation. I had a garage, a car. Bananas and papayas grew in my garden. I had a guest room, dining room, three bedrooms, and detached quarters for my servants. There I lived with Sakai, the head of the laboratory—just the two of us.

We needed to have documents available to us, so we were able to secure an exception from the army to use Dutch workers. We negotiated with the Kempeitai to use Dutch from the POW camps. The Dutch working at our research site had all been in the camps. Their families were allowed to lead normal lives outside. I went to the camp by car at ten o'clock and picked up those we needed. They worked until four, and then I took them back. It was only human to develop a relationship with such people, even though they were prisoners. We let them meet their families behind the backs of the military police. They were very appreciative. Many of their families were making their living by selling what they owned to us. Some were even high-class call girls with Japanese partners.

One day the Kempei came to pick up Tiessen. He was then chief of one of our most important technological areas. He was actually a spy. I was told he had hidden a shortwave radio in the ceiling at his home. That was June 1945.

On August 14, we were told there would be an important announcement the next day. Reception was so poor that we couldn't really make out what was coming in on the radio. We couldn't understand what the Emperor was saying, so we called the headquarters of Field Marshal Terauchi, commander of the Southern Area Army, to ask what we should do. The Southern Area Army was going to fight to the last, they told us. We should continue our work as before. The next phone call we got informed us of Japan's defeat. Give up everything. Surrender to the British-Indian Army. Orders changed completely. Things were in total confusion. That day was truly painful. Everyone was staring at us. I sensed sharp, beastlike glares. After a while, I couldn't take it anymore. I closed my door. Sakai and I just threw ourselves down on the floor and cried out loud, uncontrollably, without regard for status, position, or the consequences. Thus, overseas, I experienced the collapse of our nation.

On the sixteenth of August, Tiessen appeared before us. His form still floats before my eyes to this day. He was covered with grime and sweat. He had a strange smell. His beard was overgrown. He loomed in front of me like Niō-sama [one of the frightening guardian gods at a temple gate]. He slammed his fist down on my desk as if trying to break it. He shouted, *"Nippon kara!"*—meaning Japan's completely defeated. "Do you know what that means? Do you repent what you have done?" He told me he'd been tortured by the Kempeitai, but said, "Look at me. I'm back now!"

We fell from heaven to hell overnight. Until that moment, I had reigned with impunity as an administrator in the midst of other races. Now, I was under the British-Indian Army Command. The officers were all British. The sergeants were all Indians, mostly Gurkhas. We were taken to the camps where the Allied captives had been held. The next day, we were stripped naked, except for our shorts. Even our undershirts were taken. We were paraded down the main avenue of the town over which we had ruled, where the British were now ensconced in the high-class residences where we used to live. We were told to clean the filth from stopped-up toilets. That was the beginning of our humiliating work. Naked, we cleaned the roads, in plain sight of onlookers of all sorts. If we relaxed even a little, they kicked and beat us, called us shirkers or accused us of sabotage. It was really worse than dying. Everybody I knew in Indonesia was watching me. [*His eyes fill with tears.*]

The Indian soldiers were fairly good to us. Out of sight of their officers, they'd let us slack off at our labor, and they discreetly gave us food. They told us they, too, had suffered under the British as a colony. We understand your situation, they'd say. They were relatively generous to us Japanese from the yellow race. They were like gods of mercy. Between seven hundred and a thousand people were in our camp. I'm ashamed of myself to admit that we sank to the depths. We fought among ourselves for scraps of foods. The overseas Chinese I'd used at my home, and Indonesians, too, brought me bread and fruit. For the first time, I myself had been degraded. In that forlorn state, I came to understand the warmth of the human spirit.

It was a terrible time. We were forced by the Allies to scrub the runways of airfields with wire brushes under the scorching sun. You got so thirsty you felt you would faint, but there was no water. It was two kilometers away. To get water you had to run there, drink, and run back. Many collapsed of sunstroke every day. Our skin blistered. We told them we weren't soldiers and asked to be excused from heavy labor. We were told, "Japanese are all the same. Civilian or not. If you don't do as we say, we'll kill you." British army policy seemed to be to imbue in us the consciousness of our defeat, physically, mentally, even spiritually. We were there from August to February 1946.

Finally, we were taken to Tanjon Priak, a harbor. There a British officer questioned us, one by one. He spoke clear Tokyo dialect. He asked us the date of our arrival, our job, our rank. He already had a complete list in front of him. There was no point in lying. We were given white, blue, or red cards. I learned later that red was for war criminals, blue for those under suspicion, and white for those not guilty. I was given a white card. I got really excited, since those with white cards were going to board a ship. It was April and we would be going home!

But the ship turned out to be only a five-hundred-tonner—much too small to get to Japan. After the ship started moving, we learned we were heading for Galan Island. There were two islands, Galan and Renpan, about three hours from Singapore. Several tens of thousands of men from the armies in Malaya, Burma, and Java were being shipped to those islands. On our arrival, I was appalled by the people who met us. They were hanging onto walking sticks. Their limbs were swathed in bandages. With their rotting flesh and oozing pus, I thought they were lepers, but it turned out they were suffering from the tropical ulcers that come from extreme malnutrition and the breakdown of your circulatory system. Even if you got only a mosquito bite, the next thing you knew, you'd developed a running sore. Within five or six days I looked just like them. You don't ever really recover.

There was no natural source of water. The islands were less than ten kilometers in circumference, and located at the equator. April through June was the dry season. The weather was sweltering. No grasses or trees grew there. There was only a reef, not even a proper harbor. The British Army in Singapore delivered water in tanks once a week. People were dying. When I tried to wake my neighbor one morning, he didn't move. Dead. They had us make a road on that island. My guess is that there was no real purpose for it.

It was more hellish than hell. We were issued only seven *shaku* of rice per day, less than half a cup. We ate snakes, frogs, anything living on the island. Even the rats there were just skin and bones. From where I was, there seemed to be a beach two or three kilometers away. We heard the rumor that men from the Agriculture, Forestry, and Fisheries Ministry were there, living high by fishing. I paid them a visit, as a fellow bureaucrat. When I got there, I couldn't believe the wildness of the ocean. How could such an untamable sea exist? The edges of the reef were like razor blades. The Fisheries men had made shoes from a vine that clung to the island's few coconut palms, and wearing these they could walk out into the water. They'd catch fish with spears they'd somehow fashioned. I asked them if they could spare one for me. They just said, "Get one yourself. You can't live here by begging."

Even at night, if you had something next to you while you were asleep, it would be gone by morning. It was a matter of life and death. Scholarship, school records, career—none of that meant anything there. The strong won. Near the end, an observer team from Geneva came, after learning that such a horrible place existed. Then the food got better. We were issued combat rations. We were given only breakfast, but I thought I'd never eaten such delicious food in my life. That tiny box contained tinned corned beef, butter, cheese, four or five cigarettes, and some sugar. It was really compact. We ate with tears streaming down our faces. When I saw those rations I realized Japan's defeat had been inevitable. I was on that island for forty days until the former Japanese aircraft carrier *Hōshō* came to pick us up on May 25, 1946.

Recently I went back to Indonesia with my wife after forty-two years. I visited the site of Bandung Industrial University and the laboratory where I worked, and the place where my official residence had been. Forty years had changed everything. I'd spent four years down there. We worked hard for everybody. I'm sure there were merits and demerits to what we did, probably divided fifty-fifty. The sad thing is they don't remember us at all. When I'd ask someone if they remembered our laboratory, they'd only respond, "I don't know." Whatever I asked, they only said, "I don't know." Young and old alike. The same response. Maybe for them it was just a dirty period. But I regret that. That thought leaves me feeling desolate.

"The Army's been a good life."

TANIDA ISAMU [2]

We meet in his comfortable home in Kōenji in Tokyo. Today, the ninety-three-year-old former lieutenant general wears a dark blue linen kimono without a single wrinkle. He gestures liberally to illustrate his points, twisting imaginary mustachios, and laughing in a loud, full roar, his eyes twinkling with the humor he sees in his situation.

I was in the army for many years, but I never fought a battle. I heard the sound of the guns for a grand total of about fifty days when we landed in Hangchow Bay and occupied Nanking, and then pacified the "Triangle Area" between there and Shanghai. I never actually saw the artillery firing then, because I was always at headquarters behind the lines. When I was chief-of-staff of the Thirty-Eighth Division, before they went to the South, I both saw and listened to the guns for ten days. Small-arms fire flew by me for only two days. That's all—a couple of days in a military career of thirty-some-odd years. I was that kind of pathetic military man!

After my years in China and Manchuria, I was assigned to help head up a department on the general staff back in Tokyo, while the division I'd been with, the Thirty-Eighth, went to Guadalcanal. Almost as soon as I got back to Japan, in March 1943, I called on my former superior officers who had been forced to resign from the army at the time of the February 26, 1936, Incident. They asked me if I wouldn't say things within the army councils that their lack of position made it impossible for them to say, like "End the war at a reasonable point," or "Let's undertake maneuvers to bring about peace." I agreed and began to make the rounds, calling on senior men who still had influence to sound them out, although I was only a major general.

In May, a Kempeitai warrant officer dressed in civilian clothes came to visit me at my home. He addressed me as "Your Excellency," but then described how I'd visited Mr. So-and-So and General Such-and-Such, and had said thus-and-so, running over what I had done in the course of my peace moves. There was no point denying it, since they had it all down pat, so I said, "Yes, indeed, that's what I did." A week later I was ordered to take command of a signals unit in Rabaul on New Britain in the Southern Area.

This time I really was on the front lines! I was in charge of communications for the Eighth Area Army. For any links with the outside, we had to rely entirely on wireless communication, since our sea and air routes were so tenuous. All orders from Tokyo had to go through my units. The commander of the Eighth Area Army, General Imamura Kin, often asked me if he couldn't give my men more gasoline! It would have been all over for him if we'd run out, so they treated me very well. Since from the beginning of the war, men and material tended to concentrate there at Rabaul because of the excellent harbor. The spearhead of a unit might be sent out, but its main body and headquarters would get bottled up when they couldn't be sent on. Supplies piled up. We had more than we really needed—more than we could even use.

American broadcasts from Sydney, Australia, came in. I gathered together all the soldiers with good foreign-language and communications techniques and assembled a special group to monitor foreign broadcasts scientifically. I'm sure they were doing this back in Japan, but we who were in the forward area could pick up all the broadcasts. We sent reports back to Tokyo, and Imperial General Headquarters was pleased, as were all the specialists in that area. More immediately, my area army commander was happy with the praise it brought our unit. In Rabaul, some low-level units still had good radio receivers, but in early 1944, I sent the Kempei around to confiscate them because it was felt that it wouldn't be good if the way things were going leaked out. Only a small clutch of people in communications and headquarters then knew the situation abroad. One of them is sitting here now! My unit received all the information about the world situation for an entire area army. That meant I could saunter around glorying in my special status.

By 1944, all communication by air and sea was cut off. I was promoted to the rank of lieutenant general, but I was unable to move to another command more appropriate to my rank. The navy lost that war! Transportation lines were severed out in the middle of the Pacific Ocean. Those like me who were placed in isolated areas couldn't even change postings when they got promoted. They were just stuck wherever they were.

In August 1945, our army was preparing for enemy attack. We'd dug caves capable of withstanding direct hits from ten-ton bombs. We'd gathered and stored food for self-sufficiency. All soldiers, regardless of their branch of service or specialty, had been given combat training and drilled in hand-to-hand fighting. That was the policy of the area army commander in Rabaul. Although we weren't bombed much during the day, enemy reconnaissance planes were over us constantly. The men were keyed up and waiting for instructions to prepare for their *gyokusai* battle.

But we in communications already knew on August 12 what proposals the Allies were making to Japan, and we knew through Allied broadcasts that we would accept, although our side was still setting conditions. I felt that I would never forgive myself if I let my men die now, two or three days before surrender, yet I believed that, should I stop those final battle exercises, I'd be thought a weak commander by my officers. My regimental commander was looking to me for orders.

The broadcast announcing the end of the war was received by my section first. At 8:30 on the fifteenth. I remember it, because as I looked at my watch, the head of the special communication group responsible for monitoring foreign broadcasts—a man from the Communications Ministry—handed me a small piece of paper bearing only the words: "San Francisco Broadcast: Japan Surrenders to Us—Truman."

Thinking, "It's finally come," I ordered the men to assemble in fifteen minutes. I called over my senior staff officer, an engineering classmate of mine. I'd known him since childhood. I showed it to him, and asked. "What do we do?" When we were together, just the two of us, we spoke like friends, but when anyone else was present we spoke with language full of respect, colonel to lieutenant general. We decided not to announce this immediately.

When the men gathered again, I told them we would suspend our exercise at that point. I said not to worry about being attacked, even if they were in their cars, and ordered them to drive straight back to their units. At the same time I said, "If any disputes break out with the natives, resolve problems in favor of the natives." They all looked puzzled, but a few bright ones seemed to get my point from that clue. The meeting broke up a little after nine. At noon came the Emperor's broadcast. We used our technical power to pick it up. The radiomen at area army headquarters weren't specialists, so their radios couldn't really get it, but we at signals received it, understood it, and sent it on to them perfectly. The chief-of-staff was most pleased with our work.

As you can imagine, I still remember the moment the war ended very well. We were gathered together by area army commander General Imamura. He just came in, guided by an adjutant, read the Imperial Rescript, and then left. He's written several books about this since the war. In them he described this gathering on the night of the fifteenth of August, 1945. He always says that when he read the Rescript everyone wept bitterly and issued loud lamentations. He wrote that the one who cried loudest was Tanida. But I knew the news beforehand. Rather than weeping bitterly, I was practically laughing. It all seemed so strange to me. He's got it wrong.

General Imamura Kin calculated that it might take as long as four years for us to get home to Japan, since so many of our own ships had been sunk. In any event, General Imamura thought it would be terrible to have to just sit there for years waiting for transport home, so we started a program of job training. At Rabaul there were about twenty-five thousand navy men and about seventy-five thousand army men.

To train all these men, we gathered together teachers. There were no books on what kind of country Japan was then. According to our radio, the Communists were all coming out of prison and swaggering about, so we came up with the idea of offering our men spiritual education. Imamura told me to write a textbook on it. I didn't know anything about it, but I had a man under me who liked logic, so I made him write it. The book was completed the last day of 1945, just the day before His Highness declared that he wasn't a god anymore. In our book, we talked about how Japanese history has had no revolutions, no *coups d'état*, only "restorations"—just as I would describe it today.

In the end, we were lucky and I returned from Rabaul in November 1946. My superiors were all taken off to be investigated as war criminals, but I had nothing to do with war crimes, so I sailed home on the last repatriation ship, a Japanese destroyer, as the senior officer.

Defeated in the war, I ended up a penniless *rōnin*—a masterless samurai—but looking back on the past, I've never thought I lost anything by becoming a military man. The army's been a good life. There must be people who think they made a mistake, but not me.

21 / CRIMES AND PUNISHMENTS

Death Row at Changi Prison

ABE HIROSHI [2]

His hand-drawn pictures of Changi Prison and P Hall, where he was held when under sentence of death as a B/C class war criminal, are neatly laid out, ready for examination. So is a worn Bible. "I wrote my will in the margins of this book and it was smuggled out of prison to my father in Japan."

His voice is full of energy. "A friend of mine who fired mountain artillery at the battle of Imphal recently went to Britain and took part in a Burma War Comrades Convention with his English counterparts. I don't think they'll ever do that for the Burma–Siam Railroad."

Major Cyril Wild was liberated from the prisoners' camp where I had been when the war ended and became chief for Southeast Asia for the War Criminal Investigation Bureau. He wanted revenge. I was the first one he went after. They went right to the railway unit, staged line-ups, and looked carefully at each man, but couldn't find one. I wasn't with the unit at the end of the war. I was in a hospital in Bangkok. A year later, the night before I was to board a repatriation ship—I already had my ticket—I was informed that I would be staying. All of us pulled off were related either to the railroad unit or the Kempeitai. We were taken to Singapore. They'd finally caught the "war criminal" Abe Hiroshi!

The indictment from the War Criminal Investigation Bureau said that First Lieutenant Abe was responsible for everything. He'd violated the "Laws of War" by forcing prisoners of war to engage in war work and had placed them in improper conditions without sufficient food or medicine, resulting in the death of large numbers. Just by looking at the charges, I could see that they only wanted somebody to blame for what happened. They didn't accuse me of beating prisoners up or things like that. It was almost as if I were a Class A war criminal, responsible for plotting the whole thing. On the fourth day of my trial, Wild, now a colonel, was himself going to come to Singapore from Tokyo, where he was testifying at the Tokyo War Crimes Tribunal against the big fish.

There had been some fifty thousand POWs in all working on the Burma–Siam Railroad. Wild was in the camp known as Songkrai. That was my place. A senior staff officer under Percival, the British commander who'd surrendered Singapore, Major Wild was liaison officer at my camp. I saw his face every day, since it was to me he came to make appeals. He spoke some Japanese, as he'd once been a schoolteacher in Wakayama prefecture. Sometimes I had an interpreter. What Major Wild always said was this: "Abe-san. Using POWs for this work is against the Geneva Convention, so please stop." The same thing every day. I told him, "I have been ordered to build a bridge using you people. You're here to help. You will follow orders." I didn't really know anything about the Geneva Convention, except that something like it existed. For us Japanese, becoming a prisoner was itself the greatest shame imaginable. It was the same as death. The rail unit had a regimental commander, battalion commanders, and company commanders. I had many superior officers. I was just a second lieutenant at the time, in command of a platoon. But I was the only officer Wild knew in the Fifth Railroad Regiment.

The moment the Allied captives arrived at Songkrai, a cholera epidemic broke out. A unit dedicated to preventing infectious diseases in the water supply was brought in. I was very concerned and asked them to check all the prisoners, a process that involved an examination in which a glass bar was inserted in their rear-ends and then cultures developed. I looked into the culture dishes myself. All the prisoners, without exception, had the cholera bacillus, so every prisoner was susceptible to coming down with the disease if he grew physically weak. I recommended to my battalion commander that they be given a chance to rest. After two or three days, the answer came back, "The work can't be delayed even a single day. We must complete our assigned task. We have to keep working, even if the prisoners are reduced to the last man."

I had to build that bridge. I felt genuinely sorry for the captives, but I was in no position to actively improve their conditions. In fact, it wasn't even supposed to be of concern to me what the conditions were in the prison camps. That was the problem of the guard unit. Fukuda Tsuneo was the deputy commander of the guard unit, under Lieutenant Colonel Banno. I always went to Fukuda to ask for more prisoners to work on the bridge. Once, I actually asked Fukuda, "Don't you have any medicine?" It's true, though, that I didn't try to get medicine for them on my own initiative. We had to have human labor because we didn't have machines. One captive didn't equal one man's work, but the big shots didn't think it out. They just drew a line on a map and ordered us to finish by some date they made up.

The prisoners didn't exactly work. They resisted in silence. Officially they worked three hours in the morning, had an hour of rest, then worked four hours in the afternoon, but they were just skin and bones. They couldn't labor any more than that. Just watching them made me tired. Cholera was like having a bomb in your body. A fever would suddenly break out while you were working. Complete dehydration followed. We'd have to have them taken back to camp for treatment. If we'd been able to give saline injections they would have survived, but we had no medicine, not a bit for tens of thousands of them.

All we had for the captives' meals were a few skinny water buffalo. We gave them three a day and let them distribute it themselves. There wasn't anything there they would have wanted to eat. No beef. No eggs. No British tea. Just some unpalatable rice from us Japanese and water buffalo. There were no vegetables at all. They'd catch malaria, then cholera. Our camp was right in front of the bridge. That's where the prisoners slept. In the morning sometimes thirty corpses, wrapped in pieces of cloth made from rushes, had been rolled out from the prisoners' barracks. It rained there from morning to night, every day. There was nothing you could do but cremate them. The healthy prisoners handled the corpses. One group cut trees for the fires, another burnt the corpses. Yet they didn't always burn. Here and there, the bodies just piled up like cordwood. Sometimes the wind from those burning bodies blew toward me.

I really didn't do anything wrong. It was my fate to go there. I just worked there. I protected them. There was no reason for me to treat them cruelly and weaken them. I paid careful attention to their health. They were our source of labor. In many ways, I tried to help them. I even brought in a mobile water-purification vehicle to kill the germs in their drinking water.

If you'd beaten one of them, even once, you got ten years. Twice meant twenty. If one of them had died, it was a death sentence. If they knew your name, that was the end of you. In my case, thirty-one hundred died. I didn't have a chance. Our rail units included a lot of hot-blooded men. If a prisoner looked lazy or seemed to be loafing, he'd be beaten up. But it wasn't that we'd just kicked or punched one or two—over three thousand had *died*.

The railroad unit, the engineer unit, and the prison guard unit were all tried together. I knew immediately that they wanted each group to denounce the others so that they could convict all of us. That was the prosecution strategy. We consulted the night before the trial. Everyone was quiet. I remember the rumbling of thunder. I told Lieutenant Colonel Banno that I would say that the guard unit did their best, that things ended up the way they did simply because there wasn't any food or medicine. I asked him not to badmouth us railroad men. I said, I'm sure that if you wanted to say things about us you can find plenty to say —that we hit them, beat them, forced them to work—but I told him, "We knew you were playing mah-jongg while we were out in the river, risking our lives in rushing water up to our necks. What good would it do to repeat all of that in this trial? We did our best, all of us, didn't we? What happened was a tragedy. That should be our strategy." Banno thought about it for an hour. Finally, he said, "Let's go with that, Abe." Nobody opposed our resolution. Even the two Koreans, who'd been among the enlisted guards, went along without objection.

Death certificates, one for each individual POW, were piled up on a table at the trial. We couldn't say we didn't know. When a man died, their doctor wrote out a medical certificate, stuffed it into a bamboo stalk, and secretly buried it. When the war was over they dug all the records up. Wild had always been asking for paper every time he came to me. "Abe-san, we don't have enough paper. We don't have enough pencils." Wild's the one who told me Germany was losing the war and Japan would, too. Normally a prisoner would have had his face slapped for such a comment. "Where did you get that kind of information?" everyone would have demanded. But while I didn't like the news, I pretended I didn't hear it. There wasn't any reason for Wild to hate me.

We were given a real lawyer, Major Waite, as our defense attorney. He was a true gentleman. He could even speak some Japanese. On the first day he shook hands with all seven of us and said, "I was a prisoner on the Burma Railroad myself, but that has nothing to do with the job I've been assigned to now. I'll do my best to fight your case with all my skill as a lawyer." And he did. He asked probing questions, which touched the core of the issues at stake. For instance, some former POWs testified during our trial that some British soldiers were given impure water and came down with cholera. Waite made these witnesses admit that the responsibility for contracting cholera rested not with the Japanese, but with the British soldiers themselves. After all, they were the ones who drank the water, despite orders that no one should do so without boiling it first.

He cleared a path in this way, but the fact was that thirty-one hundred prisoners had died, nobody could deny that. Yet could they prove that the process which led to that fact was a willful one, or done maliciously, with purposeful cruelty? The judge at the trial was a British lieutenant colonel. He didn't seem to comprehend the severity of wartime conditions. He'd probably never been in the hell of a battlefield.

Wild was to appear on the fourth day of our trial, but when that day came, the court was in confusion. We were told that a plane carrying

Wild had crashed in Hong Kong. All the Japanese in Changi Prison cheered when we heard that. The court was in recess for about a week or so until they could bring in a first lieutenant from Australia. He knew nothing about the railroad. He simply said whatever they coached him to say. The trial lasted about three weeks in all.

The British army gave our trial heavy coverage. Every day, their papers carried photos of our faces with stories saying, "The evil devils of the Burma–Siam railroad of death are lined up here. Send them to the gallows." I could see those papers on my way to the court. I was sure this was sweet revenge. They didn't bother me much, but what did get to me was the way we Japanese accused each other. When my first regimental commander came all the way from Tokyo to testify at my trial, I thought the Old Man had gathered up his courage to come to our defense, but he'd been intimidated. They told him, "Whether or not you'll be indicted depends on your testimony." I couldn't really harbor ill feelings against him. Besides, he assured me again and again, "You'll be spared. You'll be saved."

I got death. Banno got three years. Fukuda got death. Tōyama, a Korean, got death. Captain Maruyama of the engineers got death. The camp doctor, a captain, only got seven years, despite three thousand deaths. The other Korean got only four or five years.

They wanted to get me. I represented the rail unit. I don't think Fukuda did anything that deserved death. Sure, he hit prisoners, even beat them. They saw him as the person with the real power. Lieutenant Colonel Banno was the boss, but the British viewed him as old and incapable of keeping things under control. But they could tell that that one Korean guard was clever, so maybe they viewed him as a sinister figure.

When we had been convicted, we were sent back to Changi Prison. The clothes we'd worn at the trial were exchanged for dirty brown prisoners' uniforms marked prominently with the letters "CD," indicating we'd been convicted and sentenced to death. I walked into P Hall October 25, 1946. Each morning at six-thirty we were rousted out to wash up. Later, we just gathered half-naked in an open space surrounded by cells under the blazing sun. Those who'd been there a while had their regular spots. There wasn't anything for us to do. We had amusements like go and shōgi and we had some things to read and we could write. The only sure thing was that we would very soon be killed.

I thought about death. Pointing to my neck, I asked Doctor Nakai, who was also in P Hall, "What's going to happen in here?" He explained to me how the bone snaps and you die instantly. It helped me to hear that. Yet I was conscious that I had developed a second-by-second approach to my fate. Could I be calm to the final instant? I didn't want to be an embarrassment, an object of ridicule, at the last moment.

"You'll love this!" said a particularly nasty guard, and opened the door leading to the gallows, letting me see into the execution room. A ramp sloped up to it for perhaps five meters, covered with straw matting, probably to prevent slipping. Execution occurred from eighty to ninety days following sentencing. When I entered P Hall, the interval between executions had grown to about a month. Soon after the end of the war executions had taken place almost every week. One time fourteen were executed on a single day.

Executions took place only once while I was in P Hall. Nine people were to die. On the eve of execution, we gave a feast for the condemned. We called it "the last supper." We sang songs to cheer them on. We didn't have any saké, but we acted drunk. Those who knew ballroom dances danced even without partners. We sang until we were so exhausted we dozed off. The morning soon came.

Three times they took groups of three from their cells and led them away. At nine o'clock, nine-thirty, and ten. They led them through the door to the gallows. That door was next to my cell. Everyone tried to avoid that particular cell, but I was a newcomer. I put my hands together and prayed for those who were dying. There was an opening high up in the cell wall for ventilation, through which I could clearly hear their last cries. The actual distance to the gallows was five or six meters. British soldiers did all the work in silence. There were no orders, no signals, nothing. Through the silence you could hear certain sounds: the turning of a chain, the trap door falling away, the horrible sound at the moment they dropped. Hanging by the neck, they probably died instantly, but they weren't taken down until a doctor confirmed their heart had stopped. You could hear footsteps of people moving around. How many, I couldn't tell.

When three were executed at once, two men were assigned to each of them, one on each side, to take each person up the scaffold to be killed. It happens so quickly. They make them stand on a fixed spot, bind their legs together, put the noose around their necks, and tighten it. They attach sandbags to those who aren't heavy enough. Between the completion of the work and the final moment, there were about twenty to thirty seconds, just time for cries of "Banzai!" At the top of the scaffold stood six people besides the condemned. Next to the gallows, one more. Others were underneath the scaffold. Altogether maybe sixteen to twenty were involved. There were witnesses invited from the outside and a coroner from the War Crimes Investigation Bureau. Press, too. But I didn't hear any talking at all.

After a while a second door opened and the next group was taken toward the room. The people who were going shouted without fail, "Thank you for your hospitality!" and "I go in good spirits." All the rest of us shouted back, "Go in high spirits." While they were saying that, hoods were being put over their heads and their hands were being tied behind their backs. They were taken by their two guards through that door. We were confined to our cells. In that room nearest to the gallows I thought I had to dare to hear everything because it was all going to fall on me eventually.

Some time after the completion of the executions, they let us out of our cells and told us to look after the possessions of those who'd been executed. They unlocked their three cells. Their rooms had all been carefully cleaned. They'd made their own posthumous name tablets, using empty cigarette boxes. These were neatly placed on their concrete pillows. The wills they had written right up to the last moment were arranged there in good order. Blankets were folded. Pencils and paper arranged precisely. "How beautiful!" I thought when I saw these things. They were spoken ill of and called war criminals and demons. They were tortured and bullied by British guards, but they realized the only thing they could do about it was to face the situation and see it through. They died splendidly. I thought, "I too, will be able to do this."

In P Hall, we didn't really ask each other why we were there. There was a man named Kimura. One night he began screaming like a madman. I asked a guard to let me go to him. He was in his cell, madly clawing at the wall, blood streaming from his fingers. I stroked his back and told him, "You're not the only one. Don't torment yourself so. Everyone must die eventually." That seemed to calm him. He was one of those who was executed while I was there. He left a letter for me. "We will never forget you. The three of us are full of gratitude. We lived with the righteousness of eternity. We will complete our lives as Japanese men. I go in good spirits." I hardly knew him, but he wrote to me. After the executions took place, for half a day or so, the inmates of P Hall were subdued. Nine of us were suddenly gone. But new ones came to take their places. When I was in P Hall there were always forty to fifty prisoners.

Around New Year's Day 1947, I knew that it was about time for me to get ready. On January 7, a Buddhist priest, Sekiguchi-san, visited me. I was sleeping under a blanket when he kicked my foot. He told me he'd seen a document which said I was to have my sentence reduced. He warned me not to say anything until it became official. A week later, on the fourteenth, the deputy commandant, an Indian, appeared. He was the deliverer of the notices of execution. Whenever he came, he always had his eyes, behind his silver frame glasses, turned up towards the sky. His first words were, "Your appeal against your conviction has been dismissed. The sentences to be executed are as follows: Fukuda—life imprisonment; Maruyama—life imprisonment; Abe—fifteen years." I'd tried so hard to be ready to die. How tiresome that I had to prepare once more to live! That's how I felt at that moment. Of course, I didn't say that to those who remained behind in P Hall. I spent two months and twenty days there.

The Changi Club meets once a year. It will be held at a Chinese restaurant in Tokyo next month. Even today, quite a few of our group don't want to pick at old wounds. Some were involved in the murder of overseas Chinese. They never reveal anything about their trials and are ready to take all their memories to their graves. We still seem to talk in hushed voices. We have to think of the families of the ones who were executed, too. We always end up talking about war-criminal issues like "victors' justice." I think it's pretty damn selfish. We can't solve anything just by saying the victors tried the defeated. We first have to talk about the wrongs we committed.

"They didn't tell me."

FUJII SHIZUE

A large black stone monument inscribed "In Memory of Fujii Hajime" stands in her garden. "It was donated by one of my husband's subordinates in the Philippines who was spared because Fujii assumed full responsibility for the crimes with which they were both charged. I agreed to let him erect it only after he asked over and over again."

When her husband, a reserve second lieutenant, was called up at the end of October 1941, they had a little girl and an infant son and lived with his mother. She maintained a fitful contact with him via letters passed through the military censors, letters that requested money, but said little and never revealed where he was. These letters nonetheless led her mother-in-law and her to conclude that he was in the Philippines and had been engaged in "punitive expeditions." There were long gaps between letters, and many she wrote never seemed to have reached him, but they were able to stay in touch until the family evacuated to the countryside in May 1945. That's where they were when the war ended. He was then a first lieutenant, commanding a company in the Thirty-Seventh Independent Garrison Infantry Battalion on Panay Island.

She has brought out a large number of letters in a wooden box and refers to them while she speaks. "They are beginning to fade. My children don't even try to read them. Perhaps, after I die, they might."

It was the fifteenth of August, 1946, that I received a letter from my husband in which he reported that he'd been sentenced to death and he was being kept in a special camp. It was a censored letter written on paper provided by America. I was plunged into despair. I can't forget that day. When night came, I still hadn't fed the children. I remember steaming sweet potatoes for them. The next morning dawned with brilliant sunlight, but for me the world was splashed in black ink. I don't know how many days I cried. I haven't wept since. Mother-in-law collapsed completely. Around this time, she told me that we didn't have any more money. Inflation was extremely severe then.

Until the middle of August 1945—practically yesterday—we'd lived under the slogan "Beat the American and English Devils!" We'd cooperated with the war. We'd endured everything for it. Suddenly, after August 15, the newspaper headlines changed: "Japanese Soldiers Are Devils." Stories of "the death march in the Philippines" in 1942 appeared in the papers. I thought, did my country really do such things? What kind of people could have committed such cruel acts? And, now, my own husband was somehow in the middle of it! I couldn't bring myself to accept that.

His letters from Manila were written on light blue letter paper like airletters today. The thing that surprised me most about them was the Scotch tape. I'd never seen that before. That's what truly convinced me Japan had lost the war. The letters always started with the line, "Is everybody well?" Then very simple things followed, like what food he had after he was sentenced. What else could he write otherwise? He knew nothing of the world outside the wire net in which he lived. He wrote at one point that he had at last achieved a serene state of mind, but then he was confused again. It must have been a terrible struggle for him to sever earthly desire. Everywhere in his letters, I saw the agonizing struggle going on in his mind. "Why?" he was asking. "Why?"

He was sentenced to death and placed in something like a bird-cage. My husband wrote about the process of his trial. His American lawyer—I think his name was Springer—was a heavy drinker. "Just like me," he wrote. Springer always appeared at court slightly intoxicated. After consulting with the lawyer, Fujii agreed to admit what he had done and to say that what he did was done under orders from his superiors. He wrote me that notification would be coming to me from Springer. Nothing ever came. He also wrote that the trial record would remain even if he died.

He said I would therefore have a record of how he fought and how he was tried. [*She sings.*] "Who doesn't think of their home town?" was his favorite song. He had a husky voice and loved singing. When he sang it there, a complete hush always fell over his fellow prisoners, he wrote to me.

The last letter I got from him was dated April 12, 1947. I didn't know for sure that my husband had died until 1950. Until then I kept wondering whether they had executed him already or whether he was still alive. I kept visiting the prefectural demobilization office. Whenever I saw a line or two in the papers which said someone had returned from that theater, I wrote immediately to see if he knew anything about Lieutenant Fujii Hajime. I kept writing, though even the cost of stamps was a burden. Nobody knew. There was no reason for anyone to know of him. He'd been dead a long time.

In 1950 I received a letter from Sugamo Prison. It was from a Mr. Kumai, my husband's comrade. He was serving a twenty-year sentence. Supervision of Sugamo shifted from the United States to Japan in 1950, and he took advantage of that opportunity to write me a letter. The fronts and backs of four sheets of straw paper were crammed full. I learned for the first time that it had happened on April 24, 1947.

I heard about his last battles from Mr. Kumai and also about the people who had fought with him. There, on the island of Panay, they were pounded from all directions, exhausted from combat and heat. Some went to town, bought women, and drank saké. Everyone was a guerrilla. Even the young girls selling saké. They were all Panay Islanders and guerrillas at the same time. Those islanders sold poisoned drinks. The Japanese sometimes saw their friends killed in terrible and cruel ways, their eyes plucked out. They vowed to avenge their friends' deaths in the next combat. My husband was accused of being involved in a series of incidents which resulted in the massacre of more than two thousand islanders.

My husband was a company commander. Under him were sergeants and corporals. They were the gods of combat, the real pros. They were trained from the beginning as soldiers. My husband was an officer in name only. One of Fujii's subordinates commented on how impressed he'd been that Fujii never drew his sword. He didn't carry a rifle, only a commander's baton. I don't believe he ever cut off anyone's head. One of his subordinates told me not to worry, he'd never done that. If I believed he did what they must have said he did, then I'd have been able to live with it. I'd have figured there was no point whimpering about it. People who knew him asked me, "Why did they kill him?" I pleaded with them not to ask me that. I told them, "He must have done something, that's why." Yet I was deeply chagrined, full of anger, shame, and resentment. But what could I do?

Panay is one hour by plane from Manila. Two of his subordinates invited me to go to the island many years later under the pretense of gathering the remains of the war dead. Whenever they discovered remains, they burned incense and prayed. I felt very uncomfortable doing so myself. I was really scared of the large eyes of the locals watching us in silence.

But I did want to meet the "Jirō" my husband had mentioned so often in his letters. He was his guide and interpreter. I was told Jirō had been accused of collaborating with the Japanese army, tried by a national court, and imprisoned for a year. Everyone said he was so ashamed that he'd gone off to live by himself in the mountains. Nobody knew how to get in touch with him. One day, he just appeared at my hotel. Jirō embraced me and we cried. We simply held each other and wept together. He said he was sorry that he had to bear witness against Fujii. Jirō had been at his side constantly. Jirō was told that if he said what they wanted him to say, he'd be forgiven because he was a native. He told me he had to say Fujii gave the order. In his last letter to me, my husband never blamed Jirō. He just mentioned that they'd been tried separately.

Mr. Kumai overheard Fujii and Jirō's interrogation, since the investigation areas were divided only by hemp curtains. Fujii admitted everything and discouraged Jirō from naming his subordinates. Fujii seemed very pleased that none of the men under him were executed. According to Mr. Kumai, a high-ranking officer came after the defeat and gave a speech, issuing instructions to all those who had been gathered in Manila and were being held on suspicion of war crimes. He was Lieutenant General Maki, if my memory is right. He said he would never forgive them were they to cause the Japanese army to lose face to foreign countries. At their trials, they should not say that they had acted on commands from superior officers and thus caused such incidents. Mr. Kumai told me that Fujii changed his mind at that point. He had been ready to tell everything at his American trial. Now he decided he shouldn't disgrace the Japanese military man and injure the honor of the Japanese nation. He decided to admit only to what he himself did and not what orders he received.

Although Fujii held officer's rank, he was nothing but an officer on loan. He acted strictly under orders. Mr. Kumai was a first lieutenant then, an adjutant to headquarters, so he knew who issued orders to whom. All superiors who were dispatched there were executed, including the ones who persisted in saying that they never issued orders. Fujii's superiors actually insisted at their trial that they never issued orders. Mr.

Kumai felt that Fujii's superiors were prepared to let Fujii die right in front of their eyes if they could escape. But America didn't allow that. It is proper, I think, for high-ranking officers to take full responsibility. At the time of the Tokyo Tribunal, I was honestly shocked. Everyone said, "Not guilty," including Tōjō. How could they say, "Not guilty"? I didn't realize those high-ranking people thought that way.

Dead men tell no tales. What choice do I have but to cry myself to sleep? I once filed a petition with the Japanese Foreign Ministry to see the records. It all came to nothing. The thing I resent most bitterly is that they never told me. He wasn't just a chicken! You don't just wring his neck! That was a man! "We killed your man. Killed him on such-and-such a date. For such-and-such a crime. Hanged him." Why couldn't America or somebody have told me? I got nothing from them. He wasn't killed by a stray bullet! That might have been acceptable. He was deliberately murdered.

I had to cross out my husband's name on our family registration certificate with my own hand. He didn't do anything for self-interest or personal gain. He did it all under orders from the state. Even if it couldn't be helped that America did nothing for me, shouldn't the Japanese state have at least notified me? It keeps me awake at night when I start remembering all this. He wasn't a particularly brilliant man, but if he were alive, he would have had no difficulty taking care of us, his family. But he never had the chance.

"War criminal" was a taboo phrase at my parents' house for a long time. We used expressions like "the ones who didn't return." I'm so grateful to my parents for that. Yet the more people were silent, the harder it was for me after a while. I didn't want to carry around a sign board marked "war criminal" anymore, so I moved to this new housing development where nobody knew anything about us.

I never spoke about him to my children. I thought I would wait until they became adults. Once my son was preparing the official papers for his high-school application when he said, "Mom, it's funny. Why did Pa die in 1947? If he'd died in the war, it should have been 1945." I failed to come up with a lie. But there's no point in talking like this anymore. I'm supposed to have forgotten all about those days. But things keep surfacing. Until I die, those memories won't fade away.

The crumbling yellowed pages of the U.S. War Department's War Crimes Office records in Suitland, Maryland, confirm that the sentence of death by hanging in U.S.A. vs. Hajime FUJII, handed down 29 July 1946, "was carried out 24 April 1947, Laguna Province, Philippine Islands."

22 / THE LONG SHADOW OF DEATH

The Emperor's Retreat

YAMANE MASAKO

"*Come with me to Matsushiro,*" she says. "*You'll understand if you see what they built for the Emperor.*" It proves to be a five-hour drive from Tokyo.

"*What first comes to mind when I think of Matsushiro are the thin white walls of the barracks in the so-called Korean Village. They were just cheap shanties of the thinnest wood, like books turned over. So many of them, they seemed to stretch on forever. It was incredible to a child's eyes. Mother told me later that there were about three hundred and eighty such units, each subdivided. We lived in one room, six mats in size, with a small earthen area at one end. Because nails were so important at that time, the floor was made only of pieces of wood resting on a frame, not even nailed down. On top of them were spread coarse, prickly rice-straw mats. It was so swampy that at night, when it froze, the ground buckled up in waves from the frost. During the day, as it melted, it grew soft and muddy. It was very unusual for my father to be home.*

"*I also remember the whores. They were painted white to the neck and they were always drunk. They walked along, spreading wide the bright-red lower parts of their kimonos. I now know they were 'comfort women,' brought here by force from Korea. I don't know why I remember those things, but small pieces of my memories are intact. I was five years old.*"

As we drive through Matsushiro, she points out the scenes and places of her childhood. "*People call Matsushiro the 'Little Kyoto of the Shinshū region.' It was the castle town of the Sanada lords. You'll find road signs for Zōzan Shrine and Sanada Clan Temple, but no directions to Matsushiro Imperial Headquarters around here. Matsushiro Station was a little larger then, and there was a substation at the site. According to my mother's testimony, they burned the dead around here, near this substation. I was brought up looking at these mountains for ten years. Togakushi is that sharp, rugged one. It has snow on the peak. The mountains are really beautiful, aren't they?*"

Finally, she parks her car in what looks like someone's backyard. Standing next to a tunnel entrance is a signboard erected by Nagano City, identifying the site as Matsushiro Zōzan Underground Shelter and providing an outline history:

> In the last stages of the Second World War, in extreme secrecy, the military built this [shelter], planning to move the Imperial General Headquarters and the government ministries to this location as the position for the Final Battle. Construction began at 11 o'clock in the morning on November 11, 1944, and lasted until August 15, 1945, the day the war ended. The construction work was pushed through, day and night, for about nine months. 3,000,000 man-days were mobilized for the enormous sum, at that time, of ¥200,000,000. Seventy-five percent of the project was completed.
>
> ... The Matsushiro Underground Imperial Headquarters comprises more than ten kilometers of tunnels, dug through Maizuruyama (today, the location of the Meteorological Agency Earthquake Observation Station), Minakamiyama, and Zōzan [mountains] like the cross-hatching of a *go* board.
>
> Statistics—Total length: 5,853.6 meters.... Approximate extent of excavation: 59,635 cubic meters. Total floor space: 23,404 square meters.

"You see, they don't even mention the Koreans who dug it. Nothing!" says Yamane Masako, who for years has almost singlehandedly been unearthing the story of what took place at Matsushiro. "I do this work, trying to discover why those Koreans were brought to Matsushiro by force and what happened to them. It's almost like Japan's Auschwitz. There are no documents saying how many Koreans were dragged here, and no figures on how many died here. There aren't even lists of the names of those who worked here. Japan lost the war, and then burnt all the documents before the American Occupation forces could arrive—or so they claim, anyway."

These underground shelters, unprecedented in their gigantic size, were prepared in expectation of an impending U.S. landing on the main islands of Japan. Special shelters for the Emperor and Empress were included. Yamane wants to expose the fate of Korean workers like her father who carved the tunnels for the shelters out of the solid rock. For her, the agonies of discrimination she suffered as a girl with a Korean father began here, while those people she feels are responsible only seek to keep the world from finding out.

"The Koreans building the Imperial chamber on August 15, 1945,

disappeared overnight. Only their number, forty-six, is known from the postwar testimony of other workers. They vanished, without a trace. If we were able to find out where they were taken, we would find they were massacred to keep the world from finding out that the Emperor was planning to flee. They were there until that moment." She is wrought up and speaks explosively, her commitment and anger boiling over. "This is the entrance," she says pointing out a dark maw leading into the mountain. "Now, they open it to the public only on Saturdays and Sundays. We'll just go through the fence."

They built these new fences so that people wouldn't be able to see the whole thing. Before, you could simply go in. Now, you're only permitted to go as far as the floor's been smoothed out, a mere fifty meters or so. You can't get the real picture from that alone. They only want to use safety as a pretext for keeping people out. [We squeeze through a narrow space between the edge of the wire net and the rock. The dim light behind us soon disappears. When she turns off her flashlight it is pitch black. It is cool and dry inside; the air is deathly still.]

This is the main shelter into which the government ministries were supposed to move for the final battle. Please watch your step. There are rough places. [Her roving light reveals sharp-edged rocks jutting up into the path and the raw face of rock on the walls.]

The tunnels are large, aren't they? A truck could drive through these shelters. It's five or six times as large as the Kōrakuen baseball stadium in Tokyo in all. My father dug this with his bare hands. They say no one was killed, no one injured during the construction. This tunnel is twice as long as the Tanna Tunnel [one of Japan's longest] and it was dug in half the time. Even in our own times, people died building that tunnel. Back then, there weren't any rock drills available. They were constantly pushed to hurry. They weren't allowed to rest even when they were injured. Twenty different horizontal shafts were dug. Each was assigned to a different group. They competed against each other. Each group had a Japanese boss, and under him a miniboss. Exploitation came down from the top, passing through many layers on the way. At war's end, they say each worker was officially paid two hundred fifty yen, but those who received the payments say they got only five yen. For them, five yen was quite a large sum, so large they feared they might be killed for it. The construction firms made great profits this way.

[Coming to an intersection, she keeps walking as if she knows every inch of these tunnels by heart. She stops. Ms. Yamane is completely still. A palm placed on the rock wall proves them dry. They are very rough. She moves the light up over the ragged rock all the way up to the ceiling.

The jagged rocks look as if they had been blasted and chiseled out just yesterday.]

I'm sorry. When I come here, I get really depressed. I realize *they* were going to survive here, while "one hundred million died together" outside. I hear the cries of agony among the rocks. I can feel the pain of whips on *my* back. These rocks maintain complete silence, but silent holes say so much. There are Hangul letters scratched by the Koreans on the walls in here. There are places where there are still ties for the mine-car tracks along the tunnel.

[*We leave the tunnels of Zōzan in silence. She drives on to the shelters where the Emperor and Empress were going to be housed.*] The Peers' School [for the sons of the nobility] was supposed to be brought to this area. That building was to be the for the Emperor and Empress's quarters, his on the right and hers on the left. [*She points at a single-story building that stretches along the mildly sloping hill.*] From the inside of that building tunnels lead underground. There is a document in the Imperial Household Agency that indicates they were about to move here when they finally accepted the Potsdam Declaration. The Imperial General Headquarters were to be in the same shelter as the Emperor himself.

When people learned that the war was over, we were hiding in our "shelter." We hadn't been able to come out for a long time. My mother then left the ditch and came back with two cucumbers. They weren't very big. We ate them with some *miso* spread on them. That's my memory of the end of the war.

I also heard adults crying out in Korean, "*Mansei! Mansei!*" "Hurrah! Hurrah!" But among the Japanese villagers there was a sense of fear. They believed that the Koreans now would attack them. There would have been no reason to fear Koreans if they hadn't done anything wrong to them. Japanese women and children were evidently told not to go out, and hid themselves in the storehouses. But the Koreans just drank saké and danced with joy. It's reasonable, don't you think? They'd been freed from labor. But from the next day on, there was no way to eat. Nobody would hire Koreans. From that time on, our struggle to live was unbelievably severe. We stayed on in those shacks until 1960. There was no place else to go. They sent most of the survivors back to North Korea. My Japanese mother, too. I got off the train at the last moment, leaving my parents and sisters to sail from Japan.

My mother is still in North Korea. People like her are unable to come home, no matter how much they might like to. They're aged and live every day in tears. Her letters, which hardly ever reach us, say only, "send this" or "send that." We'd like her to get things, but the parcels never reach her. I feel so powerless when I read letters in which she wonders why humans are unable to go home when clouds can float there freely anytime. All of them suffered so terribly during the war. It's my mission to find a way to bring the aged back to Japan. I, too, was discriminated against. I, too, tried not to disclose who I was. I only felt able to tell my own children about myself after they reached the age of twenty. I had hidden from them the fact that my father was Korean. When I ask why I continued to live like that then, and why I think the way I do now, my thoughts go back to Matsushiro.

I recently obtained a copy of the diary of a Japanese sergeant who worked here at the time. In it, he describes how Koreans were forced to work twelve hours a day on only a bowl of sorghum, while the Japanese ate well and partied. Today, of all those brought from Korea, only one man still lives in Matsushiro. He says that large quantities of spoiled rice and wheat, and piles of workmen's shoes were found in storage here after the war, while at the time Korean workers labored with their bleeding feet wrapped in rags. When asked why he hadn't gone back to Korea, he replied that he had come to Japan with so many others from his village, and now he would be ashamed to go back, the lone survivor.

Things have been concealed for such a long time, but when I've walked up to villagers working in the fields, old people—those with consciences, anyway—have told me five, maybe six people died here every day. Some say they saw the injured carried out of the tunnel on top of shutters. During that period, smoke never stopped coming out of the crematorium. What does it mean that the crematorium was kept burning in this small village? It's still there. The villagers all watched as it sent up its continuous plume.

Construction went on for about ten months, from November 1944 to August 1945. Generally, it's believed that seven thousand to ten thousand Koreans were brought by force. If five or six died every day, that means roughly one thousand to fifteen hundred died. History books don't mention those who were injured or died. Do you believe that? Nothing has been told yet of the real history of Matsushiro.

People were told that they were digging storage facilities. This copy of the document "Matsushiro Storage New Construction" proves that point. Even though it was called storage, villagers in their seventies and eighties tell me they knew from April 1945 that the Emperor would be coming because of the chrysanthemum seals on the lumber. It occurred to them that Japan must be losing the war if the Emperor was planning to escape to such a place. But back then, people wouldn't have said anything like that aloud, out of fear.

The man who had the Koreans in his hands at that time, the deputy head of the work unit of the construction company in charge, knows everything. He knows that they killed Koreans, starved them, and stole their wages. He is the only man who still knows what happened to the forty-six Koreans who disappeared on August 15. If he confesses, the whole picture will be revealed. He now lives in one of the largest houses in town. After the war, he built a fortune with hoarded goods. All the land around is his. He's not a native of this area, but after August 15, he made everything his own property. There were Koreans who dared to say that they'd kill him if they could. He ran away to Hokkaido for about three years or so and returned after the furor had cooled down. Today, he's one of the leaders of the Matsushiro Chamber of Commerce. Those who had power during the war still wield influence today.

I tried to talk to him once, assuring him I needed only five minutes of his time. He said to me "You're too beautiful. I'm unable to die although I don't want to live so long. So I don't have anything to tell." He's getting a little senile. When he dies, all the things he knows will be unknown forever. A few years ago, he had a large statue of the Goddess of Mercy built in Seisuiji Temple, facing the mountains where the shelters were dug. Its inscription reads, "To the memory of people who sacrificed their lives in the construction of the underground Imperial General Headquarters. . . . Pray for eternal peace." A man does not build such a thing without a guilty conscience.

The descendant of the last daimyo of the Sanada Clan is alive and well today. He still wields an incredibly strong influence over the town. He's been saying that the kind of thing I'm doing is a disgrace for Matsushiro. Everyone just keeps their mouth shut. Those who were there are gradually passing away, and the Koreans were never in a position to speak out. Silence was their only choice, if they wanted to live a life here. Just the other day, the authorities blocked the entrances to the underground shelters with fences, despite requests that the last Imperial General Headquarters should be preserved and left be open to the public. They're afraid it will hurt their chances to get the Olympic Games to come to Nagano! They're trying to draw down the curtain on the Shōwa era. It's inexcusable. I wonder how the Japanese today can be so undisturbed after what they did.

"My boy never came home."

IMAI SHIKE

The large flatland farmhouse is surrounded by rice fields turning yellow with the approaching harvest. Shike, eighty-five years old, is the mother of Imai Shigeo. His photograph hangs over the sliding panel doors in the main tatami room of the house. He is pictured dressed in the uniform of a heichō, *petty officer third class. Next to his photograph is one of his father, Sakuzō, who died two years ago at the age of eighty-six. Shigeo volunteered for the navy in 1942 and was killed in 1944 in the Central Pacific while on submarine Ro-36.*

Shike looks frail in her blue-and-white summer dress. Her short-cropped hair is not yet all white. The first mention of Shigeo's name brings her to tears. Her voice is high-pitched and taut. With her eyes open, her face fills with pain. Eyes closed, she seems more at peace.

Yoshio, Shigeo's younger brother and Yoshio's wife, Sayoko, join in the conversation from time to time.

SHIKE: He was good at his studies. He helped me a lot at work. He wasn't ever the best at school—always Number Two. [*She closes her eyes, brings her palms together in prayer, and sobs.*]

In two or three years it'll be fifty years that he's gone. He wouldn't listen to me about volunteering for the navy.

YOSHIO: Probably Mother opposed it in her mind, but mothers couldn't say such things openly. [*Shike moves across the room slowly to the large Buddhist altar at the center of the house.*

Shike shows us the tokonoma, *the alcove in a Japanese home usually reserved for the display of family treasures. Hanging there is a Japanese flag bearing the signatures of many of Shigeo's friends and teachers, commemorating the occasion in 1938 when he left for Manchuria to join the Manchuria-Mongolia Pioneering Youth Volunteer Corps. Beneath the flag is the preliminary notice of a serviceman's death. To its right, is the Official Notice of Death.*

Below the notices is Shigeo's last letter home. The ink is badly faded and especially difficult to make out. His letter says his thoughts are of the village rice-planting and of his brothers and sisters going to the village school and helping his parents in the fields. It also tells of his severe training in the navy, but he writes that he will do his best until the Americans and British have been destroyed and that he looks forward to the day when he will again share a meal with his brothers and sisters. He mentions at the end that he has enclosed a check for fifty yen, which he wants his parents to use to go to a hot spa to comfort their tired bodies after the physical strain of the harvest season. He closes with greetings to his whole family "from the bottom of the sea."]

SHIKE: He must have saved up all his pay to send it to us. Fifty yen was a lot of money then. I always remember him. I always think of him. I see him in my dreams. Bonya ["My little boy"] comes into my dreams. Sometimes he looks lost. Other times he's full of vigor. He always walks off, saying, "I'll go to work and be back soon." Sometimes he appears in navy uniform. At other times he's carrying our youngest on his back.

Sometimes he says, "I'm going to join the navy. I'm going on a ship." Then he's gone. No matter what I say, he's gone.

His letter, that letter there, has faded. It's almost fifty years. That picture—it used to be a tiny one, but we sent it to Tokyo and they made it large for us.

YOSHIO: The original showed him dressed in his seaman's uniform. But after he was killed, he received a posthumous promotion, so we had the photographers add the cap of a noncommissioned officer.

I'm four years younger than my brother. I'm the one who knew him best. I used to fight with him, too. They say he was killed in the middle of the Pacific Ocean. Mother dreamt of him on July 5 or 6, so we think he was killed that day. The official announcement of his death in action says July 12, 1945, but that was the date his ship was supposed to reach port. That's the official way to decide these things.

SHIKE: I've gotten this old and I don't know anything anymore, but there were people who came back. I thought my boy might come back, too, so I kept asking around. I behaved like a madwoman.

My son talked to me through a medium once. He said, "You have my brothers and sisters; don't worry about me anymore." I wonder, did he really die? I can't forget that. It's stupid, isn't it? Others no older than him came back.

YOSHIO: She went to fortunetellers.

SHIKE: Everyone has this kind of feeling when trying to separate from a child. Everyone's the same, aren't they? I had eight children. But only that one . . . All the others are well. I went to pray at his grave the other day.

We don't know anything about how he died. Only the container for his hat was sent back to us. I used to read that letter every single day. But it's faded. I can't really read it anymore. When we got it, every character was clear and dark. Also, my eyesight was better then.

YOSHIO: If Shigeo were still alive, he'd be sixty-six.

SHIKE: Even among those who went into the navy at the same time as him, there were people who came back.

YOSHIO: Three volunteered with Shigeo. One returned.

SHIKE: I only think about the person who came back. He visits us and prays before the picture of my boy.

YOSHIO: These things in the *tokonoma* are never removed, no matter what the occasion. At other households, they would have been put away in the storehouse, but here, they're always out. Always here.

SHIKE: I suffered a stroke in my seventies. These days, my legs are not strong. Once I was able to control the horses we used to plow the fields.

YOSHIO: She was really strong until then. I never could beat her at field work.

SAYOKO: When I came here as a bride, the whole house felt dark and oppressive. But I didn't have the right to say anything about it. I had come in in the middle. But our children accept the situation as it is.

YOSHIO: Three times a day she sits here for about one hour.

SAYOKO: She washes her face and combs her hair, then comes here and sits in front of him from six to seven in the morning. Breakfast is at seven. From eleven to twelve noon she comes back. Lunch is at noon. In the evening, she's here from five to six. It goes on for more than thirty minutes each time. We have a little picture of him on the altar, and sometimes she listens to a cassette of Buddhist prayers. The whole house is full of smoke and smells of incense. Sometimes the candles fall over and the *tatami* gets burnt. Her legs are so frail that when she has to get up to change the candles, I sometimes think it's a little dangerous, but . . .

SHIKE: He doesn't say a thing to me.

When I was young I had to go to the fields. Now I'm old. I only think of my little boy now. Very soon I'll be going to his side. I'm not a high priest. Maybe I won't be able to see him because I'm full of guilt. While I've been praying, I've been thinking of a lot of other things, too.

YOSHIO: Once, on a visit, he told me he was lucky to have gotten back, because so many had already been sunk. I was working at a military factory in Toyama then. That time, he told me he wouldn't be coming back anymore.

SHIKE: He never told me that.

23 / REFLECTIONS

Teaching War

IENAGA SABURŌ

One of Japan's leading historians, aged seventy-seven, he has published numerous studies of the war and modern Japan. He was a professor at Tokyo Education University in 1965 when he brought a lawsuit against the state, arguing that the Education Ministry's policy of reviewing and approving textbooks was unconstitutional. His high-school history textbook, Shin Nihonshi *[New Japanese History] was subjected to "revisions" of specific phrases and terms that were labeled critical of Japan. In a legal odyssey which is still continuing, he has argued that such interference is not merely a matter of "editing," but is a fundamental infringement on "freedom of thought and learning," thus violating the protections offered in the postwar Japanese constitution and in the Fundamental Education Law. As he puts it, "Approval of textbooks by the state prohibits the completion of the people's development as human beings. My sincere desire is to appeal this case to the world at large through the courts. The battle I have been fighting has been made possible only with the help of a growing number of concerned citizens. Some twenty thousand have now become involved." Today, the series of trials, appeals, and legal maneuvers ostensibly involving the content of textbooks, but actually contesting the nature of Japan's official remembrance of the past, are known popularly as "the Ienaga trials."*

I myself experienced the war. Although I didn't jump on the war bandwagon, I deeply regret that I did not have a hand in stopping it. That's why I so sincerely desire that we ponder that war. I graduated from university nine months before the Marco Polo Bridge Incident of 1937 that launched total war against China. I was a teacher at a higher school in Niigata at the time of Pearl Harbor in 1941, but I was not critically conscious. I really didn't understand what was happening in China at all, and had only vague feelings of uneasiness that Japan was sinking deeper and deeper into a quagmire. I knew nothing about Japan's cruel behavior. There was really no way of knowing. I honestly confess here that at that time I had no critical feelings about the war with China.

Yet I was from a generation that had been educated in the era of Taishō Democracy, so I knew, in general terms, how great the national strength of Britain and the United States really was. I knew instinctively that to fight America and England simultaneously made no sense. I had no statistical data about our relative national strength versus that of the United States of America—just the common sense of an ordinary man. When I heard the news of the opening of the war on December 8, I experienced a sense of desperation. From that time on, I simply wished that the war would end, even one day early, but I couldn't do anything to help bring that about. At least, I couldn't do anything legally. In spite of my saying that I was powerless, as an adult, as a person of that time, I must take that responsibility for simply standing by and watching the war go on.

Before the war, ordinary Japanese citizens were taught from schoolbooks compiled by the state, and were made to believe that Japan was a superior nation whose mission was to lead the world. This was particularly true of national-history and ethics textbooks, and the citizenry as a whole accepted these things as the truth. For the ruling class, I would say, political and economic needs were primary motives for the war. In the worldwide economic crisis of the 1920s and the beginning of the 1930s, Japan, too, was suffering from the Depression, and financial circles felt it was necessary to advance abroad in order to break out of economic stagnation.

From the viewpoint of the Japanese state system, the military remained above criticism. The Emperor led the military. Thus the military was seen as sacred, despite the fact that the army and navy were merely state organizations. Any criticism of the military automatically made the speaker "antimilitary." Such thoughts were said to oppose the kokutai, the national polity. The "prerogatives of the supreme command" of the armed forces remained beyond the control of the ministers of state who served the Emperor and advised him on matters pertaining to affairs of state. Neither the cabinet nor the National Diet were to be involved. There were, in fact, no institutional limitations or mechanisms to check the military in cases where it acted on its own discretion.

A temporary international trend toward arms reduction took place during the Taishō Democracy era after the First World War as demonstrated by the Washington Treaty of 1922, where nations limited the size of their fleets. These efforts culminated in the London Treaty on naval armaments of 1930. But such efforts at arms limitation were opposed by the military, who tried to recover their strength and oppose this trend by causing incidents abroad. First came the explosion that killed Chang Tso-lin, the Chinese warlord of Manchuria in 1928, an assassination that was clearly a plot by the army. Even then, a plan existed to occupy Manchuria, depending how the situation developed. It simply couldn't be immediately implemented. Several years later, however, in September 18, 1931, the Japanese forces stationed in Manchuria, the Kwantung Army, blew up a piece of railway track at Liu-t'iaou-kou. Calling this an act of Chinese soldiers, the army promptly launched an attack on the Chinese and occupied Mukden immediately. This "Manchurian Incident" lit the fuse of the Pacific War.

The military's massive organization was used consciously by the *zaibatsu*, Japan's industrial combines. It wasn't that the *zaibatsu* took the initiative in inciting the war, but that when war begins, an expansion of armaments invariably takes place. Military factories reap profits. If the *zaibatsu* and financial circles didn't start the war on their own initiative, they welcomed it when it began and made huge profits from it. So the financial circles must bear enormous responsibility for the war.

Due to the education they had received from childhood, the common people believed that the state was almighty and any act of the military was completely just. Naturally, they didn't take a critical attitude. Moreover, prior to the war, the Peace Preservation Law had restricted political activity, and all printed materials to be sold were subjected to censorship. That was why the truth was not known. At the time of the Manchurian Incident, radio was gradually emerging, but it was virtually state-owned, and it broadcast only the news announced by the authorities. Although newspapers and magazines were published by private companies, they failed to publish the truth due to the severe restrictions they were under. The assassination of Chang Tso-lin was reported as "an important happening in Manchuria"—which was, I assume, as close to the truth as they were allowed to get. Even though I'd reached the age of maturity in 1931, I knew neither the truth of Chang's assassination, nor that the Kwantung Army itself had set off that explosion outside Mukden —not at least until after 1945, when it was testified to in court at the Military Tribunal Far East. We were left that ignorant of the circumstances! We knew nothing of the Nanking massacre, nor did we know that Japanese had committed cruel acts all over China.

Although they were few in number, there were some in Japan who were awake and resisted, even if at a limited level. It isn't true that were no cases of resistance. Most resisters were Communists, though another group were the Christians. Some very radical liberals resisted, too. But despite efforts by these people up to the very last moment, there was never a real uprising from the populace, as there was in Italy. In northern

Italy, for example, there were general strikes and partisan struggles, in which Italians stood up to their government even before the arrival of the Allied forces.

The war was not brought to a conclusion by the force of the Japanese people themselves. Instead, those who led and promoted the war, faced with imminent defeat, ended it themselves. They thought that if they let the war continue, the *kokutai*—the Emperor system—would be in danger and the subjugators themselves would be jeopardized. Before the people could rise up, the ruling class took the initiative, setting the condition that the National Polity be preserved and the Emperor protected. Because the war was not concluded through the critical will of the Japanese people, I regret that it is impossible to state that a spiritual revolution occurred afterward.

Many things have now been disclosed to the people. The new democracy under a Japanese constitution brought by the American Occupation forces played a large role in improving the consciousness of the Japanese people. At bottom, however, continuity with the prewar era has been strong. There has been no true overturning of the roots of the thinking process that existed before the war. A large number of people still believe that the war was for the sake of the nation, or that Japan was driven into a corner and had no other choice. I don't know if they really believe this consciously, but they still believe in a "Japanese-style spirit," as in prewar days. There are right-wing movements that seek to apply pressure or threaten injury if one even tries to make public facts about events in that era, or voice criticism of them. This means that sometimes people refrain from speaking or writing on the subject. If someone like me, who lived thirty years before the war, and more than forty years after, compares the pre-and postwar periods, I believe one can say there have been many changes. But at the bottom of one's heart there remains a residue. This really came out at the time of the Shōwa emperor's death on January 7, 1989, and the funeral ceremony that followed. The mass media were flooded with reports on the Emperor, and tens of thousands of people went to the Imperial Palace to pay their respects.

The causes of the war were not what we were taught back then. The Chinese people consciously attempted to escape exploitation. They tried to cast off the many foreign interests in China—and with them, things like economic exploitation and extraterritoriality by which Japan had reduced China to a semicolonial status. The war resulted from the Japanese desire to prevent Japan's interests in China from being taken away.

The idea of building a Greater East Asia Co-Prosperity Sphere wasn't really there at the beginning, but was added later. There had been movements urging expansion toward the South since the Meiji period, but the idea of trying to achieve this by force came to the fore only because of the need for oil to continue waging war in China. This is an illustration of the idea that "war makes war" and "war is its own principle."

There was no reason why Japan had to fight a war against America. It was not inevitable. America implemented an economic embargo against Japan in response to China's entreaties. At the time the United States and Japan began negotiations to resolve their conflict, America accepted Chinese requests and demanded that Japan withdraw its forces from the whole of China. The army could never accept this, not after the enormous sacrifices they had made and the gains so bloodily won, so they rejected it. That's how Japan and America faced each other at the beginning of their war. But it must be remembered, everything that took place ultimately derived from *Japan's* aggression in China.

As the economic embargo by the United States, Britain, and Holland progressed, the possibility arose that Japan might not be able to continue its war in China because of a lack of oil. Japan was forced into a situation where it had to decide either to stop the war or to open a new front against those three nations in order to obtain petroleum. Stopping the war meant total withdrawal from China. That was not acceptable. The main objective of launching a war against England and America was then to control China.

It's a complete lie to say that Japan made aggressive moves in Asia in order to liberate Asians from the control of Europe and America, and that in losing, the Japanese sacrificed themselves so that the Asian peoples could become independent. It's true that by occupying China, French Indochina, the Dutch East Indies, Malaya, and Burma, Japan severed American, British, French, and Dutch control in the region. But in taking the place of those colonial powers, Japan implemented policies toward the local residents which were even more atrocious than those of the former governing countries. Revolts occurred all over. The greatest rebellions occurred in the Philippines, where people had lived under American control. In the Dutch East Indies and in Burma, the Japanese forces were welcomed at first, but the Japanese forces that came in were so violent that anti-Japanese movements soon appeared. In Vietnam, the Viet Minh, the earliest Communists, first took the Japanese side, but because of the policies of the Japanese forces, their own struggle for independence began. It completely contradicts reality to say that the Japanese made these countries independent. Japanese policies were so extreme that only in that sense may they have aided the various national people's uprisings. So it's hard to deny the idea Southeast Asians have today that Japan's economic advancement and role in the development of the South is similar in some respects to its wartime policies.

Immediately after the war, school textbooks clearly indicated Japan's responsibility for and recklessness in waging war. The first postwar history textbook, *Kuni no ayumi* [*The Course of a Country*] said, "The people suffered tremendously from the long war. The military suppressed the people and fought an unreasonable war, causing this great unhappiness." Another book, *Minshushugi* [*Democracy*], published by the Education Ministry in 1949, stated, "Japan, as well as Germany, must shoulder the greatest responsibility for the Second World War, which caused terrible suffering, pain, and shock to all the people of the world." It also declared, "The flag-waving of the military cliques, with such expressions as 'all-encompassing national defense,' held political power in their hands and trampled on the rights of the people and came to plan a reckless war."

They did not hesitate to acknowledge Japan's responsibility for the war at that time, but in 1963 the public position of the Education Ministry changed completely. In that year, my high-school history textbook failed to obtain approval. Officials of the Education Ministry pointed to a series of photographs of air raids on Japan and pictures of Hiroshima burned by the atomic bomb and the tragic pictures of disabled veterans, dressed in white clothes, begging on the streets of postwar Japan, and ruled, "As a whole, this book is too dark." The state argued with the expressions used in my textbooks, such as "The war was beautified as 'a sacred war,'" or "the cruel behavior of the Japanese army," and my reference to a "reckless war." Citing those phrases, they claimed that the book only criticized the position of Japan and Japanese behavior in the Second World War and would not bring students to a proper understanding of our country's position, caught in the whirlpool of war.

The "textbook trials" have been going on since 1965. The judgment rendered in 1970 initially conceded almost all of our assertions. The censorship of the Ienaga textbook was ruled to be unconstitutional, but we received total victory and vindication in a judgment only that once. The position was soon partially reversed on appeal. We have now had three trials. As the succeeding judgments became worse, the membership in groups supporting us has increased. This is unusual. I am nonsectarian and I do not receive any assistance from any "-ism," but am simply asserting that approval by the state is not allowed by the Constitution. I am unable to say whether this struggle has really helped or not. The state-approval system still exists today. Textbooks cannot write of Unit 731, the bacteriological unit in Manchuria where the Japanese used human beings as specimens for experiments, and where thousands were massacred at the end of the war. Students who read only school textbooks will know nothing at all about such things, though today there finally are other books on the subject one can read. We cannot let those who wish to shape our thoughts control education about the war.

One has to learn from war, but I don't necessarily think the majority learned much from that war or wants to assure that such things never happen again. Those who have forgotten about the war and those whose way of thinking has remained unchanged since the war are still with us, as was shown in the "misstatements" by Liberal Democratic Party statesmen who have declared that Japan wasn't the only country that did cruel things. Those of us who say openly that our aggression in China must be disclosed, and those who have been actively working to stop discrimination against Asians, show that Japan is a very different place from the country of the prewar era, but the numbers engaged in these activities are small. We must enlarge the number of people actively involved. This is the nature of our work. As wartime memories fade, we must ensure that the truth about the Pacific War is taught to the next generation.

Meeting at Yasukuni Shrine

KIYAMA TERUMICHI

Located a short walk from the moat surrounding the Imperial Palace, Yasukuni Shrine is an oasis of green in the concrete, steel, and asphalt of Tokyo. Two enormous torii arches soar over the expansive path coming up the hill from Kudanshita. Tall trees rise on both sides. The particular, almost indescribable sound of feet treading on the small stones of the pathway accompanies one all the way to the wooden entrance doors of the Outer Shrine gate. These bear the Imperial crest in gold. Suspended beneath the Outer Shrine's massive copper roof is the sixteen-petaled Imperial chrysanthemum on a white cloth. Beyond is the Inner Shrine.

The people who make their way to and from the shrine today are few in number, and most seem very old, their backs bent and their gaits unsteady. Except for the two black sound trucks bearing the names and slogans of right-wing patriotic organizations parked next to two huge tourist buses in a lot near the path, there are no obvious signs that the shrine is a place of controversy. Yet, since 1945 it has been at the center of often heated political arguments about the relationship between religion and the state in a democracy, centering on the role this shrine played in the last war as the resting place of the "guardian gods"—those military men who had given their lives in service of their Emperor.

Founded in 1869 to enshrine the 6,971 who had fallen in the then-recent war that ended the Tokugawa Shogun's rule and brought the Imperial family to power in the Meiji Restoration, it was given the name Yasukuni Jinja in 1879. Yasukuni means "To govern the state peacefully." As the place where all those who have perished in war to defend the Imperial state were enshrined, it became one of the most important symbols of the then official Japanese religion of State Shintō. The war dead were enshrined as kami, *meaning gods or spirits. Beginning with the Emperor Meiji, the "living god," the reigning Emperor, paid tribute to them personally. In the Second World War, to be enshrined at Yasukuni and prayed to by His Imperial Majesty was considered the highest honor that could be bestowed on a loyal subject. According to the figures provided by the Shrine, 2,465,138 "pillars" were enshrined here as of 1987. Of these, 191,074 were from the China Incident and 2,132,699 were from the Greater East Asia War.* °

The Yūshūkan, a memorial hall, was established in 1881 to exhibit items related to Japan's Imperial history. It was largely destroyed in the Great Kantō Earthquake of 1923, but rebuilt in 1931 at the present site. It was reopened in 1986, after having been used for company offices after 1945. It now contains about 30,000 historical documents or items for display. Among the more spectacular are an actual Kaiten—a human torpedo, on loan from the American Army Museum in Hawaii—an Ōka (Cherry Blossom) rocket-powered piloted flying bomb, a diorama showing the Thunder God squadron approaching Okinawa for their final attack, a Type-97 medium tank used on Saipan, and C-5631, a locomotive used on the Burma–Siam railway.

Deputy High Priest Kiyama is the Gon-no-Gūji, *the second-ranking official of Yasukuni Shrine. He wears a purple* hakama *over a pure white kimono. His office is completely Western in style. Behind his large desk is an immaculately clean glass wall, brilliant in sunlight with the autumn leaves flashing outside. The door to the hallway remains open and people pass by carrying on hushed conversations. He speaks in a voice damped down and under control. During the war he was an army air-corps reserve officer. He was in Indonesia at the end.*

The Yasukuni Shrine has followed a policy of not agreeing to interviews by journalists. The rationale for this policy is that the fundamental reason for the existence of the shrine is simply to pray to the gods.

° Yasukuni Jinja Yūshūkan, ed., *Yasukuni Jinja Yūshūkan, Shahō to sembotsusha no ihō.* [Yasukuni Jinja Yūshūkan. Shrine Treasures and Articles Left Behind by the War Dead.] Tokyo: 1987. p. 3

If we do anything else, we find ourselves involved in various political issues. After the defeat in the war, relations between Yasukuni and the state and between the shrine and the people's consciousness have been treated as if they were political issues. When the prime minister comes here to pray, it becomes an issue whether he's at the shrine as a private or a public personage. From the Yasukuni Shrine's perspective, it is not our intent to be involved in political issues. We merely pray and express our thanks to the spirits. So I will not discuss the true essence of the rites of the shrine, or how the state is involved, or the shrine's relation to the Imperial family, for the reasons I have given. I am able to speak only about my own personal experiences, as distinct from my position.

In yesterday's evening edition of the *Sankei* newspaper, a letter appeared in the "Hot Line" column addressing the issues of why people might wish to visit Yasukuni Shrine. The writer, a former medic, sixty-seven years old, was at the front on the Chinese continent. The watch-word of his unit's war-comrade association has been, "Meet you at Yasukuni," and they have been meeting annually at the shrine. This year, about three hundred of them gathered here in October. During that meeting, he says, in the shrine waiting room he met an old woman, eighty-four years old, to be exact, and the bride of her eldest son. They were from Saga prefecture, Kyushu. Her daughter had gone to the front as a military nurse and died on her repatriation trip to Japan after the war, at the age of twenty-one. Her second son died in action in the South. Because of her age, the author believed this would be her last visit to Yasukuni Shrine. The old woman tells him how good it was of the bride to bring her, and how indebted she feels to her. The bride speaks quietly about it, saying only, "It is so natural to accompany her." The letter-writer comments on how warm and comforted he felt to meet a person who still so wants to come to Yasukuni from so far away, at such an age.

In an ordinary family today, even if the old man has this desire, the young bride will oppose him. She'll just say, "Oh? So you were a victim of the war," and she'll criticize the war. "If you have that kind of money, buy toys for your grandkids." That's the typical Japanese family, today. But this Saga family! Supporting an old woman's wish so! They're proba-bly a Buddhist family. They have their own family temple, and I'm sure they have a Buddhist service at *O-Bon* [the festival of the Dead]. Yet they have the consciousness that the spirit of her daughter and her second son remain in Yasukuni Shrine.

War-bereaved families come here, pay reverence at the Outer Shrine, then proceed to the Inner Shrine, where the spirits reside. There they call out, "My son, I'm here." They believe they are able to commu-nicate directly with their dead ones. To express their feelings of gratitude, they come from far away and present the harvest of their land to them. It's as if living people are here. Don't you see? It's not a matter of religion anymore. Normally speaking, shrines conflict with temples, or exist parallel to churches. Normally, they're of this or that faith, this or that sect, this or that founder, text, secret scripture, and that's what the believers pray. But these people who come here are not thinking of secret scriptures. The sentiments of those who come to Yasukuni Shrine and of those who serve here are not religious.

I attend the rites. I often speak with such people. I myself was in the military. My war comrades and my seniors at school all perished, too. When I meet these people, I always feel I might be meeting one of their family members. I know their friends, their families, their subordinates are enshrined here. I myself am alive only by accident. If I were dead, of course, I would have been enshrined here. When I am here, the difference between the living "I" and my enshrined war comrades disappears. When these people come to worship, I feel that they might have been coming to greet me. I welcome them with that kind of deep thought. That is why the shrine values such people so highly. I deeply understand their feelings and their memories of a young daughter, a young son, who remains unchanged. I am sure that their youthful pictures are placed on the Buddhist altars in their homes. While meeting these people, I realize how serving here fills my own heart.

I dress as a Shintō priest and I conduct the rites. Sometimes various arguments are stirred up about those rites—that they are Shintō rites and Shintō is a religion—so they say. They claim that Yasukuni is one sect within a religion, but we don't think that way. We simply welcome worshipers who come here with a certain set of feelings. When we talk to those who come, we mainly speak of their remembrances. How their sons went in good spirits, or how their grandchildren are doing today. The talk rambles. Sometimes, I even meet those who were in the same war zone as I was. I'm now getting old myself, of course, but when I was younger and met parents, they would sometimes look and speak with me as if I were their son. We want them to return home satisfied.

Some people misrepresent the Yūshūkan as a war museum. In that war, teenagers and youths in their twenties perished. We are trying to decorate it with testaments written by, clothes worn by, and relics of those who perished. We endeavor to provide a background explanation for each. A human being does not have two lives. A single valuable life is extinguished in that exercise of national state authority called "war," today, just as in ancient times, in the East as in the West. To perish in war is a tragic thing, but if you assume that their spirit remains behind, then it's your duty to comfort them to the greatest extent possible. Criticism of the war comes from a time after they perished for that state-society. So we still must express our gratitude to and worship them. Today, fifty of us, including the head priest and the *miko* [vestals], have to pray to make their minds rest easy. In the world after death, they must rest as if they had died among their loved ones.

We Japanese have always been this way. Even in civil wars, battles between daimyo, they built tombstones or five-tiered gravestones for the dead, whether friend or foe. We can still view those ancient ones in the form of stone Buddhas—we Japanese have been carrying out this practice for years, just as we have been eating rice. This custom was given a national form in the Meiji period when Yasukuni Shrine was established. These feelings are connected to the deepest emotions of the Japanese. This way of living, this way of thinking, is deeply rooted in this nation. As long as we continue to live according to a Japanese way, this will not change.

Before and during the war, Shintō shrines belonged to the country. *Kokka Shintō* [State Shintō], it was called. The state was deeply involved, so priests were officials. I myself studied at the Jingū Kōgakukan, in Ise City, where they trained both people to serve the gods and teachers for girls' schools, middle schools, and normal schools. My father was a priest for the gods, but I was going to be a history teacher.

We students never really argued about the war among ourselves. We accepted it as it was, part of one great flow. We never thought differently about it. We youths had to go. The education we had received up to that point was completely dedicated to that principle. Today, there are multiple values, many parallel views of life and the world. You can think objectively, but then this wasn't so. Since Meiji times, Japan had been advancing in that direction. In order to enrich the nation, Japan had to strengthen the army. Population increased, so to increase the nation's productive capacities, the country had to expand. For the sake of the development of the race. All nations of the world would have done this. Japan was not the only nation that expanded aggressively. We were already moving in that direction. There was an ideology that served to justify this course of action. There were some partially developed ideas that conflicted with that notion, but they were merely bubbles in the great stream.

When we were ready to graduate from school in 1942, we thought, "Let's go!" For the sake of the nation, for the sake of the government. I, who was studying history, look back now and recognize that that was only one way to view things historically, but at that time we all looked and said, "Japan must take this course." Today, were my child to say, "I want to enter the military," I would reply, "Don't do it!" Of course. But at that time we didn't have that kind of choice. We only had one course open to us.

I was in the air corps, myself. I went to China, Manchuria, Manila, Luzon, the Celebes, Makassar, Java, and finally Bandung. I faced many, many occasions where I survived just by going one way rather than the other. Those days were full of hostility and hatred toward the enemy. We didn't know much about America. They were simply "the enemy." It didn't occur to us that behind the enemy there were governments, people, Christians, anything. We just thought, "they are here, we must fight them." We had no knowledge of how America was founded. What races made up America. Nothing. We just had the expression *"Kichiku Bei-Ei"* —American-English Demons. We saw them as lower animals. These terms were widespread in Japan. We would be invaded. Persecuted. Made to suffer. The race called "Japan" would be extinguished. That's the way we felt.

August 15, 1945. The Imperial Rescript came through by telegram. We all lamented the situation. The feeling that Japan faced extinction was very strong. The education I received would disappear. I drove a car up to the top of the mountain in Bandung [Indonesia], where the best astronomical observatory in Asia was located. I took my pistol with me. I really don't like to mention this. I thought Japan was done for. My life was over. I lay down on the lawn. The stars were unbelievable, overwhelming. While I was looking at the Southern Cross, the image of the shrine at Ise appeared to me. Speaking religiously, I was saved by the gods. I came down the mountain. Even today, I believe the gods of Ise called me back, "Don't throw your life away." I was a twenty-four-year-old army second lieutenant.

I feel my wartime experiences were my most valuable experiences. I dream of them even today. They are that deeply etched in my mind. I still see myself walking in Manila or driving a car in Java. I've been at Yasukuni for more than thirty years now and pretty soon I must face my retirement age. I was in the war, and I have prayed for the war dead since my return. I suppose I've been dragging the war with me all my life.

There are two million four hundred sixty-five thousand pillars of the nation enshrined here, including some from even before the Meiji Restoration, some dating back to the time when the American Commander Perry appeared off Uraga. The patriot Yoshida Shōin is here. Only the Self-Defense Forces who die on active duty do not meet our criteria. This means the list of those enshrined ends with the ones who perished in the last Pacific War.

Originally, the state established Yasukuni Shrine at the direction of the Meiji Emperor, but today it has nothing to do with the state. Under the new constitution, the state and belief are separate matters. It is not correct to say that the Emperor does not come here to pray. Though He has not done us the honor of an Imperial visit recently, the Imperial Envoy appears at the spring and autumn festivals, in proper formal attire, bringing offerings from the Emperor. Every year, twice a year, without fail. Besides, imperial family members come on their own. An emperor's last visit was in 1977.

We have eight million worshipers annually. I can probably classify them into three types. First are the mere sightseers. Then there are the war comrades and the bereaved families. Naturally, each year, membership in their associations has been dwindling. Then there is a third group, those who come here in search of some meaning. There are many in that category who feel we have to appreciate the war dead because they perished for the sake of the nation. To convey that message to history, to enshrine the war dead here means to them an assurance of the resurrection of the Japanese mind and spirit. They feel they must do that. People who have been thinking like that ideologically come here. Their numbers have gradually been increasing. Education has accomplished this.

Today, young people come here. I see many in the Yūshūkan, although today's Japan Teachers' Association has, up to now, taught that war is wrong. So they say those who died in war should just be thrown out. They have raised today's youth with those ideas. Yet despite that, quite a few youths come here to worship. Japan has established economic stability. As its educational system undergoes changes, I think the feeling that we have to value the war dead more highly will spread more and more widely. I think the official approval of textbooks exists so that there will be no mistaken schoolbooks. If a time comes when education rooted in Japanese tradition can be established, I believe the number who feel this way will grow.

Lessons

MOGAMI SADAO [2]

A 1940 graduate of the Air Officers' School of the Japanese military academy, he was a captain on the staff at central air headquarters in Tokyo, assigned as adjutant to Prince Mikasa. He was a fighter pilot, grounded by illness in the bitter last stages of the war and the futile defense of Japanese airspace, when it all ended in 1945.

Although I'd been taken out of combat early in the war because of my bad kidneys, I didn't give them a thought when I wangled a trip, through Imperial General Headquarters, to Singapore and Sumatra. I left behind my students at flight school in July 1944 and headed south. When I turned up at Third Air Corps headquarters, Lieutenant General Kinoshita was so angry at Tokyo's interference in his area of responsibility that he placed me under his direct command and ordered me to take over training for his whole corps. That was all right with me! I lived in the Raffles Hotel, in a suite in the left wing. I even had a piano in my own room. I was only a captain, but with my special allowances and one for housing, I drew eight hundred yen a month! Same as a full general. In Japan there had been severe shortages, but everything was available in Singapore. It was wonderful. No enemy around, no combat, not even a blackout. The pleasure district bars were wide open. The overseas Chinese seemed to have completely changed colors. They called out everywhere in Japanese, "Hey, Mr. Soldier!" and got on with business. Eventually, I had to return to Japan, but a one-month trip had become six months.

Back home, because of my physical condition, I was assigned only to paperwork—writing planning papers and deciding where pilots should be trained. Our pilots were being killed one after the other in great numbers. Aviation-fuel reserves were very limited. We calculated total national domestic production of aviation fuel, combined with fuel made from pine roots, was only ten thousand kiloliters a month. If we used our reserve every month exclusively for training, we'd have had no reserve at all in just four months. Training of pilots in the homeland virtually ceased.

Because of the fuel shortage, even when the B-29s came to bomb, intercepting them was prohibited. But the fighter units couldn't bear just sitting on the ground while the Americans attacked us. They wanted at least to feel they had launched some planes and perhaps disrupted the plan of the American raid, and after the terrible damage done to Tokyo March 10, 1945, we at air headquarters didn't feel we could prohibit intercepting any longer. At the very least we had to defend areas where airplane parts were manufactured. In those days, I was commuting from my home. Even my own father berated me, demanding to know what we were doing. I couldn't answer, "We don't have any fuel and our planes are made of inferior materials. They can't keep up with the Americans." I couldn't say we had to preserve our fuel for the special-attack-force planes that would be used against the huge American invasion fleets about to descend on the Homeland.

Japan no longer hoped to find a way to win, but sought some means of ending the war gracefully. That, we believed, would be accomplished when the Tokkō inflicted tremendous damage on the American fleet as they assaulted the Homeland. This supposedly offered us the best chance to get a treaty more advantageous to Japan. The Tokkō hadn't really been conceived of by the high command, but had come from more junior officers. Valuable planes would be lost, but to keep the enemy from landing on the Homeland, there seemed no other choice. The feeble firepower of our planes, even at point-blank range, could no longer force a B-29 to waver in its course. Some of my classmates died in action ramming B-29s over Ise Bay.

The young Tokkō pilots were full of fighting spirit and tried desperately to break through the enemy's defenses. Almost fifty years later, the Tokkō spirit of the Kamikazes still survives. I am today involved in the compilation of a book on the Tokkō. In the army and the navy combined, 4,668 Pillars of the Nation were awarded posthumous two-rank promotions. Due to confusion near the end of the war, some who died as Tokkō were not treated that way and never received the recognition they deserved.

The Tokkō have won the admiration of many people throughout the world. On the twenty-third of September, 1989, for example, the Turkish military attaché visited the Setagaya Kannon dedicated to the Tokkō. There, he praised General Nogi Maresuke and Admiral Tōgō Heihachirō, war gods of the Russo-Japanese War, and told us through an interpreter that he has taken the Tokkō as a model for the Turkish military.

At the end of the war, I was in Ichigaya. I had first put on my military uniform there, the original site of the military academy, and now it was there I was going to take it off for the last time. When I heard the Imperial speech on the radio, my only thought was *"Mei fa,"* that Chinese phrase for "It cannot be helped." I was lying on the *tatami* of the night-duty office thinking that when seven vice-group-leaders of the Air Officers' School burst in on me. "What are you doing!" they shouted. "Accept the Potsdam Declaration? The evil subordinates of the Emperor are thinking this. That cannot be the true mind of His Imperial Highness!" They were screaming, "If Japan accepts, Japan will perish! Keep fighting resolutely! You must do something!" They said these things menacingly, urging me on because I was their superior.

I thought for a moment and then told them that while it might be correct to rouse ourselves to action, to revolt, we first must determine the true state of His Imperial Majesty's mind. I suggested we go to the general staff headquarters, and I led them to the Military Affairs Department. The colonel there only poured oil on the flames, so I led them all to vice-chief of the general staff Kawabe. He, too, was embroiled in an argument. It seemed to me that the general staff headquarters had already given up, but the men who were with me were bubbling over with fervor. "We'll behead the evil subordinates of the Emperor!" they were threatening.

While I might have been at central headquarters, I couldn't just go and ask to meet His Imperial Majesty to find out what he thought! At that time, however, Prince Mikasa, the Emperor's younger brother, was a staff officer serving at air force headquarters. He'd been assigned there in April, since Japan's last fighting strength was in our air force, and I'd been assigned to him. He hadn't come in on that fifteenth of August, but I could think of no other way to determine His Imperial Highness's true mind than to ask Prince Mikasa.

When I got in to see him, he said a shocking thing to me. The first words out of his mouth were, "Mogami, do you know that the Manchurian Incident started because of a plot by the Kwantung Army?" I know that now, but at that time, we thought the Chinese warlord Chang Hseuh-liang had illegally resisted Japan and Japan had simply defended itself. That wasn't true, Prince Mikasa now said. He had been a staff officer with the China Garrison Army. "Mogami," he said, "you were in China, too. Even if Japan were to win this war, do you think the one billion people of Asia would follow Japan after the things we did in China?"

I felt as if I'd been hit by a bolt of lightning. At such a critical moment as this, Prince Mikasa—standing right in front of me—felt he must disclose such things even to the likes of me. It was clear His Imperial Highness felt he could trust his military no further. I was sure that was what he meant. The war had not developed the way the chief-of-staff's reports to the Throne assured him it would. I became convinced that accepting the Potsdam Declaration was indeed His Majesty's true wish, so I went around to as many units as I could to convince them. This was after my superiors had informed me that the front-line units near the capital were so worked up that they wouldn't listen to them, that high rank alone was no longer sufficient to control them, that I'd have to do it.

It was a near run thing. I told men in those units that accepting the Potsdam Declaration was certainly a gamble, but that there was absolutely no doubt that this was His Imperial Majesty's will, and I quoted Prince Mikasa to that effect. They seemed to grasp that, but the most extreme among them now began to assert that when His Imperial Highness makes a wrong decision, it was their duty as subordinates to remonstrate his decision, "even at the risk of our lives." I had to argue back, "It's outrageous to criticize him at this time, of all times. How can you say His Imperial Highness is wrong?" I appealed to their sense of duty. "Active-duty officers may be turned into slaves, they may be made to shoulder iron rails to rebuild the scorched soil of China, or they may be beaten with whips," I declared, "but even that is all right for us. With our last breaths, let us go together according to His Imperial Majesty's wishes. If he wishes to accept the Potsdam Declaration, let us join him in that."

I went around all through the sixteenth and seventeenth of August, two whole days, and even had to stare down officers ten years my senior who were loading guns from planes onto trucks so they could make a last stand in the mountains of Ōme. Looking back today, though the year 1940 saw me appointed to military rank, I did little real work during the war. But I believe that at the very end of the war I carried out one important assignment.

After the war, I entered university intending to study literature, but in my third year I joined Jardine-Matheson Trading Company. By 1968, I was involved in exporting construction materials to Southeast Asia. Our best client was the American Metal Company in Singapore, whose president was Peter Yap, nationality British. Whenever he came to Japan, I took him to hot spas in Atami. We grew very close. One day—we'd been friends for three years or so—I was at his mansion in Singapore, a house with tennis courts, a pool, and waterfalls. We started talking about the old days. We were drinking. He could really hold his liquor, let me tell you! Quite a man. He said, in English, "By the way, Mr. Mogami, my sister was killed by the Japanese army when I was sixteen years old. Her head was put on the railing at the Reservoir. I was so angry! I wanted revenge. I entered a guerrilla school, learned how to fire small arms and throw hand grenades. I was still a child, so Japanese sentries were relaxed when they saw me. Using the darkness for cover, attacking from behind, I killed more than ten people."

I sobered up immediately. I thought, "How close we've become, yet this hatred toward the Japanese army is buried deep in his bones." I didn't know what to expect, but Yap continued, "I did those things back then as an individual. Still, when I reflect on it today, the reason Singapore exists, the reason Malaysia and Indonesia exist as independent countries, is because the Japanese military fought for them. These things are all due to the Japanese army. Today's Japanese have made reparation for the crimes they committed back then. I suspect that fifty years from today Japan's military will be valued in history, or maybe it will take a century."

Until that moment I had always thought that we Japanese had done wrong and must bow down for it. I was taken aback. Mr. Yap continued, "Freedom, equality, philanthropy, these things were all only for the sake of Caucasians before. To conduct a revolution in thought, which would bring these things to everybody, to all humankind, that was the achievement of the Greater East Asia War." That was what he claimed.

Two million three hundred thousand, maybe four hundred thousand [military men] victims! Truly we fought a stupid war. The Greater East Asia War developed the way it did because we were divided between the army's northern-advance theory against the Soviet Union and the navy's idea of a move to the south. The navy asserted that without fuel they would be unable to conduct war, so the navy's first task was to secure the fuel of Indonesia. The army was pulled into a war in the South and into a war against America by the navy. America had been targeted as the navy's hypothetical enemy way back after the Russo-Japanese War, only because the navy wanted to build itself up. So this conflict started with what was essentially a grab for a bigger share of the budget. While lower-ranking officers cooperated quite freely, high-ranking ones were vicious in their battles with each other. Things started there and ended up the way they did. A nation's defense policy should never be divided.

But Japan was able to recover from the war in all respects afterwards because the people's mind was united, bound up together, and all the race's energy was combined. Today's Japan might not exist if Japan had not stood up at the time of the Japan-U.S. negotiations. If Japan had weakly submitted then, none of this might have been possible. I do not glorify war. I know you shouldn't fight war, but if it happens, what matters are the lessons you learn from it!

A Quest for Meaning

ŌTA MASAHIDE [2]

"I saw local people treated very cruelly and harshly by Japanese soldiers on the beaches of Mabuni during the Battle of Okinawa. Why was this happening, I wondered, since we'd all desperately done our best. Out of my one hundred twenty classmates, only about thirty-five survived. The battle didn't end with my friends' deaths. Among the survivors were many disabled, some maimed, and some unable to lead any life in society. They made it through the battle alive, thanks to all their efforts, but mentally they were destroyed. Such people are still here today. They were literally crippled by the war. Those are some of the reasons why I've studied the battle of Okinawa for so long and why I chase after its elusive character."

When we meet at his home in Ginowan City, Okinawa, he is a professor of journalism and sociology at the University of the Ryūkyūs.

From floor to ceiling, his study holds books on Okinawan history and culture. He has written extensively on the Battle of Okinawa.

When I was a teenager, we had no other books than those with the "Imperial-nation" view of history. For people who lived in Tokyo or Kyoto, even though some books were prohibited, somewhere secretly such books surely existed. Moreover, in the higher schools, students had a fairly advanced education. If they wanted to, they could obtain different kinds of books and listen to progressive thinkers. Such possibilities were closed to us on the islands. Okinawa was the only prefecture in all of Japan without either a technical school or a university. The goal of our education was only to create men who would fervently throw away their lives for the sake of the Emperor, men who were full of loyalty. We had no way of knowing anything other than what we knew. Therefore, we just did what we were told, and we did it believing in it.

We were really ignorant of our own history. We had a subject called Local History, but there were no lectures. We had no idea what had happened to us when the old feudal domains were eliminated and the prefectures were established.* The basis for the tragedy of the girl nurses' Lily Corps and the other student units lay in this lack of knowledge. We were a "pure culture," distilled by our education to be the Emperor's subjects. The soldiers knew the reality of war because they had participated in battles in China, so they went into the depths of the caves and stayed there. We students, and those like us who didn't know anything, were told, "This is your homeland! It is natural for you to defend your own Motherland." We had no choice but to do it. We went out without even having a healthy fear of war and ended up being slaughtered.

We must look at the Battle of Okinawa to see what distinguishes it. One of its most striking features is that soldiers of the friendly army —Japanese soldiers whom Okinawans considered to be on their side— murdered local residents, and not just a few, either. There are records that more than one thousand people were murdered because they'd engaged in "spy activities." I cannot confirm the figure, but I would say it was certainly more than eight hundred people, based on my personal investigation of the histories of various towns, cities, and villages. Moreover, a fairly large number of people were entrapped in "group suicides."

I didn't really comprehend the meaning of this kind of murder until one day I was shocked by an article I read in the *Asahi* newspaper. The killing of local residents as spies, and the group suicides took place on the

---

* Okinawa, a semi-independent kingdom, was annexed to Japan in 1879, more than a decade after the Meiji Restoration had overthrown the Tokugawa shoguns.

Kerama Islands, too. One man who was a company commander there joined the Ground Self-Defense Forces after the war, rose to the rank of major general. He taught the military history of the Okinawan battle. He now wrote that in the battle, such tragic incidents as the hanging of residents as spies did take place, but he claimed that there was no point criticizing the commanders of that time for such acts, that these only ended up becoming personal attacks, and that wasn't the main issue. Instead, he wrote, Japan's wars had been fought outside the country since Meiji, and now, "For the first time, things previously done outside the country were done inside during the battle of Okinawa. The Japanese Army did not know how to fight on its own territory, so the customs of war learned outside were brought inside the homeland. That is why such tragic incidents occurred."

My principal question to him is simply this: "What customs of war did Japan follow outside the nation?" That's really hung me up. I've been trying to clarify this. I'm writing a book called *Genocide*, and in my own way I've probed the Nanking Incident. All the top Defense Forces leaders for the Battle of Okinawa had been directly involved in the Nanking Incident—the commander Ushijima, the chief-of-staff Chō, and the staff officers. The staff officers all personally saw what happened in Nanking. I was truly stunned by this knowledge. For the first time, I thought I understood the meaning of what happened in Okinawa.

Chief-of-staff Chō Isamu held routine meetings, and at one of these on the ninth day after the American forces landed, he issued an order to the effect that from that day on, whether a person was a military man or not, speaking any language other than Japanese was forbidden. Anyone speaking Okinawan would be punished as a spy. In the War History Office of the Self-Defense Forces you can still see the daily log of orders, and that order is among them. On May 5, once again the same order was issued, bearing the signature of the chief-of-staff. People over sixty years of age here spoke nothing but the local dialect because the creation of prefectures from feudal domains took place here only in 1879. Moreover, the education level was very poor. These people used their own local language, the tongue with which they grew up, and particularly so on the battlefield, in the most extreme and difficult of all imaginable situations. Yet, merely speaking in Okinawan meant punishment as a spy.

Japanese officers and soldiers had no knowledge of Okinawa. They had never been taught anything about the place. Many Japanese thought of the Okinawans as a different race. Even after the war, one company commander's writings show that he still saw the Okinawans as a separate race. He said they had no idea where the Okinawans might dash off to if they didn't keep their eyes on them!

The particular tragedy of the battle of Okinawa may have come from the fact that Okinawans came to see themselves this way too. Because of the past history of Okinawa, various influences from Burma, Thailand, and China entered Okinawan life, and with its different habits, customs, and language, Okinawa was supposed to lack in loyalty and patriotism. Okinawans could not be true members of the pure Japanese, but only third-class Japanese. In order to become a first-class Japanese, an Okinawan had to cultivate loyalty to the Emperor, conceding nothing in the intensity of his loyalty to the Japanese of the Main Islands. When the war was lost, Japanese soldiers spread the story that the defeat was the result of Okinawans spying for the enemy. Children from Okinawa, who were evacuated to Kyushu and other areas, were told the battle was lost because Okinawans had betrayed the country. There were lots of dark incidents.

Mainland researchers, in their study of the Occupation of Japan, still treat Okinawa as if "the Ryūkyūs" weren't part of Japan. They say things like "Japan didn't have a divided Occupation" or "Japan was fortunate not to be divided like Korea or Germany." That's completely wrong. Of course Japan had a divided occupation—if, that is, you consider Okinawa a part of Japan. It's just the same as Germany. The very day the U.S. forces landed, a line was drawn at thirty degrees north latitude separating Okinawa from Japan. That division didn't officially end until March 15, 1972, when Okinawa reverted to Japan.

Today, Okinawa is the poorest prefecture in Japan. Income is only seventy-four percent of the national average. Seventy-five percent of all U.S. forces stationed in Japan are in Okinawa, which makes up only one percent of the nation's land mass. The highest-ranking Japanese often say that Japan is prospering because of the U.S.-Japan Security Treaty. I say that is fine, but I ask them, "Why don't you have a base right next to your estates? Why are the bases only in weak places like Okinawa? Share the burden of the bases equally." Shifting responsibility to the weak, while they themselves prosper comfortably—this is the policy Japan has been taking throughout Asia. It was the same towards the minorities inside the country.

POSTSCRIPT: *In 1990, Ōta Masahide was elected Governor of Okinawa on a progressive ticket, defeating the candidate backed by the conservative Liberal Democratic Party.*

24 / ENDINGS

Homecoming

TOMINAGA SHOZO [2]

A Tokyo Imperial University graduate in agriculture, trained afterward to be an army officer, he survived almost five years of war in China. A second conflict began for Captain Tominaga as that war formally ended.

Captured by the Soviets when they overran Manchuria in August 1945, he was held as a prisoner of war, and was transferred through a succession of harsh Siberian camps, encountering Germans, Rumanians, Hungarians, and Czechs, until he finally ended up in Camp 8, where he was put to mining work. "It was there I saw the full text of the Potsdam Declaration for the first time. I was shocked at Article Ten, the one which said all war criminals will be severely punished, including the ones who treated prisoners cruelly. Those lines reminded me of what I had done in China. Each day I simply did my eight hours of heavy labor and tried not to think of what those words would mean to me when I returned to camp."

The investigation of war criminals began about the time New China established itself in 1949. It was rumored that China had asked the Soviets to hand over war criminals. Some believed that we should say nothing and just tough it out. Others felt that telling what they knew was a condition for becoming a democratic man. Most of us thought then that murdering, raping, and setting fire to villages were unavoidable acts in war, nothing particularly wrong.

When I was called for investigation, Soviet officers and a Korean interpreter asked only if I was Captain Tominaga and questioned me about details of my military career. Someone else must have told about me. Some were bought by money. I remained in Siberia although trains for home departed regularly. Only one camp remained in 1950. We finally boarded a train and were told that we would be sent home via Khabarovsk.

Our train ran east along the same rail we'd taken west five years before. Farms now stood in what had been wasteland, and factories had been built where there had been open country. The waters of Lake Baikal remained the same, frozen and somehow horrifying. We were gathered at Khabarovsk. Some more prisoners joined us from Vladivostok. We conducted a ceremony in the square of the camp where we were now held. The representatives of both groups exchanged greetings and sang a "Song of Unity," hand in hand. I was told that they were the "reactionary officers." Later, one of them came up to me and said that they didn't have any desire to work for the Soviets, but would like to work to build up their physical strength in preparation for the life in prison in China. One condition they wanted to set was that they not work with men who viewed them as the enemy. I negotiated with the Soviet side and arranged work for them at wood-milling.

In June 1950 we were given new clothes by our Russian captors and told to spend all the money we had. We were taken to the station. Normally, red banners and slogans hung from the trains, but what we found were freight trains covered with barbed wire. The sight reminded me of basket cages for criminals. It was blazing hot in the cars. After two nights the train was shunted onto a siding. I read the name of the station, "Guroteko," a place on the border between the Soviet Union and Manchuria. Inside the car there was complete turmoil. Everyone knew we were going to be handed over to the Chinese. We thought we would be killed when they got their hands on us.

When the train finally started moving again, we passed through a tunnel. Soldiers of the People's Liberation Army were lined up on the other side. They were so young they looked like boy soldiers, perhaps because we were used to seeing the robust Soviets. I thought soon it would be all over. There were about 960 of us, including former police-men, military police, and men from the criminal-investigation and legal sections of Manchukuo. There were about one hundred men like that who had treated the Chinese cruelly. The others were all soldiers. The highest-ranking officers present were divisional commanders. Several of them. More than half were noncommissioned officers. There were about two or three hundred officers, but no really senior ones.

We boarded new trains in China. This time, we found ourselves in passenger cars. They gave us some bread for lunch. White bread. We'd eaten only black bread in Siberia and we feared that white bread was too refined and wouldn't provide strength enough. It was eerie. The treat-ment we received was so polite that it almost seemed like they were scared of us. Maybe they were going to treat us gently, then kill us suddenly. The train arrived at Fushun. We formed up on the platform and walked through streets lined by soldiers with guns. The machine guns on the roofs of the houses were Japanese-army issue. We were taken to Fushun Prison, which had been built by the Japanese government to hold Chinese. The former warden of the prison was now among its prisoners.

I was put into a cell with fifteen other men. The lock clanged shut behind me with a heavy noise. It was an awful feeling. A wooden board hung above the door, bearing the words "Japanese Military War Criminal Management." All of us resented that. We insisted that it didn't make any sense to call us war criminals. The war criminals were the Emperor, the cabinet ministers, and the military commanders. They were the ones who had led us into the war. They were the ones responsible. Small fish and hooligans like us weren't war criminals. Those were our complaints to our guard, who conveyed our feelings to his superior. The wooden board was replaced with one that simply said "Management."

Our first meal took us completely by surprise. We were served Chinese broccoli, with a soup of pork and radishes. It was delicious. When we ran out of fresh vegetables, they brought us more food. Our only wish in Siberia had been to get enough food. Now we did no labor. We were allowed to go out for exercise and to the lavatory for thirty minutes, morning and evening. We were confined to the cells the rest of the time. Our daily routine was to play *shōgi*, *go*, and mah-jongg, and tell pornographic stories. We had nothing to do but lie around on our backs. Sometimes the guards came by and cautioned us to sit up, but we ignored their warnings. We even spat at them. Sometimes we were given a few leaflets about the New China, but no one paid much attention to them. For the first two years, in our desperation, we were insubordinate and defiant toward our jailers. We felt we would be killed anyway. After all, every one of us was guilty of something.

They ignored our defiant attitude like willows before the wind. They never shouted at us or kicked us. When someone fell ill, they came to take care of him, even in the middle of the night. They sent the seriously ill to a special hospital outside. We began to realize that human beings should be treated this way and began to reflect on our treatment of Chinese during the war. "We acted wrongly, but we wouldn't have done it if we hadn't received the orders." That was still our thinking. In my case, I imagined I did it only because of the regiment commander's order. "Yes, the bad one was Commander Ōsawa," I'd say. "He's the one who made me kill that first one." I believed I was a victim.

We were transferred to another prison for a while in 1950 when the U.S. Army advanced to the Yalu River in the Korean War. It was confidently explained to us that the Volunteer Army from China was now participating in that war and would soon push back the Americans, that they were only moving us to protect us from American bombing. It never crossed my mind that the Chinese could defeat the U.S. forces when the Japanese military had failed to beat them. We even hoped that the U.S. forces might rescue us from captivity, but the following spring the majority of us were sent back to Fushun, though those of us over the rank of first lieutenant were moved to Harbin. Only then did we realize that the People's Liberation Army were not an ordinary army. The Korean War turned out as they told us it would, and our belief that the Chinese people were inferior and the Chinese army weak was overturned completely.

Various books were now circulated in the prison. First, novels and the like were brought in and then books on politics and economics. Books by Mao Tse-tung appeared. I reread a collection of Marx and Engels that I'd read before the war, but being in prison made it a completely different experience. The *People's Daily* was circulated. It was 1952, three years after the revolution, and a movement to criticize superiors was sweeping through China. Those who were criticized were excused if they freely admitted their actions had been wrong. If not, they were pulled through the streets wearing conical hats on their heads. The best thing to do was to voluntarily confess what one had done.

Around this time, we were summoned before a panel and asked our feelings about our treatment there and our impressions of the books we had read. The guards and soldiers didn't wear any badges of rank. Those people who came to summon us seemed to be officers and the guards were probably noncoms. We called all those who summoned and talked to us "leaders."

One day, we were given ten pages of rough paper and told to write out an account of our past. We thought that the final act had come. If we were to write, what else had we to write about but cruel acts? It meant death. The four or five of us sat apart, scattered about in one room. No one said a word, just glared at the paper on the desk. Some wrote a little and then erased it. At lunch, everyone ate in silence. I told myself that I would be executed anyway and began writing. I wrote that I killed a prisoner under direct orders, I wrote that I had made new conscripts execute prisoners when I was a company commander. I wrote that I ordered my men to shoot the Chinese soldiers who surrendered because holding prisoners was troublesome. And I wrote that I had ordered the burning of a hundred houses under direct orders.

Everybody else looked at me amazed. I rewrote this neatly and tried to give it to a guard who passed by. He just ignored me and went away. Thirty minutes later, another guard passed by. I called out to him, and after asking me if I was really done, he reluctantly accepted it. Everybody else was having difficult time writing anything, while I was now reading a magazine. A guard came and called out my prisoner number. Number

373 was my name from the beginning to the end of my prison days. The guard stood there, with a fierce expression, holding out the papers I'd submitted. It was natural, he said, not to be able to write. Writing this quickly was the epitome of an insincere attitude! I was an obstacle to the sincere students. He took me out and threw me into an underground cell.

The cell was deep underground and dark, and it had been unused for long time. It was lit by a grim, dim bulb. I convinced myself that I'd finally fallen as far to the bottom as I could go. In time my eyes got used to the darkness and I made out writing on the wall. "Down with Japanese Imperialism!" "Devils of the Orient!" All of it was abusive language about us Japanese. Written in blood. When I saw these, a chill went up my spine. They'd been written in desperate, hopeless defiance by prisoners just before being killed. For the first time, I understood the mind of those prisoners. Up to that moment, I'd excused myself from responsibility on the grounds that I was myself ordered to commit such acts by regimental commanders. From the point of view of those murdered, though, it didn't matter whether the act of killing was a voluntary one or done under orders.

I now realized that first I had to take responsibility myself, as a person who had acted. Only then could I pursue the responsibilities of the superiors, my commanders, and the Emperor. There was a notebook in the cell. I was again told to write a self-examination. About the tenth day in the cell, the blue ink turned purple, then seemed to disappear altogether. I could no longer see the letters I was writing. When I told the guard I was taken to the medical room. There, I was given a shot and ordered to stop writing. I just sat in the cell and thought. One week later they told me I could write once again, suggesting that my consciousness must have been deepened. I wrote from the viewpoint of the persons whose houses we burnt down and whom we killed. In the middle of the winter, no shelter, no food, no fuel. I wrote my self-examination based on the results of my acts.

After one month, I was allowed to leave the dungeon. Later, I was taken to the hospital attached to Harbin Medical University, a former Japanese Kwantung Army hospital with excellent facilities. I received a thorough examination and learned that I was suffering from *lumbar caries*. Hospitalized, I lay with my upper body in a plaster jacket. I couldn't sleep because of the pain, not until I was given a morphine injection. When I woke up, still in pain, I felt that this was the revenge of the victims. I was experiencing real pain for the first time. They gave me streptomycin injections, a precious substance greatly prized at that time. The pain disappeared suddenly after two weeks.

While I was hospitalized, members of my battalion made oral confessions in front of each other. It was 1954. The leaders of the "management" and the public prosecutors were present. It went on every day for several months. Whenever they were found to be hiding something, they had to repeat their stories again and again. Their lack of sincerity was criticized. The anxiety caused a loss of appetite. One of them committed suicide. When I was finally allowed to go back to the prison and rejoin the Japanese after three years in bed, I noticed their expressions had changed. They had released what they'd held in their minds. At that time, we were able to visit other rooms because the locks were not set anymore. We studied in the morning and did exercises in the afternoon.

Now, the study committee brought a new theme up for discussion. Miwa, who'd killed dozens of people, announced in front of everyone that he would request the death sentence. The idea was that the war criminal who realized his guilt shouldn't wait for a trial but should request one. We reached a level of understanding through our studies that we ought to accept any sentence. However, we were still shaken when the time for a trial came. We were now taken out of our prison on field trips. The first day we went to a machine plant. I was especially surprised by a new kind of long light bulb that I had never seen before. I was told that these were called "fluorescent lights," and that they were extremely efficient. It made me realize how long a time had passed. The second day, we visited a farming cooperative, and the third day, a mine. After we saw the mine, we were introduced to one of the survivors of a massacre in a nearby village. She described, in detail, how all of her family members and other villagers had been killed and how she felt. She explained how the Communist Party had helped her understand that Japanese militarism caused this and not the Japanese people. For the first time we directly experienced the anger of the Chinese.

Soon the trials began. It was June 1956. There were one thousand sixty-two of us altogether, including one hundred twenty who had fought with the Nationalist army. Forty-five of us were indicted and the others were given a reprieve. They told us that there was enough evidence for indictment and conviction, but that they would allow us to return to Japan because we showed clear signs of repentance and had admitted our guilt. Furthermore, Japan was no longer a militaristic nation.

When I saw the green land of Japan after two nights aboard the ship, I wasn't moved at all. I didn't even feel that I had returned to my motherland. Maybe it had just been too long. Perhaps I was overwhelmed by worries about how I would support my family and how I would adjust to the society I had yearned for so when I was in Siberia. In those days, tears came to my eyes whenever I saw the trains moving east. But I gave up on the idea of going home after I was moved to China as a war criminal.

It was more than sixteen years since I had left for China. I was a frail forty-three-year-old man wrapped up in Chinese worker's clothes, sick and weary. I couldn't help feeling empty. The pier was full of people. I got off the ship and walked past the welcoming crowd until I encountered my wife's face. "I'm back," was all I said. "Welcome home," she replied with a smile. She looked a lot older. Then she introduced a tall girl standing behind her, "This is Yumi." I touched the shoulder of the high-school student and said, "Hi." She grew tense and didn't smile. When I had last seen her, she could barely walk. The girl standing there like a stranger was my daughter.

The Face of the Enemy

SASAKI NAOKATA

He was evacuated with his Tokyo elementary-school class to Miyagi prefecture on September 2, 1944. They were staying in a small-town inn on August 15, 1945, when the war officially ended. "Many of my classmates had lost their parents. Seven of them had lost one parent, nine had lost both. Ten had had their entire families annihilated, leaving them utterly alone. This out of my eighty-five classmates in my sixth-grade class from that one Asakusa school."

The day the war ended we still did our usual morning calesthenics. You stripped to the waist, even in the middle of winter—girls, too—and shouted rhythmically in time to the exercises, "Annihilate America and England! One-Two-Three-Four! Annihilate America and England! One-Two-Three-Four!" This was at six in the morning in the inn yard close by a pond that still had carp swimming in it. We had no doubt that Japan's actions were just. We were convinced that the Americans and the British were demons. Not human beings.

We then went for our morning meal in the dining hall on the first floor of the inn and together we recited: "The blessings of the Imperial Reign on Heaven and Earth. Taste the beneficence of Parents and Supremacy." I don't even understand today what that means exactly, but maybe the "supremacy" refers to the Emperor. Then we quickly ate. The amount of food in front of us was so small we finished immediately. We were always hungry. We'd pour hot water into our bowls and gulp it down just to fill our stomachs.

That day we went to work in the mountainside pumpkin garden we had pioneered, carving it out of the woods ourselves, then back to the inn to listen to a special talk given by the Emperor. But the receiver was in such a terrible condition and the Emperor's words were so difficult we didn't understand a thing. Even our teachers didn't understand. We only learned what it meant the next day, or maybe even the day after. The thought that Japan would lose hadn't been in our thoughts. We continued to chant "Annihilate America and England! One-Two-Three-Four!" in our morning calesthenics for two more days. Finally, our teachers told us, "The war has ended." They never said, "Japan lost," just that we could go back home. That was good.

Gradually, my friends started going back to Tokyo. But not me. I couldn't yet, so there I still was, in Miyagi, on the day when word came, "The Americans are on their way! They're coming on jeeps and trucks!"

Great clouds of dust billowed up as jeeps raced down the road towards us. We peeped out through little holes we'd poked in the paper of the inn's *shōji* screens to try to catch a glimpse of them. What would they be like? Suddenly, it occurred to us, "They must have horns!" We had images of glaring demons with horns sprouting from their heads.

We were disappointed, of course. No horns at all. Later, schoolmates who'd bumped into them on the streets brought back chocolates. "Americans, they're good people," they said, but I told them that couldn't be true. I swore that they must be lying. But I never went out to see for myself, not until I got back to Tokyo, anyway.

Imperial Gifts for the War Dead

KAWASHIMA EIKO

She is the thirty-fourth in the line of masters of Shioze, a shop famed for the sweet bean-filled cakes called manjū. Their confections have been enjoyed by the Court, military rulers of Japan, masters of tea ceremony, and connoisseurs of sweets since the founder of the line arrived from China in 1349 and adapted Chinese cakes to Japanese tastes. At sixty-eight, she is the picture of the efficient businesswoman.

My father used to say, "His Imperial Highness the Emperor Meiji loved sweets. He ate our sweet jellied bean *yōkan* whenever he drank saké." Her Imperial Highness, the Empress Dowager Shōken, treated my father with favor and called him by the name of our shop, Shioze. As a child, father even played with Crown Prince Hirohito and his brothers Prince Mikasa and Prince Chichibu. Father never thought making confections for the Imperial Household was "business." We couldn't provide them free-of-charge, of course, but we made them at cost.

Early in the war, our business with the military was enormous, with large orders for events like the Imperial Military Grand Review, regimental parades, and anniversaries. Our speciality was *manjū,* but as the war grew more severe, we found it increasingly difficult to obtain raw materials, particularly enough Yamato taro for the flour. Sugar, too, was rationed. Things we'd been creating for generations—for six hundred forty years—were now hard to make.

In the end, our business was reduced to just ten employees making two things, bread for schools and *Go-monka.* This last confection, a molded cake bearing the Imperial crest, was given to bereaved families in the name of Her Imperial Highness, the Empress, to be offered to the spirits of the war dead. His Majesty presented Imperial Tobacco, also bearing the Imperial Crest. The cakes were made of flour and sugar. Pure white. We received large supplies of the materials required and kept them in our storeroom. The ingredients were mixed together by hand and then pressed into individual wooden molds shaped like the paulownia leaf. When the molds were dried in a heater, the confection became so hard that even if you dropped it off the table it wouldn't shatter. It wasn't really intended to be eaten, but to be placed on an altar in honor of the war dead. To find something black, like a burned spot, contaminating its pure surface would be a disaster, so everything was watched carefully.

Mother and I wrapped each cake in white paper and placed it in a special box covered in white paper, six to a box. A small slip of paper was attached which said, "Bestowed by the Empress." It was a rather monotonous job. But once when I dozed off, my mother scolded me severely with the words, "These cakes are given in exchange for a soldier's life. You must treat them with the respect they deserve."

The day the war ended, I listened to the Emperor's broadcast right here. We all cried. I was still a young woman. I was sad, but at the same time I felt a sense of relief. I feel rather guilty saying that even today, but the air raids were so frightening to me. There was my father next to me, though, sobbing loudly. Meiji, Taishō, Shōwa—all the emperors he had served! It must have been awfully difficult for him.

Soon, the Imperial Household sent a truck around. They wanted to recover all the supplies stored with us. They said they needed to raise money so His Majesty could tour the country, and so they could pay retirement benefits to former Imperial Household employees. My father gave them back everything. *Everything.* He didn't reserve a single bag of flour for himself. He even returned the wooden molds, saying "Please use these for the expenses of His Imperial Highness." I remember even now the moment those trucks left. My father, standing in the entrance hall, tears rolling down his cheeks. How can I forget that? He just murmured, "My service is over."

Royalties

YOKOYAMA RYŪCHI [2]

A leading Japanese cartoonist, he was living in the countryside of Nagano in 1945, having left his home in Kamakura in the face of an impending military call-up. His wife had just died and he had small children to raise.

It's funny, but the Japanese military didn't realize fully that cartoons could grab people's minds. They didn't view us as very important. As a result, we cartoonists weren't really afraid of the military, since they weren't aware of the power we wielded. The Americans knew better.

Before the war ended, they began leafleting us by air. Propaganda, included scenes from my *Fuku-chan.* They'd picked the ones that reminded you most of peaceful times, the ones which made people nostalgic for chrysanthemums. Like one that showed Little Fuku putting his umbrella over some chrysanthemums so they wouldn't get wet in the rain and then getting praised by all those around for acting so nicely. That's the kind. They never picked the ones that had Fuku-chan saying, "Luxury is our enemy. Banish desire until victory is won!" Those were the ones I drew in 1943 and '44.

Those propaganda leaflets were called "Parachute News," and they were even dropped serially! You could also see lots of actual ads in them. For things like chewing gum, Standard Oil Heaters, Lipton Tea, Eagle Milk for Babies, Libby's Corned Beef, Sunkist Raisins. The Japanese knew all these things. They'd had them before the war. You know, I almost got into trouble back in the countryside when they dropped those things over Tokyo. Someone brought one of them back after a big raid and started telling everyone, "That Yokoyama is an American spy. He's working for the Americans," and he produced Little Fuku to testify against me! It wasn't that easy to prove I wasn't doing it!

Anyway, after the war was over, I thought I'd look into this use of my cartoons, so I went down to GHQ—MacArthur's headquarters, you know—and asked to see the man in charge. I'd consulted my good friend Yoshida Ken'ichi, Prime Minister Yoshida Shigeru's son, and at his suggestion I declared they'd used my cartoons without my permission. We were hoping to get money from them if we could

Mr. Stanley—an Australian, a priest who'd studied at Tokyo Imperial University in the old days—came out to meet us at GHQ, which was across from the Palace. He told me he'd used *Fuku-chan* to study Japanese before the war. When MacArthur was advancing in the Philippines, he'd gotten some old *Asahi* newspapers and found Fuku-chan strips in them. He said it really made him nostalgic, so when it was his turn to make propaganda leaflets, he clipped Little Fuku and added in all the things he knew Tokyoites had loved in times of peace.

Now, here he was at MacArthur's headquarters talking to me. He spoke Japanese fluently. Anyway, we told him we'd come to receive our royalties. He told us to wait for a minute, saying, "I have to talk to my superiors." He soon came back, though, and informed us, "Royalties do not exist in wartime."

I told this story to my friends and they were impressed. Everybody was so scared of the Americans. "How could you go and demand money?" they all asked, rolling their eyes.

"I learned about the war from Grandma."

MIYAGI HARUMI

She has just completed compiling a history of Zamami during the Battle of Okinawa. The island lies twenty-two miles west of Naha City, in the Kerama Archipelago, where U.S. forces landed March 26, 1945, in the opening phase of the Okinawa operation. The island had a population of roughly 700 to 800 then. Its principal industries were fishing for tuna and a little agriculture. Total civilian casualties were 358, including 171 in "group suicide."

It was my grandmother, not my mother, who kindled my interest in the war. My mother only talked about the war, but my grandmother's neck had a hole in it. I wondered where it had come from. The island I come from is quite small. My aunt had a scar on her throat and others did, too. Only my grandmother had a large opening. I don't remember exactly how old I was when I first became aware of that hole, but as a child I assumed that in war everyone had their neck cut.

There was an old man in the village we used to call Murderer! Whenever he appeared, the village children used him to play a kind of tag, and when he came too near, all of us kids would run away. Later on, I learned that he had killed his whole family in one of those caves where Okinawans took shelter during the invasion. They asked him to kill them. At first, according to those who survived, he refused, tears streaming down his cheeks. But no one else had enough strength, so he killed his own children, grandchildren, everyone. Another old man who was there did the same. Then he asked this other man to kill him, but he wouldn't do it. He'd promised his grandsons he would follow them, so he tried to hang himself from a rope tied to a makeshift wooden beam that served to keep the cave's ceiling from collapsing. Many old men killed themselves this way, after they'd killed their families. But all we village children heard was "Murderer. He's nothing but a murderer."

My grandmother was very cold to my grandfather. She hardly ever talked to him. When she did, it was in a defiant way. I simply assumed he was a henpecked husband. However, that wasn't the case. She blamed him for killing his own son. In reality, she was the one who had been alarmed and had screamed, "Kill us! Kill us!" when the American forces appeared in front of their cave. She was an accomplice in the act. However, the fact that her son had died, and that her own neck had an opening, seemed to be the only things still in her mind. Grandfather had a scar on his neck, too, from where he'd tried to kill himself. I used to think Grandfather was just an extremely gentle man, but after I learned the whole situation, I realized it wasn't that simple.

First, my grandmother panicked and asked to be killed quickly. Grandfather hurriedly tried to strangle her with a rope, but failed. He hadn't the strength to wring the life out of her. Then he decided to use a blade. You know the kind of razor used in barbershops? My grandfather carried one with him because he hated to have any beard growing on his face. I remember him shaving twice or three times a day when I was a child. He carried it everywhere. With that razor, I was told, he'd cut my grandmother's throat. It still wasn't enough to kill her. She couldn't die and cried out to him to cut with more force. He did—many, many times. Next was their son, who said just one word, "Father," and died.

They had two daughters. One of them was my mother. She was away with the mayor, helping the soldiers as a leader of the women's youth group. The younger one was left there in the cave, presumed dead. That's my aunt. She later told me she noticed noises around her, regained consciousness, and opened her eyes. An American soldier was looking down at her. Their eyes accidentally met. She was shocked and closed hers in a hurry. But the American soldier poked at her eyes to get her to open them. She tried not to breathe, but it was impossible, as you can imagine. He carried her out of the cave. She was eighteen years old at the time, old enough to remember most of the things that had taken place in the cave. She said she didn't feel any pain when her throat was slashed. The blood just gushed out and her body got warm. Then she grew sleepy. It was a sea of blood. Everyone was bathed in the blood of others. For a while, when I was first eager to learn of these stories, she used to tell me, but she won't talk to me about it anymore. I wonder why? She stopped telling me after my grandmother died last year. Aunt used to say that she had those horrifying experiences because her mother was the way she was. I sensed she blamed her. Perhaps telling the stories after her mother's death seemed meaningless.

When Grandmother died, it wasn't of illness. She had a tube in her trachea in order to breathe. Her mouth was just for eating. When she spoke, she breathed the words out of the middle of her throat. Her mouth merely moved, voicelessly. Only those who were used to hearing her talk could understand what she said. The metal tube, placed in her throat by the U.S. forces during the war, remained there for forty-odd postwar years until it gradually started to disintegrate. I guess that was to be expected. The tube was replaced by one made in Japan. The new one was plastic, and it caused an inflammation. The doctors then ordered a special metal tube, but it didn't fit well. One time when it was forced in, blood filled the hole and she died of suffocation, although she was in good health.

I heard nothing about the war from her. Honestly, nothing. Only once did I ask her. She began by saying, "To tell the truth, I wanted to die! But they wouldn't let me die." She told me she wanted to apologize to her son, to die quickly and go to the place where her son is. Grandmother blamed herself for killing him. I couldn't ask more. Grandfather died about the time I entered university. I wasn't interested in the war as much then as I am now. I don't think I would be able to ask him, anyway, even if he were still alive.

Everyone used to believe that the troop commander issued an order for the killings to begin, but that order, in fact, came from men of importance within our village. A runner made the rounds of the caves and conveyed the message that all should gather in front of the monument to the war dead. Everyone assumed then that they were to kill themselves, even though there'd not been any prior arrangement or plan. It had never been decided that gathering in front of the memorial meant that. A message to gather didn't amount to an order to commit "group suicide," you know. Yet everyone knew intuitively what they were supposed to do. In a great hurry they began to "dress for death." They dressed their children in their best clothes. They ate all their remaining food. They left the caves in the midst of a late-night naval bombardment and made their way to the monument.

The site of the monument was totally unsafe. It was an open space, built for the ceremonies tied up with the twenty-six hundredth anniversary of national foundation in 1940. There, on the eighth day of every month, they prayed for success in war and sang the national anthem as the flag was raised. Gathering there meant a lot. The villagers assembled in small clusters that night. But the severity of the bombardment soon scattered everyone. Although everyone went there with the intention to die, they were unable to carry out the act. The next morning the Americans landed.

It was March 26, 1945, the Americans landed on Zamami Island. The tension in the air was unbearable at the moment the villagers actually saw American soldiers coming ashore for the first time. It was like a hair-trigger—one touch and it exploded. The villagers had received an education in not disgracing themselves as Japanese. That education centered on the Emperor and was pounded into them. "Don't use your own local dialect!" "Don't value Okinawan culture!" "Try to stand shoulder-to-shoulder with the Japanese!" This penetrated to the depths of their hearts. It was a familial education that taught that the people were the Emperor's children. This had to be stressed over and over again in Okinawa, where there had never been such a tradition. And what were they told would happen if they were caught by American soldiers? The veterans, those who'd been to China, taught the villagers what would happen if you were captured. They used things like the Nanking massacre as examples. "Japanese did things like this," they'd say. "The Americans naturally will do the same things." It's better to kill your children first and die by your own hand than be shamed and abused, disgraced and raped.

Although I was born after the war, I still feel like I'm dragging it along with me. Even some of the villagers have the impression that I lived through the war, maybe because I'm doing this kind of work. They say things like, "The Americans came like this, and we escaped. Don't you remember?"

I've interviewed many people on Zamami. When strangers go to the island, the villagers are on their guard, tight-lipped in their responses. They feel they have no control over how their answers might be used and they're worried about speaking their minds. That such deeply shameful events took place among blood relatives keeps them from talking. Moreover, all they can seem to do is blame themselves, or people already dead. There's nothing that can be done about it now.

People trust my mother. That's really helped me. She was twenty-four years old, a leader of the wartime women's youth group. Immediately after the end of the war, Mother started gathering the remains of those who had died. She organized a youth group that helped distribute what supplies they received from the Americans. During the war her group helped carry ammunition for the military at the request of the village mayor and deputy mayor. Then she and her friends prepared for their deaths and tried to kill themselves with hand grenades, but they wouldn't explode. My mother and the three most important men in the village—the mayor, deputy mayor, and school principal—went to the garrison commander to request an ammunition magazine so that they and the other villagers could kill themselves. They were turned down. "Go home," was all the garrison commander said. Perhaps it was after this that the village leaders issued that order for everybody to gather in front of the war monument. Who knows? They're all dead now, except my mother. If that commander had issued an order for group suicide I would at least feel that he had given some thought to the fate of the villagers, but even that wasn't the case.

This became clear to me when the garrison commander returned, in secret, for a visit a few years ago. In fact, I'm the one who invited him. I suggested he should meet with the villagers and speak with them about those days, if he had something important to say. He wrote to me under an assumed name and came to Okinawa. I accompanied him to Zamami Island. Mother volunteered to guide him. He wanted to see where his men had died. Whenever my mother said "A soldier died here," he immediately asked to stop the car and got out to comb through the underbrush and rocks for any sign of the lost man. He would then bring his hands together, bow his head in prayer, and sob.

"Fifty-nine villagers died here, including the village notables—the mayor, deputy mayor, and school principal," Mother said as she pointed out a monument which has been erected in their memory. "Is that so?" was his only comment. It was such a minimal response. I was shocked. "OK," he finally said, "let's get out and lay some flowers here, too." I was so surprised, I couldn't believe it. How could he take the news so lightly? Truly, fifty-nine villagers had *died*. Fifty-nine *people* had died there. And others, too, whole families together—mothers, fathers, children. He wasn't even remotely moved by that. Nothing could have convinced me more that such a man wouldn't have thought to issue an order for the villagers to kill themselves. The military were only concerned with their own units, their own commands.

On the boat back to Naha, I brought out a book of photographs by Professor Ōta Masahide called *This Is the Battle of Okinawa*. I asked the commander if he'd like to read it. "No! I don't even want to see it! I don't want to think about lost battles." He really said that! I was quiet afterwards, thinking that something I said might have been wrong. When the boat pulled into the harbor, I asked, "Are you going to visit the Southern Battlefields?" "No," he replied. "That's just the symbol of a lost war. I'm going to visit the American airbase at Kadena. I want to make sure with my own eyes that Japan's security is being guaranteed." I said to myself, "This must be what a military man was like." Nothing had changed in his mind since the war.

When I was in elementary school, new houses sprang up everywhere on our island. The money to build them came from the postwar reconstruction funds. You could borrow money at low interest rates. Most of the families put up pictures of the then Crown Prince and Princess. They said the people who *caused* the war were the bad ones, not the Emperor. Although the villagers criticize the war, they don't know where to assign the blame. They can't bear to put it on the Emperor, so it is directed elsewhere. They say, "That old man was a murderer," or "That man's father did it." The islanders were grouped into the murderers and the murdered.

It's now forty-five years since the Battle of Okinawa, and Okinawa has gone through drastic changes. First, the long American Occupation —until 1971—brought in American culture. Then suddenly Okinawa went back to Japan, and again we heard that we must walk shoulder-to-shoulder with the Japanese. In addition to the rent and subsidies for the military bases here, a great deal of money is paid to Okinawans in survivors' annuities—payments to the families of the war dead. That money has been supporting our island. It's an unhealthy way of living. We are dragging along the war even now. We are living off the dead.

The Occupiers

KAWACHI UICHIRŌ [2]

A Yomiuri newspaperman serving at Imperial General Headquarters throughout the war, he witnessed the arrival of American forces in Tokyo after Japan's surrender.

The very day the war ended, I was switched from covering the Imperial General Headquarters to the prime minister's residence, assigned to cover the cabinet. When I walked out of the Army Ministry, smoke was rising everywhere from burning documents. I glanced at the scene and then went over to the PM's residence to take up my new assignment.

The arrival of the American occupiers is something that really sticks in my mind. The first ones I saw coming into Tokyo weren't soldiers, but journalists. We Japanese couldn't conceive of that. A line of jeeps drove right into the capital, each full of reporters. Some of the Americans jumped from their jeeps when they saw familiar faces among the Japanese reporters and greeted them with cries of, "Hey, howya doing?" Newsmen who knew each other from days in Geneva or someplace else got together again. Just as if nothing had happened.

They didn't take any precautions. No guards. Nothing. They went to the Diet straight off, walked right into the House of Peers—today's House of Councillors. There's a chair for His Majesty the Emperor high up on a dais at the center of one wall of the chamber. From there the Emperor would declare the Diet open or issue proclamations. That gaggle of American newsmen rushed up the stairs to the throne and took turns having their cameramen take pictures of them on it. When I saw that, the idea of defeat really sank in! Sitting in the Emperor's seat— that's something none of us could ever have imagined.

Back at the Beginning

HAYASHI SHIGEO

He was an army engineer in eastern Manchuria and then, from 1943 on, a cameraman for Front, *a Japanese army publication intended to bolster support for the war.*

Maybe a month after the war, the Education Ministry organized a research team to go to Hiroshima and Nagasaki. At that time, Hiroshima was hardly mentioned publicly. People might say, "Hiroshima disappeared in a single blast," but that was about all. There weren't any photos, though newspapers sometimes referred to those bombings as "cruel" and "inhuman." I volunteered to go, although some of my friends tried to talk me out of it, telling me stories about how even trees would never again grow where those bombs had fallen. But my wife was three months pregnant, so I thought it was all right for me to go, as there was someone to carry on for me. As it turned out, the baby was a girl, though. It was just that I'd already faced death many times as a soldier. Whatever life was left to me seemed a bonus.

I had handled explosives every day as a soldier in the engineers in

Manchuria, so it was a snap for me to calculate how many kilograms of dynamite were required to blow up a single house, or to uproot a large tree. I felt I just had to know what had happened to Hiroshima in that single blast. If I say this now it may sound heroic and self-aggrandizing, but I felt back then that as a cameraman I wanted to take pictures of things that no one had ever seen.

What I imagined and what I saw bore no relation to each other. The scholars I accompanied placed measuring devices in the soil, attempting to determine levels of radiation. You see, they were trying to find the precise point at which the bombs had dropped. Their means were quite primitive. They measured the shadows left by buildings and the angles told them where the bomb might have been. Eventually, like an umbrella's ribs, all the rays led to a single point, and they were able to calculate the spot where the bomb had exploded. At first, the big shots on the team told me what to photograph, but eventually they got so wrapped up in their own research and calculations that they just brushed me off. "Go take pictures of anything suspicious" was all they said. So I walked around Hiroshima on my own, taking photos of whatever scenes struck my eye.

Looking at them afterwards, we could tell, for example, that a bridge had been pulled upward by the blast, or that a water main had been whipped away with the bridge. You could imagine what happened to human beings at that instant. It was all so bizarre, so eerie. "What's that? What can this be? What could have caused that?" I kept asking myself, as I took picture after picture.

Eventually we traveled to Nagasaki, and repeated the same process there. One day, I went to the Mitsubishi arsenal and was photographing the torpedo plant. I was being escorted around by a Mitsubishi man. At some point he said to me, "This is where we made the first torpedoes, the ones dropped on Pearl Harbor at the onset of the Pacific War." The wrenches and other tools used by the workers were lying there, all around me, as if they'd been set down a minute ago. I could have reached out myself and picked them up. Finally he said quietly, "Mr. Hayashi, the very first torpedo was launched from here in Nagasaki, and in the end here's where we were stabbed to death. We fought a stupid war, didn't we?" The two of us just stood there in silence.